Apostolic Church of the Pleroma
Clergy Handbook

ΕΚΚΛΗΣΙΑ ΑΠΟΣΤΟΛΙΚΟΣ ΠΛΗΡΩ-ΜΑΤΟΣ

Apostolic Church of the Pleroma

Clergy Handbook

Fox Lake, IL

Apostolic Church of the Pleroma Clergy Handbook

Fourth Edition
Published 2025

Copyright ©2014, 2025 Tau Phosphoros.
All rights reserved.

ISBN-13: 978-1-946814-01-2 (Hardcover)

ISBN-13: 978-1-946814-03-6 (Paperback)

ISBN-13: 978-1-946814-19-7 (Paperback - Black & White)

Triad Press, LLC
123 S. US 12 #33
Fox Lake, IL 60020

Triad Press, LLC

Apostolic Church of the Pleroma

Dedicated to the Memory of Tau Iohannes Harmonius, Tau Johannes XIII, Tau Philip-Μαρκος, Tau Charles Harmonius II, Tau Mikael, Tau Ioannes, and all the souls of the Holy Gnostics during the Aeons

Hear us and be near us

ΕΚΚΛΗΣΙΑ ΑΠΟΣΤΟΛΙΚΟΣ ΠΛΗΡΩΜΑΤΟΣ
Apostolic Church of the Pleroma

Record of Baptism, Chrismation, Holy Orders and other Sacraments or Ecclesiastical Appointments for:

_____

Baptism & Chrismation

Conferred on the _____ day of the month of _____, 20_____

by_____ at _____

Minor Orders

Porter: the _____ day of _____, 20_____, by _____

at _____

Lector: the _____ day of _____, 20_____, by _____

at _____

Exorcist: the _____ day of _____, 20_____, by _____

at _____

Acolyte: the _____ day of _____, 20_____, by _____

at _____

Sub-diaconate: the _____ day of _____, 20_____, by _____

at _____

Major Orders

Ordained to the Order of the Diaconate on the _____ day of the month of _____

in the Year of Our Lord 20_____, by _____ at _____

Ordained to the Order of the Presbyterate on the _____ day of the month of _____

in the Year of Our Lord 20_____, by _____ at _____

Elevated to the Office of Archpresbyter on the _____ day of the month of _____,

in the Year of Our Lord 20_____, by _____ at _____

Elected to the Office of the Episcopate on the _____ day of the month of _____,

in the Year of Our Lord 20_____, by _____ at _____

Consecrated to the Order of the Episcopate on the _____ day of the month of _____

in the Year of Our Lord 20_____, by _____ at _____

Other Ecclesiastical Activities, Appointments, etc. :

_____
_____
_____

Christian Knights of Saint-Martin

Initiation Record for:

_____

Associate: the _____ day of _____, 20____, at _____ Lodge,

N° _____, by _____

Initiate: the _____ day of _____, 20____, at _____ Lodge,

N° _____, by _____

Supérieur Inconnu: the _____ day of _____, 20____, at _____ Lodge,

N° _____, by _____, taking the Nomen Mysticum of

_____

Knight of Saint-Martin and Rose✠Croix Martinist: the _____ day of _____, 20____, at _____ Lodge, N° _____, by _____

S.I. Initiateur: the _____ day of _____, 20____, at _____ Lodge, N° _____, by _____

Initiateur Libre: the _____ day of _____, 20_____, at _____ Lodge, N° _____, by _____

Other Martinist / Martinèsist Recognitions and Appointments:

_____

_____

_____

_____

_____

_____

A la Gloire du Grand Architecte de l'Univers

Paix – Tolérance – Union

Order of Asiatic Architects

Initiation Record for:

_____

⚒ Symbolic Lodge

I°, Apprentice: the _____ day of _____, 20____, at _____ Lodge,

N° _____, Orient of _____, by _____

II°, Companion: the _____ day of _____, 20____, at _____ Lodge,

N° _____, Orient of _____, by _____

III°, Master: the _____ day of _____, 20____, at _____ Lodge, N° _____, Orient of _____, by _____

᛭ Lodge of Perfection

IV°, Perfect Architect of the Sacred Arch: the _____ day of _____, 20____, at _____ Lodge, N° _____, Orient of _____, by _____

V°, Perfect Initiate of the Starry Vault: the _____ day of _____, 20____, at _____ Lodge, N° _____, Orient of _____, by _____

Chapter

VI°, Knight of the East & West: the _____ day of _____, 20___, at _____ Lodge, N° _____, Valley of _____, by _____

VII°, Knight Rose-Croix: the _____ day of _____, 20___, at _____ Lodge, N° _____, Valley of _____, by _____

VIII°, Knight of the Red Eagle: the _____ day of _____, 20___, at _____ Lodge, N° _____, Valley of _____, by _____

Areopagus

IX°, Knight Kadosh: the _____ day of _____, 20___, at _____ Lodge, N° _____, Valley of _____, by _____

Council

X°, Prince of the Royal Secret: the _____ day of _____, 20___, at

_____ Lodge, N° _____, Valley of _____, by _____

XI°, Sovereign Grand Inspector General: the _____ day of _____, 20___,

at _____ Lodge, N° _____, Valley of _____, by _____

Hermetic College

XII°, Knight of the Sun: the _____ day of _____, 20___, at

_____ Lodge, N° _____, Zenith of _____, by _____

XIII°, Supreme Commander of the Stars: the _____ day of _____, 20___, at

_____ Lodge, N° _____, Zenith of _____, by _____

XIV°, Sublime Master of the Great Work: the _____ day of _____, 20___,

at _____ Lodge, N° _____, Zenith of _____, by _____

Supreme Consistory of Wisdom

XV°, Sublime Epopt of the A∴ A∴ : the _____ day of _____, 20___, at

_____ Lodge, N° _____, Zenith of _____, by _____

Sovereign Grand Tribunal

XVI°, Grand Inquisitor Defender of the Order: the _____ day of _____,

20___, at _____ Lodge, N° _____, Zenith of _____, by _____

Sovereign Sanctuary of the Gnosis

On the ____ day of the month of _____, Year of the True Light 60____, Corresponding to the Year of Our Lord 20___, at _____Lodge, N°____, at the Zenith of _____ was conferred upon our Very Illustrious and Worthy _____, the XVIIth and final Degree of Initiation of the Order of Asiatic Architects, Sovereign Grand Conservator of the Sanctuary of the Gnosis, at the hands of _____

Other OAA Administrative Appointments and Honorary Designations

_____

_____

_____

_____

_____

_____

Acknowledgements

The 4th edition of the ACP Clergy Handbook has been a long time coming, and we are incredibly grateful to the many people who have provided valuable feedback on earlier editions. As with the previous edition, we must first acknowledge Brother Randall Edmonston and the Most Reverend Monseigneur ☦William Michael Pierce, in ecclesia Tau Bruno II for their indispensable assistance and support from the very beginning of the ACP.

To all of our friends and colleagues old and new, your willingness to advocate our mission often in the face of severe opposition is appreciated more than you know. We thank you sincerely for your confidence in our clergy and our work.

We are forever indebted to Tau Númenor Nigredo who has worked so hard to ensure the success of the ACP and whose support and assistance has arrived at some very crucial moments.

We are extremely thankful for the extensive correspondence and very kind words of Patriarch Michael-Paul Bertiaux of the Ecclesia Gnostica Spiritualis, who has given his explicit support and blessing to our work. Bishop Bertiaux was also kind enough to provide some very thoughtful feedback on the last edition of the Clergy Handbook, offering some important additions and corrections concerning the precise history of his own consecrations as well as on the tables of Apostolic Succession. Much of this has been incorporated into this new edition.

And of course, none of the materials of the ACP would have found publication and dissemination without the tireless efforts of Michele Saridan, who has remained one of the greatest supporters of the mission of the ACP; and likewise, the efforts of Lady Betsy Howlett Adyeeri, whose work with Triad Press has been invaluable.

Finally, we must acknowledge and thank our dear friend and Brother in the Gnosis, ☦Palamas for his constant support and encouragement. ☦Palamas has long been for us a glimmering example of Christian fraternity as well as of selfless & tireless dedication to the accomplishment of the Work of Reintegration. We look forward to many more years of continued friendship and cooperation.

Τ Φωσφορος, επ. γν.
3 March, 2025

ACP Clergy Handbook

Table of Contents

Introduction to the 4th Edition xxi

Preface to the 3rd Edition xxiii

Letter of Introduction xxv

Ecclesiastical & Initiatic Schema of the ACP, CKSM, & OAA xxxi

Lesson Plan

- Porter xxxii
- Lector xliii
- Exorcist xlvii
- Acolyte liv
- Sub-diaconate lv
- Diaconate lvi

PART I-THEORY

A Theoretical Foundation for Gnostic Philosophy

- What is Gnosticism? 3
- On the Nature of God 5

Gnostic Mythology

- On the Nature of the Holy Trinity 10
- The Aeons 11
- Geradamas and Seth 12
- The Fall of Sophia and the Rise of the Demiurge 13
- The Creation and Exile of Adam 15
- Adam and Eve in the Garden 16
- Out of the Garden - Plots of the Demiurge 17
- The Incarnation of the Logos & the Redemption of Man 18

On the Sacraments of the ACP 21

The Kybalion by Three Initiates

- Introduction 24

Table of Contents

- The Hermetic Philosophy 27
- The Seven Hermetic Principles 30
- Mental Transmutation 36
- The ALL 39
- The Mental Universe 44
- The Divine Paradox 48
- "The ALL" in All 53
- Planes of Correspondence 58
- Vibration 65
- Polarity 69
- Rhythm 72
- Causation 76
- Gender 80
- Mental Gender 83
- Hermetic Axioms 88

Sepher Yetzirah

- An Introductory Note 93
- Chapter I 94
- Chapter II 96
- Chapter III 97
- Chapter IV 98
- Chapter V 100
- Chapter VI 102

PART II - PRACTICE

General Instruction

- Creating a Personal Temple and Workspace 107
- On Meditation 108
- Technique for Meditation 108
- The Sacred Art of Intonation 109
- Invocation of the Archangels 111
- Meditations of the Canonical Hours 114
- The Meditation of the Golden Orb 117
- Instructions for Censing the Temple 117

Holy Gnostic Liturgy of the Pleromic Light 119

Liturgy of St. John the Divine (Mass of the Seven Seals) 150

Liturgy of St. Peter the Gnostic 191

Theurgic Operations of the ACP

- Introduction to the Theurgic Art & Instructions for Use 221
- Formula for the Consecration of Sanctuary Items 223
- Formula for Theurgic Operations 228
- List of Theurgic Operations 235
- The 72 Spirits of the Shemhamphorasch 238

PART III - SUPPLEMENTARY DISCOURSES

On Faith and Knowledge 313

On the Eucharist 317

A Gnostic Exposition of the Three Alchemical Essentials 321

Alchemy of the Eucharist 329

The Tetragrammaton in the Three Worlds 336

The Gnostic Gospel of Luke 341

The Devil's Passion 358

Morning Star Rising 364

Theosis Through Gnosis 375

A Brief History of the Gnostic Church

- Introduction 385
- Pre-Christian and Early Christian Gnosticism 386
- Gnostic Currents in Medieval Through Renaissance Times: 12th-17th Centuries 390
- The Gnosis Restored: 18th-19th Centuries 395
- New Alliances and the Spread of the Gnostic Church: 1900s-1920s 403
- The FUDOSI Years: 1930s-1940s 407
- Post-War Reconstruction and the Emergence of the American Gnostic Churches 411
- Gnosis in the 21st Century 417

The Folly of Peter 418

Table of Contents

APPENDICES

A - The Tetragrammaton as Tetractys 425

B - Tree of Life Diagram 426

C - Sephirotic Correspondences 427

D - Hebrew Letter Correspondences 429

E - Greek Letter Correspondences 430

F – Chakras 431

G - Tables of Apostolic Succession 432

H - List of Gnostic, Catholic, and Orthodox Lines of Succession 458

I – Documents 460

J - Glossary of Ecclesiastical Terms 471

Works Cited and Selected Bibliography 479

Introduction to the 4th Edition

The ACP Clergy Handbook began as a series of lessons for new clergy, written in 2008 for a project intended to serve as a vehicle for the recently defunct Ecclesia Gnostica Catholica Hermetica. When this collaborative endeavor failed to produce a viable body, the lesson material was gathered to form the foundation of the clerical instruction of the Apostolic Church of the Pleroma, and ecclesiastical body instituted by Tau Valentinus (aka Tau Phosphoros) on May 31, 2009, at a solemn Mass at the Feast of Holy Pentecost.

The Minor Order instruction was expanded and enlarged into a Clergy Handbook, the first typescript copy of which was distributed to a few select clergy in 2009, followed by a second typescript edition a year or so later; culminating, after various additions, subtractions, and revisions, in the Third Revised Edition published in 2014 by Triad Press. The present Fourth Edition attempts to correct some errors found in previous editions, and to expand upon the work generally: The "Brief History" has been substantially updated, and additional Supplementary Discourses have been included; the Bibliography has been expanded to include references cited in the added materials, as well as to comprise a more comprehensive list of recommended reads, including those found in the Minor Order curriculum; additionally, the Mass of the Seven Seals, and the Liturgy of St. Peter the Gnostic have been included, as well as various other pieces of information in an attempt to make this Handbook as comprehensive as possible, without weighing it down with extraneous material. Everything that has been included has been with a view toward optimal usefulness; firstly for formation students, but also as a reference for all ACP clergy.

In addition, certain material from the 1st & 2nd editions have been reintroduced, namely select initiatic & ecclesiastical documents pertinent to the history of the ACP. Also, for the first time, we are presenting publicly a fully outline of the Ecclesiastical and Initiatic Schema of the ACP, CKAM, & OAA. This outline will give the neophyte or prospective adherent a clear idea of the scope of our Work. The curriculum, likewise has been greatly augmented to include the general lesson plan through the Diaconate.

Preface to the Third Edition
(2014)

The Apostolic Church of the Pleroma Clew Handbook began as a series of individual discourses distributed to Minor Order ordinands as they progressed through the formation program. These discourses were later collected together and distributed as a single Handbook in manuscript form. This present edition has been revised and expanded to include several documents not contained previously, such as: the "Lesson Plan"; the "Brief History of the Gnostic Church"; a "Glossary of Liturgical and Ecclesiastical Terms"; the "Meditations of the Canonical Hours"; and several other documents. There has also been significant revision and expansion of much of the previously existing material.

There is also much that has remained unchanged from its original state, such as the "Letter of Introduction" that accompanied the manuscript edition. Likewise, the format has been left fundamentally unaltered. This work is not intended for a mass-market audience or distribution. It is a book of instruction for students of the ACP formation program, and a reference and ritual tool for all levels of clergy. Therefore, more attention has been given to content and functionality than to marketing aesthetics.

We realize that not everyone to whom this volume will come will have access to local mentoring clergy. It is with this in mind that we have included a "Lesson Plan Outline" which had previously only been circulated to senior clergy who were taking on a mentoring role. This Lesson Plan does not replace the need for the personal attention afforded by mentoring clergy, and it has been edited to remove reference to private discourses, but it will give the student a clearer understanding of the whole formation process.

It is also with the distant student in mind that we have included the "Formula for the Consecration of Sanctuary Items," a function normally reserved for a priest or bishop, but which may be accomplished with some degree of efficacy by the sincere theurgist, regardless of ecclesiastical rank or office. Likewise, detALLed instructions are given here for the "Censing of the Temple," which would normally, and ideally, be accomplished by personal instruction.

What the reader will not find here are the private ceremonies of ordination and initiation, which may only be communicated experientially, or given in printed form to bishops and initiators. There is also much private instruction, including hundreds of pages of discourses and ceremonial work, which is reserved for those who have received Holy Order ordination and initiation into the affiliated Rites. This is not stated as a taunt or boast, but to alert the casual reader that the present volume, while certainly penetrating beyond the atrium of the Temple, is yet but a fragment of the system as a whole. It is only through ordination and initiation, and

Preface to the Third Edition

the special instructions accompanying those rites, that one may come to possess the keys necessary to unlock the full potential of this Handbook, especially the Theurgic Operations and the Holy Liturgy.

Having said that, there is yet much that may be gained by the sincere, studious, and hard-working seeker who may take up the studies laid out in these pages, but who may not have any "formal" connection with the ACP. In fact, it is possible that through the practice of the techniques and rites contained in this Handbook, the dedicated aspirant may forge a link to the egregore of the ACP and share in a portion of its Spiritual benediction. The Light of Gnosis shines ever as a beacon to all those who would partake of its life-giving rays and ascend through the realms into the Divine Pleroma. We therefore invite you to attune to the Spiritual Powers which animate our Holy Church, and join us in that highest form of worship, which is the Liberation of the Spirit, thus effecting the Regeneration of Body and Soul; and ensuring our place among the Aeons of Light, Life, Love, and Liberty.

Issued under the Seal of the Office of the Patriarchal See

Dear Brothers and Sisters,

Greetings In the Light of Gnosis!

    It is with great pleasure that we are able to present this Clergy Handbook as both an instructional guide for the Minor Orders, and a useful reference work for all levels of clergy. The purpose of this text is not to deliver lengthy dissertations on ancient history, or to dissect the myriad philosophical and theological doctrines that have, in various times and places, been labeled "Gnostic," rightly or wrongly. There are many other excellent works to which you may be referred for such studies. This present work is concerned solely with the doctrines and practices of the Apostolic Church of the Pleroma. To be sure, many ancient teachings are to be found preserved within our venerable tradition, and volumes could indeed be written to argue every minute point of doctrine. Such a work would undoubtedly be of great value; but as an instructional guide for new clergy, we want to present a succinct and cohesive course of study that focuses on the core essentials of theory and practice, and which may serve as a spiritual foundation upon which further studies and more advanced principles may be logically integrated. For, while Gnostic symbolism and mythology is, by its very nature, subject to varied interpretations, it is nevertheless crucial to present an internally logical, and unambiguous core doctrine. Without a solid philosophical and theological foundation, the tradition becomes so subjective as to become utterly meaningless. That is, although the Gnostic teachings and principles may have unique and special meanings to each individual on the path, these principles also have inherent meaning that is universal and unchanging.

Since many who are reading this will be newly ordained clergy, or perhaps as yet unordained, it is only appropriate that we should give a few introductory words on Gnosticism, the Gnostic Church, and Christian Initiation. Gnosis, from the Greek γνωσις [gnosis], meaning knowledge, does not refer to mere intellectual or even philosophical knowledge. Gnosis is an experiential knowledge that has a spiritually transformative effect upon its recipient. This transformative gnosis is discussed in many early Christian Gnostic texts, such as those discovered at Nag Hammadi, Egypt, in 1945. However, although the authors and followers of these teachings were undoubtedly seekers of gnosis, the term "Gnostic" was applied to them largely by outsiders; "orthodox" heresiologists, such as Irenaeus, who likely misunderstood the majority of the doctrines that they were attempting to expose. There is no reason to think that the earliest Christian Gnostics identified themselves as anything other than Christian. But with the multitude of sects and denominations extant today, the term "Gnostic" or "Christian Gnostic" suits the modern practitioner just fine.

It should be acknowledged that the terms "gnosis" and "gnostic" have been used throughout history to describe a number of different doctrines; not all of them compatible with our use of the terms. First of all, there is absolutely no political connotation in our usage. When we speak of "gnosis" we are referring to that transcendental knowledge of a spiritual nature that was previously mentioned. We may refer to as "gnostic" anything pertaining to this unique knowledge, or the acquiring of it. When we refer to "Gnostic" with a capital "G" we are referring to the classical Gnosticism of the ancient Christians, and those Apostolic Christians of today who self-identify as Gnostic.

One of the core precepts of the Gnostic tradition is that there is a secret doctrine that was transmitted from Jesus to His elect. This parallel tradition, communicated privately to certain of the Apostles, is alluded to throughout the gospels and epistles of the New Testament. This hidden body of knowledge is, on one level, a collection of specific teachings and instructions that were not given to the multitude, but rather to the holy elect, who in turn passed the knowledge to their students, etc. But the most profound of the teachings are hidden not by any attempt to conceal, but because by their very nature they can only be apprehended experientially, through mystical revelation.

Jesus, as the Logos incarnate, was able to reveal these mysteries directly to His disciples. But for the generations to follow, he left powerful tools by which we may also attain to the light of gnosis. These tools include the rich symbols and rituals that make up Christian Initiation. The Christian mysteries are expressed through, and communicated by, the Holy Sacraments of the Church. These sacraments may effect a spiritual transformation even when administered in a non-Gnostic, "orthodox" setting. Since the Holy Spirit is the actual agent effecting the sacrament, any validly ordained priest or bishop may equally perform the rite, regardless of their particular affiliation. The effectiveness of the sacrament, however, is due not only to the validity of its transmission, but also to the will and intent of the recipient.

It is widely known that the Eucharist is the central rite of the Church. The administration of this single sacrament could arguably be seen as the raison d'être of the Church. But in order to properly administer the sacraments, one needs to have been suitably empowered by the Holy Spirit. This empowerment is conferred through Apostolic Succession, by means of the sacrament of Holy Orders. By receiving Holy Orders, one may become a living channel for the power of the Holy Spirit. There is no greater calling than to serve humanity by helping them to come into closer communion with God. For, whatever earthly services we may render to our fellow men and women, the spiritual needs are infinitely more important. While the providing of material sustenance is necessary for the continuity of the physical body, spiritual sustenance is crucial for the well being of the soul.

The Holy Orders of the ACP, like all authentic Apostolic churches, are divided into the Minor Orders and Major Orders. The Minor Orders are: Porter, Lector, Exorcist, and Acolyte. These four orders of clergy are a period of instruction and preparation. This instruction is both theoretical and practical. In addition to this present volume, the theoretical portion may consist of studies in various academic, philosophical, and ecclesiastical works, as deemed appropriate by the clergy mentors. The practical instruction and responsibilities of Minor Order clergy include the various exercises given herein, as well as assistance in various aspects of the Holy Liturgy. Progression through the Minor Orders is influenced greatly by the aptitude and dedication of the individual, and at the discretion of his or her regional priests and bishops.

The Major Orders are: Deacon, Priest, and Bishop. Consideration for admission into the Major Orders of the ACP is at the sole determination of the Episcopal Council, and subject to approval by the Patriarch. One important criterion for admittance into the Major Orders is a sincere desire on the part of the candidate to serve the Church in whatever capacity necessary in the furtherance of the mission of the ACP. While the Minor Orders are largely "teaching" grades (though not without significant and indispensable service), the Major Orders are dedicated solely to the service of the Church, God, and our fellow Brothers and Sisters. It is within the Major Orders that the Apostolic Succession is actually transmitted; and as such, the Major Orders are the most carefully guarded of the Holy Orders, lest the profane breach her holy covenant. The Major Orders are not to be seen as a sort of reward or recompense for having advanced through Minor Orders. Many choose to serve within Minor Orders indefinitely, providing a valuable service to the Church, and serving as worthy exemplars to potential candidates to the Holy Orders. There are some, though, that sense a calling to a service and ministry within the Church. For those who may aspire toward the Diaconate or the Presbyterate, the senior clergy of the ACP will be available for counsel throughout the formation process.

In addition to the sacramental rites, the light of gnosis has been transmitted from time immemorial, through various schools of mystical and theurgic initiation. Today there exists numerous manifestations of the ancient Mystery Traditions, some authentic, and, unfortunately, some spurious. We will not comment here on these myriad societies, orders, and fraternities, leaving it for the individual seeker to discern his or her initiatic path as one's conscience dictates. We will, however, mention one such tradition that has, since the institution of the modern Gnostic tradition, operated parallel to, and in complementary concert with, the modern Gnostic Church in its divers manifestations. The venerable tradition that I am speaking of is Martinism. Martinism, and the Martinist Orders, preserve, study, and practice the teachings of the 18th century Christian mystic, Louis-Claude de Saint-Martin, and those of his theurgic master, Martinès de Pasqually. Martinism is an initiatic system of three principal degrees. It is said that Saint-Martin transmitted but a single initiation to his students, unlike Pasqually, his former master, who operated a more complex degree system based on certain Masonic models (though in fact having little to do with Freemasonry's collection of symbols and rites). This single initiation of Saint-Martin was later sub-divided into three parts by the man who would organize the Martinist teachings into a Martinist Order. That man was Dr. Gerard Encausse, known as Papus.

Papus had been the recipient of that Martinist initiation that had been transmitted successively from initiator to initiate from the time of Saint-Martin himself. In 1887, Papus and other Martinist initiates officially instituted the Ordre Martiniste (Martinist Order). In 1891, just one year after Jules Doinel instituted his restored Gnostic Church, from which the modern Gnostic Churches derive, a Martinist Supreme Council was formed for the purpose of establishing and maintaining regular Lodges. However, in addition to the Lodge system, Martinism was also spread in the traditional method of initiator to initiate, without any particular formal setting, such as a Lodge or Heptad. After one has received the three regular degrees of Martinism, the Initiateur Libre (Free Initiator) degree may be conferred, which empowers the initiate to confer the Martinist degrees upon whatever individuals she or he may see fit. As a result of the Free Initiator system, as well as divisions within the Supreme Council and Lodge system, there are today numerous Martinist Orders, as well as Free Initiators who confer the Martinist degrees without any central authority or hierarchy. The three Martinist degrees of Associate, Initiate (or Mystic), and Superieur Inconnu (Unknown Superior) transmit a spiritual lineage and form a mystic tie to the Masters of the Past; but Martinist initiation is not an end unto itself. The rites preserve a tradition, and it is that living tradition of the Way of the Heart, that inner mystical foundation of being, that is the true gem of the Martinist philosophy and practice.

In keeping with the long-standing traditional bond between Martinism and the Gnostic Church (Papus himself was consecrated as a Gnostic bishop in 1892, taking the name Tau Vincent), the ACP, through the Christian Knights of Saint-Martin, administers the Martinist degrees to those who are enrolled in the formation program, and taking Holy Orders. The Martinist doctrine of Christian mysticism and theurgy is invaluable to the Gnostic cleric. Concerning those who are entering into Holy Orders who have received Martinist Initiation from other Martinist obediences, or independent Free Initiators, those degrees will be recognized as valid, providing that sufficient evidence is produced verifying their validity. Those individuals are not required to cease their membership in any other Martinist body to which they belong, but may hold dual affiliation with the Christian Knights of Saint-Martin. There may, however, be additional programs of study within the CKSM that complement and enhance the traditional Martinist teachings.[1]

The Christian Mysteries, in both their outer, exoteric aspects of the sacrament of Holy Orders, as well as their esoteric, initiatic forms, are available to those dedicated men and women of the faith who are ready and able to devote a considerable amount of time and effort not only to their own self-improvement, but also in service to the Church and humanity. These words are not meant to discourage the sincere seeker, but merely to impress upon her, or him, the gravity and degree of commitment that is expected of each member of clergy. It is true that the dedicated aspirant may reap untold spiritual rewards, but the principal motivation for advancement through the Holy Orders and initiatic rites must always be service; and that to the glory of the Most High.

Concerning the usage and application of this Handbook, it should be understood that these materials are not listed here in order of importance, or even in the order in which they are to be studied. Rather, they are organized, as best as possible, by category and type of instruction. For instance, the entire "Theory" section would not be completed before the "Practice" section had begun. The mentoring clergy gives instruction regarding the order in which the material is to be studied. In this way, the theoretical and practical knowledge is grown and developed together, giving the student a balanced approach, and practical experience from the start.

We sincerely hope that these instructions will inspire and encourage you along your Sacramental and Initiatic Path, and help you to become as a shining beacon to those who will come after you. Remember that as ordained Clergy and Initiates we are each a link in a mystic chain that binds the Masters of the Past to the neophytes of future generations. And as links in this chain, it is required of each of us to not only uphold and preserve the principles and traditions bequeathed to us, but also to forge new paths forward, ensuring that our venerable tradition remains a living, vital organism, and not merely a shadowy apparition of the glories of the past.

---

[1] There is another initiatic body into which ACP clergy are admitted, but which has remained unmentioned in any of our public writings up until recently. While we cannot go into any detail concerning this Order, we can give its name, which is the Order of Asiatic Architects, and mention that it was instituted within the ACP in 2011 as a vehicle for several occult and Masonic currents which have been transmitted to us through various sources, including, but not limited to, the Rite Ancien & Primitif de Memphis-Misraim and the Hermetic Brotherhood of Luxor. These and other esoteric currents have long been closely associated with the Gnostic Church. Within the OAA, the initiatic and esoteric training of the ACP ordinand is supplemented with rites, exercises, and discourses not found within the ACP proper or the CKSM. - Ed. 3/2025

Introductory Letter

May the blessing of the Mystery of the Three-in-One, of God the Unknown Father, of Christ the redeeming and ever-coming Logos, and of the Holy Spirit our Celestial Mother and Consoler, descend upon you and remain with you always. Amen.

Tau Phosphoros, Ep. Gn. S∴ I∴ I.L.

13 October, 2009 A.D.

120th Year of the Gnosis Restored

Ecclesiastical and Initiatic Schema of the ACP, CKSM, & OAA

Mth	ACP	CKSM	OAA
0	Baptism		
3	Porter	Associate	I° Apprentice
5			II° Companion
7			III° Master
9	Lector	Initiate (App. Cohen)	
12			IV° Perfect Architect of the Sacred Arch
15	Exorcist	Supérieur Inconnu	
18		Philosophe Inconnu	V° Perfect Initiate of the Starry Vault
21		(Companion Cohen)	VI° Knight of the East & West
24	Acolyte	Kn. of Saint-Martin (R✠C Mart.)	VII° Knight Rose✠Croix
27	Sub-deacon		VIII° Knight of the Red Eagle
30	Deacon	S.I. Initiateur (Maître Cohen)	IX° Knight Kadosh
36			X° Prince of the Royal Secret
42	Priest	Initiateur Libre (S.G.I.G.)	XI° Sovereign Grand Inspector General
45			XII° Knight of the Sun
48		(Gr. M. Cohen)	XIII° Supreme Commander of the Stars
51			XIV° Sublime Master of the Great Work
54	Archpriest		XV° Sublime Epopt of the Arcana Arcanorum
57			XVI° Grand Inquisitor Defender of the Order
60	Bishop	(Réaux-Croix)	XVII° Sov. Gr. Conservator of the Sanctuary of the Gnosis
XX	Eparch	Grand Commander (Regional)	XVIII° Sov. Gr. Master of the Seven Seals
XX	Exarch	Dep. Sov. Gr. Commander	XIX° Master of the 19 Rays (Honorary)
XX	Patriarch	Sovereign Grand Commander	XIX° Master of the 19 Rays (Active)

Lesson Plan Outline
For Holy Orders Instruction

The following is a reproduction of the Minor Order curriculum given to students of the ACP formation program. Originally, this document was intended for Major Order clergy who were serving as mentors to those in the Minor Orders. It was decided, though, that it mt[] be beneficial for the student to have access to the entire schema of Minor Order study, in order that they might gain a better understanding of the method of instruction, and be better prepared for future tasks and responsibilities. The previously redacted materials have been restored in this edition; and the curriculum as a whole has been updated and augmented.

Porter Curriculum

Materials Needed

Books:

- *Dictionary of Gnosticism* - Andrew Smith
- *The Gnostic Bible* - Barnstone & Meyer
- *Gnosticism: New Light on the Ancient Tradition of Inner Knowing* - Stephan Hoeller
- *The Nag Hammadi Scriptures: International Edition* - Marvin Meyer
- *Gnostic Philosophy* – Tobias Churton
- Other titles as directed by clergy mentor.

Vestments:

White alb; white cincture (Cordelier); black etc.
Black robe, etc. as required for OAA

Other:

Personal sanctum items, as described in the "General Instruction" section of the Handbook.

Syllabus

Week 1

- ▶ Read "Introductory Message" in HB.
- ▶ Read "Creating a Personal Temple and Workspace" in HB, and follow instructions.
- ▶ Read CKSM Associate Lecture #1
- ▶ Read OAA Apprentice Architect Missive #1
- ▶ Begin making Journal entries concerning your studies.

Week 2

- ▶ Read "What is Gnosticism?" and "On the Nature of God" in HB
- ▶ Read "On Meditation" and "Technique for Meditation" in HB and begin exercises.
- ▶ Submit written responses to the following questions:
    - o What are some of the benefits of meditation?
    - o What is your understanding of the difference between dogma and doctrine?
    - o What are the three religious philosophies discussed in the HB? Explain them in your own words.
- ▶ Read CKSM Associate Lecture #2
- ▶ Begin reading *Gnosticism* by Stephan Hoeller.
- ▶ Continue Journal entries and exercises.

Week 3

- ▶ Read "On the Nature of the Holy Trinity," "The Aeons," and "Geradamas & Seth" in the HB.
- ▶ Read "Sacred Art of Intonation" in HB and begin exercises.
- ▶ Answer and submit the following questions:
    - o Define the term "Aeon" and discuss its possible meanings.
    - o Define the term "Pleroma" and discuss its implications.

Lesson Plan for Holy Orders

- o Who or what are Geradamas and Seth?
- o What is effected by the proper intonation of vowel sounds and names of power?
- ▶ Read OAA Apprentice Architect Missive #2
- ▶ Continue reading *Gnosticism*
- ▶ Continue Journal and exercises

Week 4

- ▶ Read "The Fall of Sophia and the Rise of the Demiurge," "The Creation & Exile of Adam," and "Adam and Eve in the Garden" in HB.
- ▶ Read and practice "Invocation of the Archangels" in the HB. This should be practiced daily until it is memorized.
- ▶ Answer the following questions:
  - o Who or what is the Demiurge?
  - o By what name is the Demiurge known in Gnostic scripture?
  - o How is the Demiurge similar to or different from the orthodox conception of Satan?
  - o What is the main difference between the Sethian and Valentinian perception of the Demiurge?
  - o What are Archons and what is their role in the Cosmos?
  - o What is meant by the "Fall of Man"?
  - o What is the Garden of Eden? Could it have more than one meaning?
  - o Who is Zoe? What is the Difference between Zoe and Eve?
  - o What is the Tree of Knowledge? What is its fruit?
  - o What is the identity of the serpent in Eden?
- ▶ Read CKSM Associate Lecture #4
- ▶ Finish reading *Gnosticism*
- ▶ Continue Journal & exercises

Week 5

- ▶ Read "Out of the Garden - Plots of the Demiurge" and "The Incarnation of the Logos & the

Redemption of Man" from the HB.

- ▶ Read and begin practicing "Meditations of the Canonical Hours" in the HB.
- ▶ Read "Introduction" and "Pre-Christian and Early Christian Gnosticism" from "A Brief History of the Gnostic Church" in the HB.
- ▶ Answer and submit the following questions:
    - o What is sin?
    - o What are the three divisions of Man?
    - o How are these applied to Humanity as a whole?
    - o What are some of the pre-Christian influences on Gnosticism?
    - o Who was Valentinus? Simon Magus? Mani?
    - o Who were the Mandaeans?
    - o What were the principal geographic areas where Gnosticism first took root?
- ▶ Read CKSM Associate Lecture #5
- ▶ Read OAA Apprentice Architect Missive #3
- ▶ Continue Journal & exercises

Week 6

- ▶ Read "On the Eucharist" in the HB.
- ▶ Read and practice the "Meditation of the Golden Orb" in HB.
- ▶ Read "Gnostic Currents in Medieval through Renaissance Times" from "A Brief History of the Gnostic Church" in HB.
- ▶ Begin reading *Gnostic Philosophy* by Tobias Churton.
- ▶ Answer the following questions:
    - o Who were the Cathars? Tell when they emerged and explain their principal tenets. What happened at Montsegur?
    - o Who were the Knights Templar? Who was their first Grand Master?
    - o Did the Templars participate in the crusades against the Cathars?
    - o Which king and which pope were responsible for the suppression of the Templars?
    - o On what day and date were the Templars in France and across Europe arrested en masse?
    - o Who was the last Grand Master of the original Order of the Temple?

- o Who was the legendary founder of the Rosicrucians?
- o What were the three Rosicrucian manifestoes, and when were they issued?
- ▶ Read CKSM Associate Lecture #6
- ▶ Continue Journal & exercises.

Week 7

- ▶ Read "The Gospel of Thomas" (NHC II,2) & comment in your Journal.
- ▶ Continue reading Gnostic Philosophy
- ▶ Read CKSM Associate Lecture #7
- ▶ Continue Journal, exercises, & special studies.

Week 8

- ▶ Finish Gnostic Philosophy
- ▶ Read "The Gospel of Philip" (NHC II,3) and comment in Journal.
- ▶ Read CKSM Associate Lecture #8
- ▶ Continue Journal, exercises, & special studies.

Week 9

- ▶ Read "The Gospel of Truth" (NHC 1,3) & comment in Journal.
- ▶ Read CKSM Associate Lecture #9
- ▶ Read OAA Companion Architect Missive #1
- ▶ Continue Journal, exercises, & special studies.

Week 10

- ▶ Begin reading "The Secret Book of John" (NHC 11,1 - also called "Apocryphon of John"), "The Nature of the Rulers" (NHC 11,4 - also called "Reality of the Rulers" or "Hypostasis of the Archons"), "On the Origin of the World" (NHC 11,5), and "The Holy Book of the Great Invisible Spirit" (NHC 111,21 - also called "Gospel of the Egyptians") and begin taking notes.
- ▶ Read CKSM Associate Lecture #10
- ▶ Read OAA Companion Architect Missive #2

- Continue Journal, exercises, & special studies.

Week 11

- Continue reading Gnostic texts begun in Week 10 and begin composing a short paper (1000-2500 words) comparing and contrasting various elements of the treatises.
- Read CKSM Associate Lecture #11
- Read OAA Companion Architect Missive #3
- Continue Journal, exercises, & special studies.

Week 12

- Finish essay and submit paper to clergy mentor.
- Read CKSM Associate Lecture #12
- Read OAA Companion Architect Missive #4
- Continue Journal, exercises, & special studies.

Week 13

- Read "Thunder" (NHC VI,2) & comment in Journal.
- Read "The Gnosis Restored" from "A Brief History of the Gnostic Church" in HB.
- Answer the following questions:
    - Who was Martinès de Pasqually?
    - Who was Bernard-Raymond Fabré-Palaprat?
    - Who was Pierre-Eugène-Vintras?
    - Who was Papus?
    - What groups, according to Papus, "form the Western chain in the transmission of occult science"?
    - What year was proclaimed to be the beginning of the "Era of the Gnosis Restored," and who made this proclamation?
    - What were some of the significant events that occurred within the French Gnostic community in 1895? In 1899?
- Read CKSM Associate Lecture #13

Lesson Plan for Holy Orders

- ▶ Continue Journal, exercises, & special studies.

Week 14

- ▶ Read "Eugnostos the Blessed" (NHC 111,3) and "The Wisdom of Jesus Christ" (NHC 111,4) and comment in Journal.
- ▶ Read CKSM Associate Lecture #14
- ▶ Read OAA Companion Architect Missive #5
- ▶ Continue Journal, exercises, & special studies.

Week 15

- ▶ Read "The Gospel of Mary" (BG 8502,1) & comment 1n Journal.
- ▶ Read CKSM Associate Lecture #15
- ▶ Work on Logic Exam
- ▶ Continue Journal, exercises, & special studies.

Week 16

- ▶ Read "Three Forms of First Thought" (NHC XIII,1 - also called "Trimorphic Protennoia") & comment in Journal.
- ▶ Read CKSM Associate Lecture #16
- ▶ Work on Logic Exam
- ▶ Continue Journal, exercises, & special studies.

Week 17

- ▶ Read "The Dialog of the Savior" (NHC III,5) & comment in Journal.
- ▶ Finish Logic Exam
- ▶ Read CK.SM Associate Lecture #17
- ▶ Continue Journal, exercises, & special studies.

Week 18

- ▶ Read "The Revelation of Paul" (NHC V,2) & comment in Journal.
- ▶ Read CK.SM Associate Lecture #18
- ▶ Read OAA Master Architect Missive #1
- ▶ Continue Journal, exercises, & special studies.

Week 19

- ▶ Read "The First Revelation of James" (NHC V,3) and "The Second Revelation of James" (NHC V,4) & comment in Journal
- ▶ Read CK.SM Associate Lecture #19
- ▶ Read OAA Master Architect Missive #2
- ▶ Continue Journal, exercises, & special studies.

Week 20

- ▶ Read "The Revelation of Adam" (NHC V,5) & comment in Journal.
- ▶ Begin writing a short essay explaining what being a Gnostic means to you. Consider such things as your perception of Gnosticism before joining the ACP, your current perceptions, etc.
- ▶ Read CK.SM Associate Lecture #20
- ▶ Read OAA Master Architect Missive #3
- ▶ Continue Journal, exercises, & special studies.

Week 21

- ▶ Read "Authoritative Discourse" (NHC VI,3) & comment in Journal.
- ▶ Work on Essay
- ▶ Read CKSM Associate Lecture #21
- ▶ Read OAA Master Architect Missive #4
- ▶ Continue Journal, exercises, & special studies.

Lesson Plan for Holy Orders

Week 22

- ▶ Read "The Prayer of the Apostle Paul" (NHC I,1) and "The Prayer of Thanksgiving" (NHC VI,7) & comment in Journal.
- ▶ Work on Essay
- ▶ Read OAA Master Architect Missive #5
- ▶ Continue Journal, exercises, & special studies.

Week 23

- ▶ Read "The Concept of Our Great Power" (NHC VI,4) & comment in Journal.
- ▶ Finish Essay & submit paper to clergy mentor.
- ▶ Read OAA Master Architect Missive #6
- ▶ Continue Journal, exercises, & special studies.

Week 24

- ▶ Read "The Paraphrase of Shem" (NHC VII,S) & comment in Journal.
- ▶ Read "New Alliances and the Spread of the Gnostic Church" from "A Brief History of the Gnostic Church" in the HB.
- ▶ Read OAA Master Architect Missive #7
- ▶ Continue Journal, exercises, & special studies.

Week 25

- ▶ Read "The Three Steles of Seth" (NHC VII,5) & comment in Journal.
- ▶ Read "The FUDOSI Years" and "Post-War Reconstruction and the Emergence of the American Gnostic Churches" from "A Brief History of the Gnostic Church" in the HB.
- ▶ Continue Journal, exercises, & special studies.

Week 26

▶ Read "The Second Discourse of Great Seth" (NHC VII,2) – also called "The Second Treatise of the Great Seth") & comment in Journal.

▶ Finish reading "A Brief History of the Gnostic Church"

▶ Continue Journal, exercises, & special studies.

Note that in addition to the above curriculum, the Porter should also be actively participating in Mass, as well as in CKSM and OAA functions. The Liturgy should be studied carefully and frequently, and the CKSM and OAA rituals should be studied with an Initiator or other senior member. The 'special studies' referenced in the Syllabus may be any additional studies assigned by the clergy mentor. These studies may be based on certain areas of deficiency in the general knowledge of the Porter, or they may be supplementary studies based on a particular area of interest. In addition to the written exercises and exams, the Porter will also be required to submit to all of the traditional oral examinations in the CKSM and OAA, and should be able to demonstrate all of the exercises taught in the curriculum with proficiency. This is not limited to the exercises taught in the Handbook, but also those taught within the CKSM and OAA.

The 26-week format of the curriculum should be seen as a guideline, not necessarily a strict structure. While it is not anticipated that the curriculum will be finished sooner, it is perfectly acceptable to extend the length of time required for satisfactory completion. In other words, this is intended as a minimum time frame, and any extension of this time frame will in no way reflect negatively upon the student.

Lesson Plan for Holy Orders

Lector Curriculum

Materials needed

Books:

- *Hermetica* – trans. Brian Copenhaver
- *The Hermetic Tradition* – Julius Evola
- *The Invisible History of the Rosicrucians* – Tobias Churton
- Other titles as directed by clergy mentor.

Vestments:

Red & White cincture; red bandolier (sash); etc.

Syllabus

Week 1

- ▶ Read "Introduction" and "The Hermetic Philosophy" from *The Kybalion*.
- ▶ Begin reading *The Invisible History of the Rosicrucians*
- ▶ Read CK.SM Initiate Lecture #1
- ▶ Maintain your Journal and other practices and exercises.

Week 2

- ▶ Read "The Hermetic Principles" and "Mental Transmutation" from *The Kybalion*.
- ▶ Continue reading *Invisible History* and take notes.
- ▶ Read CK.SM Initiate Lecture #2
- ▶ Continue Journal and exercises

Week 3

- ▶ Read "The All" and "The Mental Universe" from *The Kybalion*.
- ▶ Continue reading *Invisible History*.

- ▶ Read CKSM Initiate Lecture #3
- ▶ Continue Journal and exercises

Week 4

- ▶ Read "The Divine Paradox" and "'The All in All" from *The Kybalion*.
- ▶ Finish reading *Invisible History*.
- ▶ Read CKSM Lecture #4
- ▶ Continue Journal and exercises

Week 5

- ▶ Read "Planes of Correspondence" from *The Kybalion*.
- ▶ Read CKSM Initiate Lecture #5
- ▶ Continue Journal and exercises

Week 6

- ▶ Read "Vibration" and "Polarity" from *The Kybalion*.
- ▶ Read CKSM Initiate Lecture #6
- ▶ Continue Journal and exercises

Week 7

- ▶ Read "Rhythm" and "Causation" from The *The Kybalion*.
- ▶ Read CKSM Initiate Lecture #7
- ▶ Continue Journal and exercises

Week 8

- ▶ Read remaining chapters of *The Kybalion*.
- ▶ Begin short essay discussing the relationship between the Seven Hermetic Principles
- ▶ Read CKSM Initiate Lecture #8
- ▶ Continue Journal and exercises

Lesson Plan for Holy Orders

Week 9

- ▶ Read Introduction to *Hermetica*
- ▶ Work on essay.
- ▶ Read CKSM Initiate Lecture #9
- ▶ Continue Journal and exercises

Week 10

- ▶ Read Corpus Hermeticum I (C.H. I) & comment in your Journal.
- ▶ Work on essay.
- ▶ Read CKSM Initiate Lecture #10
- ▶ Continue Journal and exercises

Week 11

- ▶ Read C.H. II & III and comment in your Journal.
- ▶ Work on essay.
- ▶ Read CKSM Initiate Lecture #11
- ▶ Continue Journal and exercises

Week 12

- ▶ Read C.H. IV & V and comment in your Journal.
- ▶ Finish essay and submit paper to clergy mentor.
- ▶ Read CKSM Initiate Lecture #12
- ▶ Continue Journal and exercises

Week 13

- ▶ Read C.H. VI, VII, & VIII, and comment in your Journal.
- ▶ Read CKSM Initiate Lecture #13

- ▶ Read OAA Perfect Architect Missive #1
- ▶ Continue Journal and exercises

Week 14

- ▶ Read C.H. IX & X and comment in your Journal.
- ▶ Read CKSM Initiate Lecture #14
- ▶ Read OAA Perfect Architect Missive #2
- ▶ Continue Journal and exercises

Week 15

- ▶ Read C.H. XI & XII and comment in your Journal.
- ▶ Read CKSM Initiate Lecture #15
- ▶ Read OAA Perfect Architect Missive #3
- ▶ Continue Journal and exercises

Week 16

- ▶ Read C.H. XIII & XIV and comment in your Journal.
- ▶ Read CKSM Initiate Lecture #16
- ▶ Read OAA Perfect Architect Missive #4
- ▶ Continue Journal and exercises

Week 17

- ▶ Read C.H. XVI-XVIII and comment in your Journal.
- ▶ Read CKSM Initiate Lecture #17
- ▶ Read OAA Perfect Architect Missive #5
- ▶ Continue Journal and exercises

Week 18

- ▶ Read "Asclepius" in *Hermetica* and comment in your Journal.

Lesson Plan for Holy Orders

- ▶ Read CKSM Initiate Lecture #18
- ▶ Read OAA Perfect Architect Missive #6
- ▶ Continue Journal and exercises

Week 19

- ▶ Read "The Discourse on the Eighth and Ninth" (NHC VI,6) and comment in your Journal.
- ▶ Read CKSM Initiate Lecture #19
- ▶ Read OAA Perfect Architect Missive #7
- ▶ Continue Journal and exercises

Week 20

- ▶ Read "Excerpt from the Perfect Discourse" (NHC VI,8) and comment in your Journal.
- ▶ Read CKSM Initiate Lecture #20
- ▶ Read OAA Perfect Architect Missive #8
- ▶ Continue Journal and exercises

Week 21

- ▶ Begin reading *The Hermetic Tradition*
- ▶ Read CKSM Initiate Lecture #21
- ▶ Read OAA Perfect Architect Missive #9
- ▶ Continue Journal and exercises

Week 22

- ▶ Continue reading *The Hermetic Tradition*
- ▶ Read "The Sentences of Sextus" (NHC XII,1) & comment in Journal.
- ▶ Begin writing essay for S.I. Degree
- ▶ Continue Journal and exercises, & special studies

Week 23

- Finish reading The Hermetic Tradition
- Begin reading "The Tripartite Tractate" (NHC 1,5) & comment in Journal.
- Work on S.I. essay.
- Continue Journal and exercises, & special studies

Week 24

- Finish reading "The Tripartite Tractate" (NHC 1,5) & comment in Journal.
- Work on S.I. essay.
- Continue Journal and exercises, & special studies

Week 25

- Read "The Secret Book of James" (NHC 1,2 - also called "The Apocryphon of James") & comment in Journal.
- Work on S.I. essay.
- Continue Journal and exercises, & special studies

Week 26

- Read "Exegesis on the Soul" (NHC 11,6) & comment in Journal.
- Finish on S.I. essay.
- Continue Journal and exercises, & special studies

Lesson Plan for Holy Orders

Exorcist Curriculum

<u>Materials Needed</u>

Books:

- *Eastern Mysteries & Western Mysteries (The Key of it All* vols. 1 & 2) - David Allen Hulse
- *The Mystical Qabalah* - Dion Fortune
- *Q.B.L* - Frater Achad
- *The Holy Books of Thelema* - Aleister Crowley
- *Theurgy: The Art of Effective Worship* - Mouni Sadhu
- *Grand Marvelous Secrets* by Abbé Julio
- *Sacramentaire de la Rose ✠ Croix* - Robert Ambelain
- *An Anthology of Theurgic Operations of the Rose ✠ Croix d'Orient* - Demetrius Polychronis
- *Tarot of the Magicians* by Oswald Wirth
- Additional texts will be assigned as Special Studies

Vestments:
Red Cordelier
S.I. Collar
OAA material, etc.

<u>Syllabus</u>

<u>Week 1</u>

- ▶ Read the Sepher Yetzirah and begin making comments in Journal
- ▶ Read CKSM Superior Lecture #1
- ▶ Continue Journal, exercises, and special studies

Week 2

- ▶ Read "A Gnostic Exposition of the Three Alchemical Essentials" in the HB and take careful notes and comment in your Journal
- ▶ Read CKSM Superior Lecture #2
- ▶ Read "Instructions for Censing the Temple" in the HB and practice handling Thurible with your clergy mentor.
- ▶ Continue Journal, exercises, and special studies

Week 3

- ▶ Read "Alchemy of the Eucharist" in the HB and comment in Journal
- ▶ Read CKSM Superior Lecture #3
- ▶ Continue Journal, exercises, and special studies

Week 4

- ▶ Read "An Introduction to the Theurgic Art and Instructions for Use" in the HB.
- ▶ Read CKSM Superior Lecture #4
- ▶ Continue Journal, exercises, and special studies

Week 5

- ▶ Begin reading *Theurgy* by Mouni Sadhu
- ▶ Continue studying "Theurgical Operations of the ACP"
- ▶ Read CKSM Superior Lecture #5
- ▶ Continue Journal, exercises, and special studies

Week 6

- ▶ Finish reading *Theurgy*
- ▶ Continue study and practice of Theurgical Operations
- ▶ Read CKSM Superior Lecture #6
- ▶ Continue Journal, exercises, and special studies

Lesson Plan for Holy Orders

Week 7

- Begin study of the *Sacramentary of the Rose ☩ Croix* by R. Ambelain
- Continue study and practice of Theurgical Operations
- Read CKSM Superior Lecture #7
- Continue Journal, exercises, and special studies

Week 8

- Continue study of the *Sacramentary of the Rose ☩ Croix*
- Continue study and practice of Theurgical Operations
- Read CKSM Superior Lecture #8
- Continue Journal, exercises, and special studies

Week 9

- Begin study of *An Anthology of Theurgic Operations of the Rose ☩ Croix of the Orient* by Demetrius Polychronis
- Continue study and practice of Theurgical Operations
- Read CKSM Superior Lecture #9
- Continue Journal, exercises, and special studies

Week 10

- Continue study of Anthology
- Continue study and practice of Theurgical Operations
- Read CKSM Superior Lecture #10
- Continue Journal, exercises, and special studies

Week 11

- Begin reading *The Mystical Qabalah* by Dion Fortune
- Read CKSM Superior Lecture #11
- Continue Journal, exercises, and special studies

Week 12

- ▶ Continue study of *The Mystical Qabalah*
- ▶ Read CKSM Superior Lecture #12
- ▶ Continue Journal, exercises, and special studies

Week 13

- ▶ Continue study of *The Mystical Qabalah*
- ▶ Read CKSM Superior Lecture #12
- ▶ Read OAA Perf. Initiate of the Sac. V. Missive #1
- ▶ Continue Journal, exercises, and special studies

Week 14

- ▶ Continue study of *The Mystical Qabalah*
- ▶ Read CKSM Superior Lecture #14
- ▶ Continue Journal, exercises, and special studies

Week 15

- ▶ Begin reading *Q.B.L.* by Frater Achad
- ▶ Read CKSM Superior Lecture #15
- ▶ Continue Journal, exercises, and special studies

Week 16

- ▶ Continue study of *Q.B.L.*
- ▶ Read CKSM Superior Lecture #16
- ▶ Continue Journal, exercises, and special studies

Week 17

- ▶ Discuss specialized studies with your clergy mentor.

Lesson Plan for Holy Orders

- ▶ Read CKSM Superior Lecture #17
- ▶ Continue Journal, exercises, and special studies

Week 18

- ▶ Read CKSM Superior Lecture #18
- ▶ Read OAA Perf. Initiate of the Sac. V. Missive #2
- ▶ Continue Journal, exercises, and special studies

Week 19

- ▶ Read CKSM Superior Lecture #19
- ▶ Continue Journal, exercises, and special studies

Week 20

- ▶ Read CKSM Superior Lecture #20
- ▶ Continue Journal, exercises, and special studies

Week 21

- ▶ Read CKSM Superior Lecture #21
- ▶ Read OAA Perf. Initiate of the Sac. V. Missive #3
- ▶ Continue Journal, exercises, and special studies

Week 22

- ▶ Read CKSM Superior Lecture #22
- ▶ Continue Journal, exercises, and special studies

Week 23

- ▶ Read CKSM Superior Lecture #23

ACP Clergy Handbook

▶ Continue Journal, exercises, and special studies

Week 24

- ▶ Read CKSM Superior Lecture #24
- ▶ Read OAA Perf. Initiate of the Sac. V. Missive #4
- ▶ Continue Journal, exercises, and special studies

Week 25

- ▶ Read CKSM Superior Lecture #25
- ▶ Continue Journal, exercises, and special studies

Week 26

- ▶ Read CKSM Superior Lecture #26
- ▶ Continue Journal, exercises, and special studies

Week 27

- ▶ Begin study of The Holy Books of Thelema
- ▶ Read CKSM Superior Lecture #27
- ▶ Read OAA Kn. of the East & West Missive #1
- ▶ Continue Journal, exercises, and special studies

Week 28-39

- ▶ Begin study of the *Tarot of the Magicians* by Oswald Wirth
- ▶ Read CKSM Superior Lecture #28-39
- ▶ Continue Journal, exercises, and special studies

Week 40

- ▶ Take Exorcist Exam

Lesson Plan for Holy Orders

Acolyte Curriculum

<u>Materials Needed</u>

Books:

- *Basics of Biblical Greek* (Grammar & Workbook) by William D. Mounce
- Greek lexicons (BDAG, etc.) & other reference materials
- *The Gnostic Paul* & other exegetical works by Eline Pagels et al.
- Other scholarly & exegetical texts to be determined in cooperation with clergy mentor

Vestments:

- KSM Tunic, etc.
- OAA materials as directed.

<u>Syllabus</u>

<u>Weeks 1-9</u>

- Study Mounce's *Basics of Biblical Greek*
- Read CKSM R✠C Martinist/KSM special lectures
- Read OAA Knight R✠C Missives #1-9
- Continue journal, exercises, & independent study

<u>Weeks 10-13</u>

- Continue study of *Basics of Biblical Greek*
- Continue special CKSM studies.
- Discuss ideas for exegetical work with clergy mentor
- Continue journal, exercises, & independent study

Sub-diaconate Curriculum

<u>Materials Needed</u>

Discuss with clergy mentor.

<u>Syllabus</u>

<u>Weeks 1-10</u>

- Continue study of *Basics of Biblical Greek*
- Work on exegetical paper (5,000 words)
- Read OAA Knight of the Red Eagle Missives #1-10
- Continue journal, exercises, special CKSM studies, etc.

<u>Weeks 11-13</u>

- Complete study of *Basics of Biblical Greek*
- Finish exegetical paper
- Continue journal, exercises, & special studies.

Lesson Plan for Holy Orders

Diaconate Curriculum

Materials needed

Books:

- *The Science of the Sacraments* by C.W. Leadbeater
- Other works as determined with clergy mentor.

Vestments:

- Diaconate vestments
- CKSM & OAA materials as directed

Syllabus

Week 1

- ▶ Begin reading *The Science of the Sacraments*
- ▶ Read CKSM Maître Cohen Lecture #1
- ▶ Read OAA Knight Kadosh Missive #1
- ▶ Continue journal, exercises, & special studies

Week 2

- ▶ Continue reading *The Science of the Sacraments*
- ▶ Read CKSM Maître Cohen Lecture #2
- ▶ Read OAA Knight Kadosh Missive #2
- ▶ Continue journal, exercises, & special studies

Week 3

- ▶ Continue reading *The Science of the Sacraments*
- ▶ Read CKSM Maître Cohen Lecture #3 & begin practice of the "Office"
- ▶ Read OAA Knight Kadosh Missive #3
- ▶ Continue journal, exercises, & special studies

Week 4

- ▶ Continue study of *The Science of the Sacraments*
- ▶ Read CKSM Maître Cohen Lecture #4
- ▶ Read OAA Knight Kadosh Missive #4
- ▶ Continue journal, exercises, Cohen practices, etc.

Week 5

- ▶ Continue study of *The Science of the Sacraments*
- ▶ Read CKSM Maître Cohen Lecture #5
- ▶ Read OAA Knight Kadosh Missive #5
- ▶ Continue journal, exercises, Cohen practices, etc.

Week 6

- ▶ Continue study of *The Science of the Sacraments*
- ▶ Read CKSM Maître Cohen Lecture #6
- ▶ Continue journal, exercises, Cohen practices, etc.

Week 7

- ▶ Continue study of *The Science of the Sacraments*
- ▶ Read CKSM Maître Cohen Lecture #7
- ▶ Continue journal, exercises, Cohen practices, etc.

Week 8

- ▶ Continue study of *The Science of the Sacraments*
- ▶ Read CKSM Maître Cohen Lecture #8
- ▶ Continue journal, exercises, Cohen practices, etc.

Week 9

- ▶ Discuss specialized curriculum with clergy mentor
- ▶ Read CKSM Maître Cohen Lecture #9
- ▶ Continue journal, exercises, Cohen practices, etc.

Lesson Plan for Holy Orders

Weeks 10-17

- ▶ Continue specialized studies.
- ▶ Read CKSM Maître Cohen Lectures 10-17
- ▶ Continue journal, exercises, Cohen operations

Weeks 18-23

- ▶ Continue specialized studies
- ▶ Read OAA Prince of the Royal Secret Missives #1-6
- ▶ Continue journal, exercises, Cohen operations, etc.

Weeks 24-52

- ▶ Continue all studies & practices.

The curriculum associated with the Presbyterate and Episcopate, along with the studies & practices of the higher degrees of the CKSM & OAA are revealed only to those entering into these orders & degrees.

PART I

THEORY

I would that their hearts may be encouraged, having been united in agape, and in the wealth of the full assurance of Understanding in the Knowledge of the Mystery of God, Christ, in whom are all the hidden treasuries of Wisdom and Gnosis.

- Colossians 2:2-3

A Theoretical Foundation For Gnostic Philosophy

What is Gnosticism?

What at first seems to be a simple and straight forward question, necessitating a simple and straight forward answer, has in fact been answered in so many varied and divers ways so as to seem utterly meaningless to the indiscriminate researcher. Gnosticism has been described as a religious philosophy, a political philosophy, a conspiracy of the elite, an egalitarian utopianism, Christian, pre-Christian, non-Christian, anti-Christian, etc. Rather than address each of the various approaches to Gnosticism, we will instead give our own definitions, which will serve for internal consistency among the teachings, liturgies, and rites of the Apostolic Church of the Pleroma. We shall begin, then, by examining some definitions from the *American Heritage Dictionary of the English Language* (Fourth Edition. Boston: Houghton Mifflin Co. 2006).

- ▶ gnosis - n. Intuitive apprehension of spiritual truths, an esoteric form of knowledge sought by the Gnostics. (Gr. gnosis, knowledge).

- ▶ Gnosticism - n. The doctrines of certain pre-Christian pagan, Jewish, and early Christian sects that valued the revealed knowledge of God and of the origin and end of the human race as a means to attain redemption for the spiritual element in humans and that distinguished the demiurge from the unknowable Divine Being.

These are excellent definitions, and in complete concert with their usage by the ACP. They are, however, general definitions, so some expansion will be necessary to show the fullness of their meanings in the context of the ACP and the modem Gnostic Apostolic movement as a whole. Let us begin first with the word "gnosis." We are told that it means an "intuitive apprehension of spiritual truths." It is often referred to as a "revelatory knowledge." That is, a knowledge that cannot be learned through ordinary means, such as reading a book, or listening to an oration. The special type of knowledge that we call "gnosis" is revealed to the mind of the aspirant only during those rare times when the body is subdued and the soul is very nearly perfectly attuned to the higher Spiritual Mind. This condition, or state of mind, however fleeting, can have a profound and permanent impact upon the individual. It is during these times of perfect silence and clarity that the mysteries of the universe and of Self are revealed to the worthy. Remember that gnosis is attained only through your own direct experiences, and that no person or group can impart gnosis to you.

What, then, is the purpose of a Gnostic Church if not to impart gnosis? This question can be addressed through a consideration of the term, "Gnosticism." There is nothing in the dictionary definition of Gnosticism that we will disagree with. There is, though, much that we can add to the given definition. The dictionary definition mentions a set of doctrines, but offers little in the way of an explanation or elaboration of these doctrines. It is the purpose of the Gnostic Church to preserve these doctrines, and to transmit them to future generations. It is also the purpose of the Church to help lead her faithful toward the path to gnosis. She does this by means of her Holy Sacraments, as prescribed by Jesus Christ. The Church also serves to establish a community of like-minded individuals. This helps to foster a sense of fraternity, and to ensure her continuity. To be sure, our primary objective is the attainment of gnosis. But Gnosticism, as a religion, is a rich doctrinal, sacramental, and fraternal tradition, whose core principles have been passed down for millennia, but which is also a living tradition, enriched by the lives and works of those who have walked the Gnostic path and have shared with us, as best they could, their gnostic revelations.

Another point concerning Gnosticism that we should consider early on is how "pre-Christian pagan, Jewish, and early Christian" doctrines can be reconciled under a single system. This reconciliation is really not as difficult to achieve as it might first appear. These elements exist, in fact, within so-called orthodox Christianity. Firstly, it is commonly known and understood that Christianity developed directly out of certain Jewish sects. Secondly, it is also true, though perhaps somewhat less known, that Greek philosophy, especially Neo-Platonism, was fused into Christianity by the early Church fathers, including St. Augustine. These pagan and Jewish elements of Christianity are not seen as foreign or exotic additions, but rather as integral aspects of the religion. It is very much the same with Gnosticism, except that we may look to their mystical counterparts. That is, the most recognizable pagan aspect of Gnosticism is the Greco-Egyptian mystical tradition of Hermeticism. This is true not only for the ACP, but for classical Gnosticism as well, as evidenced by the presence of Hermetic texts among Gnostic collections such as the Nag Hammadi Library. The Jewish element in Gnosticism is a little more complicated. The details will become more clear as we explore the various Gnostic doctrines more in depth. Suffice it to say for now that within the doctrines of classical Gnosticism, the Jewish Gnostics held a radically different understanding of God than their mainstream counterparts. This unique understanding caused them to interpret many aspects of Scripture in a way that often seems diametrically opposed to the orthodox interpretation. These early Jewish Gnostics probably had more in common, philosophically, with the Alexandrian Hermeticists, and even certain Indo-Persian traditions, than with their mainstream Jewish counterparts. Indeed, these Hermetic and Jewish Gnostic doctrines would eventually be united in Christian Gnosticism. Another form of mystical Judaism, Qabalah, developed later, but shares many philosophical doctrines with the earlier movements; and is embraced and taught, in one form or another, by many modern Gnostic movements.

Some may wonder still how such varied and sometimes seemingly divergent ideas and philosophies can cohabitate under the roof of Gnosticism. The answer is that many religious and philosophical doctrines are not as different or contradictory as they might first appear. In fact, there are a number of fundamental principles that underlie many of the world's religions and mystical traditions. These principles will be revealed to you throughout your studies, ordinations, and initiations, and illustrated with examples from Gnostic and Hermetic scriptures, as well as from the orthodox canon.

Jesus Christ was a revealer of gnosis and is the great Reconciler and Mediator. So too is His Holy Gnostic and Apostolic Church a reconciler of many a great spiritual paradox. Just as Jesus communicated his most profound teachings in the form of parables, Gnosticism is a system of myth and symbol. It must be stated emphatically that Gnosticism is adogmatic. Certainly, Gnosticism has doctrines. And the various Gnostic churches have their own unique doctrines as well. But although these doctrines are cherished and preserved from one generation to the next, they are still but signposts; symbols of the Great Truth, but not the Truth itself. No doctrine, no matter how revered and sublime, can ever be a replacement for the Truth and Wisdom received through gnostic revelation. And as the aspirant progresses, the truth of many of our revered teachings and doctrines will be made known through the Light of Gnosis.

On the Nature of God

It may seem, upon our initial consideration, that it is a futile exercise to contemplate the nature of God; akin to counting the drops of water in the ocean. But our own nature compels us to ask questions regarding the nature and workings of Divinity. So, we approach this subject knowing that an absolute knowledge of God is not possible for us, yet reason enables us to infer certain things. To begin with, we will examine the major religious philosophies. We turn, once again, to the American Heritage Dictionary of the English Language for the definitions of certain terms. As with previous definitions, we will comment on them and elaborate upon the definitions as necessary. The terms of religious philosophy that we are looking at are: Deism, Theism, and Pantheism.

- ▶ deism - n. The belief, based solely on reason, in a God who created the universe and then abandoned it, assuming no control over life, exerting no influence on natural phenomena, and giving no supernatural revelation. (Fr. deism; Lat. deus)
- ▶ theism - n. Belief in the existence of god or gods, especially belief in a personal God as creator and ruler of the world. (Gr. theos)
- ▶ pantheism - n. A doctrine identifying the Deity with the universe and its phenomena. (Gr. pan + theos)

To determine where the Gnostic concept of God fits in, let us consider each doctrine in relation to what the Gnostic scriptures have to say on the matter. Deism asserts that God is absent in the universe, having no effect whatsoever upon its inhabitants. We may dismiss the deistic approach almost immediately, for the very idea of gnostic revelation necessitates a divine presence. The Gnostics often use the term "Unknown Father" as an appellation of the Most High which, at first glance, might seem to be in accord with the deistic view. However, the supreme God of the Gnostics is unknown because it is illimitable and ineffable, and therefore unknowable by our finite physical and mental faculties. Whereas, the deistic God is unknown because its presence in the universe simply does not exist. The relationship between a deistic God and the manifest universe may be represented by the following diagram:

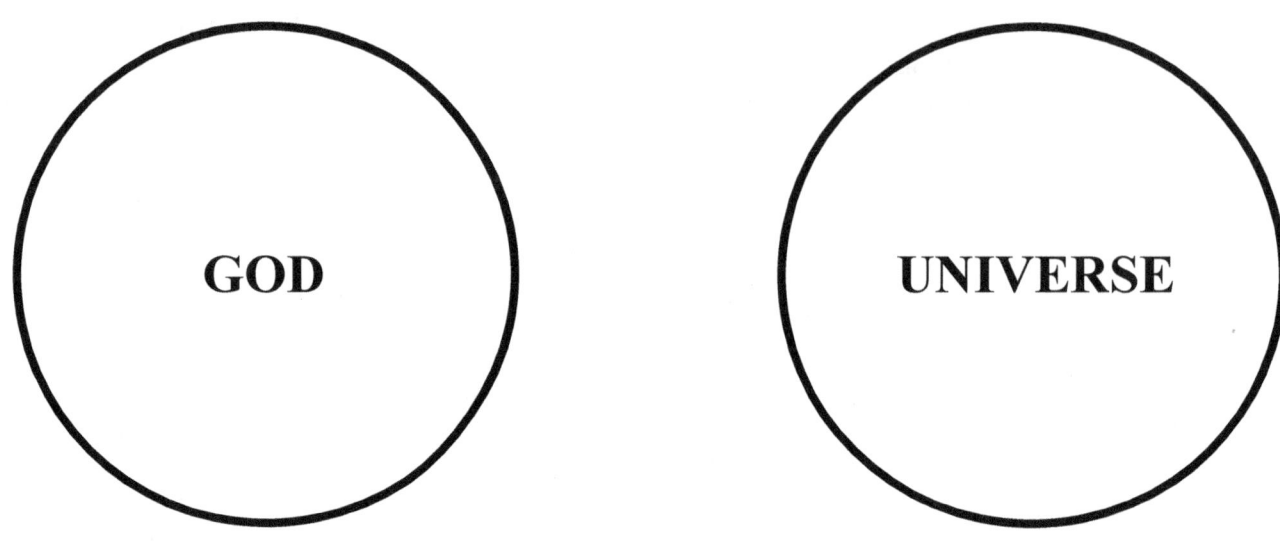

Next, we will consider theism. Theism is the predominant religious philosophy among the orthodox sects of Judaism, Christianity, and Islam. The theistic God is an anthropomorphic god, having human attributes such as jealousy, anger, wrath, and hatred. This God is seen as a being who is separate from His creation, yet who interacts regularly with the created universe. While the theistic doctrine certainly allows for mystical revelation, the God of the Gnostics bears little resemblance to this personal God of the theists. In the *Secret Book of John* (*The Gnostic Bible*. New Seeds, 2003. pp. 138-165) the Most High is called the One or Monad. We will discuss this in much greater detail a little later, but I will state here that the attributes associated with the "One" are not compatible with an anthropomorphic god. In fact, other than stating that it is an invisible spirit, and a pure and incorruptible light, it can only be described by what it is not, rather than what it is. Some of the words used are: illimitable, unfathomable, immeasurable, eternal, unutterable, and unnamable. Similar descriptions are given in the Corpus Hermeticum. So, before moving on, let us say that the relationship between the theistic God and the universe is thus:

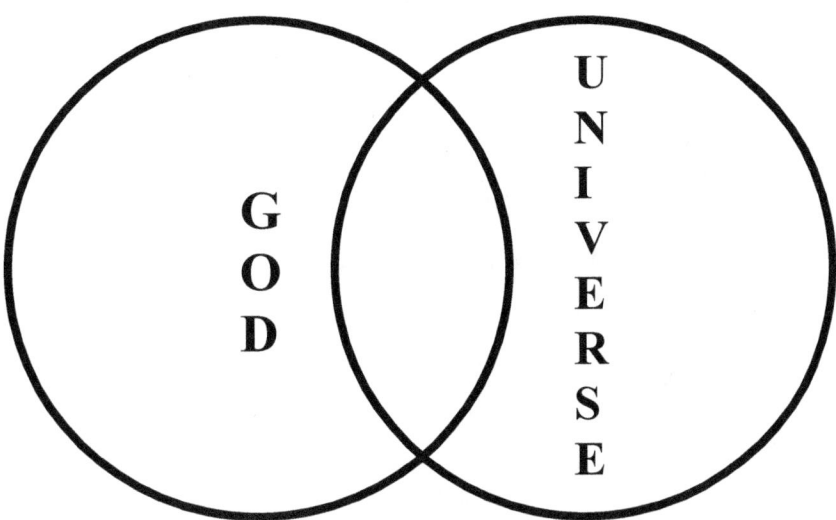

So, in our attempt to discover which religious philosophy best describes the Gnostic view of God, we have quickly eliminated deism, and with a little consideration can eliminate the theistic perspective as well. This leaves us with pantheism, which, as we shall see, will bring us much closer to the Gnostic doctrine, yet may still lack certain essential qualities. Our dictionary definition of pantheism, while not inaccurate, leaves us wanting for a more substantial explanation. The basic premise of pantheism is that all is God. That is, God is equal to the totality of the universe and the phenomena within the universe. Pantheism is most prevalent in Eastern religions such as Buddhism, and the Vedic traditions, known to us collectively as Hinduism. Do not believe, mistakenly, that Hinduism is a polytheistic religion, although it may appear so on the surface. Polytheism is a form of theism. That is, all of the characteristics of the theistic god are present in multiple gods. When there is only one such being, we call it monotheism. As we have stated, though, Hinduism is not a theistic religion, it is pantheistic. This is because the various "gods" are but really myriad manifestations of Brahman. Brahman is the name given to the all-pervading creative essence in the universe. We will not engage in an elaboration of the Vedic religions, which would be lengthy and outside the scope of this brief survey, but you will notice throughout your studies that the venerable mystical traditions of India have a great deal in common with many Gnostic teachings and doctrines. The relationship, then, between a pantheistic god, and the universe may be represented as so:

Theory: Theoretical Foundation

    Of the three major religious philosophies we have discussed, the Gnostic God of Light seems most similar to the latter, pantheism. There is, however, another word that is sometimes used that even better expresses the Gnostic perspective. It is panentheism. Panentheism is the doctrine that states that God is in all, and all is in God. It is very similar to pantheism, but does not confine God to the totality of the universe. The panentheistic God is truly without limit, being both immanent and transcendent. In this doctrine, the known universe may be but a speck in the wholeness of God. Panentheism may be seen as a subset of pantheism, just as monotheism and polytheism are subsets of theism. These designations do not, of course, offer a comprehensive view of the details of the god or gods of any particular religion, but they do provide a general description, and a basis from which a broader study can be made. Before moving on, here is a diagram that represents the panentheistic relationship of God to the Universe:

ACP Clergy Handbook

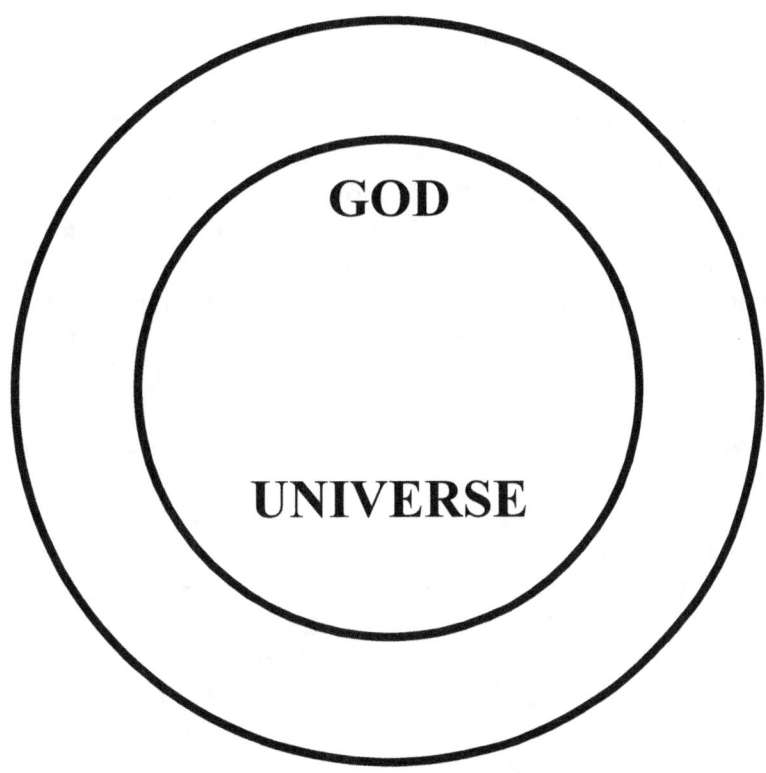

Gnostic Mythology

On the Nature of the Holy Trinity

Now that we have established a philosophical basis for the nature of God, let us delve more deeply into the specific ways that God manifests itself to the Gnostics. As mentioned previously, the supreme expression of the divine is known throughout the Gnostic and Hermetic texts as the One, the All, Incorruptible Light, Unknown Father, and other equally grand, yet ambiguous designations. One may see terms such as "Father" and believe that some anthropomorphic deity is being referred to. This is not the case, though. The term "Father" is used not to mean some sort of male being, for God, to the Gnostics, is androgynous, containing all things. The word "Father" is used to express the active, generative process of the divine. The personification of this process is used so that we mortal beings might be able to more easily comprehend the mechanics of divinity. The Father is the source of all the things that are. The Father gives all and receives nothing, for all things are in Him, and there is nothing that He lacks.

Just as there is a masculine, paternal expression of the Divine, so is there a feminine and maternal expression. This Holy Mother is known to the Gnostics as Barbelo, or the Holy Spirit. And although the Holy Spirit is considered feminine it also is sometimes designated as "triple-male" denoting its power. The Holy Spirit is the cosmic womb, and the mother of all that exists. Just as the pure Will of God issues forth from the Father, it is the Mother that, in fact, makes that Will manifest. And as the Father is the Monad, the Mother represents duality. Everything is dual in nature, and this duality is expressed through the Holy Spirit. It is for this reason that Barbelo, the Mother, is also sometimes called Mother-Father. The Gnostic text Thunder is a classic example of the duality of the feminine Deity. In Thunder, Barbelo makes a series of "I am" statements that are apparently contradictory, or in opposition to each other. What they intend to show, however, is that She is all of these things simultaneously; that one without the other is only a half-truth. This duality, and its reconciliation, is a common theme throughout the Gnostic texts. For example, the Gospel of Philip states that the "Holy Spirit is a double name."

There is one final aspect of God to consider, that is the Divine Child, also called the Logos, the Son, Savior, and Christos. First we will look at these various appellations, and why they apply. The Child is called so because He is the Seed, which is projected by the Will of God, and brought forth through the Mother. He is the Logos, or Word of God, who was one with the Father; but is also called Autogenes, or self-conceived, because the Logos issued forth by the pure Will of God, and Himself embodies the very essence and nature of the wholeness of God. And because He has been anointed by the Holy Spirit, He is called Christos, or Christ. This third aspect of God, the Son, is the means by which the host of Holy Realms, called Aeons, and the divine beings which inhabit those realms, are brought into being. The Aeons are, in fact, expressions or emanations of the Logos. The opening chapter of the Gospel According to John states: "In the beginning was the Logos, and the Logos was with God, and the Logos was God. This one was in the beginning with God. Through Him all things came to be, and without Him came to be not one thing." Likewise, Hebrews 1:2 refers to Christ as, "The Son whom he appointed the heir of all, through whom he also made the Aeons."

This, then, is the Holy Trinity. The Father sends forth His seed, His Holy Logos who, through the Holy Spirit, makes manifest the Divine Realms, which we shall discuss shortly. It is an ancient teaching which states that everything is One is essence, Dual in nature, and Triune in manifestation. This is the mystery of the Thee-in-One. The Holy Trinity can also be seen in the three alchemical Essentials: Sulphur, Mercury, and Salt. For further elaboration on these correspondences, see "A Gnostic Exposition of the Three Alchemical Essentials."

The Aeons

We will now move on to discuss the first emanations of God, which are the Holy and Eternal Realms, or Aeons. And while these supernal realms are known as Aeons, the beings that govern and reside within and among these realms are also called Aeons. In truth, these emanations are of such a pure and divine nature that both their *state of existence* and the *nature of their being*, are really indistinguishable at this stage.

Because such a perfect and primitive state cannot be known by us perfectly, and because such a state cannot be categorized without Tault, there have been a number of accounts related to us having slight (or even considerable) variations. Some accounts list many Aeons, and many Aeons within Aeons, while other accounts describe relatively few groupings. The variations can be examined through an exploration of the Gnostic scriptures, and the teachings of the Gnostic Fathers. Here we will give a simple account which is consistent with the bulk of Sethian sources; and I will avoid, for the time being, the multitudinous elaborations that may be found in various Gnostic teachings.

But before delving into descriptions of the Gnostic Aeons, let us look at the various uses of the word "Aeon" within the orthodox canon. As mentioned before, the term has meaning related to both space and time, and even personifications. At times the intended meaning may be clear, but in many cases, the ambiguity of the word serves to imply multiple readings simultaneously.

Let us look first at 1 Corinthians 2:6-7, which states, "Wisdom we speak among the initiated, though not a wisdom of this aeon, nor of the archons of this aeon, who are being brought to naught. But we speak God's wisdom in a Mystery, having been hidden, which God predestined before the aeons for our glory."

The preceding passage is rich with Gnostic symbolism and imagery, but for now let us look only at how the term "aeon" (Gr. αιωνος; - aionos) is used. The word is usually translated as "age" in this example. But we can also see how it can refer to a realm, or state of existence.

Let us look at another example, Hebrews 1:2, "At the end of these days, He spoke to us by the Son, whom he appointed heir of all, through whom he also made the aeons."

Now, in this case many translators have chosen to translate aeon as "worlds" while some others offer "ages" as their preferred translation. Neither translation is necessarily wrong, but neither one is necessarily complete either.

Here is one further example, in John 6:54, "The one feeding on my flesh and drinking my blood has aeonic life, and I will raise him up on the last day."

Here, it is common practice to translate aeonic as "eternal." This is probably the primary intention here, but given the depth of meaning of the word "aeon," we cannot really separate "eternal life" from "life in the eternal realms." Furthermore, this "aeonic life" is not merely referring to the continuity of consciousness beyond this particular incarnation. It is the state of supreme gnostic liberation that is in fact attainable in this lifetime. This phrase appears many, many times throughout the gospels as well as the epistles. As we examine the Gnostic use of the term "aeon," we will see that it may apply to entities, as well as time and space. Let us return now to our exposition of the Aeons in Gnostic thought.

After the Holy Trinity, the next Aeons to follow are grouped under four classes, or levels. These four categories, or Aeons of Aeons, are each ruled by an emissary of the Most High, called a Luminary. The first Luminary is Harmozel. The Aeons under the providence of Harmozel are called: Grace, Truth, and Form. The second Great Luminary is Oroiael. The Aeons attributed to Oroiael are: Afterthought, Perception, and Memory. The third of the four Luminaries is known as Daveithai, whose Aeons are called: Understanding, Love, and Idea. Finally, the fourth Eternal Luminary is Eleleth. The Aeons associated with Eleleth are: Perfection, Peace, and Wisdom; that is, Sophia.

These four Luminaries and the twelve Aeons associated with those Luminaries, along with the Holy Trinity, make up the Pleroma, or Fullness of God. The word "pleroma" (πληρωμα) literally means "fullness" or "that which is full of something." As used in Gnostic philosophy, the Pleroma refers to the completeness of God and the Spiritual Realms. Here are a few examples of how this term is used in the canonical scriptures:

- John 1:16 - "Because from His Pleroma we all received, even grace upon grace."
- Colossians 1:19 - "For in Him all the Pleroma was pleased to dwell."
- Colossians 2:8-9 - "Beware, lest any of you be taken captive through philosophy and empty deceit according to the tradition of men, according to the elemental spirits of the cosmos and not according to Christ. Because in Him dwells bodily, all the Pleroma of God."

Geradamas and Seth

The Luminaries and Aeons are emanations, or expressions of the Logos; the Word which is the self-conceived Divine Child. When the Aeonic hierarchies were complete, God created the Heavenly Man, known as Adamas or Geradamas (or Pigeradamas). Now remember, when we say "God" we mean the three aspects of the Trinity working together. The following account is given in the Secret Book of John, with explanatory comments in brackets: "From the Foreknowledge of the perfect mind [Holy Spirit, Barbelo, Mother], through the expressed will of the Invisible Spirit [Unknown Father] and the will of the self-conceived one [Logos, Christ, Son] came the perfect human, the First revelation, the truth." This primitive, androgynous, and perfect human is called Geradamas (or Pigeradamas or Adamas in some works) and is appointed to dwell with Harmozel in the first Aeon, or Eternal Realm.

Geradamas, through the Holy Spirit, then begets the heavenly Seth. Seth is appointed to the second Aeon with the Luminary Oroiael, and is considered to be the spiritual father of the Gnostics. The third Eternal Realm is reserved for those who seek and attain gnosis, known in the Gnostic scriptures as the "offspring of Seth." They will reside with the Luminary Daveithai. Those who remain ignorant of the Pleroma, but who eventually come to see their error and repent, will come to be with the Luminary Eleleth in the fourth Aeon. This completes, then, a basic and fundamental account of the Aeons and their inhabitants. Again, there are variations on this hierarchy; some texts and traditions elaborate greatly upon the scheme given here. At this time, though, it is really only necessary to have a grasp of the fundamental structure, as all other compatible models are based on this.

The Fall of Sophia and the Rise of the Demiurge

Now we will focus on the fall of Sophia from the Pleroma, the creation of the Demiurge and his archons, and the response of the Aeonic realms to these atrocities. According to our Gnostic scriptures, Sophia, the last of the Aeons to come into being, desired to create something similar to herself. The Secret Book of John states that her desire was considered, "without the knowledge of her partner." This implies that in her considerations, she did not utilize the proper mixture of masculine and feminine creative principles. Because of her error, the being she brought forth was imperfect. Being ashamed of having ignorantly produced an imperfect being, she sought to hide her error so that her immortal peers would not know what she had done. Sophia immediately cast her deformed creation out of her Aeon and "surrounded it with a bright cloud and put a throne in the middle of the cloud so that no one would see it." She could not, however, hide her offspring from the Holy Spirit, "who is called mother of the living." Sophia calls her creation Yaldabaoth, meaning, "child of chaos." Yaldabaoth, being ignorant of his divine origin, and assuming himself to be the sole being, is also called Sakla, meaning "foolish" and Samael, meaning "blind god" or "god of the blind."

Yaldabaoth, then, is the first being to exist outside of the Pleroma. Now, one may wonder how, if God is All, and the Pleroma is the fullness of God, anything at all can exist "outside" of that fullness. It is better to think of it as a state of being, rather than a particular location in space-time. That is, the Pleroma represents the state of perfect equilibrium. Whereas, being "outside" the Pleroma means to be out of harmony with that perfect equilibrium. And since these states of being exist outside of space-time, the Pleroma exists in potentiality in both its broken and restored states simultaneously, depending on the plane of existence from which it is observed or experienced. Thus, Yaldabaoth is a personification of the principle of unawareness due to incompletion. That is not to say that the Demiurge is fundamentally "evil," but rather incomplete, and thus falling short of perfection.

Even though the Demiurge was an imperfect creation, he nevertheless had an innate desire to create, and a flawed imprint of the divine hierarchies of the Pleroma. He had inherited this creative power from his mother, though he was ignorant of this. And like his mother, he proceeded to create by himself; imperfect creations from an imperfect creator. The appellation of "Demiurge" comes from the Greek *demiourgos* (δημιουργος), meaning builder, maker, or craftsman. The word "archon" also comes from the Greek (αρχων), and means "ruler." Yaldabaoth, then, is Demiurge and chief archon of this world, the cosmos. The following is an account of those creations.

The first creations of the Demiurge were twelve authorities, or archons. The following are the names given in the *Secret Book of John*, with the variations given in the *Gospel of the Egyptians* (or *The Holy Book of the Great Invisible Spirit*) in brackets:

1. Athoth (also called the reaper)
2. Harmas (the jealous eye) [eye of the fire]
3. Kalila-Oumbri [Galila]
4. Yabel [Yobel]
5. Adonaios (also called Sabaoth)
6. Cain (called the sun)
7. Abel
8. Abrisene [Akiressina]
9. Yobel [Yubel]
10. Armoupieel [Harmoupiael]
11. Melcheir-Adonein [Archir-Adonin]
12. Belias (who presides over the depth of Hades)

It is said that Yaldabaoth placed seven kings over the seven heavenly spheres, that is, the seven planets of the ancients; and five to reign over the depth of the Abyss. We also see a correlation here to the twelve houses of the zodiac circle; and to our musical scale which has seven whole tones and five half tones.

Seven Powers were created to rule the seven days of the week. The seven powers were united by Yaldabaoth with the archons of the seven heavenly spheres. Here are the names of the seven powers, along with the designations given them by Yaldabaoth:

1. Athoth - goodness
2. Eloaios - forethought
3. Astaphaios - divinity
4. Iao - lordship
5. Sabaoth - kingdom

6. Adonin - jealousy
7. Sabbataios – understanding

Now, it must be understood that attributes such as goodness, forethought, divinity, etc., are but shadowy imitations of the heavenly archetypes, or ideals. Because Sophia was his mother, the pattern of the original Pleroma was within the Demiurge, although he was ignorant of it. Therefore, even in his ignorance he was able to produce a grand and elaborate hierarchy of beings and realms. The realms below, then are like a distorted reflection of the realms above; that is, the Pleroma.

Sophia began to worry when she realized that her son had taken some of her power, and she became angry and ashamed. It is said that the entire Pleroma heard her prayer of repentance and plead to the Most High on her behalf. The Holy Spirit then pours forth a portion of the Pleroma unto Sophia that she might be aided. Sophia is not allowed to remain in the Pleroma, however. Rather, she is placed in the Ninth Heaven, above her son, between the worlds below and the worlds above, until she reclaims that which was taken from her. In this we see an example of a common theme which appears even in some less obviously Gnostified texts, such as the allegory of the "Hymn of the Pearl," also known as the "Hym of the Robe of Glory," found in the *Acts of Thomas*.

The Creation and Exile of Adam

Next we learn that the Holy Spirit, Barbelo, appears in the heavens, and shows Yaldabaoth and his archons the image of Geradamas, the First Human. I think we may assume that Barbelo knew exactly what Yaldabaoth would do next here, and was actually counting on it in order to fulfill the plan of the restoration of the Pleroma. When Yaldabaoth saw this, he gathered his archons and set about creating a human in the image of what he supposed was God. He did not know of the Most High because he was ignorant of the Pleroma. So, when he saw the image of a being that was greater than himself, he mistook it for the supreme God. Yaldabaoth and the archons set about creating a psychical Adam, or soul-man. The seven principal archons created seven souls as follows:

- Athoth - Soul of Bone
- Eloaios - Soul of Sinew
- Astaphaios - Soul of Flesh
- Iao - Soul of Marrow
- Sabaoth - Soul of Blood
- Adonin - Soul of Skin
- Sabbataios - Soul of Hair

These seven psychical substances were then .given to 365 lesser angels who each created a separate part of the body. The *Secret Book of John* then lists hundreds of angels and demons who create and activate the various parts and aspects of the human. After the psychical body was completed, however, it remained inanimate, for it lacked pneuma (πνευμα), which means both *spirit* and *breath*, which is the Vital Life Force.

Continuing her plan to help Sophia reclaim her usurped power, Barbelo sends five luminaries to advise Yaldabaoth to breathe some of his spirit (which is actually Sophia's) into Adam's face. He does so and unwittingly releases Sophia's stolen power into the psychical body of Adam. Adam then arises, and having been fashioned after the heavenly Man, and animated with Spirit, he is more intelligent and more powerful than Yaldabaoth or the archons that assembled him. (NB: I am referring to Adam as "him" here, but Adam is in fact androgynous, just as is the heavenly Geradamas. The use of the pronoun "he" is merely a convenience.) The archons are understandably threatened by this and promptly cast Adam into the lowest part of the material world so that he might be more easily subdued. However, Barbelo comes to Adam's aid by sending a helper, sometimes also considered to be the daughter of Sophia, called Zoe (Ζωη), meaning "life." According to the *Secret Book of John*, Zoe, "helped the whole creature, laboring with it, restoring it to its fullness, teaching it about the descent of the seed, teaching it about the way of ascent, which is the way of descent."

Remember now, that at this point Adam is still in a psychical, or soul-body form. However, the archons quickly formulate a plan to imprison Adam in the material form. It is said that they formed a body out of the four material elements: Fire, Water, Air, and Earth. This body is referred to in the *Secret Book of John* as "the fetters of forgetfulness," because the darkness of matter causes Adam to become ignorant, and to forget his origins. The archons placed Adam in a false paradise and encouraged him to eat leisurely. That is, the archons sought to keep Adam distracted with fleshly pleasures so that he would not question the nature of his being; that is to say, his essential being rather than his physical garment, which darkens the mind's eye and leads, ultimately, to decay and death. This does not mean that the physical elements are bad in and of themselves; but a preoccupation of the material to the exclusion of the spiritual is what leads to decay. Embedded within matter is the principle of entropy. Or perhaps it would be better to say that entropy is the result of divorcing spirit – the source of Eternal Life – from matter. The soul, therefore, as the mediating element, when united with spirit, has the ability to halt and even reverse physical entropy. This is the key to health and equilibrium.

Adam and Eve in the Garden

The Demiurge, Yaldabaoth, then seeks to extract Zoe, who is also called "enlightened afterthought," from Adam so that Adam will not gain full consciousness, and so that Yaldabaoth can apprehend Zoe's power for himself. So the Demiurge then removes a portion of Adam's power and puts it into a figure that he has fashioned after the form of Zoe, or Afterthought. The once-androgynous Adam is now divided into male and female. The male is called Adam after the androgynous Adam, and the female is called Eve, or Zoe (life) after the enlightened afterthought of Barbelo, the Celestial Mother. In other words, Man (humanity – male & female) has fallen into a state of forgetfulness and unawareness because of the separation of the higher Intuitive faculty (Zoe/Eve) from the Intellectual faculty (Adam). We learn in the Gnostic writings that the incorporeal Zoe is actually Sophia, or an aspect of Sophia, who has descended to reclaim that which was lost. As the demiurge is making his attempts at the apprehension of Zoe, she leaves Adam and appears in the garden as the Tree of Knowledge of Good and Evil. Now, in Gnostic mythology, it is not the Tree of

Knowledge that brings death, but rather all of the other trees in this false paradise. And the one who induces Adam and Eve to partake of the fruit is not the adversary, but rather the revealer of Gnosis. In some works the revealer is the Logos, who appears in the form of an eagle; in other works, the instructor is the serpent, who is feminine and may be related to Barbelo, the Holy Spirit. It is interesting to note that both the eagle and the serpent are symbols associated with the zodiacal sign of Scorpio, which is the sign associated with initiation into the higher mysteries. So, it is made clear that the true God of Light came, or sent emissaries, to awaken Adam and Eve from their mortal ignorance, into the Light of Gnosis. In the *Gospel of Truth* we read that Christ himself is the fruit of the Tree of Knowledge. Thus, Adam and Eve partaking of the fruit of the Tree of Knowledge is a precursor to, and typological symbol of, the sacrament of the Eucharist.

Out of the Garden - Plots of the Demiurge

After partaking of the fruit, Adam and Eve begin to awaken; and realizing their state of ignorance and imperfection, they are ashamed. Thus, their "nakedness" was in fact spiritual ignorance. Having eaten the fruit, Zoe appears in Eve. After expelling Adam and Eve from the earthly paradise Gust as he had cast Adam from the psychical realm into the hylic, or material world), the Demiurge sees that Zoe is present in Eve. Yaldabaoth moves to rape Eve in another attempt to apprehend enlightened afterthought (Zoe). But before he is able to defile her, Barbelo sends emissaries to rescue Zoe, leaving only the earthly Eve behind. The Demiurge, ignorant that Zoe has been stolen away, forces his seed upon Eve and produces two sons, who are named after the archons, Cain and Abel. The Demiurge here represents that instinctual state into which Adam had formerly been plunged. He has Intellect but no true Reason. He tries, unsuccessfully to become "wedded" to the higher Intuitive faculty (Zoe), as Adam has done. His efforts produce a tragic outcome, In this myth, Abel, who is commonly seen as the "good son" is only "good" from the perspective of the demiurgic law, for it is he who offers the burnt & bloody sacrifice. It is Cain who offers the fruit of the earth, a precursor to the sacrifice of Melchizedek; but the rejection of this offering by his "god" corrupts his heart to murderous intent.

When Adam and Eve conceive, they produce a son whom they name Seth, after the heavenly Seth. The Mother, Barbelo, blesses them by sending down her spirit so that it might raise up that spark of original light, that seed of pure goodness, to the Holy Aeons that the Pleroma might be restored. The Demiurge, however, was relentless in his plots to confound the humans, and keep them in ignorance of their origins. One of these nefarious plots was to eradicate the whole of humanity through a great flood. However, the Holy Spirit warns Noah, who in turn warns the other humans. Only those of the "unshakable race," that is, the offspring of Seth (Gnostics) heeded the warning and sought refuge. It is written that they did not hide in an ark, but rather in a "particular place," and "in a bright cloud," which would suggest, perhaps, a high mountainous region. This is reminiscent of the "Sapta Rishi" or Seven Sages of the Vedas who descended from the Himalayas and brought culture and civilization to the world.

Another of the Demiurge's plots was to send his angels, or beni-elohim (sons of the gods) to mate with human females. They made their appearance to resemble human males, and their offspring were children of darkness and ignorance; known in the scriptures as the Nephilim.

So it continued throughout the ages, that Yaldabaoth and his archons, and their angels would continue to plot and scheme against humanity. All this they have done in ignorance, even after the archon Sabaoth rose up against Yaldabaoth to worship the true God, and was exalted by Sophia to a superior position. Even then, the Demiurge did not see his erroneous ways and repent. Rather, he was cast from his realm into the Abyss, from where he now reigns. *John* 12:31 states, "Now is the judgment of this world; now the archon of this world will be cast out."

The Incarnation of the Logos & the Redemption of Man

It is because of the ceaseless attempts of the Demiurge to enslave humans in the fetters of ignorance, that it was necessary for the Logos to be incarnated in the person of Jesus. Because he is anointed by the Mother, the Holy Spirit, He is called Christos, or Christ. Jesus Christ, through his teachings, and through the sacraments he has ordained, leads the seeker to the path of gnosis, which is the path of remembrance. This is how we are saved through Christ. It was not Adam and Eve's rebellion that brought sin and wickedness into the world. Their rebellion was a necessary rebellion, a righteous rebellion. They rebelled against the archons who would keep them in darkness and ignorance. It is from that very ignorance that humanity must be saved. For, every evil act, and every sinful impulse can be directly related to humanity's ignorance of its spiritual essence, and of the Divine truth of the Fullness of God.

Concerning the nature of man, we have seen that his origins lie in the archetypal Geradamas. The soul, or psychic body, was modeled after the Heavenly man, and animated with pneuma, the breath of life. This living soul was then cast into the material, or hylic, world. So, the human condition today is such, that we have three bodies, or conditions of being: the hylic, the psychic, and the pneumatic. Of these three parts, our primary concern is with the psychic, or the soul. The pneumatic part is pure and incorruptible; the hylic is destined for dissolution. It is only the soul whose fate is indeterminate. That is, even though its nature is more subtle than that of the material world, it is nevertheless a creation of an imperfect Demiurge, and thus is itself imperfect. It is in a constant state of struggle between the lower passions of the physical, and the higher spiritual aspirations. If left to its own accord, the soul will be dragged down into the false pleasures of the material, and ultimately suffer the same fate as that of the hylic substance: utter disintegration and dissolution. However, when aided from above, the soul can rise to the heights of the spirit, wherein lies the Mind of God, the bestower of all gnosis and eternal life. According to Gnostic doctrine, those souls that have not acquired gnosis are snatched up by the archons, after the physical body perishes, and cast into another body. In other words, the soul, providing that it is striving toward the spiritual, experiences successive reincarnations until it has attained perfect memory of its origins. Then the soul can escape the cycle of incarnation, and reside eternally with the Aeons in the Pleroma. This spiritual perfection of the soul is the greatest hope and most sublime aspiration of the Gnostic. Additionally, the regenerated Soul, or enlightened consciousness, also has the ability to regenerate the physical body as well. Therefore, the key to a heathy body is a healthy soul, for the healthy soul is the one that is wedded to spirit, and this brings a regeneration and reintegration of the whole being. The "three bodies" may only be considered as such, therefore, until the reintegration, when the illusion of multiplicity gives way to unity.

Just as the human condition is divided into three aspects, so too is the human population likewise divided. The Pneumatics are those who have attained to the Light of Gnosis, and are destined to eternal life in the Pleroma. The Psychics are those Christian faithful who aspire toward the eternal, but who do not have the gift of gnosis, and therefore are not yet able to ascend to the Pleroma. The scriptures speak to this distinction between the Pneumatic and the Psychic in *1 Corinthians* 2:14-15 which states, "Now, Psychic man does not receive the things of the Spirit of God, for they are foolish to him, and he is not able to know them, because they are pneumatically discerned. But the Pneumatic man discerns all things, but he is discerned by no one." It is thus the responsibility of the Pneumatic, that is the Gnostic, to help bring the Light of Gnosis to his Psychic brethren. There is one more group of people, the Hylics, who have no inclination toward the spiritual. Their souls are immersed in materiality, and so blinded that they do not acknowledge that there is even a spiritual life toward which they might aspire. For them, it is said that their souls will perish along with their body. Just as the body dissipates into its constituent elements after the spark of life has vacated, so too will that soul that does not know the spirit of life and light, dissolve into the ethereal substance from which it was created. There is, however, a fate worse than death. Those who have attained the Light of Gnosis but have turned away from that knowledge and have willfully returned to a state of darkness and ignorance will not be allowed to regain gnosis through successive incarnations. According to the *Secret Book of John*, these unfortunate souls "will be taken to the place where the angels of misery go, where there is no repentance. They will be kept there until the day when those who have blasphemed against the Spirit will be tortured and punished eternally." Truly, it is better to have never set foot upon the path to gnosis than to have attained mastery of life, only to forsake that knowledge. This is the blaspheme of the Holy Spirit. This is what is called the unforgivable sin.

The *Pistis Sophia* also addresses this issue at length. It states in part, "All men who shall receive the mysteries of the Ineffable - blessed indeed are the souls which shall receive of those mysteries; but if they turn and transgress and come out of the body before they have repented, the judgment of those men is sorer than all the judgments, and it is exceedingly violent, even if those souls are new and it is their first ti.me for coming into the world. They will not return to the changes of the bodies from that hour onwards and will not be able to do anything, but they will be cast out into the outer darkness and perish and be non-existent forever." This concept is also discussed throughout the canonical scriptures. See "Theosis Through Gnosis" for further discussion on this.

As we near the end of our introduction to the fundamentals of Gnostic doctrine, you must understand that this is not intended to be a comprehensive discourse on Gnostic theology, but merely an introduction to some of the many ideas, principles, beliefs, and practices that make up our Gnostic tradition. Gnosticism is, and has always been, a system of myth, symbol, and ritual. And within the Gnostic doctrine you will find many literal and figurative truths. We can only point to the traditional teachings and give but the simplest of interpretation. It is up to you, and every individual on the path, to discover the various layers of truth contained within these teachings and rites. We will do our best, though, to help you develop the skills necessary to become competent clergy, and to bring you to the threshold of gnosis; a threshold you alone must cross. Our instruction is given on three levels: physical, mental, and spiritual. On the physical level, you are given training and instruction in the physical rites of the Church. This is done through written instruction, as well as personal mentoring by priests and bishops, and active participation in the Holy Liturgy and other rites of the Church. Mental assistance is given largely through the intellectual study of the philosophy, theology, and history of the Church. Spiritual assistance is given to clergy through the Sacraments, Holy Order ordination, and initiation into the esoteric degrees and orders of the ACP's appendant bodies, such as the Christian Knights of Saint-Martin and the Order of Asiatic Architects. We must stress, however, that it is up to you to perfect each of these areas; the physical through the practice and perfection of the various elements of the rites and rituals; the mental through continued independent study of the Gnostic scriptures, and in fact all areas of the arts and sciences; the spiritual through the eventual attainment of perfect knowledge and wisdom. The spirit of individual responsibility and individual attainment of salvation through gnosis is inherent in the Gnostic doctrine. And while it is true that there is a collective regeneration and reintegration of Humanity, it is up to each person, each member of the body, to fulfill his or her unique mission & function which will enable the complete restoration of the primitive androgynous Adam.

Within the Christian orthodoxy, belief in the death and resurrection of Jesus is sufficient for the remission of sins, provided of course, that the believer is sincere and contrite. To the Gnostic Christian, however, our Lord's crucifixion and resurrection, though highly significant for its symbolic value and as a means of grace or reprieve from the harshest aspects of the old demiurgic covenant, does not guarantee salvation. That is not to say that the Gnostic does not have faith. But the faith of the Gnostic is not mere belief, it is based in the inner transformative knowledge that comes from a true rebirth in Christ, which is the hallmark of Christian initiation. This fundamental difference in soteriology (doctrine of salvation) between Gnostic and so-called orthodox Christianity is due largely to the different outlooks on the topic of original sin. As we saw earlier, Adam and Eve's rebellion in Eden is completely justified from a Gnostic perspective. Whereas, from an "orthodox" perspective that rebellion is the source of all sin and wickedness in the world. From the orthodox standpoint, that wickedness has been transmitted from generation to generation through every human who has ever lived (except Jesus, of course, as well as Mary for those who hold to the doctrine of the Immaculate Conception). So, in order to cleanse this wickedness, the perfect sacrifice was necessary. To the orthodox Christian, Jesus incarnated so that he might die for our sins. To the Gnostic Christian, however, the soul of man begins as inherently good and is corrupted through ignorance, which is brought about as a result of its imprisonment in the material world. Therefore, wickedness is not an inherent condition of the soul, but exists as the offspring of ignorance. So, to the Gnostic it is from ignorance alone that we must be saved. That is why the Gnostic Christian looks not to the death of Jesus for salvation, but rather to His life, teachings, works, and most especially to His Sacraments as guideposts to the path of gnosis, which is the path of salvation. To the Gnostic, the sacrifice of Jesus is a symbol of the sacrifice we all must make. We must sacrifice the lower to the higher, so that we may give up the false life of the material world for the true life of the spiritual realms. It is only in this Spiritual attainment that the Physical can be truly known and enjoyed.

On final comment we have concerns the terms "orthodox" and "orthodoxy." You will notice that we often place the words in quotation marks, or preface them with "so-called." This is because of how the words are commonly understood. We frequently read that Gnosticism arose at a time before the establishment of an orthodoxy. So far as doctrine is concerned, this is more or less true. However, we tend to agree with Julius Evola, who said of Traditional societies that, "Orthodoxy was defined through rituals and practices and not through dogmas and theories," (*Revolt Against the Modern World*, p. 44). In this respect, I would very much consider the modern Gnostic movement to be among the orthodoxy. Nevertheless, there are certain connotations associated with the word that imply a set of "dogmas and theories." Therefore, when we speak of "orthodoxy" we are referring to that self-proclaimed "orthodoxy" of doctrinal opinion that characterizes much of the Christian world today.

On the Sacraments of the ACP

The ACP is sacramental in character. The Master Jesus instituted a number of spiritual practices to help us to attain to the salvific gnosis. He also empowered certain of His followers - the Apostles - to perpetuate these traditions which we call Sacraments. The Sacraments are seven in number; and you will notice that they all relate, in some way, to Spiritual Purification, Regeneration, and Reintegration.

The Sacraments of the ACP are as follows:

- ✓ **Baptism:** Although all of the Sacraments of the Church may be traced to pre-Christian Jewish, Egyptian, Greek, and Persian traditions, the Rite of Baptism stands out as having a clear lineage of transmission from the pre-Christian era, as Jesus himself received this Sacrament and perpetuated it among His followers. Baptism is a rite of cleansing and purifications. It generally marks the official entrance of an individual into full membership of the Church. This is true almost universally throughout Christendom, whether Catholic, Protestant, Orthodox, or Gnostic. The traditional Baptism is of Water, but may Gnostic Churches today also include Earth and Air. Also within the Baptism Rite of the ACP, and some other Gnostic churches, is the Baptism of Fire, also called Chrism.

- ✓ **Chrism:** Chrismation (known as Confirmation in the Roman Catholic Church) always follows the Baptism. In the ACP, it is conferred within the same ceremony. Our ancient Gnostic brethren placed a particular significance upon Chrism. The Gospel of Philip asserts the supremacy of Chrism over Baptism, and also associates it with the Element of Fire. The Chrism is an extension of Baptism. Just as the Baptism represents our awakening and rebirth into Pneumatic (Spiritual) truth, the Chrism recalls the Holy Fire of Pentecost that bestows Spiritual gifts. It is truly a completion of the Baptism rite.

- ✓ **Eucharist:** The Eucharist is the central rite of the ACP, and of all Apostolic Churches. The Rite of Eucharist, or Communion, is the transubstantiation of the elements of Bread and Wine into the Body and the Blood of Christ, the Logos; and then partaking of that Body and Blood - which effects a regenerative influence upon the human Soul. This is a Sacramental Grace that aids the communicant toward Spiritual Reintegration and the ultimate restoration of the Spiritual Self to the Fullness of God. The ACP practices open Communion. That is, the Sacrament of the Eucharist is open to all who wish to partake of its vivifying grace. The Sacraments of Baptism and Chrism, while encouraged for all regular congregants, are only required if one desires full membership in the Church, or if one intends to petition to receive Holy Orders. An individual who has not received Baptism and Chrism is not automatically barred from receiving Communion.

- ✓ **Bridal Chamber:** This Sacrament is mentioned throughout the Gospel of Philip, but we have no details of how it may have been practiced by the ancient Gnostics. The descriptions given by heresiologists of wanton sexual rites are very likely a misunderstanding, or an intentional perversion of the Rite of Bridal Chamber. It is generally held that this Sacrament refers to the Mystical Marriage of Spirit and Soul; the Christ and Sophia; the reintegration of the primitive wholeness. In this sense it can be seen as an extension of the Sacrament of the Eucharist. Like Redemption, this Sacrament can

Sacraments of the ACP

- ✓ only be fully realized Spiritually. Matrimony is sometimes seen as a "substitute" Sacrament, or as a temporal representation of the true Bridal Chamber.

- ✓ **Redemption:** In the Roman Catholic and Eastern Orthodox churches, this Sacrament is preserved as Confession and Absolution. The Scriptures tell us that Jesus gave His Apostles the power to forgive sins. In the Roman Rite, the priest personally offers forgiveness (e.g. "I forgive..." "etc.). In the Eastern Orthodox, the priest calls on the Holy Spirit to forgive. The Gnostic view would be more in line with the Eastern Church, though by no means identical; the principal difference, of course, being our understanding of what exactly "sin" is. A group Confession and Absolution is given within the context of the Mass, but an individualized Confession and Absolution is not mandated by the ACP unless it is desired by a member. Public Confession and Absolution is in fact more in line with the ancient Church than the sort of Confessional boxes used by the Church of Rome. True Redemption, however, is something that can only be accomplished in full reintegration and regeneration. It may be thought of as the completion of the Bridal Chamber union.

- ✓ **Holy Unction** (or Anointing of the Sick): In the Roman Church, this is called Extreme Unction or, commonly, "last rites" and has traditionally been reserved for those who are believed to be near death or terminally ill. In the Eastern Church, as in the Gnostic Church, this Sacrament may be conferred at any time. Even if one does not seem to be physically ill, we can seek alleviation from the disease of Spiritual darkness. This Sacrament is a powerful theurgic operation.

- ✓ **Holy Orders:** This is the Sacrament that transmits the Apostolic Succession, and confers the powers that Jesus first vested in His Apostles. These Spiritual Powers have been transmitted in unbroken succession - person to person, from the time of Jesus up to the present day. The ACP offers the possibility of ordination to men and women who have received Baptism and Chrismation within the ACP, or within any ecclesiastical body that is in full communion with the ACP.

ACP Clergy Handbook

The Kybalion

By Three Initiates

Annotated by Tau Phosphoros

[The Kybalion is an early 20th century treatise on Hermetic philosophy that quickly came to be considered a classic. This work, anonymously attributed to 'Three Initiates' continues to be an eloquently succinct introduction and overview of the fundamental principles that underlie the various doctrines of the Western Mystery Tradition. It is important that the clergy of the Apostolic Church of the Pleroma become intimately familiar with the seven principles outlined in the Kybalion. Do not let the brevity of this work and the simplicity of its language deceive you; for, it is but a testament to the universality and profundity of these timeless principles. We therefore offer the Kybalion in its entirety, including our own occasional comments, given italicized in brackets - such as this introductory note. We are confident that this treatise will be of the utmost benefit to the student's comprehension and application of the Gnostic doctrine in general, and the philosophy and practices of the ACP in particular.]

The Kybalion

Introduction

We take great pleasure in presenting to the attention of students and investigators of the Secret Doctrine this little work based upon the world-old Hermetic Teachings. There has been so little written upon this subject, notwithstanding the countless references to the Teachings in the many works upon occultism, that the many earnest searchers after the Arcane Truths will doubtless welcome the appearance of the present volume.

The purpose of this work is not the enunciation of any special philosophy or doctrine, but rather is to give to the students a statement of the Truth that will serve to reconcile the many bits of occult knowledge that they may have acquired, but which are apparently opposed to each other and which often serve to discourage and disgust the beginner in the study. Our intent is not to erect a new Temple of Knowledge, but rather to place in the hands of the student a Master- Key with which he may open the many inner doors in the Temple of Mystery through the main portals he has already entered.

[As stated in this paragraph, many of the teachings of the various Orders, Societies, Fraternities, and Ecclesiastical bodies of the Western Mystery Tradition can seem "apparently opposed to each other" on their surface. The reason this tends to occur is that the occult schools are not systems of dogmatic creed but rather the revealers of Universal Truths and transcendent knowledge. The medium for the transmission of these teachings is through myth, symbol and ritual. Therefore, while the individual methods of communicating the Hidden Wisdom may seem different, or even contradictory, their inner, fundamental principles on which they are based, and which are transmitted to the student, are essentially and substantially the same. The "Master-Key" referred to here is the exposition of the seven principles outlined in this book, which form the foundation for the mechanics of all the Occult Arts and Sciences, as well as the attainment of Mystical Revelation. The reference to "the main portals he has already entered" seems to suggest that it is assumed that the reader is already a student or initiate of one or more of the major branches of the Western Mystery Tradition. This is significant because although this treatise may, on its own, help the reader to understand the workings of the mind and nature of the universe, its true value is in its ability to help unlock the teachings of the Mystery Schools, and enable the student to apply those teachings for the benefit of Self and Humanity.]

There is no portion of the occult teachings possessed by the world which have been so closely guarded as the fragments of the Hermetic Teachings which have come down to us over the tens of centuries which have elapsed since the lifetime of its great founder, Hermes Trismegistus, the "scribe of the gods," who dwelt in old Egypt in the days when the present race of men was in its infancy. Contemporary with Abraham, and, if the legends be true, an instructor of the venerable sage, Hermes was, and is, the Great Central Sun of Occultism, whose rays have served to illumine the countless teachings which have been promulgated since his time. All the fundamental and basic teachings embedded in the esoteric teachings of every race may be traced back to Hermes. Even the most ancient teachings of India undoubtedly have their roots in the original Hermetic Teachings.

[Whether or not the traditional accounts of Hermes Trismegistus, Thoth in Egypt, are literally true or an allegory for a body of knowledge that has been passed down through the ages, there can be little doubt as to the antiquity and universality of the Hermetic teachings, regardless of the name under which they have been known.]

From the land of the Ganges many advanced occultists wandered to the land of Egypt, and sat at the feet of the Master. From him they obtained the Master-Key which explained and reconciled their divergent views, and thus the Secret Doctrine was firmly established. From other lands also came the learned ones, all of whom regarded Hermes as the Master of Masters, and his influence was so great that in spite of the many wanderings from the path on the part of the centuries of teachers in these different lands, there may still be found a certain basic resemblance and correspondence which underlies the many and often quite divergent theories entertained and taught by the occultists of these different lands today. The student of Comparative Religions will be able to perceive the influence of the Hermetic Teachings in every religion worthy of the name, now known to man, whether it be a dead religion or one in full vigor in our own times. There is always certain correspondence in spite of the contradictory features, and the Hermetic Teachings act as the Great Reconciler.

The lifework of Hermes seems to have been in the direction of planting the great Seed-Truth which has grown and blossomed in so many strange forms, rather than to establish a school of philosophy which would dominate the world's thought. But, nevertheless, the original truths taught by him have been kept intact in their original purity by a few men each age, who, refusing great numbers of half- developed students and followers, followed the Hermetic custom and reserved their truth for the few who were ready to comprehend and master it. From lip to ear the truth has been handed down among the few. There have always been a few Initiates in each generation, in the various lands of the earth, who kept alive the sacred flamed of the Hermetic Teachings, and such have always been willing to use their lamps to re-light the lesser lamps of the outside world, when the light of truth grew dim, and clouded by reason of neglect, and when the wicks became clogged with foreign matter. There were always a few to tend faithfully the altar of the Truth, upon which was kept alight the Perpetual Lamp of Wisdom. These men devoted their lives to the labor of love which the poet has so well stated in his lines:

"O, let not the flame die out! Cherished age after age in its dark cavern - in its holy temples cherished. Fed by pure ministers of love - let not the flame die out!"

These men have never sought popular approval, nor numbers of followers. They are indifferent to these things, for they know how few there are in each generation who are ready for the truth, or who would recognize it if it were presented to them. They reserve the "strong meat for men," while others furnish the "milk for babes." They reserve their pearls of wisdom for the few elect, who recognize their value and who wear them in their crowns, instead of casting them before the materialistic vulgar swine, who would trample them in the mud and mix them with their disgusting mental food. But still these men have never forgotten or overlooked the original teachings of Hermes, regarding the passing on of the words of truth to those ready to receive it, which teaching is stated in *The Kybalion* as follows: "Where fall the footsteps of the Master, the ears of those ready for his Teaching open wide." And again: "When the ears of the student are ready to hear, then cometh the lips to fill them with wisdom." But their customary attitude has always been strictly in accordance with the other Hermetic aphorism, also in *The Kybalion*: "The lips of Wisdom are closed, except to the ears of Understanding."

There are those who have criticized this attitude of the Hermetists, and who have claimed that they did not manifest the proper spirit in their policy of seclusion and reticence. But a moment's glance back over the pages of history will show the wisdom of the Masters, who knew the folly of attempting to teach to the world that which it was neither ready nor willing to receive. The Hermetists have never sought to be martyrs, and have, instead, sat silently aside with a pitying smile on their closed lips, while the "heathen raged noisily about them" in their customary amusement of putting to death and torture the honest but misguided enthusiasts who imagined that they could force upon a race of barbarians the truth capable of being understood only by the elect who had advanced along the path.

And the spirit of persecution has not as yet died out in the land. There are certain Hermetic Teachings, which, if publicly promulgated, would bring down upon the teachers a great cry of scorn and revilement from the multitude, who would again raise the cry of "Crucify! Crucify!"

[Even though this statement is made against the backdrop of early twentieth century societal values, the social taboos existing even today give it continued relevance, if to a somewhat lesser degree. But in every age there will be a fanaticism, whether in the majority or minority, that will seek to suppress the ancient true and hidden Wisdom.]

In this little work we have endeavored to give you an idea of the fundamental teachings of *The Kybalion*, striving to give you the working Principles, leaving you to apply them yourselves, rather than attempting to work out the teaching in detail. If you are a true student, you will be able to work out and apply these Principles -if not, then you must develop yourself into one, for otherwise the Hermetic Teachings will be as "words, words, words" to you.

THE THREE INITIATES

The Hermetic Philosophy

"The lips of Wisdom are closed, except to the ears of Understanding."
- *The Kybalion*

From old Egypt have come the fundamental esoteric and occult teachings which have so strongly influenced the philosophies of all races, nations and peoples, for several thousand years. Egypt, the home of the Pyramids and the Sphinx, was the birthplace of the Hidden Wisdom and Mystic Teachings. From her Secret Doctrine all nations have borrowed. India, Persia, Chaldea, Medea, China, Japan, Assyria, ancient Greece and Rome, and other ancient countries partook liberally at the feast of knowledge which the Hierophants and Masters of the Land of Isis so freely provided for those who came prepared to partake of the great store of Mystic and Occult Lore which the masterminds of that ancient land had gathered together.

In ancient Egypt dwelt the great Adepts and Masters who have never been surpassed, and who seldom have been equaled, during the centuries that have taken their processional flight since the days of the Great Hermes. In Egypt was located the Great Lodge of Lodges of the Mystics. At the doors of her Temples entered the Neophytes who afterward, as Hierophants, Adepts, and Masters, traveled to the four corners of the earth, carrying with them the precious knowledge which they were ready, anxious, and willing to pass on to those who were ready to receive the same. All students of the Occult recognize the debt that they owe to these venerable Masters of that ancient land.

But among these great Masters of Ancient Egypt there once dwelt one of whom Masters hailed as "The Master of Masters." This man, if "man" indeed he was, dwelt in Egypt in the earliest days. He was known as Hermes Trismegistus. He was the father of the Occult Wisdom; the founder of Astrology; the discoverer of Alchemy. The details of his life story are lost to history, owing to the lapse of the years, though several of the ancient countries disputed with each other in their claims to the honor of having furnished his birthplace - and this thousands of years ago. The date of his sojourn in Egypt, in that his last incarnation on this planet, is not now known, but it has been fixed at the early days of the oldest dynasties of Egypt - long before the days of Moses. The best authorities regard him as a contemporary of Abraham, and some of the Jewish traditions go so far as to claim that Abraham acquired a portion of his mystic knowledge from Hermes himself.

[Pre-dynastic Egypt, known as Zep-Tepi, or the "First Time," was thought to have been ruled by gods, or Masters of the Arts and Sciences, and bringers of civilization; possibly descending from an older, "lost" civilization.]

As the years rolled by after his passing from this plane of life (tradition recording that he lived three hundred years in the flesh), the Egyptians deified Hermes, and made him one of their gods, under the name of Thoth. Years after, the people of Ancient Greece also made him one of their many gods - calling him "Hermes, the god of Wisdom." The Egyptians revered his memory for many centuries - calling him "the Scribe of the Gods," and bestowing upon him, distinctively, his ancient title, "Trismegistus," which means "the thrice- great"; "the great-great"; "the greatest-great"; etc. In all the ancient lands, the name of Hermes Trismegistus was revered, the name being synonymous with the "Fount of Wisdom."

Even to this day, we use the term "hermetic" in the sense of "secret"; "sealed so that nothing can escape";

etc., and this by reason of the fact that the followers of Hermes always observed the principle of secrecy in their teachings. They did not believe in "casting pearls before swine," but rather held to the teaching "milk for babes"; "meat for strong men," both of which maxims are familiar to readers of the Christi.an scriptures, but both of which had been used by the Egyptians for centuries before the Christi.an era.

[There are, in fact, numerous similarities between primitive Christianity and the Egyptian mystery religions, not the least of which being the death / resurrection motif, and the practice of god-eating, i.e. the Eucharist. It should not surprise us then, that early Christianity, in the form of Gnosticism, should take such a foothold in Egypt and other areas of Northern Africa and Asia Minor.]

And this policy of careful dissemination of the truth has always characterized the Hermetics, even unto the present day. The Hermetic Teachings are to be found in all lands, among all religions, but never identified with any particular religious sect. This is because of the warning of the ancient teachers against allowing the Secret Doctrine to become crystallized into a creed. The wisdom of this caution is apparent to all students of history. The ancient occultism of India and Persia degenerated, and was largely lost, owing to the fact that the teachers became priests, and so mixed theology with the philosophy, the result being that the occultism of India and Persia has been gradually lost amidst the mass of religious superstition, cults, creeds and "gods." So it was with Ancient Greece and Rome. So it was with the Hermetic Teachings of the Gnostics and Early Christians, which were lost at the time of Constantine, whose iron hand smothered philosophy with the blanket of theology, losing to the Christian Church that which was its very essence and spirit, and causing it to grope throughout several centuries before it found the way back to its ancient faith, the indications apparent to all careful observers in this Twentieth Century being that the Church is now struggling to get back to its ancient mystic teachings.

[We can see now that the Twentieth Century did not bring the mainstream Christian Church back to its roots in the ancient mysteries. It did, however, spawn viable bodies of Christian mysticism within the Apostolic Tradition, namely, the development and expansion of the French Église Gnostique, established in the late Nineteenth Century by Jules Doinel. This new Gnostic Church became popular among Martinists and Egyptian Rite Freemasons. The 1945 discovery of the Nag Hammadi codices, and their subsequent translation and publication, helped to fuel an explosion of Apostolic Gnosticism in the late 20th and early 21st Centuries; our own Apostolic Church of the Pleroma being a direct descendant of these mystical and ecclesiastical bodies.]

But there were always a few faithful souls who kept alive the Flame, tending it carefully, and not allowing its light to become extinguished. And thanks to these staunch hearts, and fearless minds, we have the truth still with us. But it is not found in books, to any great extent. It has been passed along from Master to Student; from Initiate to Hierophant; from lip to ear. When it was written down at all, its meaning was veiled in terms of alchemy and astrology so that only those possessing the key could read it aright. This was made necessary in order to avoid the persecutions of the theologians of the Middle Ages, who fought the Secret Doctrine with fire and sword; stake, gibbet and cross. Even to this day there will be found but few reliable books on the Hermetic Philosophy, although there are countless references to it in many books written on various phases of Occultism. And yet, the Hermetic Philosophy is the only Master Key which will open all the doors of the Occult Teachings!

In the early days, there was a compilation of certain Basic Hermetic Doctrines, passed on from teacher to student which was known as *"THE KYBALION,"* the exact significance and meaning of the term having been lost for several centuries. This teaching, however, is known to many to whom it has descended, from mouth to ear, on and on throughout the centuries. Its precepts have never been written down, or printed, so far as we know. It was merely a collection of maxims, axioms, and precepts, which were non-understandable to outsiders, but which were readily understood by students, after the axioms, maxims, and precepts had been explained and exemplified by the Hermetic Initiates to their Neophytes. These teachings really constituted the basic principles of "The Art of Hermetic Alchemy," which, contrary to the general belief, dealt in the mastery of Mental Forces, rather than Material Elements - the Transmutation of one kind of Mental Vibrations into others, instead of the changing of one kind of metal into another. The legends of the "Philosopher's Stone" which would turn base metal into Gold, was an allegory relating to Hermetic Philosophy, readily understood by all students of true Hermeticism.

In this little book, of which this is the First Lesson, we invite our students to examine into the Hermetic Teachings, as set forth in THE KYBALION, and as explained by ourselves, humble students of the Teachings, who, while bearing the title of Initiates, are still students at the feet of HERMES, the Master. We herein give you many of the maxims, axioms and precepts of THE KYBALION, accompanied by explanations and illustrations which we deem likely to render the teachings more easily comprehended by the modem student, particularly as the original text is purposely veiled in obscure terms.

The original maxims, axioms, and precepts of *THE KYBALION* are printed herein, in quotes, the proper credit being given. Our own work is printed in the regular way, in the body of the work. We trust that the many students to whom we now offer this little work will derive as much benefit from the study of its pages as have the many who have gone on before, treading the same Path to Mastery throughout the centuries that have passed since the times of HERMES TRISMEGISTUS - the Master of Masters - the Great-Great. In the words of "*THE KYBALION*":

"Where fall the footsteps of the Master, the ears of those ready for his Teaching open wide."
- *The Kybalion*

"When the ears of the student are ready to hear, then cometh the lips to fill them with Wisdom."
- *The Kybalion*

So that according to the Teachings, the passage of this book to those ready for the instruction will attract the attention of such as are prepared to receive the truth, then will this little book come to him, or her. Such is The Law. The Hermetic Principle of Cause and Effect, in its aspect of The Law of Attraction, will bring lips and ear together - pupil and book in company. So mote it be!

The Kybalion

The Seven Hermetic Principles

"The Principles of Truth are Seven; he who knows these, understandingly, possesses the Magic Key before whose touch all the Doors of the Temple fly open."

- *The Kybalion*

[Notes to each of the seven principles will be reserved for the subsequent chapters which treat each principle to a fuller extent. This is a good place, however, to discuss the number Seven and its significance within the Hermetic doctrine. The use of the number Seven among the mystical traditions of the world is so extensive that a massive volume could treat just this one subject and still fail to be comprehensive. So, even though such a treatise cannot be given within the present work, it will greatly benefit the student to give the subject consideration, and hopefully inspire the seeker to probe farther into the mystery of the number Seven.

The first and most obvious place to look is to the natural world, specifically to the seven "planets" of the ancients: the Sun, Moon, Mars, Mercury, Jupiter, Venus, and Saturn. In the Hermetic texts we see these first referenced in the Corpus Hermeticum I.9 which calls them "seven governors" (Hermetica. Copenhaver, p. 2). C.H. I.16 discusses the sevenfold nature of humanity's original state, "...seven men [hepta anthropos], androgyne and exalted, whole natures were like those of the seven governors," (Ibid. p. 4 & 111). According to C.H. I.9, the seven heavenly bodies are created by a "craftsman" or "demiourgos," (Ibid. p. 2 & 104), an idea that is presented in more detail in the Gnostic "Secret Book of John" (Meyer, trans. Gnostic Bible. pp. 138-165), which states, "Yaldabaoth stationed seven kings, one for each sphere of heaven, to reign over the seven powers for themselves." The seven powers correspond to the seven days of the week, (Ibid. p. 148). The seven-day week is another ancient and near-universal occurrence of the number Seven, and is related inextricably to the seven planetary spheres.

C.H. I.25 suggests that humankind is currently trapped within the seven spheres and must struggle to overcome the adverse powers residing at each of the seven levels, (Copenhaver, p. 6). The striking similarities between the Hermetic texts and the Gnostic texts are certainly not coincidental, and did not go unnoticed by the ancient Gnostics. This is evidenced by the inclusion of Hermetic texts among the Nag Hammadi codices. Students of the Vedas may also wish to consider a possible connection between the "hepta anthropos" of C.H. I.16 and the Sapta Rishi, or Seven Sages, who brought culture and civilization to the Indus Valley.]

The Seven Hermetic Principles, upon which the entire Hermetic Philosophy is based, are as follows:

1. The Principle of Mentalism.
2. The Principle of Correspondence.
3. The Principle of Vibration.
4. The Principle of Polarity.
5. The Principle of Rhythm.
6. The Principle of Cause and Effect.
7. The Principle of Gender.

These Seven Principles will be discussed and explained as we proceed with these lessons. A short explanation of each, however, may as well be given at this point.

1. The Principle of Mentalism

"THE ALL IS MIND; The Universe is Mental."
- *The Kybalion.*

This Principle embodies the truth that "All is Mind." It explains that THE ALL (which is the Substantial Reality underlying all the outward manifestations and appearances which we know under the terms of "The Material Universe"; the "Phenomena of Life"; "Matter"; "Energy"; and, in short, all that is apparent to our material senses) is SPIRIT which in itself is UNKNOWABLE and UNDEFINABLE, but which may be considered and thought of as AN UNIVERSAL, INFINITE, LIVING MIND. It also explains that all the phenomenal world or universe is simply a Mental Creation of THE ALL, subject to the Laws of Created Things, and that the universe, as a whole, and in its parts or units, has its existence in the Mind of THE ALL, in which Mind we "live and move and have our being." This Principle, by establishing the Mental Nature of the Universe, easily explains all of the varied mental and psychic phenomena that occupy such a large portion of the public attention, and which, without such explanation, are non-understandable and defy scientific treatment. An understanding of this great Hermetic Principle of Mentalism enables the individual to readily grasp the laws of the Mental Universe, and to apply the same to his well-being and advancement. The Hermetic Student is enabled to apply intelligently the great Mental laws, instead of using them in a haphazard manner. With the Master-Key in his possession, the student may unlock the many doors of the mental and psychic temple of knowledge, and enter the same freely and intelligently. This Principle explains the true nature of "Energy," "Power," and "Matter," and why and how all these are subordinate to the Mastery of Mind. One of the old Hermetic Masters wrote, long ages ago: "He who grasps the truth of the Mental Nature of the Universe is well advanced on the Path to Mastery." And these words are as true today as at the time they were first written. Without this Master-Key, Mastery is impossible, and the student knocks in vain at the many doors of the Temple.

2. The Principle of Correspondence.

"As above, so below; as below, so above."
- *The Kybalion*

This Principle embodies the truth that there is always a Correspondence between the laws and phenomena of the various planes of Being and Life. The old Hermetic axiom ran in these words: "As above so below, as below, so above." And the grasping of this Principle gives one the means of solving many a dark paradox, and hidden secret of Nature. There are planes beyond our knowing, but when we apply the Principle of Correspondence to them we are able to understand much that would otherwise be unknowable to us. This Principle is of universal application and manifestation, on the various planes of the material, mental and spiritual universe - it is an Universal Law. The ancient Hermetists considered this Principle as one of the most important mental instruments by which man was able to pry aside the obstacles which hid from view· the Unknown. Its use even tore aside the Veil of Isis to the extent that a glimpse of the face of the goddess might be caught. Just as a knowledge of the Principles of Geometry enables man to measure distant suns and their movements, while seated in his observatory, so a knowledge of the Principle of Correspondence enables Man to reason intelligently from the Known to the Unknown. Studying the monad, he understands the archangel.

3. The Principle of Vibration

"Nothing rests; everything moves; everything vibrates."
- *The Kybalion*

This Principle embodies the truth that "Everything is in motion"; "everything vibrates"; "nothing is at rest"; facts which Modem Science endorses, and which each new scientific discovery tends to verify. And yet this Hermetic Principle was enunciated thousands of years ago, by the Masters of Ancient Egypt. This Principle explains that the differences between different manifestations of Matter, Energy, Mind, and even Spirit, result largely from varying rates of Vibration. From THE ALL, which is Pure Spirit, down to the grossest form of Matter, all is in vibration - the higher the vibration, the higher the position in the scale. The vibration of Spirit is at such an infinite rate of intensity and rapidity that it is practically at rest - just as a rapidly moving wheel seems to be motionless. And at the other end of the scale, there are gross forms of matter whose vibrations are so low as to seem at rest. Between these poles, there are millions upon millions of varying degrees of vibration. From corpuscle and electron, atom and molecule, to worlds and universes, everything is in vibratory motion. This is also true on the planes of energy and force (which are but varying degrees of vibration); and also on the mental planes (whose states depend upon vibrations); and even on to the spiritual planes. An understanding of this Principle, with the appropriate formulas, enables Hermetic students to control their own mental vibrations as well as those of others. The Masters also apply this Principle to the conquering of Natural phenomena, in various ways. "He who understand the Principle of Vibration, has grasped the scepter of power," says one of the old writers.

4. The Principle of Polarity

"Everything is Dual; everything has poles; everything has its pair of opposites; like and unlike are the same; opposites are identical in nature, but different in degree; extremes meet; all truths are but half-truths; all paradoxes may be reconciled."
- *The Kybalion*

This Principle embodies the truth that "everything is dual"; "everything has two poles"; "everything has its pair of opposites," all of which were old Hermetic axioms. It explains the old paradoxes, that have perplexed so many, which have been stated as follows: "Thesis and antithesis are identical in nature, but different in degree"; "opposites are the same, differing only in degree"; "the pairs of opposites may be reconciled"; "extremes meet"; "everything is and isn't at the same time"; "All truths are but half-truths"; "every truth is half- false"; "there are two sides to everything," etc., etc., etc. It explains that in everything there are two poles, or opposite aspects, and that "opposites" are really only the two extremes of the same thing, with many varying degrees between them. To illustrate: Heat and Cold, although "opposites," are really the same thing, the differences consisting merely of degrees of the same thing. Look at your thermometer and see if you can discover where "heat" terminates and "cold begins! There is no such thing as "absolute heat" or "Absolute cold" - two terms "heat" and "cold" are simply the "two poles" of that which we call "Heat" - and the phenomena attendant thereupon are manifestations of the Principle of Polarity. The same Principle manifests in the case of "Light and Darkness," which are the same thing, the difference consisting of varying degrees between the two poles of the phenomena. Where does "darkness" leave off, and "light" begin? What is the difference between "Large and Small"? Between "Sharp and Dull"? Between "Positive and Negative"? The Principle of Polarity explains these paradoxes, and no other Principle can supersede it. The same Principle operates on the Mental Plane. Let us take a radical and extreme example - that of "Love and Hate," two mental states apparently totally different. And yet there are degrees of Hate and Degrees of Love, and a middle point in which we use the terms "Like and Dislike," which shade into each other so gradually that sometimes we are at a loss to know whether we "like" or "dislike" or "neither." And all are simply degrees of the same thing, as you will see if you will but think a moment. And, more than this (and considered of more importance by the Hermetists), it is possible to change the vibrations of Hate to the vibrations of Love, in one's own mind, and in the minds of others. Many of you, who read these lines, have had personal experiences of the involuntary rapid transition from Love to Hate, and the reverse, in your own case and that of others. And you will therefore realize the possibility of this being accomplished by the use of the Will, by means of the Hermetic formulas. "Good and Evil" are but the poles of the same thing, and the Hermetist understands the art of transmuting Evil into Good, by means of an application of the Principle of Polarity. In short, the "Art of Polarization" becomes a phase of "Mental Alchemy" known and practiced by the ancient and modem Hermetic Masters. An understanding of the Principle will enable one to change his own Polarity, as well as that of others, if he will devote the time and study necessary to master the art.

5. The Principle of Rhythm

"Everything flows, out and in; everything has its tides; all things rise and fall; the pendulum-swing manifests in everything; the measure of the swing to the right is the measure of the swing to the left; rhythm compensates."

- *The Kybalion*

This Principle embodies the truth that in everything there is manifested a measured motion, to and fro; a flow and inflow; a swing backward and forward; a pendulum-like movement; a tide-like ebb and flow; a high-tide and low-tide; between the two poles which exist in accordance with the Principle of Polarity described a moment ago. There is always an action and a reaction; an advance and a retreat; a rising and a sinking. This is in the affairs of the Universe, suns, worlds, men, animals, mind, energy, and matter. This law is manifest in the creation and destruction of worlds; in the rise and fall of nations; in the life of all things; and finally in the mental states of Man (and it is with this latter that the Hermetists find the understanding of the Principle most important). The Hermetists have grasped the Principle, finding its universal application, and have also discovered certain means to overcome its effects in themselves by the use of the appropriate formulas and methods. They apply the Mental Law of Neutralization. They cannot annul the Principle, or cause it to cease its operation, but they have learned how to escape its effects upon themselves to a certain degree depending upon the Mastery of the Principle. They have learned how to USE it, instead of being USED by it. In this and similar methods, consist the Art of the Hermetists. The Master of Hermetics polarizes himself at the point at which he desires to rest, and then neutralizes the Rhythmic swing of the pendulum which would tend to carry him to the other pole. All individuals who have attained any degree of Self-Mastery do this to a certain degree, more or less unconsciously, but the Master does this consciously, and by the use of his Will, and attains a degree of Poise and mental Firmness almost impossible of belief on the part of the masses who are swung backward and forward like a pendulum. This Principle and that of Polarity have been closely studied by the Hermetists, and the methods of counteracting, neutralizing, and USING them form an important part of the hermetic Mental Alchemy.

6. The Principle of Cause and Effect

"Every Cause has its Effect; every Effect has its Cause; everything happens according to Law; Chance is but a name for Law not recognized; there are many planes of causation, but nothing escapes the Law."

- *The Kybalion*

This Principle embodies the fact that there is a Cause for every Effect; an Effect from every Cause. It explains that: "Everything Happens according to Law"; that nothing ever "merely happens"; that there is no such thing as Chance; the while there are various planes of Cause and Effect, the higher dominating the lower planes, still nothing ever entirely escapes the Law. The Hermetists understand the art and methods of rising above the ordinary plane of Cause and Effect, to a certain degree, and by mentally rising to a higher plane they become Causers instead of Effects. The masses of people are carried along, obedient to environment; the wills and desires of others stronger than themselves; heredity; suggestion; and other outward causes moving them about like pawns on the Chessboard of Life. But the Masters, rising to the plane above, dominate their moods, characters, qualities, and powers, as well as the environment surrounding them, and become Movers instead of pawns. They help to PLAY THE GAME OF LIFE, instead of being played and moved about by other wills and environment. They USE the Principle instead of being its tools. The Masters obey the Causation of the higher planes, but they help to RULE on their own plane. In this statement there is condensed a wealth of Hermetic Knowledge - let him read who can.

7. The Principle of Gender

"Gender is in everything; everything has its Masculine and Feminine Principles; Gender manifests on all planes."

- *The Kybalion*

This Principle embodies the truth that there is GENDER manifested in everything- the Masculine and Feminine Principles ever at work. This is true not only of the Physical Plane, but of the Mental and even the Spiritual Planes. On the Physical Plane, the Principle manifests as SEX. On the higher planes it takes higher forms, but the Principle is ever the same. No creation, physical, mental or spiritual, is possible without this Principle. An understanding of its laws will throw light on many a subject that has perplexed the minds of men. The Principle of Gender works ever in the direction of generation, regeneration, and creation. Everything, and every person, contains the two Elements or Principles, of this great Principle, within it, him or her. Every Male thing has the Female Element also; every Female contains also the Male Principle. If you would understand the philosophy of Mental and Spiritual Creation, Generation, and Re-generation, you must understand and study this Hermetic Principle. It contains the solution of many mysteries of Life. We caution you that this Principle has no reference to the many base, pernicious and degrading lustful theories, teachings and practices, which are taught under the fanciful titles, and which are a prostitution of the great natural principle of Gender. Such base revivals of the ancient infamous forms of Phallicism tend to ruin mind, body and soul, and the Hermetic Philosophy has ever sounded the warning note against these degraded teachings which tend toward lust, licentiousness, and perversion of Nature's principles. If you seek such teachings, you must go elsewhere for them - Hermeticism contains nothing for you along these lines. To the pure, all things are pure; to the base, all things are base.

Mental Transmutation

"Mind (as well as metals and elements) may be transmuted, from state to state; degree to degree; condition to condition; pole to pole; vibration to vibration. True Hermetic Transmutation is a Mental Art."

- *The Kybalion*

As we have stated, the Hermetists were the original alchemists, astrologers, and psychologists, Hermes having been the founder of these schools of thought. From astrology has grown modern astronomy; from alchemy has grown modern chemistry; from the mystic psychology has grown the modern psychology of the schools. But it must not be supposed that the ancients were ignorant of that which the modern schools suppose to be their exclusive and special property. The records engraved on the stones of Ancient Egypt show conclusively that the ancients had a full comprehensive knowledge of astronomy, the very building of the Pyramids showing the connection between their design and the study of astronomical science. Nor were they ignorant of Chemistry, for the fragments of the ancient writings show that they were acquainted with the chemical properties of things; in fact, the ancient theories regarding physics are being slowly verified by the latest discoveries of modern science, notably those relating to the constitution of matter. Nor must it be supposed that they were ignorant of the so-called modern discoveries in psychology - on the contrary, the Egyptians were especially skilled in the science of Psychology, particularly in the branches that the modern schools ignore, but which, nevertheless, are being uncovered under the name of "psychic science" which is perplexing the psychologists of today, and making them reluctantly admit that "there may be something in it after all."

[The spiritual renaissance of the late 19th and early 20th centuries certainly helped to promote holistic movements in various health-related fields. However, mainstream science has departed sharply from any theories or practices that so much as hint at having spiritual undertones. The Hermetic and occult traditions have never denied the physiological aspects of the psyche. In fact, it is taught that the Psyche is crucial as a mediator between the physical and spiritual qualities of the human condition. Modern science has, however, reduced the Soul (Psyche) and the Mind (Nous) to mere products of chemical and electrical reactions in the brain. The few professionals who take a more traditional and holistic view operate on the fringe of their fields, and are often shunned and ostracized by the scientific community at large. It is important to realize, then, that the occult sciences have never sought to refute or undermine the discoveries of the physical sciences, but rather to offer a more complete and universal approach to understanding the mysteries of nature and the universe.]

The truth is, that beneath the material chemistry, astronomy and psychology (that is, the psychology in its phase of "brain-action") the ancients possessed a knowledge of transcendental astronomy, called astrology; of transcendental chemistry, called alchemy; of transcendental psychology, called mystic psychology. They possessed the Inner Knowledge as well as the Outer Knowledge, the latter alone being possessed by modem scientists. Among the many secret branches of knowledge possessed by the Hermetists, was that known as Mental Transmutation, which forms the subject matter of this lesson.

"Transmutation" is a term usually employed to designate the ancient art of the transmutation of metals - particularly of the base metals into gold. The word "Transmute" means "to change from one nature, form, or substance, into another; to transform" (Webster). And accordingly, "Mental Transmutation" means the art of changing and transforming mental states, forms, and conditions, into others. So you may see that Mental Transmutation is the "Art of Mental Chemistry," if you like the term - a form of practical Mystic Psychology.

But this means far more than appears on the surface. Transmutation, Alchemy, or Chemistry on the Mental Plane is important enough in its effects, to be sure, and if the art stopped there it would still be one of the most important branches of study known to man. But this is only the beginning. Let us see why!

The first of the Seven Hermetic Principles is the Principle of Mentalism, the axiom of which is "THE ALL is Mind, the Universe is Mental," which means that the Underlying Reality of the Universe is Mind; and the Universe itself is Mental - that is, "existing in the Mind of THE ALL." We shall consider this Principle in succeeding lessons, but let us see the effect of the principle if it be assumed to be true.

If the Universe is Mental in its nature, then Mental Transmutation must be the art of CHANGING THE CONDITIONS OF THE UNIVERSE, along the lines of Matter, Force and Mind. So you see, therefore, that Mental Transmutation is really the "Magic" of which the ancient writers had so much to say in their mystical works, and about which they gave so few practical instructions. If All be Mental, then the art which enables one to transmute mental conditions must render the Master the controller of material conditions as well as those ordinarily called "mental." As a matter of fact, none but advanced Mental Alchemists have been able to attain the degree of power necessary to control the grosser physical conditions, such as the control of the elements of Nature; the production or cessation of tempests; the production and cessation of earthquakes and other great physical phenomena. But that such men have existed, and do exist today, is a matter of earnest belief to all advanced occultists of all schools. That the Masters exist, and have these powers, the best teachers assure their students, having had experiences which justify them in such belief and statements. These Masters do not make public exhibitions of their powers, but seek seclusion from the crowds of men, in order to better work their way along the Path of Attainment. We mention their existence, at this point, merely to call your attention to the fact that their power is entirely Mental, and operates along the lines of the higher Mental Transmutation, under the Hermetic Principle of Mentalism.

"The Universe is Mental" -*The Kybalion*.

But students and Hermetists of lesser degree than Masters - the Initiates and Teachers are able to freely work along the Mental Plane, in Mental Transmutation. In fact all that we call "psychic phenomena"; "mental influence"; "mental science"; "new-thought phenomena," etc., operates along the same general lines, for there is but one principle involved, no matter by what name the phenomena be called.

The student and practitioner of Mental Transmutation works among the Mental Plane, transmuting mental conditions, states, etc., into others, according to various formulas, more or less efficacious. The various "treatments," "affirmations," "denials" etc., of the schools of mental science are but formulas, often quite imperfect and unscientific, of The Hermetic Art. The majority of modern practitioners are quite ignorant compared to the ancient masters, for they lack the fundamental knowledge upon which the work is based.

Not only may the mental states, etc., of one's self be changed or transmuted by Hermetic Methods; but also the states of others may be, and are, constantly transmuted in the same way, usually unconsciously, but often consciously by some understanding the laws and principles, in cases where the people affected are not informed of the principles of self-protection. And more than this, as many students and practitioners of modem mental science know, every material condition depending upon the minds of other people may be changed or transmuted in accordance with the earnest desire, will, and "treatments" of the person desiring changed conditions of life. The public are so generally informed regarding these things at present, that we do not deem it necessary to mention the same at length, our purpose at this point being merely to show the Hermetic Principle and Art underlying all of these various forms of practice, good and evil, for the force can be used in opposite directions according to the Hermetic Principle of Polarity.

In this little book we shall state the basic principles of Mental Transmutation, that all who read may grasp the Underlying Principles, and thus possess the Master-Key that will unlock the many doors of the Principle of Polarity.

We shall now proceed to a consideration of the first of the Hermetic Seven Principles - the Principle of Mentalism, in which is explained the truth that "THE ALL is Mind; the Universe is Mental," In the words of *The Kybalion*. We ask the close attention, and careful study of this great Principle, on the part of our students, for it is really the Basic Principle of the whole Hermetic Philosophy, and of the Hermetic Art of mental Transmutation.

[Every student of mysticism and the occult should acquaint him- or herself with at least the basic principles of alchemy. The physical transmutation of metals, fascinating though it may be, is in reality but a shadowy reflection of the process of spiritual alchemy. To transmute the base elements of the human condition into the perfect spiritual being is the primary goal of the true initiate. See also, "Gnostic Exposition of the Three Alchemical Essentials" and "Alchemy of the Eucharist" for further treatment of alchemy within a Gnostic context.]

The ALL

"Under, and back of, the Universe of Time, Space and Change, is ever to be found The Substantial Reality - The Fundamental Truth."

- *The Kybalion*

Substance means "that which underlies all outward manifestations; the essence; the essential reality; the thing in itself," etc. "Substantial" means: "actually existing; being the essential element; being real," etc. "Reality" means: "the state of being real; true, enduring; valid; fixed; permanent; actual," etc.

Under and behind all outward appearance or manifestations, there must always be a Substantial Reality. This is the Law. Man considering the Universe, of which he is a unit, sees nothing but change in matter, forces, and mental states. He sees that nothing really IS, but that everything is BECOMING and CHANGING. Nothing stands still - everything is being born, growing, dying - the very instant a thing reaches its height, it begins to decline - the law of rhythm is in constant operation - there is no reality, enduring quality, fixity, or substantiality in anything - nothing is permanent but Change. He sees all things evolving from other things, and resolving into other things - constant action and reaction; inflow and outflow; building up and tearing down; creation and destruction; birth, growth and death. Nothing endures but Change. And if he be a thinking man, he realizes that all of these changing things must be but outward appearances or manifestations of some Underlying Power - some Substantial Reality.

[The concept of "God" as a Substantial Reality, containing all, ever-changing, ever-becoming, is an idea that pervades all the Hermetic writings and teachings. Considering God as Substantial Reality, take a look at a portion of one of the Hermetic hymns, "For you are whatever I am; you are whatever I make; you are whatever I say. You are everything, and there is nothing else; what is not, you are as well," (Copenhaver, p. 20). Concerning the state of nature as constantly changing and becoming, we can find an example in C.H. IX.6, which states in part, 'The sole sensation and understanding in the Cosmos is to make all things and unmake them into itself again, an instrument of God's will. In reality, God made the instrument to make all things actively in itself, taking under its protection the seeds it has received from God. In dissolving all things, the Cosmos renews them, and when things have been dissolved in this way, the Cosmos (like life's good farmer) offers them renewal through the same process of change that moves the Cosmos," (Copenhaver, p. 28).]

All thinkers, in all lands and in all times, have assumed the necessity for postulating the existence of this Substantial Reality. All philosophies worthy of the name have been based upon this thought. Men have given to this Substantial Reality many names - some have called it by the term of Deity (under many titles). Others have called it "The Infinite and Eternal Energy"; others have tried to call it "Matter" - but all have acknowledged its existence. It is self-evident, it needs no argument.

In these lessons we have followed the example of some of the world's greatest thinkers, both ancient and modern - the Hermetic Masters - and have called this Underlying Power - this Substantial Reality - the by the Hermetic name of "THE ALL," which term we consider the most comprehensive of the many terms applied by Man to THAT which transcends names and terms.

We accept and teach the view of the great Hermetic thinkers of all times, as well as of those illumined souls who have reached higher planes of being, both of whom assert that the inner nature of THE ALL is UNKNOWABLE. This must be so, for naught but THE ALL itself can comprehend its own nature and being.

[Throughout the Hermetic and Gnostic writings, the terms "All" and "One" or Monad, may be found to be used interchangeably. The All, by its very nature, containing all that is, and all that is not, may not be comprehended by anything that is not the totality of the All itself. C.H. XI.20 states, "unless you make yourself equal to God, you cannot understand God," (Ibid. p. 41). Actually, that which we call God, Father, One, or All, is in fact none of these things, yet is more. The Secret Book of John states this idea very nicely, "The One is the invisible spirit. We should not think of it as a god or like a god. For it is greater than a god, because it has nothing over it and no lord above it. It does not exist within anything inferior to it, since everything exists within it alone," (Meyer, The Gnostic Bible. pp. 139-140). The Secret Book of John goes on to describe the One with words such as: illimitable, unfathomable, immeasurable, invisible, eternal, unutterable, and unnamable. These Gnostic concepts complement perfectly the Hermetic descriptions. Before moving on, let us take one more look at the Hermetica and her description of God: "This is the God who is greater than any name; this is the God invisible and entirely visible. This God who is evident to the eyes may be seen in the Mind. He is bodiless and many-bodied; or, rather, he is all-bodied. There is nothing that he is not, for he also is all that is, and this is why he has all names, because they are of one father, and this is why he has no name, because he is father of them all," (Copenhaver, p. 20).]

The Hermetists believe and teach that THE ALL, "in itself," is and must ever be UNKNOWABLE. They regard all the theories, guesses and speculations of the theologians and metaphysicians regarding the inner nature of THE ALL, as but the childish efforts of mortal minds to grasp the secret of the Infinite. Such efforts have always failed and will always fall, from the very nature of the task. One pursuing such inquiries travels around and around in the labyrinth of thought, until he is lost to all sane reasoning, action or conduct, and is utterly unfitted for the work of life. He is like the squirrel which frantically runs around and around the circling treadmill wheel of his cage, traveling ever and yet reaching nowhere - at the end a prisoner still, and standing just where he started.

And still more presumptuous are those who attempt to ascribe to THE ALL the personality, qualities, properties, characteristics and attributes of themselves, ascribing to THE ALL the human emotions, feelings, and characteristics, even down to the pettiest qualities of mankind, such as jealousy, susceptibility to flattery and praise, desire for offerings and worship, and all the other survivals from the days of the childhood of the race. Such ideas are not worthy of grown men and women, and are rapidly being discarded.

At this point, it may be proper for me to state that we make a distinction between Religion and Theology - between Philosophy and Metaphysics. Religion, to us, means that intuitional realization of the existence of THE ALL, and one's relationship to it; while Theology means the attempts of men to ascribe personality, qualities, and characteristics to it; their theories regarding its affairs, will, desires, plans, and designs, and their assumption of the office of "middle-men" between THE ALL and the people. Philosophy, to us means the inquiry after knowledge of things knowable and thinkable; while Metaphysics means the attempt to carry the inquiry over and beyond the boundaries and into regions unknowable and unthinkable, and with the same tendency as that of Theology. And consequently, both Religion and Philosophy mean to us things having roots in Reality, while Theology and Metaphysics seem like broken reeds, rooted in the quicksands of ignorance, and affording naught but the most insecure support for the mind or soul of Man. We do not insist upon our students accepting these definitions - we mention them merely to show our position. At any rate, you shall hear very little about Theology and metaphysics in these lessons.

[We feel that some comment has to be made here concerning certain words and their definitions. The use of "Theology" here is meant to represent a dogmatic system of "beliefs," rather than knowledge, whether it be empirical or spiritual. However, the American Heritage Dictionary of the English Language defines Theology: "The study of the nature of God and religious truth; rational inquiry into religious questions." We think that this definition is not at odds with the pursuit of mystical insight. Likewise, "Metaphysics" is defined as: "The branch of philosophy that examines the nature of reality, including the relationship between mind and matter, substance and attribute, fact and value." Given these definitions, we must respectfully disagree with the authors of The Kybalion in regards to their use of terms. The disagreement, though, is purely semantic. That is, it may actually do the student a disservice to paint these words with too broad a brush. The substance of their argument, though, is a valid one. To anthropomorphize the Most High, the One, and the All is to place limits upon the illimitable.

When we see characteristics attributed to God, such as: jealousy, anger, wrath, - or other human characteristics, we know that either the writers were mistakenly imposing human qualities upon the All or that they were in fact describing some other lesser entity. At any rate, while The Kybalion *is certainly not a treatise on Theology, it nevertheless arms the student with the necessary mental and philosophical tools to make a "rational inquiry into religious questions." We would argue, however, that the Kybalion is indeed a metaphysical treatise, because examining the nature of reality is precisely the subject at hand. In our attempts to clarify, we hope that we have not farther muddled the issue. We merely felt that it was necessary to point out the commonly accepted definitions of "Theology" and "Metaphysics" compared to the rather unique interpretation of the authors of* The Kybalion.*]*

But while the essential nature of THE ALL is Unknowable, there are certain truths connected with its existence which the human mind finds itself compelled to accept. And an examination of these reports form a proper subject of inquiry, particularly as they agree with the reports of the Illumined on higher planes. And to this inquiry we now invite you.

> "THAT which is the Fundamental Truth - the Substantial Reality - is beyond true naming, but the Wise Men call it THE ALL."
>
> - *The Kybalion*

> "In its Essence, THE ALL is UNKNOWABLE."
>
> - *The Kybalion*

> "But, the report of Reason must be hospitably received, and treated with respect."
>
> - *The Kybalion*

The human reason, whose reports we must accept so long as we think at all, informs us as follows regarding THE ALL, and that without attempting to remove the veil of the Unknowable:

(1) The All must be ALL that REALLY IS. There can be nothing existing outside of THE ALL, else THE ALL would not.be THE ALL

(2) (THE ALL must be INFINITE, for there is nothing else to define, confine, bound, limit, or restrict THE ALL. It must be Infinite in Time, or ETERNAL, - it must have always

continuously existed, for there is nothing else to have ever created it, and something can never evolve from nothing, and if it had ever "not been," even for a moment, it would not "be" now, - it must continuously exist forever, for there is nothing to destroy it, and it can never "not-be," even for a moment, because something can never become nothing. It must be Infinite in Space - it must be Everywhere, for there is no place outside of THE ALL - it cannot be otherwise than continuous in Space, without break, cessation, separation, or interruption, for there is nothing to break, separate, or interrupt its continuity, and nothing with which to "fill in the gaps." It must be Infinite in Power, or Absolute, for there is nothing to limit, restrict, restrain, confine, disturb or condition it - it is subject to no other Power, for there is no other Power.

(3) THE ALL must be IMMUTABLE, or not subject to change in its real nature, for there is nothing to work changes upon it; nothing into which it could change, nor from which it could have changed. It cannot be added to nor subtracted from; increased nor diminished; nor become greater or lesser in any respect whatsoever. It must have always been, and must always remain, just what it is now - THE ALL - there has never been, is not now, and never will be, anything else into which it can change.

THE ALL being Infinite, Absolute, Eternal and Unchangeable it must follow that anything finite, changeable, fleeting, and conditioned cannot be THE ALL. And as there is Nothing outside of THE ALL, in Reality, then any and all such finite things must be as Nothing in Reality. Now do not become befogged, nor frightened - we are not trying to lead you into the Christian Science field under cover of Hermetic Philosophy. There is a Reconciliation of this apparently contradictory state of affairs. Be patient, we will reach it in time.

We see around us that which is called "Matter," which forms the physical foundation for all forms. Is THE ALL merely Matter? Not at all! Matter cannot manifest Life or Mind, and as Life and Mind are manifested in the Universe, THE ALL cannot be Matter, for nothing rises higher than its own source - nothing is evolved as a consequent that is not involved as an antecedent. And then Modem Science informs us that there is really no such thing as Matter - that what we call Matter is merely "interrupted energy or force," that is, energy or force at a low rate of vibration. As a recent writer has said, "Matter has melted into Mystery." Even Material Science has abandoned the theory of Matter, and now rests on the basis of "Energy."

[I am not a scientist, and I don't have a background in particle physics, so I will not try to make analogies between science and mysticism that may or may not be accurate. However, it is a well established scientific fact that the only real difference between particles such as photons, which compose light, and particles such as quarks, which compose matter, is their mass (measured in electron volts, or eV), and their electrical charge. These attributes cause the particles to behave in one way or another which we ultimately define in terms of matter, light, cosmic rays, etc. So, even though at the time The Kybalion *was written, science could not define the relationship between matter and energy as eloquently as the physicists of today, the fundamental principle that matter is a state of energy, a principle long held by occultists, was and is, essentially correct. In fact, it is interesting to note that while the scientific community continues to relegate the occult sciences to the realm of superstition and pseudo-science, its advances continue to support the basic tenets of the esoteric schools.]*

Then is THE ALL mere Energy or Force? Not Energy or Force as the materialists use the terms, for their energy and force are blind, mechanical things, devoid of Life or Mind. Life and Mind can never evolve from blind Energy or Force, for the reason given a moment ago: "Nothing can rise higher than its source - nothing is evolved unless it is involved - nothing manifests in the effect, unless it is in the cause." And so THE ALL cannot be mere Energy or Force, for, if it were, then there would be no such things as Life and Mind in existence, and we know better than that, for we are Alive and using Mind to consider this very question, and so are those who claim that Energy or Force is Everything.

What is there then higher than Matter or Energy that we know to be existent in the Universe? LIFE AND MIND! Life and Mind in all their varying degrees of unfoldment! "Then," you ask, "do you mean to tell us that THE ALL is LIFE and MIND?" Yes! and No! is our answer. If you mean Life and Mind as we poor petty mortals know them, we say No! THE ALL is not that! "But what kind of Life and Mind do you mean?" you ask.

The answer is "LIVING MIND," as far above that which mortals know by those words as Life and Mind are higher than mechanical forces or matter - INFINITE LIVING MIND as compared to finite "Life and Mind." We mean that which the illumined souls mean when they reverently pronounce the word: "SPIRIT."

THE ALL is Infinite Living Mind - the Illumined call it SPIRIT!

The Kybalion

The Mental Universe

"The Universe is Mental - held in the Mind of THE ALL."
- The Kybalion

THE ALL is SPIRIT! But what is Spirit? This question cannot be answered, for the reason that its definition is practically that of THE ALL, which cannot be explained or defined. Spirit is simply a name that men give to the highest conception of Infinite Living Mind - it means "the Real Essence"; it means Living Mind, as much superior to Life and Mind as we know them, as the latter are superior to mechanical Energy and Matter. Spirit transcends our understanding, and we use the term merely that we may think or speak of THE ALL. For the purposes of thought and understanding, we are justified in thinking of Spirit as Infinite Living Mind, at the same time acknowledging that we cannot fully understand it. We must either do this or stop thinking of the matter at all.

[Here, the Mind (Nous) and Spirit (Pneuma) are used interchangeably. This convention is extremely useful, especially in reconciling the use of these terms in the Gnostic scriptures and in the Hermetica. The Gnostic texts hold Spirit, or Pneuma, to be the supreme definable characteristic of God. The Hermetica, on the other hand, places Mind, or Nous, in that position. In each case, one, either Mind or Spirit, is said to flow immediately from the other. The difference is purely intellectual, rather than substantive. It is important to remember that the word is not the thing itself. This point is illustrated in the Gospel of Philip: *'The names of earthly things are illusory. We stray from the real to the unreal. If you hear the word 'God,' you miss the real and hear the unreal," (Isenberg,* Nag Hammadi Library*).]*

Let us now proceed to a consideration of the nature of the Universe, as a whole and in its parts. What is the Universe? We have seen that there can be nothing outside of THE ALL. Then is the Universe THE ALL? No, this cannot be, because the Universe seems to be made up of MANY, and is constantly changing, and in other ways it does not measure up to the ideas that we are compelled to accept regarding THE ALL, as stated in our last lesson. Then if the Universe be not THE ALL, then it must be Nothing - such is the inevitable conclusion of the mind at first thought. But this will not satisfy the question, for we are sensible of the existence of the Universe. Then if the Universe is neither THE ALL, nor Nothing, what can it be? Let us examine this question.

If the Universe exists at all, or seems to exist, it must proceed in some way from THE ALL - it must be a creation of THE ALL. But as something can never come from nothing, from what could THE ALL have created it. Some philosophers have answered this question by saying that THE ALL created the Universe from ITSELF - that is, from the being and substance of THE ALL. But this will not do, for THE ALL cannot be subtracted from, nor divided, as we have seen, and then again if this be so, would not each particle in the Universe be aware of its being THE ALL - THE ALL could not lose its knowledge of itself, nor actually BECOME an atom, or blind force, or lowly living thing. Some men, indeed, realizing that THE ALL is indeed ALL, and also recognizing that they, the men, existed, have jumped to the conclusion that they and THE ALL were identical, and they have filled the air with shouts of "I AM GOD," to the amusement of the multitude and the sorrow of sages. The claim of the corpuscle that "I am Man!" would be modest in comparison.

But, what indeed is the Universe, if it be not THE ALL, yet not created by THE ALL having separated itself into fragments? What else can it be - of what else can it be made? This is the great question. Let us examine it carefully. We find here that the "Principle of Correspondence" (see Lesson I.) comes to our aid here. The old Hermetic axiom, "As above so below," may be pressed into service at this point. Let us endeavor to get a glimpse of the workings on higher planes by examining those on our own. The Principle of Correspondence must apply to this as well as to other problems.

Let us see! On his own plane of being, how does Man create? Well, first, he may create by making something out of outside materials. But this will not do, for there are no materials outside of THE ALL with which it may create. Well, then, secondly, Man pro-creates or reproduces his kind by the process of begetting, which is self-multiplication accomplished by transferring a portion of his substance to his offspring. But this will not do, because THE ALL cannot transfer or subtract a portion of itself, nor can it reproduce or multiply itself - in the first place there would be a taking away, and in the second case a multiplication or addition to THE ALL, both thoughts being an absurdity. Is there no third way in which MAN creates? Yes, there is - he CREATES MENTALLY! And in so doing he used no outside materials, nor does he reproduce himself, and yet his Spirit pervades the Mental Creation.

Following the Principle of Correspondence, we are justified in considering that THE ALL creates the Universe MENTALLY, in a manner akin to the process whereby Man creates Mental Images. And, here is where the report of the Illumined, as shown by their teachings and writings. Such are the teachings of the Wise Men. Such was the Teaching of Hermes.

THE ALL can create in no other way except mentally, without either using material (and there is none to use), or else reproducing itself (which is also impossible). There is no escape from this conclusion of the Reason, which, as we have said, agrees with the highest teachings of the Illumined. Just as you, student, may create a Universe of your own in your mentality, so does THE ALL create Universes in its own Mentality. But your Universe is the mental creation of a finite Mind, whereas that of THE ALL is the creation of an Infinite. The two are similar in kind, but infinitely different in degree. We shall examine more closely into the process of creation and manifestation as we proceed. But this is the point to fix in your minds at this stage: THE UNIVERSE, AND ALL IT CONTAINS, IS A MENTAL CREATION OF THE ALL. Verily indeed, ALL IS MIND!

> "THE ALL creates in its Infinite Mind countless Universes, which exist for aeons of Time - and yet, to THE ALL, the creation, development, decline and death of a million Universes is as the time of the twinkling of an eye."
>
> - *The Kybalion*

> "The Infinite Mind of THE ALL is the womb of Universes."
> - *The Kybalion*

The Principle of Gender (see Lesson I. and other lessons to follow) is manifested on all planes of life, material, mental and spiritual. But, as we have said before, "Gender" does not mean "Sex." Sex is merely a material manifestation of gender. "Gender" means "relating to generation or creation." And whenever anything is generated or created, on any plane, the Principle of Gender must be manifested. And this is true even in the creation of Universes.

Now do not jump to the conclusion that we are teaching that there is a male and female God, or Creator. That idea is merely a distortion of the ancient teachings on the subject. The true teaching is that THE ALL, in itself, is above Gender, as it is above every other Law, including those of Time and Space. It is the Law, from which the laws proceed, and it is not subject to them. But when THE ALL manifests on the plane of generation or creation, then it acts according to Law and Principle, for it is moving on a lower Plane of Being. And consequently it manifests the Principle of Gender, in its Masculine and Feminine aspects, on the Mental Plane, of course.

This idea may seem startling to some of you who hear it for the first time, but you have all really passively accepted it in your everyday conceptions. You speak of the Fatherhood of God, and the Motherhood of Nature - of God, the Divine Father, and the Universal Mother - and have thus instinctively acknowledged the Principle of Gender in the Universe. Is this not so?

But, the Hermetic teaching does not imply a real duality - THE ALL is ONE - the Two Aspects are merely aspects of manifestation. The teaching is that The Masculine Principle manifested by THE ALL stands, in a way, apart from the actual mental creation of the Universe. It projects its Will toward the Feminine Principle (which may be called "Nature") whereupon the latter begins the actual work of the evolution of the Universe, from simple "centers of activity" on to man, and then on and on still higher, all according to well-established and firmly enforced Laws of Nature. If you prefer the old figures of thought, you may think of the Masculine Principle as GOD, the Father, and of the Feminine Principle as NATURE, the Universal Mother, from whose womb all things have been born. This is more than a mere poetic figure of speech - it is an idea of the actual process of the creation of the Universe. But always remember, that THE ALL is but One, and that in its Infinite Mind the Universe is generated, created and exists.

It may help you to get the proper idea, if you will apply the Law of Correspondence to yourself, and your own mind. You know that the part of You which you call "I," in a sense, stands apart and witnesses the creation of mental Images in your own mind. The part of your mind in which the mental generation is accomplished may be called the "Me" in distinction from the "I" which stands apart and witnesses and examines the thoughts, ideas and images of the "Me." "As above, so below," remember, and the phenomena of one plane may be employed to solve the riddles of higher or lower planes.

Is it any wonder that You, the child, feel that instinctive reverence for THE ALL, which feeling we call "religion" - that respect, and reverence for the FATHER MIND? Is it any wonder that, when you consider the works and wonders of Nature, you are overcome with a mighty feeling which has its roots way down in your inmost being? It is the MOTHER MIND that you are pressing close up to, like a babe to the breast.

Do not make the mistake of supposing that the little world you see around you - the Earth, which is a mere grain of dust in the Universe - is the Universe itself. There are millions upon millions of such worlds, and greater. And there are millions of millions of such Universes in existence within the Infinite Mind of THE ALL. And even in our own little solar system there are regions and planes of life far higher than ours, and beings compared to which we earth-bound mortals are as the slimy life-forms that dwell on the ocean's bed when compared to Man. There· are beings with powers and attributes higher than Man has ever dreamed of the gods possessing. And yet these beings were once as you, and still lower - and you will be even as they, and still higher, in ti.me, for such is the Destiny of Man as reported by the Illumined.

And Death is not real, even in the Relative sense - it is but Birth to a new life - and You shall go on, and on, and on, to higher and still higher planes of life, for aeons upon aeons of ti.me. The Universe is your home, and you shall explore its farthest recesses before the end of ti.me. You are dwelling in the Infinite Mind of THE ALL, and your possibilities and opportunities are infinite, both in ti.me and space. And at the end of the Grand Cycle of Aeons, when THE ALL shall draw back into itself all of its creations - you will go gladly for you will then be able to know the Whole Truth of being At One with THE ALL. Such is the report of the Illumined - those who have advanced well along The Path.

And, in the meantime, rest calm and serene - you are safe and protected by the Infinite Power of the FATHER-MOTHER MIND.

[Father-Mother is a term sometimes used by the Gnostics to describe the androgynous nature of God, the Holy Spirit in particular, in texts such as the Secret Book of John.]

"Within the Father-Mother Mind, mortal children are at home."
- *The Kybalion*

"There is not one who is Fatherless, nor Motherless in the Universe."
- *The Kybalion*

The Kybalion

The Divine Paradox

"The half-wise, recognizing the comparative unreality of the Universe, imagine that they may defy its Laws - such are vain and presumptuous fools, and they are broken against the rocks and tom asunder by the elements by reason of their folly. The truly wise, knowing the nature of the Universe, use Law against laws; the higher against the lower; and by the Art of Alchemy transmute that which is undesirable into that which is worthy, and thus triumph. Mastery consists not in abnormal dreams, visions and fantastic imaginings or living, but in using the higher forces against the lower - escaping the pains of the lower planes by vibrating on the higher. Transmutation, not presumptuous denial, is the weapon of the Master."

— *The Kybalion*

This is the paradox of the Universe, resulting from the Principle of Polarity which manifests when THE ALL begins to Create - hearken to it for it points the difference between half-wisdom and wisdom. While to THE INFINITE ALL, the Universe, its laws, its Powers, its Life, its Phenomena, are as things witnessed in the state of Meditation or Dream; yet to all that is Finite, the Universe must be treated as Real, and life, and action, and thought, must be based thereupon, accordingly, although with an ever understanding of the Higher Truth. Each according to its own Plane and Laws. Were THE ALL to imagine that the Universe were indeed Reality, then woe to the Universe, for there would be then no escape from lower to higher, divineward - then would the Universe become a fixity and progress would become impossible. And if Man, owing to half-wisdom, acts and lives and thinks of the Universe as merely a dream (akin to his own finite dreams) then indeed does it so become for him, and like a sleep-walker he stumbles ever around and around in a circle, making no progress, and being forced into an awakening at last by his falling bruised and bleeding over the Natural Laws which he ignored. Keep your mind ever on the Star, but let your eyes watch over your footsteps, lest you fall into the mire by reason of your upward gaze. Remember the Divine Paradox, that while the Universe IS NOT, still IT IS. Remember ever the Two Poles of Truth, the Absolute and the Relative. Beware of Half-Truths.

What Hermetists know as "the Law of Paradox" is an aspect of the Principle of Polarity. The Hermetic writings are filled with references to the appearance of the Paradox in the consideration of the problems of Life and Being. The Teachers are constantly warning their students against the error of omitting the "other side" of any question. And their warnings are particularly directed to the problems of the Absolute and the Relative, which perplex all students of philosophy, and which cause so many to think and act contrary to what is generally known as "common sense." And we caution all students to be sure to grasp the Divine Paradox of the Absolute and Relative, lest they become entangled in the mire of the Half-Truth. With this in view this particular lesson has been written. Read it carefully!

The first thought that comes to the thinking man after he realizes the truth that the Universe is a Mental Creation of THE ALL, is that the Universe and all that it contains is a mere illusion; an unreality; against which idea his instincts revolt.

[The paradox of the Absolute vs. Relative pervades the Hermetic writings, and can often lead to seeming contradictions, especially concerning the nature of Good and Evil. According to the Corpus Hermeticum, *as well as many Gnostic scriptures,*

the Good is in God alone (see C.H. VI, .Copenhaver, pp. 21-23), and that anything less than the One, Unknowable God, is less than good, and therefore evil. This is true, of course, but only in an Absolute sense. The Corpus Hermeticum *does address this situation, but rarely enough that the student may easily pass over the lesson without gaining its subtle truths. It is probably stated most clearly in C.H. VI.3, which states, 'With reference to humanity, one uses the term 'good' in comparison to 'evil.' Here below, the evil that is not excessive is the good, and the good is the least amount of evil here below." This passage clearly states that good and evil are relative terms in the world here below, where we live and act. Or again we read in the* Gospel of Philip, *"Light and darkness, life and death, and right and left are siblings of one another, and inseparable. For this reason the good are not good, the bad are not bad, life is not life, and death is not death." And then further goes on to say, "…the good of the world is not really good and the evil of the world is not really evil." To behave in this world as if the absolutism of the highest realm were applicable only, can lead to an extreme form of asceticism, and ultimately to nihilism. Individuals and sects who have succumbed to this type of extremism have simply followed a half-truth to its logical conclusion. It is important, then, for the student to comprehend fully this principle and how it operates on the various planes of existence. Only by looking at the whole picture can any one part of it be put into a proper perspective.]*

But this, like all other great truths, must be considered both from the Absolute and the Relative points of view. From the Absolute viewpoint, of course, the Universe is in the nature of an illusion, a dream, a phantasmagoria, as compared to THE ALL in itself. We recognize this even in our ordinary view, for we speak of the world as "a fleeting show" that comes and goes, is born and dies - for the element of impermanence and change, finiteness and unsubstantiality, must ever be connected with the idea of a created Universe when it is contrasted with the idea of THE ALL, no matter what may be our beliefs concerning the nature of both. Philosopher, metaphysician, scientist and theologian all agree upon this idea, and the thought is found in all forms of philosophical thought and religious conceptions, as well as in the theories of the respective schools of metaphysics and theology.

So, the Hermetic Teachings do not preach the unsubstantiality of the Universe in any stronger terms than those more familiar to you, although their presentation of the subject may seem somewhat more startling. Anything that has a beginning and an ending must be, in a sense, unreal and untrue, and the Universe comes under the rule, in all schools of thought. From the Absolute point of view, there is nothing Real except THE ALL, no matter what terms we may use in thinking of, or whether it be a Mental Creation in the Mind of THE ALL - it is unsubstantial, non-enduring, a thing of time, space and change. We want you to realize this fact thoroughly, before you pass judgment on the Hermetic conception of the Mental nature of the Universe. Think over any and all of the other conceptions, and see whether this be not true of them.

But the Absolute point of view shows merely one side of the picture - the other side is the Relative one. Absolute Truth has been defined as "Things as the mind of God knows them," while Relative Truth is "Things as the highest reason of Man understands them." And so while to THE ALL the Universe must be unreal and illusionary, a mere dream or result of meditation, - nevertheless, to the finite minds forming a part of that Universe, and viewing it through mortal faculties, the Universe is very real indeed, and must be so considered. In recognizing the Absolute view, we must not make the mistake of ignoring or denying the facts and phenomena of the Universe as they present themselves to our mortal faculties - we are not THE ALL, remember.

To take familiar illustrations, we all recognize the fact that matter "exists" to our senses - we will fare badly if we do not. And yet, even our finite minds understand the scientific dictum that there is no such thing as

Matter from a scientific point of view - that which we call Matter is held to be merely an aggregation of atoms, which atoms themselves are merely a grouping of units of force, called electrons or "ions," vibrating and in constant circular motion. *[As stated previously, modern science would describe this in somewhat different terms, but the principle remains the same.]* We kick a stone and we feel the impact - it seems to be real, notwithstanding that we know it to be merely what we have stated above. But remember that our foot, which feels the impact by means of our brains, is likewise Matter, so constituted of electrons, and for that matter so are our brains. And, at the best, if it were not by reason of our Mind, we would not know the foot or stone at all.

Then again, the ideal of the artist or sculptor, which he is endeavoring to reproduce in stone or on canvas, seems very real to him. So do the characters in the mind of the author or dramatist, which he seeks to express so that others may recognize them. And if this be true in the case of our finite minds, what must be the degree of Reality in the mental Images created in the Mind of the Infinite? Oh, friends, to mortals this Universe of Mentality is very real indeed - it is the only one we can ever know, though we rise from plane to plane, higher and higher in it. To know it otherwise, by actual experience, we must be THE ALL itself. It is true that the higher we rise in the scale - the nearer to "the mind of the Father" we reach - the more apparent becomes the illusory nature of finite things, but not until THE ALL finally withdraws us into itself does the vision actually vanish.

So, we need not dwell upon the feature of illusion. Rather let us, recognizing the real nature of the Universe, seek to understand its mental laws, and endeavor to use them to the best effect in our upward progress through life, as we travel from plane to plane of being. The Laws of the Universe are none the less "Iron Laws" because of their mental nature. All, except THE ALL, are bound by them. What is IN THE INFINITE MIND OF THE ALL is REAL in a degree second only to that Reality itself which is vested in the nature of THE ALL.

So, do not feel insecure or afraid - we are all HELD FIRMLY IN THE INFINITE MIND OF THE ALL, and there is naught to hurt us or for us to fear. There is no Power outside of THE ALL to affect us. So we may rest calm and secure. There is a world of comfort and security in this realization when once attained. Then "calm and peaceful do we sleep, rocked in the Cradle of the Deep" - resting safely on the bosom of the Ocean of Infinite Mind, which is THE ALL. In THE ALL, indeed, do "we live and move and have our being."

Matter is none the less Matter to us, while we dwell on the plane of Matter, although we know it to be merely an aggregation of "electrons," or particles of Force, vibrating rapidly and gyrating around each other in the formations of atoms; the atoms in turn vibrating and gyrating, forming molecules, which latter in turn form larger masses of Matter. Nor does Matter become less Matter, when we follow the inquiry still further, and learn from the Hermetic Teachings, that the "Force" of which the electrons are but units is merely a manifestation of the Mind of THE ALL, and like all else in the Universe is purely Mental in its nature. While on the Plane of Matter, we must recognize its phenomena - we may control Matter (as all Masters of higher or lesser degree do), but we do so by applying the higher forces. We commit a folly when we attempt to deny the existence of Matter in the relative aspect. We may deny its mastery over us - and rightly so - but we should not attempt to ignore it in its relative aspect, at least so long as we dwell upon its plane.

Nor do the Laws of Nature become less constant or effective, when we know them, likewise, to be merely mental creations. They are in full effect on the various planes. We overcome the lower laws, by applying still higher ones - and in this way only. But we cannot escape Law or rise above it entirely. Nothing but THE ALL can escape Law- and that because THE ALL is LAW itself, from which all Laws emerge. The most advanced Masters may acquire the powers usually attributed to the gods of men; and there are countless ranks of being, in the great hierarchy of life, whose being and power transcends even that of the highest Master among men to a degree unthinkable by mortals, but even the highest Master, and the highest Being, must bow to the Law, and be as Nothing in the eye of THE ALL. So that if even these highest Beings, whose powers exceed even those attributed by men to their gods - if even these are bound by and are subservient to Law, then imagine the presumption of mortal man, of our race and grade, when he dares to consider the Laws of Nature as "unreal"!; visionary and illusory, because he happens to be able to grasp the truth that the Laws are Mental in nature, and simply Mental Creations of THE ALL. Those Laws which THE ALL intends to be governing Laws are not to be defied are argued away. So long as the Universe endures, will they endure - for the Universe exists by virtue of these Laws which form its framework and which hold it together.

The Hermetic Principle of Mentalism while explaining the true nature of the Universe upon the principle that all is Mental, does not change the scientific conceptions of the Universe, Life, or Evolution. In fact, science merely corroborates the Hermetic Teachings. The latter merely teaches that the nature of the Universe is "Mental," while modem science has taught that it is "Material"; or (of late) that it is "Energy" at the last analysis. The Hermetic Teachings have no Tault to find with Herbert Spencer's basic principle which postulates the existence of an "Infinite and Eternal Energy, from which all things proceed." In fact, the Hermetics recognize in Spencer's philosophy the highest outside statement of the workings of the Natural Laws that have ever been promulgated, and they believe Spencer to have been a reincarnation of an ancient philosopher who dwelt in ancient Egypt thousands of years ago, and who later incarnated as Heraclitus, the Grecian philosopher who lived B.C. 500. And they regard his statement of the "Infinite and Eternal Energy" as directly in the line of the Hermetic Philosophy, the student of Spencer will be able to unlock many doors of the inner philosophical conceptions of the great English philosopher, whose work shows the results of the preparation of his previous incarnations. His teachings regarding Evolution and Rhythm are in almost perfect agreement with the Hermetic Teachings regarding the Principle of Rhythm.

So, the student of Hermetics need not lay aside any of his cherished scientific views regarding the Universe. All he is asked to do is to grasp the underlying principle of "THE ALL is Mind; the Universe is Mental - held in the mind of THE ALL." He will find that the other six of the Seven Principles will "fit into" his scientific knowledge, and will serve to bring out obscure points and to throw light in dark comers. This is not to be wondered at, when we realize the influence of the Hermetic thought of the early philosophers of Greece, upon whose foundations of thought the theories of modern science largely rest. The acceptance of the First Hermetic Principle (Mentalism) is the only great point of difference between Modem Science and Hermetic students, and Science is gradually moving toward the Hermetic position in its groping in the dark for a way out of the Labyrinth into which it has wandered in its search for Reality.

The purpose of this lesson is to impress upon the minds of our students the fact that, to all intents and purposes, the Universe and its laws, and its phenomena, are just as REAL, so far as Man is concerned, as they would be under the hypothesis of Materialism or Energism. Under any hypothesis the Universe in its outer aspect is changing, ever- flowing, and transitory - and therefore devoid of substantiality and reality. But (note the other pole of the truth) under the same hypothesis, we are compelled to ACT AND LIVE as if the fleeting things were real and substantial. With this difference, always, between the various hypotheses - that under the old views Mental Power was ignored as a Natural Force, while under Mentalism it becomes the Greatest Natural Force. And this one difference revolutionizes Life, to those who understand the Principle and its resulting laws and practice.

So, finally, students all, grasp the advantage of Mentalism, and learn to know, use and apply the laws resulting therefrom. But do not yield to the temptation which, as *The Kybalion* states, overcomes the half-wise and which causes them to be hypnotized by the apparent unreality of things, the consequence being that they wander about like dream- people dwelling in a world of dreams, ignoring the practical work and life of man, the end being that "they are broken against the rocks and torn asunder by the elements, by reason of their folly." Rather follow the example of the wise, which the same authority states, "use Law against Laws; the higher against the lower; and by the Art of Alchemy transmute that which is undesirable into that which is worthy, and thus triumph." Following the authority, let us avoid the half-wisdom (which is folly) which ignores the truth that: "Mastery consists not in abnormal dreams, visions, and fantastic imaginings or living, but in using the higher forces against the lower - escaping the pains of the lower planes by vibrating on the higher." Remember always, student, that "Transmutation, not presumptuous denial, is the weapon of the Master." The above quotations are from *The Kybalion*, and are worthy of being committed to memory by the student.

We do not live in a world of dreams, but in an Universe which while relative, is real so far as our lives and actions are concerned. Our business in the Universe is not to deny its existence, but to LIVE, using the Laws to rise from lower to higher - living on, doing the best that we can under the circumstances arising each day, and living, so far as is possible, to our biggest ideas and ideals. The true Meaning of Life is not known to men on this plane, if indeed to any - but the highest authorities, and our own intuitions, teach us that we will make no mistake in living up to the best that is in us, so far as is possible, and realizing that Universal tendency in the same direction in spite of apparent evidence to the contrary. We are all on The Path - and the road leads upward ever, with frequent resting places.

Read the message of *The Kybalion* - and follow the example of "the wise" - avoiding the mistake of "the half-wise" who perish by reason of their folly.

"THE ALL" In All

"While All is in THE ALL, it is equally true that THE ALL is in All. To him who truly understand this truth hath come great knowledge."

- *The Kybalion*

How often have the majority of people heard repeated the statement that their Deity (called by many names) was "All in All" and how little have they suspected the inner occult truth concealed by these carelessly uttered words? The commonly used expression is a survival of the ancient Hermetic Maxim quoted above. As The Kybalion says: "To him who truly understands this truth, hath come great knowledge." And, this being so, let us seek this truth, the understanding of which means so much. In this statement of truth - this Hermetic Maxim - is concealed one of the greatest philosophical, scientific and religious truths.

We have given you the Hermetic Teaching regarding the Mental Nature of the Universe - the truth that "the Universe is Mental - held in the Mind of THE ALL." As the Kybalion says, in the passage quoted above: "All is in THE ALL." But note also the co-related statement, that: "It is equally true that THE ALL is in All." This apparently contradictory statement is reconcilable under the Law of Paradox. It is, moreover, an exact Hermetic statement of the relations existing between THE ALL and its Mental Universe. We have seen how "All is in THE ALL" - now let us examine the other aspect of the subject.

The Hermetic Teachings are to the effect that THE ALL is Imminent in (remaining within; inherent; abiding within) its Universe, and in every part, particle, unit, or combination, within the Universe. This statement is usually illustrated by the Teachers by a reference to the Principle of Correspondence. The Teacher instructs the student to form a Mental Image of something, a person, an idea, something having a mental form, the favorite example being that of the author, dramatist, painter, or sculptor, is, in a sense, immanent in; remaining within; or abiding within, the mental image also. In other words, the entire virtue, life, spirit, of reality in the mental image is derived from the "immanent mind" of the thinker. Consider this for a moment, until the idea is grasped.

To take a modem example, let us say that Othello, Iago, Hamlet, Lear, Richard III, existed merely in the mind of Shakespeare, at the time of their conception or creation. And yet, Shakespeare also existed within each of these characters, giving them their vitality, spirit, and action. Whose is the "spirit" of the characters that we know as Micawber, Oliver Twist, Uriah Heep - is it Dickens, or have each of these characters a personal spirit, independent of their creator? Have the Venus of Medici, the Sistine Madonna, the Apollo Belvidere, spirits and reality of their own, or do they represent the spiritual and mental power of their creators? The Law of Paradox explains that both propositions are true, viewed from the proper viewpoints. Micawber is both Micawber, and yet Dickens. And, again, while Micawber may be said to be Dickens, yet Dickens is not identical with Micawber. Man, like Micawber, may exclaim: "The Spirit of my Creator is inherent within me - and yet I am not HE!" How different this is from the shocking half-truth so vociferously announced by certain of the half-wise, who fill the air with their raucous cries of: "I am God!" Imagine poor Micawber, or the sneaky Uriah Heep, crying: "I am Dickens"; or some of the lowly clods in one of Shakespeare's plays, eloquently announcing that: "I am Shakespeare!" THE ALL is in the earthworm, and yet the earthworm is far from being THE ALL. And still the wonder remains, that though the earthworm exists merely as a lowly thing, created and having its being solely within the Mind of THE ALL - yet THE ALL is immanent in the earthworm, and in the particles that go to make up the earthworm. Can there be any greater mystery than this of "All in THE ALL; and THE ALL IN ALL?"

[Corpus Hermeticum XII.21-23 contains a number of statements concerning the All in All:

- *"In what comes to be and has come to be, there is nothing where God is not, nothing beyond Him."*

- *"And this is God, the All."*

- *"But in the All there is nothing that He is not. Hence, neither magnitude nor place nor quality nor figure nor time has any bearing on God. For God is All. And the All permeates everything and surrounds everything."]*

The student will, of course, realize that the illustrations given above are necessarily imperfect and inadequate, for they represent the creation of mental images in finite minds, while the Universe is a creation of Infinite Mind - and the difference between the two poles separates them. And yet it is merely a matter of degree - the same Principle is in operation - the Principle of Correspondence manifests in each - "As above, so below; as below, so above."

And, in the degree that Man realizes the existence of the Indwelling Spirit immanent within his being, so will he rise in the spiritual scale of life. This is what spiritual development means - the recognition, realization, and manifestation of the Spirit within us. Try to remember this last definition - that of spiritual development. It contains the Truth of True Religion.

[The word "religion" comes from the Latin "religare," meaning literally "to bind again" (re+ligare). The Latin "ligare" means "to bind" or "to join together." The prefix "re" means "again" or "back" or "backward." So, the word "religion" means not only a joining with God, but also implies that this sought-after union is, in fact, a return to some previous state of being. This is precisely the view of the Hermeticists and Gnostics. Gnostic theology states that within every human is a spark, or a fragment of that original light. It is that same Spirit (Pneuma) which gives life and animates the human Soul (Psyche). The reintegration into the "Fullness of God" (Pleroma) is the aspirant's highest and ultimate objective: the Great Work.]

There are many planes of Being - many sub-planes of Life - many degrees of existence in the Universe. And all depend upon the advancement of beings in the scale, of which scale the lowest point is the grossest matter, the highest being separated only by the thinnest division from the SPIRIT of THE ALL. And, upward and onward along this Scale of Life, everything is moving. All are on the Path, whose end is THE ALL. All progress is a Returning Home. All is Upward and Onward, in spite of all seemingly contradictory appearances. Such is the message of the Illumined.

The Hermetic Teachings concerning the process of the Mental Creation of the Universe are that at the beginning of the Creative Cycle, THE ALL, in its aspect of Being, projects its Will toward its aspect of "Becoming" and the process of creation begins. It is taught that the process consists of the lowering of Vibration until a very low degree of vibratory energy is reached, at which point the grossest possible form of Matter is manifested. This process is called the stage of Involution, in which THE All becomes "involved," or "wrapped up," in its creation. This process is believed by the Hermetists to have a Correspondence to the mental process of an artist, writer, or inventor, who becomes so wrapped up in his mental creation as to almost forget his own existence and who, for the time being, almost "lives in his creation." If instead of "wrapped" we use the word "rapt," perhaps we will give a better idea of what is meant.

This Involution stage of Creation is sometimes called the "Outpouring" of the Divine Energy, just as the Evolutionary state is called the "Indrawing." The extreme pole of the Creative process is considered to be the furthest removed from THE ALL, while the beginning of the Evolutionary stage is regarded as the beginning of the return swing of the pendulum of Rhythm - a "coming home" idea being held in all of the Hermetic Teachings.

The Teachings are that during the "Outpouring," the vibrations become lower and lower until finally the urge ceases, and the return swing begins. But there is this difference, that while in the "Outpouring" the creative forces manifest compactly and as a whole, yet from the beginning of the Evolutionary or "Indrawing" stage, there is manifested the Law of Individualization - that is, the tendency to separate into Units of Force, so that finally that which left THE ALL as unindividualized energy returns to its source as countless highly developed Units of Life, having risen higher and higher in the scale by means of Physical, Mental and Spiritual Evolution.

[This "Outpouring" and "indrawing" can be depicted graphically as the Qabalistic Tree of Life. The Sephiroth of the Tree of Life depict a precise pattern of emanation, from the All down to the physical plane of existence. Due to the individualization that occurs on the lower planes, the path of return for each individual will be unique, determined by the unique experiences of the individual. That is why there are so many interconnected paths on the Tree. There is only one route down the Tree, but many possible paths of return.]

The ancient Hermetists use the word "Meditation" in describing the process of the mental creation of the Universe in the Mind of THE ALL, the word "Contemplation" also being frequently employed. But the idea intended seems to be that of the employment of the Divine Attention. "Attention" is a word derived from the Latin root, meaning "to reach out; to stretch out," and so the act of Attention is really a mental "reaching out; extension" of mental energy, so that the underlying idea is readily understood when we examine into the real meaning of "Attention."

The Hermetic Teachings regarding the process of Evolution are that, THE ALL, having meditated upon the beginning of the Creation - having thus established the material foundations of the Universe - having thought it into existence - then gradually awakens or rouses from its Meditation and in so doing starts into manifestation the process of Evolution, on the material, mental and spiritual planes, successively and in order. Thus the upward movement begins - and all beings to move Spiritward, Matter becomes less gross; the Units spring into being; the combinations begin to form; Life appears and manifests in higher and higher forms; and Mind becomes more and more in evidence - the vibrations constantly becoming higher. In short, the entire process of Evolution, in all of its phases, begins, and proceeds according to the established "Laws of the Indrawing" process. All of this occupies aeons upon aeons of Man's time, each aeon containing countless millions of years, but yet the Illumined inform us that the entire creation, including Involution and Evolution, of an Universe, is but "as the twinkle of the eye" to THE ALL. At the end of countless cycles of aeons of time, THE ALL withdraws its Attention - its Contemplation and Meditation - of the Universe, for the Great Work is finished - and All is withdrawn into THE ALL from which it emerged. But Mystery of Mysteries -

the Spirit of each soul is not annihilated, but is infinitely expanded - the Created and the Creator are merged. Such is the report of the Illumined!

The above illustration of the "meditation," and subsequent "awakening from meditation," of THE AIL, is of course but an attempt of the teachers to describe the Infinite process by a finite example. And, of the teachers to describe the Infinite process by a finite example. And, yet: "As Below, so Above." The difference is merely in degree. And just as THE ALL arouses itself from the meditation upon the Universe, so does Man (in time) cease from manifesting upon the Material Plane, and withdraws himself more and more into the Indwelling Spirit, which is indeed "The Divine Ego."

There is one more matter of which we desire to speak in this lesson, and that comes very near to an invasion of the Metaphysical field of speculation, although our purpose is merely to show the futility of such speculation. We allude to the question which inevitably comes to the mind of all thinkers who have ventured to seek the Truth. The question is "WHY does THE ALL create Universes?" The question may be asked in different forms, but the above is the gist of the inquiry.

Men have striven hard to answer this question, but still there is not answer worthy of the name. Some have imagined that THE ALL had something to gain by it, but this is absurd, for what could THE All gain that it did not already possess? Others have sought the answer in the idea that THE ALL "wished something to love" and others that it created for pleasure, or amusement; or because it "was lonely" or to manifest its power; - all puerile explanations and ideas, belonging to the childish period of thought.

Others have sought to explain the mystery by assuming that THE ALL found itself "compelled" to create, by reason of its own "internal nature" - its "creative instinct." This idea is in advance of the others, but its weak point lies in the idea of THE ALL being "compelled" by anything, internal or external. If its "internal nature," or "creative instinct," compelled it to do anything, then the "internal nature" or "creative instinct" would be the Absolute, instead of THE ALL, and so accordingly that part of the proposition fails. And, yet, THE ALL does create and manifest, and seems to find some kind of satisfaction in so doing. And it is difficult to escape the conclusion that in some infinite degree it must have what would correspond to an "inner nature," or "creative instinct," in man, with correspondingly infinite Desire and Will. It could not act unless it Willed to Act; and it would not Will to Act, unless it Desired to Act and it would not Desire to Act unless it obtained some Satisfaction thereby. And all of these things would belong to an "Inner Nature," and might be postulated as existing according to the law of Correspondence. But, still, we prefer to think of THE ALL as acting entirely FREE from any influence, internal as well as external. That is the problem which lies at the root of difficulty - and the difficulty that lies at the root of the problem.

Strictly speaking, there cannot be said to be any "Reason" whatsoever for THE ALL to act, for a "reason" implies a "cause," and THE ALL is above Cause and Effect, except when it Wills to become a Cause, at which time the Principle is set into motion. So, you see, the matter is Unthinkable, just as THE ALL is Unknowable. Just as we say THE ALL merely "IS" - so we are compelled to say that "THE ALL ACTS BECAUSE IT ACTS." At the last, THE ALL is All Reason in Itself; All Law in Itself; All Action in Itself - and it may be said, truthfully, that THE ALL is Its Own Reason; its own Law; its own Act - or still further, that THE ALL; Its Reason; Its Act; its Law; are ONE, all being names for the same thing. In the opinion of those who are giving you these present lessons, the answer is locked up in the INNER SELF of THE ALL, along with its

Secret of Being. The Law of Correspondence, in our opinion, reaches only to that aspect of THE ALL, which may be spoken of as "The Aspect of BECOMING." Back of that Aspect is "The Aspect of BEING" in which all Laws are lost in LAW; all Principles merge into PRINCIPLE - and THE ALL; PRINCIPLE; and BEING; are IDENTICAL, ONE AND THE SAME. Therefore, Metaphysical speculation on this point is futile. We go into the matter here, merely to show that we recognize the question, and also the absurdity of the ordinary answers of metaphysics and theology.

In conclusion, it may be of interest to our students to learn that while some of the ancient, and modem, Hermetic Teachers have rather inclined in the direction of applying the Principle of Correspondence to the question, with the result of the "Inner Nature" conclusion, - still the legends have it that HERMES, the Great, when asked this question by his advanced students, answered them by PRESSING HIS LIPS TIGHTLY TOGETHER and saying not a word, indicating that there WAS NO ANSWER. But, then, he may have intended to apply the axiom of his philosophy, the "The lips of Wisdom are closed, except to the ears of Understanding," believing that even his advanced students did not possess the Understanding which entitled them to the Teaching. At any rate, if Hermes possessed the Secret, he failed to impart it, and so far as the world is concerned THE LIPS OF HERMES ARE CLOSED regarding it. And where the Great Hermes hesitated to speak, what mortal may dare to teach?

[The question of "Why?" is indeed an ages old and seemingly futile question. However, the mere fact that we can ask the question, indeed, often feel compelled to ask the question, suggests that the question is answerable. The admonishments given here seem to serve, either intentionally or unintentionally, precisely the opposite of their stated intent. The student of the occult is a seeker of hidden wisdom. How, then, could the student turn away from the greatest, most profound, and most closely guarded secret in the history of the Universe? We are told that Hermes pressed his lips tightly together. Consider that perhaps instead of indicating that there was no answer, that this gesture may imply that the answer is to be found in silence. Or, that the answer is incommunicable. That is, that it must be learned directly through gnostic revelation, being impossible to impart any other way.]

But, remember, that whatever be the answer to this problem, if indeed there be an answer, the truth remains that: "While All is in THE ALL, it is equally true that THE ALL is in All." The Teaching on this point is emphatic. And, we may add the concluding words of the quotation: "To him who truly understands this truth, hath come great knowledge."

The Kybalion

Planes of Correspondence

"As above, so below; as below, so above." - *The Kybalion*

[This is perhaps the most famous of all Hermetic axioms. That there is a correspondence between the material, mental, and spiritual planes is a fundamental principle underlying all types of religious and magical ritual This idea is also key to understanding humanity, the Universe, and the relationship between the two, and thus, our relationship to God. The Gospel of Thomas addresses this: "But the kingdom is inside you and it is outside you. When you know yourselves, then you will be known, and you will understand that you are children of the living father," (Gnostic Bible, p. 45). Also, the Gospel of Philip suggests that the "upper" and "lower" are better thought of as the "inner" and "outer," (cf. Gospel of Philip, Gnostic Bible, p. 278). Therefore, the "uppermost" is actually the "innermost."]

The great Second Hermetic Principle embodies the truth that there is a harmony, agreement, and correspondence between the several planes of Manifestation, Life and Being. This truth is a truth because all that is included in the Universe emanates from the same source, and the same laws, principles, and characteristics apply to each unit, or combination of units, of activity, as each manifests its own phenomena upon its own plane.

For the purpose of convenience of thought and study, the Hermetic Philosophy considers that the Universe may be divided into three great classes of phenomena, known as the Three Great Planes, namely:

1. The Great Physical Plane.
2. The Great Mental Plane.
3. The Great Spiritual Plane.

These divisions are more or less artificial and arbitrary, for the truth is that all of the three divisions are but ascending degrees of the great scale of Life, the lowers point of which is undifferentiated Matter, and the highest point that of Spirit. And, moreover, the different Planes shade into each other, so that no hard and fast division may be made between the higher phenomena of the Physical and the lower of the Mental; or between the higher of the Mental and the lower of the Spiritual.

In short, the Three Great Planes may be regarded as three great groups of degrees of Life Manifestation. While the purposes of this little book do not allow us to enter into an extended discussion of, or explanation of, the subject of these different planes, still we think it well to give a general description of the same at this point.

At the beginning we may as well consider the question so often asked by the neophyte, who desires to be informed regarding the meaning of the word "Plane," which term has been very freely used, and very poorly explained, in many recent works upon the subject of occultism. The question is generally about as flows: "Is a Plane a place having dimensions, or is it merely a condition or state?" We answer: "No, not a place, nor ordinary dimension of space; and yet more than a state of condition. It may be considered as a state of condition, and yet the state or condition is a degree of dimension, in a scale subject to measurement." Somewhat paradoxical, is it not? But let us examine the matter. A "dimension," you know, is "a measure in a straight line, relating to measure," etc. The ordinary dimensions of space are length, breadth, and height, or perhaps length, breadth, height, thickness or circumference. But there is another dimension of "created things" or "measure in a straight line," known to occultists, and to scientists as well, although the latter have not as yet applied the term "dimension" to it - and this new dimension, which, by the way, is the much speculated-about "Fourth Dimension," is the standard used in determining the degrees or "planes."

This Fourth Dimension may be called "The Dimension of Vibration." It is a fact well known to modem science, as well as to the Hermetists who have embodied the truth in their "Third Hermetic Principle," that "everything is in motion; everything vibrates; nothing is at rest." From the highest manifestation, to the lowest, everything and all things Vibrate. Not only do they vibrate at different rates of motion, but as in different directions and in a different manner. The degrees of the rate of vibrations constitute the degrees of measurement on the Scale of Vibrations - in other words the degrees of the Fourth Dimension. And these degrees form what occultists call "Planes." The higher the degree of rate of vibration, the higher the plane, and the higher the manifestation of Life occupying that plane. So that while a plane is not "a place," nor yet "a state or condition," yet it possesses qualities common to both. We shall have more to say regarding the subject of the scale of Vibrations in our next lessons, in which we shall consider the Hermetic Principle of Vibration.

You will kindly remember, however, that the Three Great Planes are not actual divisions of the phenomena of the Universe, but merely arbitrary terms used by the Hermetists in order to aid in the thought and study of the various degrees and Forms of universal activity and life. The atom of matter, the unit of force, the mind of man, and the being of the archangel are all but degrees in one scale, and all fundamentally the same, the difference between solely a matter of degree, and rate of vibration - all are creations of THE ALL, and have their existence solely within the Infinite Mind of THE ALL.

The Hermetists sub-divide each of the Three Great Planes into Seven Minor Planes, and each of these latter are also sub-divided into seven sub-planes, all divisions being more or less arbitrary, shading into each other, and adopted merely for convenience of scientific study and thought.

The Great Physical Plane, and its Seven Minor Planes, is that division of the phenomena of the Universe which includes all that relates to physics, or material things, forces, and manifestations. It includes all forms of that which we call Matter, and all forms of that which we call Energy or Force. But you must remember that the Hermetic Philosophy does not recognize Matter as a thing in itself, or as having a separate existence even in the Mind of THE ALL. The Teachings are that Matter is but a form of Energy - that is, Energy at a low rate of vibrations of a certain kind. And accordingly the Hermetists classify Matter under the head of Energy, and give to it three of the Seven Minor Planes of the Great Physical Plane.

[As you read here about the Great Physical Plane, which is composed of all forms of matter and energy, keeping in mind that these divisions listed here are arbitrary and not exact, note how these sub-planes account for not only all known and observable phenomena in the physical world, but also suspected phenomena, such as dark matter and dark energy, as well as the mechanics that allow for phenomena such as quantum entanglement.]

The Seven Minor Physical Planes are as follows:

1. The Plane of Matter (A)
2. The Plane of Matter (B)
3. The Plane of Matter (C)
4. The Plane of Ethereal Substance
5. The Plane of Energy (A)
6. The Plane of Energy (B)
7. The Plane of Energy (C)

The Plane of Matter (A) comprises the forms of Matter in its form of solids, liquids, and gases, as generally recognized by the text-books on physics. The Plane of Matter (B) comprises certain higher and more subtle forms of Matter of the existence of which modem science is but now recognizing, the phenomena of Radiant Matter, in its phases of radium, etc., belonging to the lower sub-division of this Minor Plane. The Plane of Matter (C) comprises forms of the most subtle and tenuous Matter the existence of which is not suspected by ordinary scientists. The Plane of Ethereal Substance comprises that which science speaks of as "The Ether," a substance of extreme tenuity and elasticity, pervading all Universal Space, and acting as a medium for the transmission of waves of energy, such as light, heat, electricity, etc. This Ethereal Substance forms a connecting link between Matter (so-called) and Energy, and partakes of the nature of each. The Hermetic Teachings, however, instruct that this plane has seven sub-divisions (as have all of the Minor Planes), and that in fact there are seven ethers, instead of but one.

Next above the Plane of Ethereal Substance comes the Plane of Energy (A), which comprises the ordinary forms of Energy known to science, its seven sub-planes being, respectively, Heat; Light; magnetism; Electricity, and Attraction (including Gravitation, Cohesion, Chemical Affinity, etc.) and several other forms of energy indicated by scientific experiments but not as yet named or classified. The Plane of Energy (B) comprises seven sub-planes of higher forms of energy not as yet discovered by science, but which have been called "Nature's Finer Forces" and which are called into operation in manifestations of certain forms of mental phenomena, and by which such phenomena becomes possible. The Plane of Energy (C) comprises seven sub-planes of energy so highly organized that it bears many of the characteristics of "life," but which is not recognized by the minds of men on the ordinary plane of development, being available for the use on beings of the Spiritual Plane alone - such energy is unthinkable to ordinary man, and may be considered almost as "the divine power." The beings employing the same are as "gods" compared even to the highest human types known to us.

The Great Mental Plane comprises those forms of "living things" known to us in ordinary life, as well as certain other forms not so well known except to the occultists. The classification of the Seven Minor Mental Planes is more or less satisfactory and arbitrary (unless accompanied by elaborate explanations which are foreign to the purpose of this particular work), but we may as well mention them. They are as follows:

1. The Plane of Mineral Mind
2. The Plane of Elemental Mind (A)
3. The Plane of Plant Mind
4. The Plane of Elemental Mind (B)
5. The Plane of Animal Mind
6. The Plane of Elemental Mind (C)

7. The Plane of Human Mind

[The Great Mental Plane is intimately familiar to every practicing occultist. It is on these planes that every religious, magical, or Theurgical rite is primarily conducted. Upon this Great Plane resides the Soul, our conduit between the Physical and the Spiritual IT is on this plane that exist the "Elements" spoken of by the Hermeticists. When you read of the Elements of Air, Fire, Water, and Earth, it is not their gross physical nature, but rather their counterparts on this plane that are being referred to. Likewise, the Sulphur, Salt, and Mercury of the alchemists have their powers of operation on this plane. The physical counterparts of these Elements are merely tools to establish a resonance on this plane, which in turn creates a resonance on the Spiritual Planes. Mastery of this plane is the goal and objective of all initiates.]

The Plane of Mineral Mind comprises the "states or conditions" of the units or entities, or groups and combinations of the same, which animate the forms known to us as "minerals, chemicals, etc." These entities must not be confounded with the molecules, atoms and corpuscles themselves, the latter being merely the material bodies or forms of these entities, just as a man's body is but his material form and not "himself." These entities may be called "souls" in one sense, and are living beings of a low degree of development, life, and mind - just a little more than the units of "living energy" which comprise the higher sub-divisions of the highest Physical Plane. The average mind does not generally attribute the possession of mind, soul, or life, to t4e mineral kingdom, but all occultists recognize the existence of the same, and modern science is rapidly moving forward to the point-of-view of the Hermetic, in this respect. The molecules, atoms and corpuscles have their "loves and hates"; "likes and dislikes"; "attractions and repulsions"; "affinities and non-affinities," etc., and some of the more daring of modem scientific minds have expressed the opinion that the desire and will, emotions and feelings, of the atoms differ only in degree from those of men. We have no time or space to argue this matter here. All occultists know it to be a fact, and others are referred to some of the more recent scientific works for outside corroboration. There are the usual seven sub-divisions to this plane.

The Plane of Elemental Mind (A) comprises the state or condition and degree of mental and vital development of a class of entities unknown to the average man, but recognized to occultists. They are invisible to the ordinary senses of man, but, nevertheless, exist and play their part of the Drama of the Universe. Their degree of intelligence is between that of the mineral and chemical entities on the one hand, and of the plant kingdom on the other. There are seven sub-divisions to this plane, also.

The Plane of Plant Mind, in its seven sub-divisions, comprises the states or conditions of the entities comprising the kingdoms of the Plant World, the vital and mental phenomena of which is fairly well understood by the average intelligent person, many new and interesting scientific works regarding "Mind and Life in Plants" having been published during the last decade. Plants have life, mind and "souls," as well as have the animals, man, and super-man.

The Plane of Elemental Mind (B), in its seven sub-divisions, comprises the states and conditions of a higher form of "elemental" or unseen entities, playing their part in the general work of the Universe, the mind and life of which form a part of the scale between the Plane of Plant Mind and the Plane of Animal Mind, the entities partaking of the nature of both.

The Plane of Animal Mind, in its seven sub-divisions, comprises the states and conditions of the entities, beings, or souls, animating the animal forms of life, familiar to us all. It is not necessary to go into details regarding this kingdom or plane of life, for the animal world is as familiar to us as is our own.

The Plane of Elemental Mind (C), in its seven sub-divisions, comprises those entities or beings, invisible as are all such elemental forms, which partake of the nature of both animal and human life in a degree and in certain combinations. The highest forms are semi-human in intelligence.

The Plane of Human Mind, in its seven sub-divisions, comprises those manifestations of life and mentality which are common to Man, in his various grades, degrees, and divisions. In this connection, we wish to point out the fact that the average man of today occupies but the fourth sub-division of the Plane of Human Mind, and only the most intelligent have crossed the borders of the Fifth Sub-Division. It has taken the race millions of years to reach this stage, and it will take many more years for the race to move on to the sixth and seventh sub- divisions, and beyond. But, remember, that there have been races before us which have passed through these degrees, and then on to higher planes. Our own race is the fifth (with stragglers from the fourth) which as set foot upon The Path. And, then there are a few advanced souls of our own race who have outstripped the masses, and who have passed on to the sixth and seventh sub-division, and some few being still further on. The man of the Sixth Sub-Division will be "The Super-Man"; he of the Seventh will be "The Over-Man."

In our consideration of the Seven Minor Mental Planes, we have merely referred to the Three Elementary Planes in a general way. We do not wish to go into this subject in detail in this work, for it does not belong to this part of the general philosophy and teachings. But we may say this much, in order to give you a little clearer idea, of the relations of these planes to the more familiar ones - the Elementary Planes bear the same relation to the Planes of Mineral, Plant, Animal and Human mentality and Life, that the black keys on the piano do to the white keys. The white keys are sufficient to produce music, but there are certain scales, melodies, and harmonies, in which the black keys play their part, and in which their presence is necessary. They are also necessary as "connecting links" of soul-condition; entity states, etc., between the several other planes, certain forms of development being attained therein - this last fact giving to the reader who can "read between the lines" a new light upon the process of Evolution, and a new key to the secret door of the "leaps of life" between kingdom and kingdom. The great kingdoms of Elementals are fully recognized by all occultists, and the esoteric writings are full of mention of them. The readers of Bulwer's "Zanoni" and similar tales will recognize the entities inhabiting these planes of life.

Passing on from the Great Mental Plane to the Great Spiritual Plane, what shall we say? How can we explain these higher states of Being, Life and Mind, to minds as yet unable to grasp and understand the higher sub-divisions of the Plane of Human Mind? The task is impossible. We can speak only in the most general terms. How may Light be described to a man born blind - how sugar, to a man who has never tasted anything sweet - and how harmony, to one born deaf?

All that we can say is that the Seven Minor Planes of the Great Spiritual Plane (each Minor Plane having its seven sub-divisions) comprise Beings possessing Life, Mind and Form as far above that of Man of to-day as the latter is above the earthworm, mineral or even certain forms of Energy or Matter. The Life of these Beings so far transcends ours, that we cannot even thing of the details of the same; their minds so far transcend ours, that to them we scarcely seem to "think," and our mental processes seem almost akin to material processes; the Matter of which their forms are composed is of the highest Planes of Matter, nay, some are even said to be "clothed in pure Energy," What may be said of such Beings?

On the Seven Minor Planes of the Great Spiritual Plane exist Beings of whom we may speak as Angels; Archangels; Demi-Gods. On the lower Minor Planes dwell those great souls whom we call Masters and Adepts. Above them come the Great hierarchies of the Angelic Hosts, unthinkable to man; and above those come those who may without irreverence be called "The Gods," so high in the scale of Being are they, their being, intelligence and power being akin to those attributed by the races of men to their conceptions of Deity. These Beings are beyond even the highest flights of the human imagination, the word "Divine" being the only one applicable to them.

[These highest of spiritual beings are the 'eons" of the Gnostics. Their collective assembly is that fullness known to the Gnostics as the "Pleroma." Because of the Principle of Correspondence, we are able to receive the wisdom and comfort of the Aeonic beings, and glimpse the splendor of the spiritual realms, even while trapped here in the world of matter.]

Many of these Beings, as well as the Angelic Host, take the greatest interest in the affairs of the Universe and play an important part in its affairs. These Unseen Divinities and Angelic Helpers extend their influence freely and powerfully, in the process of Evolution, and Cosmic Progress. Their occasional intervention and assistance in human affairs have led to the many legends, beliefs, religions and traditions of the race, past and present. They have superimposed their knowledge and power upon the world, again and again, all under the Law of THE ALL, of course.

But, yet, even the highest of these advanced Beings exist merely as creations of, and in, the Mind of THE ALL, and are subject to the Cosmic Processes and Universal Laws. They are still Mortal. We may call them "gods" if we like, but still they are but the Elder Brethren of the Race, - the advanced souls who have outstripped their brethren, and who have foregone the ecstasy of Absorption by THE ALL, in order to help the race on its upward journey along The Path. But, they belong to the Universe, and are subject to its conditions - they are mortal - and their plane is below that of Absolute Spirit.

Only the most advanced Hermetists are able to grasp the Inner Teachings regarding the state of existence, and the powers manifested on the Spiritual Planes. The phenomena is so much higher than that of the Mental Planes that a confusion of ideas would surely result from an attempt to describe the same. Only those whose minds have been carefully trained along the lines of the Hermetic Philosophy for years - yes, those who have brought with them from other incarnations the knowledge acquired previously - can comprehend just what is meant by the Teaching regarding these Spiritual Planes. And much of these Inner Teachings is held by the Hermetists as being too sacred, important and even dangerous for general public dissemination. The intelligent student may recognize what we mean by this when we state that the meaning of "Spirit" as used by the Hermetists is akin to "Living Power"; "Animated Force"; "Inner Essence"; "Essence of Life," etc., which meaning must not be confounded with that usually and commonly employed in connection with the term, i.e., "religious; ecclesiastical; spiritual; ethereal; holy," etc., etc. To occultists the word "Spirit" is used in the sense of "The Animating Principle," carrying with it the idea of Power, Living Energy, Mystic Force, etc. And occultists know that that which is known to them as "Spiritual Power" may be employed for evil as well as good ends (in accordance with the Principle of Polarity), a fact which has been recognized by the majority of religions in their conceptions of Satan, Beelzebub, the Devil, Lucifer, Fallen Angels, etc. And so the knowledge regarding these Planes has been kept in the Holy of Holies in all Esoteric Fraternities and Occult Orders, - in the Secret Chamber of the Temple. But this may be said here, that those who have attained high spiritual powers and have misused them, have a terrible fate in store for them, and the swing of the pendulum of Rhythm will inevitably swing them back to the furthest extreme of Material existence, from which point they must retrace their steps Spiritward, along the weary rounds of The Path, but always with the added torture of having always with them a lingering memory of the heights from which they fell owing to their evil actions. The legends of the Fallen Angels have a basis in actual facts, as all advanced occultists know. The striving for selfish power on the Spiritual Planes inevitably results in the selfish soul losing its spiritual balance and falling back as far as it had previously risen. But to even such a soul, the opportunity of a return is given - and such souls make the return journey, paying the terrible penalty according to the invariable Law.

In conclusion we would again remind you that according to the Principle of Correspondence, which embodies the truth: "As Above, so Below; as Below, so Above," all of the Seven Hermetic Principles are in full operation on all of the many planes, Physical, Mental and Spiritual. The Principle of Mental Substance of course applies to all the planes, for all are held in the Mind of THE ALL. The Principle of Correspondence manifests in all, for there is a correspondence, harmony and agreement between the several planes. The Principle of Vibration manifests on all planes, in fact the very differences that go to make the "planes" arise from Vibration, as we have explained. The Principle of Polarity manifests on each plane, the extremes of the Poles being apparently opposite and contradictory. The Principle of Rhythm manifests on each Plane, the movement of the phenomena having its ebb and flow, rise and fall, incoming and outgoing. The Principle of Cause and Effect manifests on each Plane, every Effect having its Cause and every Cause having its effect. The Principle of Gender manifests on each Plane, the Creative Energy being always manifest, and operating along the lines of its Masculine and Feminine Aspects.

[Each of these remaining five principles will be addressed, individually, in the following chapters.]

"As Above, so Below; as Below, so Above." This centuries old Hermetic axiom embodies one of the great Principles of Universal Phenomena. As we proceed with our consideration of the remaining Principles, we will see even more clearly the truth of the universal nature of this great Principle of Correspondence.

Vibration

"Nothing rests; everything moves; everything vibrates."

- *The Kybalion*

[The idea of Vibration as a fundamental principle of the Universe can be found expressed in the Gospel of Thomas, *verse 50, which says in part, "If they ask you, 'What is the evidence of your father in you?' say to them, 'It is motion and rest,'" (Gnostic Bible, p. 56). What is vibration if not an alternating between motion and rest? We see, therefore, that to the Gnostics of old, the Principle of Vibration was seen as a fundamental force emanating from the Father of Light.]*

The great Third Hermetic Principle - the Principle of Vibration - embodies the truth that Motion is manifest in everything in the Universe - that nothing is at rest - that everything moves, vibrates, and circles. This Hermetic Principle was recognized by some of the early Greek philosophers who embodied it in their systems. But, then, for centuries it was lost sight of by the thinkers outside of the Hermetic ranks. But in the Nineteenth Century scientific discoveries have added additional proof of the correctness and truth of this centuries-old Hermetic doctrine.

The Hermetic Teachings are that not only is everything in constant movement and vibration, but that the "differences" between the various manifestations of the universal power are due entirely to the varying rate and mode of vibrations. Not only this, but that even THE ALL, in itself manifests a constant vibration of such an infinite degree of intensity and rapid motion that it may be practically considered as at rest, the teachers directing the attention of the students to the fact that even on the physical plane a rapidly moving object (such as a revolving wheel) seems to be at rest. The Teachings are to the effect that Spirit is at one end of the Pole of Vibration, the other Pole being certain extremely gross forms of Matter. Between these two poles are millions upon millions of different rates and modes of vibration.

Modern Science has proven that all we call Matter and Energy are but "modes of vibratory motion," and some of the more advanced scientists are rapidly moving toward the positions of the occultists who hold that the phenomena of Mind are likewise modes of vibration or motion. Let us see what science has to say regarding the question of vibrations in matter and energy.

In the first place, science teaches that all matter manifests, in some degree, the vibrations arising from temperature or heat. Be an object cold or hot - both being but degrees of the same things - it manifests certain heat vibrations, and in that sense is in motion and vibration. Then all particles of Matter are in circular movement, from corpuscle to suns. The planets revolve around suns, and many of them turn on their axes. The suns move around greater central points, and these are believed to move around still greater, and so on, ad infinitum. The molecules of which the particular kinds of Matter are composed are in a state of constant vibration and movement around each other and against each other. The molecules are composed of Atoms, which, likewise, are in a state of constant movement and vibration. The atoms are composed of Corpuscles, sometimes called "electrons," "ions," etc., which also are in a state of rapid motion, revolving around each other, and which manifest a very rapid state and mode of vibration. And, so we see that all forms of Matter manifest Vibration, in accordance with the Hermetic Principle of Vibration.

[As stated in a previous chapter, while the examples given here may not reflect the terminology of today's scientific community, the principle nevertheless stands as true today as it did for the authors of The Kybalion in the early Twentieth Century, or for the purveyors of these mystical teachings millennia ago.]

And so it is with the various forms of Energy. Science teaches that Light, Heat, Magnetism and Electricity are but forms of vibratory motion connected in some way with, and probably emanating from the Ether. Science does not as yet attempt to explain the nature of the phenomena known as Cohesion, which is the principle of Molecular Attraction; nor Chemical Affinity, which is the principle Atomic Attraction; nor Gravitation (the greatest mystery of the three), which is the principle of attraction by which every particle or mass of Matter is bound to every other particle or mass. These three forms of Energy are not as yet understood by science, yet the writers incline to the opinion that these too are manifestations of some form of vibratory energy, a fact which the Hermetists have held and taught for ages past.

The Universal Ether, which is postulated by science without its nature being understood clearly, is held by the Hermetists to be but a higher manifestation of that which is erroneously called matter - that is to say, Matter at a higher degree of vibration - and is called by them "The Ethereal Substance." The Hermetists teach that this Ethereal Substance is of extreme tenuity and elasticity, and pervades universal space, serving as a medium of transmission of waves of vibratory energy, such as heat, light, electricity, magnetism, etc. The Teachings are that The Ethereal Substance is a connecting link between the forms of vibratory energy known as "Matter" on the one hand, and "Energy or Force" on the other; and also that it manifests a degree of vibration, in rate and mode, entirely its own.

Scientists have offered the illustration of a rapidly moving wheel, top, or cylinder, to show the effects of increasing rates of vibration. The illustration supposes a wheel, top, or revolving cylinder, running at a low rate of speed - we will call this revolving thing "the object" in following out the illustration. Let us suppose the object moving slowly. It may be seen readily, but no sound of its movement reaches the ear. The speed is gradually increased. In a few moments its movement becomes so rapid that a deep growl or low note may be heard. Then as the rate is increased the note rises one in the musical scale. Then, the motion being still further increased, the next highest note is distinguished. Then, one after another, all the notes of the musical scale appear, rising higher and higher as the motion is increased. Finally when the motions have reached a certain rate the final note perceptible to human ears is reached and the shrill, piercing shriek dies away, and silence follows. No sound is heard from the revolving object, the rate of motion being so high that the human ear cannot register the vibrations. Then comes the perception of rising degrees of Heat. Then after quite a time the eye catches a glimpse of the object becoming a dull dark reddish color. As the rate increases, the red melts into an orange. Then the orange melts into a yellow. Then follow, successively, the shades of green, blue, indigo, and finally violet, as the rate of speed increases. Then the violet shades away, and all color disappears, the human eye not being able to register them. But there are invisible rays emanating from the revolving object, the rays that are used in photographing, and other subtle rays of light. Then begin to manifest the peculiar rays known as the "X Rays," etc., as the constitution of the object changes. Electricity and Magnetism are emitted when the appropriate rate of vibration is attained.

When the object reaches a certain rate of vibration its molecules disintegrate, and resolve themselves into the original elements or atoms. Then the atoms, following the Principle of Vibration, are separated into the countless corpuscles of which they are composed. And finally, even the corpuscles disappear and the object may be said to be composed of The Ethereal Substance. Science does not dare to follow the illustration further, but the Hermetists teach that if the vibrations be continually increased the object would mount up the successive states of manifestation and would in turn manifest the various mental stages, and then on Spiritward, until it would finally re-enter THE All, which is Absolute Spirit. The "object," however, would have ceased to be an "object" long before the stage of Ethereal Substance was reached, but otherwise the illustration is correct inasmuch as it shows the effect of constantly increasing rates and modes of vibration. It must be remembered, in the above illustration, that at the stages at which the "object" throws off vibrations of light, heat, etc., it is not actually "resolved" into those forms of energy (which are much higher in the scale), but simply that it reaches a degree of vibration in which those forms of energy are liberated, in a degree, from the confining influences of its molecules, atoms and corpuscles, as the case may be. These forms of energy, although much higher in the scale than matter, are imprisoned and confined in the material combinations, by reason of the energies manifesting through, and using material forms, but thus becoming entangled and confined in their creations of material forms, which, to an extent, is true of all creations, the creating force becoming involved in its creation.

But the Hermetic Teachings go much further than do those of modem science. They teach that all manifestation of thought, emotion, reason, will or desire, or any mental state or condition, are accompanied by vibrations, a portion of which are thrown off and which tend to affect the minds of other persons by "induction." This is the principle which produces the phenomena of "telepathy"; mental influence, and other forms of the action and power of mind over mind, with which the general public is rapidly becoming acquainted, owing to the wide dissemination of occult knowledge by the various schools, cults and teachers along these lines at this time.

Every thought, emotion or mental state has its corresponding rate and mode of vibration. And by an effort of the will of the person, or of other persons, these mental states may be reproduced, just as a musical tone may be reproduced by causing an instrument to vibrate at a certain rate - just as color may be reproduced in the same way. By a knowledge of the Principle of Vibration, as applied to Mental Phenomena, one may polarize his mind at any degree he wishes, thus gaining a perfect control over his mental states, moods, etc. In the same way he may affect the minds of others, producing the desired mental states in them. In short, he may be able to produce on the Mental Plane that which science produces on the Physical Plane - namely, "Vibrations at Will." This power of course may be acquired only by the proper instruction, exercises, practice, etc., the science being that of Mental Transmutation, one of the branches of the Hermetic Art.

A little reflection on what we have said will show the student that the Principle of Vibration underlies the wonderful phenomena of the power manifested by the Masters and Adepts, who are able to apparently set aside the Laws of Nature, but who, in reality, are simply using one law against another; one principle against others; and who accomplish their results by changing the vibrations of material objects, or forms of energy, and thus perform what are commonly called "miracles."

[After Mind, in the form of the extension of Will, the Principle of Vibration is the most important element of occult ritual. It is through the application of this principle that a resonance may be established among the various Planes of existence. The vibratory qualities of various colors, sounds, scents, movements, and even tastes can all serve to establish a link to the mental and spiritual planes. The Adept whose mind is resonating with the Spiritual Plane, will instantly affect those who are in the immediate presence of the Adept. The Gospel of Philip speaks to this phenomenon: "Spiritual love is wine and fragrance. Those nearby also

enjoy it from those who are anointed. But if the anointed withdraw and leave, then those unanointed, who are hanging around, remain in their bad odor." In other words, the uninitiated may experience a temporary enlightenment when in the presence of Adepts and Masters.]

As one of the old Hermetic writers has truly said: "He who understands the Principle of Vibration, has grasped the scepter of Power."

Polarity

> "Everything is dual; everything has poles; everything has its pair of opposites; like and unlike are the same; opposites are identical in nature, but different in degree; extremes meet; all truths are but half-truths; all paradoxes may be reconciled."
>
> - *The Kybalion*

The great Fourth Hermetic Principle - the Principle of Polarity embodies the truth that all manifested things have "two sides"; "two aspects"; "two poles"; a "pair of opposites," with manifold degrees between the two extremes. The old paradoxes, which have ever perplexed the mind of men, are explained by an understanding of this Principle, and has endeavored to express it by such sayings, maxims and aphorisms as the following: "Everything is and isn't, at the same time"; "all truths are but half-truths"; "every truth is half-false"; "there are two sides to everything" - "there is a reverse side to every shield," etc., etc.

The Hermetic Teachings are to the effect that the difference between things seemingly diametrically opposed to each other is merely a matter of degree. It teaches that "the pairs of opposites may be reconciled," and that "thesis and anti-thesis are identical in nature, but different in degree"; and that the "universal reconciliation of opposites" is effected by a recognition of this Principle of Polarity. The teachers claim that illustrations of this Principle may be had on every hand, and from an examination into the real nature of anything. They begin by showing that Spirit and Matter are but the two poles of the same thing, the intermediate planes being merely degrees of vibration. They show that THE ALL and The Many are the same, the difference being merely a matter of degree of Mental Manifestation. Thus the LAW and Laws are the two opposite poles of one thing. Likewise, PRINCIPLE and Principles. Infinite Mind and finite minds.

Then passing on to the Physical Plane, they illustrate the Principle by showing that Heat and Cold are identical in nature, the differences being merely a matter of degrees. The thermometer shows many degrees of temperature, the lowest pole being called "cold," and the highest "heat." Between these two poles are many degrees of "heat" or "cold," call them either and you are equally correct. The higher of two degrees is always "warmer," while the lower is always "colder." There is no absolute standard - all is a matter of degree. There is no place on the thermometer where heat ceases and cold begins. It is all a matter of higher or lower vibrations. The very terms "high" and "low," which we are compelled to use, are but poles of the same thing - the terms are relative. So with "East and West" - travel around the world in an eastward direction, and you reach a point which is called west at your starting point, and you return from that westward point. Travel far enough North, and you will find yourself traveling South, or vice versa.

Light and Darkness are poles of the same thing, with many degrees between them. The musical scale is the same - starting with "C" you move upward until you reach another "C" and so on, the differences between the two ends of the board being the same, with many degrees between the two extremes. The scale of color is the same - higher and lower vibrations being the only difference between high violet and low red. Large and Small are relative. So are Noise and Quiet; Hard and Soft follow the rule. Likewise Sharp and Dull. Positive and Negative are two poles of the same thing, with countless degrees between them.

Good and Bad are not absolute - we call one end of the scale Good and the other Bad, or one end Good and the other Evil, according to the use of the terms. A thing is "less good" than the thing higher in the scale; but that "less good" thing, in turn, is "more good" than the thing next below it - and so on, the "more or less" being regulated by the position on the scale.

And so it is on the Mental Plane. "Love and Hate" are generally regarded as being things diametrically opposed to each other; entirely different; unreconcilable. But we apply the Principle of Polarity; we find that there is no such thing as Absolute Love or Absolute Hate, as distinguished from each other. The two are merely terms applied to the two poles of the same thing. Beginning at any point of the scale we find "more love," or "less hate," as we ascend the scale; and "more hate" or "less love" as we descend this being true no matter from what point, high or low, we may start. There are degrees of Love and Hate, and there is a middle point where "Like and Dislike" become so faint that it is difficult to distinguish between them. Courage and Fear come under the same rule. The Pairs of Opposites exist everywhere. Where you find one thing you find its opposite - the two poles.

And it is this fact that enables the Hermetists to transmute one mental state into another, along the lines of Polarization. Things belonging to different classes cannot be transmuted into each other, but things of the same class may be changed, that is, may have their polarity changed. Thus Love never becomes East or West, or Red or Violet - but it may and often does turn into Hate and likewise Hate may be transformed into Love, by changing its polarity. Courage may be transmuted into Fear, and the reverse. Hard things may be rendered Soft. Dull things become Sharp. Hot things become Cold. And so on, the transmutation always being between things of the same kind of different degrees. Take the case of a Fearful man. By raising his mental vibrations along the line of Fear - Courage, he can be filled with the highest degree of Courage and Fearlessness. And, likewise, the Slothful man may change himself into an Active, Energetic individual simply by polarizing along the lines of the desired quality.

The student who is familiar with the process by which the various schools of Mental Science, etc., produce changes in the mental states of those following their teachings, may not readily understand the principle underlying many of these changes. When, however, the Principle of Polarity is once grasped, and it is seen that the mental changes are occasioned by a change of polarity - a sliding along the same scale - the latter is readily understood. The change is not in the nature of a transmutation of one thing into another thing entirely different - but is merely a change of degree in the same things, a vastly important difference. For instance, borrowing an analogy from the Physical Plane, it is impossible to change Heat into Sharpness, Loudness, Highness, etc., but Heat may readily be transmuted into Cold, simply by lowering the vibrations. In the same way Hate and Love are mutually transmutable; so are Fear and Courage. But Fear cannot be transformed into Love, nor can Courage be transmuted into hate. The mental states belong to innumerable classes, each class of which has its opposite poles, along which transmutation is possible.

The student will readily recognize that in the mental states, as well as in the phenomena of the Physical Plane, the two poles may be classified as Positive and Negative, respectively. Thus Love is Positive to Hate; Courage to Fear; Activity to Non-Activity, etc., etc. And it will also be noticed that even to those unfamiliar with the Principle of Vibration, the Positive pole seems to be of a higher degree than the Negative, and readily dominates it The tendency of Nature is in the direction of the dominant activity of the Positive pole.

In addition to the changing of the poles of one's own mental states by the operation of the art of Polarization, the phenomena of Mental Influence, in its manifold phases, shows us that the principle may be extended so as to embrace the phenomena of the influence of one mind over that of another, of which so much has been written and taught of late years. When it is understood that Mental Induction is possible, that is that mental states may be produced by "induction" from others, then we can readily see how a certain rate of vibration, or polarization of a certain mental state, may be communicated to another person, and his polarity in that class of mental states thus changed. It is along this principle that the results of many of the "mental treatments" are obtained. For instance, a person is "blue," melancholy and full of fear. A mental scientist bringing his own mind up to the desired vibration by his trained will, and thus obtaining the desired polarization in his own case, then produces a similar mental state in the other by induction, the result being that the vibrations are raised and the person polarizes toward the Positive end of the scale instead of toward the Negative, and his Fear and other negative emotions are transmuted to Courage and similar positive mental states. A little study will show you that these mental changes are nearly all along the line of Polarization, the change being one of degree rather than of kind.

A knowledge of the existence of this great Hermetic Principle will enable the student to better understand his own mental states, and those of other people. He will see that these states are all matters of degree, and seeing thus, he will be able to raise or lower the vibration at will - to change his mental poles, and thus be Master of his mental states, instead of being their servant and slave. And by his knowledge he will be able to aid his fellows intelligently and by the appropriate methods change the polarity when the same is desirable. We advise all students to familiarize themselves with this Principle of Polarity, for a correct understanding of the same will throw light on many difficult subjects.

Rhythm

"Everything flows out and in; everything has its tides; all things rise and fall; the pendulum-swing manifests in everything; the measure of the swing to the right, is the measure of the swing to the left; rhythm compensates."

- *The Kybalion*

The great Fifth Hermetic Principle - the Principle of Rhythm - embodies the truth that in everything there is manifested a measured motion; a to-and-fro movement; a flow and inflow; a swing forward and backward; a pendulum-like movement; a tide-like ebb and flow; a high-tide and a low-tide; between the two poles - manifest on the physical, mental or spiritual planes. The Principle of Rhythm is closely connected with the Principle of Polarity described in the preceding chapter. Rhythm manifests between the two poles established by the Principle of Polarity. This does not mean, however, that the pendulum of Rhythm swings to the extreme poles, for this rarely happens; in fact, it is difficult to establish the extreme polar opposites in the majority of cases. But the swing is ever "toward" first one pole and then the other.

Beginning with the manifestations of Spirit - of THE ALL - it will be noticed that there is ever the Outpouring and the Indrawing; the "Outbreathing and Inbreathing of Brahm," as the Brahmans word it. Universes are created; reach their extreme low point of materiality; and then begin in their upward swing. Suns spring into being, and then their height of power being reached, the process of retrogression begins, and after aeons they become dead masses of matter, awaiting another impulse which starts again their inner energies into activity and a new solar life cycle is begun. And thus it is with all the worlds; they are born, grow and die; only to be reborn. And thus it is with all the things of shape and form; they swing from action to reaction; from birth to death; from activity to inactivity - and then back again. Thus it is with all living things; they are born, grow, and die - and then are reborn. So it is with all great movements, philosophies, creeds, fashions, governments, nations, and all else - birth, growth, maturity, decadence, death - and then new-birth. The swing of the pendulum is ever in evidence.

[The cycle of Birth-Life-Death-Rebirth is prevalent among the ancient Mysteries. In the modern world, this cycle is seen most clearly in the Christian Mysteries of the West, and in the Vedic and Buddhist religions in the East. While all major religious philosophies contain within their mysteries examples of the cycles of life as well as an awakening from spiritual ignorance into spiritual knowledge, those traditions aforementioned seem to express this concept most clearly.]

Night follows day; and day night. The corpuscles, atoms, molecules, and all masses of matter, swing around the circle of their nature. There is no such thing as absolute rest, or cessation from movement, and all movement partakes of rhythm. The principle is of universal application. It may be applied to any question, or phenomena of any of the many planes of life. It may be applied to all phases of human activity. There is always the Rhythmic swing from one pole to the other. The Universal Pendulum is ever in motion. The Tides of Life flow in and out, according to Law.

The Principle of Rhythm is well understood by modem science, and is considered a universal law as applied to material things. But the Hermetists carry the principle much further, and know that its manifestations and influence extend to the mental activities of Man, and that it accounts for the bewildering succession of moods, feelings and other annoying and perplexing changes that we notice in ourselves. But the Hermetists by studying the operations of this Principle have learned to escape some of its activities by Transmutation.

The Hermetic Masters long since discovered that while the Principle of Rhythm was invariable, and ever in evidence in mental phenomena, still there were two planes of its manifestation so far as mental phenomena are concerned. They discovered that there were two general planes of Consciousness, the Lower and the Higher, the understanding of which fact enabled them to rise to the higher plane and thus escape the swing of the Rhythmic pendulum which manifested on the lower plane. In other words, the swing of the pendulum occurred on the Unconscious Plane, and the Consciousness was not affected. This they call the Law of Neutralization. Its operations consist in the raising of the Ego above the vibrations of the Unconscious Plane of mental activity, so that the negative-swing of the pendulum is not manifested in consciousness, and therefore they are not affected. It is akin to rising above a thing and letting it pass beneath you. The Hermetic Master, or advanced student, polarizes himself at the desired pole, and by a process akin to "refusing" to participate in the backward swing or, if you prefer, a "denial" of its influence over him, he stands firm in his polarized position, and allows the mental pendulum to swing back along the unconscious plane. All individuals who have attained any degree of self-mastery, accomplish this, more or less unknowingly, and by refusing to allow their moods and negative mental states to affect them, they apply the Law of Neutralization. The Master, however, carries this to a much higher degree of proficiency, and by the use of his Will he attains a degree of Poise and Mental Firmness almost impossible of belief on the part of those who allow themselves to be swung backward and forward by the mental pendulum of moods arid feelings.

The importance of this will be appreciated by any thinking person who realizes what creatures of moods, feelings and emotion the majority of people are, and how little mastery of themselves they manifest. If you will stop and consider a moment, you will realize how much these swings of Rhythm have affected you in your life - how a period of Enthusiasm has been invariably followed by an opposite feeling and mood of Depression. Likewise, your moods and periods of Courage have been succeeded by equal moods of Fear. And so it has ever been with the majority of persons - tides of feeling have ever risen and fallen with them, but they have never suspected the cause or reason of the mental phenomena. An understanding of the workings of this Principle will give one the key to the Mastery of these rhythmic swings of feeling, and will enable him to know himself better and to avoid being carried away by these inflows and outflows. The Will is superior to the conscious manifestation of this Principle, although the Principle itself can never be destroyed. We may escape its effects, but the Principle operates, nevertheless. The pendulum ever swings, although we may escape being carried along with it.

There are other features of the operation of the Principle of Rhythm of which we wish to speak at this point. There comes into its operations that which is known as the Law of Compensation. One of the definitions or meanings of the word "Compensate" is, "to counterbalance" which is the sense in which the Hermetists use the term. It is this Law of Compensation to which the Kybalion refers when it says: "The measure of the swing to the right is the measure of the swing to the left; rhythm compensates."

The Law of Compensation is that the swing in one direction determines the swing in the opposite direction, or to the opposite pole - the one balances, or counterbalances, the other. On the Physical Plane we see many examples of this Law. The pendulum of the clock swings a certain distance to the right, and then an equal distance to the left. The seasons balance each other in the same way. The tides follow the same Law. And the same Law is manifested in all the phenomena of Rhythm. The pendulum, with a short swing in one direction, has but a short swing in the other; while the long swing to the right invariably means the long swing to the left. An object hurled upward to a certain height has an equal distance to traverse on its return. The force with which a projectile is sent upward a mile is reproduced when the projectile returns to the earth on its return journey. This Law is constant on the Physical Plane, as reference to the standard authorities will show you.

But the Hermetists carry it still further. They teach that a man's mental states are subject to the same Law. The man who enjoys keenly, is subject to keen suffering; while he who feels but little pain is capable of feeling but little joy. The pig suffers but little mentally, and enjoys but little - he is compensated. And on the other hand, there are other animals who enjoy keenly, but whose nervous organism and temperament cause them to suffer exquisite degrees of pain and so it is with Man. There are temperaments which permit of but low degrees of enjoyment, and equally low degrees of suffering; while there are others which permit the most intense enjoyment, but also the most intense suffering. The rule is that the capacity for pain and pleasure, in each individual, are balanced. The Law of Compensation is in full operation here.

But the Hermetists go still further in this matter. They teach that before one is able to enjoy a certain degree of pleasure, he must have swung as far, proportionately, toward the other pole of feeling. They hold, however, that the Negative is precedent to the Positive in this matter, that is to say that in experiencing a certain degree of pleasure it does not follow that he will have to "pay up for it" with a corresponding degree of pain; on the contrary, the pleasure is the Rhythmic swing, according to the Law of Compensation, for a degree of pain previously experienced either in the present life, or in a previous incarnation. This throws a new light on the Problem of Pain.

The Hermetists regard the chain of lives as continuous, and as forming a part of one life of the individual, so that in consequence the rhythmic swing is understood in this way, while it would be without meaning unless the truth of reincarnation is admitted.

But the Hermetists claim that the Master or advanced student is able, to a great degree, to escape the swing toward Pain, by the process of Neutralization before mentioned. By rising on to the higher plane of the Ego, much of the experience that comes to those dwelling on the lower plane is avoided and escaped.

The Law of Compensation plays an important part in the lives of men and women. It will be noticed that one generally "pays the price" of anything he possesses or lacks. If he has one thing, he lacks another - the balance is struck. No one can "Keep his penny and have the bit of cake" at the same time. Everything has its pleasant and unpleasant sides. The things that one gains are always paid for by the things that one loses. The rich possess much that the poor lack, while the poor often possess things that are beyond the reach of the rich. The millionaire may have the inclination toward feasting, and the wealth wherewith to secure all the dainties and luxuries of the table, while he lacks the appetite to enjoy the same; he envies the appetite and digestion of the laborer who lacks the wealth and inclinations of the millionaire, and who gets more pleasure from his plain food than the millionaire could obtain even if his appetite were not jaded, nor his digestion ruined, for the wants, habits and inclinations differ. And so it is through life. The Law of Compensation is ever in operation, striving to balance and counter-balance, and always succeeding in time, even though several lives may be required for the return swing of the Pendulum of Rhythm.

[Although most of the occult schools, societies, and fraternities do not require or demand a belief in reincarnation, the principle is, nevertheless, an integral part of the Hermetic philosophy. This principle is stated quite clearly in Corpus Hermeticum X, 19, *which states, "The human soul - not every soul, that is but only the reverent - is in a sense demonic [daimonios] - and divine. Such a soul becomes wholly mind after getting free of the body and fighting the fight of reverence (knowing the divine and doing wrong to no person is the fight of reverence). The irreverent soul, however, stays in its own essence, punishing itself, seeking an earthly body to enter - a human body, to be sure. For no other body contains a human soul; it is not allowed for a human soul to fall down into the body of an unreasoning animal. This is God's law, to protect the human soul against such an outrage." We can see from this clear description, that the Hermetic concept of reincarnation differs slightly from the reincarnation doctrines of certain other Eastern religions and philosophies, in that the Hermetic view does not allow for the downward transmigration of the soul. Neither acceptance nor rejection of the principle of reincarnation will affect the ability of the student to properly apply the Hermetic laws and principles. We will comment, however, that as one works with the Hermetic system, and observes how its principles operate on multiple levels of being, the logic and plausibility of reincarnation becomes more apparent. Also, as stated previously in the "Gnostic Mythology" section, it was held among the ancient Gnostics that the soul was perfected over the course of successive incarnations.]*

Causation

"Every Cause has its Effect; every Effect has its Cause; everything happens according to Law; Chance is but a name for Law not recognized; there are many planes of causation, but nothing escapes the Law."

- *The Kybalion*

The great Sixth Hermetic Principle - the Principle of Cause and Effect - embodies the truth that Law pervades the Universe; that nothing happens by Chance; that Chance is merely a term indicating cause existing but not recognized or perceived; that phenomena is continuous, without break or exception.

The Principle of Cause and Effect underlies all scientific thought, ancient and modem, and was enunciated by the Hermetic Teachers in the Earliest days.

[The Corpus Hermeticum *is full of examples of the Principle of Causation. One such instance is found in C.H. XIV.6, "Without the maker, the begotten neither comes to be nor is, for the one without the other complete!), loses its own nature from deprivation of the other. Thus, if one agrees that there exist two entities, what comes to be and what makes it, they are one in their unification, an antecedent and a consequent. The antecedent is the god who makes; the consequent is what comes to be, whatever it may be."]*

While many and varied disputes between the many schools of thought have since arisen, these disputes have been principally upon the details of the operations of the Principle, and still more often upon the meaning of certain words. The underlying Principle of Cause and Effect has been accepted as correct by practically all the thinkers of the world worthy of the name. To think otherwise would be to take the phenomena of the universe from the domain of Law and Order, and to relegate it to the control of the imaginary something which men have called "Chance."

A little consideration will show anyone that there is in reality no such thing as pure chance. Webster defines the word "Chance" as follows: "A supposed agent or mode of activity other than a force, law or purpose; the operation or activity of such agent; the supposed effect of such an agent; a happening; fortuity; casualty, etc." But a little consideration will show you that there can be no such agent as "Chance," in the sense of something outside of Law- something outside of Cause and Effect. How could there be a something acting in the phenomenal universe, independent of the laws, order, and continuity of the latter? Such a something would be entirely independent of the orderly trend of the universe, and therefore superior to it. We can imagine nothing outside of THE ALL being outside of the Law, and that only because THE ALL is the LAW in itself. There is no room in the universe for a something outside of and independent of Law. The existence of such a Something would render all Natural Laws ineffective, and would plunge the universe into chaotic disorder and lawlessness.

A careful examination will show that what we call "Chance" is merely an expression relating to obscure causes; causes that we cannot perceive; causes that we cannot understand. The word Chance is derived from a word meaning "to fall" (as the falling of dice) [from the Latin: cadre - to fall, befall], the idea being that the fall of the dice (and many other happenings) are merely a "happening" unrelated to any cause. And this is the sense in which the term is generally employed. But when the matter is closely examined, it is seen that there is not chance whatsoever about the fall of the dice. Each ti.me a die falls, and displays a certain number, it obeys a law as infallible as that which governs the revolution of the planets around the sun. Back of the fall of the die are causes, or chains of causes, running back further than the mind can follow. The position of the die in the box; the amount of muscular energy expended in the throw; the condition of the table, etc., etc., all are causes, the effect of which may be seen. But back of these seen causes there are chains of unseen preceding causes, all of which had a bearing upon the number of the die which fell uppermost.

If a die be cast a great number of times, it will be found that the numbers shown will be about equal, that is, there will be an equal number of one-spot, two-spot, etc., coming uppermost. Toss a penny in the air, and it may come down either "heads" or "tails"; but make a sufficient number of tosses, and the heads and tails will about even up. This is the operation of the law of average. But both the average and the single toss come under the Law of Cause and Effect, and if we were able to examine into the preceding causes, it would be clearly seen that it was simply impossible for the die to fall other than it did, under the same circumstances and at the same time. Given the same causes, the same results will follow. There is always a "cause" and a "because" to every event. Nothing ever "happens" without a cause, or rather a chain of causes.

Some confusion has arisen in the minds of persons considering this Principle, from the fact that they were unable to explain how one thing could cause another thing - that is, be the "creator" of the second thing. As a matter of fact, no "thing" ever causes or "creates" another "thing." Cause and Effect deals merely with "events." An "event" is "that which comes, arrives or happens, as a result or consequent of some preceding event." No event "creates" another event, but is merely a preceding link in the great orderly chain of events flowing from the creative energy of THE ALL. There is a continuity between all events precedent, consequent and subsequent. There is a relation existing between everything that has come before, and everything that follows. A stone is dislodged from a mountain side and crashes through a roof of a cottage in the valley below. At first sight we regard this as a chance effect, but when we examine the matter we find a great chain of causes behind it. In the first place there was the rain which softened the earth supporting the stone and which allowed it to fall; then back of that was the influence of the sun, other rains, etc., which gradually disintegrated the piece of rock from a larger piece; then there were the causes which led to the formation of the mountain, and its upheaval by convulsions of nature, and so on ad infinitum. Then we might follow up the causes behind the rain, etc. Then we might consider the existence of the roof. In short, we would seen find ourselves involved in a mesh of cause and effect, from which we would soon strive to extricate ourselves.

Just as a man has two parents, and four grandparents, and eight great-grandparents, and sixteen great-great-grandparents, and so on until when, say, forty generations are calculated the numbers of ancestors run into many millions - so it is with number of causes behind even the most trifling event or phenomena, such as the passage of a tiny speck of soot before your eye. It is not an easy matter to trace the bit of soot back to the early period of the world's history when it formed a part of a massive tree-trunk, which was afterward converted into coal, and so on, until as the speck of soot it now passes before your vision on its way to other adventures. And a mighty chain of events, causes and effects, brought it to its present condition, and the latter is but one of the chain of events which will go to produce other events hundreds of years from now. One of the series of events arising from the tiny bit of soot was the writing of these lines, which caused the typesetter to perform certain work; the proofreader to do likewise; and which will arouse certain thoughts in your mind, and that of others, which in turn will affect others, and so on, and on, and on, beyond the ability of man to think further - and all from the passage of a tiny bit of soot, all of which shows the relativity and association of things, and the further fact that "there is no great; there is no small, in the mind that causeth all."

Stop to think a moment. If a certain man had not met a certain maid, away back in the dim period of the Stone Age - you who are now reading these lines would not now be here. And if, perhaps, the same couple had failed to meet, we who now write these lines would not now be here. And the very act of writing, on our part, and the act of reading, on yours, will affect not only the respective lives of yourself and ourselves, but will also have a direct, or indirect, affect upon many other people now living and who will live in the ages to come. Every thought we think, every act we perform, has its direct and indirect results which fit into the great chain of Cause and Effect.

We do not wish to enter into a consideration of Free Will, or Determinism, in this work, for various reasons. Among the many reasons, is the principal one that neither side of the controversy is entirely right - in fact, both sides are partially right, according to the Hermetic Teachings. The Principle of Polarity shows that both are but Half-Truths, the opposing poles of Truth. The Teachings are that a man may be both Free and yet bound by Necessity, depending upon the meaning of the terms, and the height of Truth from which the matter is examined. The ancient writers express the matter thus: "The further the creation is from the Centre, the more it is bound; the nearer the Centre it reaches, the nearer Free it is."

The majority of people are more or less the slaves of heredity, environment, etc., and manifest very little Freedom. They are swayed by the opinions, customs and thoughts of the outside world, and also by their emotions, feelings, moods, etc. They manifest no Mastery, worthy of the name. They indignantly repudiate this assertion, saying, "Why, I certainly am free to act and do as I please - I do just what I want to do," but they fail to explain whence arise the "want to" and "as I please." What makes them "want to" do one thing in preference to another; what makes them "please" to do this, and not do that? Is there no "because" to their "pleasing" and "wanting"? The Master can change these "pleases" and "wants" into others at the opposite end of the mental pole. He is able to "Will to will," instead of to will because some feeling, mood, emotion, or environmental suggestion arouses a tendency or desire within him se to do.

The majority of people are carried along like the falling stone, obedient to environment, outside influences and internal moods, desires, etc., not to speak of the desires and wills of others stronger than themselves, heredity, environment, and suggestion, carrying them along without resistance on their part, or the exercise of the Will. Moved like the pawns on the checkerboard of life, they play their parts and are laid aside after the game is over. But the Masters, knowing the rules of the game, rise above the plane of material life, and placing themselves in touch with the higher powers of their nature, dominate their own moods, characters, qualities, and polarity, as well as the environment surrounding them and thus become Movers in the game, instead of Pawns - Causes instead of Effects. The Masters do not escape the Causation of the higher planes, but fall in with the higher laws, and thus master circumstances on the lower plane. They thus form a conscious part of the Law, instead of being mere blind instruments. While they Serve on the Higher Planes, they Rule on the Material Plane.

But, on higher and on lower, the Law is always in operation. There is no such thing as Chance. The blind goddess has been abolished by Reason. We are able to see now, with eyes made clear by knowledge, that everything is governed by Universal law - that the infinite number of laws are but manifestations of the One Great Law - the LAW which is THE ALL. It is true indeed that not a sparrow drops unnoticed by the Mind of THE ALL - that even the hairs on our head are numbered - as the scriptures have said. There is nothing outside of Law; nothing that happens contrary to it. And yet, do not make the mistake of supposing that Man is but a blind automaton - far from that. The Hermetic Teachings are that Man may use Law to overcome laws, and that the higher will always prevail against the lower, until at last he has reached the stage in which he seeks refuge in the LAW itself, and laughs the phenomenal laws to scorn. Are you able to grasp the inner meaning of this?

Gender

"Gender is in everything; everything has its Masculine and Feminine Principles; Gender manifests on all planes."

- *The Kybalion*

The great Seventh Hermetic Principle - the Principle of Gender - embodies the truth that there is Gender manifested in everything - that the Masculine and Feminine principles are ever present and active in all phases of phenomena, on each and every plane of life. At this point we think it well to call your attention to the fact that Gender, in its Hermetic sense, and Sex in the ordinarily accepted use of the term, are not the same.

The word "Gender" is derived from the Latin root meaning "to beget; to procreate; to generate; to create; to produce." A moment's consideration will show you that the word has a much broader and more general meaning than the term "Sex," the latter referring to the physical distinctions between male and female living things. Sex is merely a manifestation of Gender on a certain plane of the Great Physical Plane - the plane of organic life. We wish to impress this distinction upon your minds, for the reason that certain writers, who have acquired a smattering of the Hermetic Philosophy, have sought to identify this Seventh hermetic Principle with wild and fanciful, and often reprehensible, theories and teachings regarding Sex.

[Since the authors are not clear here, we can only guess at what these "reprehensible theories and teachings" might be. While it is true that Sex and Gender are not the same, one being only an aspect of the other, still, sex is a representation of Gender that we can readily understand and relate to. In truth, sex, sexuality, and sexual imagery has been used for millennia to represent the Principle of Gender on all planes. In Asclepius we see Hermes describe God as "the One and the All, completely full of the fertility of both sexes and over pregnant with His own Will…," (Copenhaver, pp. 78-79). Throughout the Gnostic texts there are numerous references to sex and sexuality in order to convey the ideas of gender and generation. For instance, the Paraphrase of Shem contains a graphic sexual depiction of the creation of the cosmos (Gnostic Bible, pp. 438464). And, the Alchemical Marriage of the Rosicrucians has its origin in the Gnostic sacrament of the Bridal Chamber, which celebrates the union of the soul with the divine. This union is depicted often in sexual terms, not because of some perverse infatuation with sexual imagery, but because it is best described by analogy to the sexual act with which we are intimately acquainted. In the Gospel of Philip we read, 'Think of sex. It possesses deep powers, though its image is filthy," (Gnostic Bible, p. 275). We can see, from statements such as this that, although the popular ethics of the day regarding sex were probably not much different from our own, it is beneficial or even necessary to explore and meditate upon the mysteries of sexual union. And, though it may be true that some individuals may have exploited this great mystery solely for personal physical gratification, it must also be considered that rites of sacred sexually may serve a legitimate role in the Mystery Traditions of the East and West.]

The office of Gender is solely that of creating, producing, generating, etc., and its manifestations are visible on every plane of phenomena. It is somewhat difficult to produce proofs of this along scientific lines, for the reason that science has not as yet recognized this Principle as of universal application. But still some proofs are forthcoming from scientific sources. In the first place, we find a distinct manifestation of the Principle of Gender among the corpuscles, ions, or electrons, which constitute the basis of matter as science now knows the latter, and which by forming certain combinations form the Atom, which until lately was regarded as final and indivisible.

The latest word of science is that the atom is composed of a multitude of corpuscles, electrons, or ions (the various names being applied by different authorities) revolving around each other and vibrating at a high degree and intensity. But the accompanying statement is made that the formation of the atom is really due to the clustering of negative corpuscles around a positive one - the positive corpuscles seeming to exert a certain influence upon the negative corpuscles, causing the latter to assume certain combinations and thus "create" or "generate" an atom. This is in line with the most ancient Hermetic Teachings, which have always identified the Masculine principle of Gender with the "Positive," and the Feminine with the "Negative" Poles of Electricity (so-called).

Now a word at this point regarding this identification. The public mind has formed an entirely erroneous impression regarding the qualities of the so-called "Negative" pole of electrified or magnetized Matter. The terms Positive and Negative are very wrongly applied to this phenomenon by science. The word Positive means something real and strong, as compared with a Negative unreality or weakness. Nothing is further from the real facts of electrical phenomenon. The so-called Negative pole of the battery is really the pole in and by which the generation or production of new forms and energies is manifested. There is nothing "negative" about it. The best scientific authorities now use the word "Cathode" in place of "Negative," the word Cathode coming from the Greek root meaning "descent; the path of generation, etc." From the Cathode pole emerge the swarm of electrons or corpuscles; from the same pole emerge those wonderful "rays" which have revolutionized scientific conceptions during the past decade. The Cathode pole is the Mother of all of the strange phenomena which have rendered useless the old textbooks, and which have caused many long accepted theories to be relegated to the scrap-pile of scientific speculation. The Cathode, or Negative Pole, is the Mother Principle of Electrical Phenomena, and of the finest forms of matter as yet known to science. So you see we are justified in refusing to use the term "Negative" in our consideration of the subject, and in insisting upon substituting the word "Feminine" for the old term. The facts of the case bear us out in this, without taking the Hermetic Teachings into consideration. And so we shall use the word "Feminine" in the place of "Negative" in speaking of that pole of activity.

The latest scientific teachings are that the creative corpuscles or electrons are Feminine (science says "they are composed of negative electricity" - we say they are composed of Feminine energy). A Feminine corpuscle becomes detached from, or rather leaves, a Masculine corpuscle, and starts on a new career. It actively seeks a union with a Masculine corpuscle, being urged thereto by the natural . impulse to create new forms of Matter or Energy. One writer goes so far as to use the term "it at once seeks, of its own volition, a union," etc. This detachment and uniting form the basis of the greater part of the activities of the chemical world. When the Feminine corpuscle unites with a Masculine corpuscle, a certain process is begun. The Feminine particles vibrate rapidly under the influence of the Masculine energy, and circle rapidly around the latter. The result is the birth of a new atom. This new atom is really composed of a union of the Masculine and Feminine electrons, or corpuscles, but when the union is formed the atom is a separate thing, having certain properties, but no longer manifesting the property of free electricity. The process of detachment or separation of the Feminine electrons is called "ionization." These electrons, or corpuscles, are the most active workers in Nature's field. Arising from their unions, or combinations, manifest the varied phenomena of light, heat, electricity, magnetism, attraction, repulsion, chemical affinity and the reverse, and similar phenomena. And all this arises from the operation of the Principle of Gender on the plane of Energy.

[The modern reader may more readily understand the validity of these statements if we replace the generic term corpuscle" with more modern terms such as "quarks," "photons," and "gluons." There are, of course, many other types of particles, such as the recently discovered Higgs boson, but collectively they describe the various phenomena mentioned here.]

The part of the Masculine principle seems to be that of directing a certain inherent energy toward the Feminine principle, and thus starting into activity the creative processes. But the Feminine principle is the one always doing the active creative work - and this is so on all planes. And yet, each principle is incapable of operative energy without the assistance of the other. In some of the forms of life, the two principles are combined in one organism. For that matter, everything in the organic world manifests both genders - there is always the Masculine present in the Feminine form, and the Feminine in the Masculine form. The Hermetic Teachings include much regarding the operation of the two principles of Gender in the production and manifestation of various forms of energy, etc., but we do not deem it expedient to go into detail regarding the same at this point, because we are unable to back up the same with scientific proof, for the reason that science has not as yet progressed thus far. But the example we have given you of the phenomena of the electrons or corpuscles will show you that science is on the right path, and will also give you a general idea of the underlying principles.

Some leading scientific investigators have announced their belief that in the formation of crystals there was to be found something that corresponded to "sex-activity" which is another straw showing the direction the scientific winds are blowing. And each year will bring other facts to corroborate the correctness of the Hermetic Principle of Gender. It will be found that Gender is in constant operation and manifestation in the field of inorganic matter, and in the field of Energy or Force. Electricity is now generally regarded as the "Something" into which all other forms of energy seem to melt or dissolve. The "Electrical Theory of the Universe" is the latest scientific doctrine, and is growing rapidly in popularity and general acceptance. And it thus follows that if we are able to discover in the phenomena of electricity - even at the very root and source of its manifestations a clear and unmistakable evidence of the presence of Gender and its activities, we are justified in asking you to believe that science at last has offered proofs of the existence in all universal phenomena of that great Hermetic Principle - the Principle of Gender.

It is not necessary to take up your time with the well known phenomena of the "attraction and repulsion" of the atoms; chemical affinity; the "loves and hates" of the atomic particles; the attraction or cohesion between the molecules of matter. These facts are too well known to need extended comment from us. But, have you ever considered that all of these things are manifestations of the Gender Principle? Can you not see that the phenomena is "on all fours" with that of the corpuscles or electrons? And more than this, can you not see the reasonableness of the Hermetic Teachings which assert that the very Law of Gravitation - that strange attraction by reason of which all particles and bodies of matter in the universe tend toward each other is but another manifestation of the Principle of Gender, which operates in the direction of attracting the Masculine to the Feminine energies, and vice versa? We cannot offer you scientific proof of this at this time - but examine the phenomena in the light of the Hermetic Teachings on the subject, and see if you have not a better working hypothesis than any offered by physical science. Submit all physical phenomena to the test, and you will discern the Principle of Gender ever in evidence.

Let us now pass on to a consideration of the operation of the Principle on the Mental Plane. Many interesting features are there awaiting examination.

Mental Gender

Students of psychology who have followed the modem trend of thought along the lines of mental phenomena are struck by the persistence of the dual-mind idea which has manifested itself so strongly during the past ten or fifteen years, and which has given rise to a number of plausible theories regarding the nature and constitution of these "two minds." The late Thomson J. Hudson attained great popularity in 1893 by advancing his well-known theory of the "objective and subjective minds" which he held existed in every individual. Other writers have attracted almost equal attention by the theories regarding the "conscious and subs-conscious minds"; the "voluntary and involuntary minds"; "the active and passive minds," etc., etc. The theories of the various writers differ from each other, but there remains the underlying principle of "the duality of mind."

The student of the Hermetic Philosophy is tempted to smile when he reads and hears of these many "new theories" regarding the duality of mind, each school adhering tenaciously to its own pet theories, and each claiming to have "discovered the truth." The student turns back the pages of occult history, and away back in the dim beginnings of occult teachings he finds references to the ancient Hermetic doctrine of the Principle of Gender on the Mental Plane - the manifestation of Mental Gender. And examining further he finds that the ancient philosophy took cognizance of the phenomenon of the "dual mind," and accounted for it by the theory of mental Gender. This idea of Mental Gender may be explained in a few words to students who are familiar with the modern theories just alluded to. The Masculine Principle of Mind corresponds to the so-called Objective Mind; Conscious Mind; Voluntary Mind; Active Mind, etc. And the Feminine Principle of Mind corresponds to the so-called Subjective Mind; Sub- conscious Mind; Involuntary Mind; passive Mind, etc. Of course the Hermetic Teachings do not agree with the many modem theories regarding the nature of the two phases of mind, nor does it admit many of the facts claimed for the two respective aspects - some of the said theories and claims being very far-fetched and incapable of standing the test of experiment and demonstration. We point to the phases of agreement merely for the purpose of helping the student to assimilate his previously acquired knowledge with the teachings of the Hermetic Philosophy. Students of Hudson will notice the statement at the beginning of his second chapter of "The Law of Psychic Phenomena," that: "The mystic jargon of the Hermetic philosophers discloses the same general idea" i.e. the duality of mind. If Dr. Hudson had taken the time and trouble to decipher a little of "the mystic jargon of the Hermetic Philosophy," he might have received much light upon the subject of "the dual mind: - but then, perhaps, his most interesting work might not have been written. Let us now consider the Hermetic Teachings regarding Mental Gender.

The Hermetic Teachers impart their instruction regarding this subject by bidding their students examine the report of their consciousness regarding their Self. The students are bidden to turn their attention inward upon the Self dwelling within each. Each student is led to see that his consciousness gives him first a report of the existence of his Self - the report is "I Am." This at first seems to be the final words from the consciousness, but a little further examination discloses the fact that this "I Am" may be separated or split into two distinct parts, or aspects, which while working in unison and in conjunction, yet, nevertheless, may be separated in consciousness.

While at first there seems to be only an "I" existing, a more careful and closer examination reveals the fact that there exists an "I" and a "Me." These mental twins differ in their characteristics and nature, and an examination of their nature and the phenomena arising from the same will throw much light upon many of the problems of mental influence.

Let us begin with a consideration of the Me, which is usually mistaken for the I by the student, until he presses the inquiry a little further back into the recesses of consciousness. A man thinks of his Self (in its aspect of Me) as being composed of certain feelings, tastes, likes, dislikes, habits, peculiar ties, characteristic, etc., all of which go to make up his personality, or the "Self" known to himself and others. He knows that these emotions and feelings change; are born and die away; are subject to the Principle of Rhythm, and the Principle of Polarity, which take him from one extreme of feeling to another. He also thinks of the "Me" as being certain knowledge gathered together in his mind, and thus forming a part of himself. This is the "Me" of a man.

But we have proceeded too hastily. The "Me" of many men may be said to consist largely of their consciousness of the body and their physical appetites, etc. Their consciousness being largely bound up with their bodily nature, they practically "live there." Some men even go so far as to regard their personal apparel as a part of their "Me" and actually seem to consider it a part of themselves. A writer has humorously said that "men consist of three parts - soul, body and clothes." These "clothes conscious" people would lose their personality if divested of their clothing by savages upon the occasion of a shipwreck. But even many who are not so closely bound up with the idea of personal raiment stick closely to the consciousness of their bodies being their "Me." They cannot conceive of a Self independent of the body. Their mind seems to them to be practically "a something belonging to" their body - which in many cases it is indeed.

But as a man rises in the scale of consciousness he is able to disentangle his "Me" from his idea of body, and is able to think of his body as "belonging to" the mental part of him. But even then he is very apt to identify the "Me" entirely with the mental states, feelings, etc., which he feels to exist within him. He is very apt to consider these internal states as identical with himself, instead of their being simply "things" produced by some part of his mentality, and existing within him - of him, and in him, but still not "himself." He sees that he may change these internal states of feelings by all effort of will, and that he may produce a feeling or state of an exactly opposite nature, in the same way, and yet the same "Me" exists. And so after a while he is able to set aside these various mental states, emotions, feelings, habits, qualities, characteristics, and other personal mental belongings - he is able to set them aside in the "not-me" collection of curiosities and encumbrances, as well as valuable possessions. This requires much mental concentration and power of mental analysis on the part of the student. But still the task is possible for the advanced student, and even those not so far advanced are able to see, in the imagination, how the process may be performed.

After this laying-aside process has been performed, the student will find himself in conscious possession of a "Self" which may be considered in its "I" and "Me" dual aspects. The "Me" will be felt to be a Something mental in which thoughts, ideas, emotions, feelings, and other mental states may be produced. It may be considered as the "mental womb," as the ancients styled it - capable of generating mental offspring. It reports to the consciousness as a "Me" with latent powers of creation and generation of mental progeny of all sorts and kinds. Its powers of creative energy are felt to be enormous. But still it seems to be conscious that it must receive some form of energy from either its "I" companion, or else from some other "I" ere it is able to bring into being its mental creations. This consciousness brings with it a realization of an enormous capacity for mental work and creative ability.

But the student soon finds that this is not all that he finds within his inner consciousness. He finds that there exists a mental Something which is able to Will that the "Me" act along certain creative lines, and which is also able to stand aside and witness the mental creation. This part of himself he is taught to call his "I." He is able to rest in its consciousness at will. He finds there not a consciousness of an ability to generate and actively create, in the sense of the gradual process attendant upon mental operations, but rather a sense and consciousness of an ability to project an energy from the "I" to the "Me" - a process of "willing" that the mental creation begin and proceed. He also finds that the "I" is able to stand aside and witness the operations of the "Me's" mental creation and generation. There is this dual aspect in the mind of every person. The "I" represents the Masculine Principle of Mental Gender - the "Me" represents the Female Principle. The "I" represents the Aspect of Being; the "Me" the Aspect of Becoming. You will notice that the Principle of Correspondence operates on this plane just as it does upon the great plane upon which the creation of Universes is performed. The two are similar in kind, although vastly different in degree. "As above, so below; as below, so above."

[At the highest of spiritual planes, we see this duality represented in the eternal aspects of God that are Ever-Being and Ever-Becoming Of course, in the Mind of God, these qualities are so intertwined as to be indistinguishable to us except for our feeble attempts to classify certain phenomena.]

These aspects of mind - the Masculine and Feminine Principles - the "I" and "Me" - considered in connection with the well-known mental and psychic phenomena, give the master-key to these dimly known regions of mental operation and manifestation. The principle of Mental Gender gives the truth underlying the whole field of the phenomena of mental influence, etc.

The tendency of the Feminine Principle is always in the direction of receiving impressions, while the tendency of the Masculine Principle is always in the direction of giving out, or expressing. The Feminine Principle has much more varied field of operation than has the Masculine Principle. The Feminine Principle conducts the work of generating new thoughts, concepts, ideas, including the work of the imagination. The Masculine Principle contents itself with the work of the "Will" in its varied phases. And yet, without the active aid of the Will of the Masculine Principle, the Feminine is apt to rest content with generating mental images which are the result of impressions received from outside, instead of producing original mental creations.

Persons who can give continued attention and thought to a subject actively employ both of the Mental Principles - the Feminine in the work of the mental generation, and the Masculine Will in stimulating and energizing the creative portion of the mind. The majority of persons really employ the Masculine Principle but little, and are content to live according to the thoughts and ideas instilled into the "Me" from the "I" of other minds. But it is not our purpose to dwell upon this phase of the subject, which may be studied from any good text-book upon psychology, with the key that we have given you regarding Mental Gender.

The student of Psychic Phenomena is aware of the wonderful phenomena classified under the head of Telepathy; Thought Transference; Mental Influence; Suggestion; Hypnotism, etc. Many have sought for an explanation of these varied phases of phenomena under the theories of the various "dual mind" teachers. And in a measure they are right, for there is clearly a manifestation of two distinct phases of mental activity. But if such students will consider these "dual minds" in the light of the Hermetic Teachings regarding Vibrations and Mental Gender, they will see that the long sought for key is at hand.

In the phenomena of Telepathy it is seen how the Vibratory Energy of the Masculine Principle is projected toward the Feminine Principle of another person, and the latter takes the seed-thought and allows it to develop into maturity. In the same way Suggestion and Hypnotism operates. The Masculine Principle of the person giving the suggestions directs a stream of Vibratory Energy or Will-Power toward the Feminine Principle of the other person, and the latter accepting it makes it its own and acts and thinks accordingly. An idea thus lodged in the mind of another person grows and develops, and in time is regarded as the rightful mental offspring of the individual, whereas it is in reality like the cuckoo egg placed in the sparrow's nest, where it destroys the rightful offspring and makes itself at home. The normal method is for the Masculine and Feminine Principle in a person's mind to co-ordinate and act harmoniously in conjunction with each other, but, unfortunately, the Masculine Principle in the average person is too lazy to act - the display of Will-Power is too slight - and the consequence is that such persons are ruled almost entirely by the minds and wills of other persons, whom they allow to do their thinking and willing for them. How few original thoughts or original actions are performed by the average person? Are not the majority of persons mere shadows and echoes of others having stronger wills of minds than themselves? The trouble is that the average person dwells almost altogether in his "Me" consciousness and does not realize that he has such a thing as an "I." He is polarized in his Feminine Principle of Mind, and the Masculine Principle, in which is lodged the Will, is allowed to remain inactive and not employed.

The strong men and women of the world invariably manifest the Masculine Principle of Will, and their strength depends materially upon this fact. Instead of living upon the impressions made upon their minds by others, they dominate their own minds by their Will, obtaining the kind of mental images desired, and moreover dominate the minds of others likewise, in the same manner. Look at the strong people, how they manage to implant their seed-thoughts in the minds of the masses of the people, thus causing the latter to think thoughts in accordance with the desires and wills of the strong individuals. This is why the masses of people are such sheep-like creatures, never originating an idea of their own, nor using their own powers of mental activity.

The manifestation of Mental Gender may be noticed all around us in everyday life. The magnetic persons are those who are able to use the Masculine Principle in the way of impressing their ideas upon others. The actor who makes people weep or cry as he wills, is employing this principle. And so is the successful orator, statesman, preacher, writer or other people who are before the public attention. The peculiar influence exerted by some people over others is due to the manifestation of Mental Gender, along the Vibrational lines above indicated. In this principle lies the secret of personal magnetism, personal influence, fascination, etc., as well as the phenomena generally grouped under the name of Hypnotism.

The student who has familiarized himself with the phenomena generally spoken of as "psychic" will have discovered the important part played in the said phenomena by that force which science has styled "Suggestion," by which term is meant the process or method whereby an idea is transferred to, or "impressed upon" the mind of another, causing the second mind to act in accordance therewith. A correct understanding of Suggestion is necessary in order to intelligently comprehend the varied psychical phenomena which Suggestion underlies. But, still more is a knowledge of Vibration and Mental Gender necessary for the student of Suggestion. For the whole principle of Suggestion depends upon the principle of Mental Gender and Vibration.

It is customary for the writers and teachers of Suggestion to explain that it is the "objective or voluntary" mind which make the mental impression, or suggestion, upon the "subjective or involuntary" mind. But they do not describe the process or give us any analogy in nature whereby we may more readily comprehend the idea. But if you will think of the matter in the light of the Hermetic Teachings you will be able to see that the energizing of the Feminine Principle by the Vibratory Energy of the Masculine Principle is in a concordance to the universal laws of nature, and that the natural world affords countless analogies whereby the principle may be understood. In fact, the Hermetic Teachings show that the very creation of the Universe follows the same law, and that in all creative manifestations, upon the planes of the spiritual, the mental, and the physical, there is always in operation this principle of Gender - this manifestation of the Masculine and the Feminine Principles. "As above, so below; as below, so above." And more than this, when the principle of Mental Gender is once grasped and understood, the varied phenomena of psychology at once becomes capable of intelligent classification and study, instead of being very much in the dark. The principle "works out" in practice, because it is based upon the immutable universal laws of life.

We shall not enter into an extended discussion of, or description of, the varied phenomena of mental influence or psychic activity. There are many books, many of them quite good, which have been written and published on this subject of late years. The main facts stated in these various books are correct, although the several writers have attempted to explain the phenomena by various pet theories of their own. The student may acquaint himself with these matters, and by using the theory of Mental Gender he will be able to bring order out of the chaos of conflicting theory and teachings, and may, moreover, readily make himself a master of the subject if he be so inclined. The purpose of this work is not to give an extended account of psychic phenomena but rather to give to the student a master-key whereby he may unlock the many doors leading into the parts of the Temple of Knowledge which he may wish to explore. We feel that in this consideration of the teachings of The Kybalion, one may find an explanation which will serve to clear away many perplexing difficulties - a key that will unlock many doors. What is the use of going into detail regarding all of the many features of psychic phenomena and mental science, provided we place in the hands of the student the means whereby he may acquaint himself fully regarding any phase of the subject which may interest him. With the aid of *The Kybalion* one may go through any occult library anew, the old Light from Egypt illuminating many dark pages, and obscure subjects. That is the purpose of this book. We do not come expounding a new philosophy, but rather furnishing the outlines of a great world-old teaching which will make clear the teachings of others - which will serve as a Great Reconciler of differing theories, and opposing doctrines.

The Kybalion

Hermetic Axioms

"The possession of Knowledge, unless accompanied by a manifestation and expression in Action, is like the hoarding of precious metals - a vain and foolish thing. Knowledge, like wealth, is intended for Use. The Law of Use is Universal, and he who violates it suffers by reason of his conflict with natural forces."

— *The Kybalion*

The Hermetic Teachings, while always having kept securely locked up in the minds of the fortunate possessors thereof, for reasons which we have already stated, were never intended to be merely stored away and secreted. The Law of Use is dwelt upon in the Teachings, as you may see by reference to the above quotation from The Kybalion, which states it forcibly. Knowledge without use and Expression is a vain thing, bringing no good to its possessor, or to the race. Beware of Mental Miserliness, and express into Action that which you have learned. Study the Axioms and Aphorisms, but practice them also.

We give below some of the more important Hermetic Axioms, from The Kybalion, with a few comments added to each. Make these your own, and practiced and use them, for they are not really your own until you have Used them.

"To change your mood or mental state- change your vibration."

— *The Kybalion*

One may change his mental vibrations by an effort of Will, in the direction of deliberately fixing the Attention upon a more desirable state. Will directs the Attention, and Attention changes the Vibration. Cultivate the Art of Attention, by means of the Will, and you have solved the secret of the Mastery of Moods and Mental States.

"To destroy an undesirable rate of mental vibration, put into operation the principle of Polarity and concentrate upon the opposite pole to that which you desire to suppress. Kill out the undesirable by changing its polarity."

— *The Kybalion*

This is one of the most important of the Hermetic Formulas. It is based upon true scientific principles. We have shown you that a mental state and its opposite were merely the two poles of one thing, and that by Mental Transmutation the polarity might be reversed. This Principle is known to modem psychologists, who apply it to the breaking up of undesirable habits by bidding their students concentrate upon the opposite quality. If you are possessed of Fear, do not waste time trying to "kill out" Fear, but instead cultivate the quality of Courage, and the Fear will disappear. Some writers have expressed this idea most forcibly by using the illustration of the dark room. You do not have to shovel out or sweep out the Darkness, but by merely opening the shutters and letting in the Light the Darkness has disappeared. To kill out a Negative quality, concentrate upon the Positive Pole of that same quality, and the vibrations will gradually change from Negative to Positive, until finally you will become polarized on the Positive pole instead of the Negative. The reverse is also true, as many have found out to their sorrow, when they have allowed themselves to vibrate too constantly on the Negative pole of things. By changing your polarity you may master your moods, change your mental states, remake your disposition, and build up character. Much of the Mental Mastery of the advanced Hermetics is due to this application of Polarity, which is one of the important aspects of Mental Transmutation. Remember the Hermetic Axiom (quoted previously), which says:

"Mind (as well as metals and elements) may be transmuted from state to state; degree to degree, condition to condition; pole to pole; vibration to vibration."

- *The Kybalion*

The mastery of Polarization is the mastery of the fundamental principles of Mental Transmutation or Mental Alchemy, for unless one acquires the art of changing his own polarity, he will be unable to affect his environment. An understanding of this principle will enable one to change his own Polarity, as well as that of others, if he will but devote the time, care, study and practice necessary to master the art. The principle is true, but the results obtained depend upon the persistence, patience and practice of the student.

"Rhythm may be neutralized by an application of the Art of Polarization."

- *The Kybalion*

As we have explained in previous chapters, the Hermetists hold that the Principle of Rhythm manifests on the Mental Plane as well as on the Physical Plane, and that the bewildering succession of moods, feelings, emotions, and other mental states, are due to the backward and forward swing of the mental pendulum, which carries us from one extreme of feeling to the other. The Hermetists also teach that the Law of Neutralization enables one, to a great extent, to overcome the operation of Rhythm in consciousness. As we have explained, there is a Higher Plane of Consciousness, as well as the ordinary Lower Plane, and the Master by rising mentally to the Higher Plane causes the swing of the mental pendulum to manifest on the Lower Plane, and he, dwelling on his Higher Plane, escapes the consciousness of the swing backward. This is effected by polarizing of the Higher Self, and thus raising the mental vibrations of the Ego above those of the ordinary plane of consciousness. It is akin to rising above a thing and allowing it to pass beneath you. The advanced Hermetist polarizes himself at the Positive Pole of his Being - the "I Am" pole rather than the pole of personality and by refusing and "denying" the operation of Rhythm, raises himself above its plane of consciousness, and standing firm in his Statement of Being he allows the pendulum to swing back on the Lower Plane without changing his Polarity. This is accomplished by all individuals who have attained any degree of self-mastery, whether they understand the law or not. Such persons simply "refuse" to allow themselves to be swung back by the pendulum of mood and emotion, and by steadfastly affirming their superiority they remain polarized on the Positive pole. The Master, of course, attains a far greater degree of proficiency, because he understands the law which he is overcoming by a higher law, and by the use of his Will he attains a degree of Poise and Mental Steadfastness almost impossible of belief on the part of those who allow themselves to be swung backward and forward by the mental pendulum of moods and feelings.

Remember always, however, that you do not really destroy the Principle of Rhythm, for that is indestructible. You simply overcome one law by counter-balancing it with another and thus maintain an equilibrium. The laws of balance and counter-balance are in operation on the mental as well as on the physical planes, and an understanding of these laws enables one to seem to overthrow laws, whereas he is merely exerting a counterbalance.

> "Nothing escapes the Principle of Cause and Effect, but there are many Planes of Causation, and one may use the laws of the higher to overcome the laws of the lower."
> - *The Kybalion*

By an understanding of the practice of Polarization, the Hermetists rise to a higher plane of Causation and thus counter balance the laws of the lower planes of Causation. By rising above the plane of ordinary Causes they become themselves, in a degree, Causes instead of being merely Caused. By being able to master their own moods and feelings, and by being able to neutralize Rhythm, as we have already explained, they are able to escape a great part of the operations of Cause and Effect on the ordinary plane. The masses of people are carried along, obedient to their environment; the wills and desires of others stronger than themselves; the effects of inherited tendencies; the suggestions of those about them; and other outward causes; which tend to move them about on the chess-board of life like mere pawns. By rising above these influencing causes, the advanced Hermetists seek a higher plane of mental action, and by dominating their moods, emotions, impulses and feelings, they create for themselves new characters, qualities and powers, by which they overcome their ordinary environment, and thus become practically Players instead of mere Pawns. Such people help to play the game of life understandingly, instead of being used by it. Of course, even the highest are subject to the Principle as it manifests on the higher planes, but on the lower planes of activity, they are Masters instead of Slaves. As The Kybalion says:

> "The wise ones serve on the higher, but rule on the lower. They obey the laws coming from above them, but on their own plane, and those below them they rule and give orders. And, yet, in so doing, they form a part of the Principle, instead of opposing it. The wise man falls in with the Law, and by understanding its movements he operates it instead of being its blind slave. Just as does the skilled swimmer turn this way and that way, going and coming as he will, instead of being as the log which is carried here and there - so is the wise man as compared to the ordinary man - and yet both swimmer and log; wise man and fool, are subject to Law. He who understands this is well on the road to Mastery."
> - *The Kybalion*

In conclusion, let us again call your attention to the Hermetic Axiom:

> "True Hermetic Transmutation is a Mental Art."
> - *The Kybalion*

In the above axiom, the Hermetists teach that the great work of influencing one's environment is accomplished by Mental Power. The Universe being wholly mental, it follows that it may be ruled only by Mentality. And in this truth is to be found an explanation of all the phenomena and manifestations of the various mental powers which are attracting so much attention and study in these earlier years of the Twentieth Century. Back of and under the teachings of the various cults and schools, remains ever constant the Principle of the Mental Substance of the Universe. If the Universe be Mental in its substantial nature, then it follows that Mental Transmutation must change the conditions and phenomena of the Universe. If the Universe is

Mental, then Mind must be the highest power affecting its phenomena. If this be understood then all the so-called "miracles" and "wonder-workings" are seen plainly for what they are.

> "THE ALL is MIND; The Universe is Mental."
> - *The Kybalion*

FINIS

Sepher Yetzirah
Translated by Knut Stenring

An Introductory Note

The Sepher Yetzirah is a brief Qabalistic treatise on the creation of the universe through the emanation of the letters of the Hebrew alphabet. A cursory examination of this text may lead the reader to assume that its doctrine is contradictory to the Gnostic mythos. It must be remembered, however, that creation myths, and the like, are using a Symbolic language to express the inexpressible; to communicate the incommunicable. As your knowledge of the Mysteries deepens, and as you gain mastery of the Truth of the Hermetic philosophy, you will come to realize that the message of the Sepher Yetzirah, and the esoteric principles which underlie it, are wholly compatible with and complementary to the hidden wisdom of Christian Gnosticism.

There are many translations of this text, and even more commentaries. We encourage you to seek out and study the various opinions and exegeses of this work. But we want to present it here without comment, so that the student may confront the work at face value, without the addition of opinion or interpretation. Its exposition of the ten Sephiroth, and the twenty-two fetters of the Hebrew alphabet, makes it an immensely valuable Qabalistic work.

The translation offered here is Knut Stenring's 1923 edition. While this is not the earliest English translation of the text, it is significant in that it rectifies certain correspondences that are, almost without doubt, in error among other versions; particularly the permutations of the Tetragrammaton (ch. 1), and the correspondences of the planets and days of the week (ch. IV). There is yet much unknown about this work, including its very origin. It has been claimed by some to be a product of the first or second century after Christ; and by others to be somewhat more recent. Stenring italicizes certain phrases that he believes to be later additions to the text. This convention has been retained in the following presentation of his translation.

Regardless of its antiquity, it has served for hundreds of years as the primary basis for Qabalistic doctrine. Truly, this short essay may provide one with a lifetime of study and contemplation.

Sepher Yetzirah

Chapter I

1. In thirty-two mysterious paths of wisdom did the Lord write, *the Lord of Hosts, the God of Israel the Living Elohim, and King of the Universe, the Almighty, Merciful and Gracious God; He is great and exalted and eternally dwelling in the Height, His name is holy, He is exalted and holy.* He created His Universe by the three forms of expression: Numbers, Letters, and Words.

2. Ten ineffable Sephiroth and twenty-two basal letters: three mothers, seven double, and twelve simple (letters).

3. Ten ineffable Sephiroth, corresponding to the ten fingers, five
(over) against five and the only token of the covenant in the middle: the word of the tongue and (the circumcision) of the flesh.

4. Ten ineffable Sephiroth, ten and not nine, ten and not eleven: understand with wisdom and apprehend with care; examine by means of them and search them out; *know, count, and write.* Put forth the subject in its light and place the Formator on His throne. He is the only Creator and the only Formator, and no one exists but He: His attributes are ten and have no limits.

5. The ineffable Sephiroth: their totality is ten; they are, however, without limits: the infinity of the Beginning and the infinity of the End, the infinity of the Good and the infinity of the Evil, the infinity of the Height and the infinity of the Depth, the infinity of the East and the infinity of the West, the infinity of (the) North and the infinity of (the) South; *and only one Lord God, the trusty King, rules them all from His holy dwelling in all eternity.*

6. Ten ineffable Sephiroth: their appearance is like that of a flash of lightning, their goal is infinite. His word is in them when they emanate and when they return; at His bidding do they haste like a whirlwind; and before His throne do they prostrate (themselves).

7. Ten ineffable Sephiroth: their end is in their beginning and likewise their beginning in their end, as the flame is bound to the burning coal. *Know, count, and write.* The Lord is one and the Formator is one and hath no second (beside Him): what number canst thou count before one?

8. Ten ineffable Sephiroth: close thy mouth lest it speak and thy heart lest it think; and if thy mouth openeth for utterance and thy heart turneth toward thought, bring them back (to thy control). LMQVMf, *therefore it is written: "And the living creatures ran and returned"* (Ezekiel i.14); and hence was the covenant made.

9. Ten ineffable Sephiroth:
One - The Spirit of the Living Elohim, His throne is erected in eternity, *blessed and praised be His name, the Living God of ages, eternal and forever;* Voice, Spirit, and Word: this is the Spirit of the Holy One. His beginning hath no beginning and His end hath no ending.

10. Two - Air from Spirit: He wrote and formed therein twenty-two basal letters; three mothers, seven

double, and twelve simple.

11. Three - Water from Air: He wrote and formed therein twenty-two letters, from the formless and void - mire and clay; He designed them as a platband, He hewed them as a wall, He covered them as a building, He poured snow over them and it became earth, *even as it is written: "He saith to the snow: Be thou the earth"* (Job xxxvii.6).

12. Four - Fire from Water: and He designed and cut thereof the Throne of Glory: Seraphim, Ophanim, the Holy Animals, the Ministering Angels; and with these three he founded His dwelling. *Therefore it is written: "He maketh His angels spirits and His ministers a flaming fire"* (Ps. civ.4).

13. He chose three of the simple letters, a secret belonging to the three mothers ש מ א = A M Sh, and put them in His Great Name and sealed with them six extensions.
Five - He sealed the Height stretched upwards and sealed it with יהו = IHV.
Six - He sealed the Depth stretched downwards and sealed it with יוה = IVH.
Seven - he sealed the East stretched forwards and sealed it with, היו = HIV.
Eight- He sealed the West stretched backwards and sealed it with הוי = HVI.
Nine -He sealed the (North) stretched to the right and sealed it with ויה = VIH.
Ten - He sealed the (South) stretched to the left and sealed it with והי = VHI.

14. *These are the ten ineffable Sephiroth: one - the Spirit of the Living Elohim; two - Air from Spirit; three - Water from Air; four - Fire from Water; Height, Depth, East, West, North, and South.*

Sepher Yetzirah

Chapter II

1. Twenty-Two basal letters: three mothers, seven double, and twelve simple. *Three mothers:* אמש *= A M Sh their foundation: the scale of Merit and the scale of Guilt, and the tongue is (an) equilibrating law between the two. Three mothers: A M Sh — M is mute, Sh is sibilant, and A equilibrates the two.*

2. Twenty-two basal letters: He designed them, He formed them, He purified them, He weighed them, and He exchanged them, each one with all; He formed by means of them the whole creation and everything that should be created (subsequently).

2. Twenty-two basal letters: three mothers, seven double, and twelve simple; they are designed in the voice, farmed in the air and set in the mouth at five places.

The letters: אחהע = A H Ch O at the throat,
גיכק = G I K Q at the palate,
בטלנת = B T L N Th at the tongue,
זסצרש = Z S Tz R Sh at the teeth,
דומפ = D V M P at the lips.

4. Twenty-two basal letters: they are placed together in a ring, as a wall with two hundred and thirty-one gates. The ring may be put in rotation forwards or backwards and its token in this: Nothing excels ענג = ONG (= pleasure) in good, and nothing excels נגע = NGO (= plague) in evil.

5. How did He combine, weigh, and exchange them? A with all and all with A; B with all and all with B; G with all and all with G; and all of them turned round. Hence they go forth through two hundred and thirty-one gates, and thus it comes about that the whole creation and all language proceed from one combination of letters.

6. He created from the formless and made the non-existent exist; and He formed large columns out of intangible air. This is the token: He beheld, exchanged, and brought forth the whole creation and all objects (by means of) one combination of letters, the token of which is twenty-two objects in one body.

Chapter Ill

1. Three mothers: **שׁ מ א** = A M Sh. Their foundation is: the scale of Merit and the scale of Guilt, and the tongue is (an) equilibrating law between the two.

2. Three mothers: A M Sh. This is a great, recondite, hidden, and precious secret, sealed with six seals, and from these (A M Sh) proceeded Air, Water, and Fire. *Fathers were produced by them, and from the fathers (descend) the generations.*

3. Three mothers: A M Sh. He designed, formed, purified, weighed, and exchanged them; and by means of them He brought forth three mothers in the Universe, three mothers in the Year, three mothers in Man, *male and female.*

4. *Three mothers: A M Sh - Fire, Air, and Water. The heavens are produced from Fire, the wind is produced from Air, and the earth is produced from Water. the Fire above and the Water below, and the Air is (an) equilibrating law between the two; by them were the fathers brought forth, and by them were all things produced.*

5. Three mothers: A M Sh in the Universe -Air, Water, and Fire. The heavens were in the beginning produced from Fire, the earth from Water, and the wind from Air, which thus equilibrates the two.

6. Three mothers: A M Sh in the Year - the cold, the heat, and the temperate state. The heat was produced from Fire, the cold from Water, and the temperate state from Air, which thus equilibrates the two.

7. Three mothers: AM Sh in Man - the head, the belly, and the chest. The head was produced from Fire, the belly from Water, and the chest from Air, which thus equilibrates the two.

8. He caused the letter A to reign Air, bound a crown upon it and fused them together. He produced by means of them: the atmosphere in the Universe, the temperate state in the Year, and the chest in Man, *male and female.*

9. He caused the letter M to reign in Water, bound a crown upon it and fused them together. He produced by means of them the earth in the Universe, the cold in the Year, and the belly in Man, *male and female.*

10. He caused the letter Sh to reign in Fire, bound a crown upon it and fused them together. He produced by means of them the heavens in the Universe, the heat in the Year, and the head in Man, *male and female.*

Sepher Yetzirah

Chapter IV

1. Seven double (letters): בגדכפרת = B G D K P R Th. Their foundation is: Life, Peace, Wisdom, Wealth, Beauty, Fruitfulness, and Dominion.

2. Seven double: B G D K P R Th. They are pronounced in two ways: B B, G G, D D, K K, P P, R R, Th Th: according to the form of the soft and hard, the strong and weak breathing.

3. Seven double: B G D K P R Th, according to pronunciation and permutation: contrary to Life is Death, contrary to Peace is Misfortune, contrary to Wisdom is Folly, contrary to Wealth is Poverty, contrary to Beauty is Ugliness, contrary to Fruitfulness is Devastation, contrary to Dominion is Slavery.

4. Seven double: B G D K P R Th, Height, Depth, East, West, North, and South, and the Holy Palace in the middle, which sustains them all.

5. *Seven double: B G D K P R Th, seven and not six, seven and not eight; examine and search out by means of them, bring the subject forth into light and place the Formator on His throne.*

6. Seven double: B G D K P Th. He designed, formed, purified, weighed, and exchanged them; He produced by means of them seven planets in the Universe, seven days in the Year, and seven gateways in Man; and by means of them also He designed seven heavens, seven earths, and seven weeks. Therefore of all things under the heavens did He love the heptad.

7. These are the seven planets in the Universe: Saturn, Jupiter, Mars, Sun, Venus, Mercury, Moon. These are the seven days in the Year; the seven days of the week; seven gateways in Man - two eyes, two ears, two nostrils, and the mouth.

8. He caused the letter B to reign in Wisdom, bound a crown upon it and fused them together. He produced by means of them: (the Sun) in the Universe, Sunday in the Year, and the right eye in Man, *male and female*.

9. He caused the letter G to reign in Wealth, bound a crown upon it and fused them together; He produced by means of them: (the Moon) in the Universe, Monday in the Year, and the left eye in Man, *male and female*.

10. He caused the letter D to reign in Fruitfulness, bound a crown upon it and fused them together. He produced by means of them: (Mars) in the Universe, Tuesday in the Year, and the right ear in Man, *male and female*.

11. He caused the letter K to reign in Life, bound a crown upon it and fused them together. He produced by means of them: (Mercury) in the Universe, Wednesday in the Year, and the left ear in Man, *male and female*.

12. He caused the letter P to reign in Dominion, bound a crown upon it and fused them together. He

produced by means of them: (Jupiter) in the Universe, Thursday in the Year, and the right nostril in Man, *male and female*.

13. He caused the letter R to reign in Peace, bound a crown upon it and fused them together. He produced by means of them: (Venus) in the Universe, Friday in the Year, and the left nostril in Man, *male and female*.

14. He caused the letter Th to reign in Beauty, bound a crown upon it and fused them together. He produced by means of them: (Saturn) in the Universe, Saturday in the Year, and the mouth in Man, male and female.

15. *Seven double: B G D K P R Th. There were designed by means of them, seven earths, seven heavens, seven continents, seven seas, seven rivers, seven deserts, seven days, seven weeks, seven years, seven fallow-years, seven jubilees, and the Holy Palace: hence under all the heavens did He love the heptad.*

16. Seven double: B G D K P R Th. How did He fuse them together? Two stones build two houses, three stones build six houses, four stones build twenty-four houses, five stones build one hundred and twenty houses, six stones build seven hundred and twenty houses, seven stones build five thousand and forty houses. Make a beginning herefrom and calculate further what the mouth cannot pronounce and what the ear cannot hear.

Sepher Yetzirah

Chapter V

1. Twelve simple (letters): הוזחטילנסעצק = H V Z Ch T I L N S O Tz Q. Their foundation is: Sight, Hearing, Smell, Speech, Taste, Coition, Work, Movement, Wrath, Mirth, Meditation, Sleep.

2. Twelve simple: H V Z Ch T I L N S O Tz Q twelve and not eleven, twelve and not thirteen. Their foundation corresponds to the twelve oblique angles (or directions): the North-East angle, the South-East angle, the above-East angle, the below-East angle, the above-North angle, the below-North angle, the North-West angle, the South-West angle, the above-West angle, the below-West angle, the above-South angle, the below-South angle. And they stretch out and diverge into infinity: *these are the arms of Universe.*

3. Twelve simple: H V Z Ch T I L N S O Tz Q. He designed, formed, purified, exchanged, and weighed them, and produced by means of them twelve zodiacal signs in the Universe, twelve months in the Year, and twelve chief (members) in Man, *male and female.*

4. Twelve zodiacal signs in the Universe: Aries, Taurus, Gemini, Cancer, Leo, Virgo, Libra, Scorpio, Sagittarius, Capricornus, Aquarius, Pisces.

5. Twelve months in the Year: Nisan, Ijar, Sivan, Tamuz, Abh, Elul, Tišri, Marhešvan, Kislev, Ṭebeth, Šebath, Adar.

6. Twelve chief (members) in Man, *male and female*: two hands, two feet, two kidneys, the liver, the spleen, the gall, the stomach, the colon, the bowels. *He made them according to the order of a battle, even one against the other made God.*

7. He caused the letter H to reign in Sight, bound a crown upon it and fused them together; He produced by means of them: Aries in the Universe, Nisan in the Year, and the right hand in man, *male and female.*

8. He caused the letter V to reign in Hearing, bound a crown upon it and fused them together; He produced by means of them: Taurus in the Universe, Ijar in the Year, and the left hand in man, *male and female.*

9. He caused the letter Z to reign in Smell, bound a crown upon it and fused them together; He produced by means of them: Gemini in the Universe, Sivan in the Year, and the right foot in man, *male and female.*

10. He caused the letter Ch to reign in Speech, bound a crown upon it and fused them together; He produced by means of them: Cancer in the Universe, Tamuz in the Year, and the left foot in man, *male and female.*

11. He caused the letter T to reign in Taste, bound a crown upon it and fused them together; He produced by means of them: Leo in the Universe, Abh in the Year, and the right kidney in man, *male and female.*

12. He caused the letter I to reign in Coition, bound a crown upon it and fused them together; He produced by means of them: Virgo in the Universe, Elul in the Year, and the left kidney in man, *male and*

female.

13. He caused the letter L to reign in Work, bound a crown upon it and fused them together; He produced by means of them: Libra in the Universe, Tišri in the Year, and the liver in man, *male and female.*

14. He caused the letter N to reign in Movement, bound a crown upon it and fused them together; He produced by means of them: Scorpio in the Universe, Marhešvan in the Year, and the spleen in man, *male and female.*

15. He caused the letter S to reign in Wrath, bound a crown upon it and fused them together; He produced by means of them: Sagittarius in the Universe, Kislev in the Year, and the gall in man, *male and female.*

16. He caused the letter O to reign in Mirth, bound a crown upon it and fused them together; He produced by means of them: Capricornus in the Universe, Tebeth in the Year, and the stomach in man, *male and female.*

17. He caused the letter Tz to reign in Meditation, bound a crown upon it and fused them together; He produced by means of them: Aquarius in the Universe, Šebath in the Year, and the colon in man, *male and female.*

18. He caused the letter Q to reign in Sleep, bound a crown upon it and fused them together; He produced by means of them: Pisces in the Universe, Adar in the Year, and the bowels in man, *male and female.*

19. He made them according to the art of warfare, arranged them as a wall, and armed them as for battle.

Sepher Yetzirah

Chapter VI

1. There are three mothers, that are three fathers-, from them proceed Fire, Air, and Water. Three mothers, seven double, and twelve simple.

2. (A M Sh, B G D K P R Th, H V Z Ch T I L N S O Tz Q). These are the twenty-two letters by means of which the Holy (One), *blessed be He, the Lord of Hosts, the Living Elohim, the God of Israel, hath founded (everything). He is great and exalted, the One Who dwelleth (in the Height) eternally. His name is exalted and holy; He is exalted and holy.*

3. A proof of this and true tokens are: the Universe, the Year, and Man. Twelve are beneath, seven upon these, and three upon the seven. From the three He founded His dwelling and everything proceeds from one. This is a token that He is One and hath no second (beside Him). He is the only King in the Universe, He is one and His name is One.

4. The numbers of the Universe are ten (and twelve); a proof of this and true tokens are: *the Universe, the Year, and Man*; Fire, Air, and Water, seven planets and twelve zodiacal signs.

5. *These are the three mothers: A M Sh; from these proceeded fathers, and from the fathers (descend) generations. Three fathers and their generations, seven planets and their hosts, and twelve oblique angles. A proof of this and true tokens are: the Universe, the Year, and Man.*

6. A law is: the dodecad, the heptad, and the triad; their commissioners are: the dragon, the (celestial) sphere, and the heart.

7. *Three mothers, A M Sh - Air, Water, and Fire; Fire above, Water below, and the Air is an equilibrating law between the two. The token is: the Fire carries the Water; M is mute, Sh is sibilant, and A is an equilibrating law between the two.*

8. The dragon in the Universe is like a king on his throne; the (celestial) sphere in the Year is like a king in a province; the heart (in Man) is like a king in warfare.

9. God hath also set one thing against the other; the good against the evil and the evil against the good, good from good and evil from evil; the good marks out the evil and the evil marks out the good; good is reserved for the good ones and evil is reserved for the evil ones.

10. Three: each one stands alone for himself; one merited, one loaded with guilt, and one equilibrating between the two.

11. Seven are divided, three against three and one is equilibrating between the two groups.

12. Twelve are in warfare, *three friends and three enemies, three life-givers, three destroyers.*

13. *Three friends: the heart and the ears; three enemies: the gall, the tongue, and the liver; three life-givers: the two nostrils and the spleen; three destroyers: the two (lower) apertures and the mouth; and God, a trusty King, ruleth them all from His holy*

place in all eternity.

14. One over three, three over seven, seven over twelve, and all are joined one to the other, a token of which is twenty-two objects in one body.

15.

(A M Sh
B G D K P R Th
H V Z Ch T I L N S O Tz Q.)

These are the twenty-two letters by means of which אהיה = AHIH, יה = IH, יהוה = IHVH, אלהים = ALHIM, , אלהים יהוה = ALHIM IHVH, יהוה צבאות = IHVH TzBAVTh, אלהים צבאות = ALHIM TzBAVTh, שדי = ShDI, יהוה אדני = IHVH ADNI, hath designed (all); He made three numbers of them and formed His whole world of them; by means of them He formed the whole creation and all that shall yet be created.

16. *And when our father Abraham, peace be with him, had come, he beheld, contemplated, studied, and understood this; he formed and designed till he had reached it, then the Lord of the Universe, blessed be His name, appeared to him. He took him to His bosom and kissed him on his head and called him Abraham His friend; He made a covenant with him and his children, therefore it is written: "He had faith in the Lord." This was ascribed to him justly. He (the Lord) put the token of the covenant between his (Abraham's) hands, that is, the tongue; and between the feet, that is, the circumcision. He bound the twenty-two letters of the Thora to his tongue, and the Holy One, blessed be He, unveiled to him His secret. He let them (the letters) soak in Water, burn in Fire, and sway in the Air; He let them shine in the seven stars and lead in the twelve zodiacal signs.*

PART II

PRACTICE

Because God, the one who said, "Out of darkness, light will shine," is he who shone in our hearts with the light of the gnosis of the glory of Jesus Christ.

- 2 Corinthians 4:6

General Instruction

Creating a Personal Temple and Workspace

It will be necessary for you to create a personal temple space. Nothing elaborate is required; in fact, if absolutely necessary, nearly all temple work may be completely visualized mentally. It is beneficial, though, and preferable to maintain a modest physical temple space. Your altar may simply be a table or desk at which you may conduct basic meditation and ritual workings. We are not concerned here with the more elaborate requirements of the Liturgy, or the Theurgical Operations, but merely with the simple but effective exercises and techniques that may be practiced by individuals privately; exercises and techniques that are crucial to the effective celebration of the Mass, as well as other sacramental and initiatic rites.

Your altar should include one or more candles. Simple white tapers will suffice. Beeswax or liturgical wax is ideal, but paraffin will serve your purposes if the others are not available. Incense should also be present. A powdered incense, or chopped resin, over charcoal is traditionally preferred. If this method is not available to you, then a solid incense, or even a stick incense will be acceptable. It is not absolutely crucial that you use any one particular type of incense, but if possible, you should prepare the following ancient formula upon which the liturgical incense of the ACP is also based:

(Measurements based on weight)
2 parts Frankincense
1 part Myrrh
½ part Sumatran Benzoin

If this mixture is unavailable, then pure teardrop Frankincense may be used, or else Sandalwood if necessary.

In order to provide a balance to the Elements of Fire and Air, already present in the burning incense, you should also have a small dish of water and one of salt present during your study or practice sessions, to represent the Elements of Water and Earth. There should also be a mirror present at the altar that you may use to gaze into during certain meditation techniques. These are the basic elements required for your temple space. However, since this will be your personal sanctum where you can come to study, meditate, and practice various rites and techniques, you may wish to adorn the area with additional items that may help to foster a sense of sanctity and solemnity. Such items might include: an altar cloth, a cross, icons, or other religious or spiritual items. Finally, it would be advantageous for you to keep a journal in which you take notes on your studies, and record observations related to your various spiritual exercises.

Practice: General Instruction

On Meditation

Meditation is one of the most simple, yet most sublime of all spiritual practices. The practice is found in all religious systems, and many systems of philosophy as well. Its origin lies, undoubtedly, in the dawn of humanity. In fact, it would not be surprising to learn that the predecessors of modem Homo Sapiens had similar practices as well. As many cultures as there are on earth, there are as many techniques for meditation, and more. We will not tell you that one method is better than another, for many methods have proven their effectiveness for countless practitioners. There are, however, certain practices that will be recommended for the sake of uniformity. By ritualizing the practice of meditation, the practitioner is brought into attunement with other members of the Church, and with the egregore of the Church.

Concerning what to expect during meditation, the results may vary depending upon a number of circumstances, individually and collectively. For example, the act of meditation itself is really a clearing of the mind, or the establishing of a state of mind that is void of conscious thought, and receptive to the impressions from the higher Mind. Often, one may contemplate a certain subject before attempting to reach this clarity of mind. Depending on the nature of the contemplation, the resulting meditation can have different results for different people. Another factor that may influence the results or effectiveness of meditation is the degree of ability, on the part of the practitioner, to properly reach a meditative state. Unfortunately, there is no short cut, or immediate route to the perfect state of meditation. There is only dedication and practice. There is no doubt, though, that through repeated efforts and a sincerity of heart and mind, you will reap great benefits from this ancient practice that is integral to our Gnostic tradition, and key to receiving the gnostic insights toward which we all strive. In fact, you will receive benefits from every meditation session, from your very first onward, even if you do not immediately perceive those benefits objectively. It is also recommended that you incorporate a period of meditation into each of your study session.

Technique for Meditation

While seated before your altar in your personal temple space, light a single candle and place it before you at the center of the altar. Next, light some incense and allow it to permeate the area in which you will be meditating. Make sure that you maintain a good upright posture, with both feet placed flat on the floor, and your hands resting in your lap. Your spine should be erect, but the shoulders relaxed, not tense.

Once you have attained the correct posture, begin regulating your breathing. Do this by drawing long, slow, deep breaths in through the nose, followed by long, slow, complete exhalations through the mouth. At the points of maximum breath capacity and maximum breath evacuation, hold the state for a few moments before proceeding. After taking several breaths in this manner, slowly allow your breathing to return to a normal rhythmic state. Then, while gazing into the candle's flame, contemplate the given topic for your session.

We will give an example here that may be used at any time, or replaced with other topics for meditation. For this particular meditation, contemplate what it means to be part of a *tradition*, specifically the Gnostic Apostolic tradition. Think about those who have come before you; who have helped to establish the Gnostic tradition; whose legacy we have inherited. Think also about those who will come after, to perpetuate the tradition after we are gone, for generations to come. Think about the bond that ties the past, present, and future together. Visualize this connection as a golden thread, stretching through space and time to tie together all of the seekers of gnosis; tethering them in an infinite string forward and backward through time. Think now about your place as a link in this chain, connecting the Masters of the Past to the neophytes of the future. Contemplate appreciation for our inheritance and realize your responsibility to ensure the continuity of the tradition.

After you have spent several minutes in silent contemplation, release the thoughts from your mind. It may be helpful to visualize them being consumed by the flame of the candle. As the thoughts dissipate, allow a vacuum to form in their absence. In the vacuum, allow yourself to be receptive to any impressions you might experience. Do not force thoughts out, but do not cling to them either. Simply allow the impressions to pass through. Do not become frustrated if you cannot maintain this ideal state. The Perfect Silence is something attained only after regular and frequent practiced of meditation techniques. As stated previously, however, there will be beneficial and productive changes occurring from the very first meditation. Over time you will come to recognize those subtle changes and learn to properly interpret the myriad impressions received.

For each meditation session, just follow the ritualized procedure given here, inserting whatever topic is appropriate for that session. There is no specific amount of time that each session needs to be. Just let the meditation itself guide you, and the conclusion will come naturally. When your meditation has ended, conclude with the following brief prayer of thanksgiving:

"O, Father of Light and Mother of Eternal Wisdom, thank you for the gifts you have bestowed upon me this day. Through Christ our indwelling Lord, and the revealer of the Holy Gnosis. Amen."

Then extinguish the candle and retire from your sanctum. For future meditations you may wish to consider some of the following topics:

- What does it mean to be a seeker of Truth and hidden wisdom?
- Why do you seek gnosis?
- Think of a time when ignorance of a situation has caused you to err. Think of a situation where your knowledge and awareness has enabled you to act correctly and beneficially.

The Sacred Art of Intonation

We have seen the creative power of the Logos in the emanations of the Aeons and the creation of Geradamas. And just as the spiritual Word is the creative expression of the pure will of the Father, so is the logos of man the creative expression of the human will. It is, in fact, the same creative Word flowing through human vessels as that which created the Aeons. But even at their best, human actions are flawed and imperfect. That does not stop us, of course, from seeking and striving for a more perfect state.

One of the most apparent manifestations of the Word in man is the spoken word itself. For, sound embodies the most primitive form of manifestation, which is Vibration. Everything that is, is in motion. Everything vibrates according to a particular frequency. In the *Gospel of Thomas*, Jesus says, "If they ask you, 'What is the evidence of your father in you?' say to them, 'It is motion and rest.'" And what is vibration but "motion and rest"? This fundamental truth has been known since long before the dawning of what we call civilization. It is for this reason that prayer, chanting, intonations, or other vocalizations are to be found as integral to every system of spirituality.

Intonations are used extensively throughout the liturgies of the ACP. Through the proper use of intonation, we may call forth the powers of the Aeons and the Archangels to assist us in our work; and we can also use those intonations to affect certain energy centers within ourselves, so that we might become more susceptible to the subtle spiritual powers to which we hope to attain. So, this instruction will focus on some of the intonations found in the ACP liturgy. Keep in mind, however, that this instruction is not intended as a replacement for personal training and mentorship, but rather as a reminder of, and supplement to, the instruction already given. Nevertheless, if you find yourself without a clergy mentor, following these instruction will do much to help guide you toward efficacious intonation.

Foremost in being able to properly intone vowel sounds and names of power, is being able to breathe properly. Breath control is necessary for the proper polarization of energies in your body, as well as for proper vocal control of the vibratory quality of your intonations. For these exercises, you should prepare your temple space as previously instructed, and establish your posture and breathing techniques, as given in the section on meditation. It is important to be physically relaxed and mentally focused so that the intonations can flow from you in a natural manner, rather than being strained or forced. Concerning the proper tonal qualities of your intonations, it will be necessary for you to witness them performed; either live or via recording. We can, however, give a basic description of pronunciations. In fact, if these intonations are performed as instructed here, they should be very similar to those within the context of the Mass, even if you have not personally witnessed them.

The first sounds we will intone are the opening intonations of the Mass. We will begin with IAO. In this, "I" is pronounced with a long "ee" sound, as in "pita" or "kiwi." And when intoned, you should feel a resonance in the "third eye" region of your head. That is, between and slightly above your brows. The "A" is pronounced "ah" as in "father." The resonance should be felt in your chest area. Finally, the "O" is pronounced with a long "oh" sound, as in "row." The "O" should be felt vibrating in the center of your throat.

Just before you perform your intonation you should draw a deep breath, vibrating your intonation as you exhale. As your intonation moves from I to A to O, you should feel the vibratory resonance shift to each of the physical regions described above. Each of the regions stimulated by intonation correspond to various energy centers in the body. And different combinations of energy centers can produce a variety of effects. For example, the IAO intonation should have the net effect of the building up and focusing of the creative spiritual principle. The Pistis Sophia has this to say regarding the mystical significance of IAO: "Iota, because the universe hath gone forth; Alpha, because it will turn back again; Omega, because the completion of all the completeness will take place."

The next intonation is very similar, but having a slightly different effect. In the I-A-UM intonation, the first two sounds are the same as those in I-A-O, except that they may be intoned at a higher pitch. The "UM" is pronounced as "oom" as in "loom" or "room." UM, though it is a single syllable, is actually a composite tone, in that it contains two phonemes and affects two different energy centers successively. The "U" part should be felt in the throat, similar to the "O" of I-A-O. The "M" sound, however, should resonate the entire head, emanating out of the top of the skull. Just as I-A-O has the effect of focusing the creative spiritual power, I-A-UM should have the effect of releasing or expressing that same power.

The third opening intonation of the Mass is A-U-M. The individual sounds of this intonation are similar to those given above. It should be noted, though, that here the "U" and "M" sounds are intoned as two separate syllables. So, as you intone A-U-M you can visualize a spiritual energy radiating from your heart and rising straight up through the throat, into the head, and expanding out into the farthest reaches of the universe. In this way, the A-U-M intonation links the core of the individual with the macrocosm of the universe. This trio of intonations, I-A-O, I-A-UM, and A-U-M, can be an effective introduction to any number of spiritual and religious rites, from the Mass, to the Theurgic Operations, to your own personal study and meditation sessions.

It should probably be mentioned here that what we have been referring to as "energy centers" are sometimes called "chakras." The word "chakra" is derived from a Sanskrit word "cakram" meaning "circle" or "wheel." This is the same root from which we get the Greek word "kuklos," also meaning "circle" or "wheel." This is where we get words such as "cycle," "cyclone," and "epicycle." Indeed, the very word "circle" itself comes from this very same root. The Vedic Indian concept of the chakras as seven spiritual energy centers within the human body is nearly identical with our own understanding of these energy centers. Now, it may be argued that an element of Indian Vedic spirituality has no place within a Christian Gnostic framework. To that charge we must respond that although as Christians we look to Jesus Christ as our revealer of gnosis, as Gnostics we must always be receptive to the truth wherever it may be found. The validity of the chakra doctrine has long been acknowledged and affirmed within the Western Mystery Tradition, which has been the preserver and transmitter of the ancient principles of gnosis. Gnosticism has, from its very beginning, looked to find truth wherever it may be hidden; unceasingly knocking at every door, and leaving no stone unturned. When the seeker applies him- or herself to the pursuit of Wisdom, one will find her abiding among the varied peoples, cultures, and religious traditions of the world. So then our study and application of the energy centers, or chakras, though it comes to us through a non-Christian source, is nevertheless wholly compatible with our Christian Gnostic doctrine and practices. And the practice of intonation is inextricably linked to the stimulation and activation of the various energy centers. (See the Appendices for a table of chakra correspondences.)

Invocation of the Archangels

The rite of the Invocation of the Archangels is really a simplification of a ritual developed in the late 19th century by the Hermetic Order of the Golden Dawn called the Lesser Banishing Ritual of the Pentagram. It is called a banishing ritual because its intention is to purify and cleanse an area by banishing unclean and unwanted entities or energies. In fact though, this is much more than a purification ritual. It is the summoning of powerful Archangelic beings to protect and assist the operator in his or her works. And though this invocation is used within the context of the Mass, it is also useful in other applications, or as a stand-alone rite. After you have prepared your personal sanctum, you will be ready to begin. You may also wish to open

Practice: General Instruction

this work with the three intonations from the Invocation of the Aeons, as discussed earlier.

The Invocation of the Archangels begins with a brief rite called the Qabalistic Cross. Begin by facing "Temple East." This may or may not correspond with geographical east. As you stand before your altar, facing it, this will be considered "Temple East." Now, with your right forefinger, touch your forehead and say "Ateh," which you may pronounce, AH-TAH. Now bring your finger down in a straight line to below your navel and say, "Malkuth," pronounced MAL-KOOT. Now bring your finger up to touch your right shoulder, saying, "Ve'Geburah," pronounced VEG-BOO-RAH. Then move your finger straight across to touch your left shoulder and say, "Ve'Gedulah," pronounced VEG-DOO-LAH. Now place your palms together before you, in front of your heart, and say, "Le Olam," pronounced LEH-OH- LAHM. Finally, cross your arms over your chest in an X formation and intone A-U-M. The words given here in the Qabalistic Cross are transliterations of the Hebrew words meaning roughly, "Thine is the Kingdom, the Power, and the Glory forever. Amen." In our version "amen" is replaced with AUM, because of its unique vibratory qualities. Now, using your forefinger again, or a ceremonial dagger if you have one, continue facing East and draw a pentagram in the air in front of you. The pentagram should be drawn starting from the lower left, thus:

Visualize the star as glowing Yellow. Now draw a deep breath and step forward with your right foot, thrusting your arms forward, and say, "In the Name of YODH-HEH-VAHV-HEH (יהוה) we (or I) invoke thee, Archangel of the East, RAH-PHAY-EL (Raphael).

Now step back to your former position. Point with your finger, or dagger, to the center of the pentagram you drew and, with your arm extended, turn your body 90° until you are facing South. Once again, draw the pentagram as before, but this time visualize it as glowing Red. Indraw your breath; step forward with your right foot; extend your arms and say, "In the Name of AH-DOH-NAI (Adonai - אדני) we invoke thee, Archangel of the South, MEE-CHAI-EL (Michael)."

Now, again, step back; point to the center of the star and turn 90° to face West. Draw a Blue pentagram; take your breath; step forward, arms extended, and say, "In the Name of EH-HEH-YA Y (Eheieh - אהיה) we invoke thee, Archangel of the West, GAH-BREE-EL (Gabriel)."

Repeat the motions that will bring you 90° to face North; repeat the motions, as you did for the other directions, drawing a dark Green pentagram, and say, "In the Name of AH-GL-AH (AGLA - אגלא) we invoke thee, Archangel of the North, AUR-EE-EL (Auriel)."

Again, step back, point to the center of the star, and turn 90° so that you are once again facing East. Close the ceremony by repeating the Qabalistic Cross that you opened with. We should also note that during this ceremony, the God names and the Archangelic names should be intoned and vibrated rather than merely spoken. If this rite is performed as a stand-alone ceremony, you may wish to follow it with a period of meditation, so that you may contemplate the invocations, and open yourself up to any further revelation. You may then record any thoughts or impressions in your journal.

Practice: General Instruction

Meditations of the Canonical Hours

The following readings may be performed daily, as you are able; The ACP celebrates seven Canonical Hours: Matins, Prime, Tierce, Sext, Nones, Vespers, and Complin. We realize that it may not be practical for all clergy to perform the readings at every appointed hour, every day. But you are encouraged to attempt this exercise, in its entirety, for six consecutive days, followed by the Holy Liturgy of the Pleromic Light on the seventh. This exercise is especially appropriate during the season of Lent, but may be repeated at any time. In addition, any part (that is, any Hour) may be performed on any day that you are able, as often as you are able. This exercise is also particularly useful when preparing to perform a Theurgic Operation.

Each of the Canonical Hours corresponds to the hours of the day as follows (times should be in local standard time):

- Matins - Midnight
- Prime - 6:00AM
- Tierce - 9:00AM
- Sext - NOON
- Nones - 3:00PM
- Vespers - 6:00 PM
- Complin - 9:00 PM

Each reading should begin with the performance of the Invocation of the Archangels. If time does not permit, then at least perform the Qabalistic Cross portion. You will also perform the Qabalistic Cross to close the session. So, the order of operations is thus:

o Qabalistic Cross
o Invocation of the Archangels
o Canonical Reading
o Qabalistic Cross

The readings for the Canonical Hours are as follows:

Matins (Matthew 25:1-13)

"Then the Kingdom of Heaven will be compared to ten virgins who took their lamps and went out to meet the bridegroom. Now, five of them were foolish and five wise. For, the foolish took their lamps but did not take oil with them. But the wise took containers of oil with their lamps. The bridegroom was delayed, and they all became drowsy and fell asleep. At midnight there was a shout, 'Behold, there is the bridegroom! Go out to meet him.' Then all the virgins awakened and trimmed their lamps. The foolish said to the wise, 'Give us some of your oil, for our lamps are going out.' But the wise ones answered, saying, 'There should certainly not be enough for us and you. Go instead to those selling and buy some for yourselves.' And while they were away buying oil, the bridegroom came, and the ones prepared entered with him into the wedding celebration; and the door was shut. The other virgins came later saying, 'Lord, lord, open the door for us.' But he answered saying, 'Truly I say to you, I do not know you.' Keep alert, therefore, for you do not know the day nor the hour."

Prime (Luke 1:68-79)

"Blessed be the Lord God of Israel, because he visited and redeemed his people, and he raised up a horn of salvation for us in the house of David his servant, just as he spoke through the mouth of his Holy Prophets from the Aeons, salvation from our enemies and from the hand of all those who hate us, to demonstrate mercy to our fathers and to remember his holy covenant, the path which he swore to Abraham our father, to grant us, having been delivered from the hand of our enemies, to serve him fearlessly in holiness and righteousness before him, all our days. And you also, child, will be called a prophet of the Most High; for you will go before the Lord to prepare his ways, to give salvific gnosis to his people by a forgiveness of their sins through the tender mercies of our God, by which the Sun rising from on high will break upon us, to appear to the ones sitting in darkness and in the shadow of death, to direct our feet into the way of peace."

Tierce (1 Thessalonians 5:1-6)

But concerning the times and the seasons, brothers, you have no need for anything to be written to you, for you yourselves know well that the day of the Lord comes as a thief in the night. Whenever they say, "We are in peace and security," then sudden destruction comes upon them, as birth pains come to her with a child in her womb, and they cannot escape. But you, brothers, are not in darkness, that the day should overtake you as a thief; for you are all children of Light and children of the day. We are not of night or of darkness; therefore, let us not sleep as the rest, but let us keep awake and be sober.

Sext (Acts 22:6-16)

"And it happened to me as I was traveling and drawing near to Damascus at about noon; suddenly a bright light from heaven shone around me, and I fell to the ground and heard a voice saying to me, 'Saul, Saul, why are you persecuting me?' And I answered, 'Who are you, Lord?' And he said to me, 'I am Jesus, the Nazorean, whom you are persecuting.' Those who were with me saw the light, but they did not hear the voice speaking to me. And I said, 'What may I do, Lord?' And the Lord said to me, 'Arise and go into Damascus; there you will be told about everything that has been assigned for you to do.' And because I had been blinded by the glory of that light, I entered Damascus being led by the hand by those who were with me.

And a certain Ananias, a devout man according to the law, who was well spoken of by all the Jews living there, came to me and stood by me, and said to me, 'Brother Saul, receive your sight!' And in that hour I looked up and saw him. And he said, 'The God of our fathers appointed you to know his will and to see the Righteous One, and to hear the call from his mouth because you will be a witness to him to all men of what you have seen and heard. Now what are you going to do? Arise, be baptized, and wash away your sins, calling upon his name.'"

Nones John 9:1-11)

And passing along, he saw a man blind from birth. His disciples asked of him, "Who sinned, this man or his parents, that he was born blind?" Jesus answered, "Neither this man sinned, nor his parents, but that the works of God may be manifested in him. It is necessary for us to do the work of He who sent me while it is day. Night is coming, when no one is able to work. While I am in the world, I am the light of the world." Having said this, he spat on the ground and made clay out of the saliva, and he anointed the man's eyes with the clay, and said to him, "Go and wash in the pool of Siloam" (which means "Sent"). He went, therefore, and washed, and returned able to see. Then his neighbors and those who had seen him before as a beggar, were saying, "Is this not the man who sits and begs?" Some were saying, "This is he." Others were saying, "No, but he resembles him." The man was saying, "I am." Then they said to him, "How were your eyes opened?" The man answered, "That man, the one called Jesus, made clay and anointed my eyes and said to me, 'Go into Siloam and wash.' Then I went, and when I washed, I saw."

Vespers (Matthew 24:23-31)

"If someone says to you, 'Look, here is the Christ,' or 'there he is,' do not believe. For false Christs and false prophets will arise, and they will give great signs and wonders so as to deceive, if possible, even the elect. Behold, I have told you beforehand. If, then, they say to you, 'Look, he is in the desert,' do not go out there. 'Look in the inner rooms,' do not believe them. For as the lightning flashes from the East, shining unto the West, thus will be the coming of the Son of Man. Wherever the corpse may be, there the Eagles will be gathered together. Immediately after the tribulation of those days, the Sun will be darkened, and the Moon will not give its light, and the Stars will fall from heaven, and the Powers of the heavens will be shaken. And then will appear the Sign of the Son of Man coming on the clouds of heaven, with power and great glory. And he will send his angels with a loud trumpet call, and they will gather together his Elect from the Four Winds, from one end of the heavens to the other."

Complin (Romans 13:8-10)

Owe no one anything, except to Love one another; for the one who Loves another has fulfilled the Law. For, "You shall not commit adultery; You shall not murder; You shall not steal; You shall not covet," and any other commandment, is summed up in this word, "You shall Love your neighbor as yourself." Love does not work evil toward your neighbor; Love, therefore, is the Fullness of the Law.

ACP Clergy Handbook

Meditation of the Golden Orb

For this meditation, prepare you sanctum as usual, including the intonations and invocations. Place your lighted candle in front of you; and as you gaze into its flame, visualize its golden aura growing larger and larger. With each indrawn breath, visualize the golden sphere of light expanding outward until it completely engulfs you. As you bask in its golden glow, feel its warmth enter you through your breath, and circulate throughout your body with every beat of your heart.

With each of your rhythmic breaths, sense the golden orb expanding, growing outward in all directions. It fills the room, the whole house…your neighborhood, your city…inflating exponentially. The warm, healing, golden light encompasses the globe of the Earth, pulsing, bathing all in its rejuvenating glow.

Now slowly draw the light back to yourself. Just as the light gradually flowed out, allow it to ebb in a natural, comfortable manner. When the light has returned to you, forming a golden orb around you, visualize it compressing smaller and smaller, withdrawing into you until it is as a golden seed resting in your breast until you choose to expand it. outward once again.

Instructions for Censing the Temple

These are instructions for censing the Temple for a Eucharistic Celebration or Theurgic Operation. You may adapt this technique, if you wish, for use in your personal Sanctum.

The Thurifer should be ordained up to the Order of Exorcist. He, or she, while still in the ante-chamber, places a copious amount of Blessed Incense upon the charcoal in the Thurible. After entering the Temple, he proceeds to face the East, where the following diagram is traced out before him with the fuming Thurible.

Starting at the level of the "third eye," move the Thurible down to the left at a 60° angle to about the level of the Solar Plexus, then horizontally across to the right, then back up to the point of origin, so that you have drawn an equilateral triangle, thus:

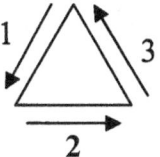

117

Now, start again at the level of your left shoulder. Pull the Thurible horizontally across to the level of your right shoulder, then down to the left at a 60° angle to the level of your groin, then back up to the point of origin at your left shoulder, thus:

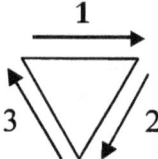

Now draw a line from top to bottom through the vertical axis of the hexagram:

Next draw a line from left to right through the horizontal axis:

To complete the diagram, you will make three circles encompassing everything. The first two are drawn, from the top-most point, clockwise; and the third is drawn counterclockwise, thus:

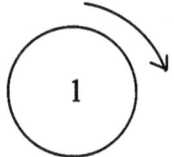 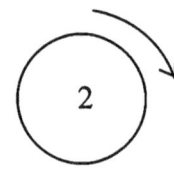 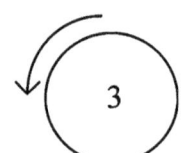

The Thurible is then positioned in the center of the figure, and the Thurifer walks in a 90° arc to the South of the Temple or Sanctuary, where the above figure is made again. The same procedure continues in the West and North, and then the Thurifer returns full circle to the East before returning to the antechamber for procession.

The Holy Gnostic Liturgy of the Pleromic Light

Introductory Note

The Holy Gnostic Liturgy of the Pleromic Light is the central rite of the Apostolic Church of the Pleroma. While the principal celebrant of the Mass is the priest or bishop, there are crucial roles for every level of clergy. It will benefit you greatly to learn not only your own unique role, but to study and become intimately familiar with every aspect of the liturgy. The Holy Mass has many truths to impart, and many mysteries to reveal to the one who carefully studies, contemplates, and meditates upon its many-faceted teachings. The better acquainted you are with the liturgy, the more you will get out of each celebration of the Most Holy Eucharist, and the better prepared you will be to fulfill your own ecclesiastical duties. Within the Liturgy of the Pleromic Light, you will find expressed the highest of Hermetic and Qabalistic principles, as well as the most sublime formulas of alchemical and theurgic operations. Just as Christ is the great Mediator, so too is His Holy Sacrament the means by which all doctrines are reconciled, and the soul itself may experience regeneration and reintegration into the fullness of God.

Practice: Liturgy of the Pleromic Light

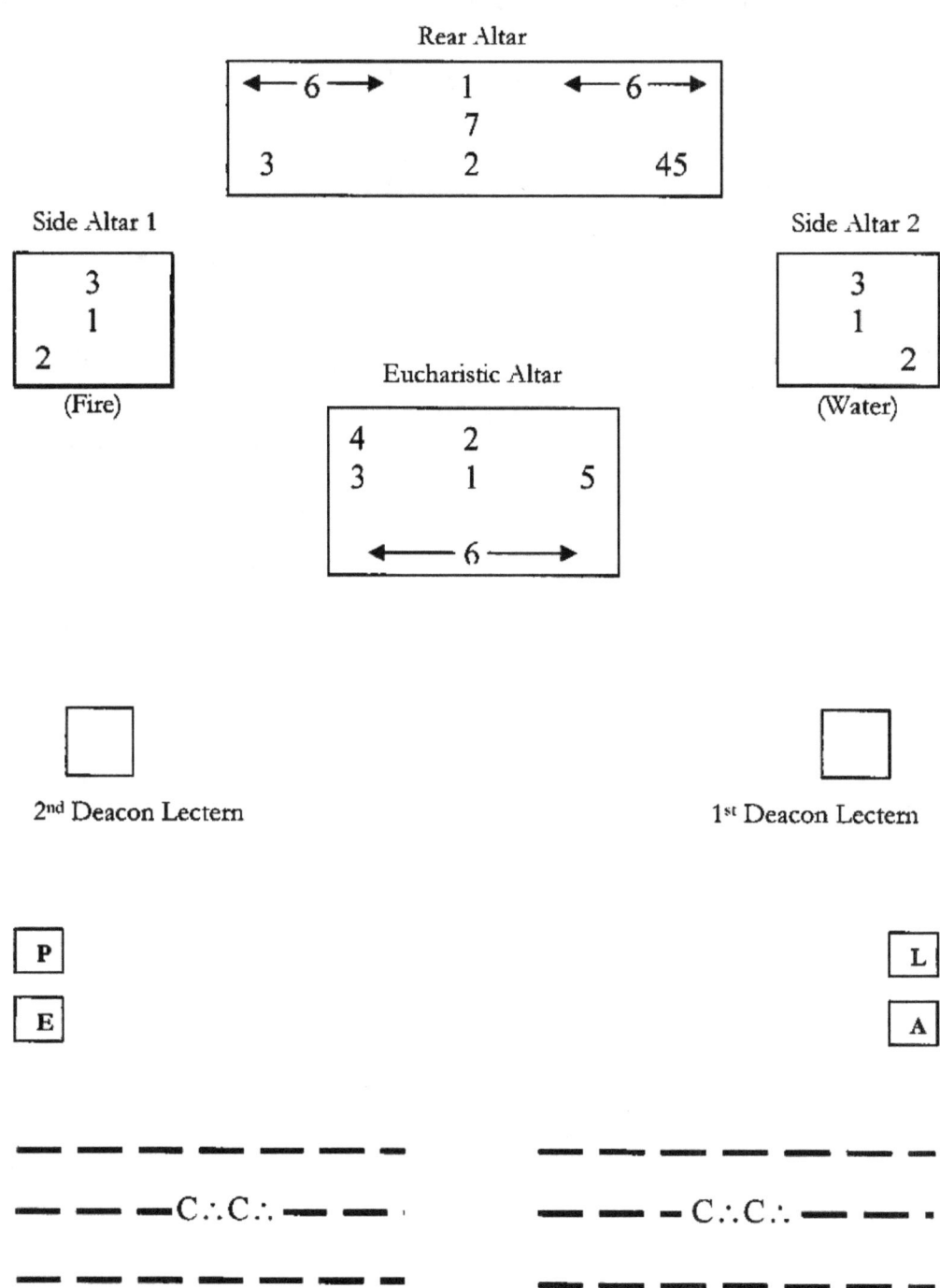

Temple Layout Key

Rear Altar

1. Seven-stick candelabra
2. Lectionary
3. Thurible
4. Aspergillum
5. Lavabo font
6. Icons
7. Sword (pointing North)

Eucharistic Altar

1. Altar stone, Chalice, etc.
2. Scripture (open to Gosp. Jn.)
3. Ceremonial Dagger
4. Bell
5. Ciborium
6. Altar Cross & Icons

Side Altar 1

1. Perpetual Luminary
2. Other special or occasional items
3. Icons

Side Altar 2

1. Wine & Water cruets
2. Other special or occasional items
3. Icons

P = Porters
L = Lectors
E = Exorcists
A = Acolytes
C∴ C∴ = Congregants

Practice: Liturgy of the Pleromic Light

Preliminary Rites

Before each celebration of the Holy Liturgy, the participating clergy shall assemble in the antechamber for certain preliminary rites, prayers, and meditation. Before vesting, each of the clergy should make the following prayer over his or her vestments:

"Our help is in the Name of the Lord. Bless these cloths, and make for me a robe of your Incorruptible Light. Amen."

Next, an Acolyte should enter the Temple proper and light the Perpetual Luminary. When the Acolyte returns, the Thurifer - who should be an Exorcist - proceeds to cense the Temple as he or she has been previously instructed. The Thurifer then returns to the antechamber with the thurible and prepares for procession. The Porter then calls the clergy to order thus:

"My Brothers and Sisters, come to order and prepare yourselves for our procession into the Temple of the Most High God."

The clergy will then line up in the following order:

- Porters (principal Porter acting as Conductor and carrying Sword)
- Lectors (principal Lector carrying Gospel)
- Exorcists (principal Exorcist carrying Altar Cross)
- Acolytes (principal Acolyte carrying Eucharistic elements)
- Deacons
- Priests
- Bishops
- Visiting Bishops
- Eparchs
- Exarch
- Patriarch
- Thurifer (should be of the rank of Exorcist)

Once the clergy has lined up for procession, they shall place their right hand over the heart while the Lector offers the following Invocation of the Paraclete:

"O Mother-Father of the Aeons,
O Paraclete!
Spirit of Truth,
Omnipresent and filling everything, Giver of Life!
Come to dwell in us,
Purify us of all iniquities
And save our souls,
O Merciful God!"

Then all clergy together say:

"Through our Lord Jesus, Christos, Soter, Logos. Amen."

The officiating Priest then calls for a moment of silent meditation and reflection. After a couple of minutes, the Porter says:

"My Brothers and Sisters, let us now enter the Temple of the Most High with the reverence due the Sovereign Architect of All Worlds."

Procession

The clergy processes single file into the Temple, circum-ambulating the Eucharistic Altar three times clockwise. On the first circuit, the Holy Bible is placed on the Altar open to the Gospel According to John. On the second circuit, the Altar Cross is placed in position. On the third circuit, the Eucharistic elements are placed on their appropriate altars. After the third circuit, the clergy lines up a few feet in front of the Eucharistic Altar. However, the Porter bearing the Sword remains standing centered behind the clergy line, and the Exorcist who is acting as Thurifer stands directly behind the Porter, continuing to swing the thurible from side to side while the opening invocations are recited.

Invocation of the Aeons

PRIEST:
In the Name of the Lord of all Worlds.

Priest and Deacons place right hand over heart.

PRIEST:
I...

1st DEACON:
A...

2nd DEACON:
O...

Priest and Deacons place hands, right over left, over the Solar Plexus.

Practice: Liturgy of the Pleromic Light

PRIEST:
I…

1ˢᵗ DEACON:
A…

2ⁿᵈ DEACON:
UM…

Priest & Deacons cross their arms across chest, right over left, palms open.

PRIEST:
A…

1ˢᵗ DEACON:
U…

2ⁿᵈ DEACON:
M…

Clergy now place their hands in front of them, palms together, as in prayer.

PRIEST:
Lord of the Past

PRIEST & DEACONS: *(As all take one step forward)*
We hail thee!

PRIEST:
Lord of the Present

PRIEST & DEACONS: *(As all take one step forward)*
We hail thee!

PRIEST:
Lord of the Future

PRIEST & DEACONS *(As all take one step forward)*
We hail thee!

CLERGY: *(Kneeling before the Eucharistic Altar)*
O Ineffable Light, Father of Resplendent Glory, Mother of Eternal Wisdom, we, being assembled together on the path of Light to manifest the Power of the Logos, the Christ within, and to participate in the offering

of that great sacrifice which was, and is, and is to come, do hail Thee as the Great Architect of the Universe, and the Source of all Light, Life, Love, and Liberty.

Clergy rise and proceed to their stations. Porter places Sword on Rear Altar, pointing North, and proceeds to station at the Temple entrance. Thurifer replaces thurible on Rear Altar and proceeds to station.

PRIEST:
In the Name of the Unknown One who reveals His Mysteries out of the Treasuries of Light to them that call upon Him, and who mercifully bestows His Secrets of Gnosis upon us without measure.

May He always grant to us, through Christ the Eternal Logos, and the Divine Sophia, the revealer of His Gnosis, His eternal blessings that we may worthily perform the mysteries of the Mass. Help us to reveal the greatest Secrets which are lawful for man to know, and use them without offence unto God. Amen.

PRIEST:
For what purpose do we congregate?

1st DEACON:
To seek Truth.

PRIEST:
What shall we use to aid us in our search for Truth?

2nd DEACON: *(using a small taper, extracts flame from Perpetual Luminary)*
The Light of Gnosis!

PRIEST: *(receives lit taper from Deacon and lights candles reciting…)*
O Pure Light! Symbol of Divine Essence! Light of the Empyrean Realm! Make thy radiant & pure fire purge and sanctify this, thy holy altar, and my lips for the words that we are to proclaim for the greater glory of the Eternal. Amen.

As these flames lighten our way in the earthly realm, so are the great Luminaries of the Aeons ever present to illumine and enlighten our spiritual path. Come, join us now, O great Luminaries, emissaries of the Most High!

HARMOZEL
OROIAEL
DAVEITHAI
ELELETH

Come now and witness as we praise the Most High, and prepare for the celebration of the Most Holy Eucharist.

Practice: Liturgy of the Pleromic Light

PRIEST:
Our Help is in the Lord, secret center, heart and tongue.

1st DEACON:
Whose Pure Will hath created Worlds, and fitly framed the heavens hung.

PRIEST:
Our Love is in the continuity of the Queen of Infinite Space.

2nd DEACON:
Who from Her womb hath brought all things, yet knoweth neither time nor place.

PRIEST:
Trust ye in the Pure Will.

1st DEACON:
For He gives the Mind that understandeth.

PRIEST:
Abide in the Love of Sophia forever.

2nd DEACON:
For that Beauty is above comparison, and that Good is inimitable, as God Himself.

PRIEST:
Blessed are the knowers of the Truth.

1st DEACON:
For they shall ascend to the Light.

PRIEST:
Blessed are those of the loving heart.

2nd DEACON:
For Love and Truth will make them free.

PRIEST:
The Truth and Love of God be with you.

CLERGY & CONGREGANTS:
And with thy spirit.

PRIEST: (intones)
O glorious Godhead of the Aeons, Thou, secret center, Who art surrounded by the radiant presence of the host of holy angels and messengers of Light, hear our prayers and listen to our thoughts which rise from this world of shadows, toward Thy abode of unsearchable, unspeakable, and unending Light. Amen.

Invocation of the Archangels

PRIEST:
Please rise for the Invocation of the Archangels.

ALL: *(using the forms as previously instructed)*
Ateh. Malkuth. Ve'Geburah. Ve'Gedulah. Le Olam. A-U-M
In the Name of יהוה we invoke thee, Archangel of the East, RAPHAEL!
In the Name of אדני we invoke thee, Archangel of the South, MICHAEL!
In the Name of אהיה we invoke thee, Archangel of the West, GABRIEL!
In the Name of אגלא we invoke thee, Archangel of the North, AURIEL!
Ateh. Malkuth. Ve'Geburah. Ve'Gedulah. Le Olam. A-U-M

Asperges

PRIEST: *(sprinkles blessed water while reciting…)*
Purify us, O Lord, that in Thy Power we may worthily perform the Great Work. In Thy strength, O Indwelling Lord, do we expel all forces of darkness from this, Thy Holy Altar and Sanctuary, and from this house and our own human temples wherein we worship Thee; and we pray Thee Heavenly Father, that Thou wilt command the Rulers of the Four Regions, your mighty Archangels, Lords of the Air, Water, Fire, and Earth, to build for us a Spiritual Temple through which Thy Strength and Blessing may be poured forth upon Thy people. Through Christ our Indwelling Lord.

ALL:
So Mote It Be!

Prayer

PRIEST:
When we enter herein with all humility, let God the Almighty One enter into this Sanctuary of the Gnosis by the entrance of an eternal happiness, of a Divine prosperity, of a perfect joy, of an abundant charity, and of an eternal salutation. Let all the demons fly from this place, especially those who are opposed unto this work, and let the Angels of Peace assist and protect this Sanctuary, from which let discord and strife fly and depart. Magnify and extend upon us, O Lord, Thy most Holy Name, and bless our conversation and our assembly.

Practice: Liturgy of the Pleromic Light

Sanctify, O Lord our God, our humble entry herein, Thou the Blessed and Holy One of the Eternal Ages! Amen.

I beseech Thee, O Lord God, the All Powerful and the All Merciful, that Thou wilt deign to bless this Sanctuary, and all this place, and all those who are herein, and that Thou wilt grant unto us, who serve Thee, and rehearse nothing but the wonders of Thy Law, a good Angel for our Guardian; remove from us every adverse power; preserve us from evil and from trouble; grant, O Lord, that we may rest in this place in all safety, through Thee, O Lord, Who livest and reignest unto the Ages of the Ages.

O Lord God, All Powerful and All Merciful, Thou who desirest not the death of a sinner, but rather that he may turn from his ignorance and live; give and grant unto us Thy Grace, by ✠ Blessing and ✠ Consecrating this Altar and this Sanctuary, which is here marked out with the most powerful and holy Names of God. And may God bless this place with all the virtues of Heaven, so that no obscene or unclean spirit may have the power to enter into this Sanctuary, or to annoy any person who is therein; through our Lord Jesus, Christos, Soter, Logos, Who liveth eternally unto the Ages of the Ages. Amen.

ALL:
Amen.

Censing of the Altar

PRIEST: *(Puts incense into thurible and blesses it…)*
Creature of incense, be thou blessed in the Name of the ✠ Father, and of the ✠ Son, and of the ✠ Holy Spirit.

Priest censes the alter center, left, right.

Purify this place, O Divine and Eternal One, and make of us one mystical Body, growing into the Pleroma of your Gnosis. Make us a Spiritual Temple of living stones, through which your infinite Light may flow. Let the Holy Angels of Light join with us and assist us in this act of divine transformation. We unite now to celebrate, knowing that we all come from the Original Light, which is the Source of everything visible and invisible.

May the Lord be with you ✠

ALL:
And with thy spirit.

Confiteor

ALL:
O Lord, that which is mortal cometh not into a body immortal; but that which is immortal cometh into that which is mortal. Thou art Thou, all that is made, and all that is not made. Thou art all things, and there is

nothing else Thou art not. I beseech Thee that I may never err from the Knowledge of Thee. For Thou art what I am, Thou art what I do, Thou art what I say. Amen.

PRIEST:
O Lord All Powerful, Eternal God and Father of ALL, shed upon me the Divine Influence of Thy Mercy, for I am Thy Creature. I beseech Thee to defend me from mine enemies, and to confirm in me true and steadfast faith. O Lord, I commit my Body and my Soul unto Thee, seeing I put my trust in none beside Thee; it is on Thee alone that I rely. O Lord my God aid me. O Lord hear me in the day and hour wherein I shall invoke Thee. I pray Thee by Thy Mercy not to put me into oblivion, nor to remove me from Thee. O Lord be Thou my succor, Thou Who art the God of my salvation. O Lord make me a new heart according unto Thy loving Kindness. These, O Lord, are the gifts which I await from Thee, O my God and my Master, Thou who livest and reignest unto the Ages of the Ages. Amen.

O Lord God the All Powerful One, who hast formed unto Thyself great and Ineffable Wisdom, and Co-Eternal with Thyself before the countless Ages; Thou Who before the birth of Time hast created the Aeons, and the things that they contain; Thou who hast vivified all things by Thy Holy Breath, I praise Thee, I bless Thee, I adore Thee, and I glorify Thee. Be Thou propitious unto me who am but a miserable sinner, and despise me not; save me and succor me, even me that work of Thine hands. I conjure and entreat Thee by Thy Holy Name to banish from my Spirit the darkness of Ignorance, and to enlighten me with the Fire of Thy Wisdom; take away from me all evil desires, and let not my speech be as that of the foolish. O Thou, God the Living One, whose Glory, Honor, and Kingdom shall extend unto the Ages of the Ages. Through our Lord Jesus, Christos, Soter, Logos. Amen.

DEACONS:
Amen.

Absolution

PRIEST:
God the Father ✠ God the Son ✠ God the Holy Spirit ✠ Bless ✠ Strengthen ✠ Preserve ✠ and Sanctify ✠ you. May the Lord in His loving kindness look down upon you that you may win the victory over your lower selves and receive the Grace and Comfort of the Holy Spirit.

Hear me, O Father, father of all fatherhood. I invoke you, ye forgivers of sins, ye purifiers of iniquities. Forgive the sins of the souls of these disciples, and purify their iniquities and make them worthy to be reckoned with the Kingdom of the Father of the Treasury of the Light.

Now, therefore, O Father, father of all fatherhood, let the forgivers of sins come, whose names are these:

Σιφιρψνιχευ ζενει βεριμου σοχαβριχηρ ευθαρι να ναι φιεισβαλμηριχ μευνιπος χιριε ενταιρ μουθιορ σμουρ πευχηρ οουσχους μινιονορ ισοχοβορθα.

Hear me invoking you, forgive the sins of these souls and blot out their iniquities. Let them be worthy to be reckoned with the Kingdom of the Father of the Treasury of Light.

I know the great powers and invoke them:

Αυηρ βεβρω αθρονι η ουρεφ η ωνε σουφεν κνιτουσοχρεωψ
μαυωνβι μνευωρ σουωνι χωχωετεωφ χωχε ετεωφ μεμωχ ανημφ.

Forgive the sins of these souls, blot out their iniquities which they knowingly and unknowingly have committed; forgive them then and make them worthy to be reckoned with the Kingdom of the Father, so that they are worthy to receive this Eucharistic Offering which we have come to make, Holy Father. Through our Lord Jesus, Christos, Soter, Logos. Amen.

The Lord has put away all your sins. Abide in the peace and love of the Holy Spirit.

ALL:
Amen.

Sign of Peace

PRIEST:
My Brothers and Sisters in the Gnosis, the Lord of Agape binds us with a bond of Love that cannot be broken. Therefore we invoke the indwelling Christos, Who does ever say to Thy disciples: "Peace I leave with you, My peace I give unto you." Grant us that peace and unity which are agreeable to Thy Holy Will and Commandment. In the Name of our Lord Jesus Christ, Savior and Logos, may the peace of the Lord be with you always.

CONGREGANTS:
And also with you.

Clergy & Congregants exchange Sign of Peace.

First Hermetic Discourse: Psalm of Wisdom and Praise

PRIEST:
Which way shall I look when I praise Thee? Upward? Downward? Outward? Inward? For about Thee there is no manner, nor place, nor anything else of all things that are. But all things are in Thee; all things from Thee; Thou givest all things and takest nothing, for Thou hast all things and there is nothing that Thou hast not.

1st DEACON:
He that shall learn and study the things that are, and how they are ordered and governed, and by whom, and for what cause, or to what end, will acknowledge thanks to the Great Architect. And he that gives thanks shall be of the spirit. And he that is of the Spirit shall know both where the Truth is and what it is; and learning that, he will be yet more and more of the Spirit.

2nd DEACON:
For never shall or can that soul which, while it is in the body, lightens and lifts up itself to know and comprehend that which is Good and True, slide back to the contrary; for it is infinitely enamored thereof and forgetteth all evils; and when it hath learned and known its Father and Progenitor, it can no more apostatize or depart from that Good. That which is Good desireth to be set at liberty; but the things that are Evil love slavery.

PRIEST:
I give praise and blessing unto God the Father.

1st DEACON:
Who art everywhere the center of the sphere.

PRIEST:
I give praise and blessing unto the Mighty Mother.

2nd DEACON:
Whose circumference is nowhere found.

PRIEST:
Wisdom is to be understood in silence, and the Seed is the true Good, sown by the Will of God.

1st DEACON:
The Child of God is the Author of Regeneration. The One Man by the Will of God.

2nd DEACON:
Things of this kind are not taught, but are by God, to whom he pleaseth, brought to remembrance.

PRIEST:
I give praise and blessing unto the One.

1ˢᵗ DEACON:
Holy is God whose Will is performed and accomplished by his own powers.

2ⁿᵈ DEACON:
Holy is God that determineth to be known and is known of His, or those that are His.

PRIEST & DEACONS:
Holy art Thou, that by Thy Word hast established all things. Holy art Thou, of Whom all Nature is the image.
Holy art Thou, Whom Nature hath not formed.
Holy art Thou, that art stronger than all power.
Holy art Thou, that art greater than all excellency.
Holy art Thou, Who art better than all praise.
O Thou unspeakable, unutterable, be praised with silence!

Pause for a moment of silent reflection.

First Reading

PRIEST:
The First Reading is taken from…

The First Lectionary Reading of the day is read by Priest.

PRIEST:
Give ear unto us, O Indwelling One, while we sing Thy praises. Thou Mystery before all uncontainables and impassables, Who did shine forth in Thy Mystery, in order that the Mystery that is from the beginning be completed in us. Hear us, O Father of boundless Light, Mother of Eternal Wisdom! All has come forth from Thee, and will return unto Thee, when the consummation of all consummations has taken place.

ALL:
Amen.

Second Hermetic Discourse: The Secret Song

2ⁿᵈ DEACON:
Let all the Nature of the World entertain the hearing of this Hymn.

1st DEACON:
Praise ye the Lord of the Creation, and the All, and the One; the Name of the Most High be praised.

PRIEST:
Let us altogether give him blessing which rideth upon the heavens; the Creator of all Nature. This is he that is the eye of the mind, and will accept the praise of my powers.

2nd DEACON:
O all ye powers that are in me, praise the One and the All.

1st DEACON:
Sing together with my will, all you powers that are in me.

PRIEST:
O Holy Knowledge, being enlightened by thee I magnify the intelligible Light, and rejoice in the joy of the Lord. By me the Truth sings praise to the Truth, the Good praiseth the Good. O Life, O Light, from us unto You comes this Praise and Thanksgiving.

2nd DEACON:
I give thanks to Thee, the Operation of my powers.

PRIEST & DEACONS: *(with arms crossed over chest)*
A-U-M

1st DEACON:
I give thanks to Thee, the Power of my operations.

PRIEST & DEACONS: *(arms crossed)*
A-U-M

PRIEST:
By me Thy Word sings praise unto Thee. Receive by me this verbal sacrifice.

PRIEST & DEACONS: *(arms crossed)*
A-U-M

2nd DEACON:
The powers that are in me cry these things, they praise the All, they fulfill Thy Will; Thy Will and Counsel is from Thee unto Thee.

1st DEACON:
O All, receive a reasonable sacrifice from all things; O Life save all that is in us; O Light, enlighten, for the Mind guideth the Word.

PRIEST:
Thou art God, Thy child crieth these things unto thee, by the Fire, by the Air, by the Earth, by the Water, by the Spirit, by Thy Creatures.

PRIEST & DEACONS:
So Mote It Be!

Gnostic Canticle

PRIEST:
Faith is our Earth in which we take root.

ALL:
Amen.

PRIEST:
Hope is the Water with which we are nourished.

ALL:
Amen.

PRIEST:
Love is the Air through which we grow.

ALL:
Amen.

PRIEST:
Knowledge is the Light by which we ripen.

ALL:
Amen.

PRIEST:
It is Christ who standeth at the door of every heart. Open ye your heart unto Him that ye may be One. For as the One is in the All, so is the All in the One. Thus the Logos sayeth: As I am One with the Father, so ye are One with me. Then may ye enter that Supernal Sphere, and dwell in that great celestial mansion whose pillars are: WISDOM, STRENGTH, and BEAUTY.
Ring bell three times.

PRIEST & DEACONS: *(intone)*
Amen.

Epistle

LECTOR:
The Epistle (or Second Reading) is taken from...

The Second Lectionary Reading of the day is read by Lector.

Here endeth the Lesson.

ALL:
Thanks be to God.

Gradual

PRIEST:
He that loveth the Holy Sophia loveth Life; and they that seek her early shall be filled with Joy.

Teach me, O Lord, the way of Thy statutes, and I shall keep it unto the end. Give me understanding, and I shall keep Thy law; yea I shall keep it with my whole heart. The path of the just is as the shining light, shining more and more unto the perfect day.

Munda Cor Meum

DEACON:
Cleanse my heart and lips, O God who by the hands of Thy Seraph didst cleanse the lips of Thy prophet Isaiah with a burning coal from Thine altar, and in Thy loving kindness, so purify me that I may worthily proclaim Thy Holy Gospel. Through Christ, our Indwelling Lord. Amen.

PRIEST: *(blesses Deacon with the following words...)*
May the Lord be in thy heart and on thy lips, that through thy heart the love of God may shine forth, and through thy lips His power be made manifest. Amen.

Gospel

DEACON:
Please rise for the reading of the Gospel. The Lord be with you.

Practice: Liturgy of the Pleromic Light

ALL:
And with thy spirit.

DEACON:
The Gospel is taken from...

> *As the Deacon announces the Gospel he makes the sign of the cross with the right thumb successively upon the forehead, lips, and heart.*

ALL:
Glory be to Thee, O Lord.

> *Deacon censes the Gospel, then Gospel is read.*

DEACON:
Here endeth the Gospel.

ALL:
Praise be to Thee, O Christ.

DEACON:
Be ye doers of the Word, and not hearers only.

> *Deacon bids people to be seated and censes the Priest, then returns to his position.*

> *Homily and Parish announcements are given by Priest or other designated speakers.*

Act of Faith

PRIEST:
Please all join me in the Act of Faith.

ALL: *(while placing right hand over heart)*
I believe in the Ineffable, Unknowable Father, incorruptible Spirit, Lord of All Worlds, Architect of all things visible and all things invisible. Light of Light.

And in the Pure Will of the Father which sends forth the Seed, which is the true Good. Life of Life.

And I believe in the Holy Spirit, Sublime Mother of the Aeons, from whose womb all things are made manifest and to which they shall return. Love of Love.

And I believe in the incarnation of our Lord Jesus Christ, self-generated and alone-begotten; creative essence of the Father; Logos of the Eternal Aeon; the Author of Regeneration, through which we may loosen the bonds of matter and recall our own divine nature, and become one in the fullness of God. Liberty of Liberty.

And I believe in the communion of the Holy Saints and Prophets.

And I believe in the miracle of the Eucharist, whereby the elements of Bread and Wine are transmuted into the Body and Blood of Christ the Logos, giving us Spiritual sustenance, and a visible means of grace.

And I believe in One Universal and Apostolic Church of Light, Life, Love, and Liberty.

A-U-M A-U-M A-U-M

Invocation of the Holy Guardian Angel

PRIEST:
O You, divine Spirit! Spirit of Wisdom, Strength, and Beauty; powerful Being of Light, with whom I desire to accomplish the most intimate union!

I call you! I invoke you! Come to my assistance; guide my steps on the Path of Regeneration during this whole day. Vivify me with that Divine Love that enflames you; send me continually your intellect; give me the weapons that I need in order to vanquish my spiritual enemies.

Guide my steps toward the Truth; I abandon myself to your direction with total confidence.

Divine Logos, that have deigned to send Your Angels to guard and guide us, help me profit from their powerful operations; help me be preserved from any fall during this day.

Let me come to know intimately this Spirit, to which you have particularly entrusted me.

I ask this Grace by Your Holy Blood, that has become the sigil of my reconciliation with you. Amen.

Offertorium

PRIEST: *(removes veil, pall, etc.)*
Come Thou Holy Name of Christ, Name above all names; come power from above and come highest gift; Thou Knower of the Chosen's Mysteries descend; Thou Who dost share in all noble strivers' struggles; Come! Come Thou Who givest joy to all who are at one with Thee; come and commune with us in this Eucharist which we are about to make in Thy Name, in this Sacrament to which we have assembled at Thy call.

Practice: Liturgy of the Pleromic Light

Αεηιουω ιαω αωι ωια ψινωθερ θερνωψ νωψιθερ ζαγουρη παγουρη νεθμομαωθ νεψιομωθ μαραχαχθα θωβαρραβαυ θαρναχαχαν ζοροκοθορα ιεου Σαβαωθ.

Priest elevates paten with both hands.

Blessed are You, O God, who art the Source of all things visible and invisible; the Lord of Light, Life, Love, and Liberty. We offer this bread, grain of the Earth, transformed by human hands, as a token of our terrestrial nature. May it transform us and be the BODY OF CHRIST.

ALL:
Blessed be God forever.

Priest returns paten. Acolyte pours wine and a little water into the Chalice.

PRIEST:
Remembering the psychic and pneumatic natures of the Master Jesus, and our own psychic and pneumatic natures, we mix water with this wine, praying that we may abide in His Consciousness and He in us.

Priest elevates Chalice with both hands.

Blessed are you O God who art the source of all things visible and invisible, the Lord of Light, Life, Love, and Liberty. We offer this wine, fruit of the Earth, transformed by human hands, as a token of our celestial nature. May it transform us and be the BLOOD OF CHRIST.

ALL:
Blessed be God forever.

Second Censing

PRIEST: *(places more incense on charcoal)*
Be thou blessed in the Name of the ✠ Father, and of the ✠ Son, and of the ✠ Holy Spirit.

God the Father, seen of none, God the Co-Eternal Son, and God the Holy Spirit who givest us life, pour forth Thy three-fold power into these our oblations.

As this incense rises before Thee, O Lord, so let our prayer ascend Thy Holy Realms.

Glory be to the Unknown Father ✠ to the Son the Divine Logos ✠ and to the Holy Spirit ✠ our Celestial Mother and Consoler.

Lavabo

PRIEST: *(washes hands)*
O Heavenly Father, as Your rains cleanse and purify the earth, I wash my hands so that they too may be cleansed of the impurities of this world.

Asperges me hyssopo - et mundabor. Lavabis me aqua et super nivem dealbabor!

Orate Fratres

PRIEST:
My Brothers and Sisters, we have built a temple for the distribution of the power of the Logos. Let us prepare these gifts as a channel for its reception. Receive, O Source of all things visible and invisible, this Sacrifice of bread and wine. And may our lives be forever sanctified in Your service by the power of Christ, our Indwelling Lord. Amen.

Prayer Over the Gifts

PRIEST:
May we who partake of this Holy sacrament receive the power of Your Light and Life and be forever joined in Your Holy Wisdom.

ALL:
Amen.

Prayer to the Holy Spirit

PRIEST:
O Holy Spirit, Barbelo, Divine Mother of All, may you receive us with your Glorious Embrace. Thou Who hast made Thyself known to us through your emissaries of Light and Life, of Love and Liberty; Your Aeon Sophia and her daughter Zoe, whose heavenly archetypes have been mirrored here on earth in the persons of Eve, Norea, the Virgin Mary, and Mary Magdalene; and known in the celestial realm as the Woman Clothed with the Sun; may You open our ears that we may hear Your voice of Understanding, and open our hearts that we may pour forth Thy Love.

Practice: Liturgy of the Pleromic Light

Eucharistic Prayer

PRIEST:
O Most High God, You are holy indeed, and all creation rightly gives You praise. All life, all holiness comes from You through Christ, our Lord, Logos of the Eternal Aeon. From age to age, You reveal Your perennial Wisdom to Your Holy Elect, and call forth those that might partake of Your Divine Mystery.

Joins hands, holding them outstretched over the offerings.

Epiclesis

PRIEST:
And so, Most High God, we bring You these gifts. We ask You to make them holy by Your power to bless ✠ to approve ✠ and to ratify ✠ that they may become the Body ✠ and Blood ✠ of Christ, the Logos.

Raises bread slightly.

Institution

PRIEST:
Following the example set forth by Melchizedek, the eternal High Priest, the Master Jesus, took bread and gave You thanks and praise. He blessed and broke the bread and gave it to His disciples, and said:

Bows slightly.

Take and eat ye all of this, for THIS IS MY BODY.

Shows consecrated host to the people, places on paten and genuflects in adoration.

In like manner, when the supper was ended, he took the noble Chalice.

Raises Chalice a little.

Again he gave You thanks and praise, blessed it and gave it to His disciples, and said:

Bows slightly.

Take and drink ye all of this, for THIS IS MY BLOOD. Do this in remembrance of me.

Shows Chalice; returns Chalice and genuflects in adoration.

Extends hands.

Father, we celebrate the memory of Christ, the Eternal Logos, the repairer and our restorer of Gnosis. We, Your people and Your Priests offer unto You, O Most High God, this perfect sacrifice: the bread of Life and the cup of eternal Salvation.

Look with favor on these offerings and accept them as once You accepted the gifts of our patriarch in the Gnosis, the bread and wine offered by Your priest Melchizedek.

Almighty God, we pray that this sacrifice be borne to thine altar, there to be offered by Him who, as the eternal High Priest, forever offers Himself as the eternal sacrifice.

And as He has ordained that the heavenly sacrifice shall be mirrored here on earth through the ministry of mortals, to the end that Your holy people may be brought more closely into fellowship with You, we do pray for them who serve at this altar, that rightly celebrating the mysteries of the Most Holy Body ✠ and Blood ✠ of the Christ, they may be filled ✠ with Your mighty power and blessing, O Lord of Light, Life, Love, and Liberty.

Litany

The Litany may be shortened or lengthened as required.

PRIEST:
Let us now in due and ancient fashion call upon the powers of the Most High and on all the Holy Ones who were and are and are to come, that united with them we may bravely strive for and ultimately attain to the Gnosis of Light, Life, Love, and Liberty.

All face West and kneel

PRIEST:
I-A-O

DEACONS:
Shed thy glory upon us.

PRIEST:
Sabaoth

DEACONS:
Shed thy glory upon us.

PRIEST:
Abraxas

DEACONS:
Shed thy glory upon us.

PRIEST:
Sophia

DEACONS:
Shed thy glory upon us.

PRIEST:
All the souls of the Holy Gnostics during the Aeons.

DEACONS:
Hear us and be near us.

Practice: Liturgy of the Pleromic Light

PRIEST:
Holy Mary Magdalene

DEACONS:
Hear us and be near us.

PRIEST:
Holy John the Baptist

DEACONS:
Hear us and be near us.
PRIEST:
Holy John the Evangelist

DEACONS:
Hear us and be near us.

PRIEST:
Holy Thomas

DEACONS:
Hear us and be near us.

PRIEST:
Holy Philip

DEACONS:
Hear us and be near us.

PRIEST:
Holy Simon Magus

DEACONS:
Hear us and be near us.

PRIEST:
Holy Dositheus

DEACONS:
Hear us and be near us.

PRIEST:
Holy Menander

DEACONS:
Hear us and be near us.

PRIEST:
Holy Saturninus

DEACONS:
Hear us and be near us.

PRIEST:
Holy Basilides
DEACONS:
Hear us and be near us.

PRIEST:
Holy Valentinus

DEACONS:
Hear us and be near us.

PRIEST:
Holy Bardaisan

DEACONS:
Hear us and be near us.

PRIEST:
Holy Clement of Alexandria

DEACONS:
Hear us and be near us.

PRIEST:
Holy Origen

DEACONS:
Hear us and be near us.

PRIEST:
Holy Hypatia

DEACONS:
Hear us and be near us.

PRIEST:
Holy Esclaremonde & all Cathar Martyrs

DEACONS:
Hear us and be near us.

PRIEST:
Holy Joachim

DEACONS:
Hear us and be near us.

PRIEST:
Holy Jacque de Molay & all the Blessed Templars

DEACONS:
Hear us and be near us.

PRIEST:
Holy Martinès de Pasqually

DEACONS:
Hear us and be near us.

PRIEST:
Holy Louis Claude de Saint-Martin

DEACONS:
Hear us and be near us.

PRIEST:
Holy Jean-Baptiste Willermoz

DEACONS:
Hear us and be near us.

PRIEST:
Holy Bernard-Raymond Fabré-Palaprat

DEACONS:
Hear us and be near us.

PRIEST:
Holy Lady Caithness

DEACONS:
Hear us and be near us.

PRIEST:
Holy Tau Valentin II

DEACONS:
Hear us and be near us.

PRIEST:
Holy Mar Timotheus I

DEACONS:
Hear us and be near us.

PRIEST:
Holy Jean Sempé

DEACONS:
Hear us and be near us.

PRIEST:
Holy Abbé Julio

DEACONS:
Hear us and be near us.

PRIEST:
Holy Tau Vincent

DEACONS:
Hear us and be near us.

PRIEST:
Holy Jean II

DEACONS:
Hear us and be near us.

PRIEST:
Holy Tau Harmonious

DEACONS:
Hear us and be near us.

Practice: Liturgy of the Pleromic Light

PRIEST:
Holy Tau Jean III

PRIEST:
Holy Tau Ogdoade Orfeo I

DEACONS:
Hear us and be near us.

PRIEST:
Holy Tau Ogdoade Orfeo III

DEACONS:
Hear us and be near us.

PRIEST:
All the Apostles, Prophets, Bishops, Priests, & Martyrs of the Gnosis.

DEACONS:
Hear us and be near us, now and forever.

DEACONS:
Hear us and be near us.

PRIEST:
Holy Tau Johannes XIII

DEACONS:
Hear us and be near us.

PRIEST:
Holy Tau Iohannes Harmonius

DEACONS:
Hear us and be near us.

Kyrie

PRIEST:
Kyrie Eleison

ALL:
Kyrie Eleison

PRIEST:
Christe Eleison

ALL:
Christe Eleison

PRIEST & ALL:
Kyrie Eleison

PRIEST:
Welcome into Your kingdom, O Lord, our departed brothers and sisters in the Gnosis.

Mother and Father united as one;
Wisdom and Strength through Your eternal Son;
We are divided for Love's sake;
That through our union we may make
Ourselves as symbols of Heaven on Earth;
In life, in death, and in rebirth!
O Christ our Lord who gives us all these gifts, bless them and make them holy.

Pater Noster

PRIEST:
Let us pray with confidence to the Father in the words the Master Jesus gave us.

ALL:
Our Father who art in Heaven, hallowed by Thy Name; Thy kingdom come, Thy will be done,
On Earth as it is in Heaven. Give us this day, our daily bread,
And forgive us our debts, as we have also forgiven our debtors. And leave us not in temptation, but deliver us from evil,
For Thine is the Kingdom, and the Power, and the Glory, forever and ever. Amen.

PRIEST: *(with hands extended)*
Deliver us Lord from the evil of ignorance, and grant us peace, love, and light in our day.

Breaking of the Bread

PRIEST:
O Divine Light, You show Yourself this day upon countless altars and yet are one and indivisible. In token of Thy great Sacrifice, we rend *(break bread)* this, Thy Holy Body, that we may be as Thou art.

Through this ancient and sacred tradition, all Heaven and Earth are united in Thy Consciousness, Thy Love, and Thy Will. And as the One became many, only to restore all to the Pleroma, so too, in the breaking of this bread, we are one with Thee, as Thou art one with the Father.

> *Breaks off small piece of bread from the left half, makes sign of the cross over the Chalice, and places piece in Chalice; then blows three crosses of air over Chalice.*
>
> *Intones...*

Through Him, and with Him, and in Him;

Practice: Liturgy of the Pleromic Light

In the Unity of the Holy Spirit;
All glory and honor are Yours Almighty Father,
Forever and ever.

ALL: *(intone)*
Amen.

PRIEST:
Let us pray. Adoration be to Thee, O Most High God, Father of all Fatherhood, and to Thee, O Mother of all, who in the incarnation of Your Logos have mystically provided us with the Sacrament of His Body and Blood, that by partaking of this Mystery, we may reunite within ourselves the fragments of Your Divinity dispersed throughout the Cosmos. Holy, Holy, Holy, are You, the Father and Mother of the Treasury of the Light, now and unto the countless ages. Amen.

Theurgic Consecration

Priest takes Dagger, faces East, and draws the letter YOD in the air with Dagger as it is pronounced, then intones the Holy Name, thus:

By the virtue of י I call forth the power of IAO to join in this Holy Sacrifice.

Priest travels to the South via the North and West, that is, by walking 270° counterclockwise, draws the letter HE, and intones the Holy Name, thus:

By the virtue of ה I call forth the power of SABAOTH to join in this Holy Sacrifice.

Priest continues 270° counterclockwise to the West, draws the letter VAV, and intones the Holy Name, thus:

By the virue of ו I call forth the power of ABRAXAS to join in this Holy Sacrifice.

Priest continues 270° to the North, draws the letter HE, and intones the Holy Name, thus:

By the virtue of ה I call forth the power of SOPHIA to join in this Holy Sacrifice.

Priest travels 270° counterclockwise again to return to the East for the third complete circuit. He faces the Eucharistic Altar, and with arms outstretched and holding the Dagger in the right hand...

The Son would not be the Father without wearing the Father's Name. So by the Power of the Holy Tetragrammaton, and by the virtue of the Tri-Unity of the Holy Letter ש *(draws Hebrew letter with Dagger in the air above Chalice)*, I call forth the power of the Author of Regeneration, the Repairer of Souls, the Destroyer of Death...

Intones while slowly lowering Dagger with both hands into Chalice.

יהשוה to pour forth Thy powers into this Holy Sacrifice and transmute these elements of bread and wine into the Divine Body and Blood of the Logos.
Makes three crosses in Chalice with Dagger.

Communion

PRIEST: *(Elevating the Body and Blood)*
Behold the Divine Light which lighteth every man that cometh into the world. May the communion of these Holy Mysteries be to the regeneration of both soul and body. Let us draw nigh and receive this most Holy Sacrament.

Ablutions and silent meditation.

Post Eucharistic Prayer

ALL:
May we, who in this Holy Mystery have entered into the all-pervading strength and love of Christ our Indwelling Lord, be guided by the Divine Presence into the fullness of Truth, that we may attain to that mount of vision whereon we may see the boundless light unveiled in the wholeness of its Divine Glory. Amen.

Third Hermetic Discourse: Concluding Rite

PRIEST:
If thou wilt not equal thyself to God, thou canst not understand God. Increase thyself unto an immeasurable greatness, leaping beyond every body and transcending all time; become eternity and thou shalt understand God. If thou believe in thyself that nothing is impossible, but accountest thyself immortal, thou canst understand all things; every art, every science, and the manner and custom of every living thing.

1st DEACON:
Become higher than all height, lower than all depths, comprehend in thyself the qualities of all the Creatures of the Fire, the Water, the Dry and Moist; and conceive likewise, that thou canst at once be everywhere in the Sea, in the Earth, in the Air.

2nd DEACON:
Thou shalt at once understand thyself, not yet begotten, in the womb, young, old, to be dead, the things after

death, and all these together; as also times, places, deeds, qualities, quantities; or else thou canst not yet understand God.

PRIEST & DEACONS:
For the Light is One and its Mystery is a hiddenness beyond our senses and beyond the vision of our eyes.

PRIEST:
In all things that are, are the senses, because they cannot be without them.

1st DEACON:
But Gnosis differs much from sense; for sense is of the things that surmount it, but Gnosis is the end of sense.

2nd DEACON:
Gnosis is the gift of God; for all Gnosis is unbodily, but useth the Mind as an instrument, as the Mind uses the body.

PRIEST & DEACONS:
Therefore I believe Thee, and bear witness and go into the Life and Light.

PRIEST:
The Life and Light of God be with you.

ALL:
And with thy spirit.

Dismissal

PRIEST:
From our sanctuary here, may the Light be spread throughout the world. May Christ the Logos of the Eternal Aeon, show you the Light that you seek, give you His comfort and compassion, and lead you to true Wisdom.

Solomon in his great wisdom said to his son: Do thou, O my son Roboam, remember, that the fear of the Lord is only the beginning of Wisdom. Keep and preserve those who have not Understanding in the Fear of the Lord, which will give and will preserve unto thee my crown. But learn to triumph thyself over Fear by Wisdom, and the Spirits will descend from Heaven to serve thee.

I, Solomon, thy father, King of Israel and Palmyra, I have sought out and obtained in my lot the Holy Chokmah, which is the Wisdom of Adonai. And I have become King of the Spirits, as well of Heaven as of Earth, Master of the Dwellers of the Air, and of the Living Souls of the Sea, because I was in possession of the Key of the Hidden Gates of Light.

There is a peace that passes all understanding; it abides in the hearts of those who live in the eternal now. There is a power that makes all things new; it lives and moves in those who know themselves as one.

May that peace abide with you; may that power lift you up to the awareness wherein dwells the Christ, so that you may look with your eyes unveiled upon His most Holy Countenance and there see your true self revealed.

And may the blessing of the Mystery of the Three-in-One, of God the Unknown Father ✠ of Christ the redeeming and ever-coming Logos ✠ and of the Holy Spirit our celestial Mother and Consoler ✠ descend upon you and remain with you always. Amen.

Ite, missa est.

ALL:
Deo Gratias.

Practice: Mass of the Seven Seals

Liturgy of Saint John the Divine

or

Mass of the Seven Seals

This Liturgy of St. John the Divine or Mass of the Seven Seals is not to be seen as a replacement for the Liturgy of the Pleromic Light. Rather, it is an alternate liturgy, based upon Apocalyptic imagery and related to the Alchemical process. As to how the Alchemical process is related to the Mass, please refer to our discourse: "Alchemy of the Eucharist." Concerning how the writings of the Apocalypse of St. John relate to the Alchemical operations, we do not have space here for a full treatment. But we may say a few words concerning the imagery found in some of the passages utilized in this liturgy, especially those concerning the seven seals and the seven angels.

The first seal and the first angel give us a couple of essential symbols. The first is the Crown. This is to us a symbol of the Royal Art: Alchemy. We also see the image of "fire cast upon the earth." This is related to the *Calcination* of the First Matter.

The second seal and angel yield further symbolic elements related to the Alchemical process. We see herein a "burning mountain, cast into the sea," which is emblematic of the *Dissolution* of the Calcinated First Matter. We also have here the Sword, symbol of the *Separation*. We see it separating in thirds, indicative of the three Essentials: *Sulphur, Mercury and Salt*.

With the third seal and third angel we are presented with symbols of the *Conjunction*. First, we have the balances, representing the Equilibrium of the Conjunction. Next we have the star Wormwood, which is the very *Agent of Transformation*, without which the Conjunction could not occur. Our initiates of a certain degree, within one of our affiliated bodies, will better understand the significance of this. But these are higher teachings that cannot be given in a public and cursory document such as this.

The fourth seal and fourth angel reveal the elements of *Putrefaction*, the process of decay that indicates the beginning of *Fermentation*. We have here Death, the darkening of the Sun, Moon and Stars, and other imagery related to the impurities that are brought to the surface - the Caput Mortem - which will be severed in order to continue the Fermentation process.

The fifth seal and angel bring us into the Fermentation proper. We are presented with a robe, made white by being washed in blood. This signifies, in part, the transition from one phase of the work to another. We also read that "no green thing" should be hurt. This refers to the new substance being created through Fermentation.

The sixth seal and angel contain many mysteries, but the one symbol that stands out to us in this particular context is the Moon turning to blood. This is indicative of the process of *Distillation*, and the emergence of the *Philosopher's Stone*.

The seventh seal and seventh angel bring Silence, and the completion of the Mystery of God. In other words, it is the alchemical *Coagulation*, the full realization of the *Lapis Philosophorum*, which is represented as a little book that is sweet when eaten, but becomes bitter upon digestion. This is because the Body and Blood of our Lord is indeed sweet to us. But it also initiates the process of enlightenment and self-knowledge, which means that our myriad faults and weaknesses will begin to make themselves known to us. We can no longer live in the darkness of ignorance. And these realities are indeed often bitter when "digested." We must nevertheless continue to partake of this fruit of self-knowledge if we wish for it to eventually transform us into beings worthy of entrance into the new Jerusalem - the Pleroma of Light.

That was a very brief synopsis of how we relate some of the Apocalyptic imagery to Alchemy. In addition to the "Alchemy of the Eucharist" aforementioned, we also encourage you to read our poetic treatment, "Ora et Labora: A poetic exploration of the Royal Art," which addresses Alchemical imagery in a more intuitive way, as well as *The Pleromic Light Unveiled*, which gives a more detailed analysis of the symbolism as it relates to the Holy Gnostic Liturgy of the Pleromic Light. But all of these things only scratch the surface. It is only through study, practice, and undergoing mystical states through meditation, initiation, and gnostic revelation that will bring you to an inner comprehension of these Mysteries. Part of that practice, though, can be in the performance of this liturgy.

Although there are considerable differences between this present liturgy and the Liturgy of the Pleromic Light, there are also certain key similarities which will make it instantly recognizable to the egregore of the ACP as one of its own. First, the overall structure and formula of this Mass is the same as the Pleromic Light Mass, which was necessary not only for the sake of consistency, but also in order to maintain the same relationship to the Alchemical phases and operations. Secondly, certain key elements remain which identify it unmistakably as an ACP liturgy.

As we stated in the beginning of this introduction, this is not a replacement for our standard liturgy, and should not be adopted as such by any of our parishes or clergy. But it is a powerful Eucharistic service that may be employed for certain appropriate feast days, for celebration of the Eucharist in addition to the stated Masses, and even as the occasional replacement for the standard liturgy. But as you work with this Mass you will come to realize that it is better suited for special occasions than as the norm.

Should any non-ACP clergy wish to utilize this liturgy, you are certainly free to do so, as is or modified to suit your particular church. We only advise you to consider what we have said so far.

The temple arrangement for this Mass is basically the same as our standard Temple Layout found in the ACP Clergy Handbook and elsewhere. There are, however, a couple of modifications worth mentioning. First, if possible, there should he banners posted in the four quarters bearing images of the Bull, Lion, Eagle and Man. These correspond to the four Fixed Signs of the Zodiac and to the four Elements. In the ACP we use the following arrangement:

Practice: Mass of the Seven Seals

```
East  - Air   - Man   (Aquarius)
South - Fire  - Lion  (Leo)
West  - Water - Eagle (Scorpio)
North - Earth - Bull  (Taurus)
```

The other recommended modification is that each of the seven candles in the candelabra upon the Rear Altar have inscribed or affixed to them the initials of each of the seven churches of the Apocalypse:

Other appropriate decorations could include an image or hanging of the heptagram, or other apocalyptic imagery or appropriate icons, etc. Alchemical images are also appropriate.

The Mass of the Seven Seals begins with the Preliminary Rites and Procession, as given in the Liturgy of the Pleromic Light. They are therefore not reproduced here in the interest of space. Unlike our standard Mass, the PRIEST functions as sole operator in all but a few parts of this liturgy. It is therefore possible, with very slight modification, to perform this as a solitary rite. We always encourage, of course, an open and public Eucharist, but because of the special nature of this Mass it may be suitable to celebrate it as a private, clergy-only, or, again, in a solitary fashion.

We hope that this Mass will prove to be inspiring and transformative for all its celebrants and communicants. We encourage our clergy, colleagues and friends to notify us of the efficacy of this rite and to report to us any particular phenomena associated with its celebration.

Τ Φωσφορος, επ. γν.
Patriarch,
Apostolic Church of the Pleroma
30 January, 2016

ACP Clergy Handbook

Liturgy of Saint John the Divine

or

Mass of the Seven Seals

FIRST PHASE: NIGREDO

CALCINATION

Preliminary Rites

See Liturgy of the Pleromic Light

Procession

See Liturgy of the Pleromic Light

Invocation of the Aeons

PRIEST:
In the Name of the Lord of all Worlds.

Priest and Deacons place right hand over heart.

PRIEST:
I…

1st DEACON:
A…

2nd DEACON:
O…

Practice: Mass of the Seven Seals

Priest and Deacons place hands, right over left, over the Solar Plexus.

PRIEST:
I…

1st DEACON:
A…

2nd DEACON:
UM…

Priest & Deacons cross their arms across chest, right over left, palms open.

PRIEST:
A…

1st DEACON:
U…

2nd DEACON:
M…

Clergy now place their hands in front of them, palms together, as in prayer.

PRIEST:
Lord of the Past

PRIEST & DEACONS: *(As all take one step forward)*
We hail thee!

PRIEST:
Lord of the Present

PRIEST & DEACONS: *(As all take one step forward)*
We hail thee!

PRIEST:
Lord of the Future

PRIEST & DEACONS *(As all take one step forward)*
We hail thee!

CLERGY: *(Kneeling before the Eucharistic Altar)*
O Ineffable Light, Father of Resplendent Glory, Mother of Eternal Wisdom, we, being assembled together on the path of Light to manifest the Power of the Logos, the Christ within, and to participate in the offering of that great sacrifice which was, and is, and is to come, do hail Thee as the Great Architect of the Universe, and the Source of all Light, Life, Love, and Liberty.

> *Clergy rise and proceed to their stations. Porter places Sword on Rear Altar, pointing North, and proceeds to station at the Temple entrance. Thurifer replaces thurible on Rear Altar and proceeds to station.*

PRIEST:
In the Name of the Unknown One who reveals His Mysteries out of the Treasuries of Light to them that call upon Him, and who mercifully bestows His Secrets of Gnosis upon us without measure.

May He always grant to us, through Christ the Eternal Logos, and the Divine Sophia, the revealer of His Gnosis, His eternal blessings that we may worthily perform the mysteries of the Mass. Help us to reveal the greatest Secrets which are lawful for man to know, and use them without offence unto God. Amen.

PRIEST:
For what purpose do we congregate?

1st DEACON:
To seek Truth.

PRIEST:
What shall we use to aid us in our search for Truth?

2nd DEACON: *(using a small taper, extracts flame from Perpetual Luminary)*
The Light of Gnosis!

PRIEST: *(receives lit taper from Deacon and lights candles reciting…)*
O Pure Light! Symbol of Divine Essence! Light of the Empyrean Realm! Make thy radiant & pure fire purge and sanctify this, thy holy altar, and my lips for the words that we are to proclaim for the greater glory of the Eternal. Amen.

As these flames lighten our way in the earthly realm, so are the great Luminaries of the Aeons ever present to illumine and enlighten our spiritual path. Come, join us now, O great Luminaries, emissaries of the Most High!

HARMOZEL
OROIAEL
DAVEITHAI
ELELETH

Come now and witness as we praise the Most High, and prepare for the celebration of the Most Holy Eucharist.

Practice: Mass of the Seven Seals

Invocation of the Seven Churches

PRIEST:

Extracts a flame from the Perpetual Luminary with a taper; holds lit taper in right hand with arms outstretched before the candelabra, saying:

I was in the Spirit on the Lord's day, and heard behind me a great voice, as of a trumpet, saying, I am Alpha and Omega, the first and the last: and, What thou seest, write in a book, and send it unto the seven churches which are in Asia; unto Ephesus, and unto Smyrna, and unto Pergamos, and unto Thyatira, and unto Sardis, and unto Philadelphia, and unto Laodicea.

And I turned to see the voice that spake with me. And being turned, I saw seven golden candlesticks; And in the midst of the seven candlesticks one like unto the Son of Man, clothed with a garment down to the foot, and girt about the paps with a golden girdle. His head and his hairs were white like wool, as white as snow; and his eyes were as a flame of fire; And his feet like unto fine brass, as if they burned in a furnace; and his voice as the sound of many waters.

And he had in his right hand seven stars: and out of his mouth went a sharp two- edged sword: and his countenance was as the sun shineth in his strength. And when I saw him, I fell at his feet as dead. And he laid his right hand upon me, saying unto me, Fear not; I am the first and the last: I am he that liveth, and was dead; and, behold, I am alive for evermore, Amen; and have the keys of hell and of death.

Write the things which thou hast seen, and the things which are, and the things which shall be hereafter; The mystery of the seven stars which thou sawest in my right hand, and the seven golden candlesticks. The seven stars and the angels of the seven churches: and the seven candlesticks which thou sawest are the seven churches.

Light the candle of Ephesus while saying:

Unto the angel of the church of Ephesus write; These things saith he that holdeth the seven stars in his right hand, who walketh in the midst of the seven golden candlesticks; I know thy works, and thy labour, and thy patience, and how thou canst not bear them which are evil: and thou hast tried them which say they are apostles, and are not, and hast found them liars: And hast borne, and hast patience, and for my name's sake hast laboured, and hast not fainted. Nevertheless I have somewhat against thee, because thou hast left thy first love. Remember therefore from whence thou art fallen, and repent, and do the first works; or else I will come unto thee quickly, and will remove thy candlestick out of his place, except thou repent. He that hath an ear, let him hear what the Spirit saith unto the churches; To him that overcometh will I give to eat of the Tree of Life, which is in the midst of the paradise of God.

Light the candle of Smyrna while saying:

And unto the angel of the church in Smyrna write; These things saith the first and the last, which was dead and is alive; I know thy works, and tribulation, and poverty, (but thou art rich) and I know the blasphemy of them which say they are Jews, and are not, but are the synagogue of Satan. Fear none of those things which thou shalt suffer: behold, the devil shall cast some of you into prison, that you may be tried; and ye shall have tribulation ten days: be thou faithful unto death, and I will give thee a crown of life. He that hath an ear, let him hear what the Spirit saith unto the churches; He that overcometh shall not be hurt of the second death.

Light the candle of Pergamos while saying:

And to the angel of the church in Pergamos write; These things saith he which hath the sharp sword with two edges; I know thy works, and where thou dwellest, even where Satan's seat is: and thou boldest fast my name, and hast not denied my faith, even in those days wherein Antipas was my faithful martyr, who was slain among you, where Satan dwelleth. But I have a few things against thee, because thou hast there them that hold to the doctrine of Balaam, who taught Balac to cast a stumblingblock before the children of Israel, to eat things sacrificed to idols, and to commit fornication. Repent; or else I will come unto thee quickly, and will fight against them with the sword of my mouth. He that hath an ear, let him hear what the Spirit saith unto the churches; To him that overcometh will I give to eat of the hidden manna, and will give him a white stone, and in the stone a new name written, which no man knoweth saving he that receiveth it.

Light candle of Thyatira while saying:

And unto the angel of the church in Thyatira write; These things saith the Son of God, who hath his eyes like unto a flame of fire, and his feet are like fine brass; I know thy works, and charity, and service, and faith, and thy patience, and thy works; and the last to be more than the first. Notwithstanding I have a few things against thee, because thou sufferest that woman Jezebel, which calleth herself a prophetess, to teach and to seduce my servants to commit fornication, and to eat things sacrificed unto idols. And I gave her space to repent of her fornication; and she repented not. Behold, I will cast her into a bed, and then that commit adultery with her into a great tribulation, except they repent of their deeds. And I will kill her children with death; and all the churches shall know that I am he which searcheth the reins and hearts; and I will give unto every one of you according to your works. But unto you I say, and unto the rest in Thyatira, as many as have not this doctrine, and which have not known the depths of Satan, as they speak; I will put upon you none other burden. But that which ye have already hold fast till I come. And he that overcometh, and keepeth my works unto the end, to him will I give power over the nations: And he shall rule them with a rod of iron; as the vessels of a potter shall they be broken to shivers: even as I received of my Father. And I will give him the Morning Star. He that hath an ear, let him hear what the Spirit saith unto the churches.

Light candle of Sardis while saying:

And unto the angel of the church in Sardis write; These things saith he that hath the seven Spirits of God, and the seven stars; I know thy works, that thou hast a name that thou livest, and art dead. Be watchful, and strengthen the things which remain, that are ready to die: for I have not found thy works perfect before God. Remember therefore how thou hast received and heard, and hold fast, and repent. If therefore thou shalt not watch, I will come on thee as a thief, and thou shalt not know what hour I will come upon thee. Thou hast a few names even in Sardis which have not defiled their garments; and thy shall walk with me in white: for they are worthy. He that hath an ear, let him hear what the Spirit saith unto the churches.

Light candle of Philadelphia while saying:

And to the angel of the church in Philadelphia write; These things saith he that is holy, he that is true, he that hath the key of David, he that opined, and no man shutteth; and shutteth, and no man openeth. I know thy works: behold, I have set before thee an open door, and no man can shut it: for thou hast a little strength, and hast kept my word, and hast not denied my name. Behold, I will make them of the synagogue of Satan, which say they are Jews, and are not, but do lie; behold, I will make them to come and worship before thy feet, and to know that I have loved thee. Because thou hast kept the word of my patience, I also will keep thee from the hour of temptation, which shall come upon all the world, to try them that dwell upon the earth. Behold, I come quickly; hold that fast which thou hast, that no man take thy crown. Him that overcometh will I make a pillar in the temple of my God, and he shall go no more out: and I will write upon him the name of my God, and the name of the city of my God, which is new Jerusalem, which cometh down out of heaven from my God: and I will write upon him my new name. He that hath an ear, let him hear what the Spirit saith unto the churches.

Light candle of Laodicea while saying:

And unto the angel of the church of the Laodiceans write; These things saith the Amen, the faithful and true witness, the beginning of the creation of God; I know thy works, that thou art neither cold nor hot: I would thou wert cold or hot. So then because thou art lukewarm, and neither cold nor hot, I will spue thee out of my mouth. Because thou sayest, I am rich, and increased with goods, and have need of nothing; and knowest not that thou art wretched, and miserable, and poor, and blind, and naked: I counsel thee to but of me gold tried in the fire, that thou mayest be rice; and white raiment, that thou mayest be clothed, and that the shame of thy nakedness do not appear; and anoint thine eyes with eyesalve; that thou mayest see. As many as I love,

I rebuke and chasten; be zealous therefore and repent. Behold, I stand at the door, and knock: if any man hear my voice, and open the door, I will come in to him, and will sup with him, and he with me. To him that overcometh will I grant to sit with me in my throne, even as I also overcame, and am set down with my Father in his throne. He that hath an ear, let him hear what the Spirit saith unto the churches.

Prayer for Peace

PRIEST: *(Again facing the Eucharistic Altar)*
Blessed be the Kingdom of the Father, and of the Son, and of the Holy Spirit, now and forever and from all ages to all ages.

ALL:
Amen.

PRIEST:
The Lord be with you.

ALL:
And with thy spirit.

PRIEST:
Let us pray. For the peace from the Holy Pleroma, and for the regeneration of our souls, let us pray to the Lord.

ALL:
Lord, hear our prayer.

PRIEST:
For the peace of the whole world, the stability of the Holy Gnostic, Catholic, and Apostolic Churches of God and for the union of all humanity, let us pray to the Lord.

ALL:
Lord, hear our prayer.

PRIEST:
For this holy House, and for those who enter it with faith and reverence, let us pray to the Lord.

Practice: Mass of the Seven Seals

ALL:

Lord, hear our prayer.

PRIEST:

For our Patriarch Tau... and Exarch Tau..., for the venerable episcopate and presbyterate, the diaconate, for all the Clergy and the people, let us pray to the Lord.

ALL:

Lord, hear our prayer.

PRIEST:

For the President of the United States..., and for all the American people, let us pray to the Lord.

ALL:

Lord, hear our prayer.

PRIEST:

For this city and for this Community, for every city and country, and for the Faithful who dwell therein, let us pray to the Lord.

ALL:

Lord, hear our prayer.

PRIEST:

For the seasonable weather, for the abundance of the fruits of the earth, and for peaceful times, let us pray to the Lord.

ALL:

Lord, hear our prayer.

PRIEST:

For those who travel by water and by land and by air, for the sick, for the afflicted, for the captives, and for their salvation, let us pray to the Lord.

ALL:

Lord, hear our prayer.

PRIEST:
For our deliverance from all affliction, wrath, danger and necessity, let us pray to the Lord.

ALL:
Lord, hear our prayer.

PRIEST:
Help us, heal us, enlighten us and protect us, O God, by Thy Grace.

Intone:
O glorious Godhead of the Aeons, Thou, secret center, Who art surrounded by the radiant presence of the host of holy angels and messengers of Light, hear our prayers and listen to our thoughts which rise from this world of shadows, toward Thy abode of unsearchable, unspeakable, and unending Light. Amen.

Invocation of the Archangels

PRIEST:
Please rise for the Invocation of the Archangels.

ALL: *(Using the forms as previously instructed.)*
Ateh. Malkuth. Ve'Geburah. Ve'Gedulah. Le Olam. A-U-M...
In the Name of n יהוה, we invoke thee, Archangel of the East, RAPHAEL!
In the Name of אדני, we invoke thee, Archangel of the South, MICHAEL!
In the Name of אהיה, we invoke thee, Archangel of the west, GABRIEL!
In the Name of אגלא, we invoke thee, Archangel of the North, AURIEL!
Ateh. Malkuth. Ve'Geburah. Ve'Gedulah. Le Olam. A-U-M...

Asperges

PRIEST: *(Sprinkles blessed water while reciting...)*

Purify us, O Lord, that in Thy Power we may worthily perform the Great Work. In Thy strength, O Indwelling Lord, do we expel all forces of darkness from this, Thy Holy Altar and Sanctuary, and from this house and our own human temples wherein we worship Thee; and we pray Thee Heavenly Father, that Thou wilt command the Rulers of the Four Regions, your mighty Archangels, Lords of the Air, Water, Fire, and Earth, to build for us a Spiritual Temple through which Thy Strength and Blessing may be poured forth upon Thy people. Through Christ our Indwelling Lord.

ALL:
So mote it be!

Prayer

PRIEST:
When we enter herein with all humility, let God the Almighty One enter into this Sanctuary of the Gnosis by the entrance of an eternal happiness, of a Divine prosperity, of a perfect joy, of an abundant charity, and of an eternal salutation. Let all the demons fly from this place, especially those who are opposed unto this work, and let the Angels of Peace assist and protect this Sanctuary, from which let discord and strife fly and depart. Magnify and extend upon us, O Lord, Thy most Holy Name, and bless our conversation and our assembly. Sanctify, O Lord our God, our humble entry herein, Thou the Blessed and Holy One of the Eternal Ages! Amen.

I beseech Thee, O Lord God, the All Powerful and the All Merciful, that Thou will deign to bless this Sanctuary, and all this place, and all those who are herein, and that Thou wilt grant unto us, who serve Thee, and rehearse nothing but the wonders of Thy Law, a good Angel for our Guardian; remove from us every adverse power; preserve us from evil and from trouble; grant, O Lord, that we may rest in this place in all safety, through Thee, O Lord, Who livest and reignest unto the Ages of the Ages.

O Lord God, All Powerful and All Merciful, Thou who desirest not the death of a sinner, but rather that he may turn from his ignorance and live; give and grant unto us Thy Grace, by ✠ Blessing and ✠ Consecrating this Altar and this Sanctuary, which is here marked out with the most powerful and holy names of God. And may God bless this place with all the virtues of Heaven, so that no obscene or unclean spirit may have the power to enter into the Sanctuary, or to annoy any person who is therein; through our Lord Jesus, Christos, Soter, Logos, Who liveth eternally unto the Ages of the Ages. Amen.

ALL:
Amen.

Censing of the Altar

PRIEST:

And I saw when the Lamb opened one of the seals, and I heard, as it were the noise of thunder, one of the four beasts saying, Come and see. And I saw, and behold a white horse: and he that sat on him had a bow; and a crown was given unto him: and he went forth conquering and to conquer. The first angel sounded, and there followed hail and fire mingled with blood, and they were cast upon the earth: and the third part of trees was burnt up and all green grass was burnt up.

ALL:

Amen.

PRIEST: *(Puts incense into thurible and blesses it...)*

Creature of incense, be thou blessed in the Name of the ✠ Father, and of the ✠ Son, and of the ✠ Holy Spirit.

Priest censes the altar center, left, right.

Purify this place, O Divine and Eternal One, and make of us one mystical Body, growing into. the Pleroma of your Gnosis. Make us a Spiritual Temple of living stones, through which you infinite Light may flow. Let the Holy Angels of Light join with us, and assist us in this act of divine transformation. We unite now to celebrate, knowing that we all come from the Original Light, which is the Source of everything visible and invisible.

May the Lord be with you ✠

ALL:

And with thy spirit.

Confiteor

ALL:

O Lord, that which is mortal cometh not into a body immortal; but that which is immortal cometh into that which is mortal. Thou art Thou, all that is made, and all that is not made. Thou art all things, and there is nothing else Thou art not. I beseech Thee that I may never err from the Knowledge of Thee. For Thou art what I am, Thou art what I do, Thou art what I say. Amen.

PRIEST:

Practice: Mass of the Seven Seals

O Lord All Powerful, Eternal God and Father of ALL, shed upon me the Divine Influence of Thy Mercy, for I am Thy Creature. I beseech Thee to defend me from mine enemies, and to confirm in me true and steadfast faith. O Lord, I commit my Body and my Soul unto Thee, seeing I put my trust in none beside Thee; it is on Thee alone that I rely. O Lord my God aid me. O Lord hear me in the day and hour wherein I shall invoke Thee. I pray Thee by Thy Mercy not to put me into oblivion, nor to remove me from Thee. O Lord be Thou my succor, Thou Who art the God of my salvation. O Lord make me a new heart according unto Thy loving Kindness. These, O Lord, are the gifts which I await from Thee, O my God and my Master, Thou who livest and reignest unto the Ages of the Ages. Amen.

O Lord God the All Powerful One, who hast formed unto Thyself great and Ineffable Wisdom, and Co-Eternal with Thyself before the countless Ages; Thou Who before the birth of Time hast created the Aeons, and the things that they contain; Thou who hast vivified all things by Thy Holy Breath, I praise Thee, I bless Thee, I adore Thee, and I glorify Thee. Be Thou propitious unto me who am but a miserable sinner, and despise me not, save me and succor me, even me the work of Thine hands. I conjure and entreat Thee by Thy Holy Name to banish from my Spirit the darkness of Ignorance, and to enlighten me with the Fire of Thy Wisdom; take away from me all evil desires, and let not my speech be as that of the foolish. O Thou God the Living One, whose Glory, Honor, and Kingdom shall extend unto the Ages of the Ages. Through our Lord Jesus, Christos, Soter, Logos. Amen.

DEACONS:
Amen.

Absolution

PRIEST:
God the Father ✠ God the Son ✠ God the Holy Spirit ✠ Bless ✠ Strengthen ✠ Preserve ✠ and Sanctify ✠ you. May the Lord in His loving kindness look down upon you that you may win the victory over you lower selves and receive the Grace and Comfort of the Holy Spirit.

Hear me, O Father, father of all fatherhood. I invoke you, ye forgivers of sins, ye purifiers of iniquities. Forgive the sins of the souls of these disciples, and purify their iniquities and make them worthy to be reckoned with the Kingdom of the Father of the Treasury of the Light.

Now, therefore, O Father, father of all fatherhood, let the forgivers of sins come, whose names are these:

Σιφιρψνιχευ ζενει βεριμου σοχαβριχηρ ευθαρι να ναι φιεισβαλμηριχ
μευνιπος χιριε ενταιρ μουθιορ σμουρ πευχηρ οουσχους μινιονορ

ισοχοβορθα.

Hear me invoking you, forgive the sins of these souls and blot out their iniquities. Let them be worthy to be reckoned with the Kingdom of the Father of the Treasury of Light.
I know the great powers and invoke them:

Αυηρ βεβρω αθρονι η ουρεφ η ωνε σουφεν κνιτουσοχρεωψ
μαυωνβι μνευωρ σουωνι χωχωετεωφ χωχε ετεωφ μεμωχ ανημφ.

Forgive the sins of these souls, blot out their iniquities which they knowingly and unknowingly have committed; forgive them then and make them worthy to be reckoned with the Kingdom of the Father, so that they are worthy to receive this Eucharistic Offering which we have come to make, Holy Father. Through our Lord Jesus, Christos, Soter, Logos. Amen.

The Lord has put away all your sins. Abide in the peace and love of the Holy Spirit.

ALL:
Amen.

Sign of Peace

PRIEST:
My Brothers and Sisters in the Gnosis, the Lord of Agape binds us with a bond of Love that cannot be broken. Therefore we invoke the indwelling Christos, Who does ever say to Thy disciples: "Peace I leave with you, My peace I give unto you." Grant us that peace and unity which are agreeable to Thy Holy Will and Commandment. In the Name of our Lord Jesus Christ, Savior and Logos, may the peace of the Lord be with you always.

ALL:
And with thy spirit.

Clergy and congregants exchange Sign of Peace.

Practice: Mass of the Seven Seals

DISSOLUTION

First Reading

PRIEST:
The First Reading is taken from...

The First Lectionary Reading of the day is read by Priest.

PRIEST:
Give ear unto us, O Indwelling One, while we sing Thy praises. Thou Mystery before all uncontainables and impassables, Who did shine forth in Thy Mystery, in order that the Mystery that is from the beginning be completed in us. Hear us, O Father of boundless Light, Mother of Eternal Wisdom! All has come forth from Thee, and will return unto Thee, when the consummation of all consummations has taken place.

ALL:
Amen.

PRIEST:
And the second angel sounded, and as it were a great mountain burning with fire was cast into the sea: and the third part of the sea became blood; And the third pard of the creatures which were in the sea, and had life, died; and the third part of the ships were destroyed.

ALL:
Amen.

Gnostic Canticle

PRIEST:
Faith is our Earth in which we take root.

ALL:
Amen.

PRIEST:
Hope is the Water with which we are nourished.

ALL:
Amen.

PRIEST:
Love is the Air through which we grow.

ALL:
Amen.

PRIEST:
Knowledge is the Light by which we ripen.

ALL:
Amen.

PRIEST:
It is Christ who standeth at the door of every heart. Open ye your heart unto Him that ye may be One. For as the One is in the All, so is the All in the One. Thus the Logos saith: As I am One with the Father, so ye are One with me. Then may ye enter that Supernal Sphere, and dwell in that great celestial mansion whose pillars are WISDOM, STRENGTH, and BEAUTY.

Ring bell three times.

PRIEST & DEACONS: *(Intone)*
Amen.

Epistle

LECTOR:
The Epistle *(or* Second Reading*)* is taken from...

The Second Lectionary Reading of the day is read by Lector.

Here endeth the lesson.

ALL:
Thanks be to God.

Gradual

PRIEST:
He that loveth the Holy Sophia loveth Life; and they that seek her early shall be filled with joy.
Teach me, O Lord, the way of Thy statutes, and I shall keep it unto the end. Give me understanding, and I shall keep Thy law; yea I shall keep it with my whole heart. The path of the just is as the shining light, shining more and more unto the perfect day.

Munda Cor Meum

DEACON:
Cleanse my heart and lips, O God who by the hands of Thy Seraph didst cleanse the lips of Thy prophet Isaiah with a burning coal from Thine altar, and in Thy loving kindness, so purify me that I may worthily proclaim Thy Holy Gospel. Through Christ, our Indwelling Lord. Amen.

PRIEST: *(Blesses Deacon with the following words...)*
May the Lord be in thy heart and on thy lips, that through thy heart the love of God may shine forth, and through thy lips His power be made manifest. Amen.

Gospel

DEACON:
Please rise for the reading of the Gospel.
The Lord be with you.

ALL:
And with thy spirit.

DEACON:
The Gospel is taken from...

> *As the Deacon announces the Gospel all make the sign of the cross with the right thumb successively upon the forehead, lips, and heart.*

ALL:
Glory be to Thee, O Lord.

> *Deacon censes the Gospel, then Gospel is read.*

DEACON:
Here endeth the Gospel.

ALL:
Praise be to Thee, O Christ.

DEACON:
Be ye doers of the Word, and not hearers only.

> *Deacon bids people to be seated and censes the Priest, then returns to his position. Homily and Parish announcements are given by Priest or other designated speakers.*

Practice: Mass of the Seven Seals

Act of Faith

PRIEST:
Please all join me in the Act of Faith.

ALL: *(While placing right hand over heart)*
I believe in the Ineffable, Unknowable Father, Incorruptible Spirit, Lord of All Worlds, Architect of all things visible and all things invisible. Light of Light.

And in the Pure Will of the Father which sends forth the Seed, which is the true Good. Life of Life.

And I believe in the Holy Spirit, Sublime Mother of the Aeons, from whose womb all things are made manifest and to which they shall return. Love of Love.

And I believe in the incarnation of our Lorde Jesus Christ, self-generated and alone-begotten; creative essence of the Father; Logos of the Eternal Aeon; the Author of Regeneration, through which we may loosen the bonds of matter and recall our own divine nature, and become one in the fullness of God. Liberty of Liberty.

And I believe in the communion of the Holy Saints and Prophets.

And I believe in the miracle of the Eucharist, whereby the elements of Bread and Wine are transmuted into the Body and Blood of Christ the Logos, giving us Spiritual sustenance, and a visible means of grace.

And I believe in One Universal and Apostolic Church of Light, Life, Love and Liberty.

A-U-M A-U-M A-U-M

Invocation of the Holy Guardian Angel

PRIEST:
An Angel of peace, a faithful guide, a guardian of our souls and bodies, let us ask of the Lord.

ALL:
To Thee, O Lord.

PRIEST:
O You, divine Spirit! Spirit of Wisdom, Strength, and Beauty; powerful Being of Light, with whom I desire to accomplish the most intimate union!

I call you! I invoke you! Come to my assistance; guide my steps on the Path of Regeneration during this whole day. Vivify me with that Divine Love that enflames you; send me continually your intellect; give me the weapons that I need in order to vanquish my spiritual enemies.

Guide my steps toward the Truth; I abandon myself to your direction with total confidence.

Divine Logos, that have deigned to send Your Angels to guard and guide us, help me profit from their powerful operations; help me be preserved from any fall during this day.

Let me come to know intimately this Spirit, to which you have particularly entrusted me.

I ask this Grace by Your Holy Blood, that has become the sigil of my reconciliation with you. Amen.

Practice: Mass of the Seven Seals

SECOND PHASE: ALBEDO

SEPARATION

Offertorium

PRIEST:
And when he had opened the second seal, I heard the second beast say, Come and see. And there went out another horse that was red: and power was given to him that sat thereon to take peace from the earth, and that they should kill one another: and there was given unto him a great Sword.

ALL:
Amen.

PRIEST: *(Removes veil, pall, etc.)*
Come Thou Holy Name of Christ, Name above all names; come power from above and come highest gift; Thou Knower of the Chosen's Mysteries descend; Thou Who dost share in all noble strivers' struggles; Come! Come Thou Who givest joy to all who are at one with Thee; come and commune with us in this Eucharist which we are about to make in Thy Name, in this Sacrament to which we have assembled at Thy call.

Αεηιουω ιαω αωι ωια ψινωθερ θερνωψ νωψιθερ ζαγουρη παγουρη νεθμομαωθ νεψιομωθ μαραχαχθα θωβαρραβαυ θαρναχαχαν ζοροκοθορα ιεου Σαβαωθ.

CONJUNCTION

PRIEST: *(elevates paten with both hands)*
Blessed are You, O God, who art the Source of all things visible and invisible; the Lord of Light, Life, Love and Liberty. We offer this bread, grain of the Earth, transformed by human hands, as a token of our terrestrial nature. May it transform us and be the BODY OF CHRIST.

ALL:
Blessed be God forever.

Priest returns paten. Acolyte pours wine and a little water into Chalice.

PRIEST:

Remembering the Divine and human natures of the Master Jesus, and our own Divine and human natures, we mix water with this wine, praying that we may abide in His Consciousness and He in us.

Priest elevates Chalice with both hands.

Blessed are you, O God, who art the Source of all things visible and invisible; the Lord of Light, Life, Love and Liberty. We offer this wine, fruit of the Earth, transformed by human hands, as a token of our celestial nature. May it transform us and be the BLOOD OF CHIRST.

ALL:

Blessed be God forever.

PRIEST:

And when he had opened the third seal, I heard the third beast say, Come and see. And I beheld, and lo a black horse; and he that sat on him had a pair of balances in his hand. And I heard a voice in the midst of the four beasts say, A measure of wheat for a penny, and three measures of barley for a penny; and see thou hurt not the oil and the wine. And the third angel sounded; and there fell a great star from heaven, burning as it were a lamp, and it fell upon the third part of the rivers, and upon the fountains of waters; And the name of the star is called Wormwood.

ALL:

So mote it be!

Practice: Mass of the Seven Seals

THIRD PHASE: RUBEDO

FERMENTATION (PUTREFACTION)

Second Censing

PRIEST: *(Places more incense on charcoal)*
Be thou blessed in the Name of the ✠ Father, and of the ✠ Son, and of the ✠ Holy Spirit.

God the Father, seen of none, God the Co-Eternal Son, and God the Holy Spirit who givest us life, pour forth Thy three-fold power into these our oblations.

As this incense rises before Thee, O Lord, so let our prayer ascend Thy Holy Realms.

Glory be to the Unknown Father ✠ to the Son the Divine Logos ✠ and to the Holy Spirit ✠ our Celestial Mother and Consoler.

Lavabo

PRIEST:
And when he had opened the fourth seal, I heard the voice of the fourth beast say, Come and see. And I looked, and behold a pale horse: and his name that sat on him was Death, and Hell followed with him. And power was given unto them over the fourth part of the earth, to kill with sword, and with hunger, and with death, and with the beasts of the earth. And the fourth angel sounded, and the third part of the sun was smitten, and the third part of the moon, and the third part of the stars; so as the third part of them was darkened, and the day shone not for a third part of it, and the night likewise.

Priest washes hands.

O Heavenly Father, as Your rains cleanse and purify the earth, I wash my hands so that they too may be cleansed of the impurities of this world.

Asperges me hyssopo - et mundabor. Lavabis me aqua et super nivem dealbabor!

Orate Fratres

PRIEST:

My Brothers and Sisters, we have built a temple for the distribution of the power of the Logos. Let us prepare these gifts as a channel for its reception. Receive, O Source of all things visible and invisible, this Sacrifice of bread and wine. And may our lives be forever sanctified in Your service by the power of Christ, our Indwelling Lord. Amen.

Prayer Over the Gifts

PRIEST:

May we who partake of this Holy sacrament receive the power of Your Light and Life and be forever joined in Your Holy Wisdom.

ALL:

Amen.

Preface

PRIEST:

The Grace of our Lord Jesus Christ, and the love of God the Father, and the communion of the Holy Spirit be with you all.

ALL:

And with thy spirit.

PRIEST:

Let us lift up our hearts.

ALL:

we lift them up to the Lord.

PRIEST:

Let us give thanks unto the Lord.

ALL:
It is meet and right so to do.

PRIEST:
It is meet and right to hymn Thee, to bless Thee, to praise Thee, to give thanks unto Thee, and to worship Thee in every place of Thy dominion. For thou art God ineffable, inconceivable, invisible, incomprehensible, ever existing and eternally the same, Thou and Thy Only-begotten Son and Thy Holy Spirit. Thou didst bring us into being, and when we had fallen away didst raise us up again, and didst not cease to do all things until Thou hadst brought us back to your Pleroma, and hadst endowed us with Thy Kingdom which is to come. For all these things we give thanks to Thee, and to Thy Only-begotten Son, and Thy Holy Spirit, for all the things we know and we do not know, for the benefits conferred upon us, both seen and unseen. We render thanks to Thee also for this liturgy which Thou dost deign to receive from our hands, although there stand beside Thee myriads of Angels and Archangels, the Cherubim and the Seraphim, six-winged, many-eyed, soaring aloft on wings, chanting, voicing, shouting and saying the triumphal hymn:

Trisagion

ALL:
Holy, holy, holy, Lord of Sabaoth, heaven and earth are full of Thy glory.

Benedictus Qui Venit

ALL:
Blessed is He that cometh in the Name of the Lord. Hosanna+ in the Highest.

Prayer to the Holy Spirit

PRIEST:
o Holy Spirit, Barbelo, Divine Mother of All, may you receive us with your Glorious Embrace. Thou Who hast made Thyself known to us through your emissaries of Light and Life, of Love and Liberty; Your Aeon

Sophia and her daughter Zoe, whose heavenly archetypes have been mirrored ere on earth in the persons of Eve, Norea, the Virgin Mary, and Mary Magdalene; and known in the celestial realm as the woman clothed with the Sun; may You open our ears that we may hear Your voice of Understanding, and open our hearts that we may pour forth Thy Love.

Practice: Mass of the Seven Seals

FERMENTATION (PROPER)

Eucharistic Prayer

PRIEST:
O Most High God, You are holy indeed, and all creation rightly gives You praise. All life, all holiness comes from You through Christ, our Lord, Logos of the Eternal Aeon. From age to age, You reveal Your perennial Wisdom to Your Holy Elect, and call forth those that might partake of Your Divine Mystery.

Joins hands, holding them outstretched over the offerings.

And so, Most High God, we bring You these gifts. We ask You to make them holy by Your power to bless ✠ to approve ✠ and to ratify ✠ that they may become the Body ✠ and Blood ✠ of Christ, the Logos.

Raises bread slightly.

Following the example set forth by Melchizedek, the eternal High Priest, the Master Jesus, took bread and gave You thanks and praise. He blessed and broke the bread and gave it to His disciples, and said:

Bows slightly.

Take and eat ye all of this, for THIS IS MY BODY.

Shows consecrated host to the people, places on paten and genuflects in adoration.

In like manner, when the supper was ended, he took the noble Chalice.

Raises Chalice a little.

Again he gave You thanks and praise, blessed it and gave it to His disciples, and said:

Bows slightly.

Take and drink ye all of this, for THIS IS MY BLOOD. Do this in remembrance of me.

Shows Chalice; returns Chalice and genuflects in adoration. Extends hands.

Father, we celebrate the memory of Christ, the Eternal Logos, the repairer and our restorer of Gnosis. We, Your people and Your Priests offer unto You, O Most High God, this perfect sacrifice: the bread of Life and the cup of eternal Salvation.

Look with favor on these offerings and accept them as once You accepted the gifts of our patriarch in the Gnosis, the bread and wine offered by Your priest Melchizedek.

Almighty God, we pray that this sacrifice be borne to thine altar, there to be offered by Him who, as the eternal High Priest, forever offers Himself as the eternal sacrifice.

And as he has ordained that the heavenly sacrifice shall be mirrored here on earth through the ministry of mortals, to the end that Your holy people may be brought more closely into fellowship with You, we do pray for them who serve at this altar, the rightly celebrating the mysteries of the Most Holy Body ✠ and Blood ✠ of the Christ, they may be filled ✠ with Your mighty power and blessing, O Lord of Light, Life, Love, and Liberty.

Litany

PRIEST:
And when he had opened the fifth seal, I saw under the altar the souls of them that were slain for the word of God, and for the testimony which they held: And white robes were given unto every one of them.

Let us now in due and ancient fashion call upon the powers of the Most High and on all the Holy Ones who were and are and are to come, that united with them we may bravely strive for and ultimately attain to the Gnosis of Light, Life, Love, and Liberty.

All face West and kneel.

PRIEST:
I-A-O

DEACONS:
Shed thy glory upon us.

PRIEST:
Sabaoth

DEACONS:
Shed thy glory upon us.

PRIEST:
Abraxas

DEACONS:
Shed thy glory upon us.

Practice: Mass of the Seven Seals

PRIEST:
Sophia

DEACONS:
Shed thy glory upon us.

PRIEST:
All the souls of the Holy Gnostics during the Aeons.

DEACONS:
Hear us and be near us.

PRIEST:
Holy Mary Magdalene

DEACONS:
Hear us and be near us.

PRIEST:
Holy John the Baptist

DEACONS:
Hear us and be near us.

PRIEST:
Holy John the Evangelist

DEACONS:
Hear us and be near us.

PRIEST:
Holy Thomas

DEACONS:
Hear us and be near us.

PRIEST:
Holy Philip

DEACONS:
Hear us and be near us.

PRIEST:
Holy Simon Magus

DEACONS:
Hear us and be near us.

PRIEST:
Holy Dositheus

DEACONS:
Hear us and be near us.

PRIEST:
Holy Menander

DEACONS:
Hear us and be near us.

PRIEST:
Holy Saturninus

DEACONS:
Hear us and be near us.

PRIEST:
Holy Basilides

DEACONS:
Hear us and be near us.

PRIEST:
Holy Valentinus

DEACONS:
Hear us and be near us

PRIEST:
Holy Bardaisan

DEACONS:
Hear us and be near us.

PRIEST:
Holy Clement of Alexandria

DEACONS:
Hear us and be near us.

PRIEST:
Holy Origen

DEACONS:
Hear us and be near us.

PRIEST:
Holy Esclaremonde & all Cathar Martyrs

DEACONS:
Hear us and be near us.

PRIEST:
Holy Prophet Joachim

DEACONS:
Hear us and be near us.

PRIEST:
Holy Jacque de Molay & all the Blessed Templars

DEACONS:
Hear us and be near us.

PRIEST:
Holy Martinès de Pasqually

DEACONS:
Hear us and be near us.

PRIEST:
Holy Louis Claude de Saint-Martin

DEACONS:
Hear us and be near us.

PRIEST:
Holy Bernard Raymond Fabré-Palaprat

DEACONS:
Hear us and be near us.

PRIEST:
Holy Tau Valentin II

DEACONS:
Hear us and be near us.

PRIEST:
Holy Tau Synésius

DEACONS:
Hear us and be near us.

PRIEST:
Holy Mar Timotheos

Practice: Mass of the Seven Seals

DEACONS:
Hear us and be near us.

PRIEST:
Holy Paolo Miraglia Gulotti

DEACONS:
Hear us and be near us.

PRIEST:
Holy Jean Sempé

DEACONS:
Hear us and be near us.

PRIEST:
Holy Abbe Julio

DEACONS:
Hear us and be near us.

PRIEST:
Holy Tau Jean II

DEACONS:
Hear us and be near us.

PRIEST:
Holy Tau Harmonius

DEACONS:
Hear us and be near us.

PRIEST:
Holy Tau Jean III

DEACONS:
Hear us and be near us.

PRIEST:
Holy Tau Ogdoade Orfeo I

DEACONS:
Hear us and be near us.

PRIEST:
Holy Tau Ogdoade Orfeo III

DEACONS:
Hear us and be near us.

PRIEST:
Holy Tau Iohannes Harmonius

DEACONS:
Hear us and be near us.

PRIEST:
Holy Tau Johannes XIII

DEACONS:
Hear us and be near us.

PRIEST:
All the Apostles, Prophets, Bishops, Priests & Martyrs of the Gnosis.

DEACONS:
Hear us and be near us, now and forever.

Kyrie

PRIEST:
Kyrie Eleison

ALL:
Kyrie Eleison

PRIEST:
Christe Eleison

ALL:
Christe Eleison

PRIEST & ALL:
Kyrie Eleison

PRIEST:
Welcome into Your kingdom, O Lord, our departed brothers and sisters in the Gnosis.

Mother and Father united as one;
Wisdom and Strength through Your Eternal Son;
We are divided for Love's sake;
That through our union we may make
Ourselves as symbols of Heaven on Earth;
In life, in death, and in rebirth!

O Christ our Lord who gives us all these gifts, bless them and make them holy.

PRIEST:
And the fifth angel sounded, and I saw a star fall from heaven unto the earth: and to him was given the key of the bottomless pit. And he opened the bottomless pit; and there arose a smoke out of the pit, as the smoke of a great furnace; and the sun and the air were darkened by reason of the smoke of the pit. And there came out of the smoke locusts upon the earth: and unto them was given power, as the scorpions of the earth have power. And it was commanded them that they should not hurt the grass of the earth, neither any green thing, neither any tree; but only those men which have not the seal of God in their foreheads.

Practice: Mass of the Seven Seals

Pater Noster

PRIEST:
Let us pray with confidence to the Father in the words the Master Jesus gave us.

ALL:
Our Father who art in Heaven, hallowed be Thy Name;
Thy kingdom come, Thy will be done,
On Earth as it is in Heaven.
Give us this day, our daily bread,
And forgive us our debts, as we have also forgiven our debtors.
And leave us not in temptation, but deliver us from evil,
For Thine is the Kingdom, and the Power, and the Glory, forever and ever. Amen.

PRIEST: *(With hands extended)*
Deliver us Lord from the evil of ignorance, and grant us peace, love, and light in our day.

DISTILLATION

Breaking of the Bread

PRIEST:
And I beheld when he had opened the sixth seal, and, lo, there was a great earthquake; and the sun became black as sackcloth of hair; and the moon became as blood; And after these things I saw four angels standing on the four corners of the earth, holding the four winds of the earth, that the wind should not blow on the earth, nor on the sea, nor on any tree. And I saw another angel ascending from the East, having the seal of the living God: and he cried with a loud voice to the four angels, to whom it was given to hurt the earth and the sea, saying, Hurt not the earth, neither the sea, nor the trees, till we have sealed the servants of our God in their foreheads. And I heard the number of them which were sealed: and there were sealed an hundred and forty and four thousand of all the tribes of the children of Israel. After this I beheld, and, lo, a great multitude, which no man could number, of all nations, and kindreds, and people, and tongues, stood before the throne, and before the Lamb, clothed with white robes, and palms in their hands; These are they which came out of great tribulation and have washed their robes, and made them white in the blood of the Lamb.

ALL:
Amen.

PRIEST:
O Divine Light, You show Yourself this day upon countless altars and yet are one and indivisible. In token of Thy great Sacrifice, we rend *(break bread)* this, Thy Holy Body, that we may be as Thou art.

Through this ancient and sacred tradition, all Heaven and Earth are united in Thy Consciousness, Thy Love, and Thy Will. And as the One became many, only to restore all to the Pleroma, so too, in the breaking of this bread, we are one with Thee, as Thou art one with the Father.

> *Breaks off small piece of bread from the left half, makes sign of the cross over the Chalice, and places piece in Chalice; then blows three crosses of air over Chalice.*
>
> *Intones...*

Through Him, and with Him, and in Him;
In the Unity of the Holy Spirit;
All glory and honor are Yours Almighty Father,

Practice: Mass of the Seven Seals

Forever and ever.

ALL: *(intone)*
Amen.

PRIEST:
And the sixth angel sounded, and I heard a voice from the four horns of the golden altar which is before God, saying to the sixth angel which had the trumpet, Loose the four angels which are bound in the great river Euphrates. And the four angels were loosed, which were prepared for an hour, and a day, and a month, and a year, for to slay the third part of men. And the number of the army of the horsemen were two hundred thousand thousand: and I heard the number of them. And thus I saw the horses in the vision, and them that sat on them, having breastplates of fire, and of jacinth, and brimstone: and the heads of the horses were as the heads of lions.

Let us pray. Adoration be to Thee, O most High God, Father of all Fatherhood, and to Thee, O Mother of all, who in the incarnation of Your Logos have mystically provided us with the Sacrament of His Body and Blood, that by partaking of this Mystery, we may reunite within ourselves the fragments of Your Divinity dispersed throughout the Cosmos. Holy, Holy, Holy, are You, the Father and Mother of the Treasury of the Light, now and unto the countless ages. Amen.

Theurgic Consecration

Priest takes Dagger, faces East, and draws the letter YOD in the air with Dagger as it is pronounced, then intones the Holy Name, thus:

By the virtue of י I call forth the power of IAO to join in this Holy Sacrifice.

Priest travels to the South via the North and West, that is, by walking 270° counterclockwise, draws the letter HE, and intones the Holy Name, thus:

By the virtue of ה I call forth the power of SABAOTH to join in this Holy Sacrifice.

Priest continues 270° counterclockwise to the West, draws the letter VAV, and intones the Holy Name, thus:

By the virue of ו I call forth the power of ABRAXAS to join in this Holy Sacrifice.

Priest continues 270° to the North, draws the letter HE, and intones the Holy Name, thus:

By the virtue of ה I call forth the power of SOPHIA to join in this Holy Sacrifice.

Priest travels 270° counterclockwise again to return to the East for the third complete circuit. He faces the Eucharistic Altar, and with arms outstretched and holding the Dagger in the right hand...

The Son would not be the Father without wearing the Father's Name. So by the Power of the Holy Tetragrammaton, and by the virtue of the Tri-Unity of the Holy Letter ש *(draws Hebrew letter with Dagger in the air above Chalice)*, I call forth the power of the Author of Regeneration, the Repairer of Souls, the Destroyer of Death...

Intones while slowly lowering Dagger with both hands into Chalice.

יהשורה to pour forth Thy powers into this Holy Sacrifice and transmute these elements of bread and wine into the Divine Body and Blood of the Logos.

Makes three crosses in Chalice with Dagger.

Communion

PRIEST: *(Elevating the Body and Blood)*
And I took the little book out of the angel's hand, and ate it up; and it was in my mouth sweet as honey: and as soon as I had eaten it, my belly was bitter. And he said unto me, Thou must prophesy again before many peoples, and nations, and tongues, and kings. And there was given me a reed like unto a rod: and the angel stook, saying, Rise, and measure the temple of God, and the altar, and them that worship therein. But the court which is without the temple leave out, and measure it not; for it is given unto the Gentiles: and the holy city shall they tread under foot forty and two months. And I will give power unto my two witnesses,
and they shall prophesy a thousand two hundred and threescore days, clothed in sackcloth. And when they shall have finished their testimony, the beast that ascendeth out of the bottomless pit shall make war against them, and shall overcome them, and kill them. And their dead bodies shall lie in the street of the great city, which spiritually is called Sodom and Egypt, where also our Lord was crucified. And they of the people and kindreds and tongues and nations shall see their dead bodies three days and a half, and shall not suffer their dead bodies to be put in graves. And they that dwell upon the earth shall rejoice over them, and make merry, and shall send gifts one to another; because these two prophets tormented them that dwelt on the earth. And after three days and a half the Spirit of life from God entered into them, and they stood upon their feet; and great fear fell upon them which saw them. And they heard a great voice from heaven saying unto them, Come up hither. And they ascended up to heaven in a cloud; and their enemies beheld them.

Practice: Mass of the Seven Seals

Behold the Divine Light which lighteth every man that cometh into the world. May the communion of these Holy Mysteries be to the regeneration of both soul and body. Let us draw nigh and receive this most Holy Sacrament.

Ablutions and silent meditation.

ACP Clergy Handbook

COAGULATION

Post-Communio

PRIEST:
And when he bad opened the seventh seal, there was silence in heaven about the space of half an hour. And the seventh angel sounded; and there were great voices in heaven, saying, The kingdoms of this world are become the kingdoms of our Lord, and of his Christ; and he shall reign for ever and ever. And the four and twenty which sat before God on their seats, fell upon their faces, and worshipped God, saying, We give thee thanks, O Lord God Almighty, which art, and wast, and art to come; because thou hast taken to thee thy great power, and hast reigned. And the nations were angry, and thy wrath is come, and the time of the dead, that they should be judged, and that thou shouldest give reward unto thy servants the prophets, and to the saints, and them that fear thy name, small and great; and shouldest destroy them which destroy the earth. And the temple of God was opened in heaven, and there was seen in his temple the ark of his testament: and there were lightnings, and voices, and thunderings, and an earthquake, and great hail. And there appeared a great wonder in heaven; a woman clothed with the sun, and the moon under her feet, and upon her head a crown of twelve stars: And she being with child cried, travailing in birth, and pained to be delivered. And there appeared another wonder in heaven; and behold a great red dragon, having seven heads and ten horns, and seven crowns upon his heads. And his tail drew the third part of the stars of heaven, and did cast them to the earth: and the dragon stood before the woman which was ready to be delivered, for to devour her child as soon as it was born. And she brought forth a man child, who was to rule all nations with a rod of iron: and her child was caught up unto God, and to his throne. And the woman fled into the wilderness, where she hath a place prepared of God, that they should feed her there a thousand two hundred and threescore days. And there was war in heaven: Michael and his angels fought against the dragon; and the dragon fought and his angels, and prevailed not; neither was their place found any more in heaven.

May we, who in this Holy Mystery have entered into the all-pervading strength and love of Christ our Indwelling Lord, be guided by the Divine Presence into the fullness of Truth, that we may attain to that mount of vision whereon we may see the boundless light unveiled in the wholeness of its Divine Glory. Amen.

Practice: Mass of the Seven Seals

Dismissal

PRIEST:

And I saw a new heaven and a new earth: for the first heaven and the first earth were passed away; and there was no more sea. And I John saw the holy city, new Jerusalem, coming down from God out of heaven, prepared as a bride adorned for her husband. And I heard a great voice out of heaven saying, Behold, the tabernacle of God is with men, and he will dwell with them, and they shall be his people, and God himself shall be with them, and be their God. And God shall wipe away all tears from their eyes; and there shall be no more death, neither sorrow, nor crying, neither shall there be any more pain: for the former things are passed away. And he that sat upon the throne said, Behold, I make all things new. And he said unto me, Write: for these words are true and faithful. And he said unto me, It is done. I am Alpha and Omega, the beginning and the end. I will give unto him that is athirst of the fountain of the water of life freely. He that overcometh shall inherit all things; and I will be his God, and he shall be my son. And he saith unto me, Seal not the sayings of the prophecy of this book: for the time is at hand. He that is unjust, let him be unjust still: and he which is filthy, let him be filthy still: and he that is righteous, let him be righteous still: and he that is holy, let him be holy still. And behold, I come quickly; and my reward is with me, to give every man according as his work shall be. I am Alpha and Omega, the beginning and the end, the first and the last. Blessed are they that do his commandments, that they may have right to the Tree of Life, and may enter in through the gates into the city. I Jesus have sent mine angel to testify unto you these things in the churches. I am the root and the offspring of David, and the bright and Morning Star. And the Spirit and the bride say, Come. And let him that heareth say, Come. And let him that is athirst come. And whosoever will, let him take the water of life freely. The grace of our Lord Jesus Christ be with you all.

ALL:

And with thy spirit.

PRIEST:

Ite, missa est.

ALL:

Deo gratias.

ACP Clergy Handbook

Liturgy of St. Peter the Gnostic

The role of St. Peter within Gnostic scriptures and sects has often been as a stand-in for the psychic Church, that is, the non-Gnostic, so-called "orthodoxy." Within certain Gnostic texts, such as the *Pistis Sophia* and the *Gospel of Thomas*, Peter is depicted as ignorant of, and even outright hostile toward, the higher pneumatic teachings. And, while this may be a useful literary device by which to criticize the purely psychic interpretation of Christ, it is by no means the final word on the matter.

Among the Gnostic writings are a number of pieces which portray Peter as a recipient and transmitter of Gnostic teachings and revelations, most notably the Apocalypse of Peter and the Letter of Peter to Philip, and to a lesser extent the Acts of Peter and the Twelve, works which appear all in the Nag Hammadi Codices. And within the canonical texts, the Second Epistle of Peter is of a particularly mystical, and I would go so far as to say gnostic, character (cf. our "Theosis Through Gnosis"). And, as modern Gnostics who hold and value the Apostolic Succession which emits principally from St. Peter, it seems wise to do a little to rehabilitate his name, and to bring to light the deeply pneumatic teachings of the Petrine tradition.

Therefore, we have arranged the following liturgy which, while following the basic format of our principal Liturgy of the Pleromic Light, incorporates aspects of the aforesaid Petrine tradition. This is done in two manners: 1st, by incorporating text from the canonical Petrine epistles, as well as from the specifically Petrine works from the Nag Hammadi Codices; 2nd, by incorporating the Latin text of certain aspects of the Mass, so as to invoke a connection with the ancient Roman Church, being a principal expression of the Petrine tradition. The Latin text is drawn primarily from that given by Abbé Julio in *Liturgical Prayers*, wherein also its translation may be found. In the case of the small Latin excerpt from 2 Peter, it has been taken from the *Nova Vulgata*, Ed. XXVII.

As with our other alternate liturgies, the present work is not intended to replace the Holy Gnostic Liturgy of the Pleromic Light, but to supplement it. In the future we may have specific recommendations as to particular feast days to which this Mass is especially suited, but for now we simply encourage our priests and friends of the Church to experiment with it and inform us of their experiences with it.

The layout of the Temple is the same as that used for our standard Mass, with the following exceptions:

Rear Altar: Draped in red; icon(s) of St. Peter.
Eucharistic Altar: Draped in white, with Cross of St. Peter in red; Cross of St. Peter may be displayed as Altar Cross as well.

Practice: Liturgy of St. Peter the Gnostic

1st Deacon's lectern: Draped in red, with Cross of St. Peter in black.
2nd Deacon's lectern: Draped in black, with Cross of St. Peter in white. All other items as usual.

The Preliminary Rites and Procession are the same as found in the standard liturgy, and therefore are not reproduced here. Likewise, the Recession is as described in The Pleromic Light Unveiled.

† Φωσφορος, επ. γν.
Patriarch
Apostolic Church of the Pleroma
14 February, 2019
Feast of Holy Valentinus

Invocation of the Aeons

PRIEST:
In the Name of the Lord of all Worlds.

Priest and Deacons place right hand over heart.

PRIEST:
I…

1st DEACON:
A…

2nd DEACON:
O…

Priest and Deacons place hands, right over left, over the Solar Plexus.

PRIEST:
I…

1st DEACON:
A…

2nd DEACON:
UM…

Priest & Deacons cross their arms across chest, right over left, palms open.

PRIEST:
A…

1st DEACON:
U…

2nd DEACON:
M…

Clergy now place their hands in front of them, palms together, as in prayer.

PRIEST:
Lord of the Past

Practice: Liturgy of St. Peter the Gnostic

PRIEST & DEACONS: *(As all take one step forward)*
We hail thee!

PRIEST:
Lord of the Present

PRIEST & DEACONS: *(As all take one step forward)*
We hail thee!

PRIEST:
Lord of the Future

PRIEST & DEACONS *(As all take one step forward)*
We hail thee!

CLERGY: *(Kneeling before the Eucharistic Altar)*
O Ineffable Light, Father of Resplendent Glory, Mother of Eternal Wisdom, we, being assembled together on the path of Light to manifest the Power of the Logos, the Christ within, and to participate in the offering of that great sacrifice which was, and is, and is to come, do hail Thee as the Great Architect of the Universe, and the Source of all Light, Life, Love, and Liberty.

Clergy rise and proceed to their stations. Porter places Sword on Rear Altar, pointing North, and proceeds to station at the Temple entrance. Thurifer replaces thurible on Rear Altar and proceeds to station.

PRIEST:
In the Name of the Unknown One who reveals His Mysteries out of the Treasuries of Light to them that call upon Him, and who mercifully bestows His Secrets of Gnosis upon us without measure.

May He always grant to us, through Christ the Eternal Logos, and the Divine Sophia, the revealer of His Gnosis, His eternal blessings that we may worthily perform the mysteries of the Mass. Help us to reveal the greatest Secrets which are lawful for man to know, and use them without offence unto God. Amen.

PRIEST:
For what purpose do we congregate?

1ˢᵗ DEACON:
To seek Truth.

PRIEST:
What shall we use to aid us in our search for Truth?

2ⁿᵈ DEACON: *(using a small taper, extracts flame from Perpetual Luminary)*
The Light of Gnosis!

PRIEST: *(receives lit taper from Deacon and lights candles reciting…)*
O Pure Light! Symbol of Divine Essence! Light of the Empyrean Realm! Make thy radiant & pure fire purge and sanctify this, thy holy altar, and my lips for the words that we are to proclaim for the greater glory of the Eternal. Amen.

As these flames lighten our way in the earthly realm, so are the great Luminaries of the Aeons ever present to illumine and enlighten our spiritual path. Come, join us now, O great Luminaries, emissaries of the Most High!

HARMOZEL
OROIAEL
DAVEITHAI
ELELETH

Come now and witness as we praise the Most High, and prepare for the celebration of the Most Holy Eucharist.

2nd **DEACON:**
Father

1st **DEACON:**
Father

PRIEST:
Father of Light, who possesses incorruption, hear us, as you have taken pleasure in your Holy Son Jesus Christ.

2nd **DEACON:**
Son of life.

1st **DEACON:**
Son of immortality.

PRIEST:
You who are in the Light, Son, Christ of immortality, our Redeemer and Repairer, give us strength.

PRIEST & DEACONS:
Blessed are those who belong to the Father, for they are above the heavens.

PRIEST:
All things for life and godliness have been given to us by the Divine Power.

Practice: Liturgy of St. Peter the Gnostic

1ˢᵗ DEACON:
Through the knowledge of the one who called us to his own glory and virtue.

2ⁿᵈ DEACON:
Through which he has given to us great and precious promises.

PRIEST & DEACONS:
That through these we may become sharers of the divine nature.

PRIEST: *(intones)*
O glorious Godhead of the Aeons, Thou, secret center, Who art surrounded by the radiant presence of the host of holy angels and messengers of Light, hear our prayers and listen to our thoughts which rise from this world of shadows, toward Thy abode of unsearchable, unspeakable, and unending Light. Amen.

Invocation of the Archangels

PRIEST:
Please rise for the Invocation of the Archangels.

ALL: *(using the forms as previously instructed)*
Ateh. Malkuth. Ve'Geburah. Ve'Gedulah. Le Olam. A-U-M
In the Name of יהוה we invoke thee, Archangel of the East, RAPHAEL!
In the Name of אדני we invoke thee, Archangel of the South, MICHAEL!
In the Name of אהיה we invoke thee, Archangel of the West, GABRIEL!
In the Name of אגלא we invoke thee, Archangel of the North, AURIEL!
Ateh. Malkuth. Ve'Geburah. Ve'Gedulah. Le Olam. A-U-M

Asperges

PRIEST: (sprinkles blessed water while reciting…)
Purify us, O Lord, that in Thy Power we may worthily perform the Great Work. In Thy strength, O Indwelling Lord, do we expel all forces of darkness from this, Thy Holy Altar and Sanctuary, and from this house and our own human temples wherein we worship Thee; and we pray Thee Heavenly Father, that Thou wilt command the Rulers of the Four Regions, your mighty Archangels, Lords of the Air, Water, Fire, and Earth, to build for us a Spiritual Temple through which Thy Strength and Blessing may be poured forth upon Thy people. Through Christ our Indwelling Lord.

ALL:
So Mote It Be!

Prayer

PRIEST:
When we enter herein with all humility, let God the Almighty One enter into this Sanctuary of the Gnosis by the entrance of an eternal happiness, of a Divine prosperity, of a perfect joy, of an abundant charity, and of an eternal salutation. Let all the demons fly from this place, especially those who are opposed unto this work, and let the Angels of Peace assist and protect this Sanctuary, from which let discord and strife fly and depart. Magnify and extend upon us, O Lord, Thy most Holy Name, and bless our conversation and our assembly. Sanctify, O Lord our God, our humble entry herein, Thou the Blessed and Holy One of the Eternal Ages! Amen.

I beseech Thee, O Lord God, the All Powerful and the All Merciful, that Thou wilt deign to bless this Sanctuary, and all this place, and all those who are herein, and that Thou wilt grant unto us, who serve Thee, and rehearse nothing but the wonders of Thy Law, a good Angel for our Guardian; remove from us every adverse power; preserve us from evil and from trouble; grant, O Lord, that we may rest in this place in all safety, through Thee, O Lord, Who livest and reignest unto the Ages of the Ages.

O Lord God, All Powerful and All Merciful, Thou who desirest not the death of a sinner, but rather that he may turn from his ignorance and live; give and grant unto us Thy Grace, by ✠ Blessing and ✠ Consecrating this Altar and this Sanctuary, which is here marked out with the most powerful and holy Names of God. And may God bless this place with all the virtues of Heaven, so that no obscene or unclean spirit may have the power to enter into this Sanctuary, or to annoy any person who is therein; through our Lord Jesus, Christos, Soter, Logos, Who liveth eternally unto the Ages of the Ages. Amen.

ALL:
Amen.

Censing of the Altar

PRIEST: *(Puts incense into thurible and blesses it…)*
Creature of incense, be thou blessed in the Name of the ✠ Father, and of the ✠ Son, and of the ✠ Holy Spirit.

Priest censes the alter center, left, right.

Purify this place, O Divine and Eternal One, and make of us one mystical Body, growing into the Pleroma of your Gnosis. Make us a Spiritual Temple of living stones, through which your infinite Light may flow. Let the Holy Angels of Light join with us and assist us in this act of divine transformation. We unite now to celebrate, knowing that we all come from the Original Light, which is the Source of everything visible and invisible.

Practice: Liturgy of St. Peter the Gnostic

May the Lord be with you ✠

ALL:
And with thy spirit.

Confiteor

ALL:
O Lord, that which is mortal cometh not into a body immortal; but that which is immortal cometh into that which is mortal. Thou art Thou, all that is made, and all that is not made. Thou art all things, and there is nothing else Thou art not. I beseech Thee that I may never err from the Knowledge of Thee. For Thou art what I am, Thou art what I do, Thou art what I say. Amen.

PRIEST:
O Lord All Powerful, Eternal God and Father of ALL, shed upon me the Divine Influence of Thy Mercy, for I am Thy Creature. I beseech Thee to defend me from mine enemies, and to confirm in me true and steadfast faith. O Lord, I commit my Body and my Soul unto Thee, seeing I put my trust in none beside Thee; it is on Thee alone that I rely. O Lord my God aid me. O Lord hear me in the day and hour wherein I shall invoke Thee. I pray Thee by Thy Mercy not to put me into oblivion, nor to remove me from Thee. O Lord be Thou my succor, Thou Who art the God of my salvation. O Lord make me a new heart according unto Thy loving Kindness. These, O Lord, are the gifts which I await from Thee, O my God and my Master, Thou who livest and reignest unto the Ages of the Ages. Amen.

O Lord God the All Powerful One, who hast formed unto Thyself great and Ineffable Wisdom, and Co-Eternal with Thyself before the countless Ages; Thou Who before the birth of Time hast created the Aeons, and the things that they contain; Thou who hast vivified all things by Thy Holy Breath, I praise Thee, I bless Thee, I adore Thee, and I glorify Thee. Be Thou propitious unto me who am but a miserable sinner, and despise me not; save me and succor me, even me that work of Thine hands. I conjure and entreat Thee by Thy Holy Name to banish from my Spirit the darkness of Ignorance, and to enlighten me with the Fire of Thy Wisdom; take away from me all evil desires, and let not my speech be as that of the foolish. O Thou, God the Living One, whose Glory, Honor, and Kingdom shall extend unto the Ages of the Ages. Through our Lord Jesus, Christos, Soter, Logos. Amen.

DEACONS:
Amen.

Absolution

PRIEST:

God the Father ✠ God the Son ✠ God the Holy Spirit ✠ Bless ✠ Strengthen ✠ Preserve ✠ and Sanctify ✠ you. May the Lord in His loving kindness look down upon you that you may win the victory over your lower selves and receive the Grace and Comfort of the Holy Spirit.

Hear me, O Father, father of all fatherhood. I invoke you, ye forgivers of sins, ye purifiers of iniquities. Forgive the sins of the souls of these disciples, and purify their iniquities and make them worthy to be reckoned with the Kingdom of the Father of the Treasury of the Light.

Now, therefore, O Father, father of all fatherhood, let the forgivers of sins come, whose names are these:

Σιφιρψνιχευ ζενει βεριμου σοχαβριχηρ ευθαρι να ναι φιεισβαλμηριχ μευνιπος χιριε ενταιρ μουθιορ σμουρ πευχηρ οουσχους μινιονορ ισοχοβορθα.

Hear me invoking you, forgive the sins of these souls and blot out their iniquities. Let them be worthy to be reckoned with the Kingdom of the Father of the Treasury of Light.

I know the great powers and invoke them:

Αυηρ βεβρω αθρονι η ουρεφ η ωνε σουφεν χνιτουσοχρεωψ μαυωνβι μνευωρ σουωνι χωχωετεωφ χωχε ετεωφ μεμωχ ανημφ.

Forgive the sins of these souls, blot out their iniquities which they knowingly and unknowingly have committed; forgive them then and make them worthy to be reckoned with the Kingdom of the Father, so that they are worthy to receive this Eucharistic Offering which we have come to make, Holy Father. Through our Lord Jesus, Christos, Soter, Logos. Amen.

The Lord has put away all your sins. Abide in the peace and love of the Holy Spirit.

ALL:
Amen.

Sign of Peace

PRIEST:

My Brothers and Sisters in the Gnosis, the Lord of Agape binds us with a bond of Love that cannot be broken. Therefore we invoke the indwelling Christos, Who does ever say to Thy disciples: "Peace I leave with you, My peace I give unto you." Grant us that peace and unity which are agreeable to Thy Holy Will and Commandment. In the Name of our Lord Jesus Christ, Savior and Logos, may the peace of the Lord be with you always.

CONGREGANTS:
And also with you.

Clergy & Congregants exchange Sign of Peace.

Discourse of Peter

PRIEST:
The day of the Lord will come as a thief in the night, in which the heavens shall pass away with a suddenness, and the elements shall be dissolved in fire, and the earth and the works that are therein shall be disclosed.

1st DEACON:
Seeing then that all these things shall be dissolved, what manner of persons ought ye be in holy conversation and godliness, awaiting and hastening the coming of the day of God, wherein the heavens being set ablaze shall be dissolved and the elements shall dissolve with fire.

2nd DEACON:
But we, according to his promise, await new heavens and a new earth, wherein dwelleth righteousness.

PRIEST:
Therefore, beloved, seeing that ye await such things, strive to be found by him at peace, spotless and unblemished, and account the longsuffering of our Lord as salvation.

1st DEACON:
So too hath our beloved brother Paul, according to the wisdom given unto him, written unto you, speaking of these things as he does in all his epistles.

2nd DEACON:
In them are some things hard to understand, which they that are unlearned and unstable wrest, as they do also other scriptures, unto their own destruction.

Ye, therefore, beloved, seeing ye know these things before, beware lest ye also, being led away with the error of the wicked, fall from your own stability.

1st DEACON:
But grow in grace, and in the gnosis of our Lord and Savior Jesus Christ.

PRIEST:
To him be glory, both now and unto the day of the aeons.

PRIEST & DEACONS:
Amen.

First Reading

PRIEST:
The First Reading is taken from...

The First Lectionary Reading of the day is read by Priest.

PRIEST:
Give ear unto us, O Indwelling One, while we sing Thy praises. Thou Mystery before all uncontainables and impassables, Who did shine forth in Thy Mystery, in order that the Mystery that is from the beginning be completed in us. Hear us, O Father of boundless Light, Mother of Eternal Wisdom! All has come forth from Thee, and will return unto Thee, when the consummation of all consummations has taken place.
ALL:
Amen.

Te Deum Laudamus

PRIEST: *(chants)*
Te Deum laudamus, te Dominum confitemur.
Te reternum Patrem omnis terra veneratur.
Tibi omnes Angeli, tibi cœli, et universre Potestates,
Tibi Cherubim et Seraphim incessabili voce proclamant:
Sanctus, Sanctus, Sanctus, Dominus Deus Sabaoth.
Pleni sunt cœli et terra Majestatis gloriæ tuæ,
Te gloriousus Apostolorum chorus,
Te prophetarum laudabilis numerus.
Te Martyrum candidatus laudat exercitus.

Practice: Liturgy of St. Peter the Gnostic

Te per orbem terrarum sancta confitetur Ecclesia,
Patrem immensæ majestatis,
Venerandum tuum verum et unicum Filium,
Sanctum quoque Paraclitum Spiritum.
Tu Rex gloriæ, Christe.
Tu Patris sempiternus es Filius.
Tu ad liberandum suscepturus hominem, non horruisti Virginis uterum.
Tu, devicto mortis aculeo, aperuisti credentibus regna crelorum.
Tu ad dexteram Dei sedes in gloria Patris.
Judex crederis esse venturus.
Te ergo quæsumus, tuis famulis subveni, quos pretioso sanguine redemisti.
Æterna fac cum sanctis tuis in gloria numerari.
Saluum fac populum tuum, Domine, et benedic hæreditati, tuæ.
Et rege cos, et extolle illos usque in æternum,
Per singulos dies benedicimus te.
Et laudamus nomen in sæculum, et in sæculum sæculi.
Dignare, Domine, die isto, sine peccato nos custodire.
Miserere nostri, Domine, miserere nostri.
Fiat misericordia tua, Domine, super nos, quemadmodem speravimus inte.
In te, Domine, speravi, non confundar in æternum.
Benedicamus Patrem, et Filium, cum Sancto Spiritu.

ALL:
Laudemus et superexaltemus eum in sæcula.

PRIEST:
Oremus. Deus cujus misericordiæ non est numerus, et bonitas infinitus est thesaurus, piissimæ majestati tuæ pro collatis donis gratias agimus, tuam semper clementiam exorantes: ut, qui petentibus postulata concedis, eosdem non desceras, et ad præmia futura disponas. Per Christum Dominum nostrum.

ALL:
Amen.

Gnostic Canticle

PRIEST:

Faith is our Earth in which we take root.

ALL:

Amen.

PRIEST:

Hope is the Water with which we are nourished.

ALL:

Amen.

PRIEST:

Love is the Air through which we grow.

ALL:

Amen.

PRIEST:

Knowledge is the Light by which we ripen.

ALL:

Amen.

PRIEST:

It is Christ who standeth at the door of every heart. Open ye your heart unto Him that ye may be One. For as the One is in the All, so is the All in the One. Thus the Logos sayeth: As I am One with the Father, so ye are One with me. Then may ye enter that Supernal Sphere, and dwell in that great celestial mansion whose pillars are: WISDOM, STRENGTH, and BEAUTY.

Ring bell three times.

PRIEST & DEACONS: *(intone)*

Amen.

Practice: Liturgy of St. Peter the Gnostic

Epistle

LECTOR:
The Epistle (or Second Reading) is taken from...
The Second Lectionary Reading of the day is read by Lector.

Here endeth the Lesson.

ALL:
Thanks be to God.

Gradual

PRIEST:
He that loveth the Holy Sophia loveth Life; and they that seek her early shall be filled with Joy.
Teach me, O Lord, the way of Thy statutes, and I shall keep it unto the end. Give me understanding, and I shall keep Thy law· ye I shall keep it with my whole heart. The path of the just is as the shining light, shining more and more unto the perfect day.

Munda Cor Meum

PRIEST:
Munda cor meum ac labia mea, omnipotens Deus, qui labia Isaiæ Prophetæ calculo mundasti ignitoi ita mea tua grata miseratione, dignare mundare, ut sanctum Evangelum tuum aigne valeam nuntiare. Per Christum Dominum nostrum. Amen.

Jube, Domine, benedicere.

Dominus sit in corde me et in labiis meis, ut digne et competenter annuntiem Evangelium suum. Amen.

Gospel

DEACON:
Please rise for the reading of the Gospel. The Lord be with you.

ALL:
And with thy spirit.

DEACON:
The Gospel is taken from...

> *As the Deacon announces the Gospel he makes the sign of the cross with the right thumb successively upon the forehead, lips, and heart.*

ALL:
Glory be to Thee, O Lord.

> *Deacon censes the Gospel, then Gospel is read.*

DEACON:
Here endeth the Gospel.

ALL:
Praise be to Thee, O Christ.

DEACON:
Be ye doers of the Word, and not hearers only.

> *Deacon bids people to be seated and censes the Priest, then returns to his position.*
>
> *Homily and Parish announcements are given by Priest or other designated speakers.*

Act of Faith

PRIEST:
Please all join me in the Act of Faith.

ALL: *(while placing right hand over heart)*
I believe in the Ineffable, Unknowable Father, incorruptible Spirit, Lord of All Worlds, Architect of all things visible and all things invisible. Light of Light.

And in the Pure Will of the Father which sends forth the Seed, which is the true Good. Life of Life.

And I believe in the Holy Spirit, Sublime Mother of the Aeons, from whose womb all things are made manifest and to which they shall return. Love of Love.

And I believe in the incarnation of our Lord Jesus Christ, self-generated and alone-begotten; creative essence of the Father; Logos of the Eternal Aeon; the Author of Regeneration, through which we may loosen the bonds of matter and recall our own divine nature, and become one in the fullness of God. Liberty of Liberty.

And I believe in the communion of the Holy Saints and Prophets.

And I believe in the miracle of the Eucharist, whereby the elements of Bread and Wine are transmuted into the Body and Blood of Christ the Logos, giving us Spiritual sustenance, and a visible means of grace.

And I believe in One Universal and Apostolic Church of Light, Life, Love, and Liberty.

A-U-M A-U-M A-U-M

Invocation of the Holy Guardian Angel

PRIEST:
O You, divine Spirit! Spirit of Wisdom, Strength, and Beauty; powerful Being of Light, with whom I desire to accomplish the most intimate union!

I call you! I invoke you! Come to my assistance; guide my steps on the Path of Regeneration during this whole day. Vivify me with that Divine Love that enflames you; send me continually your intellect; give me the weapons that I need in order to vanquish my spiritual enemies.

Guide my steps toward the Truth; I abandon myself to your direction with total confidence.

Divine Logos, that have deigned to send Your Angels to guard and guide us, help me profit from their powerful operations; help me be preserved from any fall during this day.

Let me come to know intimately this Spirit, to which you have particularly entrusted me.

I ask this Grace by Your Holy Blood, that has become the sigil of my reconciliation with you. Amen.

Offertorium

PRIEST: *(removes veil, pall, etc.)*
Come Thou Holy Name of Christ, Name above all names; come power from above and come highest gift;

Thou Knower of the Chosen's Mysteries descend; Thou Who dost share in all noble strivers' struggles; Come! Come Thou Who givest joy to all who are at one with Thee; come and commune with us in this Eucharist which we are about to make in Thy Name, in this Sacrament to which we have assembled at Thy call.

Αεηιουω ιαω αωι ωια ψινωθερ θερνωψ νωψιθερ ζαγουρη παγουρη νεθμομαωθ νεψιομωθ μαραχαχθα θωβαρραβαυ θαρναχαχαν ζοροκοθορα ιεου Σαβαωθ.

Priest elevates paten with both hands.

Blessed are You, O God, who art the Source of all things visible and invisible; the Lord of Light, Life, Love, and Liberty. We offer this bread, grain of the Earth, transformed by human hands, as a token of our terrestrial nature. May it transform us and be the BODY OF CHRIST.

ALL:
Blessed be God forever.

Priest returns paten. Acolyte pours wine and a little water into the Chalice.

PRIEST:
Remembering the psychic and pneumatic natures of the Master Jesus, and our own psychic and pneumatic natures, we mix water with this wine, praying that we may abide in His Consciousness and He in us.

Priest elevates Chalice with both hands.

Blessed are you O God who art the source of all things visible and invisible, the Lord of Light, Life, Love, and Liberty. We offer this wine, fruit of the Earth, transformed by human hands, as a token of our celestial nature. May it transform us and be the BLOOD OF CHRIST.

ALL:
Blessed be God forever.

PRIEST: *(bows)*
In spiritu humilitatis, et in animo contrito suscipiamur ate, Domine: et sic facitat sacrificium nostrum in conspectu tuo hodie, ut placeat tibi, Domine Deus.

Raises hands toward the heavens.

Veni, sanctificator omnipotens, æternæ Deus, et benedic hoc sacrificium tuo sancto nomini præ paratum.

Practice: Liturgy of St. Peter the Gnostic

Second Censing

PRIEST: *(places more incense on charcoal)*
Be thou blessed in the Name of the ✠ Father, and of the ✠ Son, and of the ✠ Holy Spirit.

God the Father, seen of none, God the Co-Eternal Son, and God the Holy Spirit who givest us life, pour forth Thy three-fold power into these our oblations.

As this incense rises before Thee, O Lord, so let our prayer ascend Thy Holy Realms.

Glory be to the Unknown Father ✠ to the Son the Divine Logos ✠ and to the Holy Spirit ✠ our Celestial Mother and Consoler.

Lavabo

PRIEST: *(washes hands)*
O Heavenly Father, as Your rains cleanse and purify the earth, I wash my hands so that they too may be cleansed of the impurities of this world.

Asperges me hyssopo - et mundabor. Lavabis me aqua et super nivem dealbabor!

Orate Fratres

PRIEST:
My Brothers and Sisters, we have built a temple for the distribution of the power of the Logos. Let us prepare these gifts as a channel for its reception. Receive, O Source of all things visible and invisible, this Sacrifice of bread and wine. And may our lives be forever sanctified in Your service by the power of Christ, our Indwelling Lord. Amen.

Prayer Over the Gifts

PRIEST:
Come to the Lord a living stone, rejected by men, but among God's precious elect, you who are yourselves as living stones being built into a pneumatic house, for a holy priesthood, to offer acceptable pneumatic sacrifices to God through Jesus Christ. For it stands in Scripture: Behold, I place in Zion a cornerstone, honored and elect, and the one believing in him shall never be ashamed.

You are an elect race, a kingly priesthood, a holy nation, a people for possession, that you may express the virtues of the one who called you out of darkness into his marvelous light.

May we who partake of this Holy sacrament receive the power of Your Light and Life and be forever joined in Your Holy Wisdom.

ALL:
Amen.

Preface

PRIEST:
Dominum vobiscum.

ALL:
Et cum spiritu tuo.

PRIEST:
Sursum corda.

ALL:
Habemus ad Dominum.

PRIEST:
Gratias agamus Domino Deo nostrum.

ALL:
Dignum et justum est.

> *The following is the Preface of the Apostles; other Prefaces may be utilized according to the season and/or purpose of the Mass. See Abbé Julio's* Liturgical Prayers *for alternate Preface readings, as well as their translations.*

PRIEST:
Vere dignum et justum est, æquum et salutare, te, Domine suppliciter exorare, ut gregem tuum Pastor æterne, non deseras, sed beatos Apostolos continuo protectione custodias. Ut iisdem rectoribus gubernetur, quos

Practice: Liturgy of St. Peter the Gnostic

operis tui vicarios eidem contulisti præesse Pastores. Et ideo cum Angelis et Archangelis, cum Thronis et Dominationibus, cumque omni militia cœlestis, exercitus, hymnum ·gloriæ tuæ canimus, sine fine dicentes:

Trisagion

ALL:
Sanctus, Sanctus, Sanctus, Dominus Deus Sabaoth. Pleni cœli et terra gloria tua.

Benedictus Qui Venit

ALL:
✠ Benedictus qui venit in nomine Domini. Hosanna in excelsis!

Prayer to the Holy Spirit

PRIEST:
O Holy Spirit, Barbelo, Divine Mother of All, may you receive us with your Glorious Embrace. Thou Who hast made Thyself known to us through your emissaries of Light and Life, of Love and Liberty; Your Aeon Sophia and her daughter Zoe, whose heavenly archetypes have been mirrored here on earth in the persons of Eve, Norea, the Virgin Mary, and Mary Magdalene; and known in the celestial realm as the Woman Clothed with the Sun; may You open our ears that we may hear Your voice of Understanding, and open our hearts that we may pour forth Thy Love.

Eucharistic Prayer

PRIEST:
O Most High God, You are holy indeed, and all creation rightly gives You praise. All life, all holiness comes from You through Christ, our Lord, Logos of the Eternal Aeon. From age to age, You reveal Your perennial Wisdom to Your Holy Elect, and call forth those that might partake of Your Divine Mystery.

Joins hands, holding them outstretched over the offerings.

Quam oblationem tu, Deus, in omnibus, quæ sumus ✠ benedictam, ✠ adscriptam, ✠ ratam, rationabliem, acceptabilemque facere digneris: ut nobis ✠ Corpis et ✠ Sanguis fiat dilectitissimi Filii tui Domini nostri Jesu Christi Verbum.

Raises bread slightly.

Following the example set forth by Melchizedek, the eternal High Priest, the Master Jesus, took bread and gave You thanks and praise. He blessed and broke the bread and gave it to His disciples, and said:

Bows slightly.

Accipite, et manducate ex hoc omnes:

HOC EST ENIM CORPUS MEUM

Show the consecrated host to the people, places on paten and genuflects in adoration.

In like manner, when the supper was ended, he took the noble Chalice.

Raises Chalice a little.

Again he gave You thanks and praise, blessed it and gave it to His disciples, and said:

Bows slightly.

Accipite, et bibite ex eo omnes:

HIC EST ENIM CALIX SANGUINIS MEA, NOVI TESTAMENTUM, MYSTERIUM FIDE!

Hæc quoties cumque feceritis, in mei memoriam facietis.

Shows Chalice; returns Chalice and genuflects in adoration. Extends hands.

Practice: Liturgy of St. Peter the Gnostic

Father, we celebrate the memory of Christ, the Eternal Logos, the repairer and our restorer of Gnosis. We, Your people and Your Priests offer unto You, O Most High God, this perfect sacrifice: the bread of Life and the cup of eternal Salvation.

Look with favor on these offerings and accept them as once You accepted the gifts of our Patriarch in the Gnosis, the bread and wine offered by Your priest Melchizidek.

Almighty God, we pray that this sacrifice be borne to thine altar, there to be offered by Him who, as the eternal High Priest, forever offers Himself as the eternal sacrifice.

And as He has ordained that the heavenly sacrifice shall be mirrored here on earth through the ministry of mortals, to the end that Your holy people may be brought more closely into fellowship with You, we do pray for them who serve at this altar, that rightly celebrating the mysteries of the Most Holy Body ✠ and Blood ✠ of the Christ, they may be filled ✠ with Your mighty power and blessing, O Lord of Light, Life, Love, and Liberty.

Litany

The Litany may be shortened or lengthened as required.

PRIEST:
Let us now in due and ancient fashion call upon the powers of the Most High and on all the Holy Ones who were and are and are to come, that united with them we may bravely strive for and ultimately attain to the Gnosis of Light, Life, Love, and Liberty.

All face west and kneel.

PRIEST:
I-A-O

DEACONS:
Shed thy glory upon us.

PRIEST:
Sabaoth

DEACONS:
Shed thy glory upon us.

PRIEST:
Abraxas

DEACONS:
Shed thy glory upon us.

PRIEST:
Sophia

DEACONS:
Shed thy glory upon us.

PRIEST:
All the souls of the Holy Gnostics during the Aeons.

DEACONS:
Hear us and be near us.

PRIEST:
Holy John the Baptist

DEACONS:
Hear us and be near us.

PRIEST:
Holy Apostle Peter

DEACONS:
Hear us and be near us.

PRIEST:
Holy John the Evangelist

DEACONS:
Hear us and be near us.

PRIEST:
Holy Thomas

DEACONS:
Hear us and be near us.

PRIEST:
Holy Philip

DEACONS:
Hear us and be near us.

PRIEST:
Holy Mary Magdalene

DEACONS:
Hear us and be near us.

PRIEST:
Holy Simon Magus

DEACONS:
Hear us and be near us.

PRIEST:
Holy Dositheus

DEACONS:
Hear us and be near us.

PRIEST:
Holy Menander

DEACONS:
Hear us and be near us.

PRIEST:
Holy Saturninus

DEACONS:
Hear us and be near us.

PRIEST:
Holy Basilides

DEACONS:
Hear us and be near us.

Practice: Liturgy of St. Peter the Gnostic

PRIEST:
Holy Valentinus

DEACONS:
Hear us and be near us.

PRIEST:
Holy Bardaisan

DEACONS:
Hear us and be near us.

PRIEST:
Holy Clement of Alexandria

DEACONS:
Hear us and be near us.

PRIEST:
Holy Origen

DEACONS:
Hear us and be near us.

PRIEST:
Holy Hypatia

DEACONS:
Hear us and be near us.

PRIEST:
Holy Esclaremonde & all Cathar martyrs

DEACONS:
Hear us and be near us.

PRIEST:
Holy Prophet Joachim

DEACONS:
Hear us and be near us.

PRIEST:
Holy Jacque de Molay & all Blessed Templars

DEACONS:
Hear us and be near us.

PRIEST:
Holy Martines de Pasqually

DEACONS:
Hear us and be near us.

PRIEST:
Holy Louis-Claude de Saint-Martin

DEACONS:
Hear us and be near us.

PRIEST:
Holy Jean-Baptiste Willermoz

DEACONS:
Hear us and be near us.

PRIEST:
Holy Bernard Raymond Fabré-Palaprat

DEACONS:
Hear us and be near us.

PRIEST:
Holy Marie, Countess of Caithness, Duchess of Pomar

DEACONS:
Hear us and be near us.

PRIEST:
Holy Tau Valentin II

DEACONS:
Hear us and be near us.

PRIEST:
Holy Mar Timotheos

DEACONS:
Hear us and be near us.

PRIEST:
Holy Jean Sempé

DEACONS:
Hear us and be near us.

PRIEST:
Holy Abbe Julio

DEACONS:
Hear us and be near us.

PRIEST:
Holy Tau Jean II

DEACONS:
Hear us and be near us.

PRIEST:
Holy Tau Harmonius

DEACONS:
Hear us and be near us.

PRIEST:
Holy Tau Jean III

DEACONS:
Hear us and be near us.

PRIEST:
Holy Tau Ogdoade Orfeo I

DEACONS:
Hear us and be near us.

PRIEST:
Holy Tau Ogdoad Orfeo III

DEACONS:
Hear us and be near us.

PRIEST:
Holy Tau Charles

DEACONS:
Hear us and be near us.

PRIEST:
Holy Tau Johannes XIII

DEACONS:
Hear us and be near us.

PRIEST:
Holy Tau Iohannes Harmonius

DEACONS:
Hear us and be near us.

Practice: Liturgy of St. Peter the Gnostic

PRIEST:
All the Apostles, Prophets, Bishops, Priests & Martyrs of the Gnosis.

DEACONS:
Hear us and be near us, now and forever.

Kyrie

PRIEST:
Kyrie Eleison

ALL:
Kyrie Eleison

PRIEST:
Christe Eleison

ALL:
Christe Eleison

PRIEST & ALL:
Kyrie Eleison

PRIEST:
Welcome into Your kingdom, O Lord, our departed brothers and sisters in the Gnosis.

Mother and Father united as one;
Wisdom and Strength through Your eternal Son;
We are divided for Love's sake;
That through our union we may make
Ourselves as symbols of Heaven on Earth;
In life, in death, and in rebirth!

O Christ our Lord who gives us all these gifts, bless them and make them holy.

Pater Noster

PRIEST:
Let us pray with confidence to the Father in the words the Master Jesus gave us.

ALL:
Our Father who art in Heaven, hallowed be Thy Name;
Thy kingdom come, Thy will be done,
On Earth as it is in Heaven.
Give us this day, our daily bread,
And forgive us our debts, as we have also forgiven our debtors.
And leave us not in temptation, but deliver us from evil,
For Thine is the Kingdom, and the Power, and the Glory, forever and ever. Amen.

PRIEST: *(with hands extended)*
Deliver us Lord from the evil of ignorance, and grant us peace, love, and light in our day.

Breaking of the Bread

PRIEST:
O Divine Light, You show Yourself this day upon countless altars and yet are one and indivisible. In token of Thy great Sacrifice, we rend (break bread) this, Thy Holy Body, that we may be as Thou art.
Through this ancient and sacred tradition, all Heaven and Earth are united in Thy Consciouness, Thy Love, and Thy Will. And as the One became many, only to restore all to the Pleroma, so too, in the breaking of this bread, we are one with Thee, as Thou art one with the Father.
Breaks off small piece of bread from the left half, makes sign of the cross over the Chalice, and places piece in Chalice; then blo1,1s three crosses of air over the Chalice.
Hæc commixtio et consecratio Corporis et Sanguinis Domini nostri Jesu Christi fiat accipientibus nobis in vitam æternam. Amen.

Intones...

Through Him, and with Him, and in Him;
In the Unity of the Holy Spirit;
All glory and honor are Yours Almighty Father,
Forever and ever.

ALL: *(intone)*
Amen.

Practice: Liturgy of St. Peter the Gnostic

PRIEST:

Let us pray. Adoration be to Thee, O Most High God, Father of all Fatherhood, and to Thee, O Mother of all, who in the incarnation of Your Logos have mystically provided us with the Sacrament of His Body and Blood, that by partaking of this Mystery, we may reunite within ourselves the fragments of Your Divinity dispersed throughout the cosmos. Holy, Holy, Holy, are You, the Father and Mother of the Treasury of the Light, now and unto the countless ages. Amen.

Theurgic Consecration

Priest takes Dagger, faces East, and draws the letter YOD in the air with Dagger as it is pronounced, then intones the Holy Name, thus:

By the virtue of י I call forth the power of IAO to join in this Holy Sacrifice.

Priest travels to the South via the North and West, that is, by walking 270° counterclockwise, draws the letter HE, and intones the Holy Name, thus:

By the virtue of ה I call forth the power of SABAOTH to join in this Holy Sacrifice.

Priest continues 270° counterclockwise to the West, draws the letter VAV, and intones the Holy Name, thus:

By the virue of ו I call forth the power of ABRAXAS to join in this Holy Sacrifice.

Priest continues 270° to the North, draws the letter HE, and intones the Holy Name, thus:

By the virtue of ה I call forth the power of SOPHIA to join in this Holy Sacrifice.

Priest travels 270° counterclockwise again to return to the East for the third complete circuit. He faces the Eucharistic Altar, and with arms outstretched and holding the Dagger in the right hand...

The Son would not be the Father without wearing the Father's Name. So by the Power of the Holy Tetragrammaton, and by the virtue of the Tri-Unity of the Holy Letter ש *(draws Hebrew letter with Dagger in the air above Chalice)*, I call forth the power of the Author of Regeneration, the Repairer of Souls, the Destroyer of Death...

Intones while slowly lowering Dagger with both hands into Chalice.

יהשוה to pour forth Thy powers into this Holy Sacrifice and transmute these elements of bread and wine into the Divine Body and Blood of the Logos.

Makes three crosses in Chalice with Dagger. Then, arms outstretched, palms up, chants...

Et habemus firmiorem propheticum sermonem, cui bene factis attendentes quasi lucernæ lucenti in caliginoso loco, donec dies illucescat, et Lucifer oriatur in cordibus vestris.

Communion

PRIEST: *(Elevating the Body and Blood)*
Behold the Divine Light which lighteth every man that cometh into the world. May the communion of these Holy Mysteries be to the regeneration of both soul and body. Let us draw nigh and receive this most Holy Sacrament.

After the communion has been administered...

First Ablution

PRIEST: *(Pours a little wine & water into Chalice)*
Quod ore sumpsimus. Domine, pura mente capiamus: et de munere temporali fiat nobis remedium sempiternum.

Drinks.

Second Ablution

PRIEST: *(Joins thumbs & forefingers over the Chalice & has Acolyte or other assistant pour some water only over them into the Chalice)*
Corpus tuum, Domine, quod sumpsi, et Sanguis quern potavi, adhæreat visceribus meis: et præsta, ut in me non remaneat sclerum macula, quern pura et sancta refecerunt sacramenta. Qui vivis et regnas in sæcula sæculorum. Amen.

Drinks.

Practice: Liturgy of St. Peter the Gnostic

Post Eucharistic Prayer

ALL:

May we, who in this Holy Mystery have entered into the all-pervading strength and love of Christ our Indwelling Lord, be guided by the Divine Presence into the fullness of Truth, that we may attain to that mount of vision whereon we may see the boundless light unveiled in the wholeness of its Divine Glory. Amen.

Dismissal

PRIEST:

Be strong, for these mysteries have been given to you so that you might know through a revelation that the one they crucified is the firstborn, the abode of demons, the stone vessel in which they live, the man of Elohim, the man of the cross, who is under the law. But the one who is standing near him is the living Savior, who was in him at first, and was arrested but set free. He is laughing at their lack of perception, knowing that they were born blind. The one capable of suffering must remain, since the body is the substitute, but what was set free was the bodiless body, the Spirit of Thought filled with radiant light.

Present what you have seen to those who are strangers, who are not of this aeon. For there will be no grace among those who are not immortal, but only among those elect because of their immortal nature, which has shown it can receive the one who gives in abundance.

For this reason it is said, Whoever has will be given more, and shall have it abundantly. But whoever has not - that is to say the man of this aeon who completely is as one who is dead, who derives from creation and procreation, who thinks he can lay hold of someone else of immortal nature when such a person appears - this will be taken away from that person and added to whatever exists.

So be courageous and fear nothing. For יהשורה shall be with you, that none of your enemies may prevail over you. May grace and peace be multiplied to you in the knowledge of God and our Lord יהשורה.

Pax Vobis.

ALL:

Et cum spiritu tuo.

PRIEST:

Ite missa est.

ALL:

Deo gratias.

Theurgical Operations of the ACP

An Introduction to the Theurgic Art

Theurgy, like prayer, is a means of obtaining healing, benedictions, intercession, and protection. The principal difference between theurgy and prayer, is that while prayer is mainly focused inwardly, and relies upon personal attunement with God, theurgy, though incorporating prayer and mystical attunement, invokes helpful spirits, which are commanded by the theurgic operator to perform certain tasks that are complementary to their character.

The Theurgic Art is similar, in some ways to what is commonly called "ceremonial magic." However, theurgic invocation is much safer, and more reliable, generally speaking, than magical evocation. Both invocation and evocation concern the calling forth of spiritual powers or entities. However, invocation calls forth the powers to be present within the operator's direct working environment, or even within his or her self at times. On the other hand, evocation calls forth the powers to a space outside the protected working environment of the operator. Theurgy deals with beneficent spirits that, when properly invoked, serve the theurgists in accordance with its nature; joyfully, and to the glory of God. Many of the spirits dealt with in magical evocation, however, are of a contrary nature, and must be compelled through the use of violent exorcisms. Because of these spirits' volatile nature, the magical operator must perform extensive purifications and protection rites, and take every possible precaution in order to prevent physical or psychological harm. The ACP Formula for Theurgic Operations is designed for *invocative* operations, and should not be used for operations which require *evocation*. Our advanced students should consult the Maître Cohen lectures for instructions in evocation.

The Theurgical Operations of the Apostolic Church of the Pleroma are based upon the seventy-two spirits of the Shemhamphorasch. The names of these spirits are derived from a special arrangement of the Hebrew letters which compose the three verses of Exodus 14:19-21. Each of the seventy-two names are associated with certain spiritual, astrological, and practical attributes, as well as a Psalm that traditionally accompanies each name.

In order to utilize this system, the operator of the Theurgic Art should first become thoroughly familiarized with the Formula for Theurgic Operations. This formula is based upon the structure of the Mass, but is tailored specifically for theurgic invocation. After the Formula is a list of the Theurgic Operations. In this list, each operation is followed by a number or numbers. These numbers correspond to the Spirit that is to be invoked for that operation. You will notice that many of the Operations list multiple Spirits. This is due to the unique qualities and characteristics of each Spirit, which may overlap one another at times. When operations list multiple numbers, it does not mean that all of those Spirits should be called upon. Rather, the Operator should determine which Spirit is best suited for the Operation at hand. For example, it is beneficial to perform these Operations on the day and hour that are most conducive and complementary to the nature of the particular Spirit as determined by its zodiacal attributes. If, however, there is a pressing need, such as an emergency healing or an urgent need for protection, it is acceptable to perform the Operation during a

Practice: Theurgical Operations

less-than-ideal time, but its efficacy may be weakened, and if possible it should be repeated at a more suitable time. It is not beneficial, however, to attempt the invocation of multiple Spirits during the same Operation.

The Theurgic Operations may be performed by a single person or in a group. If performed as group work, though, there is still only a single Operator. The Operator should, at the very least, have been ordained into the Holy Order of Exorcist, and have received the Martinist degree of Initiate. Ideally, the Operator should be ordained into the Diaconate, and should be a Martinist S::: I:::. These levels of ordination and initiation are not *requirements*, per se. A theurgical operation is not a Sacrament, so it does not depend upon the sacerdotal powers conferred through the priesthood. Rather, the efficacy of the operator of High Theurgy depends solely upon one's personal inner development. While the Sacraments are effected under the principle of *ex opere operato*, or "from the work done," Theurgy is accomplished under the principle of *ex opere operantis*, or "from the work of the one working." In *The Magic of Catholicism*, Brother A.D.A. writes: "This means that the efficacy of the work is determined by the virtue and merit of the operator." Therefore, even though ecclesiastical and initiatic empowerments can be extremely helpful to the practicing theurgist, they in no way guarantee the efficacy of the work. This is accomplished only through a deep knowledge and inner connection to the work. In addition, even though the Spirits of the Shemhamphorasch are of a beneficent nature, they are still incredibly powerful forces, and the Operator should thoroughly prepare oneself beforehand through prayer, meditation, and abstinence from any excessive indulgence. When properly executed, these theurgic operations will prove to be most efficacious in providing prompt and powerful aid.

We also should make a brief comment on the 72 names and their relationship to the zodiac, the calendar year, and Jesus Christ. You will notice that while each name has a three-letter root, the name itself is of five letters. Notice, also, that each name represents 5° of the zodiac circle, for a total of 360° (72 x 5°). However, our calendar year is actually 365 days, instead of a perfect 360. The ancients rectified this by maintaining a 360-day year, and acknowledging five "intercalary days"; that is, days that lie outside the calendar year proper. It will serve us well to make a similar observance. To the ancient Egyptians, the five intercalary days represented their five principal deities. The intercalary days of the Shemhamphorasch are March 15-19; at the end of Pisces in the calendar year, but at the beginning of Pisces in the Precessional year (which moves backwards through the zodiac). In our case, therefore, the "73rd" pentad is represented by Christ himself, the Logos and World-Teacher of the Age of Pisces. In the five letters of the name of Jesus, יהשוה [YHShVH], we have the supreme Pentagrammaton. And just as there are five days that lie outside the calendar year, Jesus Christ is ever-present among us, yet exists outside space-time itself. Truly, the Mystery of Christ is the Master-Key to the Theurgic Operations, for it is in His Name that the Spirits submit to us. Thus, we also see that the Holy Liturgy, specifically the rite of the Eucharist, is in fact the Supreme Theurgic Operation.

Formula for the Consecration of Sanctuary Items

In the following formulas, as well as within the Theurgical Rite and the Liturgy, the presence of a "✶" or "✠" in the text indicates that the Operator is to make with his or her hand (unless otherwise indicated) a Banishing Pentagram of Earth or Sign of the Cross respectively.

All Sanctuary items, for both the Eucharistic celebration and Theurgic Operations, should be consecrated by a priest or bishop. However, the following formula may be used by all clergy for the blessing and consecration of ritual items in your personal Sanctum, or when a priest or bishop is unavailable. The following Invocations, Blessings, and Consecrations are derived largely from the works of Mouni Sadhu, Robert Ambelain, and other traditional sources.

For the preparation of Holy Oil, combine 2 parts finely powdered Cinnamon, 1 part Myrrh, and ½ part Galanga Root into 2 parts Virgin Olive Oil. The preparation should be sealed and left to sit for six months, after which it may be strained and bottled for use. (Alternatively, the respective extracts or oils may be mixed to use immediately.)

The formula for the standard liturgical incense, as given elsewhere, is 2 parts Frankincense, 1 part Myrrh, and ½ part Sumatran Benzoin. This formula will be sufficient for most Theurgical operations. However, if you would like to customize your incense for a particular operation, consult the following table of Planetary Correspondences:

- Sun - Frankincense
- Moon - Myrrh
- Mars - Galbanum
- Jupiter - Siamese Benzoin
- Mercury - Sumatran Benzoin
- Venus - Sandalwood
- Saturn - Storax

The first step in any Blessing or Consecration is a General Invocational Blessing, as follows:

"Our help is in the Name of the Lord, who created the Holy Aeons of Light. Lord, hear my prayer, and let my cry ascend to thee!"

"O God, in whose light all our actions and even the smallest thoughts are sanctified! We beseech Thee to extend Thy blessing upon us, according to Thy will and Thy law, who alone, in Thy goodness, can grant it. Through the invocation of Thy Most Holy Name, grant health of body, salvation of soul, and everything necessary for this life, which we beseech with devotion and faith. Through our Lord Jesus, Christos, Soter, Logos. Amen!"

The next step is to exorcize and bless the Water that will be used for the consecration of items. You must first bless the Salt, thus:

"I exorcize thee ✣, creature of Salt, through the Living ✠ God, through the True ✠ God, through the Holy ✠ God, who ordered that thou will be thrown into water by Elisha the prophet, in order to cure the sterility of water; in order that thou bring to all who partake of thee, health of body and soul, and in order that from every place where thou may be spread, all illusion and evil will disappear along with the maliciousness or subterfuge of every devil. I also conjure every impure spirit in the name of Him, who will come to judge the living and the dead, annihilating the world by fire. Amen."

"Ineffable Light, Lord my God, by Your Omnipotent Logos, bless this Salt. Ineffable Light, Lord my God, by Your Omnipotent Logos, bless this Salt. Ineffable Light, Lord my God, by Your Omnipotent Logos, bless this Salt!"

"Deign to grant ✠ Blessing and ✠ Sanctifying of this creature of Salt, which Thou hast created for human use; so that all who will use it will receive salvation of soul and health of body, and everything touched by Thee will be purified from all uncleanliness and the invasion of the evil spirit. Through our Lord Jesus, Christos, Soter, Logos. Amen!"

We now continue with the Blessing of the Water:

"I exorcize thee ✣, creature of water, in the Name of ✠ God the Unknown Father, ✠ Son, redeeming and ever-coming Logos, and the virtue of the ✠ Holy Spirit, our Celestial Mother and Consoler, in order that thou become exorcized and blessed water, which will disperse all the enemy's forces and in order that thou will extract and eradicate the enemy himself, together with his apostate angels. Through our Lord Jesus, Christos, Soter, Logos. Amen."

"Ineffable Light, Lord my God, by Your Omnipotent Logos, bless this Water. Ineffable Light, Lord my God, by Your Omnipotent Logos, bless this Water. Ineffable Light, Lord my God, by Your Omnipotent Logos, bless this Water!"

"My God, who has established for the benefit of human beings the greatest sacraments with the substance of water, be pleased with our prayers and with this element of Water, which must serve for purification; shed the boon the Thy ✠ Blessing so that Thy creature used in Thy Mysteries, will serve through divine Grace, for defeating the demons, and the expulsion of sickness; let every place where it may be sprinkled such as the dwellings of the faithful and everywhere else, become free from all impurity and harmful matter. May there never remain any pest or contamination of the air, and let all the hidden snares of the enemy be dispersed."

"And if there is anything which could harm the health or peace of the inhabitants of these places, let the sprinkling with this water dissipate all these influences. Let all health asked for and invoked in Thy Holy Name remain beyond the reach of all attacks. Through our Lord Jesus, Christos, Soter, Logos. Amen."

Sprinkle the Blessed Salt into the Water in the form of a cross three times, and say:

"May this mixture of Salt and Water become united as One, in the Name of the ✠ Father, and ✠ Son, and ✠ Holy Spirit. Amen."

Blow three times in the form of a cross upon the Saline Water ✠ ✠ ✠.

"By the Power of the Holy Trinity, let this mixture of water and salt be consecrated through our Lord Jesus, Christos, Soter, Logos. Amen."

The Blessing of the Incense is a simple invocation as found in the "Censing of the Altar" section of the Liturgy. We will repeat it here, however, for the sake of convenience:

"Creature of incense, be thou blessed in the Name of the ✠ Father, and of the ✠ Son, and of the ✠ Holy Spirit. Amen."

No exorcism is necessary for the incense, as it is purified by the fire itself. For all other items, such as the Altar Cloth, Candles, Oil, Dagger, Sword, or any other ritual item, you may use the following simple rite. Remember to have your Blessed Water and Incense on hand, and to always begin with the General Invocational Blessing.

Then continue with this Blessing of a Special Item:

"Lord the Omnipotent, look on Thy people who are praying to Thee, and deign to look with a gracious eye upon our service at this moment, and deign to ✠ Purify, ✠ Bless, and ✠ Sanctify this (name of item), that through Thy gracious will, it may become a symbol of our good intentions and Your righteousness."

"Ineffable Light, Lord my God, by Your Omnipotent Logos, bless this (name of item)." *(Recite three times.)*

"Through our Lord Jesus, Christos, Soter, Logos. Amen."

Sprinkle item three times with Blessed Water; cense item three times each: center, left, and right, and make the sign of the cross over item three times.

One more consecration that may be useful is the Consecration of a Photograph or Symbolic Representation of a Patient. This type of item is especially useful when performing a Theurgic Operation for an individual who is not present. As usual, begin with the General Invocational Blessing, then:

"Lord the Omnipotent, deign to look down unto this image of Your Servant (name of patient), and bless it so that it constitutes a bond between him/her and me, and it symbolizes his/her presence here."

"Bless, Lord, this image, so that it becomes a true and real symbol of the presence of Your represented Servant in front of me. Let every expression of my logos to this image be transferred to Your represented Servant, and let every Operation of me towards him/her be thus facilitated."

"Ineffable Light, Lord my God, by Your Omnipotent Logos, bless this image." *(Recite three times.)*

"Through our Lord Jesus, Christos, Soter, Logos. Amen."

Practice: Theurgical Operations

Sprinkle image three times with Blessed Water; cense image three times each: center, left, right; make sign of cross three times over image; then place your hands in the form of an open triangle, and blow through unto the image to establish the link between your logos and that of the recipient or patient.

Before beginning any operation to invoke one of the 72 Spirits, you should create and consecrate a talisman to represent the Spirit. This is traditionally drawn on virgin parchment, but any plain, unlined paper that has not been used for any other purpose may suffice. Upon a square piece of this paper, draw in black ink a pentagram enclosed by a double circle. In the center of the pentagram, in red ink, draw the appropriate seal. Next, draw the five-lettered name of the Spirit (in Hebrew), also in red ink, in the points of the pentagram, beginning in the upper-right point, and going around counter-clockwise (since Hebrew is written from right to left). Still using your red ink, write the Latin version of the associated Psalm inside the double circle (though you may pronounce the English during the actual operation). Finally, in the spaces between the points of the pentagram, you may draw the symbols for the various alchemical and astrological attributes (i.e. Element, Essential, Planetary Ruler, Zodiac sign) in black or in the proper corresponding colors if you know them. In addition to these four attributes, you may inscribe in the fifth space a unique sigil of your own design that represents you as the operator. Here is an example of what the talisman for the 1st Spirit – Vehuiah – might look like:

Once your parchment is constructed, you must consecrate it before using it in an Operation. The consecration of the pentacle should take place at a day and hour appropriate to the nature of the Spirit. For the consecration you should prepare your altar with a red altar cloth, upon which should rest a thurible burning appropriate incense in the North-West corner, a dish of consecrated Saline Water in the South-West corner, and a burning consecrated Taper in the East. In the center of the altar should be the Martinist Pantacle. Place the parchment on the center of the Pantacle. Hold a burning taper in your hand (not the one on the Altar), stand before the Altar facing East, and recite the following:

"Thus said Adonai, The heaven is my throne, and the earth my footstool: where is the house that ye build unto me? And where is the place of my rest? For all those things hath mine hand made. Thus said Adonai: I was glad also when they said unto me, Let us go into the house of the Lord. Our feet shall stand within thy gates, O Jerusalem. Jerusalem is builded as a city that is compact together, Peace be within thy walls, and prosperity within thy palaces. For except Adonai build the house, they labor in vain that build it; except Adonai keep the city, the watchman waketh but in vain."

"Father of Power and Greatness, Being of Beings, Almighty Sanctifier, who created all things from Nothing, despise not Thy servant, but let it please Thee to purify, consecrate, and sanctify this place dedicated to Thy service; command Thy angel *(name of Spirit)* to descend, reside, and remain for Thy Glory and Service. Through our Lord Jesus, Christos, Soter, Logos. Amen."

Next, sprinkle the parchment with the consecrated Water while reading Psalms 98 and 102. Finally, place the burning taper (the one you're holding) on the parchment and leave it there while you focus your attention on the flame for several minutes. The sigil is now activated and may be utilized in an Operation.

Practice: Theurgical Operations

Formula for Theurgic Operations

The Operation proper should be conducted at a day and hour conducive to the properties of the Spirit invoked. Concerning the day, there are a number of specific dates throughout the year that are particularly efficacious to each Spirit. Each Spirit governs 5 degrees of the zodiac, beginning with the Spring Equinox. Therefore, for example, the first Spirit, Vehuiah, governs approximately the first five days in Spring (slightly more actually, since 1° equals about 24 hours, 20 minutes). There are also five days ruled by this Spirit throughout the year. These days are spaced evenly throughout the year, so that if you were to draw out a calendar in the shape of a circle and draw a line between the five days, it would form a nearly perfect pentagram (not entirely perfect because of the intercalary days). If none of these days are near to when the Operation must be performed (such as in the case of a pressing need for healing), then at the very least it should be performed on the day of the week corresponding astrologically. Thus, in our example of Vehuiah, being under the influence of Mars, it would be appropriate to invoke him on a Tuesday. Concerning the hour of invocation, the most propitious time for the Spirit in our example is at precisely 12:00 midnight until 12:20 AM. If the stated time is not possible, then an hour should be chosen that best corresponds to the Spirit's attributes.

During the Operation, the parchment is placed upon the Martinist Pantacle in the center of the Altar, as in the Consecration of the Parchment. Concerning the Temple arrangement for the Theurgic Operations, it should be similar to that of the Liturgical Celebration. However, certain items that are particular to the Eucharist may be absent, such as the Chalice, Water & Wine cruets, etc. However, if any of these elements correlate to the Elemental attributes of the Spirit with which you are working, then you may wish to have them present as a symbolic representation. For example, the Chalice could be present during an Operation involving a Spirit with a Water attribute. You may use any items which appropriately represent the Elemental or Alchemical Essential properties of the particular Spirit. A parchment may be created to represent the Recipient of the aid of the Theurgic Operation if that person is not present and if no photograph is available (a photograph being preferable). Such an item should be consecrated as instructed in the "Formula for the Consecration of Sanctuary Items" section above.

Also, make sure that all ritual items have been properly consecrated and dedicated for their intended use. If the items have already been consecrated for Liturgical use, they do not need to be re-consecrated for Theurgic use, since, as we have already stated, the Eucharistic Rite is itself the highest of Theurgical Operations.

The Operations contained herein should suffice for nearly every instance. However, there are a number of additional operations approved for clergy use by the Patriarchate. These include certain privately distributed operations (such as the Élus-Cohen operations distributed by the Christian Knights of Saint-Martin), as well as any of the operations found in the following works:

- *Sacramentaire de la Rose✠Croix* by Robert Ambelain
- *Grand Marvelous Secrets* by Abbé Julio
- *Liturgical Prayers* by Abbé Julio
- *The Secret Book of Grand Exorcisms and Benedictions* by Abbé Julio
- *An Anthology of Theurgic Operations of the Rose✠Croix of the* Orient by Demetrius Polychronis
- *Theurgy* by Mouni Sadhu

The above-mentioned works contain numerous operations that may be used as instructed in each work, or that may be adapted for use within the Theurgic Formula of the ACP.

Before the Operation begins, perform the Preliminary Rites as found in the Liturgical celebration, then proceed:

OPERATOR:
In the Name of the Lord of All Worlds!

OPERATOR & ASSISTANTS:
I-A-O
I-A-UM
A-U-M

OPERATOR: *(Lights candle while reciting...)*
O Pure Light! Symbol of Divine Essence! Light of the Empyrean Realm! Make thy radiant & pure fire purge and sanctify this, thy holy altar, and my lips for the words that we are to proclaim for the greater glory of the Eternal. Amen.

As these flames lighten our way in the earthly realm, so are the great Luminaries of the Aeons ever present to illumine and enlighten our spiritual path. Come, join us now, O great Luminaries; emissaries of the Most High!

HARMOZEL OROIAEL DAVEITHAI ELELETH

Come now and witness as we praise the Most High, and petition the aid of His holy angels.

Invocation of the Archangels

OPERATOR & ASSISTANTS: *(using the forms as previously instructed)*
Ateh. Malkuth. Ve'Geburah. Ve'Gedulah. Le Olam. A-U-M

In the Name of יהוה, we invoke thee, Archangel of the East, RAPHAEL!
In the Name of אדני, we invoke thee, Archangel of the South, MICHAEL!
In the Name of אהיה, we invoke thee, Archangel of the West, GABRIEL!
In the Name of אגלא, we invoke thee, Archangel of the North, AURIEL!
Ateh. Malkuth. Ve'Geburah. Ve'Gedulah. Le Olam.
A-U-M

Practice: Theurgical Operations

Asperges

OPERATOR: *(sprinkles blessed water while reciting...)*
Purify us, O Lord, that in Thy Power we may worthily perform the Great Work. In Thy strength, OIndwelling Lord, do we expel all forces of darkness from this, Thy Holy Altar and Sanctuary, and from this house and our own human temples wherein we worship Thee; and we pray Thee Heavenly Father, that Thou wilt command the Rulers of the Four Regions, your mighty Archangels, Lords of the Air, Water, Fire, and Earth, to build for us a Spiritual Temple through which Thy Strength and Blessing may be poured forth upon Thy people. Through Christ our Indwelling Lord.

OPERATOR & ASSISTANTS:
So Mote It Be!

Prayer

OPERATOR:
When we enter herein with all humility, let God the Almighty One enter into this Sanctuary of the Gnosis by the entrance of an eternal happiness, of a Divine prosperity, of a perfect joy, of an abundant charity, and of an eternal salutation. Let all the demons fly from this place, especially those who are opposed unto this work, and let the Angels of Peace assist and protect this Sanctuary, from which let discord and strife fly and depart. Magnify and extend upon us, O Lord, Thy most Holy Name, and bless our conversation and our assembly. Sanctify, O Lord our God, our humble entry herein, Thou the Blessed and Holy One of the Eternal Ages! Amen.

I beseech Thee, O Lord God, the All Powerful and the All Merciful, that Thou wilt deign to bless this Sanctuary, and all this place, and all those who are herein, and that Thou wilt grant unto us, who serve Thee, and rehearse nothing but the wonders of Thy Law, a good Angel for our Guardian; remove from us every adverse power; preserve us from evil and from trouble; grant, O Lord, that we may rest in this place in all safety, through Thee,) Lord, Who livest and reignest unto the Ages of the Ages. Amen.

Censing of the Altar

OPERATOR: *(Puts incense into thurible and blesses it...)*
Creature of incense, be thou blessed in the Name of the ✠ Father, and of the ✠ Son, and of the ✠ Holy Spirit. Priest censes the alter center, left, right.

Purify this place, O Divine and Eternal One, and make of us one mystical Body, growing into the Pleroma of your Gnosis. Make us a Spiritual Temple of living stones, through which your infinite Light may flow. Let the Holy Angels of Light join with us, and assist us in this act of divine transformation. We unite now to celebrate, knowing that we all come from the Original Light, which is the Source of everything visible and invisible. Amen.

Confiteor

OPERATOR & ASSISTANTS:
O Lord, that which is mortal cometh not into a body immortal; but that which is immortal cometh into that which is mortal. Thou art Thou, all that is made, and all that is not made. Thou art all things, and there is nothing else Thou art not. I beseech Thee that I may never err from the Knowledge of Thee. For Thou art what I am, Thou art what I do, Thou art what I say. Amen.

OPERATOR:
O Lord All Powerful, Eternal God and Father of ALL, shed upon me the Divine Influence of Thy Mercy, for I am Thy Creature. I beseech Thee to defend me from mine enemies, and to confirm in me true and steadfast faith. O Lord, I commit my Body and my Soul unto Thee, seeing I put my trust in none beside Thee; it is on Thee alone that I rely. O Lord my God aid me. O Lord hear me in the day and hour wherein I shall invoke Thee. I pray Thee by Thy Mercy not to put me into oblivion, nor to remove me from Thee. O Lord be Thou my succor, Thou Who art the God of my salvation. O Lord make me a new heart according unto Thy loving Kindness. These, O Lord, are the gifts which I await from Thee, O my God and my Master, Thou who livest and reignest unto the Ages of the Ages. Amen.

O Lord God the All Powerful One, who hast formed unto Thyself great and Ineffable Wisdom, and Co-Eternal with Thyself before the countless Ages; Thou Who before the birth of Time hast created the Aeons, and the things that they contain; Thou who hast vivified all things by Thy Holy Breath, I praise Thee, I bless Thee, I adore Thee, and I glorify Thee. Be Thou propitious unto me who am but a miserable sinner, and despise me not; save me and succor me, even me that work of Thine hands. I conjure and entreat Thee by Thy Holy Name to banish from my Spirit the darkness of Ignorance, and to enlighten me with the Fire of Thy Wisdom; take away from me all evil desires, and let not my speech be as that of the foolish. O Thou, God the Living One, whose Glory, Honor, and Kingdom shall extend unto the Ages of the Ages. Through our Lord Jesus, Christos, Soter, Logos. Amen.

Invocation of the Holy Guardian Angel

OPERATOR:
O You, divine Spirit! Spirit of Wisdom, Strength, and Beauty; powerful Being of Light, with whom I desire to accomplish the most intimate union!

I call you! I invoke you! Come to my assistance; guide my steps on the Path of Regeneration during this whole day. Vivify me with that Divine Love that enflames you; send me continually your intellect; give me the weapons that I need in order to vanquish my spiritual enemies.

Guide my steps toward the Truth; I abandon myself to your direction with total confidence.

Divine Logos, that have deigned to send Your Angles to guard and guide us, help me profit from their powerful operations; help me be preserved from any fall during this day.

Let me come to know intimately this Spirit, to which you have particularly entrusted me.

I ask this Grace by Your Holy Blood, that has become the sigil of my reconciliation with you. Amen.

Invocation of the Barbarous Names

OPERATOR & ASSISTANTS:
Αεηιουω ιαω αωι ωια ψινωθερ θερνωψ νωψιθερ ζαγουρη παγουρη νεθμομαωθ νεψιομωθ μαραχαχθα θωβαρραβαυ θαρναχαχαν ζοροκοθορα ιεου Σαβαωθ.

Operation of the Art

OPERATOR:
I conjure thee in the name of the Twenty-Four Elders, in the name of the Nine Choirs to which you belong, O *(name of Spirit)*! I conjure thee in the name of Angles, Archangels, Thrones, Dominions, Powers, Virtues, Cherubim and Seraphim! In the name of the Four Mysterious Powers which carry the Throne of the Most High, and who have eyes before and behind; in the name of the all that contributes to our Regeneration.

I conjure thee, Spirit of Light, in the Name of the Living God, the True God, the Holy God! In the name of the Seven Mysterious Candlesticks in the right hand of God! In the name of the Seven Churches of Asia! In the name of Ephesus, Smyrna, Pergamum, Thyatira, Sardis, Philadelphia, and Laodicea.

I conjure thee by Heaven and Earth, by Sun and Moon, by Day and Night; by all that exists and all the Virtues therein encompassed; by the Four Primordial Elements; by all which may be said or thought by the Sovereign Creator, through His Supreme Will and the Celestial Court in which he reigns; through Him who has produced all from Nothing; through the Glorious Phalanxes to which you belong; through the Saints; through all those who night and day, endlessly cry: "Holy, Holy, Holy, Lord God of Hosts. Heaven and Earth are full of Thy Glory. Glory be to Thee, O Lord Most High."

I conjure thee, Illuminating Intelligence, Messenger of Light! I conjure thee in the name of Auriel, Guardian of the North! I conjure thee in the name of Michael, Guardian of the South! I conjure thee in the name of Raphael, Guardian of the East! I conjure thee in the name of Gabriel, Guardian of the West! I conjure thee, O Divine Messenger, by the Seven Golden Candlesticks, which burn before the Altar of God; by the Company of the Blessed who follow the footsteps of the Immaculate Lamb! I conjure thee, O Celestial *(name of Spirit)* in the name of all the Saints whom God has chosen from and before the Creation of the World, because of their merits, which are agreeable to God! I conjure thee, O Invisible yet Immanent Power, and I conjure thee through the Redoubtable Power of the Lord's Name; through the Glory of His Divine Name, manifested in the World, where the most beautiful attributes of God find expression.

I conjure and implore thee, O *(name of Spirit)* in the Name of these Attributes! May you quit the Celestial Abode at the call of their syllables! May you deign, O Illuminating Power, when they are invoked, to descend to this place, there to instruct thine Unworthy Servant. I conjure thee in the name of Adonai Melech, Master of the Realm of Form! I conjure thee in the name of Shaddai, Mirror of Truth and Cornerstone of Stability! I conjure thee in the name of Hod, Principle of the Realm of Glory! I conjure thee in the name of Netzach, Master of Life over Death. I conjure thee in the name of Tiphareth, Sovereign Essence of Beauty! I conjure thee in the name of Geburah, Principle of Infinite and Absolute Justice! I conjure thee in the name of Chesed, Divine Mercy! I conjure thee in the name of Binah, Active Intelligence and Supreme Understanding! I conjure thee in the name of Chokmah, Uncreated Wisdom! I conjure thee in the name of Kether, the Horizon of Eternity!

I conjure thee, O Celestial Teacher, in the Name of יהוה! I conjure thee in the Name of אדני! I conjure thee in the Name of אהיה! I conjure thee in the Name of אגלא! May it be thus in the Blessed Name of the Lord. ✠ ✠ ✠

Holding Dagger in one hand and the parchment in the other...

By the virtue of the Holy Trigram ... *(pronounce while drawing Trigram in air with Dagger)* whose attribute is ... and by the power of the Holy Spirit which has been conferred upon me, I call forth the presence of the Spirit... *(intone name of Spirit)* to obey this servant of the Most High and lend your assistance in ... *(state specific purpose of function of the Operation)*. We bid thee to work swiftly and surely, and ever to the glory of the Most High God. In the Name of יהשוה, Christos, Soter, Logos, So Mote It Be!

Pater Noster

OPERATOR & ASSISTANTS:
Our Father who art in Heaven, hallowed by Thy Name;
Thy kingdom come, Thy will be done,
On Earth as it is in Heaven.
Give us this day, our daily bread,
And forgive us our debts, as we have also forgiven our debtors.
And leave us not in temptation, but deliver us from evil,
For Thine is the Kingdom, and the Power, and the Glory, forever and ever. Amen.

Dismissal

OPERATOR:
Solomon in his great wisdom said to his son: Do thou, O my son Roboam, remember, that the fear of the Lord is only the beginning of Wisdom. Keep and preserve those who have not Understanding in the Fear of the Lord, which will give and will preserve unto thee my crown. But learn to triumph thyself over Fear by Wisdom, and the Spirits will descend from Heaven to serve thee.

Practice: Theurgical Operations

I, Solomon, thy father, King of Israel and Palmyra, I have sought out and obtained in my lot the Holy Chokmah, which is the Wisdom of Adonai. And I have become King of the Spirits, as well of Heaven as of Earth, Master of the Dwellers of the Air, and of the Living Souls of the Sea, because I was in possession of the Key of the Hidden Gates of Light.

We, therefore, being in possession of the Keys, have conjured and compelled the Spirits in accordance with our Holy Work, and now, or when their work is complete, do bless and release those Spirits to their ethereal abodes until such time as their services may be again required. All this we do by the authority of our Lord Jesus, Christos, Soter, Logos, in whose Name all Spirits do humbly submit. And we pray that the blessing of the Mystery of the Three-in-One, of God the Unknown Father ✠ of Christ the redeeming and ever-coming Logos ✠ and of the Holy Spirit our celestial Mother and Consoler ✠ descend upon us and remain with us always. Amen.

List of the Theurgical Operations

Operations of Spiritual Grace and Benediction

To Obtain Spiritual Illumination: 1

To Obtain the Benediction of God: 8

To Obtain the Grace of God: 19, 24

To Obtain the Mercy of God: 9, 24, 50, 54, 66

For Spiritual Inspiration: 8

For the Praising of God for Having Been Enlightened: 47

For the Exaltation of Oneself for the Benediction & Glory of God: 49

For the Acquisition of Wisdom: 25, 51, 62, 65, 67

For the Acquisition of Heavenly Treasures: 38

For the Discovery of the Truth of Hidden Mysteries: 12, 25, 47, 67

To Discover the Secret of the Philosopher's Stone: 51

For Spiritual Conversion: 20, 41, 63

For Premonitions: 48

To Procure Revelations: 46, 48

For Revelations in Dreams: 12, 17, 25, 46 For the Acquisition of Patience: 7, 30

Operations of Healing

To Cure Diseases of Every Kind: 6, 10, 28, 39, 58, 63, 68

To Cure Afflictions of the Eyes: 58

To Cure Diseases of the Liver: 6

To Cure Diseases of the Gall Bladder: 10

To Cure Diseases of the Kidneys: 28

To Cure Digestive and Intestinal Diseases: 39

To Cure Diseases of the Heart and Lungs: 63

To Cure Epilepsy: 66

Practice: Theurgical Operations

For the Health of Men and Children: 39

For the Health of Women: 68

To Cure Mental Illness: 60

For Peace, Contentment, and the Alleviation of Mental Stress: 4, 17, 30, 34, 50, 58

To Live In Peace With Others: 5

For the Preservation of Peace: 35, 48 For Familial Harmony: 39, 48, 59

To Prevent Sterility and Encourage Fruitfulness: 2, 55, 59

Operations of General Intercession

To Learn the Secrets of Nature: 1, 5, 7, 21, 37, 46, 70

To Acquire Intellectual Knowledge: 1, 5, 6, 19, 31, 53

To Acquire Good Memory: 32

To Acquire Bravery: 16, 71

To Bear Adversity With Patience and Courage: 19, 52, 57, 67

For the Obtainment of Victory in General: 11, 16, 37, 52

To Obtain Victory Over Unjust Attacks: 2, 32

For the Identification of Traitors: 4, 33

For the Discovery of Conspiracies: 42

To Confound the Wicked: 27, 45

To Find Lost or Stolen Objects and Person Responsible: 69

For Deliverance From Bondage and Oppression: 14, 16, 27, 29, 36, 40, 43, 52, 57, 60

To Make Truth Known in Law Suits: 18, 26, 47

To Preserve One's Means of Livelihood: 36

For Prosperous Business and Commerce: 22, 59, 63

For Prosperous Agricultural Production: 8, 23, 31, 68

For General Prosperity: 57, 72

For the Success of a Useful Undertaking: 44, 65

For the Accomplishment of Difficult Tasks: 1, 7

For Friendship and Favor: 9, 13, 35, 61

For the Fulfillment of One's Request: 56

Operations of Protection

Protection of Those Who Wish to Progress Spiritually: 25, 26, 70

Protection in Mysterious Operations: 72

Protection Against Black Magic and Evil Spirits: 8, 21, 38, 65

Protection Against Adversity: 3, 12, 64

Protection Against Those Who Attack us in Court: 32

Protection Against Those Who Seek to Usurp Fortunes of Others: 14

Protection From Thieves and Assassins: 24

Protection Against the Impious and Enemies of Religion: 15, 20, 29, 41

Protection Against Traitors: 16

Protection Against Armies: 44 Protection of Heads of State: 54

Protection From Wild Animals: 3, 24, 38, 64

Protection Against Weapons: 3, 23, 38

Protection Against Lightning: 11 Protection Against Fire: 28, 71

Protection Against Floods: 23

Protection Against Storms and Shipwreck: 22

For Safety in Sea Travel: 4

For Safety in Travel in General: 4, 23, 42, 61

Protection Against Accidents: 63

Protection Against Fraud: 38

General Protection: 48, 71

Practice: Theurgical Operations

The 72 Spirits of the Shemhamphorasch

1st Spirit

Holy Trigram: VHV - Vehu

Name: VHVIH - Vehuiah

Gematria Value: 17/32

Assisting Angel: Chontare

Attribute: God exalted above all.

Zodiac: 1-5° Mars in Aries 1-5°

Planetary Ruler: Mars Alchemical

Element: Fire Alchemical

Essential: Sulphur

Time of Invocation: Midnight - 12:20 AM

Ruling Days: March 20, May 31, August 11, October 22, January 2

Psalm 3.3: But thou, O Lord, art my helper; my glory and the one that lifts up my head.

Latin: Et tu Domine susceptor meus es Gloria mea et exaltans caput meum.

ACP Clergy Handbook

2nd Spirit

Holy Trigram: ILi - Yeli

Name: ILIAL- Yeliel

Gematria Value: 50/81

Assisting Angel: Asican

Attribute: Helpful God.

Zodiac: 6-10° Mars in Aries 6-10°

Planetary Ruler: Mars

Alchemical Element: Fire

Alchemical Essential: Sulphur

Time of Invocation: 12:20 AM - 12:40 AM

Ruling Days: March 21, June 1, August 12, October 23, January 3

Psalm 22.19: But thou, O Lord, remove not my help afar off; be ready for mine aid.

Latin: Et tu Domine ne elongareris auxilijum tuum a me, ad defensionem meam conspice.

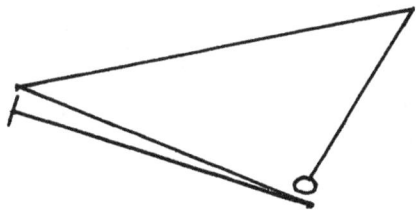

Practice: Theurgical Operations

3rd Spirit

Holy Trigram: SIT - Sit

Name: SITAL - Sitael

Gematria Value: 79/ 110

Assisting Angel: Chontachre

Attribute: God, help of all creatures.

Zodiac: 11-15° Suns in Aries 11-15°

Planetary Ruler: Mars

Alchemical Element: Fire

Alchemical Essential: Sulphur

Time of Invocation: 12:40 AM - 1:00 AM

Ruling Days: March 22, June 2, August 13, October 24, January 4

Psalm 91.2: He shall say to the Lord, thou art my helper and my refuge; my God; I will hope in him.

Latin: Dicam Domino susceptor meus es tu, et refugium meum Deus sperabo in sum.

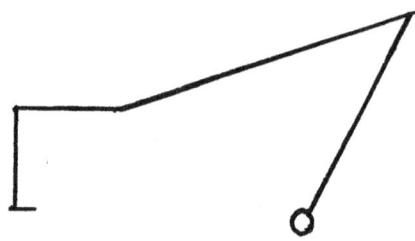

ACP Clergy Handbook

4th Spirit

Holy Trigram: OLM - Aulem

Name: OLMIH - Aulemiah

Gematria Value: 140/155

Assisting Angel: Senacher

Attribute: Hidden God.

Zodiac: 16-20° Sun in Aries 16-20°

Planetary Ruler: Mars

Alchemical Element: Fire

Alchemical Essential: Sulphur

Time of Invocation: 1:00 AM - 1:20 AM

Ruling Days: March 23, June 3, August 14, October 25, January 5

Psalm 6.4: Return, O Lord, deliver my soul; save me for thy mercy's sake.

Latin: Convertere Domino, et eripe animam meam, salvum me fac propter misericordiam tuam

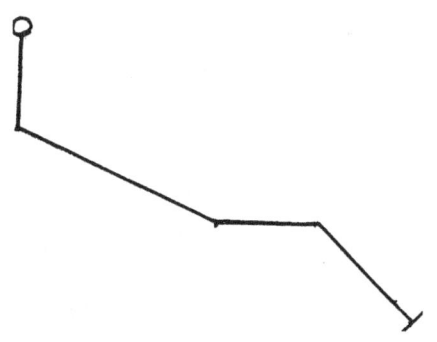

Practice: Theurgical Operations

5th Spirit

Holy Trigram: MHSh - Mahash

Name: MHShIH - Mahashiah

Gematria Value: 345/360

Assisting Angel: Seket

Attribute: God the Savior.

Zodiac: 21-25° Venus in Aries 21-25°

Planetary Ruler: Mars

Alchemical Element: Fire

Alchemical Essential: Sulphur

Time of Invocation: 1:20 AM - 1:40 AM

Ruling Days: March 24, June 4, August 15, October 26, January 6

Psalm 34.4: I sought the Lord diligently, and he hearkened to me, and delivered me from all my sojournings.

Latin: Ex qui sive Dominum et exaudivit me, et ex omnibus tribulationibus eripuit me.

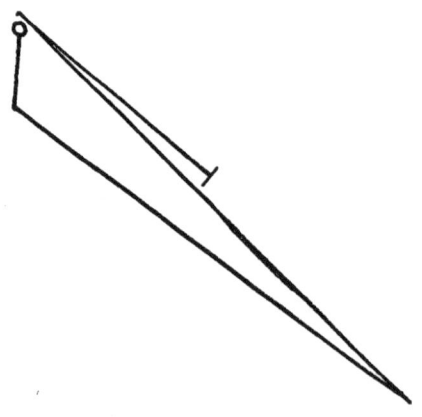

ACP Clergy Handbook

6th Spirit

Holy Trigram: LLH - Lelah

Name: LLHAL - Lelahael

Gematria Value: 65/96

Assisting Angel: Asentacer

Attribute: Praiseworthy God.

Zodiac: 26-30° Venus in Aries 26-30°

Planetary Ruler: Mars

Alchemical Element: Fire

Alchemical Essential: Sulphur

Time of Invocation: 1:40 AM - 2:00 AM

Ruling Days: March 25, June 5, August 16, October 27, January 7

Psalm 9.11: Sing praises to the Lord, who dwells in Zion; declare his dealings among the nations.

Latin: Psallite Domino qui habitat in Sion annunciate inter gentes studia eius.

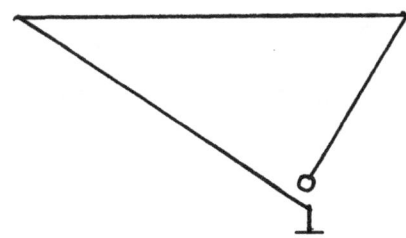

Practice: Theurgical Operations

7th Spirit

Holy Trigram: AKA - Aka

Name: AKAIH - Akaiah

Gematria Value: 22/37

Assisting Angel: Chous

Attribute: Good and patient God.

Zodiac: 31-35° Mercury in Taurus 1-5°

Planetary Ruler: Venus

Alchemical Element: Earth

Alchemical Essential: Salt

Time of Invocation: 2:00 AM - 2:20 AM

Ruling Days: March 26, June 6, August 17, October 28, January 8

Psalm 103.58: The Lord is compassionate and merciful, long-suffering, and full of mercy.

Latin: Miserator et misericors Dominus, longanimus et multum nusencors.

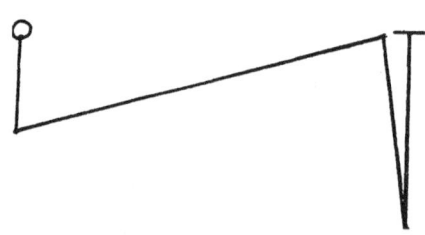

ACP Clergy Handbook

8th Spirit

Holy Trigram: KHTh - Kahath

Name: KHThAL - Kahathael

Gematria Value: 435/456

Assisting Angel: Asicat

Attribute: Adorable God.

Zodiac: 36-40° Mercury in Taurus 6-10°

Planetary Ruler: Venus

Alchemical Element: Earth

Alchemical Essential: Salt

Time of Invocation: 2:20 AM - 2:40 AM

Ruling Days: March 27, June 7, August 18, October 29, January 9

Psalm 95.6: Come, let us worship and fall down before him; and weep before the Lord that made us.

Latin: Venite, adoremus, et procidamus ante Dominum qui ferit nos.

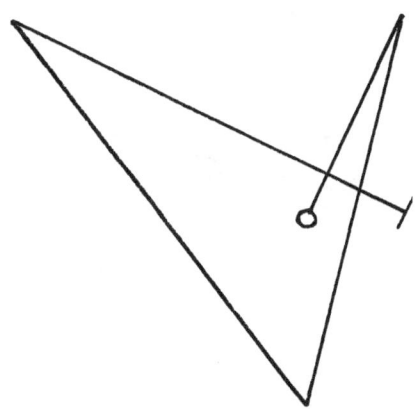

Practice: Theurgical Operations

9th Spirit

Holy Trigram: HZI - Hezi

Name: HEZIAL - Heziel

Gematria Value: 22/ 53

Assisting Angel: Ero

Attribute: God of Mercy.

Zodiac: 41-45° Moon in Taurus 11-15°

Planetary Ruler: Venus

Alchemical Element: Earth

Alchemical Essential: Salt

Time of Invocation: 2:40 AM - 3:00 AM

Ruling Days: March 28, June 8, August 19, October 30, January 10

Psalm 25.6: Remember thy compassions, O Lord, and thy mercies, for they are from everlasting.

Latin: Reminiscere miserationum tuarum Domine et miserationum tuarum quæ a sæculo sunt.

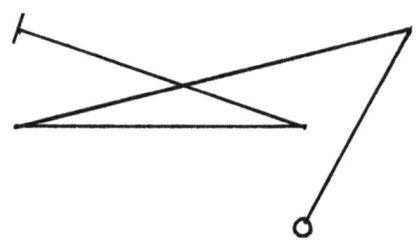

ACP Clergy Handbook

10th Spirit

Holy Trigram: ALD - Elad

Name: ELADIH - Eladiah

Gematria Value: 35/ 50

Assisting Angel: Viroaso

Attribute: Propitious God.

Zodiac: 46-50° Moon in Taurus 16-20°

Planetary Ruler: Venus

Alchemical Element: Earth

Alchemical Essential: Salt

Time of Invocation: 3:00 AM - 3:20 AM

Ruling Days: March 29, June 9, August 20, October 31, January 11

Psalm 33.22: Let thy mercy, O Lord, be upon us, according as we have hoped in thee.

Latin: Fiat misericordiam tua super nos, quemadmodu speravimus in te.

Practice: Theurgical Operations

11th Spirit

Holy Trigram: LAV - Lav

Name: LAVIH - Laviah

Gematria Value: 37/52

Assisting Angel: Rombomare

Attribute: God exalted and praised.

Zodiac: 51-55° Saturn in Taurus 21-25°

Planetary Ruler: Venus

Alchemical Element: Earth

Alchemical Essential: Salt

Time of Invocation: 3:20 AM - 3:40 AM

Ruling Days: March 30, June 10, August 21, November 1, January 12

Psalm 18.46: The Lord lives; and blessed be my God; and let the God of my salutation be exalted.

Latin: Vivit Dominus et benedictus Deus meus et exaltatur Deus salutis meæ.

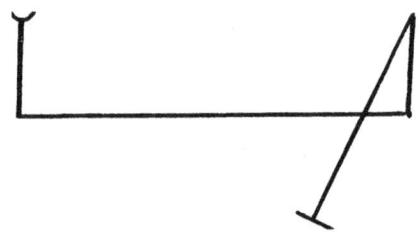

ACP Clergy Handbook

12th Spirit

Holy Trigram: HHO - Hahau

Name: HHOIH-Hahauiah

Gematria Value: 80/95

Assisting Angel: Atarph

Attribute: God the refuge.

Zodiac: 56-60° Saturn in Taurus 26-30°

Planetary Ruler: Venus

Alchemical Element: Earth

Alchemical Essential: Salt

Time of Invocation: 3:40 AM - 4:00 AM

Ruling Days: March 31, June 11, August 22, November 2, January 13

Psalm 10.1: Why standest thou afar off, O Lord? Why dost thou overlook us in times of need, in affliction?

Latin: Ut quid Domine recessisti longe desperis in opportunitatibus in tribulation.

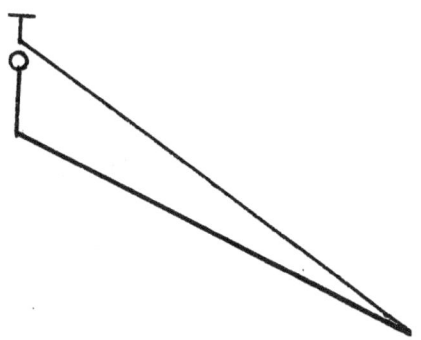

Practice: Theurgical Operations

13th Spirit

Holy Trigram: IZL - Yezel

Name: IZLAL- Yezelael

Gematria Value: 47/78

Assisting Angel: Theosolk

Attribute: God glorified above all things.

Zodiac: 61-65° Jupiter in Gemini 1-5°

Planetary Ruler: Mercury

Alchemical Element: Air

Alchemical Essential: Mercury

Time of Invocation: 4:00 AM - 4:20 AM

Ruling Days: April 1, June 12, August 23, November 3, January 14

Psalm 98.4: Shout to God, all the earth; sing, and exult, and sing psalms.

Latin: Jubilate Domino omnis Terra, Cantate, et exultate, et Psallite.

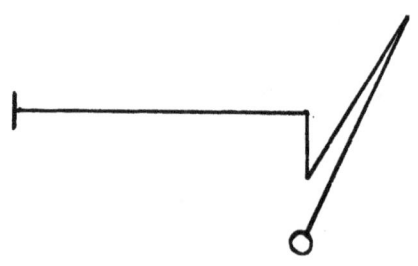

ACP Clergy Handbook

14th Spirit

Holy Trigram: MBH - Mebha

Name: MBHAL - Mebhael

Gematria Value: 47/78

Assisting Angel: Thesosgar

Attribute: Preserving God.

Zodiac: 66-70°Jupiter in Gemini 6-10°

Planetary Ruler: Mercury

Alchemical Element: Air

Alchemical Essential: Mercury

Time of-Invocation: 4:20 AM - 4:40 AM

Ruling Days: April 2, June 13, August 24, November 4, January 15

Psalm 9.9: The Lord also is become a refuge for the poor, a seasonable help in affliction.

Latin: Et factus est mihi Dominus refugium pauperis; adjutor in opportunitatibus, in tribulation.

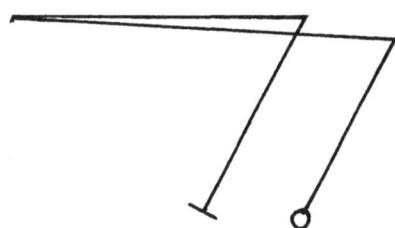

Practice: Theurgical Operations

15th Spirit

Holy Trigram: HRI - Heri

Name: HRIAL- Heriel

Gematria Value: 215/246

Assisting Angel: Ouere

Attribute: God the Creator.

Zodiac: 71-75° Mars in Gemini 11-15°

Planetary Ruler: Mercury

Alchemical Element: Air

Alchemical Essential: Mercury

Time of Invocation: 4:40 AM - 5:00 AM

Ruling Days: April 3, June 14, August 25, November 5, January 16

Psalm 94.22: But the Lord was my refuge; and my God the helper of my hope.

Latin: Et factus est mihi Dominus in refugium et Deus meus in adjutorium spei meæ.

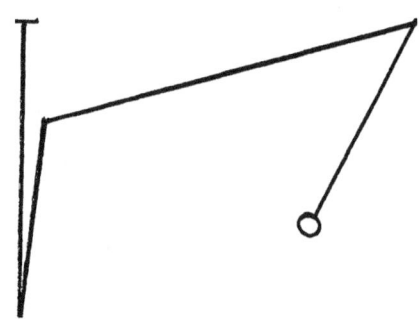

ACP Clergy Handbook

16th Spirit

Holy Trigram: HQM - Haqem

Name: HQMIH - Haqemiah

Gematria Value: 145/160

Assisting Angel: Verasua

Attribute: God who erects the universe.

Zodiac: 76-80° Mars in Gemini 16-20°

Planetary Ruler: Mercury

Alchemical Element: Air

Alchemical Essential: Mercury

Time of Invocation: 5:00 AM - 5:20 AM

Ruling Days: April 4, June 15, August 26, November 6, January 17

Psalm 88.1: O Lord God of my salvation, I have cried by day and in the night before thee.

Latin: Domine Deus salutis meæ in die clamavi et nocte coram te.

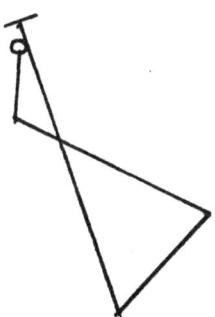

Practice: Theurgical Operations

17th Spirit

Holy Trigram: LAV - Lau

Name: LAVIH - Lauiah

Gematria Value: 37/ 52

Assisting Angel: Phuor

Attribute: Admirable God.

Zodiac: 81-85° Sun in Gemini 21-25°

Planetary Ruler: Mercury

Alchemical Element: Air

Alchemical Essential: Mercury

Time of Invocation: 5:20 AM - 5:40 AM

Ruling Days: April 5, June 16, August 27, November 7, January 18

Psalm 8.1: O Lord, our Lord, how wonderful is thy name in all the earth! For thy magnificence is exalted above the heavens.

Latin: Domine Dominus noster quam admirabile est nomen tuum in universa terra.

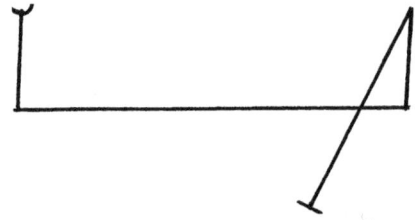

ACP Clergy Handbook

18th Spirit

Holy Trigram: KLI - Keli

Name: KLIAL - Keliel

Gematria Value: 60/91

Assisting Angel: Tepistatosa

Attribute: God prompt to fulfill.

Zodiac: 86-90° Sun in Gemini 26-30°

Planetary Ruler: Mercury

Alchemical Element: Air

Alchemical Essential: Mercury

Time of Invocation: 5:40 AM - 6:00 AM

Ruling Days: April 6, June 17, August 28, November 8, January 19

Psalm 35.24: Judge me, O Lord, according to thy righteousness, O Lord my God; and let them not rejoice against me.

Latin: Iudica me Domine secundum misericordiam et iustitiam tuam Domine Deus meus et non supergaudeant mihi.

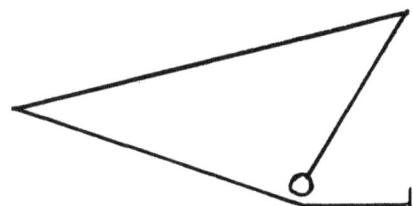

Practice: Theurgical Operations

19th Spirit

Holy Trigram: LLV - Levo

Name: LLVIH - Levoiah

Gematria Value: 42/57

Assisting Angel: Sortis

Attribute: God who hears sinners.

Zodiac: 91-95° Venus in Cancer 1-5°

Planetary Ruler: Moon

Alchemical Element: Water

Alchemical Essential: Sulphur

Time of Invocation: 6:00 AM - 6:20 AM

Ruling Days: April 7, June 18, August 29, November 9, January 20

Psalm 40.1: I waited patiently for the Lord; and he attended to me, and hearkened to my supplication.

Latin: Expectans expectavi Dominum et intendit mihi.

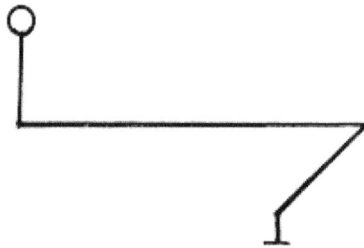

ACP Clergy Handbook

20th Spirit

Holy Trigram: PHL - Pahel

Name: PHLIH - Paheliah

Gematria Value: 115/ 130

Assisting Angel: Sortis

Attribute: God the Redeemer.

Zodiac: 96-100° Venus in Cancer 6-10°

Planetary Ruler: Moon

Alchemical Element: Water

Alchemical Essential: Sulphur

Time of Invocation: 6:20 AM - 6:40 AM

Ruling Days: April 8, June 19, August 30, November 10, January 21

Psalm 116.4: I shall call upon the name of the Lord, O Lord free my soul.

Latin: Et nomen Domini invocabo O Domine libera animam meam.

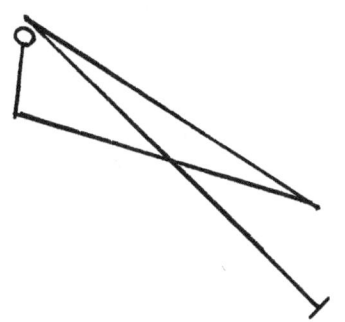

Practice: Theurgical Operations

21st Spirit

Holy Trigram: NLK- Nelak

Name: NLKAL - Nelakael

Gematria Value: 100/131

Assisting Angel: Sith

Attribute: God unique and alone.

Zodiac: 101-105° Mercury in Cancer 11-15°

Planetary Ruler: Moon

Alchemical Element: Water

Alchemical Essential: Sulphur

Time of Invocation: 6:40 AM - 7:00 AM

Ruling Days: April 9, June 20, August 31, November 11, January 22

Psalm 31.14: But I hoped in thee, O Lord; I said, Thou art my God, my lots are in thy hands.

Latin: Ego autem in te speravi Domine dixi Deus meus es tu.

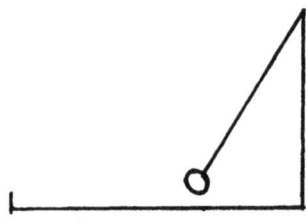

ACP Clergy Handbook

22ⁿᵈ Spirit

Holy Trigram: III - Yiai

Name: IIIAL - Yiaiel

Gematria Value: 30/ 61

Assisting Angel: Syth

Attribute: The right hand of God.

Zodiac: 106-110° Mercury in Cancer 16-20°

Planetary Ruler: Moon

Alchemical Element: Water

Alchemical Essential: Sulphur

Time of Invocation: 7:00 AM - 7:20 AM

Ruling Days: April 10, June 21, September 1, November 12, January 23

Psalm 121.5: The Lord shall keep thee; the Lord is thy shelter upon thy right hand.

Latin: Dominus custodit te, Dominus protection tua super manum dextram tuam.

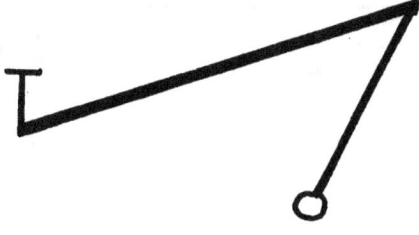

Practice: Theurgical Operations

23rd Spirit

Holy Trigram: MLH - Melah

Name: MLHAL - Melahel

Gematria Value: 75/ 106

Assisting Angel: Chumis

Attribute: God who delivers from evil.

Zodiac: 111-115° Moon in Cancer 21-25°

Planetary Ruler: Moon

Alchemical Element: Water

Alchemical Essential: Sulphur

Time of Invocation: 7:20 AM - 7:40 AM

Ruling Days: April 11, June 22, September 2, November 13, January 24

Psalm 121.8: The Lord shall keep thy coming in, and thy going out, from henceforth and even forever.

Latin: Dominus custodit introitum tuum et exitum tuum ex nunc et usque in sæculum.

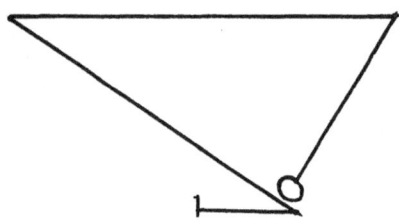

24th Spirit

Holy Trigram: ChHV - Chaho

Name: ChHVIH - Chahoiah

Gematria Value: 19/34

Assisting Angel: Thuimis

Attribute: God good in himself.

Zodiac: 116-120° Moon in Cancer 26-30°

Planetary Ruler: Moon

Alchemical Element: Water

Alchemical Essential: Sulphur

Time of Invocation: 7:40 AM - 8:00 AM

Ruling Days: April 12, June 23, September 3, November 14, January 25

Psalm 33.18: Behold, the eyes of the Lord are on them that fear him, those that hope in his mercy.

Latin: Ecce oculi Domini super metuentes eum et in eis qui spirant in misericordiam ejus.

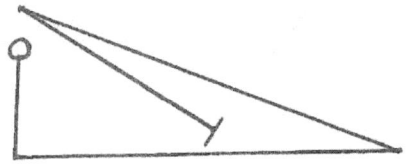

Practice: Theurgical Operations

25th Spirit

Holy Trigram: NThH - Nethah

Name: NThHIH-Nethahiah

Gematria Value: 455/470

Assisting Angel: Charcumis

Attribute: God who gives Wisdom.

Zodiac: 121-125° Saturn in Leo 1-5°

Planetary Ruler: Sun

Alchemical Element: Fire

Alchemical Essential: Salt

Time of Invocation: 8:00 AM - 8:20 AM

Ruling Days: April 13, June 24, September 4, November 15, January 26

Psalm 9.1: I will give thanks to thee, O Lord, with my whole heart; I will recount all thy wonderful works.

Latin: Confitebor tibi Domine in tote corde meo varrabo omnia mirabilia tua.

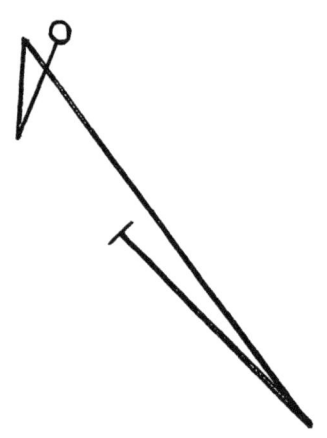

ACP Clergy Handbook

26th Spirit

Holy Trigram: HAA - Haa

Name: HAAIH - Haaiah

Gematria Value: 7/22

Assisting Angel: Aphruimis

Attribute: Hidden God.

Zodiac: 126-130° Saturn in Leo 6-10°

Planetary Ruler: Sun

Alchemical Element: Fire

Alchemical Essential: Salt

Time of Invocation: 8:20 AM - 8:40 AM

Ruling Days: April 14, June 25, September 5, November 16, January 27

Psalm 119.145: I cried with my whole heart; hear me, O Lord; I will search out thine ordinances.

Latin: Clamavi in toto corde meo, exaudi me Domine, iustificationes tuas requiram.

Practice: Theurgical Operations

27th Spirit

Holy Trigram: IRTh – Yereth

Name: IRThAL - Yerethael

Gematria Value: 610/ 641

Assisting Angel: Hepe

Attribute: God who punishes the wicked.

Zodiac: 131-135° Jupiter in Leo 11-15°

Planetary Ruler: Sun

Alchemical Element: Fire

Alchemical Essential: Salt

Time of Invocation: 8:40 AM - 9:00 AM

Ruling Days: April 15, June 26, September 6, November 17, January 28

Psalm 140.1: Rescue me, O Lord, from the evil man; deliver me from the unjust man.

Latin: Eripe me Domine ab homine malo a viro iniquio eripe me.

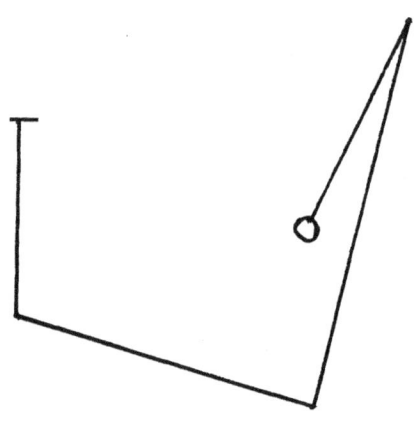

ACP Clergy Handbook

28th Spirit.

Holy Trigram: ShAH - Shaah

Name: ShAHIH- Shaahiah

Gematria Value: 306/321

Assisting Angel: Sithacer

Attribute: God who heals the sick.

Zodiac: 136-140° Jupiter in Leo 16-20°

Planetary Ruler: Sun

Alchemical Element: Fire

Alchemical Essential: Salt

Time of Invocation: 9:00 AM - 9:20 AM

Ruling Days: April 16, June 27, September 7, November 18, January 29

Psalm 71.12:0 God, go not far from me, O my God, draw nigh to my help.

Latin: Deus ne elongeris a me Deus meus in auxilium meum respice.

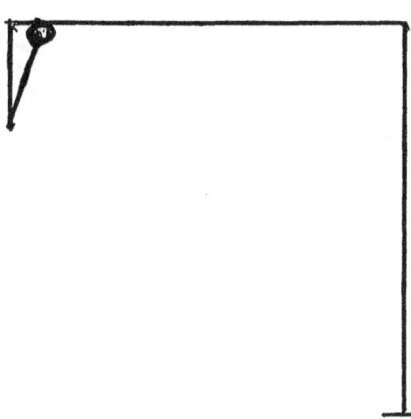

Practice: Theurgical Operations

29th Spirit

Holy Trigram: RII - Riyi

Name: RIIAL - Riyiel

Gematria Value: 220/251

Assisting Angel: Phupe

Attribute: God prompt to aid.

Zodiac: 141-145° Mars in Leo 21-25°

Planetary Ruler: Sun

Alchemical Element: Fire

Alchemical Essential: Salt

Time of Invocation: 9:20 AM - 9:40 AM

Ruling Days: April 17, June 28, September 8, November 19, January 30

Psalm 54.4: For lo! God assists me; and the Lord is the helper of my soul.

Latin: Ecce Deus adiuvat me et Dominus susceptor est animæ meæ.

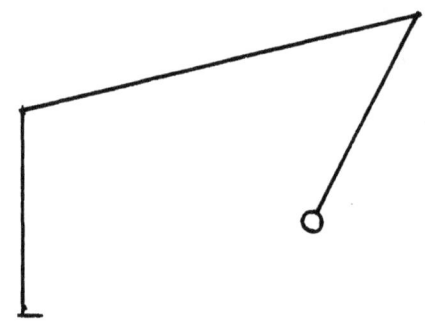

ACP Clergy Handbook

30th Spirit

Holy Trigram: AVM - Aum.

Name: AVMAL - Aumael

Gematria Value: 47/78

Assisting Angel: Phuonisie

Attribute: Patient God.

Zodiac: 146-150° Mars in Leo 26-30°

Planetary Ruler: Sun

Alchemical Element: Fire

Alchemical Essential: Salt

Time of Invocation: 9:40 AM - 10:00 AM

Ruling Days: April 18, June 29, September 9, November 20, January 31

Psalm 71.5: For thou art my support, O Lord; O Lord, thou art my hope from my youth.

Latin: Quoniam tues potentia mea Domine. Domine spes mea a iuventute mea.

Practice: Theurgical Operations

31st Spirit

Holy Trigram: LKB - Lekab

Name: LKBAL - Lekabael

Gematria Value: 52/83

Assisting Angel: Tomi

Attribute: God who inspires.

Zodiac: 151-155° Sun in Virgo 1-5°

Planetary Ruler: Mercury

Alchemical Element: Earth

Alchemical Essential: Mercury

Time of Invocation: 10:00 AM - 10:20 AM

Ruling Days: April 19, June 30, September 10, November 21, February 1

Psalm 71.16: I will go on in the might of the Lord; O Lord, I will make mention of thy righteousness only.

Latin: Introibo in potentia Domini, Deus meus memorabor iustitiæ tuæ solius.

ACP Clergy Handbook

32nd Spirit

Holy Trigram: VShR - Vesher

Name: VShRIH - Vesheriah

Gematria Value: 506/521

Assisting Angel: Thumis

Attribute: God the just.

Zodiac: 156-160° Sun in Virgo 6-10°

Planetary Ruler: Mercury

Alchemical Element: Earth

Alchemical Essential: Mercury

Time of Invocation: 10:20 AM - 10:40 AM

Ruling Days: April 20, July 1, September 11, November 22, February 2

Psalm 33.4: For the word of the Lord is right; and all his works are faithful.

Latin: Quia rectum est verbum Domini, et omni opera eius in fide.

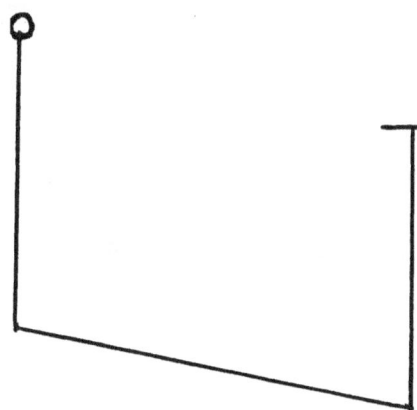

Practice: Theurgical Operations

33rd Spirit

Holy Trigram: IChV - Yecho

Name: YChVIH- Yechoiah

Gematria Value: 24/39

Assisting Angel: Ouestucati

Attribute: God who knows all things.

Zodiac: 161-165° Venus in Virgo 11-15°

Planetary Ruler: Mercury

Alchemical Element: Earth

Alchemical Essential: Mercury

Time of Invocation: 10:40 AM - 11:00 AM

Ruling Days: April 21, July 2, September 12, November 23, February 3

Psalm 94.11: The Lord knows the thoughts of men, that they are vain.

Latin: Dominus scit cogitations hominum quoniam vana sunt.

ACP Clergy Handbook
34th Spirit

Holy Trigram: LHCh- Lehach

Name: LHChIH - Lehachiah

Gematria Value: 43/58

Assisting Angel: Thopitus

Attribute: God the clement.

Zodiac: 166-170° Venus in Virgo 16-20°

Planetary Ruler: Mercury

Alchemical Element: Earth

Alchemical Essential: Mercury

Time of Invocation: 11:00 AM - 11:20 AM

Ruling Days: April 22, July 3, September 13, November 24, February 4

Psalm 131.3: Let Israel hope in the Lord, from henceforth and forever.

Latin: Speret Israel in Domino ex hoc nunc et usque in sæculum.

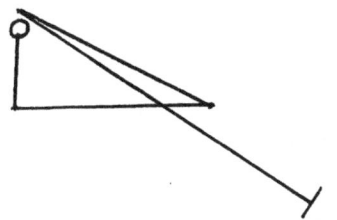

Practice: Theurgical Operations

35th Spirit

Holy Trigram: KVQ - Kaveq

Name: KVQIH-Kaveqiah

Gematria Value: 126/141

Assisting Angel: Aphoso

Attribute: God who gives joy.

Zodiac: 171-175° Mercury in Virgo 21-25°

Planetary Ruler: Mercury

Alchemical Element: Earth

Alchemical Essential: Mercury

Time of Invocation: 11:20 AM - 11:40 AM

Ruling Days: April 23, July 4, September 14, November 25, February 5

Psalm 116.1: I am well pleased because the Lord will hearken to the voice of my supplication.

Latin: Dilexi quoniam exaudi Dominus vocem orationis meæ.

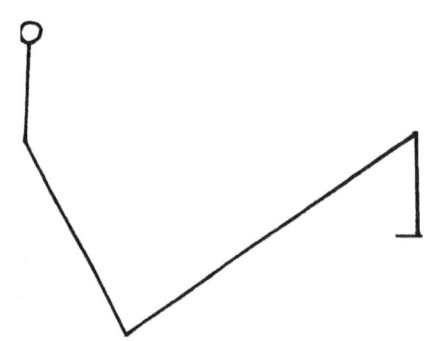

ACP Clergy Handbook

36th Spirit

Holy Trigram: MND - Menad

Name: MNDAL-Menadael

Gematria Value: 94/125

Assisting Angel: Aphut

Attribute: Divine God.

Zodiac: 176-180° Mercury in Virgo 26-30°

Planetary Ruler: Mercury

Alchemical Element: Earth

Alchemical Essential: Mercury

Time of Invocation: 11:40 AM-12:00 NOON

Ruling Days: April 24, July 5, September 15, November 26, February 6

Psalm 26.8:0 Lord, I have loved the beauty of thy house, and the place of the tabernacle of thy glory.

Latin: Domini dilexi decorum domus tuæ et locem habitationis gloriæ tuæ.

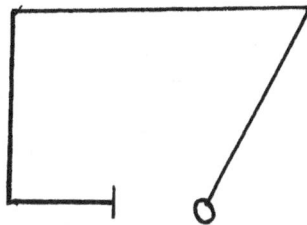

Practice: Theurgical Operations

37th Spirit

Holy Trigram: ANI - Ani

Name: ANIAL - Aniel

Gematria Value: 61/92

Assisting Angel: Souchoe

Attribute: God of Virtues.

Zodiac: 181-185° Moon in Libra 1-5°

Planetary Ruler: Venus

Alchemical Element: Air

Alchemical Essential: Sulphur

Time of Invocation: 12:00 NOON - 12:20 PM

Ruling Days: April 25, July 6, September 16, November 27, February 7

Psalm 80.7: Turn us, 0 Lord God of hosts, and cause thy face to shine; and we shall be saved.

Latin: Domini Deus virtutum converte nos et ostende faciem tuam et salvi erimus.

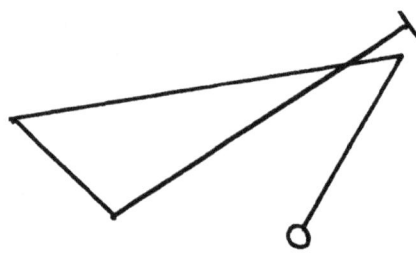

ACP Clergy Handbook

38th Spirit

Holy Trigram: ChOM - Chaum

Name: ChOMIH-Chaumiah

Gematria Value: 118-133

Assisting Angel: Serucuth

Attribute: God the hope of all children of the earth.

Zodiac: 186-190° Moon in Libra 6-10°

Planetary Ruler: Venus

Alchemical Element: Air

Alchemical Essential: Sulphur

Time of Invocation: 12:20 PM-12:40 PM

Ruling Days: April 26, July 7, September 17, November 28, February 8

Psalm 91.9: For thou, O Lord, art my hope; thou, my soul, hast made the Most High thy refuge.

Latin: Quoniam tu es Domine spes mea altissimum profuisti refugium tuum.

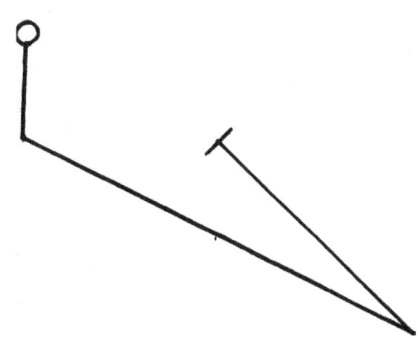

Practice: Theurgical Operations

39th Spirit

Holy Trigram: RHO - Rehau

Name: RHOAL - Rehauel

Gematria Value: 275/306

Assisting Angel: Techout

Attribute: God who receives sinners.

Zodiac: 191-195° Saturn in Libra 11-15°

Planetary Ruler: Venus

Alchemical Element: Air

Alchemical Essential: Sulphur

Time of Invocation: 12:40 PM - 1:00 PM

Ruling Days: April 27, July 8, September 18, November 29, February 9

Psalm 30.10: The Lord heard, and had compassion upon me; the Lord is become my helper.

Latin: Audivit Dominus et misertus est mihi Dominus factus est adiutor meus.

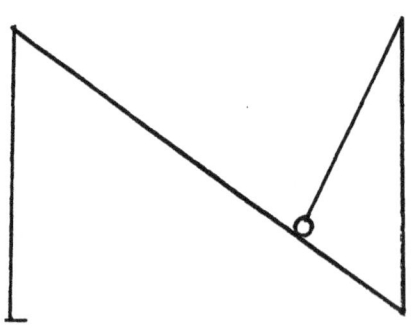

ACP Clergy Handbook

40th Spirit

Holy Trigram: IIZ - Yeiz

Name: IIZAL - Yeizael

Gematria Value: 27/ 58

Assisting Angel: Aterchinis

Attribute: God who rejoices.

Zodiac: 196-200° Saturn in Libra 16-20°

Planetary Ruler: Venus

Alchemical Element: Air

Alchemical Essential: Sulphur

Time of Invocation: 1:00 PM - 1:20 PM

Ruling Days: April 28, July 9, September 19, November 30, February 10

Psalm 88.14: Wherefore, O Lord, dost thou reject my prayer, and turn thy face away from me.

Latin: Ut quid Domine repellis animam meam, avertis faciem tuam a me.

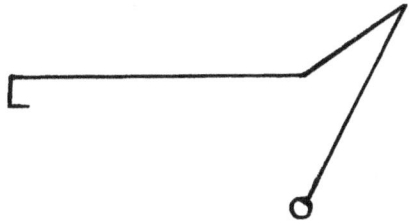

Practice: Theurgical Operations

41st Spirit

Holy Trigram: HHH - Hahah

Name: HHHAL - Hahahel

Gematria Value: 15/ 46

Assisting Angel: Chontare

Attribute: God in three persons.

Zodiac: 201-205° Jupiter in Libra 21-25°

Planetary Ruler: Venus

Alchemical Element: Air

Alchemical Essential: Sulphur

Time of Invocation: 1:20 PM - 1:40 PM

Ruling Days: April 29, July 10, September 20, December 1, February 11

Psalm 120.2: Deliver my soul, O Lord, from unjust lips and from a deceitful tongue.

Latin: Domine libera animam meam a labiis iniquis et a lingua dolosa.

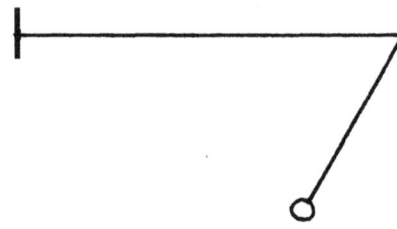

ACP Clergy Handbook

42nd Spirit

Holy Trigram: MIK - Mik

Name: MIKAL - Mikael

Gematria Value: 70/101

Assisting Angel: Arpien

Attribute: Virtue of God, House of God, Like unto God.

Zodiac: 206-210° Jupiter in Libra 26-30°

Planetary Ruler: Venus

Alchemical Element: Air

Alchemical Essential: Sulphur

Time of Invocation: 1:40 PM - 2:00 PM

Ruling Days: April 30, July 11, September 21, December 2, February 12

Psalm• 121.7: May the Lord preserve thee from all evil; the Lord shall keep thy soul.

Latin: Domine custodit te ab omni malo et custodiet animam tuam.

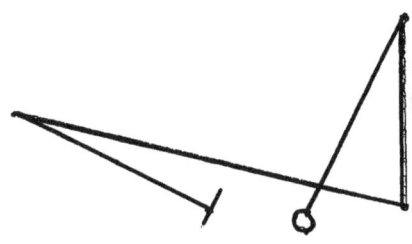

Practice: Theurgical Operations

43rd Spirit

Holy Trigram: VVL - Veval

Name: VVLIH - Vevaliah

Gematria Value: 42/ 57

Assisting Angel: Stochene

Attribute: Ruling King.

Zodiac: 211-215° Mars in Scorpio 1-5°

Planetary Ruler: Mars

Alchemical Element: Water

Alchemical Essential: Salt

Time of Invocation: 2:00 PM - 2:20 PM

Ruling Days: May 1, July 12, September 22, December 3, February 13

Psalm 88.13: But I cried to thee, O Lord; and in the morning shall my prayer come before thee.

Latin: Et ego ad te Domine clamavit, et mane oratio meæ prævenit te.

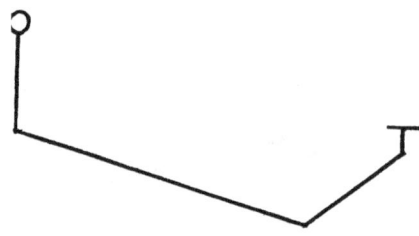

ACP Clergy Handbook

44th Spirit

Holy Trigram: ILH - Yelah

Name: ILHIH- Yelahiah

Gemattia Value: 45/60

Assisting Angel: Sentacer

Attribute: Eternal God.

Zodiac: 216-220° Mars in Scorpio 6-10°

Planetary Ruler: Mars

Alchemical Element: Water

Alchemical Essential: Salt

Time of Invocation: 2:20 PM - 2:40 PM

Ruling Days: May 2, July 13, September 23, December 4, February 14

Psalm 119.108: Accept, I pray thee, O Lord, the freewill offerings of my mouth, and teach me thy judgments.

Latin: Volutaria eris mei beneplacita fac Domine et Judicia tua doce.

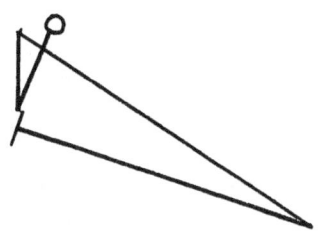

Practice: Theurgical Operations

45th Spirit

Holy Trigram: SAL - Sael

Name: SALIH - Saeliah

Gematria Value: 91/106

Assisting Angel: Sesme

Attribute: Mover of all things.

Zodiac: 221-225° Sun in Scorpio 11-15°

Planetary Ruler: Mars

Alchemical Element: Water

Alchemical Essential: Salt

Time of Invocation: 2:40 PM - 3:00 PM

Ruling Days: May 3, July 14, September 24, December 5, February 15

Psalm 94.18: If I said, My foot has been moved; thy mercy, O Lord, helped me.

Latin: Si dicebam motus est pes meus misericordiam tua Domine adiuvabit me.

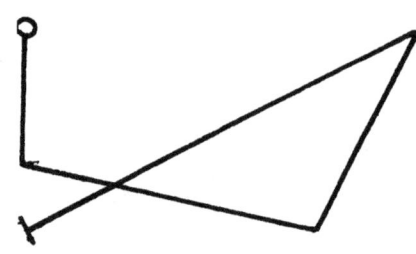

ACP Clergy Handbook

46th Spirit

Holy Trigram: ORI - Auri

Name: ORIAL - Auriel

Gematria Value: 280/311

Assisting Angel: Tepiseuth

Attribute: Revelatory God.

Zodiac: 226-230° Sun in Scorpio 16-20°

Planetary Ruler: Mars

Alchemical Element: Water

Alchemical Essential: Salt

Time of Invocation: 3:00 PM - 3:20 PM

Ruling Days: May 4, July 15, September 25, December 6, February 16

Psalm 145.9: The Lord is good to those that wait; and his compassions are over all his works.

Latin: Suavis Dominus universis et miserationes super omnia opera ems.

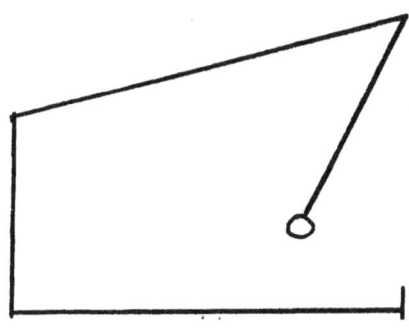

Practice: Theurgical Operations

47th Spirit

עשליה

Holy Trigram: OShL - Aushal

Name: OShLIH - Aushaliah

Gematria Value: 400/ 415

Assisting Angel: Sieme

Attribute: God, the just, who shows the truth.

Zodiac: 231-235° Venus in Scorpio 21-25°

Planetary Ruler: Mars

Alchemical Element: Water

Alchemical Essential: Salt

Time of Invocation: 3:00 PM - 3:20 PM

Ruling Days: May 5, July 16, September 26, December 7, February 17

Psalm 104.24: How great are thy works, O Lord! In wisdom hast thou wrought them all; the earth is filled with thy creation.

Latin: Quam magnificata sunt opera tua Domine! Omnia in sapientia fecisti: impleca est terra possentione tua.

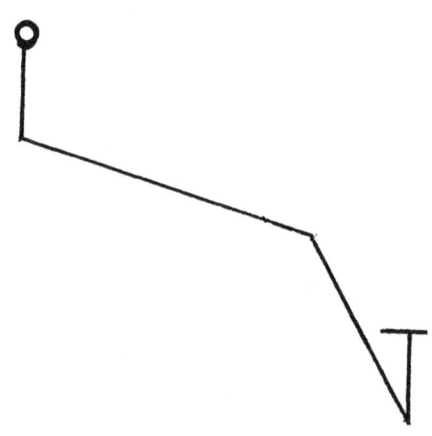

ACP Clergy Handbook

48th Spirit

Holy Trigram: MIH - Miah

Name: MIHAL - Miahel

Gematria Value: 55/86

Assisting Angel: Senciner

Attribute: God, helpful father.

Zodiac: 236-240° Venus in Scorpio 26-30°

Planetary Ruler: Mars

Alchemical Element: Water

Alchemical Essential: Salt

Time of Invocation: 3:40 PM - 4:00 PM

Ruling Days: May 6, July 17, September 27, December 8, February 18

Psalm 98.2: The Lord has made known his salvation, he has revealed his righteousness in the sight of the nations.

Latin: Notum fecit Dominus salutare tuum in conspectus gentium, revelabit justitiam suam.

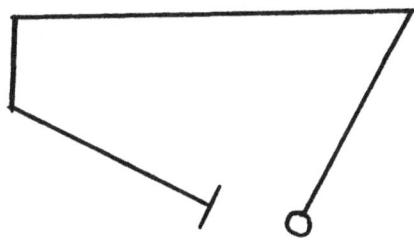

Practice: Theurgical Operations

49th Spirit

Holy Trigram: VHV - Vaho

Name: VHVAL - Vahoel

Gematria Value: 17/ 48

Assisting Angel: Reno

Attribute: God, great and exalted.

Zodiac: 241-245° Mercury in Sagittarius 1-5°

Planetary Ruler: Jupiter

Alchemical Element: Fire

Alchemical Essential: Mercury

Time of Invocation: 4:00 PM - 4:20 PM

Ruling Days: May 7, July 18, September 28, December 9, February 19

Psalm 145.3: The Lord is great, and greatly to be praised; and there is no end of his greatness.

Latin: Magnus Domine et laudabilis et magnitudinis eius non est finis.

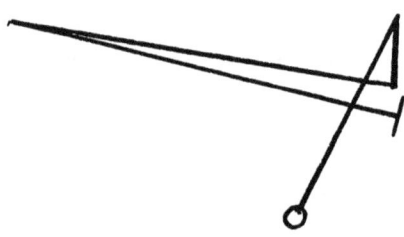

ACP Clergy Handbook

50th Spirit

Holy Trigram: DNI - Doni

Name: DNIAL - Doniel

Gematria Value: 64/95

Assisting Angel: Eregbuo

Attribute: The sign of Mercy. The Angel of confession.

Zodiac: 246-250° Mercury in Sagittarius 6-10°

Planetary Ruler: Jupiter

Alchemical Element: Fire

Alchemical Essential: Mercury

Time of Invocation: 4:20 PM - 4:40 PM

Ruling Days: May 8, July 19, September 29, December 10, February 20

Psalm 103.8: The Lord is compassionate and merciful, long-suffering and full of mercy.

Latin: Miserator et misericors Dominus, patiens et multum misericors.

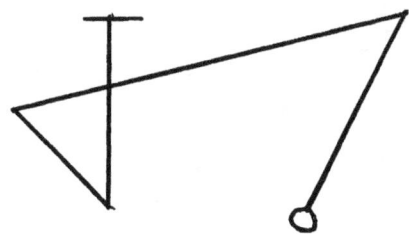

Practice: Theurgical Operations

51st Spirit

Holy Trigram: HChSh - Hachash

Name: HChShIH - Hachashiah

Gematria Value: 313/328

Assisting Angel: Sesme

Attribute: Hidden God.

Zodiac: 251-255° Mercury in Sagittarius 11-15°

Planetary Ruler: Jupiter

Alchemical Element: Fire

Alchemical Essential: Mercury

Time of Invocation: 4:40 PM - 5:00 PM

Ruling Days: May 9, July 20, September 30, December 11, February 21

Psalm 104.31: Let the glory of the Lord be forever; the Lord shall rejoice in his works.

Latin: Sit Gloria Dominus in sæcula lætabitur Dominus in operibus suis.

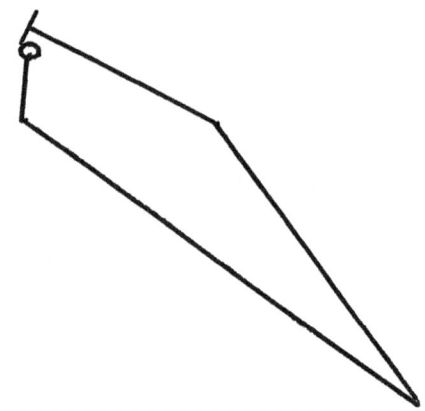

ACP Clergy Handbook

52nd Spirit

Holy Trigram: OMM - Aumem

Name: OMMIH - Aumemiah

Gematria Value: 150/165

Assisting Angel: Sagen

Attribute: God elevated above all things.

Zodiac: 256-260° Moon in Sagittarius 16-20°

Planetary Ruler: Jupiter

Alchemical Element: Fire

Alchemical Essential: Mercury

Time of Invocation: 5:00 PM - 5:20 PM

Ruling Days: May 10, July 21, October 1, December 12, February 22

Psalm 7.17: I will give thanks to the Lord according to his righteousness; I will sing to the name of the Lord Most High.

Latin: Confitebor Domino sacundum justitiam eius et Psallam nomini Domini altissimi.

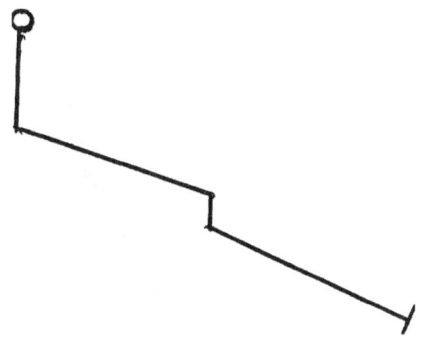

Practice: Theurgical Operations

53rd Spirit

Holy Trigram: NNA - Nena

Name: NNAAL - Nenael

Gematria Value: 101/132

Assisting Angel: Chomine

Attribute: God elevated who humbles the proud.

Zodiac: 261-265° Saturn in Sagittarius 21-25°

Planetary Ruler: Jupiter

Alchemical Element: Fire

Alchemical Essential: Mercury

Time of Invocation: 5:20 PM - 5:40 PM

Ruling Days: May 11, July 22, October 2, December 13, February 23

Psalm 119.75: I know, O Lord, that thy judgments are righteousness, and that thou in truthfulness hast afflicted me.

Latin: Cognari Domine quia æquitas judicia tua et in veritate tua humiliasti me.

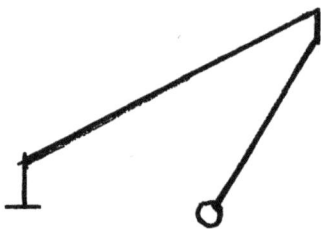

ACP Clergy Handbook

54th Spirit

Holy Trigram: NITh - Neith

Name: NIThAL - Neithael

Gematria Value: 460/491

Assisting Angel: Chenon

Attribute: God King of the heavens.

Zodiac: 266-270° Saturn in Sagittarius 26-30°

Planetary Ruler: Jupiter

Alchemical Element: Fire

Alchemical Essential: Mercury

Time of Invocation: 5:40 PM - 6:00 PM

Ruling Days: May 12, July 23, October 3, December 14, February 24

Psalm 103.19: The Lord has prepared his throne in the heavens; and his kingdom rules over all.

Latin: Dominus in Cœlo paravit sedem suam et Regnum suum omnibus dominabitur.

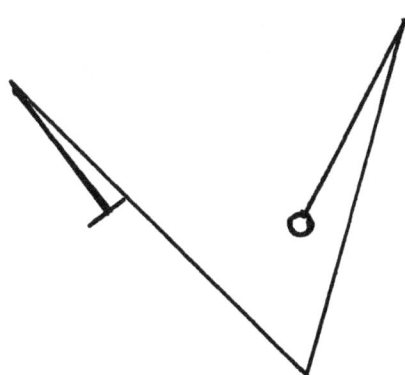

Practice: Theurgical Operations

55th Spirit

Holy Trigram: MBH - Mebeh

Name: MBHIH - Mabehiah

Gematria Value: 47/ 62 Assisting Angel: Smat

Attribute: Eternal God.

Zodiac: 271-275° Jupiter in Capricorn 1-5°

Planetary Ruler: Saturn

Alchemical Element: Earth

Alchemical Essential: Sulphur

Time of Invocation: 6:00 PM - 6:20 PM

Ruling Days: May 13, July 24, October 4, December 15, February 25

Psalm 102.12: But thou, Lord, endures forever, and thy memorial to generation and generation.

Latin: Tu autem Domine in æternum permanes et memorial tuum in generationem et generationem.

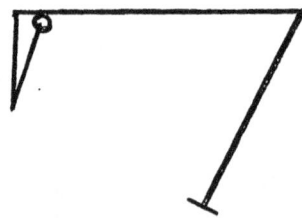

ACP Clergy Handbook

56th Spirit

Holy Trigram: PVI - Poi Name: PVIAL - Poiel

Gematria Value: 96/127

Assisting Angel: Themeso

Attribute: God who supports the universe.

Zodiac: 276-280° Jupiter in Capricorn 6-10°

Planetary Ruler: Saturn

Alchemical Element: Earth

Alchemical Essential: Sulphur

Time of Invocation: 6:20 PM - 6:40 PM

Ruling Days: May 14, July 25, October 5, December 16, February 26

Psalm 145.14: The Lord supports all that are falling, and sets up all that are broken down.

Latin: Allevat Dominus omnes qui corrunt, et erigit omnes elisos.

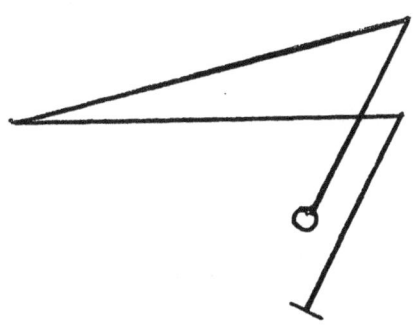

Practice: Theurgical Operations

57th Spirit

Holy Trigram: NMM - Nemem

Name: NMMIH - Nememiah

Gematria Value: 130/145

Assisting Angel: Sro

Attribute: Praiseworthy God.

Zodiac: 281-285° Mars in Capricorn 11-15°

Planetary Ruler: Saturn

Alchemical Element: Earth

Alchemical Essential: Sulphur

Time of Invocation: 6:40 PM - 7:00 PM

Ruling Days: May 15, July 26, October 6, December 17, February 27

Psalm 115.11: They that fear the Lord trust in the Lord; he is their helper and defender.

Latin: Qui timent Dominum speraverunt in Domino, adiutor eorum et protector eorem est.

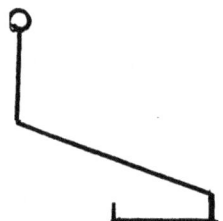

ACP Clergy Handbook

58th Spirit

Holy Trigram: IIL - Yeil

Name: IILAL - Yeilael

Gematria Value: 50/81

Assisting Angel: Epima

Attribute: God who hears the generations.

Zodiac: 286-290° Mars in Capricorn 16-20°

Planetary Ruler: Saturn

Alchemical Element: Earth

Alchemical Essential: Sulphur

Time of Invocation: 7:00 PM - 7:20 PM

Ruling Days: May 16, July 27, October 7, December 18, February 28

Psalm 6.3: My soul is greviously vexed; but thou, O Lord, how long?

Latin: Et anima mea turbata est valde sed tu Domine usque quo.

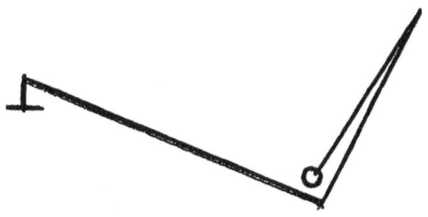

Practice: Theurgical Operations

59th Spirit

Holy Trigram: HRCh - Harach

Name: HRChAL - Harachael

Gematria Value: 213/244

Assisting Angel: Irso

Attribute: God who knows all things.

Zodiac: 291-295° Sun in Capricorn 21-25°

Planetary Ruler: Saturn

Alchemical Element: Earth

Alchemical Essential: Sulphur

Time of Invocation: 7:20 PM - 7:40 PM

Ruling Days: May 17, July 28, October 8, December 19, March 1

Psalm 113.3: From the rising of the sun to his setting, the name of the Lord is to be praised.

Latin: Ab ortu solis usque ad occasum laudabile nomen Domine.

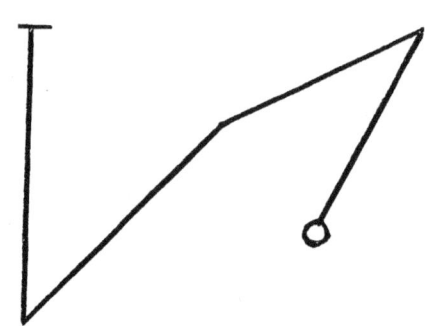

ACP Clergy Handbook

60th Spirit

Holy Trigram: MTzR,. Metzer

Name: MTzRAL - Metzerael

Gematria Value: 330/361

Assisting Angel: Hometh

Attribute: God who comforts the oppressed.

Zodiac: 296-300° Sun in Capricorn 26-30°

Planetary Ruler: Saturn

Alchemical Element: Earth

Alchemical Essential: Sulphur

Time of Invocation: 7:40 PM - 8:00 PM

Ruling Days: May 18, July 29, October 9, December 20, March 2

Psalm 145.7: The Lord is righteous in all his ways, and holy in all his works.

Latin: Iustus Dominus in omnibus viis suis et sanctus in omnibus operibus eius.

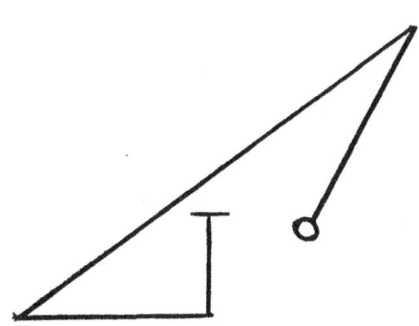

Practice: Theurgical Operations

61st Spirit

Holy Trigram: VMB - Vameb

Name: VMBIH- Vamebiah

Gematria Value: 48/ 63

Assisting Angel: Ptiau

Attribute: God above all things.

Zodiac: 301-305° Venus in Aquarius 1-5°

Planetary Ruler: Saturn

Alchemical Element: Air

Alchemical Essential: Salt

Time of Invocation: 8:00 PM - 8:20 PM

Ruling Days: May 19, July 30, October 10, December 21, March 3

Psalm 113.2: Let the name of the Lord be blessed, from this present time and forever.

Latin: Sit nomen Domini benedictum ex hoc nunc et usque in sæculum.

ACP Clergy Handbook

62nd Spirit

Holy Trigram: IHH - Yehah

Name: IHHAL- Yehahel

Gematria Value: 20/ 51

Assisting Angel: Oroasoer

Attribute: Supreme Being.

Zodiac: 306-310° Venus in Aquarius 6-10°

Planetary Ruler: Saturn

Alchemical Element: Air

Alchemical Essential: Salt

Time of Invocation: 8:20 PM - 8:40 PM

Ruling Days: May 20, July 31, October 11, December 22, March 4

Psalm 119.159: Behold, I have loved thy commandments, O Lord; quicken me in thy mercy.

Latin: Vide quoniam mandata tua dilexi Domine, in misericordiam tua vivifica me.

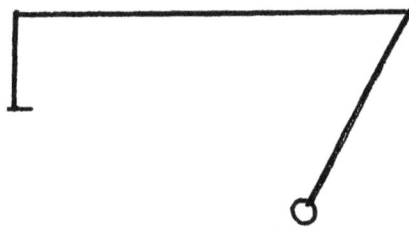

Practice: Theurgical Operations

63rd Spirit

Holy Trigram: ONV - Aunu

Name: ONVAL -Aunuel

Gematria Value: 126/157

Assisting Angel: Asau

Attribute: God, infinitely good.

Zodiac: 311-315° Mercury in Aquarius 11-15°

Planetary Ruler: Saturn

Alchemical Element: Air

Alchemical Essential: Salt

Time of Invocation: 8:40 PM - 9:00 PM

Ruling Days: May 21, August 1, October 12, December 23, March 5

Psalm 100.2: Serve the Lord with gladness; come before his presence with exultation.

Latin: Servite Domino in Lætite, introite in conspectus eius in exultatione.

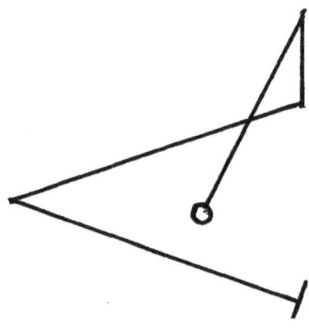

ACP Clergy Handbook

64th Spirit

Holy Trigram: MChl - Machi

Name: MChlAL- Machiel

Gematria Value: 58/98

Assisting Angel: Astiro

Attribute: God who gives life to all things.

Zodiac: 316-320° Mercury in Aquarius 16-20°

Planetary Ruler: Saturn

Alchemical Element: Air

Alchemical Essential: Salt

Time of Invocation: 9:00 PM - 9:20 PM

Ruling Days: May 22, August 2, October 13, December 24, March 6

Psalm 33.18: Behold, the eyes of the Lord are on them that fear him, those that hope in his mercy.

Latin: Ecce oculi Domini super metuentes eum et in eis qui spirant super misericordiam eius.

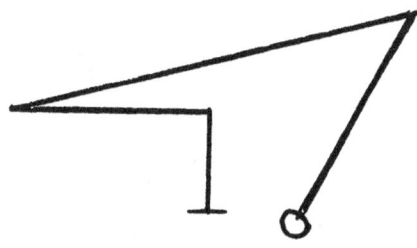

Practice: Theurgical Operations

65th Spirit

Holy Trigram: DMB – Dameb

Name: DMBIH – Damebiah

Gematria Value: 46/61

Assisting Angel: Ptebiou

Attribute: God, fountain of wisdom.

Zodiac: 321-325° Moon in Aquarius 21-25°

Planetary Ruler: Saturn

Alchemical Element: Air

Alchemical Essential: Salt

Time of Invocation: 9:20 PM – 9:40 PM

Ruling Days: May 23, August 3, October 14, December 25, March 7

Psalm 90.13: Return, O Lord, how long? And be entreated concerning thy servants.

Latin: Convertere Domine, et usque qua? Et deprecabilis esto super savos tuos.

ACP Clergy Handbook

66th Spirit

Holy Trigram: MNQ – Menaq

Name: MNQAL – Menaqael

Gematria Value: 190/221

Assisting Angel: Tepisatras

Attribute: God who supports and maintains all things.

Zodiac: 326-330° Moon in Aquarius 26-30°

Planetary Ruler: Saturn

Alchemical Element: Air

Alchemical Essential: Salt

Time of Invocation: 9:40 PM – 10:00 PM

Ruling Days: May 24, August 4, October 15, December 26, March 8

Psalm 38.21: Forsake me not, O Lord my God; depart not from me.

Latin: Ne dereliquas me Dominus Deus meus ne discesseris a me.

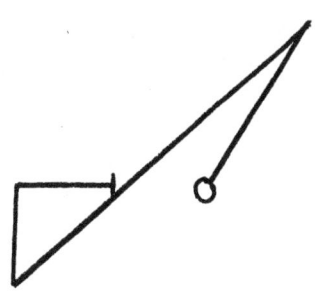

Practice: Theurgical Operations

67th Spirit

Holy Trigram: AIO – Aiau

Name: AIOAL – Aiauel

Gematria Value: 81/112

Assisting Angel: Abiou

Attribute: God, delight of the children of men.

Zodiac: 331-335° Saturn in Pisces 1-5°

Planetary Ruler: Jupiter

Alchemical Element: Water

Alchemical Essential: Mercury

Time of Invocation: 10:00 PM – 10:20 PM

Ruling Days: May 25, August 5, October 16, December 27, March 9

Psalm 37.4: Delight thyself in the Lord; and he shall grant thee the requests of thine heart.

Latin: Delectar in Domino et dabit tibi petitiones cordis tui.

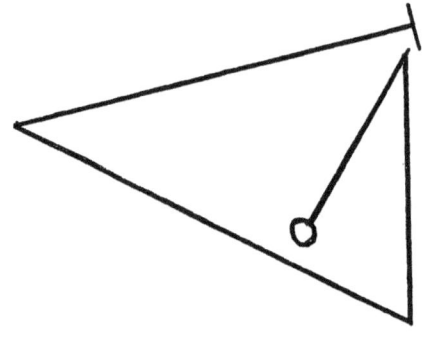

ACP Clergy Handbook

68th Spirit

Holy Trigram: ChBV – Chebo

Name: ChBVIH – Cheboiah

Gematria Value: 16/31

Assisting Angel: Archatapias

Attribute: God who gives liberally.

Zodiac: 336-340° Saturn in Pisces 6-10°

Planetary Ruler: Jupiter

Alchemical Element: Water

Alchemical Essential: Mercury

Time of Invocation: 10:20 PM – 10:40 PM

Ruling Days: May 26, August 6, October 17, December 28, March 10

Psalm 106.1: Give thanks to the Lord; for he is good; for his mercy endures forever.

Latin: Confitemini Dominoquoniam bonus, quoniam in æternum misericordiam eius.

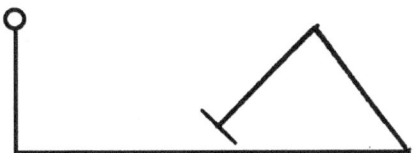

Practice: Theurgical Operations

69th Spirit

Holy Trigram: RAH – Raah

Name: RAHAL – Raahel

Gematria Value: 206/237

Assisting Angel: Chontare

Attribute: God who sees all.

Zodiac: 341-345° Jupiter in Pisces 11-15°

Planetary Ruler: Jupiter

Alchemical Element: Water

Alchemical Essential: Mercury

Time of Invocation: 10:40 PM – 11:00 PM

Ruling Days: May 27, August 7, October 18, December 29, March 11

Psalm 16.5: The Lord is the portion of mine inheritance and of my cup; thou art he that restores my inheritance to me.

Latin: Dominus pars hæreditatis meæ et calicis meæ tues qui restitutes hæreditatem meum mihi.

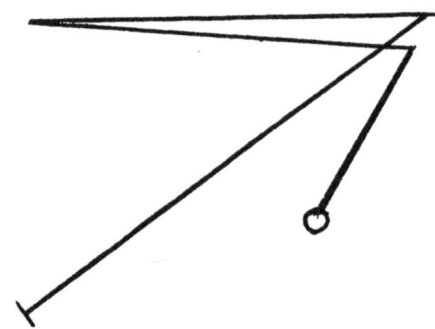

ACP Clergy Handbook

70th Spirit

Holy Trigram: IBM – Yebem

Name: IBMIH- Yebemiah

Gematria Value: 52/67

Assisting Angel: Thopibui

Attribute: Word which produces all things.

Zodiac: 346-350° Jupiter in Pisces 16-20°

Planetary Ruler: Jupiter

Alchemical Element: Water

Alchemical Essential: Mercury

Time of Invocation: 11:00 PM – 11:20 PM

Ruling Days: May 28, August 8, October 19, December 30, March 12

Genesis 1.1: In the beginning God created the Heavens and the Earth.

Latin: In principio creavit Deus Cœlum et Terram.

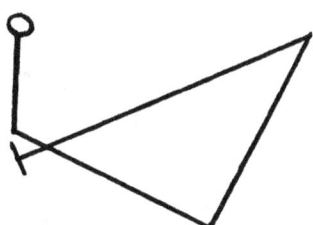

Practice: Theurgical Operations

71st Spirit

Holy Trigram: HII – Haiai

Name: HIIAL – Haiaiel

Gematria Value: 25/56

Assisting Angel: Ptibiou

Attribute: God, master of the universe.

Zodiac: 351-355° Mars in Pisces 21-25°

Planetary Ruler: Jupiter

Alchemical Element: Water

Alchemical Essential: Mercury

Time of Invocation: 11:20 PM – 11:40 PM

Ruling Days: May 29, August 9, October 20, December 31, March 13

Psalm 109.30: I will give thanks to the Lord abundantly with my mouth; and in the midst of many I will praise him.

Latin: Confitebor Domino nimis in ore meo, et in media multorum laudabo eum.

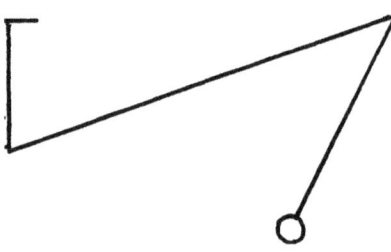

ACP Clergy Handbook

72nd Spirit

Holy Trigram: MVM – Mourn

Name: MVMIH – Moumiah

Gematria Value: 86/101

Assisting Angel: Atembui

Attribute: Alpha and Omega.

Zodiac: 356-360° Mars in Pisces 26-30°

Planetary Ruler: Jupiter

Alchemical Element: Water

Alchemical Essential: Mercury

Time of Invocation: 11:40 PM – 12:00 Midnight

Ruling Days: May 30, August 10, October 21, January 1, March 14

Psalm 116.7: Return to thy rest, O my soul; for the Lord has dealt bountifully with thee.

Latin: Convertere anima mea in requiem tuam quoniam Dominus benefaciet tibi.

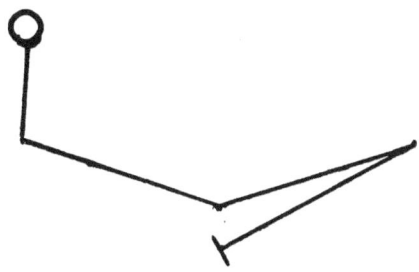

PART III
SUPPLEMENTARY DISCOURSES

O the depth of the riches and wisdom and gnosis of God! How unsearchable are His judgments and untraceable His ways!

- Romans 11:33

On Faith and Knowledge

In this essay, I want to examine two terms that are often heard in discussions about Gnosticism: Pistis, from the Greek, meaning "faith"; and Gnosis, also from the Greek, meaning "Knowledge." When I was ordained into the Minor Orders of the Gnostic Church over a decade ago, I remember, during my studies, participating in many discussions about Gnostic theology wherein a sharp distinction was often made between "pistic" Christianity, which seeks salvation through faith in the death and resurrection of Jesus Christ, and "gnostic" Christianity, which seeks salvation through the revelatory knowledge of Jesus Christ. This distinction is an accurate one, owing to the contrasting soteriological doctrines of original sin. That is, one element of Christendom views humanity as being utterly depraved due to its rebellion against God, and helpless concerning its own salvation. It is therefore only through absolute and unquestioning faith in the salvific quality of the passion that one may have hope of salvation. The "gnostic" Christian, however, views man as an essentially divine being, but ignorant of his true nature because of the slumber induced by the false god against whom he once rebelled. To the Gnostic, then, Jesus Christ came to awaken humanity to its own latent potential, whereby it may effect its own salvation. These definitions are gross over-simplifications, but nevertheless serve to show the fundamental philosophical difference between Gnosticism and non-gnostic Christianity.

Because of the clear distinction between the two theological camps mentioned above, the concepts of pistis and gnosis are routinely pitted against one another as if they are irreconcilably opposed. However, to place faith in opposition to knowledge is a false dichotomy, and leads away from the spiritual reintegration sought by Gnostics. Faith, in fact, is an integral part of the spiritual regenerative process. This process is expressed poetically in the following excerpt from The Gospel of Philip:

Faith is our earth in which we take root.

Hope is the water with which we are nourished.

Love is the air through which we grow.

Knowledge is the light by which we ripen.

In this agricultural analogy we see that faith is at the very foundation of the Christian Gnostic doctrine. But we may ask what, then, is the foundation of our faith? The answer is "knowledge." Now this may seem to be somewhat circular reasoning, since knowledge is also the end result. But it must be understood that there are various levels or degrees of knowledge. The very lowest form of knowledge is the simple accumulation of facts and data. This type of knowledge is indispensable to the productive functioning in the material world, but does little to effect spiritual transformation. The faith based upon this knowledge is the surety of the physical laws of the universe. The hope arising from this type of faith is the sort of expectation we have that the atoms of our body will not spontaneously dissipate; or that all of the air in a room will not suddenly collect in one corner, leaving a vacuum. With this basic expectation met – that the laws of nature are stable and consistently reliable – there arises a very primitive form of love. This love is not the agape that leads to the salvific gnosis; rather, it is the base desires of the physical nature: nourishment, shelter, sex, etc. This level of love also includes emotional attachments and aesthetic value judgments.

This level of functioning is seen in those many people who go about their lives seeking nothing but the fulfillment of the most basic human needs as mentioned above. These individuals are "sinners" not because they are acting with malicious intent, but because they are acting blindly; without knowledge of their true Nature – in fact, without even suspecting that there is any nature of man higher than the animal nature to which they might aspire. Because this type of individual has little control over the many factors influencing his life, and seems to be tossed about - for better or worse – by the tides of Fortune, he is referred to by our beloved 18th century mystic, Louis-Claude de Saint-Martin, as l'Homme du Torrent, or the Man of the Stream. This state of being is characterized by rote behavior and the lack of philosophical inquiry or introspection.

These lowest forms of knowledge, faith, hope, and love make possible a somewhat higher form of knowledge based upon philosophical reasoning. It is this type of knowledge upon which we may establish our faith in the existence of a God. This faith, based upon reason rather than empirical data, thus represents our first step out of the personal, material realm and toward the eternal or spiritual realm. That is why it is "our earth in which we take root." Faith is crucial to the fulfillment of liturgical life. It is from this faith that the priest derives the intent necessary to effect the transmission of the sacraments. Likewise, it is our faith in the efficacy of those sacraments that allows them to produce the desired results.

With faith in a divine and eternal realm comes the hope for our attainment of that ultimate glory. The canonical scriptures are filled with references to the hope of eternal or aeonic life. One interesting example of this is in the introduction of the Letter of Paul to Titus, which expresses this in the context of faith and knowledge:

> Paul, a servant of God, apostle of Jesus Christ, according to the faith of the elect of God and the knowledge of truth according to godliness, on the hope of aeonic life promised by the truthful God before the aeons of time.

The individual who aspires to spiritual grace corresponds to what Saint-Martin called l'Homme de Désir – the Man of Desire. This desire is not like the primitive material urges of the Man of the Stream, but a yearning of the soul for its spiritual home. When one has set oneself upon this path, she, or he, begins to develop a concern for the general upliftment of humanity. This movement away from the immediate concerns of self-preservation and gratification toward a more universal ideal is best expressed in the Greek concept of agape. The Latin, caritas, from which we get the word "charity," conveys a similar sentiment. This love, therefore, is not at all like the self-centered demands of the Man of the Stream. It is what the Buddhists call compassion; which is not an emotional outpouring, but a genuine altruism toward one's fellow brothers and sisters on the path – humanity.

This path of faith, hope, and love makes possible the bestowal of the higher knowledge, or gnosis, upon those who have spiritually matured. The first glimpses of gnosis may come through dreams, intuitive flashes, or premonitions. This phenomena often pertains to specific facts, persons, or events, and may be referred to as personal gnosis. That is, its significance is relative to the one who experiences it. But this same process of enhanced awareness is also the vehicle for divine gnosis, or knowledge of God. This divine knowledge is revealed through the intuitive faculties. Therefore, it is not subject to quantification, such as the lowest form of knowledge discussed previously; neither is it subject to logical reasoning, because it is higher than the laws governing normal logic and critical thinking.

In other words, in normal deductive reasoning, the truth of an idea or principle is dependent upon certainties which often necessitate the falsehood of some other principle. An example of a deductive argument would go something like this:

If A is true, then B is not true.

A is true. Therefore, B is not true.

Or,

Either A or B is true.

A is true. Therefore B is not true.

You would never find a valid deductive argument that states:

If A is true then A is not true.

For, this would create an irreconcilable paradox. Neither could you state:

Either A is true, or A is not true.

A is true. Therefore A is not true.

In this example, the argument would be valid if we had stopped at "A is true." However, the statement that "A is not true" does not logically follow from the previous statements. But gnosis comes from a plane that is above the laws of nature which state that an idea must be either true or not true; that a thing must be of one nature but not another. In gnosis, paradoxes are reconciled; the circle squared. We are not talking here about mere probability or inductive reasoning, which states that as one thing becomes more likely, something else must become less likely. No, gnosis is a revelatory knowledge that allows all seeming contradictions to simultaneously coexist. This elevation of the consciousness above the duality of either/or is indicative of the process of reintegration into the One from which all apparent divisions extend.

With this higher level of gnostic awareness, there is the emergence of what Saint-Martin called Le Nouvelle Homme – the New Man. This is the same "New Man" that St. Paul, in his Letter to the Colossians (3:10-11), tells us is "being renewed in knowledge." And, "in that renewal there is not Greek and Jew, circumcision and uncircumcision...etc.; but Christ is all and in all." The faith of the New Man is unshakable because it is founded upon a surety that can come from neither empirical data, nor philosophical reasoning. The knowledge gained from empirical study must necessarily be falsifiable; that is the scientific method.

That is, no matter how well-tested a theory or law of physics may be, there must exist the possibility of discovering new evidence that could alter or even reverse our views on the matter. Likewise, with logic and critical thinking, new ideas may be presented that are more plausible than those previously held. But true gnosis comes from the innermost depths of the human psyche, or soul, which is that elusive and vivifying pneumatic spark. Truly, as it was said in ancient times, to know oneself is to know the universe and the gods.

The hope arising from this faith is no longer mere expectation, but a certainty of one's place among the aeons and of one's role on earth in service to humanity. And love is the means by which the Great Work is accomplished. This highest form of agape is a regenerative and sanctifying grace that the high priest of the gnosis radiates toward all within his sphere of influence. This love has the ability to instantly liberate the divine spark from even the densest and basest of matter. The adept who has discovered this ultimate secret is a true Gnostic; a living Master and demiourgos. This accomplishment is identical to the creation of the fabled Philosopher's Stone of the alchemists. It is the Elixir of Life; the Fountain of Youth. This is what Saint-Martin referred to as l'Homme-Esprit, or Spirit-Man. Beyond this, what more can be said? We have already tried to express the inexpressible; to articulate that which is ineffable. If there are higher planes of attainment, they are known only to those who have experienced them directly, and are surely wholly incommunicable. Here, the differences between Faith, Hope, Love, and Knowledge melt away into an undifferentiated state of pneumatic luminescence.

So, when we speak of "pistic" Christians and "gnostic" Christians, let us not suppose that we, as Gnostics, are somehow above the need for faith, but let us be thankful that our faith has matured. And let us not take pride in calling ourselves "Gnostics," for that designation is on loan to us on the hope of our eventual attainment. There are not likely many living today who can wear that name deservingly. There are more people than ever, though, who are aspiring toward this worthy goal. Faith and Gnosis, therefore, are not opposing philosophic doctrines, but are each a form of salvific grace, bestowed by the Holy Spirit to aid us in our quest for spiritual perfection. If we can learn to integrate the concepts of Faith, Hope, Love, and Knowledge into our theological worldview, then we will be well on our way toward reconciling the myriad dualities struggling within each of us. We may look forward to that hour when the Law of Agape brings all seemingly contrary forces into a symphony of complementarity.

On the Eucharist

The sacrament of the Eucharist is the central rite of the Apostolic Church of the Pleroma. The entire ceremony of the Mass has but one ultimate function: to rightly celebrate the Mystery of the Eucharist. First of all, let us look at the definition of the word "Eucharist." The word comes from the Greek ευχαριστος (eukharistos) meaning "grateful" or "thankful." According to the *American Heritage Dictionary of the English Language*, the Eucharist is, "a sacrament and the central act of worship in many Christian churches which was instituted at the Last Supper and in which bread and wine are consecrated and consumed in remembrance of Jesus."

Sometimes the terms "Eucharist" and "Communion" are used interchangeably, but we will make the following distinction between the two: that the term "Communion" refers specifically to the act of consuming the consecrated Eucharistic elements. This is because the actual communing with God is through the consuming of the Body and Blood of Jesus Christ. This ritual transformation is called "transubstantiation." According to the *American Heritage Dictionary*, transubstantiation is, "The doctrine holding that the bread and wine of the Eucharist are transformed into the body and blood of Jesus, although their appearances remain the same." We are going to address here the various elements and conditions that are necessary to effect the Eucharistic transformation. The requisite elements are three-fold, being physical, mental, and spiritual.

Let us begin with the physical requirements. First of all there must be a celebrant to perform the rite. The Eucharist is performed by either a priest or a bishop. These are the levels of clergy that have the power to cause the transubstantiation. The origin of these powers will be addressed in the section concerning the spiritual requirements. The other physical requirements are the **matter** and **form**. The *matter* is the bread and wine that are to be consecrated. The bread, also called the "Host," used by the ACP, as well as by other Apostolic churches, is a flat, unleavened bread. There are some Eastern traditions, however, that use a leavened loaf instead. But although we share certain Eastern ecclesiastical philosophies, there are sound esoteric reasons (which go beyond the scope of this paper) for utilizing the unleavened wafer. The wine, in our Apostolic tradition, should be a fermented grape wine. Now, there are many wines that contain additional fruits or spices. This is acceptable as long as it is a principally grape wine. Non-fermented wine, though inferior, may also be substituted if absolutely necessary, though it should still be grape-based. Just as the wine is representative of the blood of Jesus, the water mixed with the wine represents the Holy Spirit which anoints and sanctifies.

The *form* consists of the words of institution, or the words of consecration, that must be pronounced. These words vary slightly among the different Apostolic traditions, but all are similar and are derived from the words spoken by Jesus at the Last Supper. There are accounts given of these words in the three synoptic gospels of Matthew, Mark, and Luke. You may find these in Matthew 26:26-28, Mark 14:22-24, and Luke 22:17-20. Words similar to those found in the aforementioned passages are spoken by the priest or bishop in conjunction with other prayers and blessings to consecrate the bread and wine, and cause them to become the Body and Blood of Christ. Now, it may be asked whether subtractions from, or additions to the sacramental form will in any way affect the validity of a sacrament;. On this topic we must concur with the renowned alchemist and theologian St. Thomas Aquinas, who addresses this very issue in his *Summa Theologica*. He rightly points out that:

> Certain words are inserted by some in the sacramental forms which are not inserted by others; thus the Latins baptize under the form: I baptize thee in the name of the Father, and of the Son, and of the Holy Ghost, whereas the Greeks use the following form: The servant of God, N... is baptized in the name of the Father, etc. Yet both confer the sacrament validly. Therefore it is lawful to add something to or to take something from, the sacramental forms.

He goes on to say, however:

> If he intends by such addition or suppression to perform a rite other from that which is recognized by the Church, it seems that the sacrament is invalid, because he seems not to intend to do what the Church does.

Aquinas also uses the following example, "Thus, in the form of the Eucharist, - For this is My Body, the omission of the word 'for' does not destroy the due sense of the words, nor consequently cause the sacrament to be invalid." We see then that the form, or words of institution, need not be exactly the same among all Apostolic traditions, but that their meaning and substance does need to be maintained.

This brings us to the mental conditions required for the consecration of the Eucharist. This requirement is simple, yet it is vitally important: **Intent**. The priest or bishop must have the proper intent in order to validly consecrate the Eucharist. This means that not only must the priest intend for the transubstantiation to occur, but that he or she be a vehicle for the power of Christ to act. Looking again to Aquinas, he says that, "his intention is required, whereby he subjects himself to the principal agent; that is, it is necessary that he intend to do that which Christ and the Church do." Intent is required of all sacraments; indeed, of all religious or spiritual rites. The form is closely associated with the intent. Without intent, the form is empty and meaningless. Without proper form, the intent cannot be articulated and realized.

Having addressed, then, the physical and mental requirements for the consecration of the Eucharist, we are left with the spiritual requirement. The spiritual requirement is the **Apostolic Succession**. This is, according to the *American Heritage Dictionary*, "Of or relating to a succession of spiritual authority from the twelve Apostles, regarded by the Anglicans, Roman Catholics, Eastern Orthodox, and some others, to have been perpetuated by successive ordinations of bishops and to be requisite for valid Orders and administration of sacraments." In Apostolic traditions such as ours, we hold to the doctrine that Jesus imparted special powers to His disciples, including: the power to heal the sick, the power to cast out and control evil spirits, and the power to effect the transformation of bread and wine into His Body and Blood.

The sacrifice of bread and wine was an extremely ancient rite even in the time of Jesus, for we read in Genesis 13:18, "And Melchizedek, king of Salem, brought forth bread and wine; and he was the priest of the most high God ..." Concerning this passage from Genesis and the transmission of this sacrificial tradition to

Jesus and from Jesus to His Apostles, bishop Robert Ambelain writes in Spiritual Alchemy:

> This phrase, innocent enough in appearance, has however an unsuspected depth in the context of Judeo-Christian Tradition. For if, when Melchizedek transmitted the sacrificial rite of Bread and Wine – of *Corn* and *Vine* – to Abraham, he had the powers of the *Most High* God, this shows that Gnosis existed already, and that certain people knew there was *another God* besides the common gods. Moreover, this initiation into a secret Rite which was new to Abraham, when he received it from Melchizedek, Abraham transmitted it to all his posterity, to the whole of the future Israel. Indeed, because of this, in the heart of Solomon's Temple, alongside the propitiatory bloody sacrifices of animals, we meet again the offering of azyme bread and wine. This has been perpetuated in the rite of *Seder*, which includes the presences of *Matzoh*, or azyme bread; and the rite of *Kiddush*, the blessing of the cup of wine. When the Christ made it the basis of all Christian ritual he called himself the "Sacrificer after the Order of Melchizedek." So his Apostles and their Disciples received an "ordination" from him dating back to a certain origin in the time of Abraham which, according to history, was around the twelfth Egyptian dynasty, nineteen centuries B.C., during the time of the Middle Empire. In fact, this mysterious rite descended from occult elements and traditions *as old as four millennia!*

The first bishops were those who were ordained by the original Apostles. They received those same spiritual powers as were conferred to the Apostles. These powers have been regularly transmitted down through the generations to the present day. The lines of Apostolic succession have been meticulously recorded and preserved, so that every bishop alive today can trace his Apostolic lineage all the way back to Jesus and the original twelve Apostles. In addition to the bishops, the priesthood also receives the Apostolic succession. In fact, a priest's powers are similar in almost every way to those of the bishop. However, a priest is not able to ordain another priest. Although a priest may, with special perrmss1on, ordain an individual into the Minor Orders of the Church, only the bishop has the spiritual authority to confer the major Orders of Deacon, Priest, and Bishop, wherein the Apostolic Succession is actually transmitted.

We have seen, then, that the Eucharist is much more than a symbolic meal. It is a carefully formulated ritual, requiring specific physical, mental, and spiritual conditions to be met for the effective administration of the rite. Again, the physical conditions are: the **priest** or **bishop**; the **matter**, which is the bread and wine; and the **form**, which consists of the words of institution. The mental condition is the **intent** to be an instrument of the power of Christ for the transformation of the Eucharistic elements into His Body and Blood. And finally, it is necessary that the priest or bishop has a valid line of **Apostolic succession**, so he will have received the requisite spiritual power and authority to effect the transubstantiation.

To those of us who adhere to the Apostolic tradition, the Eucharist is a means of receiving God's grace. The Gospel of John, 6:54, says, "Whoso eateth my flesh and drinketh my blood, hath eternal life." When we partake of this sacrament by consuming the body and blood of Christ, we become one with Christ. John 6:56 tells us, "He that eateth my flesh and drinketh by blood, dwelleth in me, and I in him." The *Gospel of Truth* tells us that Jesus himself is the fruit of the Tree of Knowledge. Therefore, we partake of Him so that the veils of ignorance might be lifted from our eyes. By communing with the divine and human natures of Jesus, we commune with and reconcile our own divine and human natures; and through this communion receive the grace and comfort of the Holy Spirit. To be sure, when Jesus said, "Do this in remembrance of Me," he was not merely suggesting that we recall his earthly being and works. He was also speaking as the Logos of God; that divine seed through which everything was made, and which resides within us as a treasure awaiting to be discovered and remembered. And in that treasure is the secret of our origin, and therefore the keys of life and death. To partake of His Body and Blood is to invite the Holy Spirit upon us, so that the Seed may be awakened, and restored to the Pleroma.

Let us close this brief analysis with another quote from Ambelain's *Spiritual Alchemy*:

> With the Eucharist, we absorb an occult and mystic "charge," a *philter of immortality* which, if we impregnate ourselves with it sufficiently and often enough during the course of our terrestrial life, could transmute us little by little, year by year. For this "charge," assimilated by our organism like all regular nourishment, nevertheless passes from the physiological plane to the psyche, and from the psyche into the *nous*, or spirit.

A Gnostic Exposition of the Three Alchemical Essentials

The venerable Art and Science of Alchemy has been associated with Gnosticism and Hermeticism since the earliest days of these religious and philosophical systems. Alchemy could probably be said to be more directly related to the Egyptian Hermetic tradition than to the religious doctrines of the Gnostics proper; but Gnostic and Hermetic doctrines have been so inextricably linked from antiquity until the present day, that it seems reasonable to consider it as a single system, at least for our purposes here. It is not the purpose of this brief article to examine the historical aspects of alchemy, or to get bogged down with academic categorization or arbitrary labels. In fact, whatever historical connection may have existed between alchemy and Gnosticism would have effectively ceased with the suppression of Gnosticism by the emerging "orthodoxy." Alchemy, however (and for that matter, the entire Hermetic Tradition), has managed to find a way to continue to develop and thrive among numerous cultures and civilization. So, in the present day we find the situation to be that as Gnosticism has re- emerged as a viable system of spirituality, alchemy has evolved in a way that, while complementary to Gnosticism in its core principles, does not quite match up in language and symbolism as neatly as one might like. I will elaborate upon this shortly.

I must also state that I do not intend to give a comprehensive introduction to alchemical symbolism. This article supposes that the reader has at least a general understanding of some of the basic alchemical principles. What is intended here is an examination of the Three Alchemical Essentials: Sulphur, Mercury, and Salt, and their correspondences within a specifically Gnostic framework. I am speaking here, of course, with regard to the spiritual and philosophical aspects of alchemy, not the physical chemical properties. I am specifically concerned here with how the Essentials correlate with the Gnostic symbolic philosophy and mythos; especially the relationship between Divinity and Humanity. Because the Alchemical Triad may be so conveniently compared to the myriad instances of triplicity in nature and in esoteric philosophy, there have been many writings on the subject, often contradicting one another. One commonly misunderstood and confused issue is the relationship between Spirit and Soul, and whether they should correspond respectively to Sulphur and Mercury, or to Mercury and Sulphur. There has been no little confusion regarding this matter, largely due to the fact that alchemists and mystical philosophers over the centuries have interchanged the two in their charts and discourses, seemingly arbitrarily at times. I am not going to go too far down this rabbit hole right now, except to say that both attributes are correct, depending upon the context in which they are viewed.

As Gnostics, we have very precise definitions of Spirit and Soul, but these terms have also been used in many mystical and alchemical writings to describe other aspects of duality or polarity, such as Fixity and Changeability, Active and Passive, Masculine and Feminine, Outer and Inner, etc. We can, however, address this within a Gnostic context so that these symbols are relevant to our particular language, methods, and work. That is, the esotericism that has been passed down as the Western Mystery Tradition need not be at odds with the neo-Sethianism or neo-Valentinianism that is practiced by many ecclesiastical Gnostics such as ourselves.

Supplement: Three Alchemical Essentials

But if we are to attempt a workable synthesis, we must define our terms in such a way that it is internally consistent.

In addition to the Spirit/Soul dichotomy, another critical issue which needs to be addressed concerns the various attempts made in many works to associate Sulphur, Mercury, and Salt with the aspects of the Holy Trinity. Many of these works throughout the centuries tend to make what I find to be a peculiar and, if not entirely erroneous, at the very least incomplete attribution of Salt to the Holy Spirit. A typical example of this can be seen in the tables given in Manly P. Hall's *The Secret Teachings of All Ages*:

World of	Father	Son	Mother
1. God	Father	Son	Holy Ghost
2. Man	Spirit	Soul	Body
3. Elements	Air	Fire	Water
4. Chemicals	Mercury	Sulphur	Salt

Alternative renderings of 3 and 4 are:

World of	Father	Son	Mother
3. Elements	Fire	Air	Water
4. Chemicals	Sulphur	Mercury	Salt

Hall goes on to list Paracelsus' arrangement as another alternative, though it omits the Holy Trinity. Regardless, I will list it here so that we have another point of reference:

1. Man	Spirit	Soul	Body
2. Elements	Air	Water	Earth
3. Chemicals	Sulphur	Mercury	Salt

In the charts above we can see examples of the concerns I mentioned previously. In addition, we see discrepancies with the Elemental attributes as well. Standard rules of logic tell us that all of these tables of correspondences cannot be simultaneously true; that one or another of these combinations must be the right one. Well, the real enigma of this subtle Art is that all of these attributes, as well as additional permutations, are in fact correct. The reason for this is that all of the properties of Sulphur, Mercury, and Salt are present in each of the three Essentials individually. Georg von Welling, in his Opus Mago- Cabbalisticum et Theosophicum, emphasizes this point repeatedly in statements such as: "We have sufficiently proved that Sulphur is also in its essence Salt and Mercury, just as Salt is essentially Sulphur and Mercury, and Mercury is Salt and Sulphur," (p. 166). Therefore, simple correspondence charts, like those referenced above, cannot give an adequate representation of the complex dynamic at play here. So, rather than offering refutations of the commonly accepted correspondences, I will instead propose a new set of attributes that takes into account the triune nature of each of the three Essentials, and that may align more closely with Gnostic doctrine. I therefore offer you the following chart with explanatory notes for each of the nine divisions:

Supplement: Three Alchemical Essentials

⊕ (circle/triangle/square/circle)	🜍 (Salt-fire symbol)	☿ (Mercury)	Θ (Earth)
🜍 Pneumatic Realm (Pleroma)	1. Unknown Father of Light; Divine Mind (Nous); Divine Will & Seed; Primum Mobile; Adam (Fire / Æsch)	2. Holy Spirit; Barbelo; Mother-Father; Aeons & Syzygies; Eve / Zoe (Water / Schamajim)	3. Son – Christos – Logos; Archetype of Rectified First Matter; Geradamas; 4 Luminaries; Sophia; Body of Light; Seth (Archetypal Form)
☿ Psychic Realm	4. Vital Life Force; Animating Principle; Pneumatic Spark (Fire)	5. Mind in Man; Rose unfolding upon the Cross; Christ Consciousness in the New Man (Air)	6. Ethereal / Astral Substance (Water)
Θ Hylic Realm	7. Brain; Nervous system; Genitalia; Creative & Generative principle; Neurotransmitters; Sperm & Egg (Fire)	8. Lungs; Heart; Respiratory & Circulatory systems; Blood & Oxygen (Water / Air)	9. Prima Materia (First Matter); Physical Substance; Digestive & Excretory Organs; Urea & Feces (Earth)

As illustrated in the chart, the Realms are divided into Pneumatic, Psychic, and Hylic. The Pneumatic, or Spiritual Realm, being considered a realm of Pure Light, is most similar to the Fiery aspects of Sulphur; although each of the three Essentials is represented therein. The psychic Realm, being caught in a struggle between what is Above and what is Below, is principally similar to the dual nature of Mercury. But just like the Pneumatic Realm, Sulphur, Mercury, and Salt are each represented in the Psychic. Likewise, the Hylic, or Material Realm, contains the most base forms of the alchemical principles; though as a whole it is most closely associated with Salt, and the Prima Materia which it represents.

Having given an overview of the basic structure and major divisions, let us now look more closely at each of the nine squares of the grid:

1. As the Divine Mind (Nous), that is, the Source of All, the Father can be represented by the alchemical Sulphur. The Unknown Father of Light is that primal Fire (1.Esch) from which all ultimately emanates. It is also the Divine Will which sends forth the Seed, and also the Seed itself. This is the Unity, or Monad.

2. The Holy Spirit, Barbelo, the Divine Mother of All, being a polar complement to the Father, is represented by Mercury. The dance of Sulphur and Mercury is represented in all such polar complements, such as the Sun and Moon, or in the Yin and Yang of the Tao. Mercury, however, in addition to being the polar complement to Sulphur, is known to have a unique polar characteristic of its own. This double nature is sometimes depicted in alchemical artwork as a human with two heads, or a man holding a red and white flower, or some other such imagery. This correlates well with the characteristics ascribed to the Holy Spirit, which is principally considered Feminine in relation to the Father, but who is also called Mother-Father; the embodiment of duality. Elementally, the Holy Spirit can be seen as Water (Majim) as compared to the Father, but being of a Pneumatic nature, this Philosophical Mercury is actually the Fiery Waters, Æsch-Majim, or Schamajim of the alchemists. Von Welling confirms this, stating that the Schamajim is, "generally called Mercury by the philosophers," (p. 6). In the Pleroma, Mercury can also be seen in the Valentinian syzygies, as well as the androgynous spiritual beings of Eugnostos, who have both male and female names, (cf. "Eugnostos the Blessed," *The Nag Hammadi Scriptures*, pp. 279-280).

3. Just as the lower Salt is representative of the unrefined Prima Materia, or First Matter, the Pneumatic Salt is the archetype of the Rectified First Matter. The union of Sulphur and Mercury is the alchemical Salt. In the Holy Trinity, this is the Divine Child, Christ himself. It is Christ alone who is able to transform the Lead of our sinful natures into the pure Spiritual Gold and give to us eternal, or Aeonic life. Von Welling states that Christ is, "Our savior and mediator, himself the divine eternal Salt, Fiat, or Word, eternally begotten and born from the divine fire of love for our eternal salvation. Unless

we really and truly partake of this salt, we can never withstand either in this world or the next, the cleansing fire of his majesty," (p. 7). He also states that this Salt, "is the origin, beginning and end of all creatures, and from which all creatures were created," (p. 65). We can see a parallel to this in the *Gospel According to John*, which tells us that, "Through him all things came to be, and without him came to be not one thing," (1:3). We also have here the Logos/ Sophia syzygy. Just as the alchemical Salt is both the substance being transformed (Lead) and that which it is transformed into (Gold), it is also the agent of transformation as seen in the relationship between the Logos and Sophia. In Sophia's descent from the Pleroma, she becomes that which must be redeemed and reconciled to her former estate. In the descent of the Logos we can see the agent of the redemption and reintegration. We can also see how these roles are reversed from time to time. In the Pleroma we also see this principle of Pneumatic Salt represented in Geradamas, the perfect and archetypal Anthropos. The lower psychic and hylic forms of man are like dim reflections of this perfect Body of Light. It is this glorious and luminous garment that every soul will don which has ascended to the Aeons. There could also be an argument made for an association here with the four Luminaries as archetypes of the four Elements.

4. As we enter into the Psychic Realm, we must assign the Vital Life Force to the position of Sulphur. The VLF is that Active and Spiritual essence that animates all life. It is the divine Pneumatic spark that was breathed into Psychic Adam to make him a Living Soul (Psyche). Thus, even though it is found here in the Psychic Realm, it is actually of a purely Pneumatic nature.

5. The infusion of Pneuma into the Psychic body of Adam gave rise to consciousness. When Adam was in Psychical form, this consciousness caused him to be instantly enlightened, (cf. "The Secret Book of John" *The Nag Hammadi Scriptures*, p. 125). But since being trapped in the material world, the mind is in a constant struggle between the Mind of God and the temporal passions of the physical which lead only to decay and death. This dual nature of the mind places it squarely within the Mercurial column of the Psychic Realm, which is itself Mercurial in nature. It is the Rose unfolding upon the Cross. This is where the New Man, the enlightened human, may experience Christ Consciousness. Elementally, it is the Airy aspect of Mercury, since it is a product of the Sulphuric heat of the Pneumatic spark acting upon the Saline fluidity of the etheric substance of which the Psychic is composed.

6. In the Salt column we place the etheric, or Psychic substance previously mentioned. While the Psychic body is not of the dross nature of the physical or Hylic Body, it yet requires further purification and refinement so that it might be transmuted into pure Spiritual Gold, the Lapis Philosophorum. Only then may the Soul find Eternal Life in the Pleroma. It corresponds elementally to Water because of its elastic nature. This is the fluid, or plastic envelope that characterizes the Soul.

7. In the Hylic, or Material Realm, the principle of Sulphur is to be found in the creative and generative aspects of man. This Sulphuric Fire is associated with the brain and the genitalia, which are the organs of creation and generation. The entire nervous system would also be included in this category, for the electrochemical neural impulses are a type of Fire.

8. The Mercurial aspects of the human body are the lungs, which draw in the air, and with the air, the Vital Life Force; and the heart and circulatory system, which distributes the VLF throughout the body via the blood and lymphatic systems. Thus, the Elements represented here are both Air and Water.

9. This brings us, finally, to the First Matter, that dross substance, or Hyle, from which the entire material world is constructed. But as everything has ultimately emanated from the One, which is the All, even this corrupt state of being contains within it the Seed of Goodness. In the body, this corresponds to the digestive and excretory organs, as well as the urea and feces. This is the Element of Earth in its most base form.

Hopefully these attributes given here have not further complicated an already perplexing matter. I have tried, as much as possible, to limit this study to the relationship between God and man, within a specifically Gnostic frame of reference. However, I am also aware that these correspondences are far from complete. Nevertheless, I believe that by using this system as a basis, many other associations may be extrapolated. We can also see how this system begins to rectify apparent contradictions found in earlier descriptions. For instance, this table addresses the Spirit / Soul problem rather neatly. From a purely Gnostic perspective, the Psychic and Pneumatic are given their own categories wherein we can see how all of the Essentials relate to one another. If we are looking at Spirit and Soul from a more classical alchemical perspective of the dualities of Active-Passive, Being- Becoming, etc., then we can see that in the Pneumatic Realm, the Divine Mind, the "Soul" in this case, is Sulphur, and Barbelo as "Spirit" is Mercury. However, if we look at the dynamics of the Psychical Realm, then we see the mind, or "Soul" in the position of Mercury, while "Spirit" in the form of the Vital Life Force, is Sulphur. The apparent dichotomy therefore, has been reconciled. Martinists and other students of Qabalah will also see how the divisions of man, including the Elemental correspondences as expressed in the Sepher Ietzirah, have been reconciled to both the Western Hermetic / alchemical tradition, as well as to the schema of the ancient Gnostics.

The one area where reconciliation among systems does no" seem possible is in the correspondences to the Holy Trinity. While it is true that the characteristics of all three Essentials may be identified in each aspect of the Trinity, it seems inescapable that the principal correspondence of the Son is Salt. This seems to be borne out in the sacrament of the Eucharist, wherein the Sacred Marriage of Spirit and Soul, symbolized by the mixing of the Wine and Water (Sulphur and Mercury), ultimately gives rise to the Child of the Conjunction, the Body of Christ, which is the alchemical Salt. Thus, the Eucharistic bread is the Prima Materia which, throughout the ritual of the Mass, is passed through the various alchemical operations and is eventually transformed into the Lapis Philosophorum. By partaking of the Eucharist, then, the Lead of our Hylic nature is transformed into the Pure Spiritual Gold. Our realization of this transformation, though – the attainment of Christ Consciousness – occurs through the Mind in man as stated in our fifth point above. It is likely for this reason that the –on is often attributed to Mercury. We can see now, though, that the Archetypal Logos is the Pneumatic Salt, whereas the Christ-in-Man manifests as Psychic Mercury.

Before concluding, I want to spend just a little more time examining this crucial Fifth position which sits at the crossroads of all worlds. We have already discussed the horizontal row of the Psychic Realm, and how the Vital Life Force acts upon the Astral body to animate the Soul-Man. We may also see a similar occurrence in the vertical column. Here, the VLF (from the Holy Spirit) is acting upon the Physical body (through the respiratory and circulatory systems) to animate the Animal-man. Diagonally, we see another interesting dynamic occurring. The Unknown Father of Light, as the Primum Mobile and the Source of all Spiritual emanation, is opposed to (or complementary to) the Prima Materia, from which all material edifices are constructed. Likewise, the Logos of God is opposed to (or, again, complementary to) the creative and generative functions of the human body that give rise to the logos of man. And our Mercurial Quintessence is at the crux of the whole scheme, connecting what is Above to what is Below. Qabalists will undoubtedly see a relationship here to the Tiphareth sephirah. And students of Freemasonry may also wish to consider that when we add the numbers of the squares in the patterns given above, we arrive at that mysterious and mystical number 15, whether we add vertically, horizontally, or diagonally. And we can further extrapolate that when we realize that the perfected human will, symbolized here by the number 5, exists simultaneously in all three worlds, we arrive at an additional, hidden 15 in the form of 555, which can be found in many 3° Tracing Boards on the coffin of Hiram Abiff.

There are many other patters and associations to be observed in this system I have proposed; but I will refrain from further comment and leave it to the student to put this system to the test, and hopefully discover hidden treasures that I have not yet imagined. Again, this is not so much a new system that I am proposing, but rather a reconciliation of ancient and modern symbolic philosophies. In this way, our Western Hermetic Tradition may be understood within the context of Christian Gnostic cosmological and ontological language and mythos; naturally, without being forced, and while maintaining an historical honesty and integrity.

Alchemy of the Eucharist

Alchemy is widely thought of in the sense of attempts to transmute Lead, or other metals, into Gold. It is often depicted as the fruitless efforts of superstitious and misguided exercises in primitive chemistry. Indeed, there were those who sought to make financial gains, and wasted many an hour at the bellows. These types were referred to derogatorily as "puffers" by other alchemists who, while still performing certain physical operations, were more concerned with the internal mental and spiritual processes. That is, the alchemical language was seen as a metaphor for the refinement of one's own imperfections, and the fulfillment of one's potential. It was a mental and spiritual practice above all else; though, many scientific advancements were made which led to the present discipline of chemistry.

In this discourse we are going to look at how the alchemical operations function within the Liturgy of the Pleromic Light. The Transubstantiation is, of course, a direct parallel to alchemical transmutation. This much has been acknowledged for centuries. We will see, though, how our venerable liturgy closely follows the entire alchemical process. I will not delve too deeply into the infinite complexities of alchemy (many of which, due to their paradoxical nature, are incommunicable), but rather I will address certain general elements and processes as they specifically relate to the mass. If you have not done so already, you may wish to read the "Gnostic Exposition of the of the Three Alchemical Essentials" before proceeding with this discourse.

Alchemy utilizes a richly symbolic language. Some of the principal aspects of alchemical symbolism include the Four Elements: Earth, Air, Fire, and Water; and the Three Essentials: Sulphur, Mercury, and Salt. Most people have at least heard of the Four Elements, although their nature has often been misunderstood. Remembering that the alchemical language is a symbolic language, it must be understood that these Elements do not necessarily refer to the literal chemical compounds form which their names are derived. They are to be thought of as categories, or classes of substances and phenomena. According to Aristotle, these Elements are derived from the dynamic interaction between more basic principles, namely: Heat, Coldness, dryness, and Moistness, thus:

Supplement: Alchemy of the Eucharist

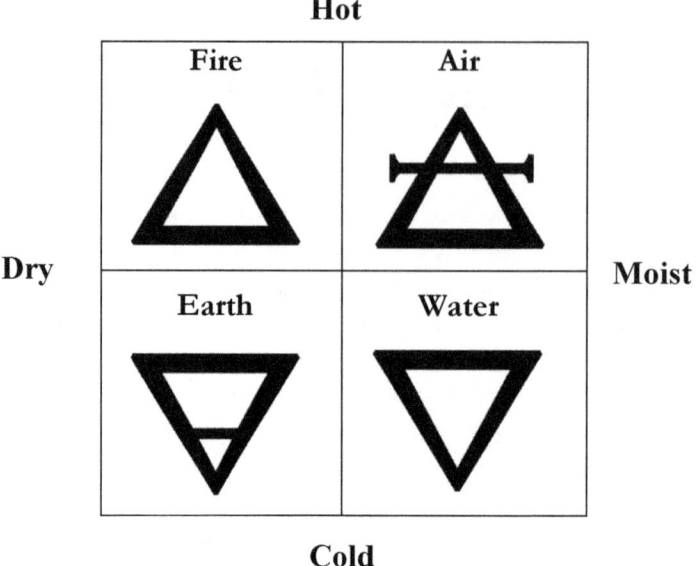

The previous diagram illustrates how the Elements are derived from the interaction between characteristics, such as heat and Dryness to produce Fire, or Moisture and Coldness to produce Water, etc. To the ancients, Fire and Water were considered to be the "pure," or primary Elements from which all nature was formed. This is because heat and Moisture were seen as being the only true attributes. Coldness and Dryness were merely their absence. Thus, Fire was pure Hotness, lacking the presence of any Moisture. Likewise, Water was pure Moisture, lacking any Heat. The bars crossing the symbols for Air and Earth are to show their secondary nature. This view is to be found throughout many ancient mystical traditions, including the Hebrew Qabalah, whose words for fire (Æsch) and Water (Majim) are joined in the principle of Schamajim, or Fiery Waters, from which all ultimately emanates.

Let us look then at the Temple layout itself (found in the *ACP Clergy Handbook*). We find, on the various altars, multiple Elemental tools and symbols. Most prevalent are representations of the "pure" Elements of Fire and Water, which each have altars representing these primal forces. We will examine each Element in turn, beginning with Fire.

The Celestial Fire is best represented by the Perpetual Luminary on Side Altar 1, which could also rightly be called the Fire Altar. This flame represents the One, Eternal and ineffable Father of Light. The Source of All.

The Central Fire is seen in the seven-stick candelabra on the Rear Altar. Like the seven prismatic rays, it reminds us that the Logos of God is present within the core of all things. It is a goal common to both the Gnostic and the alchemist to release the inner essence that has been obscured by the darkness of matter. The number seven is also significant alchemically, because it represents the seven principal alchemical operations, which correspond to the seven planets of the ancients, as well as to the seven metals.

The Elementary Fire is expressed in the Thurible. The purpose of the Elementary Fire Is to produce heat.

In the alchemical laboratory, this would be the fire of the furnace. And its purpose here is similar in that it is not intended to represent the Divine light, neither does it provide any light to see by. Its sole function is to burn with raw, destructive heat.

Another tool representing Fire is the Sword, which rests upon the Rear Altar, facing north. And, one final place that Fire is represented is in the open Scripture on the Eucharistic Altar. Scripture is a symbol of the Light of the Eternal logos, manifested in the world. That is, what we call the "word of God," is a temporal representation of the Word (Logos) of God.

The Element of Water appears in a number of prominent places as well. On the Side Altar 2, which we may also call the Water Altar, we find the cruets containing the water and wine for the Eucharist. I will examine the alchemical significance of these elements more fully later on, but suffice it to say for now that they are representative of the Water Element, in a general sense.

On the Rear Altar we have both the Aspergill, and the Lavabo Font. Both of these tools of Water are used for purification purposes throughout the Mass. The water here, of course, has been blessed. Water has always been a useful tool in ritual operations because of its ability to absorb and retain the subtle spiritual qualities directed toward it. So, when the blessed holy Water is scattered about the Temple during the Asperges, the Spiritual Power of that blessing is being distributed throughout.

Finally, the Chalice, on the Eucharistic Altar, is our most prominent Water symbol. Except for the Cross, it is probably the most widely recognized Christian symbol. It is also a symbol of the Sacred Feminine; the Cosmic Womb from which all came, and to which all will return.

The primary Earth Element is the Eucharistic bread itself. Earth is also represented by the Altar Stone, which may bear an image of the Seal of the ACP, or some other appropriate diagram or Pantacle. Air is represented by the Ceremonial Dagger. Both Earth and Air are also represented in the incense for the Thurible. The dual nature of the incense is made manifest in its Separation by the Elementary Fire of the burning coal. And all four Elements are embodied in the Priest.

The four Elements are also seen throughout the liturgy, both explicitly and implicitly. Wherever there is a quaternary, the four-fold Elemental nature is implied. Likewise, wherever a triad is apparent, they represent the principles of the Three Essentials: Sulphur, Mercury, and Salt. All polarities are symbolic of the duality of Sulphur and Mercury. The Salt is the mediating term of those two polar Essences, whether stated or implied. The Salt is both the thing being transformed, and that which it is transformed into; likewise, it is the transforming agent itself. It is the First Matter (Prima Materia) of Lead, and the Lapis Philosophorum of Gold; the Ros and the Rose. The four Elements and three Essentials are also represented in the Holy Orders; the Minor Orders corresponding to the Elements, and the major Orders, the Essentials.

Having looked at the symbolism of some of the various items in the Temple, let us now examine the liturgy itself, so that we may identify the alchemical phases and operations. Over the centuries, writers on the subject have divided the process into varying numbers of individual operations. Some have claimed there to be seven, while others list twelve, and still others may list fourteen, etc. It is not the case (typically) that the experts are disagreeing about the processes a whole, but rather where certain arbitrary lines are drawn. You see, many of the operations proceed quite seamlessly, one into the next. Also, there may be sub- processes within each operation. For the sake of simplicity and clarity, I will describe the process in the three classical phases which contain seven operations.

The first phase is known as the Black Phase, or by the Latin, *Nigredo*. The Black Phase is the stage in which impurities are brought to light and ultimately confronted. There are two operations in this phase: *Calcination* and *Dissolution*. Calcination involves burning off, or otherwise removing the dross material, leaving a dry bone-like, or ashy matter that has become impervious to fire. This basic substance is known to the alchemists by the Latin term, *Prima Materia*, or First Matter. This corresponds directly with the alchemical Salt, representing the skeletal structure or framework that underlies all constructed edifices, whether material, mental, or spiritual. As stated previously, in its lowest expression, Salt is the "Lead" that must be refined and perfected. It is also, however, in its Rectification, the spiritual "Gold." The Dissolution is the liquefaction of the Calcined material in a solvent, such as water. This solution then becomes the basis for the remainder of the operations. It also represents, to the alchemical operator, the stripping away of undesirable habits, desires, or other personal traits that may impede spiritual development.

The Calcination begins in the antechamber, during the period of preparation, and silent meditation and reflection. It continues throughout the opening invocations and purification rituals such as the Asperges and the Censing of the Altar; culminating in the Confiteor and Absolution, wherein the celebrants and participants are made pure by the power of Christ, thus preventing contamination of the Eucharistic Operation; and concluding with the Sign of Peace.

Dissolution begins with the First Hermetic Discourse. The substance extracted from the Calcination is dissolved in the thoughtful meditations on the One, which continues throughout the Second Hermetic Discourse and the reading of the Gospel. The Dissolution concludes with the Act of Faith. At this point, the dross has been thoroughly exorcized, and all participants and celebrants are brought together under a single, inseparable consciousness and belief.

The second phase is known as the White Phase, or *Albedo*. Now that the purifications of the Black Phase are complete, the White Phase begins a spiritualization of the elements, and of the celebrant himself. There are, as previously, two operations in this phase: the Separation and the *Conjunction*. Both operations occur during the Offertorium.

The Separation is the dividing of a substance into its essential parts. In the rite of the Eucharist, this is symbolized by the priest removing the veil and paten from the Chalice at the beginning of the Offertorium, and the displaying of the water and wine cruets. At this point, the bread, wine, and water are representative of the Three Essentials: Salt, Sulphur, and Mercury respectively. It is by the proper manipulation of these three Essentials that the celebrant, who is in fact an alchemical operator, hopes to eventually "Rectify" the First Matter; that is, transform these Eucharistic elements into the Body and Blood of Christ, the Logos.

The Conjunction is concerned with the dynamic between Sulphur and Mercury. The Mercury is that fluid nature which is always *becoming*, ever changing. Sulphur represents *being*, that Fiery will that imposes fixity.

Sulphur and Mercury are a polar dynamic, similar to that represented in the Yin-Yang symbol of the Taoists. They also represent Spirit and Soul, and the Conjunction is often called the Sacred marriage of Spirit and Soul. In the Eucharist, this is symbolized by the mixing of the water (Mercury) with the wine (Sulphur). The bread (Salt) will eventually become the *Child of the Conjunction*, that is, the *Lapis Philosophorum*, or Philosopher's Stone, in the Red Phase.

The Red Phase, or *Rubedo*, is a continuation of the White Phase that culminates, if successful, in the creation of the Philosopher's Stone; or in the case of the Eucharistic celebration, the Body and Blood of Christ. The Red phase consists of three operational stages: *Fermentation*, *Distillation*, and *Coagulation*.

Fermentation is the stage in which our elements begin to transform into an entirely new substance. The beginning of Fermentation involves a process called Putrefaction, which is somewhat like a miniature Black Phase, in that it is a final purification and purgation of any impurities that may have been previously missed, and inadvertently carried over. Spiritually and psychologically, this stage represents what the Christian mystical theologian, St. John of the Cross, referred to as the "dark night of the soul." Emotionally, it may be deep-seated baggage which the mind kept suppressed until this more advanced stage had been developed. In the Mass, this stage is represented by the Second Censing and the Lavabo, wherein the priest ritually washes his hands with blessed water, and continues through the Prayer to the Holy Spirit.

The Fermentation process continues with the Eucharistic Prayer. And with the Words of Institution, we can see the Eucharistic elements coming to life. For the alchemist in the laboratory, this is a ti.me of intense prayer and meditation; for the alchemical workshop is both Laboratory and Oratory. In the Liturgy, this continues throughout the Litany, Kyrie, and the Pater Noster.

Distillation is a process of repeated separation and recombination of the fermented substance, so that its perfected form might eventually emerge. This process begins with the Breaking of the Bread. The small piece of bread that is placed in the Chalice is symbolic of the emergence of the Rectified First Matter. The section just before the actual Communion, the Theurgic Consecration, may seem redundant, because the bread and wine have already been consecrated. But redundancy is a part of the Distillation process. Remember that this process is just as much a transformation of the celebrant and participants as it is of the Eucharistic elements themselves. This last section, then, is really more concerned with the psychological transformation of the individuals, as well as being the final crucial step of the Supreme Theurgic Operation.

The Coagulation is the final operation in the process of alchemical transmutation, or in the case of the Eucharist, transubstantiation. It is the Logos made flesh, and the spiritualization of our own bodies and minds. It is the Resurrection in Christ. The completion of this operation can be best seen in the Communion proper. When the priest elevates the Body and Blood, he is displaying the Philosopher's Stone. Therefore, by partaking of the Eucharist, we are symbolically transforming the Lead of our lower "sinful" natures into the pure Gold of Divine union with Christ.

Robert Ambelain, in his *Spiritual Alchemy*, states

> *And it is here we find the true Philosophical Stone of Spiritual Alchemy: the Eucharist, in which Water, image of the Mercury of the Wise and of the Church, is united in the Chalice, image of the crucible, with Wine, symbol of*

Supplement: Alchemy of the Eucharist

Sulphur of the Wise and Christ. Moreover, from this union of the Philosophical Sun (the Wine) and the Philosophical Moon (the Water), of these newlyweds called the "*Red Bridegroom*" and the "*White Bride*," according to the treatise by Ripley, joins together as the Philosophical Earth (the Com), symbol of the Salt of the Wise. It is the fusion of these three terms which then constitute the Spiritual Chrysopage, by which man is identified with God, as Lead becomes Gold in the heart of the matras [an alchemical vessel].

The concluding prayers and rites of the Mass are not a part of the alchemical process proper except perhaps in the sense of the *Projection*, as they encourage and instruct us in how to live in the Light we have just experienced, to remain free from the impurities of the world, and to spread that Light. For even though the efficacy of the Eucharist is assured, our continual union with Christ is dependent upon our remaining free from the myriad contaminants of this world. The difficulty of this task necessitates that we partake of the Eucharist often. In this way we may attain the final Reintegration. Referring again to Ambelain, he states:

Reintegration, or the reconstitution of the pleroma, consists of the slow and progressive working out of the Preexistent Church dispersed by the Fall. Now, this Church is the Mystic Body of Christ. It is represented by the Eucharistic bread. To absorb it is to build our own mystic body, represented by the "Vestment of Glory" of which the Palestinian Kabbalists and the Fathers of the Church spoke. *Without this "Vestment," our Father tells us, nothing can bridge the Fire principle separating the Created from the Uncreated...*

There are many details that I was not able to mention in this brief discourse, such as the significance of the various astrological correspondences and attributes. But I will at least give a brief chart illustrating how the alchemical operations correspond to certain planetary influences, and the metals associated with them:

Operation	Planet	Metal
Calcination	Saturn	Lead
Dissolution	Jupiter	Tin
Separation	Mars	Iron
Conjunction	Mercury	Mercury (Quicksilver)
Fermentation	Venus	Copper
Distillation	Moon	Silver
Coagulation	Sun	Gold

Now that you have seen how the alchemical processes are present and active within the liturgy, try to identify these processes and operations within your own life. Keep in mind, though, that many of these processes tend to be cyclical, and also may not occur precisely in that order that they are performed in the lab, or in this case, the Temple.

These are fluid processes for which we have set arbitrary boundaries, in order to understand them better, and to utilize them more efficiently. That is not to say that there are not distinct phases and operations; there are. But often one process may pass into another so seamlessly, that it would be quite impossible to say with any certainty, where the one ends and the other begins. But by identifying these general stages in one's life, the individual will be in a better position to try to take the steps necessary for a successful personal transmutation. Students of the ACP formation program may refer to their private course material for an overview of the relationship between alchemical principles and psychological or personality traits. All who wish a more in-depth exploration of this spiritual practice should study Ambelain's Spiritual Alchemy at length.

The Tetragrammaton in the Three Worlds

As modern Gnostics, we are inheritors not only of the Gnostic traditions and teachings of our ancient forebears, but also of those teachings and practices known to us as the western Mystery Tradition. The Western Mysteries, as they have come down to us in the present day, consist principally of Hermeticism and the Qabalah. By the term Hermeticism we mean both the doctrines expounded in the Hermetic scriptures and the practices and disciplines that derive from the Hermetic principles, such as astrology and alchemy. Likewise, by Qabalah we mean the mystical interpretation of the Hebrew scriptures, especially the Torah, and the writings and practices that have derived from that doctrine, such as the Tarot, pathworking along the Tree of Life, and certain forms of theurgy or ceremonial magic. In modern Gnosticism we find ourselves wedding these doctrines and practices to the older forms of Gnosticism, such as is found among the Nag Hammadi texts. The problem that arises, as we briefly alluded to in our treatise, "A Gnostic Exposition of the Three Alchemical Essentials," is that while Hermeticism and Qabalah have had centuries to develop and mature together, on complement to one another, the Gnostic doctrine is largely frozen in time, in the 4th century when it was definitively suppressed.

One of the challenges that arises when syncretizing these various theosophies into a workable, coherent system, is how we are able to reconcile doctrinal elements of each that are different or even seemingly contradictory to one another. In the aforementioned treatise we attempted to do a little toward this effort of reconciliation as concerns - as the title suggests - the three alchemical essentials and their relation to Gnostic terminology. In the present work we are going to try to advance this reconciliation a little further by looking at the Tetragrammaton - יהוה - in the light of Gnostic philosophy and language. This is why the title of this paper is "The Tetragrammaton in the *Three Worlds*" as opposed to the traditional Qabalistic concept of *Four Worlds*.

An immediate difficulty we face is that to the ancient Gnostics, the god of the Old Testament is not the true God of Light, but an inferior Demiurge. Even modern Gnostics generally adhere to this concept, though we also recognize that the Qabalah opens up a new level of interpretation of the Torah that often flatly contradicts the surface message and reinforces the older Gnostic viewpoints. Over the years I have had many discussions about the nature of the Tetragrammaton, and how it should be interpreted by Gnostics. Some argue that it represents the Demiurge and should not be confused with the True God of Light. Others state that it does indeed refer to the True God and was merely misappropriated by the Demiurge or misapplied to him by ignorant mortals. Still others argue that it represents the four Elements of the physical world. All of these viewpoints have merit, yet none of them, alone, seem to encompass the whole picture. What we shall attempt, then, is to posit a workable theory that accounts for all of these viewpoints, without being self-contradictory, and while being reconciled to both Gnostic and Qabalistic doctrine.

Let us begin by looking at a very general Qabalistic concept of the four-letter Name. Upon the Tree of Life, the Tetragrammaton can be arranged so that each letter corresponds to each of the four "worlds." As mentioned above, we will be looking at the Gnostic "three worlds" model, but we are beginning here because it shows from a Qabalistic perspective that the Tetragrammaton is present within all worlds or realms, from the archetypal down to the material. This gives us a starting point, and the hope and expectation that the various viewpoints may be reconciled and rectified under a single philosophy. Let us look, then, at how the Tetragrammaton manifests on the pneumatic, psychic, and hylic planes. We must state here that the letters YOD-HE-VAV-HE, while composing what we consider to be a "Name," is actually more akin to a formula than to a name in any conventional sense of the word. We nevertheless call it a Name because of the intimacy implied by that word. Regardless, let us start with the pneumatic realms and work our way down.

The whole of the Pleroma - the Fullness - can be summed up in the Tetragrammaton. In this, YOD corresponds to the Father; the first HE corresponds to the Mother, that is, Barbelo, the Holy Spirit; and VAV corresponds to the Son, the Logos. The final HE may be seen as a type of the first, best represented by the aeon Sophia. This gives us a view of the Pleroma that is not nearly as comprehensive and complex as the descriptions given in the Gnostic texts, but one that succinctly encapsulates the prime forces at work.

According to our Gnostic scriptures, the perfect equilibrium that we call the Pleroma was disturbed when Sophia attempted to create, according to the Secret Book of John, "without consent of her partner." In other words, just as the masculine and feminine principles represented by YOD and HE were united to issue forth the VAV and final HE, so would the secondary feminine principle, in order to produce a perfect offspring, have had to have been united with the masculine principle - VAV. Sometimes we call this the Logos/Sophia syzygy. As we know, this disruption caused an imbalance or "breaking" of the Pleroma, resulting in the creation of the psychic and hylic planes, and the Demiurge. It also placed Sophia "outside" the Pleroma - that is, our of harmony - until such time as the equilibrium can be restored.

We thus have the Demiurge as the lord and ruler of the lower realms, for although Sophia is outside the Pleroma, she has not descended so far as to become enmeshed in her creation. We are told, therefore, that she resides in the veil between what is above and what is below. The Demiurge, being an offspring of Sophia, bears within himself an image, albeit imperfect, of the whole Pleroma. We may see, therefore, how the Tetragrammaton is represented in the psychic realm as the Demiurge. But this expression of the Tetragrammaton is a distortion of the pneumatic archetype. And his creations are likewise distortions of the pneumatic aeons.

Supplement: Tetragrammaton in the 3 Worlds

In the hylic, or material, world, we see that Tetragrammaton manifest as the four elements. In this (not to be confused with the attributes given in the Sepher Yetzirah of the archetypal Elements represented by ALEPH, MEM, and SHIN), YOD corresponds to Fire, and HE corresponds to Water. As we have discussed elsewhere, these are the two "pure" or primary elements. The secondary elements of Air and Earth are represented by the VAV and final HE respectively. That is, the heat of YOD and the moisture of HE unite to produce the VAV, and the dryness of YOD unites with the coldness of HE to produce the final HE (see "Alchemy of the Eucharist" for a discussion on how the elements are derived from the more basic principles of heat, moisture, coldness, and dryness). The Tetragrammaton is also expressed on this plane in the form of the natural reproductive cycle: Father, Mother, Son, and Daughter.

We can see, therefore, that attributing the Tetragrammaton to either the psychic or hylic planes is not incorrect, but that this attribution - this formula - is based upon a pneumatic archetype. And let us return to a discussion of this archetype in Gnostic mythology so we can look at how this broken Pleroma may be ultimately restored. When the Demiurge fashioned a creature from the psychic substance to resemble the heavenly, or Pleromic Man (Geradamas), he could not cause it to live. Barbelo, the Holy Spirit, then instructs the ignorant Demiurge (who remains ignorant of this divine assistance) on how to infuse the psychic Adam with pneuma (spirit or breath) to make him a living soul. This descent of Spirit into the psychic realm is represented by the VAV, which we connected earlier to the Logos. But before the psychic Adam, enlivened by the power of the Logos, is able to accomplish the mission of the restoration of the Pleroma, the androgynous Adam is cast into the hylic realm, there to be imprisoned in matter, and no longer whole, but divided among myriad cages of flesh.

With this further degradation, man is no longer capable of uniting the male principle directly with the fallen Sophia (who is still above the psychic realm). But another aspect of Sophia is sent into the lowest realm to find Adam before he is completely trapped in matter. That is, while Adam is yet in the psychical form, a *type* of Sophia, referred to as Zoe (Life) is joined to him and, according to the *Secret Book of John*, "helped the whole creature, laboring with it, restoring it to its fullness, teaching it about the descent of the seed, teaching it about the way of ascent, which is the way of descent." But when Adam is finally imprisoned in a body of flesh, the once-androgynous nature is divided into male and female. The feminine spiritual component, Zoe, returns to the Pleroma, and the masculine component becomes dormant once again.

This entire Gnostic tragedy is but an elaborate explanation of the breaking of the divine equilibrium and the need for its restoration. It is also to show the significance of the coming of Jesus Christ as the great Reconciler. And it is to the very name of Jesus that we must look for a clue to his true nature. We render this Name, in the Hebrew, as יהשוה - transliterated as Yeheshuah, or some similar pronunciation. But what we notice immediately in the Hebrew is that the name consists of the Tetragrammaton with the letter SHIN placed in the center. This configuration is significant to us on multiple planes.

Let us consider, for a moment, the letter SHIN. In its very shape we can see the image of three VAVs. Now, we have already associated the letter VAV with the Logos and have shown that the Logos resides within each of us as the life-giving, vivifying force and our link to the divine gnosis. But wait, you may say, isn't Jesus Christ the Logos incarnate? How is this so if the Logos is already present within? Perhaps here would be a good place to borrow some terminology from our Orthodox brethren. In Eastern Orthodoxy they distinguish between divine energy and divine essence. Now, we are not using the words here in exactly the same way as the Orthodox usage, but they are convenient terms to describe what we are talking about. That is, it could be said that the energy of the Logos is present within every person, giving rise to the personal logos. In Jesus, however, we have not merely the energy or power of the Logos, but an embodiment of the very essence itself. It is this essential or archetypal Logos that manifested in the world, wearing the body of the psychic Christ, who is the son of the Demiurge, the messiah promised by the prophets of old (see "The Devil's Passion" for a discussion of the union of the pneumatic Logos with the psychic Christ). Again, if you look at this letter SHIN, we see not only the VAV, but in fact a representation of the YOD and HE as well. It is really a perfect hieroglyph for the triune power of God.

We are also told of Jesus that, "in Him all the Pleroma was pleased to dwell," (*Col.* 1:19), and then in chapter 2 of the same text, "In Him dwells bodily, all the Pleroma of God." Now remember that we said the "Pleroma" is representative of the divine equilibrium. This is possible because Jesus is the embodiment of that equilibrium. He is both *Logos* and *Sophia*, or as she is known when descending to the lower planes, *Zoe* - Life. The Gospels bear out this truth, for in the 14th chapter of *John*, Jesus states: "I am the Way, the Truth, and the Life [Zoe]." And Paul writes in *1 Corinthians*, "Christ is God's Power and God's Wisdom [Sophia]." So it is through the vehicle of Jesus Christ that Zoe is reintroduced into the cosmos, as it states in the prologue to John: "In Him was Life [Zoe], and the Life was the Light of men."

Now let us consider the placement of the letter SHIN within this Holy Name. YOD and HE are to one side, while VAV and HE are to the other. The YOD and HE to the right are emblematic of the supernal masculine and feminine aspects remaining in the Pleroma; while the VAV and HE to the left are representative of the fallen Sophia and the power of the Logos that was sent to redeem her but ultimately became trapped itself and fragmented. The SHIN between them, then, represents the Logos united with Zoe in perfect equilibrium, full of the power of the whole Pleroma, which can awaken the logos in Man so that it can reunite with Sophia and accomplish the restoration of the Pleroma. The SHIN is therefore appropriately placed as the reconciler and restorer of the divine equilibrium. This is acknowledged in our Eucharistic rite when the Priest says, "by partaking of this Mystery, we may reunite within ourselves the fragments of Your Divinity dispersed throughout the Cosmos."

There is also a significance on the psychic plane of this Name. Remember that the Tetragrammaton manifests on the psychic plane as the Demiurge, the father of the psychic Christ. Thus, when we read in the *Gospel of Philip* that, "The Son would not be the Father without wearing the Father's name," we can see that it is referring simultaneously to both the psychic and pneumatic "father." And when Jesus says, "I and the Father are one," he is telling us: 1) that he is one with the Unknown Father of Light, from which the Logos proceeds; and 2) that his psychic and pneumatic natures have been reconciled and rectified.

On the hylic plane we see this Name most recognizably in the image of Jesus crucified. It is also portrayed more mystically as the rose blooming upon the cross. In some of our theurgical workings, this image is presented even more blatantly as a cross with the Tetragrammaton inscribed upon its arms and the letter SHIN placed in the very center. It is, in fact, this latter arrangement that is dramatically enacted during the "Theurgic Consecration" section of our Mass. Truly, the manifestations of the Holy Pentagrammaton on the physical plane are nearly infinite, for it is the Name by which all is reconciled. St. Paul, in his Letter to the Philippians, calls it, "The Name above every name," and that in this Name, "every knee should bend, those in heaven and on earth, and under the earth." It is the power of this Name that effects the miracle of transubstantiation, and to which angels and archons alike humbly submit in service to the Most High.

We must acknowledge that this short paper does not provide a complete reconciliation of Qabalistic principles to historic Gnosticism. But it does go a little way towards showing how the creation, breaking, and reconstitution of the Pleroma can be expressed within the Tetragrammaton (and, ultimately, the Pentagrammaton). We have shown also how this Name is in fact a formula that manifests on all planes. And we have tried, wherever possible, to illustrate our assertions with reference to both Gnostic scripture and the orthodox canon.

This paper is not intended to be the final word on the matter, but rather to begin a conversation. We therefore invite our friends and colleagues to use these ideas as a springboard for further explorations into the subject, and help to ensure that ours remains a living tradition.

ACP Clergy Handbook

The Gnostic Gospel of Luke:

A Gnostic-Hermetic Exegesis of the Tenth Chapter of the Gospel According to Luke

by Reginald Freeman

This essay was originally published in The Gnostic 3 *(Dublin: Bardic Press, 2010), and is reprinted here with permission of the author.*

In this essay, I will attempt to show that the tenth chapter of the Gospel According to Luke contains elements of Gnostic and Hermetic philosophy, including a Græco-Egyptian astrological tradition. Among the canonical scriptures, the *Gospel According to John* is usually considered to be the one favored by the Gnostics. This idea has been written on extensively. Therefore, I will not elaborate upon what is readily available in multiple works. But, it is nevertheless important to at least mention this fact, because of the far reaching influence of the Johannine works on Gnostic tradition and scriptures. For example, the prologue to the gospel contains peculiar language that is not common to the synoptic gospels, but is more reminiscent of Gnostic scriptures. The *Gospel of John* also emphasizes the spiritual nature of Jesus, and stresses the supremacy of the spiritual over the material. This is made obvious in statements such as *John* 6.63a: "It is the spirit that makes a thing live. The flesh benefits nothing." The *Gospel According to Luke*, however, while conforming largely to the gospel narratives found in *Matthew* and *Mark*, also contains a number of unique sayings and parables that suggest a secret knowledge that is to be bestowed upon God's elect, using language that would have been recognized by Gnostics and Hermeticists. Of course, to the Gnostic, and other Christian mystics, all of the scriptures may have multiple layers of meaning which, when taken together collectively, may offer a broader, richer, and fuller understanding of the text than what might be immediately apparent on the surface. And perhaps we should not be surprised to find evidence of Gnostic mysticism within Luke's writings, especially given his close companionship with Paul, whose teachings were highly valued by the early Gnostics, and whose writings share much of the same terminology as the Gnostics. In fact, concerning the Gnostic teacher Valentinus, Elaine Pagels writes, "Paul communicated his pneumatic teaching to his disciple Theudas, and Theudas, in turn, to Valentinus; and Valentinus to his own disciples," (*The Gnostic Paul*, p. 5). In addition, if we accept that Luke was a physician, a commonly held view, then we may probably safely assume that he had studied the Hermetic texts over the course of his education, as many of those works were known to have dealt extensively with medicine and healing; particularly "tracts on astrological medicine, such as the *Book of Asclepius Called Myriogenesis,*" (Copenhaver, Hermetica, p. xxxiii).

Let me be clear at the outset that this is primarily a Gnostic theological work, though it may have some academic implications as well. The ancient Gnostics were arguably the Church's first theological exegetes. In modern times, however, it has been left largely to the secular academia to provide insight into a belief system that they themselves do not necessarily share. To be sure, many excellent works have been produced by the academic community, and I do not wish to diminish their efforts in any way. There are some excellent

Supplement: The Gnostic Gospel of Luke

historical works available, and without the superb translation efforts of the last several decades, most of the original Gnostic scriptures would still be lost to us. On the other hand, the modem Gnostic cannot help but to notice a deficiency in some of the commentaries and attempts at exegesis. This deficiency is not due to poor scholarship; rather, it is due to the fact that they are written from an outside perspective, trying to make sense of a religious tradition that, by its very nature, can only be understood experientially. While it is my intention to present scholarly and reasonable hypotheses, I do not want to mislead the reader by supposing some impartiality, or theological neutrality that does not exist. In spite of my admitted bias, however, I think that there is ample evidence to support the bulk of my ideas in those cases where empirical, or strong circumstantial evidence, may confirm or support the hypothesis.

The structure of this essay is as follows: After this brief introduction, the first part of our exegesis will cover *Luke* 10.1-24, followed by a second section addressing verses 25-37. These two sections comprise the main body of this work. Finally, the conclusion will attempt to anticipate certain questions, and to briefly survey other sections of Luke and place them in a Gnostic context consistent with the analysis offered in the main body. The reader may notice that the first section of this exegesis is disproportionately longer than the second section. This imbalance is regrettable, but necessary due to the natural divisions of the text. In the early stages of the development of this exegesis, these two sections existed as two separate essays. It seemed beneficial, however, to combine them into a single work. It is only by treating them together that a comprehensive conclusion may be offered. For, without placing these passages in a proper context, the analyses offered herein may be seen as anomalous, or could too easily be dismissed as fanciful speculation. A scriptural anomaly might be interesting to comment upon, but would not necessarily demand a rigorous investigation. What I intend to show here is that there is a pattern of esoteric symbolism scattered throughout *Luke*, but especially concentrated in the tenth chapter.

Translations of New Testament texts throughout this essay are my own, being translated from the Greek New Testament, Fourth Corrected Edition (USB4), which contains the same text as the Novum Testamentum Græce, 27th Edition (NA27), which was also consulted throughout the translation process. The translations found here are not substantially different from many others, but they do illustrate certain variances among the source texts, and certain wording that lends itself more easily to the type of exegetical treatment that is to follow.

This first passage from Luke that I have selected for this paper is perhaps the most overlooked example of Gnostic and Hermetic philosophy among the canonical scriptures. I believe that this oversight may be largely due to the available translations of the Geek text, which seem to favor a particular variation of the text that does not lend itself as well to the interpretation that is to be put forth here shortly. I must admit, however, that I am surprised that, (to my knowledge) this subject matter has not been addressed by scholars and students of early Christian literature who are familiar with the Greek sources. It is equally possible, of course, that there are such extant works, of which I am merely ignorant. Regardless, I hope that this brief treatise can offer a fresh perspective on the matter. Here, then, is the *Gospel According to Luke*, 10.1-24:

> 23. And after these things, the Lord appointed seventy-two others, and he sent them two by two before his face into every city and place where he was about to go. 2. And he was saying to them, "Indeed, the harvest is great, but the workers few; ask then, the Lord of the harvest that he might send out workers into his

harvest. 3. Go! Behold, I send you as lambs in the midst of wolves. 4. Do not carry a purse, nor a wallet, nor sandals, and greet no one along the way. 5. And into whatever house you enter, first say, 'Peace to this house.' 6. And if there is a son of peace, your peace will rest upon him; otherwise, on you it will return. 7. And in the same house remain eating and drinking the things with them; for the worker is worthy of his wage. Do not move from house to house. 8. And into whichever city you enter and they receive you, eat the things being set before you 9. And heal the ones in it who are sick and say to them, 'The Kingdom of God has come near to you.' 10. But into whatever city you enter and they do not receive you, go out into its streets and say, 11. 'Even the dust from your city that has clung to our feet we shake off against you; but know this that the Kingdom of God has come near.' 12. I say to you that for Sodom in that day it will be more bearable than with that city. 13. Woe to you Chorazin, woe to you Bethsaida; because if the miracles that have happened in you had occurred in Tyre and Sidon, they would have repented long ago, sitting in sackcloth and ashes. 14. But for Tyre and Sidon it will be more bearable in the judgment than for you. 15. And you Capernaum, will you not be exalted up to heaven? No, you will come down to Hades."

16. "The one listening to you, listens to me, and the one rejecting you rejects me; but the one rejecting me, rejects the one who has sent me."

17. And the seventy-two returned with joy saying, "Lord, even the demons submit to us in your name." 18. And he said to them, "I watched Satan fall like lightning from heaven. 19. Behold, I have given to you the authority to walk on snakes and scorpions, and over all the power of the adversary, and nothing at all may hurt you. 20. However, do not rejoice in this that the spirits submit to you, but rejoice that your names have been recorded in the heavens."

21. In the same hour he was full of joy in the Holy Spirit and he said, "I praise you, Father, Lord of heaven and earth, that you concealed these things from the wise and intelligent and revealed them to young children; yes, Father, for thus it was well-pleasing before you. 22. Everything was handed over to me by my Father and no one knows who the Son is except the Father, and who the Father is except the Son and to whom the Son wishes to reveal Him."

23. And having turned toward the disciples privately he said, "Blessed are the eyes seeing what you see. 24. For I say to you that many prophets and kings desired to see what you see and they did not see, and to hear what you hear and they did not hear."

You will notice in the very first verse of this chapter a small, but significant difference from other translations. I am referring specifically to the statement that, "the Lord appointed seventy-two others." Many translations read "seventy" rather than "seventy-two." The reason for this seems to be due to a discrepancy among the ancient manuscripts; some reading "seventy," while others having "seventy-two." The text I have translated from, the *Greek New Testament* (UBS4), is considered by many students of New Testament (Koine) Greek to be the foremost edition. This edition contains the Greek, "hebdomekonta duo," that is, "seventy-two." Likewise, the Latin *Nova Vulgata* (Stuttgart Vulgate, Fourth Edition), contains "septuaginta duos," (*Novum Testamentum*, p. 190). I stress this point because much of my argument, as you will see, is dependent upon this particular reading of the text. Taken at face value, it really makes little difference which interpretation is used. But, when we apply the "seventy-two" reading, mystical depths are opened up to us.

It is entirely possible, and in my opinion probable, that "seventy- two" was at some point abbreviated to "seventy," either for convenience, or by inadvertent omission. The abbreviation of "seventy- two" into "seventy" would not be unique to this particular passage. For example, the legend regarding the development of the Septuagint (the Greek Old Testament) states that the Hebrew Scriptures were translated into Greek by seventy-two scholars, over a period of seventy- two days. However, the word "Septuagint" comes from the Latin, meaning "seventy." And when the Septuagint is reference in academic works, it is usually represented by the Latin numerals for seventy, "LXX." While this usage may have been adopted for convenience, it loses the numerological significance of the number seventy-two.

In the number seventy-two, we see an allusion to the Jewish tradition that there were seventy-two nations with seventy-two different languages in the world. Therefore, the seventy-two disciples are representatives of the whole of the known world, and thus representative of the Universal Kingdom of Christ; that is, the Church. As we shall see, though, this symbolism of universality extends far beyond the four corners of the Earth. The unique wording and peculiar phraseology of this passage suggests that the reign of Christ's power extends throughout the whole of the cosmos. The number seventy-two also suggests a connection to Jewish mystical and numerological traditions, such as the Shemhamphorasch [see the "Theurgical Operations" section of this *Handbook*], and the sum of the values of the Hebrew letters of the Tetragrammaton when arranged as the Pythagorean Tetractys [see Appendix A]. However, while these traditions are not wholly unrelated to the subject at hand, a more in-depth exploration of them lies outside the scope of the present work.

The seventy-two disciples are sent out in pairs, so that there are thirty-six groups of two. These thirty-six pairs suggest a connection to the thirty-six decans of Egyptian astrology. In the introduction to his translation of the *Hermetica*, Brian P. Copenhaver writes, "The most important of the astrological Hermetica known to us is the *Liber Hermetis*, a Latin text whose Greek original contained elements traceable to the third century BCE. This *Book of Hermes* describes the decans, a peculiarly Egyptian way of dividing the zodiacal circle into thirty-six compartments, each with its own complex of astrological attributes," (*Hermetica*, p. xxxiii). The decans are called so because they each represent ten degrees of the zodiacal circle. The 20th century scholar of mystical and esoteric philosophical traditions, Manly P. Hall, has described it thus: "The early star gazers, after dividing the zodiac into its houses, appointed the three brightest stars in each constellation to be the joint rulers of that house. Then they divided the house into three sections of ten degrees each, which they called decans," (*The Secret Teachings of All Ages*, p. 159). (In a certain form of the Egyptian calendar, this translated into twelve months, each month having three ten-day weeks. At the end of the 360-day year, there were five additional days that corresponded to certain principal Egyptian deities, and lied outside of the calendar year proper.) Even the philosophical Hermetica, such as *Asclepius*, (which was quoted from liberally by early Church Fathers such as Lactantius in his *Divine Institutes*, in defense of Christian doctrine) acknowledges, "the thirty-six ... the stars that are always fixed in the same place," (*Hermetica*, p. 78).

We may find similar references in early Gnostic writings as well. For example, in the proto-Sethian text, *Eugnostos the Blessed*, we read, "Then the twelve powers... consented with each other. Six males each and six females each were revealed, so that there are seventy-two powers. Each one of the seventy-two revealed five spiritual powers, which together are the three hundred sixty powers," (*Nag Hammadi Library*, p. 233). This establishes a pattern in the spiritual realm, which is later imitated in the physical cosmos. This pattern is confirmed further on in *Eugnostos*, "The twelve months came to be as the type of the twelve powers. The three hundred sixty days of the year came to be as the type of the three hundred sixty powers who appeared from Savior," (Ibid. p. 234). As explained previously, this type of calendar system is uniquely Egyptian; a fact that does not go unnoticed by Douglas M. Parrott, the translator of the Eugnostos text. For he comments in his introduction to the text, "Egyptian religious thought also appears to have influenced its picture of the supercelestial realm," (Ibid. p. 231).

Another early Gnostic example of this type of cosmology may be found in the *Gospel of Judas*, in a discourse of Jesus to Judas which states, "And the twelve aeons of the twelve luminaries constitute their Father, with six heavens for each aeon, so that there are 72 heavens for the 72 luminaries, and for each of them five firmaments, for a total of 360 firmaments," (*The Gospel of Judas*, pp. 44-45). This reference is also noticed by Bart D. Ehrman in his analysis of the Judas text, wherein he draws a connection to a variation of the same Egyptian tradition previously mentioned. His analysis states in part, "These numbers are not accidental, of course. The text doesn't explain them, but they appear to be astronomical references: there are twelve months of the year and twelve signs of the zodiac; in Egyptian lore there are seventy- two 'pentads'(stars) that reside over the days of the week, and so seventy-two luminaries; and there are 360 degrees in the zodiac (and 360 days in some calendars of the year) and so 360 firmaments," (*The Lost Gospel of Judas Iscariot*, p. 94).

The numbers seventy-two and thirty-six are, by themselves, enough to consider a likely astrological connection. For, we have seen that the pattern for the decans was present in the Aeons, or eternal realms. To the Gnostics, though, the physical cosmos is not a direct emanation of the Most High, as the Aeons are, but instead have been fashioned by an imperfect demiurge. Therefore, the decans of the material world are but imperfect reflections; shadowy images of their supercelestial counterparts, requiring the purification and perfection that can be brought only by the Son, whom we are told in the *Letter to the Hebrews* is, "appointed heir of all things, through whom He also made the Aeons." Granted, the occurrence of these numbers here could be coincidental, or lack the specific implications that I am suggesting. But, fortunately, we have additional clues throughout the passage that make the possibility of mere coincidence seem much less likely. Looking at verses 5-7 we find further curious language, suggestive of an astrological connection. The thirty-six pairs are instructed to take up residence in various "houses," to offer peace upon the inhabitants of each house, and to "not move from house to house." Anyone with even a passing familiarity with astrology will recognize that "house" is a term used to designate each of the twelve major divisions of the zodiac circle. And, according to Gnostic and Hermetic sources, the inhabitants, or rulers, of the zodiac are demons, or spirits, that influence the lives of humans. The fact that verse 6 mentions, "if there are sons of peace," would seem to indicate that there may be a number of "sons" who are not "of peace." Also, the use of the term "sons" in verse 6 should not be seen as arbitrary. Referring again to Copenhaver, he states, "Excerpt VI [of Stobaeus' *Anthology*] deals with astrology, in particular with the decans and their 'sons,' the star demons," (*Hermetica*, p. xxxvii). For one description of these demons of the zodiac, we may look to the pseudo-Solomonic grimoire, *The Testament of Solomon*, which has a number of similarities to other Gnostic, Hermetic, and Jewish magical texts of the period, and which may well have been in circulation in some form at the time Luke was written. In the Testament of Solomon, Solomon compels the demons of the zodiac to help build his temple. When he calls them forth, they announce, "We are the thirty-six elements, the world-rulers of this darkness." When he begins to interrogate the demons, the first says, "I am the first decans of the zodiac circle." Solomon continues to question each of the thirty-six, causing each to reveal its name, its powers, and its weaknesses. The powers of these demons include a broad range of nefarious acts; from leading people into error and heresy, to breaking up the harmony among families, to causing blindness and deafness in unborn children. The banishing of the demons typically consists of invoking certain divine or angelic names, and performing certain ritual actions. After subjugating the entire assembly, Solomon sets them to work at building his temple. The idea is that the possessor of this grimoire will likewise be able to compel the spirits. But if this is the power of Solomon, how much greater is the power of Christ, who is known throughout the scriptures As one "greater than Solomon," (*Luke* 11:31)? Indeed, as great as the power of Solomon was, when he fell into apostasy he states that, "At once the Spirit of God departed from me, and I became weak as well as foolish in my words." As we will see, Christ's power over the world-rulers will be perfect, complete, and unlike Solomon, eternal.

In verses 8 and 9, Jesus indicates that those archons that do not resist the messengers of Christ should be treated respectfully, and that their sickness should be healed. Their sickness, of course, is their spiritual darkness, or ignorance. And while those zodiacal rulers may never be granted access into the realms of eternal light and life, since their origin is with the demiurge, rather than the True God of Light, they may still occupy an exalted position in the cosmos, and help to bring Christ's love into the world, and into the hearts of men. Verses 10-16, on the other hand, constitute an admonishment and warning to all those who would oppose the power of Christ, (cf. *Matthew* 11:21-24). The message to them is that God's reign will extend throughout the cosmos, with or without their cooperation; and that if they choose to resist, they will, by their own actions, remove themselves from the grace of Christ.

In verse 17 we learn that the seventy-two (thirty-six pairs) have been successful. They are full of joy and declare, "Lord, even the demons submit to us in your name." Given our elaboration on the nature of the decans, this statement takes on a richer, and clearer meaning. The explanation offered in this analysis casts light on an otherwise vague and cryptic statement. That is, given our celestial / spiritual interpretation, their ordeal has been nothing less than the subjugation of the entire assembly of the "world-rulers." Since these demons control and influence the personalities and affairs of humanity, then we can see that the disciples' ordeals actually represent the mastery of self as much as they represent mastery over external forces. So, the joy of the disciples is due to the fact that, through Christ, they have attained to a perfect understanding of the order of things, and thus have learned to overcome their lower, sinful natures.

Jesus' reply in verse 18 is equally as cryptic, claiming to have "watched Satan fall like lightning from heaven." The very nature of this statement suggests that we are not dealing with real-time events here. Depictions of the fall of Satan are generally placed in the "beginning," or at the "end of days." Since Christ is the "Alpha and the Omega, the first and the last, the beginning and the end," (*Apocalypse of John* 22:13), we can say that His position is above, or outside of, our normal space-time experience. That is, the fall of Satan is not a fixed point in space-time, but rather an event occurring in perpetuity. To the Christian faithful, the fall of Satan is seen from a relative perspective. To those who reject Christ and His message, the Devil is lording above them, and ruling their world. But those who, through the grace of Christ, have found the knowledge of the Father, and the comfort of the Holy Spirit, are raised above the· adversarial powers. So to them, from their particular vantage point, Satan is seen to fall.

Let us take a look at some of the Gnostic scriptures for similar accounts of the adversary and his fall; in this case, the demiurge, Yaldabaoth. In the *Reality of the Rulers*, (or *Hypostasis of the Archons*) we read of such a fall, "She [Zoe] breathed into his faced, and her breath became a fiery angel for her; and that angel bound Yaldabaoth and cast him down into Tartaros, at the bottom of the abyss," (*Gnostic Bible*, p. 176). Then a bit further down, we read about one of Yaldabaoth's "sons" who rejects evil: "He [Sabaoth] loathed her [matter], but he sang songs of praise up to Sophia and her daughter Zoe. And Sophia and Zoe found him and put him in charge of the seventh heaven, below the veil between above and below," (Ibid. p. 176). Thus, this "son of peace" has been elevated because of his righteousness, and his rejection of the things of this world. In *On the Origin of the World*, there is yet another account of Sabaoth's worship of Sophia, who raises him up to the seventh sphere and, with the aid of archangels, "established the kingdom for him above everyone so that he might dwell above the twelve gods of chaos," (*Gnostic Bible*, p. 421). These "twelve gods of chaos" are the principal zodiacal archons created by Yaldabaoth in the *Secret Book of John*, (*Gnostic Bible*, p. 147) and in other Gnostic sources.

Returning now to our passage in *Luke*, Jesus continues to address the seventy-two who have returned. In the reference to "snakes and scorpions" we have symbols of the adversary, and of death itself. But, we also see what seems to be yet another astrological reference, indicating well-known constellations. With Draco in the Northern Hemisphere, and Scorpius in the Southern Hemisphere, together they can be seen to represent the poles of the cosmos. This authority given to the disciples to "walk on snakes and scorpions, and over all the power of the adversary," suggests an elevation over the planetary and zodiacal influences, and is strikingly similar to the elevation of Sabaoth over the powers of the demiurge and his archons. This verse also reminds us of Solomon's subjugation of the demons discussed earlier and, together with verse 21, bears a strong resemblance in wording to the following passage from *The Testament of Solomon*: "And when I saw the prince of demons [Beelzeboul], I glorified the Lord God, Maker of heaven and earth, and I said: 'Blessed art thou, Lord God Almighty, who hast given to Solomon thy servant wisdom, the assessor of the wise, and hast subjected unto me all the power of the devil,'"(*The Testament of Solomon*).

It is also possible that rather than referring to two separate constellations, that both the snake and the scorpion are referring to the zodiacal sign of Scorpio. According to Manly P. Hall, the sign of Scorpio, "has three different symbols," or forms. The first is that of the Scorpion, representing "deceit and perversion." The second form is that of the Serpent, "often used by the ancients to symbolize wisdom." The third form, interestingly, is that of the Eagle, representing, "the highest and most spiritual type of Scorpio, in which it transcends the venomous insects of the earth," (*The Secret Teachings of All Ages*, p. 156). In this sense, then, it becomes a symbol of the process of initiation: the Scorpion symbolizing that degree, or stage, of initiation wherein the passions are subdued, which begins the process of the purification of the soul; the Serpent representing the stage of growth and maturation, wherein various knowledge is accumulated, though largely of a material or temporal sort; and finally the Eagle, which is not named here, but whose presence would be implied to the initiated reader. The Eagle represents the completion of the initiation process, where the spiritually perfected initiate is raised up above all worldly things, and all temporal knowledge.

Even if we were to concede that *Luke* is the more ancient of the texts (which is not at all certain), and that the Gnostic and Hermetic authors were influenced by *Luke*, rather than the other way around, it is nevertheless clear that the Gnostic and Hermetic authors would have seen in this account, an allusion to the spirits of the zodiac. The Valentinian Gnostic certainly recognized a compatible theology here, since we read in the "Valentinian Liturgical Readings" a direct reference to verse 19: "It is fitting for you at this time to send your son Jesus the Anointed and anoint us, so we can trample on snakes and the heads of scorpions and all the power of the devil, since He is the shepherd of the seed," (*Gnostic Bible*, p. 336). Verse 20 concludes Jesus' discussion with the seventy-two by reminding them that their true reward is not the ability to compel spirits, but rather that they have had their place in the eternal realms secured for them by his grace; that is, the divine gnosis.

Verses 21 and 22 constitute a prayer of Jesus to the Father, (cf. *Matthew* 11:25-27. This prayer reinforces the concept of Jesus as the revealer of divine knowledge, or gnosis. That the Father has, "concealed these things from the wise and intelligent," indicates that this special knowledge can be gained neither through philosophical reasoning, nor through academic pursuits, but only by "young children"; that is, those who have been reborn in the spirit. It is made clear in verse 22 that this knowledge of God is revealed through the Son, to whom he pleases. The idea of a secret or hidden knowledge, revealed only to the elect, is carried over in verses 23-24, (cf. *Matthew* 13:16-17). The fact that Jesus is speaking to his disciples privately is a further indication that He is imparting a special knowledge, not intended for the multitude. In verse 24, the "prophets and kings" refer to those who seek power and glory from a sense of self-importance, and those who have incomplete, or imperfect knowledge. To them the real power, and the true knowledge is not given. But to those who come as little children, to them is given the Kingdom of God.

This completes, then, this first section of our interpretive analysis of the tenth chapter of *Luke*. It is, however, far from being the final word on the subject. Of the several points addressed here, many have merely skimmed the surface, and a number of questions remain unanswered. For example, why was this allegory devised to begin with? Is this an historical account or teaching of Jesus? Or is it an invention of the author of Luke? Perhaps it is a bit of both. As the reader will have undoubtedly noticed, this passage bears an uncanny resemblance to the accounts given in *Mark* 6.7-11, *Matthew* 10, and Luke 9.1-6, of Jesus sending out the twelve Apostles, as well as similarities to various other scriptural elements as noted throughout this exegetical work. Why were these various elements put together in this way? Perhaps the author of Luke drew a connection between the twelve Apostles and the twelve houses of the zodiac, then reworked the account in order to stress this connection, and to elaborate on the premise using Gnostic and hermetic literature and traditions that would have been well-known to the literate Greek-speaking world at that time. Perhaps this allegory comes to us from some other source, now lost. For now, we can only speculate as to the origin of this passage. I think we can be fairly certain, though, that this Gnostic-Hermetic, astrological connection is real and not merely coincidental. The unique and specific language that is used throughout the passage gives us a preponderance of evidence that cannot be easily dismissed. After our analysis of the second section of Luke 10, perhaps we can return to some of these questions and gain a better understanding and insight into the inner workings of this enigmatic gospel. Before continuing, let me recap some of the major points of this analysis thus far:

- The seventy-two are sent out in thirty-six pairs, corresponding to the thirty-six decans of Egyptian astrology.

- The "houses" referred to are the twelve houses of the zodiac.

- The "sons" are the star demons of the Hermeticists, the Archons of the Gnostics, and the thirty-six world-rulers of the *Testament of Solomon*.

- Sabaoth, in Gnostic mythology, is one of the "sons of peace" who renounced evil.

- Jesus watching Satan fall is further evidence that this entire passage is dealing with celestial and spiritual events.

- The "authority to walk on snakes and scorpions" refers to the elevation of the disciples above the powers of the planetary and zodiacal rulers; and the disciples' ability to cause said rulers to submit to them in the name of Jesus Christ.

- Jesus' prayer to the Father in verses 21-22 shows Jesus in the roll of the "revealer of gnosis."

- Jesus' private discussion indicates that the disciples· have received a special or secret knowledge, reserved for God's elect.

The next section of this essay deals with *Luke* 10.15-37, which contains the parable of the "Good Samaritan." You will notice that this section is less academic in nature, and more strictly theological. This is due, in part, to the fact that we do not have to wrestle with the complex astrological symbolism contained in the first section. The parable of the Good Samaritan lends itself to a fairly straight forward Gnostic interpretation. That is, if we approach the story from a traditional Gnostic perspective, we will see that there is a message beyond the moral admonishment to judge people by who they actually are, and what they do, rather than by our preconceptions of them. Even the lesson of selflessly helping those who are in need is, at best, incomplete. The moral message is not doubt useful; but from a Gnostic perspective, it is the lesser meaning. The greater meaning of this parable concerns the salvation of the spirit from its hylic imprisonment.

In order for the reader to have a greater appreciation for a Gnostic interpretation of the text, I will give a very brief description of Gnostic ontology and soteriology. While some details differ among the various Gnostic schools of thought (Valentinian, Sethian, etc.), they mostly agree upon certain foundational premises. First of all, regarding the nature of human existence, Gnostics view man as having three bodies, or conditions of being. The Spiritual, or pneumatic, body is the part of man that is pure and incorruptible; the Vital Life Force that animates the psychic and hylic bodies. The pneumatic body descended from the original spiritual fullness (Pleroma), and seeks a return to its divine origin. The material, or hylic, body comes not from the True God, but from the imperfect demiurgic creator of the cosmos. The hylic body is often compared to a prison because it binds and conceals the pneumatic spark. The soul, or psychic body, resembles a comingling of the hylic and pneumatic bodies. The psychic body contains the passions as well as reasoning; thoughts as well as feelings. The lower regions of the psyche, then, belong to the hylic; containing the passions and what would be considered the "sinful" nature of man. The higher regions of the psyche, however, are associated with the pneumatic body, and contain the sublime aspects of mind (nous) such as the mystical revelations of divine gnosis. Thus, our human experience is realized largely by the soul, which, if left untended, will be wholly consumed by our hylic nature. For the Christian who seeks the knowledge of God (gnosis), however, the psychic body may align itself to the pneumatic and help to restore the pneumatic body to the Pleroma, and thus itself be saved from dissolution into matter. This is the meaning of *Luke* 9.24, which states, "For whoever wants to save his soul will lose it, but whoever loses his soul on account of me will save it." That is, if the lower self clings to the soul, then the soul will suffer the same fate as the flesh. But if the soul is given up to the higher, spiritual nature of Christ, then it will be preserved for eternal life in the Holy Realms.

Just as the human condition may be divided into three categories, or bodies, so too can the human population be likewise divided, (more especially in the Valentinian school). Those who have attained spiritual perfection, or who are destined to attain perfection, are designated as Pneumatics. The Psychics are those who are striving toward spiritual enlightenment, but have not yet attained the perfect understanding that comes with the gift of gnosis. And finally, there are the Hylics, who are wholly ignorant of their own spiritual darkness, and therefore are not aspiring toward spiritual knowledge. There are some Gnostics, both past and present, who are not entirely comfortable with this type of classification, seeing it as either elitist, or as supporting a doctrine of predestination that infringes upon free will. This is not the place to debate the merits of the various approaches, but I will say that these classifications are not without canonical support. *John* 6.64 tells us that, "Jesus had known from the beginning who the non-believers were." And the differences between the Psychic and the Pneumatic are stated quite plainly in *1 Corinthians* 2.14-15: "Psychic man does not receive the things of the Spirit of God, for they are foolish to him, and he is not able to know them, because they are pneumatically discerned. Now the Pneumatic man discerns all things, but he is discerned by no one."

Having given this brief introduction to Gnostic thought, then, let us proceed with our analysis of the parable of the Good Samaritan:

Luke 10.26-29:

> And he said to him, "What has been written in the Law? How do you read it?"
>
> And he answered saying, "You will love [agape] the Lord your
>
> God from the whole of your heart, and in the whole of your soul, and in the whole of your strength, and in the whole of your mind, and your neighbor as yourself."
>
> And he said to him, "You have answered correctly. Do this and you will live."
>
> But wanting to justify himself, he said to Jesus, "And who is my neighbor?"

Jesus tests the lawyer by asking him how he interprets the (demiurgic) Law. The Valentinians believed that the demiurge, and his laws, were not wholly evil, but imperfect. In this respect, their doctrine of the demiurge seems to be closer to the views held by the Hermeticists and Neoplatonists, than that of their more traditional Sethian counterparts, who tended to view the demiurge as more nefarious than merely imperfect. In his "Letter to Flora," Ptolemy, a successor of Valentinus, writes, "The law of god [that is, the demiurgic god, not the True God of Light], pure and not mixed with inferiority, is the Decalogue, those ten sayings engraved on two tables, forbidding things not to be done and enjoining things to be done. These contain pure but imperfect legislation and required the completion made by the savior. There is also the law interwoven with injustice, that an eye should be cut out for an eye and a tooth for a tooth, and that a murder should be avenged by a murder. The person who is the second one to be unjust is no less unjust than the first; he simply changes the order of events while performing the same action," (*Gnostic Bible*, p. 303). We can see therein the imperfection of the demiurge, and the Mosaic Law. In order to enforce his laws of justice, he must require a second injustice. So, how the lawyer responds to this inquiry will reveal much to Jesus about his character. That is, Jesus is testing him to determine whether he is oriented toward the just aspects of the law, or toward the imperfections of the law. When the lawyer responds that one must "love the Lord your God," and "your neighbor as yourself," Jesus seems satisfied with this response. This is because even though the man's faith may be misplaced in the demiurge, the quality of complete and unconditional love (agape) is an attribute that emanates from the True God of Light. In other words, the act of love is in itself salvific to an extent; or it may lead toward the salvific gnosis. Notice, though, that Jesus' response seems to be somewhat lacking. While he tells the man that he will live, he does not specifically guarantee the eternal, or Aeonic, life that he is seeking. Perhaps sensing that there is a greater truth to be gained, the man asks of Jesus who the neighbor is, that he should love as himself. This, of course, opens the door for Jesus to relate the parable.

Luke 10.30:

> Jesus replied, "A certain man was coming down from Jerusalem into Jericho and fell upon some highwaymen, who having both stripped and beat him, went away leaving him half dead."

The man coming down from Jerusalem represents the spark of divine spirit (Pneuma) descending from the eternal realms, or aeons, into the cosmos. Upon entering this world, the Spiritual man is confronted by the demiurge and his archons, represented here as highwaymen. What they strip him of is the knowledge and memory of who he is and where he came from. Ignorance of divine knowledge is often depicted as nakedness in Gnostic scripture and exegesis. For instance, in the Gnostic interpretation of Genesis, Adam and Eve's nakedness represents their spiritual ignorance. This is stated quite plainly and clearly in the *Reality of the Rulers*, when they eat the fruit of the Tree of Knowledge, "And their imperfections become apparent in their lack of knowledge. They recognized that they were naked of the spiritual," (*Gnostic Bible*, p. 171). Their shame, then, is due to the fact that they had forgotten their origin in the realms of light. This spiritual amnesia is not only a common Gnostic theme, it is the very condition from which we must be redeemed. The reason that our Spiritual or Pneumatic man is now "half dead" is because his true nature has been mixed with, and obscured by, the hylic and psychic natures of this world.

Luke 10.31-38

> "And coincidentally a certain priest was coming down that road and having seen him, passed by on the other side. And likewise, a Levite also came upon the place, and having seen him, passed by on the other side. But a certain Samaritan came upon him while traveling and having seen him, was moved with compassion. And having approached, he bandaged his wounds, pouring oil and wine over them, and having set him upon his own animal, brought him to an inn and cared for him. And the next day he took out two denarii and gave them to the inn-keeper and said, 'Take care of him, and whatever else you spend, I will repay you when I return.'"

Supplement: The Gnostic Gospel of Luke

When the man encounters the priest and the Levite, they are unwilling, and in fact unable, to help him because they themselves are priests of the demiurge, not of the True God of Light. The demiurgic Law of Moses is an imperfect law. While it serves to preserve Jewish customs, identity, and a semblance of order, its strict adherence leads to isolationism and contradiction rather than the upliftment of humanity. The law of the True God of Light, however, is the Law of Agape; the very same Law that Christ came to bear witness to. It is a Samaritan, a stranger and foreigner, who ultimately rescues our battered traveler. It is a common theme among Gnostic myths for the Pneumatic, or true Gnostic, to be depicted as a stranger; alien to this world, (cf. "Allogenes," *Nag Hammadi Library*, pp. 290-300). This image is confirmed by Jesus himself, who often depicts himself as being a stranger to this world, (cf. John 17:14-18). The symbol of the Samaritan as one of God's elect is also found later in *Luke*, in chapter 17, where the only one to give praise to God for his healing was the foreigner (Allogenes), a Samaritan, (*Luke* 17:11-19). It is interesting to note that while the Allogenes is a hero of several Gnostic texts, its only canonical usage is in *Luke*.

Luke 10.36-67:

"Who, of these three, seems to you to have become a neighbor to the one who fell upon the highwaymen?"
And he said, "The one who showed him compassion."
And Jesus said to him, "Depart and do likewise."

When Jesus asks the lawyer which of the three is the neighbor to the fallen traveler, the man responds that, of course, it is the one who has shown compassion. When Jesus tells him to depart and do likewise, he is not only telling him to be compassionate to his fellow man, but in fact, to be a stranger to this world; as Christ himself is. This parable also tells us that we are unable to raise ourselves up out of ignorance on our own. It requires an intervention from a spiritual force outside of ourselves to remind us of our origins, and to be restored to the Pleroma, or fullness of God, from which we came. So, the Samaritan here is representative of Christ, the redeemer, as well as of our own potential perfected self; that is, our spiritual, or pneumatic self that has been liberated from the bonds of matter and the lower mental states by the grace and compassion of Jesus Christ. So, just as Jesus healed the sick and raised the dead, that is, brought the ignorant into spiritual awareness, so too is the enlightened Christian called upon to help raise up his fallen brethren into the light of gnosis, and to tend to them until they are able to walk on their own, clothed in the robe of the glory of Christ; and in turn help to raise up yet others who have fallen prey to the darkness of this world.

In this parable of the Good Samaritan we can see that the attainment of gnosis and the elevation of the soul above the influence of its hylic imprisonment is not some selfish or elitist entitlement. In fact, we cannot even say that spiritual enlightenment is the destination of the Gnostic path. Rather, the attainment of enlightenment, or gnosis, can be more accurately depicted as a process than as a single event. Gnosis is not the end; it is the means by which the fragments of spiritual light will be ultimately restored to the Pleroma. The path of the living gnosis, therefore, leads inevitably to acts of compassion, and to the general upliftment of humanity. For, as it is written in the Gnostic scriptures, "Each one by his deeds and gnosis will reveal his nature," (*Gnostic Bible*, p. 437).

Speaking of "Good Samaritans," I could hardly discuss Gnosticism and Luke without addressing the only overt canonical reference to the Gnostics, the appearance of Simon Magus of Samaria in *Acts*. Given our hypothesis of a Gnostic undercurrent in *Luke*, we would expect a more sympathetic treatment of Simon Magus than we find in Luke's *Acts of the Apostles*. On the other hand, given the Church's later harsh suppression of Gnosticism, one might expect to find a more vehement denouncement than we see in Luke's casual dismissal. Perhaps, though, there is more this account than meets the eye. Let us take a look at these events from *Acts*, and then consider how this account might be reconciled with our previous hypotheses.

In the eighth chapter of *Acts*, Simon is introduced as a magician who is, "amazing the people of Samaria, saying to be someone great," (*Acts of the Apostles* 8:9b). This passage goes on to say that Philip converted the people of Samaria, and that "Simon himself also believed and, having been baptized, was following Philip, and seeing signs and great works being done, was amazed," (Ibid. 8:13). Later, Simon witnesses Peter and John conferring the power of the Holy Spirit upon people through the laying on of hands. Simon offers money for this Apostolic power, and is roundly rebuked and chastised by Peter, (Ibid. 8:18-24).

On the surface, this seems to be merely the rejection of the teachings and works of a pretender to the messianic throne. For instance, Simon's miracles are relegated to mere magic, while the miracles wrought by Philip are, "signs and great works." Likewise, for Simon to attempt to purchase Apostolic authority is to reduce him to a mere charlatan. While it is a common tactic to diminish the importance of one's adversary, in order to raise one's own perceived worth, such fraudulence as is attributed to Simon here, does not match up well with what we know of his lofty philosophical doctrines. Anyone reading this account, at the time, who was familiar with Simon's Gnostic doctrine, would likely have seen right through this weak attempt at refutation. Luke, the author of *Acts*, who is thought to have been highly educated, certainly would have realized the weakness of his straw man argument. In fact, it should not surprise us at all if Luke had at least a professional respect for Simon, considering Luke's profession, and the fact that Simon was known to have produced works on anatomy and the circulatory system, (*The Arcane Schools*, p. 157). What if, however, instead of trying to outright dismiss the Gnostics, he was actually embracing them, while saving face for the fledgling Christian Church?

We have already seen examples of the Samaritan as a symbol for the Gnostic. Perhaps this "conversion" of the Samaritans is actually a thinly veiled account of the absorption of the Samaritan Gnostics into the Christian fold. This would explain Luke's superficial dismissal of Simon Magus (after all, Christ can be the only leader of the Church), while embracing Simon's followers, as well as a fair amount of his philosophy. We do not have any surviving works today, to which we may turn for a comprehensive description of Simon's Gnostic philosophy. We do know, however, through fragments, and from the heresiologists (Irenaeus, Hippolytus, et at.), some of his core doctrines. One of his principal teachings was that the First Thought (Ennoia) of God was separated from her masculine counterpart, and eventually imprisoned in the material world, from which she must be liberated, and restored to her heavenly estate, (Hoeller, *Gnosticism*, p. 95). This forms one of the bases for both the Gnostic Sophia myth, as well as the gnostic concept of the soul's descent into matter. How can we possibly see as coincidence, then, that the tenth chapter of Luke contains a parable about a Samaritan that, as we have seen, follows a story line that is nearly identical to the philosophy espoused by Simon Magus, the greatest Samaritan spiritual leader of the time? The Good Samaritan parable seems to be a wink and a nod to those early Christian Gnostics of Samaria; just as the account of the seventy-two disciples seems to acknowledge the Alexandrian Gnostics and Hermeticists. It also seems that the reputation of Simon Magus, one of the most profound Gnostic philosophers of the first century AD, has been an unfortunate casualty of the early Church's battle for supremacy. (We see this also with the downgrading of John the Baptist, though with less animosity.)

We have seen, I believe, that the tenth chapter of Luke contains elements, and an overall air, of an unmistakably Gnostic and Hermetic character. This is confirmed by the fact that we have nothing quite like these accounts in all the rest of the canonical scriptures, but that we do, however, find similarities in a number of outside texts. As noted throughout this essay, nearly all of the allegorical images, and even much of the specific language may be found in numerous Hermetic and Gnostic sources.

It is also interesting to note that many of the themes and images introduced in the tenth chapter, at the beginning of Jesus' journey toward Jerusalem, are carried throughout the journey, over the next several chapters. Even in cases where we have parallels between Luke and other synoptic passages, the wording in Luke is often altered ever so slightly, so as to reflect its unique character. For example, in Luke 11.9-13 we have a passage that mirrors, nearly identically, a similar excerpt from Matthew 7.7-11. There are a couple of differences in Luke, however, that while seemingly insignificant, actually serve to provide a semantic continuity from the previous chapter, and to illustrate the spiritual nature of the work as a whole. Let us examine, then these two passages, and briefly discuss these minor but significant discrepancies.

Matthew 7.7-11:

"Ask and it will be given to you, seek and you will find, knock and it will be opened to you. For everyone asking receives, and the one seeking finds, and to the one knocking it will be opened. What man is among you who, if his son asks for bread, will give a stone to him? Or if he asks for a fish, surely you will not give to him a snake? If, therefore, you being evil know to give good gifts to your children, how much more will your Father in heaven give good things to those asking him!"

Luke 11.9-13:

"And I say to you, Ask and it will be given to you, seek and you will find, knock and it will be opened to you. For everyone asking receives, and the one seeking finds, and to the one knocking it will be opened. But what father among you, whose son asks for a fish, will give him a snake instead of a fish? Or if he will ask for an egg, will give to him a scorpion? If, therefore, you being evil ones, know to give good gifts to your children, how much more will the Father from heaven give the Holy Spirit to those asking Him!"

There are a couple of variances in the above passages that should be immediately apparent. The first concerns the requests of the hypothetical son, and the responses. Both *Matthew* and *Luke* have the son requesting a fish, which is negatively juxtaposed with a snake. In both passages the symbolism is readily apparent. The fish is an obvious symbol for Christ, which is quite naturally contrasted with the serpent, representing the adversary. Beyond that, we have a discrepancy between the two texts. In *Matthew*, we have an image of bread, contrasted with a stone. This too seems to be a natural comparison. The bread is the bread of life, Christ himself, and the life-giving law he brings. The stone is representative of the old Law, that which does not nourish the soul. In *Luke*, we are presented with a different set of symbols. There is the egg, which is a natural symbol for life and rebirth. The egg is contrasted with the scorpion, which is certainly a symbol of death, but is also significant in that it mirrors the "snakes and scorpions" imagery from chapter ten. It seems obvious, then, that this passage has been specifically reworded in order to maintain a continuity of symbolism, and perhaps as a subtle reminder of the underlying esotericism.

If the subtlety of the word play in the previous example was not enough to illustrate this point, it is made obvious at the end of the passage in *Luke*. In *Matthew*, the passage concludes with the Father giving "good things" to those who ask. This concept is in agreement with the Jewish view of God as the provider of material sustenance. This is consistent with the prevailing hypothesis that Matthew's target audience is Jewish. Luke, however, makes a small, but theologically significant, alteration to the text. The passage in *Luke* concludes with the Father giving the "Holy Spirit" to those who ask. I think this tells us something about the intended audience of Luke's gospel. It is generally speculated that Luke's audience is primarily Greek. I will not dispute that, but would posit, additionally, that many aspects of the gospel, especially elements of the journey toward Jerusalem, are targeted specifically at Neoplatonists, Hermeticists, and even early Gnostics. To those groups I just mentioned, for the Father (that is, the True God, not an inferior demiurge) to give anything except spiritual gifts would be unthinkable. So, to state that the Father gives the Holy Spirit, acknowledges Him as the True God of Light, and not the demiurgic creator of the cosmos.

Another curious aspect of this gospel is the fact that the author basically states that he is merely retelling what has already been recorded. Let us look at his specific wording at the beginning of the gospel, and then discuss some of the implications.

Luke 1.1-4

Seeing that many have attempted to compile their recollections about the events that have been fulfilled among us, just as they were handed down to us by those who from the beginning had been eyewitnesses and servants of the Logos, it also seemed good to me, having investigated everything carefully from the start, to write to you in an orderly manner, most noble Theophilus, that you may know with assurance the words about which you have been instructed.

In the first verse, Luke states that there have been "many" compilations of the gospel. If we go by the traditional number and ordering of the gospels, then that would place *Luke* as the third to compile a gospel of Jesus Christ. Even if we were to place *Luke*'s authorship after the *Gospel According to John*, that would still only place it fourth in line according to tradition. Two or three prior works can hardly be considered "many" by any stretch of the imagination. We must assume, then, that there were a number of works circulating at the time, that never found their way into the official canon of the Church. Some of these works undoubtedly vanished from the pages of history. Others, however, may be with us, but not previously suspected as having influenced our modem canon.

When we examine the various sayings, narratives, and parables of *Luke*, much of the material finds its parallel in the other "synoptic" gospels of *Matthew* and *Mark*. We are left, however, with a significant amount of material that is present nowhere else in the official canon. This creates an interesting dilemma, because if we accept the orthodox canon, then the gospels are complete, as we now have them. If, however, we accept Luke's opening statements at face value, that he is retelling what has already been recorded, then we cannot accept that the orthodox canon is complete. We have already seen that there are a number of concepts in the tenth chapter that seem to have their origin in Hermetic and proto-Gnostic doctrines. But there are a number of other passages among the chapters that comprise the "journey toward Jerusalem" section, that seem to have their parallel in the Thomasine literature. I will mention but a few here briefly, merely to illustrate the point. *Luke* 14.15-24 tells the parable of the "Great Supper." A remarkably similar version also exists as saying number 64 of the *Gospel of Thomas*, (*Gnostic Bible*, pp. 60-61). Saying number 107 of that same work contains a version of the "Lost Sheep" parable, (Ibid. p. 68) found in *Luke* 15.3-7. There are also shorter passages, such as *Luke* 17.20-21, that are elaborated upon in sayings 3 and 113 in the *Gospel of Thomas* (Ibid. pp. 45, 69). And verse 22 of that same chapter in *Luke* is echoed in saying 38 (Ibid. p. 54). It may be argued that the author of the Gospel of Thomas may merely be retelling the accounts found in *Luke*. We do not have any definitive proof, one way or the other. But we do have Luke's admission that he is using other sources for the compilation of his gospel. So, while we cannot, with absolute certainty, establish a chronology for these documents (since we do not have the original source texts), we can nevertheless reasonably infer a relationship between the two works.

The above examples, while not exhaustive analyses, serve to show, I think, that we must look to the Gnostic scriptures to find parallels to many of the otherwise unique passages throughout Luke. Though the principal theme and purpose of this essay is an exegesis of the tenth chapter, it was necessary to illustrate that a Gnostic and Hermetic interpretation is not out of place in a broader context of Luke, specifically within the "journey toward Jerusalem" section of the text. Indeed, far from being anomalous, these mystical tendencies seem to form a pattern running throughout the text as a sort of sub-current to the standard gospel narrative.

There is still much left unsaid regarding the hypotheses set forth in this essay. To be sure, there is much additional material that could be brought into discussion on the topic. And hopefully, a more exhaustive analysis of the text will eventually be accomplished; whether by this author or another. Doubtless, many among the Christian orthodoxy will be inclined to refute my conclusions on principle alone. Likewise, secular biblical scholars may feel that I have drifted too far from the academic into the speculative and theological. But, as stated in the introduction to this essay, this is intended to be a primarily theological work, which may have certain academic implications. I certainly have attempted to use academically sound reasoning in my analyses. In the end, I simply ask the reader to contemplate the work with an open mind and, having carefully examined all of the supporting material that I have presented, to give serious consideration to the ideas articulated here. For what I am advocating here is not a radical redefinition of Christianity, but rather a return to a more universal and encompassing Christianity that recognizes that the scriptures at once speak on multiple literal and symbolic levels, and to multiple audiences; and that one of the primary audiences of early Christianity was the Gnostic in his varied forms, whether Jewish, Neoplatonic, or Hermetic. We now know that many among these Gnostic groups were in fact Christianized and thrived within the pre-Nicene Christian community. Many of these early Christian Gnostics were not operating outside of the Apostolic tradition, as is so often depicted today in popular writings and television programs. In fact, most of the Gnostic teachers claimed to have received their teachings from one or another of the Apostolic schools; whether it be from

Matthew, John, Paul, or others. Many of the early Gnostics represented an Apostolic tradition that ran parallel to, and sometimes overlapped, the Apostolic tradition that was to survive as the "orthodoxy." It is my hope that this short work will add to the mounting evidence that the canonical scriptures are filled with fragments of an underlying secret mystical tradition that may rightly be called, "Gnostic"; as well as add to the ever-growing body of modem Apostolic Gnostic literature and research.

For a parting thought, I leave the reader with the words of the Apostle:

> Awake, sleeper!
> And arise from the dead,
> And the Christos will shine upon you.
>
> - *Ephesians* 5:14b

Supplement: The Devil's Passion

The Devil's Passion
A Gnostic View of the Crucifixion

The Crucifixion of Jesus of Nazareth is central to the beliefs and practices of nearly the whole of Christendom. For nearly two thousand years, Christians the world over have joyously exclaimed, "Jesus died for our sins!" But what is really meant by this statement? Why did Jesus have to die? And what, exactly, was salvific in this action? These are questions that have been asked since the time of Christ, and questions that are worth exploring in our own day. And of course, we must not be afraid to inquire as to what sort of god it is that requires human sacrifice for the atonement of sins. These are some of the questions we intend to address here. The answers to these questions, found in both canonical and extra-canonical sources, and through logical extrapolation, will show that the god who demands human sacrifice is not the true God of Light, but an inferior Demiurge; and that the Crucifixion of Christ is in fact a sacrifice to this demi-god.

It is no great secret that to the Gnostics, the "God" of the old covenant is not really God at all, but rather an imposter. We can go straight to the Old Testament scriptures to examine the character of this "God." In Exodus 20:5, this entity states, "...for I the Lord God am a jealous God, visiting the iniquity of the fathers upon the children unto the third and fourth generation of them that hate me." In Isaiah 45:7, this same god states, "I form the light, and created darkness. I make peace, and create evil. I the Lord do all these things." We could go on for pages with such examples. But in just these two brief passages we can already see a petty, vengeful god who has no qualms about admitting to being the author of evil.

The Chief prophet and spokesman for this god, this imperfect fashioner of the worlds, was Moses. Through Moses was given his Law, which included that animals be sacrificed unto this lord of the cosmos. It is evident from the Christian canon that the Demiurgic law was imperfect and in need of rectification. In John 1:17 we read, "The law indeed was given through Moses; grace and truth came through Jesus Christ. No one has ever seen God. It is God the only Son who is close to the Father's heart, who has made him known." This is a scathing criticism of the Demiurgic law and the god of the Old Testament. It suggests that the law given through Moses was not that of Truth, and that Moses was never really in communication with God at all, for it is only the Son "who has made him known."

Now, Paul's approach is more diplomatic and less abrasive, but he comes to the same point - that those who follow the law of Moses are not in accord with the will of God. For, he says in Romans 10:1-8,

> Brothers and sisters, my heart's desire and prayer to God for them is that they may be saved. I can testify that they have a zeal for God, but it is not enlightened. For, being ignorant of the righteousness that comes from God, and seeking to establish their own, they have not submitted to God's righteousness. For Christ is the end of the law so that there may be righteousness for everyone who believes.

Moses writes concerning the righteousness that comes from the law, that "the person who does these things will live by them." But the righteousness that comes from faith says, "Do not say in your heart, 'Who will ascend into heaven?'" (that is, to bring Christ down) "or 'Who will descend into the abyss?'"(that is, to bring Christ up from the dead). But what does faith say? "The word is near you, on your lips and in your heart" (that is, the word of faith that we proclaim).

In the above quote, we clearly see that those who seek the so-called righteousness of the law of Moses are "ignorant of the righteousness that comes from God." In other words, the law given through Moses cannot have been given by God. If the god that gave the law had been the true God, the law would have been perfect. Paul says of Christ in Ephesians 3:15, that "He has abolished the law with its commandments and ordinances... " If the law had come from the true Father of Light, it would not have had to have been abolished.

So far we have sought the identity of the god of the law in both the Old and New Testaments of the Christian canon. Let us now look at what the Gnostics of old had to say of this nefarious character. In The Testimony of Truth we find an echo of the sorts of questions and observations we have just made:

> What kind of god is this? First, he begrudged Adam's eating from the tree of knowledge. Second, he said, "Adam, where are you?" God does not have foreknowledge; otherwise, wouldn't he have known from the beginning?

> Great is the blindness of those who read such things, and they don't know him. He said, "I am the jealous God; I will bring the sins of the fathers upon the children up to three and four generations." He also said, "I will make their heart thick, and I will cause their minds to become blind, that they might not understand or comprehend the things that are said." But these are things he says to those who believe in him and worship him! (Pearson, p. 623).

Our present view, therefore, is in complete concert with the Gnostic fathers. We see that they did not posit any new doctrine, but merely revealed what is plainly written in the scriptures. The author of The Second Revelation of James makes the following observations:

> His inheritance, which he boasted about, claiming it was great, will prove to be insignificant. His gifts are not blessings and his promises are evil intrigues. You are not of the children of his compassion, but he does violence against you. He wants to do injustice against us. And he will have dominion for a period of time appointed for him, (Funk, p. 377).

Although there are many, many more examples we could present that show the true nature of the Demiurge, The *Gospel of Philip* sums up the whole of his character pretty well in this statement: "God is a man-eater, and so humans are sacrificed to him," (Meyer, *Gosp. Phil.*, p. 170).

Having established, then, the identity of the false god of the law, let us seek to establish the identity and purpose of Jesus Christ. The entirety of the Christian scriptures, both canonical and extra-canonical, serve to show his divinity and his redemptive, restorative mission. One point of commonality among nearly every branch of the Christian Church, whether Catholic or Protestant, Orthodox or Gnostic, is that Jesus Christ was the Logos incarnate. This doctrine is nowhere more beautifully and aptly described than in the prologue to The Gospel According to John:

> In the beginning was the Logos, and the Logos was with God, and the Logos was Divine. He was in the beginning with God. All things came into being through him, and without him not one thing came into being that has come into being. In him was Life, and the Life was the Light of Man. And the light shines in the darkness and the darkness did not overcome it.

> The Gospel goes on to identify Christ as "the true light, which enlightens everyone." And concerning His mission, we have already seen that He is "the end of the law so that there may be righteousness … "; and that he has come to bring "grace and truth."

In Gnostic thought, Man is divided into three states, or bodies: the physical, or hylic body; the soul, or psychic body; and the spirit, or pneumatic body. Some of the ancient Gnostics claimed that Christ only had psychic and pneumatic bodies, and that the physical body was merely an illusion projected by the psychic body. That is an interesting debate, but one that does not really concern us here. For, if he did have a physical body, it was no doubt transformed into a more subtle form at the time of the ascension. So, for the sake of this present work, let us primarily consider the psychic and pneumatic aspects of Jesus. But this should not be taken as an outright denial of a physical Jesus.

In order to ascend into the spiritual realms, one must become pure spirit. For nothing less can withstand the perfection of those realms. So it was for Jesus Christ. In order for the Word, the Logos, to return to the bosom of the Father, any lesser, extraneous elements needed to be discarded. Jesus predicts this in the following statement from The Gospel According to Matthew 20:17-19, using a richly symbolic language:

> While Jesus was going up to Jerusalem, he took the twelve disciples aside by themselves, and said to them on the way, "See, we are going up to Jerusalem, and the Son of Man will be handed over to the chief priests and scribes, and they will condemn him to death, then they will hand him over to the Gentiles to be mocked and flogged and crucified, and on the third day he will be raised."

Whenever we see Jesus speaking to the twelve apostles "aside" or "in private," we should take this as a cue that a symbolic account is to follow, which requires spiritual discernment to properly interpret. The phrase "going up to Jerusalem" is indicative of ascending into the Pleroma, the Aeonic realms. In order to do that, the lower bodies must be shed. Therefore, the "Son of Man will be handed over… " Notice that he does not say that the "Son of God" will be handed over. For, the pneumatic Son, the Logos of the Eternal Aeon, can only be delivered unto the Unknown Father of Light. But the Son of Man, that is the psychic Christ, is handed over to the "chief priests and scribes." This refers to the Demiurge and his archons. The psychic Christ is then mocked, flogged, and crucified by the minions of the Demiurge (Gentiles). Although the physical crucifixion happened once, at a certain point in space and time, the psychical crucifixion occurs in perpetuity. This is why the Eucharistic Prayer in our holy liturgy states that Christ "forever offers Himself as the eternal sacrifice."

Concerning the psychic Christ, let us look at a passage from "Excerpts from Theodotus," a collection of notes compiled by Clement of Alexandria concerning Valentinian doctrine:

> Now the Saviour became the first universal creator. "But Wisdom," the second, "built a house for herself and hewed out seven pillars" and first of all she put forth a god, the image of the Father and through him she made heaven and earth, that is, "heavenly things and the earthly" - the things on the right hand and on the left. This, as an image of the Father, then became a father and put forth first the psychic Christ, an image of the Son... (Casey, p. 171)

So, we see here that the psychic Christ is the first creation of the Demiurge. But his psychic Christ is only an image of the pneumatic Savior, just as the Demiurge himself is only a pale reflection of the true Father. Further on in "Theodotus" we find an account of the spiritual Jesus putting on the psychic Christ:

> And when he came into Space, Jesus found Christ, whom it was foretold that he would put on, whom the Prophets and the Law announced as an image of the Saviour. But even this psychic Christ whom he put on, was invisible, and it was necessary for him when he came into the world to be seen here, to be held, to be a citizen, and to hold on to a sensible body, (Casey, p. 173).

Thus, we see that the Christ prophesied by the law is the psychic Christ. Therefore, the incarnation of Jesus Christ fulfills both the law of the Demiurge and the will of God, reconciling the one to the other.

Since we have now examined the nature of, and established the identity of, the god who demands human sacrifice, and since we have likewise studied the nature of Jesus Christ, let us look at the significance of the Crucifixion itself. We have already seen in Matthew 20:17-19 that Jesus has full knowledge of what must transpire. This conversation between Jesus and his disciples is recorded in all three of the synoptic gospels. It is interesting to note that in Luke, after the conversation, it states, "But they understood nothing about these things, in fact, what he said was hidden from them, and they did not grasp what was said." The language used by Jesus in this passage seems quite straightforward. It is impossible to believe that the surface message was not grasped. It is therefore only logical that the message that was not grasped was some other, deeper interpretation, just as we posited earlier.

This is not the only place where we see Jesus speaking cryptically about the various bodies or natures returning to their origin. We find just such a discourse within a well-known parable that occurs in each of the synoptic gospels that seems, on the surface, to be talking about paying taxes to Caesar, but which is actually expounding the principle we have been discussing. Here is the version from The Gospel According to Luke 20:22-25,

> "Is it lawful for us to pay taxes or not?" But he perceived their craftiness and said to them, "Show me a Denarius. Whose head and whose title does it bear?" They said, "Caesar's." He said to them, "Then give to Caesar the things that are Caesar's, and to God the things that are God's."

In the above parable, it seems obvious that "Caesar" is the Demiurge. Therefore, not only has Jesus acknowledged that things of a psychic nature are rendered unto the Demiurge, lord of the psychic realm, and the things of a spiritual nature are returned to the true God, but he also through this parable seems to suggest that it is proper to perform the rites demanded by the Demiurge - that is, to "pay taxes." At the same time, though, it cautions not to give unto the Demiurge the things that belong to God, which is our worship and dedication. In other words, this suggests that harmony and balance is to be sought on all planes of existence. Jesus is telling us, simply, to "give the devil his due."

The crucifixion, then, separates the constituent parts of Jesus Christ so that the Demiurge may have his sacrifice, and the Logos may return to the Pleroma. But what, exactly, is salvific in the Crucifixion? We are often told, "Jesus died for our sins." But what should we really take from that statement? It would seem that this statement is true insofar as his death was a consequence of his incarnation, which was necessitated by Man's insistence upon the worship of a false god. But does that mean that his death was really the salvific action? The New Testament scriptures seem to indicate otherwise. We earlier examined Romans 10:1-8. If we look at the very next verse, we read, "Because if you confess with your lips that Jesus is Lord and believe in your heart that God raised him from the dead, you will be saved." This seems very clear that it is faith in the *resurrection* that has a salvific effect.

This is not to say, however, that the Crucifixion is without significance. The image of the crucifixion gives us a powerful symbol, and adds to the importance of the resurrection. Truly, the Crucifixion and Resurrection are as two sides of the same coin. The Crucifixion fulfills an obligation to the Demiurge, and the Resurrection opens the path to the. Tree of Life; it restores Humanity to its primitive wholeness. This duality is expressed perfectly in the celebration of the Eucharist.

The Eucharist is both psychic and pneumatic. The psychic Eucharist is the offering up of the Body and Blood of Christ. Through transubstantiation, the psychic Christ is sacrificed anew at every Eucharistic celebration. And this sacrifice is indeed a sacrifice to the Demiurge. It is a renewal of the new covenant made with the Demiurge. For, the true God of Light does not need to make deals or contracts with Man. The Most High God gives of his grace freely to all who would partake.

This brings us, then, to the pneumatic Eucharist. We read in *The Gospel of Truth*:

> He was nailed to a tree, and he became fruit of the knowledge of the Father. This fruit of the tree, however, did not bring destruction when it was eaten, but rather it caused those who ate of it to come into being. They were joyful in this discovery, and he found them within himself and they found him within themselves, (Meyer, *Gosp. Truth*, p. 37).

We thus see that Jesus is the fruit of the Tree of Knowledge, and that by partaking of the Communion, we have been given the opportunity to eat from that Tree. This assimilation of the pneumatic Logos is the Gnostic Communion.

The Eucharist unites the mysteries of the Crucifixion with the mysteries of the Resurrection. In doing so, the practitioner finds therein an atonement for sin of two types. Through the sacrifice of Christ, the bloodthirsty Demiurge is appeased, and one is absolved of the "sin" caused by falling short of the mandates of the old law. By partaking of the Eucharistic elements, the Body and Blood of the pneumatic Logos, we eat from the Tree of Knowledge. This gnosis alleviates the real sin, which is ignorance of the Father of Light.

Let us look, finally, at some of the consequences of the Crucifixion. First, it is interesting to note that blood sacrifices ceased within Judaism within a generation of Christ's Crucifixion. Ostensibly, this is because of the destruction of the Temple. But to consider this as mere coincidence seems to stretch beyond the plausible. A careful analysis of the myth, legend, and facts surrounding the birth, life, death, and resurrection of Jesus Christ leaves one little choice but to acknowledge that he was indeed the fulfillment of the prophecies of old.

Although Jesus brought the opportunity for true redemption through gnosis, the majority of worshippers still venerate the Demiurge. These are the psychic Christians. Some of the ancient Gnostics were quite derisive toward the psychic Church. We read of the psychics in *The Second Discourse of Great Seth*, "They proclaim the doctrine of a dead man, along with false teachings that mock the freedom and purity of the perfect assembly," (Meyer, *Sec. Disc.*, p. 482). But the psychic Christians do indeed have their psychic Christ. We read again in "Excerpts from Theodotus": "Now the psychic Christ sits on the right hand of the Creator, as David says, 'Sit thou on my right hand' and so on. And he sits there until the end 'that they may see him whom they pierced,'" (Casey, p. 174).

But Christ has compassion for those still in error and ignorance. This is evident in the fact that the psychics and pneumatics are reconciled under one Church. Returning to the passage quoted earlier from Ephesians 2:15, let us re-examine it and read on a bit further:

> He has abolished the law with its commandments and ordinances, that he might create in himself one new humanity in place of the two, thus making peace, and might reconcile both groups to God in one body through the cross, thus putting to death that hostility through it.

Through this act of divine charity, the psychics - the worshippers of the Demiurge and his son, the psychic Christ - have the opportunity to become pneumatics and ascend to the Unknown Father of Light. In fact, it is held by many modern Gnostics that the elevation of the psychics to the pneumatic realm is practically assured, whether it be by means of a sudden, transcendental revelation, or through a slow, steady evolution of faith into gnosis; extending, perhaps, over several incarnations. The message of Christ is one of perpetual hope and of eternal salvation. It is in this spirit of fraternity and reconciliation that all Christians should conduct themselves toward all of their brothers and sisters, without judgment, but striving ever toward the highest and purest ideals. It is only through these lofty aspirations and the drive to attain to them, that one may gain liberty from not only the old law, which Christ has indeed abolished, but also from the new covenant of the psychic Christ which, though for now remains a "necessary evil," is still but a blood pact with the Demiurge. It is only in the final liberation that one may attain oneness with the Logos of the Unknown Father.

So we have the prophetic message more fully confirmed. You will do well to be attentive to this as to a lamp shining in a dark place, until the day dawns and the Morning Star rises in your hearts."

- 2 Peter 1:19

Supplement: Morning Star Rising

Morning Star Rising
Further considerations on the Gnostic Eucharist

Και εχομεν βεβαιοτερον τον προφητικον λογον, ᾧ καλως ποιει τε προσεχ ὡς λυχνω φαινοντι εναυχμηρω τοπω, ἕως οὗ ἡμερα διαυγαση και Φωσφορος ανατειλη εν ταις καρδιαις ὑμων.

- ΠΕΤΡΟΥ Β 1:19

Et habemus firiorem propheticum sermonem, cui bene facitis attendentes quasi lucemae lucenti in caliginoso loco, donec dies illucesat, et Lucifer oriatur in cordibus vestris.

- EPISTULA PETRI II 1:19

So we have the prophetic message more fully confirmed. You will do well to be attentive to this as to a lamp shining in a dark place, until the day dawns and the Morning Star rises in your hearts.

- 2 Peter 1:19

In our previous paper, "The Devil's Passion," we illustrate that the Eucharistic celebration contains both psychic and pneumatic elements. That is, it celebrates the ritual sacrifice of the psychic Christ to his father, the Demiurge; and also the Holy Communion with the pneumatic Logos by partaking of His spiritual Body and Blood. Now, one may wonder why a psychic Eucharist is practiced at all, since gnosis is our ultimate goal. And it is true that one who has attained to a perfect knowledge of God, which is a perfect knowledge of Self, and has perfectly wedded spirit and soul, would no longer need to partake in any sacramental or theurgic rite whatsoever. But for those who have not yet received Perfection, the sacrament of the Eucharist is one of the means by which we gradually spiritualize the psychic body.

But this still does not address why we continue to celebrate a psychic Eucharist, instead of a solely pneumatic rite. The answer is that we are still under the influence of the Demiurge and his Archons; it is simply a condition of the natural world. Christ's sacrificial blood did indeed purchase our freedom from the old Law of the Demiurge. But until we obtain that perfect liberation through gnosis, we are subject to the terms of our contract with the Demiurge, the New Covenant established by Christ on our behalf. The Law of Vengeance was replaced by the Law of Agape (Love), which is a law of Grace, but at a great cost – Christ's sacrifice of himself; not once, but in perpetuity, until all of humanity is restored to the Pleroma, the Oneness of God.

This final liberation is mentioned in the conclusion of "The Devil's Passion," which states that, "one may gain liberty from not only the old law, which Christ has indeed abolished, but also from the new covenant of the psychic Christ which...is still but a blood pact with the Demiurge. It is only in the final liberation that one may attain oneness with the Logos of the Unknown Father." This "final liberation" is the rising of the Morning Star in one's heart spoken of in the passage from 2 Peter which concludes "The Devil's Passion" and which introduces the present work.

Let us consider, then, the nature of this Morning Star, and the meaning of this verse. The "prophetic message" that is "more fully confirmed" is the Good News of the incarnation of the psychic Christ, which had been foretold by the Prophets. His sacrifice to the Demiurge, renewed at each celebration of the Holy Eucharist, is what must be tended to as "a lamp shining in a dark place, until the day dawns and the Morning Star rises in your hearts." That is, if we wish to live under the grace of the Law of Love, the Demiurgic rites must be performed in good faith until one has fully assimilated the pneumatic Logos; in other words, "until the day dawns and the Morning Star rises in your hearts." The rising of the Morning Star - Lucifer or Phosphoros - in one's heart is a reference to the emergence of the Light of Gnosis within the individual. To the Gnostic, this deification of the individual - called *Theosis* by our Orthodox brethren, represented by Paul as the *New Man*, and by the venerable Louis-Claude de Saint-Martin also as the *Spirit Man* - is the real Good News, or Gospel. The Masonic Blazing Star with the "G" in the center is a graphic representation of this very principle.

The grace that comes from Christ's sacrifice is accessible through faith. But the Morning Star is obtainable only through gnosis, to those who conquer their lower natures by a concerted act of Will, and who accomplish the Work of Jesus, as we read in the *Revelation of St. John*:

> To everyone who conquers and continues to do my works to the end, I will give authority over the nations... even as I also received authority from my Father. To the one who conquers I will also give the Morning Star. Let anyone who has an ear listen to what the Spirit is saying to the churches, (Rev. 2:26, 28-29).

We are told near the end of Revelation that the Morning Star is in fact Jesus Christ himself:

> It is I, Jesus, who sent my angel to you with this testimony for the churches. I am the root and the descendant of David, the bright and Morning Star, (Rev. 22:16).

This is a most intriguing statement, and one that requires comment on a couple of fronts. First, as we have just said, it definitively identifies the Morning Star with Jesus himself. But we must look at this title as more than a mere epithet of Christ. Given its other canonical usage in *2 Peter*, wherein it is described as something to arise within, and in the second chapter of *Revelation* wherein it is something that is granted from on high to "the one who conquers," we must conclude that this title refers to a state of being, of existence, which may be attained by the initiate who overcomes the trials and Ordeals. Indeed, we must conclude that the "Morning Star" refers to the very state of Christhood. To put this into a Qabalistic context, it is the consciousness that has ascended to Tiphareth and furthermore has attained the Knowledge and Conversation of the Holy Guardian Angel. This is not to say that the consciousness has achieved reintegration into the Pleroma, but that reintegration is now possible. In other words, the arising of the Morning Star is that Gnostic illumination sought by every initiate of the Mysteries; true Salvation.

Another interesting aspect of the quote from *Revelation* 22 is Jesus' stated relationship to David. As shown by Bishop William Pierce in his paper, "A Brief Gnostic Interpretation of the Gospel According to Matthew," David is a symbol or representation of the Demiurge (a sentiment corroborated by the Valentinians of old such as Theodotus). Therefore, for Jesus to say that he is the root *and* the descendent of David (the Demiurge) shows the dual nature of Jesus Christ as discussed in "The Devil's Passion"; that is, the pneumatic Logos who *preceded* the Demiurge and through whom all things were created, and the psychic Christ who is the creation or *descendent* of the Demiurge. In man this refers to the logos in man, or the pneumatic spark, and the soul or psychic substance. The Morning Star, therefore, is the catalyst of reconciliation between the two - the alchemical marriage of Spirit and Soul.

Now that we have more clearly identified the goal of the Gnostic, and the nature of the pneumatic Eucharist as opposed to the psychic Eucharist, let us address a topic long held as taboo amid the public discussions of Gnostic Christians, but upheld as sacred doctrine in the secret inner conclaves of many of those same Christian Gnostic communities: Θελημα (Thelema - Will) - the philosophy expounded by the poet, adventurer and mystic, Aleister Crowley. We do not fault any person or group for not publicly espousing the Thelemic philosophy, for it is surrounded by controversy; often unfairly criticized by those who do not understand it, and defended by those equally ignorant of the deeper truths of the Thelemic doctrine, and even more ignorant of classical Gnosticism, which is fundamentally Christian. Let us therefore examine some of the core Thelemic doctrines, and we shall attempt to illustrate that the apparent opposition of Thelema and Christianity is in fact a false dichotomy. We wish to show further that the principal doctrines of Thelema are a natural extension of, and complement to, Christianity.

The entire Thelemic doctrine may be summed up in the following statements, known as the Law of Thelema: "Do what thou wilt shall be the whole of the Law. Love is the law, love under will." The student of the early Church fathers will notice immediately the similarity to St. Augustine's famous injunction, "Love, and do what you will." But this statement, in a Thelemic context, is much more profound than the narrow views of Augustine, who turned from his Gnostic Manichean origins to adopt the politically correct views of the emerging Christian orthodoxy. Looking at the first statement, "Do what thou wilt shall be the whole of the Law," we must not see herein a license to succumb to every passing whim. It is actually instructing the very opposite. It involves the concept of True Will - i.e. that it is the responsibility of every initiate to discover his or her True Will, the innermost raison d'être, and to *do* that Will. In other words, it is not enough to ascend to the heights of the proverbial mountaintop. If what one has received is not put into action, then the whole work was for naught.

This brings us then to the second part of the Law of Thelema: "Love is the law, love under will." This Love (Αγαπη - Agape) is not some fleeting sentimental attachment as the profane suppose. We should see it rather as a technical term referring, in part, to the putting into action of the Will. Love is a powerful force; it is *the* powerful force, making all emanation and creation possible. But it is only a force for Good (again, a technical term, in the Platonic sense) when it is guided by the Divine Will. When we read in *Romans* 13:10 that "Love (Agape) is the fulfillment of the law," we will immediately see that the Thelemic caveat "love under will" is but an elaboration and explanation of the former. This Law of Love is the very same that Jesus came to establish for humanity.

The Thelemic law is therefore nothing but a pure application of the Law of Agape instituted by Jesus Christ. One of the "hang-ups" that many Christian Gnostics have with Thelema, however, is that it seems, on its surface, to have nothing to do with Christianity, being non-Christian at best, or anti-Christian at worst. This is true, but only in part, and only superficially. As to that which seems anti-Christian, we must look closely at what Crowley says, and who exactly these "Christians" are that he rails against. In "The World's Tragedy" Crowley makes the following observation:

> I therefore hold the legendary Jesus in no wise responsible for the trouble ... what I am trying to get at is the religion which makes England to-day a hell for any man who cares at all for freedom. That religion they call Christianity; the devil they honour they call God... it is their God and their religion that I hate and will destroy.

It seems abundantly clear here that the Christianity that Crowley so despises is that false so-called Christianity that is the bane of every true initiate. Crowley's disdain for what passed as "Christianity" in his day (and mostly in our own day as well, unfortunately) provided the impetus for a non-Christian approach to the Mysteries, at least in the outer. The principal vehicle for the revelation of the Thelemic doctrine is *Liber AL vel Legis - The Book of the Law*. This work was "revealed" to Crowley and his wife Rose in Cairo, Egypt over three days -April 8, 9, & 10, 1904. It is a short work in three chapters. Each of the three chapters purports to be from the perspective of each of a pseudo- Egyptian trinity: Nuit, Hadit, and Ra-Hoor-Khuit. This triad corresponds fairly closely with other trinities and the Law of the Triangle in general. Nuit and Hadit are described in terms of the Hermetic Point-within-the-Circle: Nuit as an infinite sphere, encompassing all; Hadit as the omnipresent center, as expressed in *Liber AL* 11:3, "In the sphere I am everywhere the center, as she the circumference, is nowhere found." Ra-Hoor-Khuit, the protagonist of Chapter III, is the product or synthesis of the former two, known as the "Crowned and Conquering Child."

In this third chapter of *The Book of the Law* is found a single verse that has been the go-to passage for "proving" that Thelema is antithetical to any form of Christianity: "With my Hawk's head I peck at the eyes of Jesus as he hangs upon the cross," (*Liber AL* 111:51). This phrase is almost always quoted to illustrate the incompatibility between Thelema and Christianity. But as with all sacred scripture, we must look beyond the apparent. We must move beyond a surface interpretation and apply our knowledge of the language of symbolism. First, we must look at who is speaking here. Ra-Hoor-Khuit, the Crowned and Conquering Child, corresponds directly to the Son, or Logos, of the Christian Trinity. In order to understand this passage, or *Liber AL* in general, or any sacred scripture for that matter, it is vitally important to understand the principle of the Trinity, the Mystery of the Three-in- One.

In Christianity we have the Father, Holy Spirit, and Son. In Gnosticism we refine these terms further as the Unknown Father of Light; Barbelo, the Mother of the Aeons; and the Logos, self-begotten of the Father. We see this trinity reflected throughout the phases of emanation and creation, such as in Adam, Eve, and Seth. In *Liber AL*, as mentioned above, we see these principles represented by Hadit, Nuit, and Ra-Hoor-Khuit (or more properly, Heru-Ra-Ha, who is represented in a passive form: Hoor-paar-kraat; and an active form: Ra-Hoor-Khuit). It is important, therefore, not to attach ourselves too strongly to the images by which these principles are represented. Rather, we need to be able to recognize the occult doctrine of the Law of Three, which underlies all such Trinities such as the Sulphur, Mercury, and Salt of the alchemists, or Brahma,

Shiva, and Vishnu of the Hindus.

So, in regards to the quote from *AL* III:51, we see that the speaker is the active principle of the Logos, in the form of the Hawk-headed Ra-Hoor-Khuit. Since birds are often used to symbolically represent a divine messenger, this ornithomorphization of the Logos is not inappropriate. Next we must look at the actions being performed. He is "pecking at the eyes of Jesus as he hangs upon the cross," a gruesome image to be sure. This is a destructive action. But esoterically, death and destruction mean *transition* and *transformation*. The destructive, or transformative action is being performed upon the eyes, the organs of *sight* or *perception*. Finally, we must take into account the image of "Jesus as he hangs upon the cross," the Crucifixion. We can see this image in a couple of ways: that of the physical vehicle, which is temporary and useless without its animating principle; and that of the crucifixion of the psychic Christ which, as we have previously indicated, is but a sacrifice to the Demiurge.

Looking at the entire verse, and reading it with the alphabet of symbolism, we see that the pneumatic Logos is making an effort to transform our perception of the "dying god." It is an attempt to show that the true Logos is something that is distinct from any of the temporal images through which it may be manifested. It is really no different than the portrayal of Jesus who, in the following Gnostic scriptures, laughs at those who mistakenly believe that they are crucifying him (the Logos), when in fact they are merely nailing up an image:

> Though they punished me, I did not die in actuality but only in appearance ... The death they think I suffered they suffered in their error and blindness. They nailed their man to their death... someone else, their father, drank the gall and the vinegar; it was not I. .. Someone else wore the crown of thorns. And I was on high, poking fun at all the excesses of the rulers and the fruit of their error and conceit. I was laughing at their ignorance, ("The Second Discourse of the Great Seth," p. 480).

> I said, "What do I see, Lord? Is it really you they are seizing, and are you holding on to me? And who is the one smiling and laughing above the cross?"

> The Savior said to me, "The one you see smiling and laughing above the cross is the living Jesus. The one into whose hands and feet they are driving nails in his fleshly part, the substitute for him. They are putting to shame the one who came into being in the likeness of the living Jesus."

> He said to me " ... the one they crucified is the firstborn, the abode of demons, the stone vessel in which they live, the man of Elohim, the man of the cross who is under the law. But the one who is standing near him is the living Savior ... He is standing and observing with pleasure that those who did evil to him are divided among themselves. And he is laughing at their lack of perception, knowing that they were born blind," ("The Revelation of Peter," pp.496-7).

In divorcing itself from Christian imagery, Thelema may be accused of (in the words of Lon Milo DuQuette, as stated at a 2001 lecture at the Occult Bookstore in Chicago) "throwing out the baby Jesus with the bathwater." This is a legitimate criticism, and one that has been made by many occultists over the past century. Nevertheless, Thelemic Gnostic scriptures, as Christian Gnostic scriptures, show themselves to be of the religion of the Logos. The Law of Thelema, however, dares at last to sweep away every trace of the oppressive bonds of the Demiurge and his prophets, including the psychic Christ. Perhaps, though, it was necessary to deliver the message of Thelema (which is really not a new message at all) outside the context of the Christian narrative in order for it to be properly understood - without any of the biases that inevitably come along with the Christian language. But that has not stopped esotericists from seeking to reconcile Thelema with Christian gnosis. This was true in Crowley's lifetime, as evidenced by the works, rites, and philosophies of such individuals as Theodor Reuss, Arnoldo Krumm-Heller, and perhaps even Jean Bricaud, among many others. And it is true in modem times as well. The language and apocalyptic imagery of *Liber AL* seem, in fact, to encourage this. Remember that according to *Revelation*, the Morning Star will be given to "the one who conquers." And we read in The Book of the Law that "this is the Law of the Battle of Conquest," and "Conquer! That is enough," (*Liber AL* 111:9, 11). Through careful study and contemplation, it will be found that those Gnostic and Hermetic principles found veiled in the language of the Christian scriptures are the very same as what is later veiled in the language of *Liber AL vel Legis*. The attainment of the Morning Star, the principle of Gnostic illumination, lies at the core of both Christian and Thelemic deification. And if we still doubt the fundamentally Christian (that is, Gnostic) nature of Thelema, we need only look at the secret teachings of the OTO, which become increasingly Christianized as the degrees advance, until at last, in the key document of the IX°, *Liber Agape*, we are given a purely Christian language, having no traces at all of the Trinity of *Liber AL*: Nuit, Hadit, and Ra-Hoor-Khuit. For, as useful as the non-Christian terminology may be in separating the inner message from the symbols whose meanings have become corrupted, the High Adept is able to return to the pure Christian Gnosis, whose language, in the end, is far superior to that of any other scripture in its depth and sublimity. In order to illustrate what we mean, here is a brief excerpt from *Liber Agape*:

> Now there are three that bear witness in Heaven: the Father, the Word, and the Spirit; and these Three are One. And there are Three that bear witness on earth: the Spirit, the Water, and the Blood; and these Three are One.
>
> In that Trinity IAO, I is the Father, A the Spirit, O the Word; and in this A [א] the Spirit, M [מ] the Water, Sh [ש] the Blood; and in all these are 358, MShICh [משיח], the Messiah, our Lord and Saviour Jesus Christ, in His death who gave up the Spirit, the Water, and the Blood, as St. John beareth witness in his Evangel. Hence is Jesus Christ Alpha and Omega, the symbol of the union of GOD and man.
> Here then is a second Trinity: GOD, GOD-man, man. And to this GOD-man our ancient brethren have given many names.
>
> And though this name of Jesus Christ hath been universally blasphemed by Christians, yet this name hath been acknowledged by the true Brothers of the Rosie Crosse; and this which is written of Him in the Evangels and in the Epistles and in the Apocalypse is true, if it be interpreted in light by the Adepts of the Stone.

The process of deification, be it under the aegis of Thelema or Christianity, is facilitated sacramentally through the Eucharistic transubstantiation. Among the Christian Gnostic churches there are a number of liturgies extant, differing in style but agreeing almost universally in their ability to confer validly the sacrament of the Eucharist, provided it is administered by one holding the proper sacramental authority. The principal Thelemic Eucharist rite is the one written by Crowley, *Liber XV*. This liturgy has been harshly criticized by some members of the Christian Gnostic community, especially by the Right Reverend Stephan A. Hoeller (Tau Stephanus), who attacks the liturgy on two fronts: 1) that it is unable to confer a validly consecrated

Eucharist; and 2) that the priests and bishops of the Ecclesia Gnostica Catholica (the liturgical branch of the OTO) do not possess the necessary apostolic authority to effect the transubstantiation. Now, we do not mean any disrespect toward Bishop Hoeller, who has done so much to advance the cause of Christian Gnosis, and for whom we have nothing but the utmost reverence and respect. But we do disagree with him on certain of his points outlined in his "Ecclesia Gnostic Position Paper Concerning the Thelemite or Crowleyan Gnostic Churches." Many of his criticisms rest on the assumption that neither Crowley nor Reuss held valid Holy Orders, a non-issue for the current EGC clergy, which we shall address a bit further on. And even though this argument doesn't really bear on the over-all point we are trying to make here, let us spend a little time and consideration upon it regardless, as it may help to place everything in its proper context.

The question of Crowley's valid Holy Orders (or lack thereof) relies, in part, on the validity of the Holy Orders received by Theodor Reuss, Crowley's initiator in the Ordo Templi Orientis. Reuss received Episcopal consecration from Papus (Dr. Gerard Encausse) in 1908. With this authority he established a German branch of the Gnostic Church: Gnostische Katholische Kirche. Reuss incorporated his branch into the OTO, of which order he was the head. It is supposed then that this Episcopal authority was likewise passed to Aleister Crowley, who then passed it to his initiates. Bishop Hoeller comments that, "Neither Papus nor Crowley had a valid apostolic succession to pass on because they had none in the first place." He states that, "Papus only received the unquestionably valid succession from Bricaud after July 1913." We can agree with this only in part. It is true that Bricaud's 1913 consecration by Louis-Marie-François Giraud did bring an "unquestionably valid" apostolic succession. But it is very likely that a valid succession was already held. It has been asserted that in 1895 Tau Synésius, Patriarch of the Église Gnostique, incorporated the Episcopal lineage of Fabré-Palaprat's Johannite Church via bishop Chatel. However, even if the 1895 event did not occur, in 1907 the Johannite succession was received again by Papus and Jean Bricaud via Bernard Clement. Although the Johannite Church claimed its apostolic authority through a ridiculously contrived Templar lineage, it did in fact possess a perfectly valid succession via the Scipione Rebiba line (cf. "Successio Apostolica"). We therefore must concede the likelihood that Papus at least *did* have a valid apostolic succession to pass on.

Hoeller then criticizes the very ability for either Reuss or Crowley to receive Holy Orders. He points out the possible lack of intent and proper form. He states, as concerns Papus' conferral of the Episcopate upon Reuss, "While there may be honorary degrees of Masonic orders conferred at a distance or 'on sight,' this cannot be done in an ecclesiastical succession. Thus even if Papus may have wished to pass on some kind of an ecclesiastical succession to Reuss, the manner of conferring it would have been enough to render it very suspect indeed." He goes on to illustrate that if either Reuss or Crowley had not been validly baptized and confirmed, then "even if the consecrator possessed a valid succession and held the proper intention" they could not have been capable of receiving valid Holy Orders. With these criticisms we find little to disagree. Thus, on the point of the validity of Crowley's Holy Orders and his ability to pass on any sacramental authority, we agree that it is extremely unlikely that Crowley possessed any such authority; and whatever other occult currents may have been passed on to his initiates, the apostolic succession was not one of them.

With our little diversion concerning Crowley's succession out of the way, let us turn to Hoeller's criticism of liber XV. He states that it "does not contain many of the essential features which make up a Mass in any and all branches of the church catholic whether in East or West. Although it does contain the necessary formula of consecration in Greek ('this is my body' and 'this is my blood') the formula of consecration is taken out of the traditional context wherein it is identified as spoken by Jesus the Christ." He goes on to say that *Liber XV* "is clearly not a Mass in any sense of the Christian and catholic mythos." But if we look at the words of institution in *Liber XV*, we find that the bread and wine of the Eucharistic elements are transformed into the Body and Blood of the Logos. So, disregarding for a moment the symbolic and mythological context in which we find the Thelemic Eucharist, the only substantive difference we find between the consecration of the elements in the Christian Mass and that found in the Thelemic Mass is that in the former the Eucharistic elements are transformed into both the psychic Christ and the pneumatic Logos; whereas in the latter ritual the psychic element has been eliminated, leaving only a pneumatic transubstantiation. It seems to us, then, that while *Liber XV* may not contain a valid *Christian* transubstantiation, in the sense of evoking the presence of the psychic Christ, it nevertheless perpetuates a perfectly valid *Gnostic* sacrament.

Hoeller accuses Crowley of having not any "shred of sympathy for the catholic sacramental mythos even in its most esoteric aspect." Now, we have already shown in the brief passage from *Liber Agape* that Crowley did indeed have an intimate understanding of the esoteric Christian doctrine. In *Liber DCCCLXXXVIII* Crowley further shows his familiarity with the occult laws which underlie the philosophy behind the Eucharist, stating, "It is a perfectly rational idea that, by taking a divine substance, and making it part of oneself by the miracle of assimilation, the eater should become possessed of the qualities of the substance." He then goes on to state:

> It is not a question of nutriment alone, the replacing of the tissues to repair their expenditure. It is the actual entrance into the body of some subtle substance, or, as the ancients would have said, divine substance, which manifests itself in the eater as abundance of life and joy. It is also impossible to doubt that Catholics obtain real spiritual sustenance from the Host.

So, as concerns Crowley's knowledge of and appreciation for the esoteric Christian doctrines and sacramental formulae, we must respectfully disagree with the opinions of bishop Hoeller. For many years, the opinions articulated by Hoeller in regards to Thelema and the Thelemic "Gnostic Mass" represented a sort of "orthodoxy" for the Christian Gnostic community – at least on the surface. The truth behind the relationship between Thelema and Christian Gnosticism is obviously much more complex.

Just as bishop Hoeller and those of his school of thought claim that *Liber XV* is not a valid Mass, and that the EGC contains no valid apostolic authority, the Thelemites of the "Caliphate" OTO and their Ecclesia Gnostica Catholica have claimed that they do not require the apostolic succession for the validity of their sacraments; that the only succession they need be concerned with is that of their prophet, Aleister Crowley. Tau Apiryon (David Scriven), in his "History of the Gnostic Catholic Church," states:

> When the E.G.C. converted from Christianity to Thelema, it ceased to be an institution dedicated to the administration of Christian sacraments. Therefore, a valid apostolic succession was no longer of critical relevance.

In this respect, the views of both the Christian and Thelemic Gnostics would seem to be complementary. The Christian Gnostics of the persuasion of Tau Stephanus claim there is no Christian transubstantiation in

Liber XV. The Thelemic Gnostics of the persuasion of Tau Apiryon & co. claim that no such transubstantiation is necessary or even desired since their sacraments are purely Thelemic. Case closed!

But behind the scenes the bishops of the OTO's EGC went to great lengths to ensure that they held all of the relevant lines of apostolic succession. Why would this be done if it were not considered vital to the ecclesia? Apiryon states that Hymenaeus Alpha (Grady McMurtry - former head of the "Caliphate" OTO) and "for a time" Hymenaeus Beta (William Breeze - current Outer Head of the Order) held that, "A valid traditional apostolic succession would increase the prestige of the E.G.C. and help it to achieve recognition from the civil authorities." This may be the case, but the line of reasoning sounds suspicious at least. First, civil authorities do not recognize a church based on apostolic succession. If they did, we would not have the plague of Protestantism that infects every corner of this nation. That assertion therefore seems flatly ridiculous to me. As to the question of prestige, there may be a legitimate argument there, but again, why? The only ones who would lend further credibility or prestige to the EGC based on their possession of a valid line of apostolic succession would be other apostolic churches who might acknowledge the validity of the EGC sacraments. Curiously, it is only after securing those lines of succession that they are suddenly no longer "of critical relevance."

To illustrate the significance placed on the apostolic succession within the EGC, even in the 21st century, let us look at a sentence from a letter from James Graeb to William Breeze in 2004. To give a brief background on this correspondence, James Graeb was the IX° initiator of William Breeze and also consecrated him as a bishop. In an act of apparent initiatic patricide, Breeze (Hymenaeus Beta) attempted to (or did) expel Graeb from the OTO and excommunicate him from the EGC, thereby seeming to sever his own link, or at least his primary one, to McMurtry & Crowley, the OTO, and the EGC. This is stated only to give context to the following statement by Graeb in his response to Breeze's seemingly bizarre actions: "As to any apostolic successions that you hold from me, they too are hereby revoked and you are apostolically excommunicated from the Ecclesia Gnostica Catholica."

Now, we have no desire to comment on the convoluted relationship between Messrs. Breeze and Graeb. But we can infer from the language used here that in spite of the adoption of the Law of Thelema, the EGC remains, as it has always been, an essentially Christi.an institution. It may not be so in the psychic sense, but it is most certainly in the pneumatic sense. And it is from the apostolic succession that it draws its sacramental authority.

However, it is not only that the Thelemites are clamoring after the apostolic succession. Conversely, the majority of Christi.an Gnostic bishops have sought out Thelemic initiations and successions. Why is this? Are all of these Thelemites secret Christians? Are all these Christian Gnostics secret Thelemites? Well, yes; at least at the level of the episcopate. By the time one has become a bishop, if they have gone through the appropriate channels of training and initiation, the underlying unity of initiatic systems and sacred scriptures will have become obvious. But this is not to say that one must reach the episcopacy to appreciate this unity. If the initiate has been trained properly, without having to "keep up appearances," and without succumbing to silly superstitions, then one may recognize and appreciate and embrace the fundamental unity of esoteric doctrine that emanates from different, *seemingly* contradictory sources.

To be perfectly candid about the matter, political correctness has no place in the search for Truth. It is only with the full liberty of conscience that one may rightly explore Truth's many facets. Ecumenism is a good thing, so long as it helps churches, orders, societies, and individuals to unite under a common goal, doctrine, or belief, and such relationships are crucial to the general reintegration. But often such relationships can cease to be unifying elements and become limiting factors. For example, a Gnostic church may wish to establish a formal relationship with another church, non-Gnostic but liberally oriented, because of their shared values and the importance of the sacraments. Now, that same Gnostic church may wish to associate with some non-Christian sect or society on the basis of a shared goal of spiritual illumination. Now let us suppose that the non-Gnostic Christian church becomes uncomfortable having associations with a church who will associate with non-Christian bodies in an ecumenical fashion. The hypothetical Gnostic church then faces a crisis of conscience. Should it break off relations with the non-Christian body in order to conform to a perceived Christian orthodoxy? We say, resoundingly, No! It should exercise its full liberty of conscience, and if any of its associates are unable to accept that freedom, it should be upon *them* to either sever relationships or not, as their own conscience dictates. If a church, order, or society declares itself to be Gnostic while simultaneously attempting to portray itself as belonging to some more mainstream orthodoxy, it will lose it way entirely.

It must be understood that the nature of Gnosticism, from its very inception, has been syncretic. The original Gnostic sects of the first centuries A.D. were highly syncretic, as are the Gnostic churches of today. The doctrines of the early Gnostic fathers contain obvious influences of Hermeticism, and Greek and Egyptian mystery traditions, not to mention the inherent Platonic and Pythagorean philosophical bases. We have some interesting literary examples of the transition from pre-Christian Gnosticism into Christianized forms in such texts as "Eugnostos the Blessed" and "The Sophia [Wisdom] of Jesus Christ," the latter being a Christianization of the former. There are also many similarities between Christian scriptures, both canonical and non- canonical, and some of the language used in the Greek and Demotic Magical Papyri. There is ample evidence in both the writings and ritual practices of early Christianity that it is a direct perpetuation of the older mystery traditions.

In this paper, together with our former treatise, "The Devil's Passion," we have examined the nature of the Gnostic Eucharist, in both its Christian and Thelemic forms. We have demonstrated that the Thelemic philosophy emphasizes the liberation of conscience and the ultimate freedom from the mandates of the Demiurge. In this sense, *Liber XV* represents a more purely Gnostic Eucharist. We have compared various aspects of Christian and Thelemic doctrine, and have shown that the former may easily accommodate the latter into a syncretic Gnosticism that is in complete accord with the Gnostic Fathers of old. Gnosticism has always been with us in one form or another, and it has usually been perpetuated as a syncretic system; for only syncretism may adequately express the universality of Gnostic doctrines, which underlie all true schools of occult philosophy. As Gnostics we have but a single mandate: to attain to the Light of Gnosis, that Man might be restored to his primitive and archetypal form in the Pleroma. It is in this higher mandate - that of conquering the lower, impermanent self to win the glory of the Morning Star - that we may find the applicability of the Thelemic philosophy. Many Christian Gnostics will continue to dismiss Thelema out of hand because of preconceptions based on the statements of critics, or because of unenlightened literal readings of the Thelemic scriptures. But as initiates we must look ever to the message behind the message. If we look for the occult truths behind the surface of the Christian scriptures, why would we not utilize the same process of symbolic interpretation for any other scripture? As Gnostics, we hold that Truth must be sought in all places, and that she must not be rejected regardless of the form in which she may be clothed. In our examination, therefore, of the principles of Thelema and their relationship to the message of Christ and to our Gnostic doctrine, we see that Thelema represents a natural progression from the Age of the Son to the Age of the Holy Spirit, just as the Christian message represents a progression from the Age of the Father (the Demiurge, that is) to the Age of the Son.

In conclusion, therefore, we acknowledge the Gnostic validity of the Thelemic sacraments, so long as one possessing the necessary empowerments performs them. But do not think that we are advocating in any way for the *supremacy* of the Thelemic Eucharist. As we have demonstrated amply in this paper and elsewhere, there is good reason to preserve the ancient and traditional Christian Eucharist, including the psychic aspects of that rite. Just as the Gnostic Eucharist is necessary for the gradual transmutation of the soul into spirit, the psychic Eucharist is necessary to preserve the balance of power between the Children of Light and the Powers of the Demiurge. As the earth is populated with more and more enlightened souls, there may come a time when the psychic Eucharist is no longer necessary, but that time has not yet arrived. The frequent renewal of the New Covenant is needed more today than ever before. The daily unrest in this country and around the world is no doubt it part due to the decline in Eucharistic services and the rise of Protestantism and atheism. I do not include other traditional religions in this statement, such as Islam, Hinduism, Buddhism, etc., because they each have their own unique relationship with the Demiurge and his archons, as well as their own methods of Gnostic liberation. But make no mistake, we live in the Christian era; and the Demiurge and his psychic Christ are the rulers and preservers of this world. Through the sacrifice of the psychic Christ, we may experience a form of grace, a reprieve from the harsh and unjust Law of yore. The Thelemic philosophy may aid us on our quest toward Gnosis, but it simply does not supplant the Christian era or its rites. It is, at best, a supplement to them and a guiding light toward the Age of the Spirit.

So in the end, as in the beginning, we turn to the admonishment of *2 Peter* to attend to this prophetic message until the Morning Star rises in your heart. Leave no door un-knocked and no stone unturned. Do not let fear and insecurity keep you from the Truth. But know also that our Lord Jesus Christ, in all His aspects, is Lord of All Worlds, and the reconciler and rectifier of all planes.

Theosis Through Gnosis
Gnostic Considerations on Deification

Theosis is a term employed largely by the Eastern Orthodox church to describe the divinization of Man (i.e. humanity). This doctrine of divinization or deification is derived from the Second Epistle of Peter, chapter 1, verse 4, which exhorts us to "become partakers of the divine nature." Within Eastern Orthodoxy this doctrine is of such vital and central importance that it is often equated with salvation and the very purpose of Life itself. We, as Gnostic Christians, of course have no quarrel with this worthy pursuit. In fact, in this regard the ultimate aims of the Gnostic and Orthodox Christian are fundamentally identical. This is not to say that our theological doctrines are identical, but our approaches to theology are similar in that they derive from mystical revelation rather than the pure rational speculation of Catholic Scholasticism. Let us, therefore, look at this process known as theosis through the lens of Gnosticism, as well as its scriptural sources and means of attainment.

According to the doctrine of theosis, deification is attained through a three stage process: Catharsis (καθαρσις) or Purification; Theoria (θεωρια) or Illumination; and Theosis (θεωσις), which term thus describes the process as a whole, as well as the final stage of that process. This final stage represents the regeneration of humanity to its primitive estate, which is divine. This, however, poses some challenges to Orthodox theology, for they hold that God is transcendent and that His essence is unknowable. But the genuine mystical experience proves to the participant empirically that there is a divinity immanent in Man. In order to reconcile these seemingly contradictory views, theologians such as Gregory Palamas have posited that there is a distinction between the "essence" of God - which remains unknowable, and the "energies" or "operations" of God, through which it is possible to obtain an experiential knowledge of God. This is not an altogether bad explanation, as it is easily relatable to the principles of the *fixed* and the *volatile* as in the alchemical Sulphur & Mercury. In the Orthodox schema, the "essence" would be the Sulphuric or *fixed* aspect of God; that is, it remains within Himself, unchangeable and immovable. The "energies" would be the Mercurial or *volatile* aspect, with which we may participate and ultimately unite our consciousness. Many western theologians, however - especially those who adhere to the school of Scholasticism - have viewed this as an irreconcilable division within God.

The Gnostic, on the other hand, asserts the fundamental unity of God. One may still use the words "essence" and "energies" as semantic conventions if it seems helpful, but the doctrines of Gnosticism show that there is a solution that is both simple and elegant. Most branches of modern Gnosticism, while having very little dogma to speak of, mostly agree on two fundamental doctrines: the doctrine of emanation; and salvation through gnosis. We will address the second doctrine a little further on. But let us now look briefly at the doctrine of emanation.

Emanation means a pouring or issuing forth as a means of generation, as opposed to *creation* which is the forming and fashioning of a thing using some outside medium. The concept of creation works fine on the lower planes. For example, humans create by fashioning things of a material nature, utilizing the elements of the material universe. Even seemingly incorporeal things, such as music, consist of generating particular vibratory patterns within the medium of air. If there were no air, liquid, or solid medium through which these vibrations could be generated, then it would be impossible to create sound or music. We may even extend this analogy to the astral or psychic realm wherein the Demiurge and his archons create worlds using substances of which they themselves are not the source. But this theory becomes problematic once we have worked our way back to the source, i.e. God Himself. God, as the ultimate Source of all, cannot have created in the sense of the manipulation of some outside material, since He must necessarily be the very source of any such material. This paradox is resolved in creation doc- trine by the introduction of the concept of *creatio ex nihilo*, creation from nothing.

Emanation on the other hand, posits a process of the issuing forth of the Aeons - the whole of the Pleroma. In Gnostic thought, God - who is sometimes called the One - reflects upon itself, resulting in the emanation of Thought, or First Thought (Protennoia). This is the Holy Spirit of the Trinity. Through this Thought, the One then issues forth the Logos. The Logos, just as the Thought, was pre-existent in the Father (Propator), and is in fact the creative power of the Father. The Logos, therefore, is seen to issue forth of its own accord, and is thus not only Monogenes (alone-born, or only begotten), but also Autogenes (self-generated). It is by means of the Logos, then, that all subsequent realities or hypostases are brought forth. The Trinity, therefore, existed in union with the Father, or the One, for all eternity; and their emanation or issuing forth makes them no less substantively or essentially divine, but it does make that divinity accessible, as we shall attempt to explain.

Adam was made a "living soul" through the infusion of *pneuma*, or spirit - the very essence of the divine. And it is only because of the immanence of the divine essence in Man that we may hope to gain an experiential knowledge (gnosis) of the transcendent Father. If, therefore, we see God as *both* transcendent and immanent, we no longer need to draw any substantive distinction between the "essence" and "energies" of God, except as semantic conveniences to help better explain our relative and conditional experience of God in contrast to the fullness of God in His boundlessness.

Before we get ahead of ourselves, let us return to an examination of the three stages of Theosis: Catharsis, Theoria, and Theosis proper. Catharsis, as previously stated, is a stage of purification. Orthodox theology holds that this purification is most importantly the purification of consciousness. This purification is effected through various means of asceticism. Among the advanced initiates of the Mystery Traditions, this purification through asceticism constitutes a phase of spiritual alchemy. Among the Orthodox, this purification is brought about chiefly through the practice of Hesychasm. In both instances the practitioner seeks to cultivate "ceaseless prayer" (cf. *1 Thess.* 5:17), which is also known as "Prayer of the Heart." This contemplative prayer arises from a state of perpetual watchfulness, or nepsis (Gr. νεψις).

The basis of Hesychasm, from-the Greek *hesuchos* (ἠσυχος, quiet, silent), is found in *Matthew* 6:6, "Whenever you pray, go into your hidden room and shut the door and pray to your Father who is in secret." This is understood to mean that one is to retire unto oneself, the heart being that "hidden room." This doctrine is not at odds with the Gnostic *Gospel of Philip* which states, "He said, 'Go into your room, shut the door behind you, and pray to your Father who is in secret,' that is, the one who is innermost. What is innermost is the Fullness, and there is nothing further within. And this is what they call the uppermost."

Hesychasm involves asceticism and repetitive prayer, usually the so-called Jesus Prayer: "Lord Jesus Christ, Son of God, have mercy on me, a sinner." Through the repeated recitation of the Jesus Prayer, one may be brought to the awareness and experience of the true inner prayer, or Prayer of the Heart. Another prayer utilized since antiquity is the one given by St. John Cassian (c. 360-435): "O God, make speed to save me. O Lord, make haste to help me." Hesychasm also involves adopting certain postures and breathing techniques. Students of the ACP formation program - all initiates in fact - should appreciate the use of breathing, posture, and intonation as a means toward inner illumination. These practices, of course, do not actually cause the state of inner illumination. They are merely part of the preparatory and purgative process that allows for the eventual liberation of conscience from the fetters of the temporal passions. The actual inner illumination is known as theoria, which we shall now discuss.

Theoria is the word from which our word "theory" is derived. It is from the verb *theorein*, meaning "to look at, consider, speculate, contemplate." Its meaning in Orthodox theology, however, as well as within Neoplatonism, is closer to the Latin *contemplatio* than *speculatio*. That is, it is understood to refer to the inner, contemplative, primary experiential knowledge that leads to divine union, rather than the speculative, secondary or tertiary knowledge that arises through rational inquiry. The theological conception of theoria moves even beyond its use by the Neoplatonists, from whom it was borrowed. According to Thomas Keating, the Church Fathers viewed theoria as being akin to the Hebrew word *da'ath* implying an experiential knowledge not of the mind alone, but of the mind united with the heart, involving the whole being. In short, theoria should be understood to have the sense of "beholding" rather than merely "thinking of."

One of the chief proponents and defenders of Hesychasm and the doctrine of theosis in general was St. Gregory Palamas (1296-1359), who taught that theoria is the state of beholding the uncreated Light of God, the "Tabor Light." This doctrine states that the light that shone at the transfiguration of Jesus on Mount Tabor (Mt. 17, Mk. 9, Lk. 9:28-), identified also with the light seen by St. Paul at his conversion, is that very uncreated Light of God which is not the essence of God, but emanates perpetually from that essence, and is inseparable from the divine essence itself. Palamas went to great lengths to emphasize the distinction between the essence of God, which is eternal and uncreated and transcendent, and the energies of God, which are also eternal and uncreated and, as we have seen, inseparable from the essence, but accessible. Furthermore, Palamas theorized that the Tabor Light is one and the same as the promised Kingdom of Heaven. In fact, this is one of the theses of Palamas that was canonized by the Orthodox church.

Luke 17:20b-21 states: "The Kingdom of God is not coming with that which can be observed; nor will they say 'Behold, here it is!' or 'There it is!' For behold, the Kingdom of God is within you!" If, therefore, the Tabor Light is one and the same as the Kingdom (as affirmed by Orthodox canon), and if the Kingdom is within, that is, immanent (as affirmed by the very words of Jesus), then it follows that that uncreated Light which shone forth from Jesus at the Transfiguration is in fact immanent within every human.

Orthodoxy, while allowing for the possibility of a "true gnosis," most often likes to distance itself from the term "gnosis" or at least to accord it a rank lower than theoria. The following passage from the "Palamism" entry in Wikipedia describes this pretty well:

> Gnosis and all knowledge are created, as they are derived or created from experience, self-awareness and

spiritual knowledge. Theoria, here, is the experience of the uncreated in various degrees, i.e. the vision of God or to see God. The experience of God in the eighth day or outside of time therefore transcends the self and the experiential knowledge or gnosis. Gnosis is most importantly understood as a knowledge of oneself; theoria is the experience of God, transcending the knowledge of oneself.

This idea is summed up succinctly in the Wiki for "Theoria" which states: "Knowledge is derived from experience, but experience is not derived from knowledge." In other words, theoria, or experience of God, is seen as the primary or causative event, and gnosis - however genuine and pure it may be - can only be a secondary event; an effect of the experience. This is a very clever argument, and one that initially appears quite convincing. But this definition of gnosis is rather limiting, not only according to a Gnostic interpretation, but even within orthodox circles, such as the statements by Thomas Keating previously mentioned which readily equate theoria with da'ath (knowledge). The problem is that the term gnosis is used by the theologians to mean different things at different times. In one instance it may mean the intellectual knowledge gained through rational inquiry; in another case it may refer to the knowledge of oneself; and yet again it may be used to refer to spiritual knowledge, but which is separate from and subsequent to the spiritual experience itself. But Gnosis, to the Gnostic, is a revelatory knowledge which is indistinguishable from the experience itself. Gnosis, therefore, to the Gnostic, is in fact the same phenomenon as that called theoria by the Orthodox.

Of the three types of knowledge referred to above, the first is dealing with a mundane form of knowledge. The third form refers only to the memory of an experience. But the second type - knowledge of oneself - comes closer to what we, as Gnostics, mean by the term gnosis. Gnostics often distinguish, however, between personal gnosis and divine gnosis. It is generally held that personal gnosis is but a step toward the divine gnosis. We have already shown that theoria, or divine gnosis, is the vision or realization of the immanence of the divine. So, if God is immanent, or "innermost" as stated in the *Gospel of Philip*, then the knowledge of oneself, through maturation and cultivation, may lead to the experience of God - divine gnosis/theoria, which in turn leads ultimately to theosis, or union with God.

While we feel that we have successfully argued in favor of equating gnosis with theoria, it will be better to offer additional scriptural support for our assertions. Let us turn, then, to *2 Peter* - the very scripture on which the entire doctrine of theosis is based. This epistle is a particularly mystical text in which references to gnosis are found throughout. In fact, gnosis is one of the very first things mentioned, and one of the very last things mentioned. And sandwiched in between among these three short chapters are a number of mystical treasures.

As early as the 2nd verse of the first chapter, we read: "May grace and peace be multiplied unto you in knowledge of God and Jesus our Lord." So, right from the start we are reading of the "knowledge of God." The text continues in verse 3:

> All things for life and godliness have been given to us by His divine power through the knowledge of the One Who called us to His own glory and virtue.

We see here, then, that lest there be any mistake concerning the value of the knowledge mentioned in verse 2, it is nothing less than the "divine power" that comes to us "through knowledge." And this divine power enables us to receive life (ζωη - zoe; not mere *bios*) and godliness. We therefore now see the context in which the following verse occurs - the verse, as stated previously, which constitutes the scriptural basis for the doctrine of theosis:

> Through which things he has given us the precious and great promises, that through these you may become participants of the divine nature, having escaped the cosmos which has been corrupted by lust.

It now becomes clear that the "things he has given us" that allow us to "become participants of the divine nature" are the "knowledge of God" and the "divine power" that comes through that knowledge. Therefore, if theosis is participation in the divine nature, and if theoria is the means by which theosis is attained, then we must conclude that theoria consists of the knowledge of God and the divine power that comes through this knowledge. But let us continue with our study of the text.

The next verses show us that knowledge does not operate in a vacuum. Rather, it is part of a process that culminates in deification, the crowning virtue of which is agape. Thus we read in verses 5-7:

> And for this very reason, you must with due diligence support faith with virtue, and virtue with knowledge, and knowledge with self-control, and self-control with endurance, and endurance with godliness, and godliness with brotherly love (φιλαδελφια - philadelphia), and brotherly love with agape (αγαπη).

We must therefore always remember that gnosis, however precious it may be, is not an end unto itself, but a part of the process toward divinization. We do posit, however, that it is the central and key experience of the divinization process. And our scripture seems to bear this out, for we read in the very next verses (8-9):

> For these things being in you and multiplying keep you from becoming un- productive and unfruitful in the knowledge of our Lord Jesus Christ. For anyone in whom these things are not present is shortsighted and blind, having forgotten the purification [καθαρισμου] of his past shortcomings [ἁμαρτιων].

We have thus once again returned to our central theme of knowledge, which comes after a period of purification or catharsis. This gives us even further evidence to identify gnosis as the principal experience of theoria. Now, we will not here provide an exegesis of every verse of this epistle, but let us continue on for a while, for the next two verses (10-11) offer continued support to our thesis:

> Therefore, brothers, be diligent to confirm your calling and election, for in doing these things you will not ever fall. For thus will be richly provided for you the entrance into the eternal kingdom [αιωνιον βασιλειαν] of our Lord and Savior Jesus Christ

There are a number of interesting points contained in these verses. First, in verse 10 we see reference to the "calling and election." We don't wish to go too far into this here, but these terms are significant to Gnostic theology, as they are seen to represent the psychic church and the pneumatic church, sometimes referred to as the Church Suffering and the Church Triumphant. In verse 11, though, we find concepts directly pertinent to our study. Here the text speaks of entry into the eternal kingdom. You will recall that the Kingdom has already been identified with the uncreated Light of God (according to Orthodox canon), and that the Kingdom is immanent (according to *Luke* 17:20-21). If we look at the Greek words which we translate as

Supplement: Theosis Through Gnosis

"eternal kingdom" αιωνιον βασιλειαν – we could also read this as "the Kingdom of the Aeons." In other words, through gnosis we may access the Pleroma. Recall the previously quoted text from the *Gospel of Philip*: "What is innermost is the Fullness [i.e. Pleroma], and there is nothing further within. And this is what they call the uppermost."

As if to reaffirm the correctness of this doctrine, verses 17-18 tell us:

> He [Jesus] received honor and glory from God the Father when that voice was conveyed to him by the Majestic Glory, saying, "This is my Son, my Beloved, with whom I am well pleased." We ourselves heard this voice come from heaven, while we were with him on the holy mountain.

The text, in recalling here the Tabor event, does indeed seem to confirm the whole doctrine of theosis, in both its Orthodox and Gnostic aspects. But it is within the next verse (19) that we find the summation of this process so beautifully expressed:

> So we have the prophetic message more fully confirmed. You will do well to be attentive to this as a lamp shining in a dark place, until the day dawns and the Morning Star rises in your hearts.

We have written elsewhere concerning this passage and the meaning of the Morning Star. In our treatise, "Morning Star Rising" we have stated that the "rising of the Morning Star...in one's heart is a reference to the emergence of the Light of Gnosis within the individual." Let us expand on this concept a bit further by revisiting a longer excerpt from that work:

> The grace that comes from Christ's sacrifice is accessible through faith. But the Morning Star is obtainable only through gnosis, to those who conquer their lower natures by a concerted act of Will, and who accomplish the Work of Jesus, as we read in the Revelation of St. John:
>
>> To everyone who conquers and continues to do my works to the end, I will give authority over the nations...even as I also received authority from my Father. To the one who conquers I will also give the Morning Star. Let anyone who has an ear listen to what the Spirit is saying to the churches, (Rev. 2:26, 28-29).
>
> We are told near the end of Revelation that the Morning Star is in fact Jesus Christ himself:
>
>> It is I, Jesus, who sent my angel to you with this testimony for the churches. I am the root and the descendant of David, the bright and Morning Star, (Rev. 22:16).
>
> This is a most intriguing statement, and one that requires comment on a couple of fronts. First, as we have just said, it definitively identifies the Morning Star with Jesus himself. But we must look at this title as more than a mere epithet of Christ. Given its other canonical usage in *2 Peter*, wherein it is described as something to rise within, and in the second chapter of *Revelation* wherein it is something that is granted from on high to "the one who conquers," we must conclude that this title refers to a state of being, of existence, which may be attained by the initiate who overcomes the trials and Ordeals. Indeed, we must conclude that the Morning Star refers to the very state of Christhood. To put this into a Qabalistic context, it is the consciousness that has ascended to Tiphareth, and furthermore has attained the Knowledge and Conversation of the Holy Guardian Angel. This is not to say that the consciousness has achieved reintegration into the Pleroma, but that reintegration is now

possible. In other words, the arising of the Morning Star is that Gnostic illumination sought by every initiate of the Mysteries; true Salvation.

Certainly, more could be said on this verse alone (2 Peter 1:19), but we need to move along with the study of our topic. The second chapter of 2 Peter is de- voted largely to admonishments to stay upon the true path and warning of the dire consequences of straying. But the profundity of this chapter reaches its climax toward the final verses. Before examining these verses, though, let us turn to Luke 12:10, wherein we read of the enigmatic "blaspheme of the Holy Spirit":

> Everyone who speaks a word against the Son of Man will be forgiven, but whoever blasphemes against the Holy Spirit will not be forgiven.

You may wonder why, in the midst of our study of theosis, we would turn to such an obscure and puzzling topic as the blaspheme of the Holy Spirit, or the "unforgivable sin." But it is in fact directly related to our topic, and is explained in *2 Peter* 2:20-21, thus:

> If, after they have escaped the defilements of the cosmos through knowledge of our Lord and Savior Jesus Christ, they are again entangled in them and defeated, for them the last state has become worse than the first. For it was better for them not to have known the way of righteousness than, having known it, to turn away from the holy commandment that was passed on to them.

We see, therefore, the singular importance placed on the attainment and retention of the "knowledge of our Lord." So central is it to the process of salvation (deification) that to obtain it and then reject it puts the soul in a mortal danger worse than its original spiritual ignorance. The Gnostics of old held this precise view, for we read in the *Secret Book of John*:

> I said, "Lord, where will the souls go of people who had knowledge but turned away?"
>
> He said to me, "They will be taken to the place where the angels of misery go, where there is no repentance. They will be kept there until the day when those who have blasphemed against the Spirit will be tortured and punished eternally."

This passage shows us that the ancients viewed this phenomenon as being identical to the blaspheme of the Holy Spirit. The *Pistis Sophia* also addresses this:

> All men who shall receive the mysteries of the Ineffable - blessed indeed are the souls which shall receive of those mysteries; but if they turn and transgress and come out of the body before they have repented, the judgment of those men is sorer than all the judgments, and it is exceedingly violent... they will be cast into the outer darkness and perish and be non-existent forever.

Truly, it is difficult to imagine how such a transgression could even occur; to attain to such limitless heights only to be dragged back into a state of willful ignorance. But the emphasis given to this phenomenon in both canonical and Gnostic scriptures assures us that this is a very real condition, and that we must maintain our watchfulness diligently. This is the same watchfulness, or sobriety - nepsis - spoken of previously that leads to the contemplative "Prayer of the Heart."

Supplement: Theosis Through Gnosis

The third chapter of *2 Peter* deals mainly with the dawning of the awaited illumination. It speaks of the burning away of the temporal, or elemental things of the world, and the coming of the "day of the Lord" and the "new heavens and new earth." These are terms used to refer to the coming of the Kingdom of God which, of course, does not refer to the destruction of the physical cosmos, but to the transformation of consciousness brought about by beholding the Light of Christ. Again, we are not going to give an exegesis of this final chapter, but we do want to draw your attention to the final verse of the text:

> Grow in the grace and knowledge of our Lord and Savior Jesus Christ. To him be the glory both now and to the day of eternity. Amen.

We really only want to make a couple of comments on this verse. First, we find the concept of gnosis reiterated once again. The text really could not be more clear on the matter. It opens in the first chapter with a discussion of knowledge as the means by which we receive divine power and partake in the divine nature. The theme of the knowledge of God is then reiterated throughout the whole text. And then we find it emphasized once again in the concluding verse, as if to re-mind us that it is the beginning and ending of all spiritual works. As a secondary comment on this verse, it is interesting to note that the phrase translated as "day of eternity" or "day of the age" is more appropriately rendered: as the "day of the Aeon" (Gr. ἡμεραν αιωνος).

We have nearly exhausted our study of theoria, but before moving on let us examine another aspect. Up to this point we have mentioned the path of asceticism or the Prayer of the Heart, as a means toward theoria or illumination. But there is also the sacramental path, which is equally important to the attainment of illumination and eventual deification. Referring once again to the "Theoria" Wiki, it states:

> While theoria is possible through prayer, it is attained in a perfect way through the Eucharist. Perfect vision of the deity, perceptible in its uncreated light, is the "mystery of the eighth day." The eighth day is the day of the Eucharist but it also has an eschatological dimension as it is the day outside of the week i.e. beyond time. It is the start of a new eon of human history. Through the Eucharist people experience the eternity of God who transcends time and space.

This is also a doctrine held by many modern Gnostics. Robert Ambelain (Tau Jean III), late Patriarch of the Église Gnostique Apostolique (Gnostic Apostolic Church), states in his work *Spiritual Alchemy*:

> With the Eucharist, we absorb an occult and mystic "charge," a *philter of immortality* which, if we impregnate ourselves with it sufficiently and often enough during the course of our terrestrial life, could transmute us little by little, year by year. For this "charge," assimilated by our organism like all regular nourishment, nevertheless passes from the physiological plane to the psyche, and from the psyche into the *nous*, or spirit.

We see, therefore, that the sacramental life is not supplanted by the ascetic life, but neither does it supplant the ascetic life. But through adherence to both ascetic and sacramental practices, one may hope to obtain the perfect vision of God. And it is this vision, this beholding of the Tabor Light, that leads one into full theosis - the regenerated Man.

So what is meant, precisely, by deification or divinization? A simple answer would be that it is to become one with God. This answer would not be disputed by either the Orthodox or the Gnostic. It does, however, have certain implications that could suggest an incompatibility with Orthodox dogma. For example, Orthodoxy emphasizes that becoming divine through theosis is not the same as the doctrine of apotheosis, or becoming "a God" such as may be found within Mormonism and some forms of Satanism (e.g. Setianism - not to be confused with Sethianism!). Apotheosis is considered as a heresy in the Orthodox church, and I am inclined to agree with that position. The goal of every true mystic is to achieve union with the divine. The erroneous doctrine of apotheosis asserts that the individual may be raised, or may raise oneself, to such a stature that he becomes for all intents and purposes co-eternal and co-omnipotent with God, or the divine essence, yet remaining as an utterly unique hypostasis, divorced from the influences of the supreme creative principle. Hence, in this doctrine any union with the divine is merely a steppingstone by which one may increase his or her power and knowledge in order to ultimately break free of the natural order. This doctrine is precisely (if over-simplified) that of the Temple of Set, an off-shoot of the Church of Satan.

Many Gnostics, if not most (certainly those who have been educated and trained in the mystical orders and societies traditionally associated with the Gnostic Church) will recognize immediately the fallacies contained within the above doctrine. This Satanic philosophy mistakenly holds that if one surrenders his will to the will of God, then that one would become a mere automaton, devoid of any self-awareness. But the exact opposite is in fact true. Through willfully uniting with God, one attains the supreme self-realization. In order to understand this, it is first necessary to understand the divisions of Man, i.e. the hylic, or physical; the psychic, or soul; and the pneumatic, or spiritual. When we speak of salvation, or divinization, we are really talking about the spiritualization of the soul. The pneumatic essence in Man is that pure, uncreated light. But only that which is pneumatic can behold the pneumatic. It is therefore through the gradual purification of the soul - the spiritualization of the psychic substance - that the pneumatic is realized, and that regeneration and reintegration can occur.

Amazingly, though, there is at least one fairly well-known so-called Christian Gnostic church that adheres to the childish and unenlightened Setian/Satanic philosophy. It is childish because it is based on the primal childhood fear of the dark, of death, of non-being. It is unenlightened because every true student of the Mysteries knows that to be initiated is to learn how to die. Those who yet hold to this fear have not yet received the Wisdom of initiation. This doctrine of the unenlightened is lacking because it stagnates at the rational, unable to grasp the trans-rational, or mystical. The church I have referred to, which shall remain unnamed, seems in its outer manifestations to adhere to the ancient and traditional doctrines of the gnosis. But within the teachings of the highest level of its inner order are found the erroneous doctrines we have mentioned. I know this to be true because I myself was admitted into its highest ranks and served for a time in an administrative position. While I will not quote directly from the documents of this church, you can find the general doctrine discussed throughout Stephen Flowers' Lords of the Left-Hand Path.

This idea of possibly losing one's identity is terrifying not only to Satanists and Setian-derived Gnostic churches, but to the Roman Catholic church as well. There has long been an aversion in the West to the mysticism of the Eastern church. And even though Catholicism has been slowly warming up to the Eastern doctrines and practices, the cloud of rational scholasticism still looms large. While the Eastern Orthodox church fears the heresy of apotheosis, the Catholic fears tend toward the other direction. A recent article in the Catholic magazine "Inside the Vatican" states:

> The true Christian understanding of *Theosis* rejects any form of pantheism and any idea that all individuals cease, becoming fused into one single identity, or swallowed up (as some Eastern religions hold) into the deity. Rather, the individual remains a person in integrity, in fact, truly becoming [the] person [he] is created to be.

This sounds suspiciously similar to the Satanic philosophy previously mentioned, and is tending toward a view that is inconsistent with the experience of mystics throughout history. As Gnostics, theosis consists of the reintegration of the Pleroma, as explained in Ambelain's Spiritual Alchemy:

> *Reintegration*, or the reconstitution of the pleroma, consists of the slow and progressive working out of the Preexistent Church dispersed by the Fall. Now, this Church is the Mystic Body of Christ.

This concept of the reuniting of the divine fragments dispersed by the Fall is central to both ancient and modern Gnostic theology. While Gnosticism may not hold much in the way of dogma, there are nevertheless a number of doctrines which are held almost universally. Reintegration into the divine Fullness is one such doctrine. It is therefore our opinion that the Gnostic character of any individual or church who expounds a doctrine contrary to this traditional teaching must be considered suspect at least.

In summary, we can say that the Orthodox doctrine of theosis may be shared in almost every respect by the Gnostic. The practical methods of attaining illumination and theosis - asceticism and sacramental participation - are substantially the same for the Orthodox and the Gnostic. Gnosticism's doctrine of emanation, however, allows for the natural immanence of God, which is validated through the genuine mystical experience. Orthodox doctrine suffers in part from having to try to reconcile the mystical experience with codified dogma. The Orthodox, therefore, must create complicated definitions and clever word play in order to justify the undeniable experience of the mystics while escaping the label of "heretic" - i.e. Gnostic, Bogomil, etc. The Gnostic merely states plainly what is understood by the mystic who has attained to the Vision. To be sure, the Gnostic is not without a set of relatively complicated doctrines and definitions, but there is no need for him to rationalize his experience in a way that is not seen to violate dogma.

It is only because of the immanence of divinity that we are able to participate fully in the divine nature. For divinization represents a sort of spiritual evolution. And nothing can *evolve* which was not already *involved*. This process of spiritual evolution is effected through gnosis, by which the veils of obscurity may be lifted, revealing the divine inner light. And it is through this immanent light that we are connected to the unknowable and transcendent Father. I would encourage all of our Gnostic brothers and sisters to thoroughly acquaint themselves with the doctrines and practices of theosis, including the Hesychastic method. Even though the ancient Gnostics were suppressed long ago, the gnosis itself can never be extinguished. We can learn much from our Orthodox brethren, and even those in the Roman church who have developed such worthy methods as the *lectio divina* system of contemplative scripture reading. By learning about and utilizing those ideas and methods which are good from Orthodox and Catholic sources, we will do much to further the Great Work of the reintegration of the Preexistent Church.

A Brief History of the Gnostic Church

The history of the traditional Apostolic churches (i.e. Eastern Orthodox, Roman Catholic, etc.) has been well-documented throughout the ages; albeit typically from a point of view that is sympathetic to the "correctness" of Church doctrine and policy. Nevertheless, the Apostolic tradition remains as one of the oldest continually perpetuated spiritual systems. With very little discrepancy, the Apostolic lineage may be traced back to the original followers of Jesus, known as "Apostles" or "messengers." What is less well documented, however, is the equally ancient Apostolic tradition known to us as Gnosticism. It is true that there are many books now available on the subject, offering a clearer view of the Gnostic movements and traditions than has ever been available. But these works, for the most part, are painstaking reconstructions of Gnostic history, taken largely from the biased accounts of the early heresiologists, scattered accounts and traditions, and newly discovered ancient documents.

This short treatise, while briefly addressing the ancient and medieval movements, is largely concerned with the modem Gnostic traditions and the Orders and Societies which often form their inner circles. Today's Gnostic churches derive largely from 19th century Masonic, Rosicrucian, Templar, Theosophic, and Martinist groups in France. These esoteric Orders and Societies have been crucial in preserving and transmitting the Gnostic doctrine, and inner spiritual traditions. Likewise, the exoteric Apostolic churches have played a vital role in preserving the succession of bishops. The reunification of the sacramental with the initiatic represents a true restoration of the Gnosis.

The 20th century brought many hardships and struggles to the Gnostic and esoteric movements, but it also saw many rich rewards. In spite of two World Wars, collapsing economies, and other sorts of social and political upheaval around the globe, the sacred flame of Truth was never extinguished. The advent of personal computing helped usher in the Information Age, which has also helped to facilitate the reconnecting of the disparate facets of the Gnostic gem. In these early years of the 21st century, Gnosticism has grown exponentially, yet remains firmly rooted in the ancient traditions and customs.

Supplement: A Brief History of the Gnostic Church

Pre-Christian and Early Christian Gnosticism

There are three principal components which seem to have most influenced Christian Gnosticism: Persian, Semitic, and Græco-Egyptian mysticism. This, of course, is an oversimplification of the matter, but I merely want to introduce the general concepts here, not to elaborate upon their myriad intricacies. That is, our survey will begin in around the 6th century B.C., and examine some of the prominent movements that have left the strongest echo in Gnosticism. Know, however, that these traditions are tied to even older ones originating in Egypt, Sumeria, Akkadia, et al. In fact, tradition unites all ancient theosophies in the legends of Atlantis and Lemuria. But, let us limit our discussion to more verifiable historic eras.

By the 6th century B.C., several sophisticated religious and philosophical systems were thriving in Persia, Palestine, and northern Africa (and much of Asia as well, but that is beyond the scope of our present study). The Persian prophet Zoroaster (Zarathustra) founds a religion that emphasizes the dualities of nature: good/evil; light/darkness; summer/winter; heat/cold. This duality was personified in the perpetual conflict between Ahura-Mazda, who represented the True God, and Ahriman, the adversarial deity who would seek to bring darkness and suffering into the world (but who ultimately loses to the True God of Light). The Zoroastrian teachings are, of course, much more complicated, but this fundamental duality underlies the whole system. This type of duality is prevalent throughout ancient Gnostic doctrines. Although Gnosticism, in most of its forms, is not dualistic in an absolute sense, it strongly emphasizes the relative duality as observed from a corporeal perspective.

In mystical and apocalyptic Judaism of the 6th century B.C., we can find the roots of both Gnostic, and later Qabalistic doctrine. Ezekiel's vision of the Son of Man becomes the prototype for the Gnostic Geradamas, as well as the Adam Qadmon of the Qabalists. By the 2nd century B.C., this figure has made it into *Daniel*, and appears in later apocalyptic texts. At this time, the Qabalah does not yet exist as a fully developed doctrine, such as its current state. But, Merkavah mysticism certainly exists, as well as an inner, oral tradition from which the Qabalah derives its name.

Meanwhile, in 6th century Greece, Pythagoras is teaching a system of mystical philosophy which includes the study of reincarnation, mystical numerology, and emanationist cosmology, as well as the practice of theurgy. Pythagoras is said to have been initiated into the Mysteries of Egypt, and those of the Chaldean Magi. Pythagoras taught that geometry was the basis of all creation, and is said to have referred to God as the "Grand Geometrician." Outside of the students of mysticism and ancient philosophy, Pythagoras is probably best known for his theorem which states that in a right triangle, the sum of the square of two sides is equal to the square of its hypotenuse ($a^2+b^2=c^2$). This is also sometimes referred to as the 47th Proposition of Euclid, but Pythagoras was the first to expound it. Pythagoras also made an in-depth study of the relationship between the intervals of musical tones and harmonies. Both the scientific and mystical aspects of Pythagoras' doctrine (which were inextricably linked) would greatly influence later Greek philosophers, such as Plato, and would blend harmoniously with Gnostic and Hermetic doctrines in Alexandria, Egypt.

By the 3rd century B.C., the Astrological Hermetica was emerging in Alexandria. While the Greek influence on the Hermetic doctrine cannot be denied., the underlying principles, especially concerning the astrological schema, are undoubtedly of a purely Egyptian origin. It seems fitting that the greatest mystical and philosophic doctrines of the Greek philosophers, who claimed to have received secret teachings from the Egyptian priesthood, would find their greatest expression in Alexandria in the form of Hermetic philosophy.

In the 1st century A.D., Neoplatonism, Pythagoreanism, Hermeticism, and apocalyptic Judaism meet and mix in Alexandria to form the basis of Gnostic doctrine and philosophy. In Palestine, the Essenes practice a form of apocalyptic Judaism that may have also contributed proto-Gnostic elements. John the Baptizer likely taught some form of these doctrines, as evidenced by the teachings of Jesus, as well as those of the Mandaeans, whose very name translates to "gnostic."

Certain traditions hold that another disciple of John the Baptizer was Simon Magus of Samaria. Simon taught a Gnostic doctrine concerning the descent of Spirit into matter, and its ultimate liberation and return to the Light; themes echoed throughout nearly all of the Gnostic writings. Although Simon is spoken of disparagingly in the *Acts of the Apostles*, I don't think we can take this as much more than a petty rivalry. This is really no stretch of the imagination when we consider the situations that exist in the present day, with individuals and groups denouncing one another as "inauthentic" while teaching identical doctrines; or doctrines so similar as to be virtually indistinguishable, one from the other. Some of the well-known successors of Simon Magus include Menander, who established himself in Antioch, and whose teachings spread throughout Asia Minor (roughly, the area occupied by modem-day Turkey); and Saturninus, a student of Menander who further refined and expanded upon the Gnostic doctrine.

Another 1st century teacher to contribute much to the terminology and philosophic basis for Gnosticism is St. Paul. The letters attributed to Paul are full of examples of this, such as the distinction made between the psychic and pneumatic; and many other elements both subtle and blatant. Much of this is exposed in Elaine Pagels' work, *The Gnostic Paul*.

The 2nd century can rightly be seen as the Golden Age of Gnosticism. At this time, Gnosticism is widely spread throughout Christendom. There is, as yet, no distinct "orthodoxy." There are numerous Christian sects from North Africa, through the Middle East, Asia Minor, and into the Mediterranean. Basilides was an extremely important and influential teacher of Gnosis in Alexandria. He claimed to have received his Gnostic doctrine from Glaucias, a follower of St. Peter, and from Matthias. Shortly after, or perhaps during the period Basilides was teaching, the North African, Valentinus, was receiving his education in Alexandria. Valentinus moved to Rome, where he very nearly became Bishop of Rome; the office now referred to as Pope. The Valentinian school produced sublime texts of Gnostic teaching and exegesis, and has continued to influence Gnostic groups throughout history, up to the present day.

St. Thomas is credited with bringing Christianity to Syria. From this school came many important mystical tests and teachers, such as the luminous Bardaisan (Bardesanes) of Edessa, who taught a Gnostic doctrine containing many elements similar to those of Simon Magus, Basilides, and Valentinus. He also wrote many early hymns, including, very likely, the "Hymn of the Robe of Glory" found in the Ads of Thomas. Although many modern scholars attempt to dissociate Thomasine Christianity from Gnosticism proper, I think that the early writings and practices of Syrian Christians suggest otherwise.

Around 180 A.D., the "orthodox" heresiologist Irenaeus (in truth there is yet no true orthodoxy at the time, but Irenaeus represents the doctrinal school which will ultimately establish itself by force) composes *Adversus Hæresus*, denouncing various Gnostic sects. Ironically, his work, and those of later heresiologists, will unwittingly preserve many key Gnostic doctrines. Through, because the works are decidedly biased against Gnosticism, the doctrines are often preserved imperfectly; containing both errors and outright fabrications. This has become especially evident as more ancient Gnostic texts have come to light. Still, these damning tomes of the early heresiologists are a wealth of information about various forms of early Christian thought.

At the dawn of the 3rd century, Clement of Alexandria develops a type of Christian Neoplatonism and self-identifies as Gnostic. He advocates for the supremacy of gnosis over mere faith, but does not seem to have taught a doctrine of the Demiurge, or many other elements of classical Gnosticism. It is probably for this reason that he was never denounced as a heretic by the "orthodoxy."

The 3rd century brought continued development and growth of Gnostic doctrine and literature; but, also continued and growing opposition from the emerging orthodoxy. While Hippolytus was composing venomous tirades against the Gnostics and other "heretics," the Persian prophet Mani begins having angelic visions instructing him to found a new faith. Mani's system has many Gnostic elements, such as the liberation of the Divine Spark from the darkness of matter, but is more radically dualistic than other Gnostic sects. Mani's syncretic system incorporates elements of Judaism, Zoroastrianism, Buddhism, and Christianity. Mani's religion spread far and wide, and survived in east Asia for centuries.

The 4th century would bring the eventual suppression of the vast majority of Christian Gnosticism. An orthodoxy was established with the support and strength of the state. The Nag Hammadi scriptures date from this period; though, these Coptic texts are translations of older Greek texts. This vast collection, which lay undiscovered for over 15 centuries, shows the unique mixture of Christian, Jewish, Hermetic, and Neoplatonic sources that make up the Gnostic tradition. Ironically, considering the harsh suppression of Gnosticism, the Hermetic texts gain a wider acceptance throughout mainstream Christianity.

During the 5th century, Iamblichus and Proclus perpetuate a form of Gnostic/Hermetic theurgy; and Pseudo-Dionysus composes the work, Celestial Hierarchies, largely influenced by Gnostic cosmology, but eventually to be accepted by St. Thomas Aquinas as orthodox theology. But, as the Dark Ages descend upon Europe, the dissemination of the genuinely Gnostic teachings is greatly inhibited. Many Gnostic themes are found in superstitious practices and beliefs, but the Gnostic current is largely preserved in the East among Jewish and Islamic mysticism. If the Mysteries survive at all during this period in Europe, it is deep within the confines of the monasteries or secreted away in the Masons' guilds.

Supplement: A Brief History of the Gnostic Church

Gnostic Currents In Medieval Through Renaissance Times: 12th – 17th Centuries

The 12th century saw the emergence of the Cathars in the Languedoc region, with a Christian dualism that was similar, in many ways, to ancient Gnosticism and Manichæism. It is widely held that the Cathars were inheritors of the "heretic" faith brought to the area by Bulgarian Bogomil clerics; and, while the Bogomil influence is not generally disputed, there also seems to be some evidence suggesting a pre-existent Cathar movement into which the Bogomil doctrine was incorporated. In any case, their teachings included certain Gnostic elements, such as the distinction between the True God of Light, and an imperfect demiurgic god, in this case, Lucifer. They also taught that souls had been trapped in the material world by Lucifer, and required liberation through successive incarnations. Although revered by local populations, and even many mainstream clergy, these heretical teachings (which often denounced the opulence of the Roman Church) incurred the wrath of the Papacy. Edicts were issued against the Cathars, and in the early 13th century, Pope Innocent III commissions "St." Dominic to wage spiritual (and literal) warfare against the Cathars. These efforts culminated in the infamous massacre at Montsegur, where, on the 16th of March, 1244, hundreds of Cathar Perfecti (those who had received the sacrament of the Consolamentum) were burned alive. Cathars in other parts of Europe are forced into secrecy, re-emerging later among the Rosicrucians.

Another important 12th century movement developed within the very bosom of the Roman Catholic Church. I am referring to the founding of the Poor Fellow Soldiers of Jesus Christ, on Christmas Day in the year 1118 (or 1119 by some accounts). This religious military order was formed under papal decree in Jerusalem for the purpose of protecting Christian pilgrims during their voyage to the Holy Land. They became known as the Knights of the Order of the Temple, or Knights Templar, because of their association with the old Temple mount. While in the Holy Land, the Templars encountered mystical Isma'ili sects, as well as "Johannites" who were quite probably Mandaeans. The teachings of these groups were said to be preserved and perpetuated in secret by the Templar Order. It is interesting to note that the Templars were composed largely of Frenchmen. The French have a long and mysterious history of being the conservators of the ancient Wisdom Traditions. While it is difficult to know the absolute truth about the claims of the various Templar esoteric activities, it is important to keep in mind that the lines between legend and historically verifiable fact often become so blurred as to be considered virtually non-existent.

Later, in the early 14th century, King Philippe IV (le bel) of France would seize upon the rumors of the Templars' mysterious rites and amplify them with outright fabrications. The true motive of the king's denouncement of the Templars had less to do with heresy than with greed for the Order's vast wealth. Pope Clement V, to whom the Templars answered directly and solely, allowed their harsh suppression through either collaboration or complacency. On Friday, October 13th, 1307, Jacque de Molay (the last Grand Master of the Order of the Temple) and all of the Templars in France were arrested. Many Knights throughout the rest of Europe managed to escape the arrest orders. They found refuge in countries less sympathetic to the Papacy, such as Scotland; and continued on in other countries under different names, such as the Knights of Christ in Portugal. Legend maintains that when de Molay was burned at the stake, he called out for the Pope and King to join him before the throne of God within one year. Indeed, both the King and the Pope were dead within one year's time. The Templars, and their rites, emerge later among the Masonic and occult bodies all across Europe.

While the Cathars were struggling for their very existence, and the Templars were receiving secret initiations in the Holy Land, and possibly Persia, the Spanish Moors and Jews (under Moorish protection) were introducing all forms of Arts and Sciences into Europe; including Alchemy, which had been preserved within the Islamic sects since the suppression of the ancient Gnostics, and Qabalism, which thrived within the Jewish communities of Moorish Spain. These philosophies and practices, along with Astrology, Theosophy, and other mystical Arts and Sciences, would form the foundation for the doctrine known generally as Rosicrucianism. They are the same elements that had come together over a millennium prior to give rise to Gnosticism.

It is impossible to say, with absolute certainty, when exactly the rose and cross began to be used together in such a way as to represent the Hermetic Tradition. One can be certain, though, that the history of the Hermetic Tradition is, in essence, the history of Rosicrucianism. According to John Yarker, in *The Arcane Schools:*

> It may be mentioned here that the Syrian Mysteries of Adonis represented the slain God as changed by Venus into a red rose; and Theodoratus, Bishop of Cyrus in Syria, asserts that the Gnostics deemed *Ros* to be a symbol of regeneration and love, and as the Latin word Rosa is derived from Ros, the dew, it has a relation with baptism; hence the rose-tree in Christian symbolism is the symbol of the regenerated, whilst dew is the symbol of regeneration.

Some of the famous alchemists of the period, who would be considered forefathers of Rosicrucianism include: Roger Bacon, Albertus Magnus, Raymond Lulli, and Nicholas Flamel. The founding of the Rosicrucian Fraternity is traditionally attributed to one Christian Rosenkreutz. Rosenkreutz is said to have been born to a German Cathar family in 1378. The story of Christian Rosenkreutz (also called the Father C.R.C.) is often thought to be purely allegorical; but, although the name of the legendary founder is undoubtedly symbolic, there may very well have been an actual personality behind the myth.

Whatever the literal truth may be of the Rosicrucian tales, there can be no doubt that there were several alchemists and initiates of the Ancient Mysteries who worked quietly throughout the 15th century to bring together the elements of a true Rosicrucian Fraternity. By the early 16th century, Henri Cornelius Agrippa had established Communities of the Magi in Paris and elsewhere throughout Europe. There is a record of the establishment of such a Community in London in 1510. This Society was concerned with things such as Alchemy, Qabalah, and Theurgy; in other words, Gnostic-Hermetic-Rosicrucian Arts and Sciences. According to Michael Maier, alchemist and physician to Emperor Rudolph II, the German branch of the Community of the Magi reorganizes as the Brethren of the Golden Rosycross in 1570. Another society is formed in Germany around the same time called Militia Crucifera Evangelica. The founder of the MCE is said to be Simon Studion, who wrote a book entitled *Naometria* in about 1604, and mentions the Rose and Cross in connection to the MCE. Within a year of the publication of this work, the MCE seems to have officially adopted the Rose-Cross as a symbol of the Order.

The 17th century would be extremely important to the shaping and structuring of the schools of the Western Mystery Tradition as we know them today. At the crux of the whole Tradition is the Rose+Croix. In the years 1614-1615, three Rosicrucian manifestos appeared: *Fama Fraternitatis*, *Confessio Fraternitatis*, and The *Chymical Wedding of Christian Rosencreutz*. The Fama deals primarily with the initiatic journey of "The Highly Illuminated Father C.R.C." who, like the Buddha, was of noble birth, but renounced material wealth and traveled the world in search of true wisdom. Eventually, C.R.C. returns to his native Germany where he quietly established a small "Fraternity of the Rose Cross" to preserve the knowledge imparted to him. In short, the *Fama* consists of the traditional, or legendary, founding of the Rosicrucian Order. The *Confessio* lays out many of the aims of the Fraternity, and strongly denounces the Papacy, as well as those so-called alchemists who were only interested in the transmutation of base metals, without gaining the inner knowledge, which is the true Work. The *Chymical Wedding* is an allegory of the Alchemical Conjunction - the mystical union of Spirit and Soul; a fascinating topic, but one that strays from our present discourse.

Perhaps the single most important society to emerge in the 17th century is the Order of Unknown Philosophers, formed in 1643. Associated with this Order, we find some of the most illustrious names: Jacob Boehme, the Gnostic and Qabalist whose works influence Louis-Claude de Saint-Martin as much as, if not more than, his master, Martinès de Pasqually; Heinrich Khunrath; Alexander Sethon "the Cosmopolite"; Michael Sendivogius; Rudolph Salzman; etc., etc. Louis-Claude himself becomes connected with this Order, and so embodies it principles that the term "Unknown Philosopher" came to represent all that he stood for and taught.

One last topic that we should touch upon before moving on, is the origin of the relationship between the Rosicrucians and Freemasonry. The earliest connection remains shrouded in mystery and speculation. But, there is one individual who can be connected to both Rosicrucianism and "Speculative" Masonry; that is, Philosophic Masonry, as opposed to Operative Masonry. That person is Elias Ashmole, who, with others in 1645, formed a society that was outwardly dedicated to the study of Nature, but actually transmitted a secret, occult teaching, oriented toward mysticism, Qabalah, and Gnosticism. In 1646, Ashmole receives Masonic initiation as an "Accepted" (i.e. Speculative/Philosophic) Mason, and requests that the society of the Rose+Croix be allowed to meet at the guild's headquarters. This Rose+Croix society eventually gives birth to various other societies dedicated to mysticism and to the phenomena of the natural world, such as the Royal Society which received a charter from King Charles II.

Supplement: A Brief History of the Gnostic Church

The Gnosis Restored: 18th - 19th Century

In the year 1705, there was supposedly a Templar Convention held in Versailles wherein Philippe, Duc d'Orleans, was elected as the 40th Grand Master of the "Ordre du Temple." This succession of Grand Masters is based upon the so-called "Larmenius Charter" of 1324. In this Charter, John-Marc Larmenius is designated as the successor to Jacque de Molay, last Grand Master of the old Templar Order. Both the Larmenius Charter and the 1705 revival have had their authenticity called into question frequently. I do not intend to revisit this controversy here. I only mention it because it will serve as the basis for another Templar revival a century later, as we shall see a little further on. What is certain is that in the early 18th century, various forms of Templarism and the Rose+Croix were popular throughout Europe, and were becoming very influential in the Fraternity of Freemasons.

Beginning with this period, Freemasonry becomes the conduit which will channel the transmission of the various branches of the Mystery Schools. Papus (Dr. Gerard Encausse) states in his *The Tarot of the Bohemians*, "The Gnostic sects, the Arabs, Alchemists, Templars, Rosicrucians, and lastly the Freemasons, form the Western chain in the transmission of occult science." As we have seen, the truth of this statement is borne out upon an examination of the historical evidence. And, as we continue our journey through the 18th, 19th, and 20th centuries, up to the present day, we shall see not only the modem influence of Freemasonry, but also the resurgence of those original Gnostic principles, and how all of these worthy elements come together in the modem Gnostic churches.

Returning now to the 18th century, let us take a look at how the Rose+Croix influenced Freemasonry and was perpetuated through Masonic rites. The Master Mason degree, added in 1723, is based upon a death and resurrection rite of Rosicrucian inspiration. Even the Opening and Closing rituals are full of alchemical symbolism. I cannot give details of these rites, but there are some aspects which are commonly observed, even in public ceremonies. For instance, it is no real secret that the staves of the Jr. and Sr. Deacons bear the images of the Moon and the Sun. These officers move about the Lodge in such a way that the true Initiate cannot help but to see therein the dance of Mercury and Sulphur; the alchemical Conjunction. In fact, a careful study (including experiential study, not just academic) of the Masonic rituals will reveal the whole essence of the Hermetic Tradition.

It is likely for this reason that Masters of the Qabalah, Theurgy, and the Magical Arts and Sciences in general, such as Martinès de Pasqually, would couch their teachings in the system of Freemasonry Pasqually is named in a Masonic Patent issued to his father by Charles Stuart in either 1738 or 1758 (the '58 date is considered by many scholars to be the more likely). In this Patent, Pasqually is to receive authority as "Deputy Grand

Master" upon his father's death. During the late 1750s through the early '60s, Pasqually travels throughout France recruiting followers and opening Lodges. In 1760 he forms a chapter of "Le Temple Cohen"; and in 1761 opens the Lodge "La Perfection Élue Écossaise" in Bordeaux. On March 21, 1767, Pasqually founds the Sovereign Tribunal of l'Ordre des Chevaliers Maçons Élus-Coëns de l'Univers with de Lusignan, de Loos, de Grainville, Jean-Baptiste Willermoz, Fauger d'Ignéacourt, and Bacon de la Chevalerie as his Deputy.

This Order was open only to Master Masons, and taught a peculiar system of Theurgy, or Ceremonial magic. Louis-Claude de Saint-Martin was initiated a year later by Pasqually himself. Saint-Martin, and the other disciples of Pasqually, would attest to the miraculous and phantasmagorical nature of Pasqually's Theurgic Operation. An entity, referred to as the Unknown Agent, appeared often during the workings to give instruction. Few of Pasqually's students would ever be able to repeat his works, but all would testify to the veracity of the claims. Pasqually left for Santo Domingo in 1772 to claim an inheritance, but he would never return to Europe. Pasqually died on September 20, 1774, in Port-au-Prince, Haiti, after founding Élus-Coëns Temples throughout the country.

It is interesting to note that the West Indies, and Haiti in particular, have been instrumental as a port of entry into the New World for the old French rites. The mere fact that it was a French colony does not seem to account for the mysterious magnetism that has drawn to it every major stream of the Mystery Tradition. The Masonic Rite of Perfection of 25° came to San Domingo and Kingston, Jamaica in the 1760s, and is finally brought to the United States at the beginning of the 19th century, where it was transformed into the Ancient and Accepted Scottish Rite of 33°. So, in an environment of High-Grade Masonry, it is not surprising that Pasqually's Élus-Coëns would thrive. Even after the white European colonists were ousted from Haiti, the Cohen Temples continued to influence the secret initiatory rites of the black Haitians, and became integrated into some esoteric Voudoo practices.

After the death of Pasqually, the work of the Élus-Coëns in Europe was primarily carried on by Jean-Baptiste Willermoz and Louis-Claude de Saint-Martin. The approach of Willermoz was to incorporate the rites into a Strict Observance Lodge (a German Masonic Templar rite) from which emerged the Chevaliers Bienfaisant de la Cité Saint (Knights Beneficent of the Holy City) in 1778. It is said that later in his life, Willermoz began to develop some of the powers possessed by his former master.

Saint-Martin, on the other hand, seeks to perfect his master's work by shedding extraneous elements that he feels are not essential to the goal of the Work, which is Reintegration and Regeneration. Saint-Martin never speaks disparagingly of Pasqually, nor does he doubt the efficacy of his methods. He feels, however, that the complex ritual and phantasmagoric projections are not necessary to the attainment of gnosis. The works of Jacob Boehme becomes a second master to him. From 1777 to 1790, Saint-Martin travels Europe extensively, gaining disciples and becoming connected to the aforementioned Order of Unknown Philosophers. Saint-Martin develops a system that has but a single initiation, having stripped away much of the Masonic and Theurgic pageantry. His system comes to be known as the "Way of the Heart," because it is a path of inner contemplation, reflection, and rectification. When Louis-Claude de Saint-Martin dies in 1803, he leaves behind many initiated disciples in numerous countries.

A year later, in 1804, Bernard-Raymond Fabré-Palaprat and others found a "restored" Ordre du Temple, based on the Larmenius Charter. This Templar Order was said to be a reconstitution of the Duc d'Orleans' Templar revival of 1705. As stated previously, there was, and continues to be, much controversy regarding the legitimacy of this Templar lineage. It does indeed seem difficult to believe, even if the 1705 revival did occur, that de Molay would have been in any sort of position to issue rights of succession before his execution. It is not impossible, of course, as we know that the Knights were able to secret away the vast treasures of the Order, thus foiling the French King's plans to usurp the Order's wealth. But, even if we remove the question of succession from the equation, we find that the Ordre du Temple has many other interesting connections, especially to Freemasonry, even though it was not a specifically Masonic rite. A number of historians have traced the Order's foundation to the hidden influence of certain prominent Freemasons and High-Grade Masonic rites. In any case, we should probably not judge its value solely upon the legitimacy of the so-called Larmenius Charter.

What interests us more than Palaprat's Ordre du Temple at the moment, however, is the foundation of his Johannite Church, or l'Église Johannite des Chrétiens Primitif. Although the Church was not officially formed until 1828 or 1830, its foundation goes back to several years previous. In 1810, Fabré-Palaprat received valid apostolic episcopal consecration from Guillaume Mauviel. Mauviel himself had been consecrated ten years prior into the Rebiba succession (Scipione Cardinal Rebiba), from which over 90% of current Roman Catholic bishops derive their succession. The fact that Mauviel had been consecrated as "Constitutional Bishop of Cayes in Haiti" I think draws another interesting link between Haiti and the transmission of the Mysteries. On the same day that Palaprat received his episcopal consecration July 29, 1810), he consecrated Jean Machault. It is these three, Palaprat, Mauviel and Machault, that would found the Johannite Church upon the principles of a version of the Gospel of john and its commentary called the *Levitikon*. This church was Gnostic in character, and tied into the Ordre du Temple. The church claimed an apostolic succession from St. John through a Templar lineage - the same lineage that was supposed to have preserved the succession of Grand Masters. This lineage, however, is almost certainly a fabrication. There are Johannite successions that are valid - such as the one derived from Polycarp - but this contrived Templar lineage is not one of them. Even if we admit the possibility of an actual succession of Templar Grand Masters from Larmenius, which is highly suspect at least, the idea that this succession additionally transmitted a valid apostolic succession of any kind seems to be beyond the realm of serious consideration. Nevertheless, the Johannite Church of Primitive Christians did, as we have seen, possess a valid apostolic succession; even if it was not as they claimed.

Machault was a Primate of the Church, and in 1831 he consecrated François-Ferdinand Toussaint Chatel (1795-1857) to the episcopacy with the title of "Primate of the Gauls." It is known that Chatel had created his own church, l'Église Catholique Français (not to be confused with the church of René Vilatte having the same name). It is widely understood that his time with the Johannite Church was short-lived, but some historians have posited that he went on to lead the Church after Palaprat's death in 1838. It would also seem that the Templar Order had schisms while Palaprat was yet alive. Apparently, some members of the Knighthood were not willing to accept the Johannite faith which Palaprat, as Patriarch of the Church and Grand Master of the Order, required of them.

A couple of the well-known survivals of the succession from the Johannite Church include the line that was incorporated into Jean Bricaud's Église Catholique Gnostique of 1907 (which will be discussed further on), and the line that became fused with a Spanish neo-Albigensian church with connections to the esoteric Egyptian Masonic obedience of The Ancient and Primitive Rite of Memphis-Misraïm. This latter succession comes to be when Michel Henri d'Adhémar (1801-1900, who had been consecrated by Chatel in 1836 (two years before Palaprat's death), consecrates Manuel Lopez de Brion (1830-1874) under the episcopal nomen of Orfeo V in 1857. Then, in 1860, de Brion (who is also a Memphis-Misraïm initiator) consecrates Paul Pierre de Marraga (1823-1901) as Orfeo VI and initiates de Marraga into Memphis-Misraïm. We shall see, later, how these currents have come to us in the present day.

A year after Palaprat's death, Pierre-Eugène-Michel Vintras (1807- 1875) has visions of St. Michael, St. Joseph, the Virgin Mary, and the Holy Spirit. He is told of the coming of the Paraclete, and of the Age of the Holy Spirit. This principle echoes concepts found in ancient Gnosticism, such as is found in the work, *Tripartite Tractate* (which was unknown at the time) and the doctrines of Joachim of Fiore, a 12th century Christian monk who, like the ancient Gnostic work mentioned above, divided history into three "Ages": the Age of the Father, which referred to the era before Christ; the Age of the Son, referring to the period of time since the incarnation of Jesus; and the Age of the Holy Spirit, which was an Age yet to come.

Vintras then founded a movement based upon these visions called l'Oeuvre de la Misericorde (Work of Mercy), which apparently attracted a number of Roman Catholic Priests. It seems also that numerous people witnessed many instances of "miracles" of bleeding hosts, wine turning to blood, apparitions, and the like. The popularity of Vintras' movement incurred the ire of the Papacy. His work was denounced by Pope Gregory XVI in 1841, and again, ten years later, by Pope Pius IX. Around the time of the second condemnation, Vintras was traveling Europe, founding several branches of his work which he had now organized as the Sanctuaire Interieur du Carmel d'Élie, or the "Church of Carmel."

After Eugène Vintras' death in 1875 (the same year in which the Russian mystic Madame Helena Petrovna Blavatsky and the American Colonel Henry Steel Olcott would found the Theosophical Society in New York) the Carmelite Church would survive in a fractured form, owing to disagreements over the succession of leadership. The splinter groups seem to have been just as controversial as Vintras' initial movement, involving individuals such as the Abbé de Boullan (Joseph-Antoine Boullan) and Louis Van Haeckel. At least one branch of the Carmelite Church was later incorporated into Bricaud's church mentioned previously.

Beginning in about 1880, a series of very important events begins to unfold that will help shape the face of the Western Mystery Tradition for the foreseeable future. In this year, Dr. Gerard Encausse (1865-1916), better known as "Papus" receives the initiation transmitted by Louis-Claude de Saint-Martin from Henri Delaage. At the time, there was no formal school or Order of Martinists; only individuals who were linked through the Initiatic Chain to Saint-Martin, who gave but a single initiation, that of the Superieur Inconnu (Unknown Superior). One day, not long after receiving this initiation, while discussing esoteric and occult topics with some of his peers in a Paris café, Papus discovered another man, Pierre-Augustin Chaboseau, who had also received this special initiation, via Amélie de Boisse-Mortemart.

Papus and Chaboseau exchanged initiations in order to solidify the Martinist initiatic lineage, and began seeking out other SS∴ II∴. The two desired to gather these Initiates into an organized group that could serve as a vehicle for the transmission of the Martinist Initiation, as well as the preservation and perpetuation of the Martinist doctrine. In 1884, a Constitution was drafted adopting the name l'Ordre Martiniste (Martinist Order). By 1891, a Supreme Council had been formed consisting of 12 members: Papus (President and Grand Master), Augustin Chaboseau, Stanislas de Guaïta, Chamuel (Lucien Mauchel), Paul Sédir (Yvon Le Loup, 1871-1926), Paul Adam, Maurice Barres, Jules Lejay, George Montière, François-Charles Barlet, Jacques Burget, and Joséphin Péladan. Barres and Péladan are soon replaced by Dr. Marc Haven and Victor-Emile Michelet. This new Martinist Order conferred Saint-Martin's Initiation in three degrees instead of just one, as Saint-Martin had done.

Péladan's departure from the Ordre Martiniste also coincided with his departure from l'Ordre Kabbalistique de la Rose+Croix, which had been founded by Péladan (1858-1918) and Stanislas de Guaïta (1861-1897) in 1888. The same year (1891), Péladan forms the Ordre de la Rose+Croix Catholique et Esthetique du Temple et du Graal, and adopted the mystical nomen of Sâr Merodack. And a year later, he inherited the Grand Mastership of Palaprat's Ordre du Temple. All of these Orders continue to be relevant and important in the years to come for the French neo-Gnostic revival.

In the same year as the founding of the OKR+C, Jules-Benoit Stanislas Doinel du Val-Michel (1842-1903), known commonly as Jules Doinel, has a vision of the "Aeon Jesus" and is spiritually consecrated as "Bishop of Montsegur and Primate of the Albigensians." He adopted the episcopal nomen Tau Valentin II, in honor of the great second- century Gnostic teacher, Valentinus. The "Tau" is a reference to the Tau cross, which has been used since remote antiquity to represent the mystical; especially in Egypt, where it appears in the simple tau (I) form, and also as a component of the ankh. In another such vision, he had been instructed to re-establish the Gnostic Church. These visions occurred at the residence of Maria de Mariategui, Lady Marie Caithness, Duchess of Pomar (1842-1895), a friend of Madame Blavatsky and an early member of the Theosophical Society. It is widely believed that Doinel's visions occurred during seances hosted by Lady Caithness, but Bishop Stephan Hoeller (Tau Stephanus) refutes this assertion in his work, *Gnosticism: New Light on the Ancient Tradition of Inner Knowing*. No reason is given for his correction, but one should consider the fact that the French word "seance" merely means "session" or "meeting" and was not necessarily a Spiritualist seance. On the other hand, it is reported that a system of pendulum divination was used to commune with the spirits at these sessions. In any case, Doinel believed in the message he received from Sophia-Achamoth to "establish my Gnostic Church."

In 1890, Doinel fulfilled his mandate by officially founding the Church (which existed under various names during his Patriarchate, but which is generally known as l'Église du Paraclet or l'Église Gnostique) and proclaimed 1890 to be the beginning of the "Era of the Gnosis Restored." (Incidentally, this would make 1890 "Year One" of the Era of the Gnosis Restored. I have seen several documents and certificates misdated because the author has merely counted the number of intervening years between 1890 and the present. For example, there is before me a Bull of Election that was issued "on the second of October, of the year of our Lord, two-thousand and two, the Feast of All Holy Souls, the One Hundred and Twelfth year of the Era of the Gnosis Restored..." Since 1890 would have been "the First year of the Era..." then 2002 would be the 113th year.) By 1892, Doinel had consecrated the following bishops: Gerard Encausse (Papus) - Tau Vincent, Bishop of Toulouse; Paul Sédir (Yvon Le Loup, 1871-1926) - Tau Paulus, Coadjutor of Toulouse, Bishop of Concorezzo; Chamuel (Lucien Mauchel) - Tau Bardesanes, Bishop of La Rochelle & Saintes; Louis-Sophrone Fugairon (b. 1848) – Tau Sophronius, Bishop of Béziers; Albert Jounet (1863-1929) - Tau Theodotus, Bishop of Avignon; Marie Chauvel de Chauvigny (1842-1927) - Esclarmonde, Sophia of Warsaw; Léonce-Eugène Joseph Fabre des Éssarts - Tau Synésius, Bishop of Bordeaux; François-Charles Barlet; and Jules Lejay. You will notice that many of these names are identical to those of the Martinist Supreme Council. This is no coincidence. The Gnostic Church and the Martinist Order quickly formed a relationship that has endured for over a century. Doinel himself was appointed by Papus to the Martinist Supreme Council, sometime after 1892. To emphasize this intimate relationship, in 1893 the "Holy Gnostic Synod" of Doinel's Église Gnostique publishes a list of decrees in the Martinist journal, L'Initiation, Article Seven of which states: "The Martinist Order is declared to be of gnostic

essence." There are also several rights and privileges given to those who have attained the Superieur Inconnu degree of the Martinist Order. It is also interesting to note that Article Eight states that, "The Gospel of John is the only Gnostic Gospel." This illustrates the recurring importance of the Johannine tradition within Gnosticism. It should also be stated, though probably needlessly, that Doinel and others in that circle, were Freemasons; and it is well-known that Masonic Lodges are dedicated to the Holy Saints John; that is, the Evangelist and the Baptizer. Freemasonry, of one sort or another, has always been closely associated with the Gnostic Church, which has often been referred to as a Church of Initiates.

The year 1894 would bring many changes to the Gnostic Church. As the "fin de siècle" was drawing to a close, the currents flowing within the Gnostic Church would become rather tumultuous. Doinel suddenly abdicates the Gnostic Patriarchate, and converts to Roman Catholicism! Doinel seems to have succumbed to paranoia, induced largely by the Masonophobic ravings of Leo Taxil (G.A. Jogand-Pages). This, evidently, caused a crisis of faith in Doinel, severe enough that he would renounce Gnosticism, Freemasonry, and all things esoteric. It has also been suggested that Doinel never actually left his faith, but merely put on the appearance in order to expose the exposé, so to speak. Doinel did finally seek re-admission to the Gnostic Church in 1900, and was re-consecrated as Tau Jules, but would never return to the patriarchal throne.

In order to fill the vacancy left by Doinel's defection, the Synod of Bishops held an election in 1895. The High Synod would elect Léonce-Eugène Joseph Fabre des Essarts - Tau Synésius - to the Gnostic Patriarchate. Fabre des Éssarts was a close friend and personal student of Abbé Julio (Julien-Emest Houssay, 1844-1912). Abbe Julio was a Roman Catholic priest until he was strong-armed out in 1885 for openly criticizing the corrupt Roman Catholic clergy. The Abbe became a close associate to the mystical healer Jean Sempé, who seems to have based his teachings upon those of Origen, and the occult value of the Psalms for healing and Spiritual attunement. Abbe Julio would also become associated with the Syro-Jacobite bishop, Joseph-René Vilatte (1854-1929), and receive episcopal consecration from him; but we will return to that at a later point.

Returning to the 1895 election of Tau Synésius, this occurred at the oratory of Lady Caithness, where Doinel first had his visions some years prior. The Duchess would die later that year, as would Monseigneur Chatel of the Église Johannite. It has been stated that the 1895 Synod included the incorporation of the lineage of Fabre-Palaprat's church from Mgr. Mauviel and Mgr. Chatel. Since bishop Mauviel had died some 80 years prior, I think we can assume that he did not personally transmit this lineage. Likewise, Mgr. Chatel had died in 1857. Whatever the source, if that transmission occurred at that time, then the Gnostic Church under Synésius had a valid apostolic succession; although they may not have realized it at the time, especially due to the Johannite Church's insistence upon the contrived Templar succession.

1895 is also the year that the Pistis Sophia was first translated into French. This becomes an important document in establishing a firm doctrine for the Church. Under Doinel, the Church had been more oriented toward a pseudo-Catharism than a true Gnosticism. This re-organization was accomplished with the help of

Tau Sophronus (Louis-Sophrone Fugairon), who wrote the "Catéchisme Expliqué de l'Église Gnostique" in 1899. This was one of many changes that the turn of the century would bring to the Gnostic Church.

The year 1899 also saw the French and Spanish Gnostic successions passed to the Haitian Lucien-François Jean-Maine. Jean- Maine was born in 1869, in Léogane, Haiti. He had received the highest Voudoo initiations in his father's temple before traveling to Europe in search of additional Gnostic and occult currents. The Voudoo of his father and grandfather had been interwoven with the remnants of the Élus-Coëns work established there by Pasqually, so it is quite natural that those initiatic currents would lead him to seek out like currents. Having been previously ordained into the subdiaconate, diaconate, and priesthood by Orfeo VI (Paul-Pierre de Marraga), he received episcopal consecration in 1899 by both Orfeo VI and Tau Synésius, thus uniting the Spanish Memphis-Misraïm / Johannite succession with that of the French Gnostic Church. Jean-Maine took the episcopal nomen of Tau Ogdoade Orfeo I. He spent the next several years working with various followers of Pascal Beverly Randolph's (1825-1875) Fraternitas Lucis Hermetica in France. The Jean-Maine line of succession will be of the utmost importance in transmitting the Gnostic and Apostolic current to many of the modern-day Gnostic churches, including our own Apostolic Church of the Pleroma.

Pascal Beverly Randolph

New Alliances and the Spread of the Gnostic Church: 1900s-1920s

As we progress along our time-line into the 20th century, we find that Jean Bricaud (1881-1934) is consecrated by Tau Synésius in 1901 as Tau Johannes, Bishop of Lyon. Two years later, in 1903, the year of Doinel's death, Bricaud receives the Martinist S::: I::: degree. Bricaud, who had studied for a time in the Seminary of the Roman Catholic Church, had also worked with Vintras' "Work of Mercy" and "Church of Carmel" as well as Palaprat's Église Johannite.

In 1906, Synésius drafted a Constitution and Bylaws for his reformed Église Gnostique. It seems, however, that not everybody was entirely happy with the changes instituted by Synésius. For instance, he never received Martinist initiation, nor does it seem that he ever desired it; therefore, the Gnostic Church, under his direction, no longer enjoyed the close relationship with Martinism it had under Doinel. Needless to say, this did not set well with those who held to the original principles laid out in the Decrees of 1893; especially the ones having to do with the special connection existing between Martinism and the Gnostic Church. The result was that Bricaud, with the assistance of Papus and Fugairon (who had written the 1899 Catéchisme) founded his own branch, the Église Catholique Gnostique, in 1907. According to Le Forestier in Occultism in France in the 19th and 20th centuries: L'Église Gnostique, "Bricaud has the idea to invite the Primates of the various Churches to a General Conference at Lyon. At what was then called the Council of Lyon of 1907, participated Sophronius, to be sure, the Primate of Russia, the Cathar primate of the United States (His Grace B. Clemens who was at the same time Primate of the Église Johannite), Mgr. Breton (1822-1908), Pontiff of Prudence of the Carmel Eliaque. Vincenzo Soro, great admirer of Bricaud and Italian representative of his Church, said the 'His Grace Synésius (Fabre des Essarts) did not respond' to the invitation." The new Catholic Gnostic Church of Bricaud, Papus, and Tau Sophronus, incorporated successions from Palaprat's Johannite Church via Bernard Clement, and Vintras' Carmelite Church via Marius Breton and Edouard Souleilon, two of the "Pontiffs" consecrated by Vintras himself. In 1908, Bricaud was elected Patriarch of the new Church, and adopted the new episcopal nomen, Tau Jean II.

The momentum created by the intense spiritual activities of those couple of years culminated in a very important "Congress Maçonnique Spiritualiste" organized by Papus and his secretary, an influential Martinist of the time, Victor Blanchard. Some of the visitors, participants, and Orders represented at the Congress: Charles Henri Detre (Teder), René Guénon (Tau Palingenius), Theodor Reuss (co-institutor of the Ordo Templi Orientis, which was in essence a condensation of the Memphis-Misraïm Rite), Edgardo Frosisi (of the Italian M-M), Henri Durville (representing Péladan and his Rose+Croix Order), Albert Jounet, Arnoldo Krumm-Heller, and several others. Many Masonic and esoteric Orders and Rites were represented at the Congress, including (in addition to what has already been mentioned) Le Droit Humain (who hosted the Congress), the Swedenborgian Rite, various Masonic Grand Lodges from across Europe, the Sons of Ismael (Arabic Masonry), and of course, the Ordre Martiniste and the Ordre Kabbalistique de la Rose+Croix.

Supplement: A Brief History of the Gnostic Church

The Congress was intended to create an "International Esoteric Federation," which it did not really accomplish. But, many important connections were made, and there were a number of significant events. One interesting occurrence was that Bricaud changed the name of his church from l'Église Catholique Gnostique to l'Église Gnostique Universelle. Some of the other events, though, were more substantive. For instance, among the many lecturers was Fabre des Essarts, Tau Synésius, who reasserted his position as the sole Patriarch of the Gnostic Church, and denounced Bricaud's church as "a schism and a heresy." One can imagine that the tension in the room must have been palpable. Although Synésius' church had been fairly radically modified, in comparison to the Church under Doinel, Bricaud's and Papus' EGU became the first real break (in France) from the Patriarchal authority. That is, although Synésius' EG looked very different from Doinel's EG, Synésius was, nevertheless, Doinel's elected successor. The EGU, therefore, represents a truly new and unique Gnostic Church; carrying the episcopal succession of the EG, but in no way perpetuating its authority. This should be remembered when evaluating any claims of a direct Primatial or Patriarchal line from Doinel to Bricaud to the present. In other words, from at least 1907 onward (actually much earlier when considering the Spanish, Haitian, and other branches), the "Gnostic Church" has not referred to a single Church, but rather a collection of independent and autocephalous churches which together represent the modern Gnostic Tradition. Sometimes this tradition is called the "French Gnostic Church" but, in fact, is an assembly of bodies that have emerged from a common source. Unfortunately, this simple principle has been misunderstood, ignored, or even willfully suppressed by some who have wished to subtly twist historical fact into a scenario that supports their claims to authority and power, to the exclusion of others equally qualified. Alas, such is the nature of the human animal, which threatens all works of the Spirit.

Another important event of the 1908 Congress was the exchange of authorities between Papus and Theodor Reuss (Peregrinus). Papus received a charter for a Supreme Grand Council of France for the Ancient and Primitive Rite of Memphis-Misraïm (33°-90°-96°), authorized by Reuss and John Yarker, as well as X0 authorization for Reuss' OTO. In return, Papus grants Reuss episcopal and primatial authority in Bricaud's Gnostic Church. Based upon this episcopal authority, Reuss forms his own German branch, Gnostiche Katholische Kirche, which he would incorporate into the OTO.

Reuss had also issued an OTO charter to Dr. Arnoldo Krumm-Heller at the '08 Congress. Krumm-Heller also received Martinist initiation from Papus, and was associated with the Hermetic Brotherhood of Luxor, Memphis-Misraïm, and other traditional orders and societies, including the Theosophical Society, into which he had been personally initiated by Henry Steel Olcott in 1897. Dr. Krumm-Heller, under the authority of Papus and Reuss, spread Martinism, Memphis-Misraïm, the OTO, and later, the Gnostic Church and his own Fraternitas Rosicruciana Antiqua, throughout South America and the Spanish and Portuguese-speaking world. His organizations still have many thriving branches throughout South America.

George Lagrèze, who had received Martinist initiation from Teder in 1906, also received a Memphis-Misraïm charter from Yarker in 1909. This is the same year that the American, Harvey Spencer Lewis, claims to have founded the Ancient Mystical Order Rosæ Crucis; though it would be several years before the Order would gain recognition by the European Orders. Although Lewis claimed to have received initiation in Toulouse in this year, the story probably belongs more to the realm of myth than of historical fact. He could also have been referring to some sort of astral initiation, or psychic attunement, which would not have been an unusual claim for the period.

It is said that Papus met with the Haitian, Lucien-François Jean-Maine (who, as previously stated, had been consecrated as a bishop by Tau Synésius and P-P de Marraga in 1899) in 1910, and conferred upon him the X0 of Reuss' OTO "for Haiti and the French West Indies." Reciprocally, Jean-Maine conferred additional high degrees upon Papus of de Marraga's Spanish Memphis-Misraïm rite. It is possible that they also may have exchanged Martinist initiation. The transmission of these rites and successions to Jean-Maine is significant, not only because of their increased accessibility to people of African descent, but in their preservation and eventual transmission to the United States; a topic to which we shall return later.

The next major advancement within the French Gnostic Tradition would come in 1913, when Jean Bricaud would receive an additional episcopal consecration from Louis-Marie-François Giraud (1876-1951). This consecration brings the "Vilatte Succession" into the Gnostic Church. Joseph-Rene Vilatte (1854-1929) had received episcopal consecration as Mar Timotheos in 1892 by Mar Julius I (Antonio Francis Xavier Alvares), Bishop of the Syrian Jacobite Orthodox Church, and Metropolitan of the Independent Catholic Church of Ceylon, Goa, and India. Vilatte makes the acquaintance of several prominent clerics and occultists of the day and is well-known and respected throughout France and America. We have already mentioned that Abbe Julio had become associated with Vilatte. In 1904, Abbe Julio is consecrated as a bishop by Mgr. Paolo Miraglia Gulatti, who had himself been consecrated by Vilatte in 1900. It is Abbe Julio who passes the Apostolic Succession to Giraud, Bricaud's consecrator. This consecration was significant in that it brought a recognized, valid Apostolic Succession into the EGU. This is also further evidence that the French Gnostics at the time were unaware that they already held a valid succession through Palaprat's Johannite Church. In any case, this succession, and the Church's official relationship to the Martinist Order, would definitively unite the inner, secret, initiatic Tradition with the exoteric, sacramental Tradition as preserved through the Apostolic Succession of bishops. Thus, the Initiatic and Sacramental are functioning within the same church, a Gnostic Church, for the first time since the suppression of the ancient Gnostics; except perhaps in isolated pockets of activity throughout history.

But, just as if the Demiurge himself had reached out to take vengeance upon those who would dare to restore the Light of Gnosis, the first World War broke out, disrupting activities and taking the life of the Very illustrious Papus. Dr. Encausse was serving as a medical doctor on the front lines in the French Army. He died in 1916 after contracting tuberculosis in the trenches. There were other deaths to follow during the years of the War (1914-1918). And, while many of them may not be obviously attributable to the War, not all effects have immediately apparent causes. Some of the others to die during this period include: Tau Synésius (1917), Teder (1918), and Josephin Péladan (1918).

With the death of Papus, Teder (Charles Detre) would succeed him, briefly, as Grand Master of the Ordre Martiniste (with Victor Blanchard as Deputy Grand Master), as well as the French sections of Memphis-Misraïm and the OTO. Lucien-François Jean-Maine continues his own branch of the French OTO which, upon his return to Haiti in 1921, he will transform into the Ordo Templi Orientis Antiqua (OTOA); which expands the OTO into a system of XVI° and is incorporated within Jean-Maine's M-M rite and his Ecclesia Gnostica Spiritualis. However, before returning to Haiti, he travels once more from France to Spain in order to consecrate his European successor, Martin Ortiere de Sanchez y Marraga as Tau Ogdoade Orfeo II on December 27, 1918. Sanchez y Marraga is then appointed Primate of the Ecclesia Gnostica Spiritualis for Spain in 1921. In 1922 Jean-Maine created an order of esoteric Voudoo, "La Couleuvre Noire" (Cult of the Black Snake). These various currents, the OTOA, the EGS, La Couleuvre Noire, and the Fraternitas Lucis Hermetica, were organized within the Memphis-Misraïm Rite and, collectively, are commonly referred to as the Franco-Haitian Gnostic Tradition. And the descendants of this Tradition are often referred to as "Jean-Maine bishops." While in Haiti, Jean-Maine married (1921) and had a son in 1924, Hector-François Jean-Maine.

Returning now to the activities in France, when Fabre des Éssarts (Tau Synésius) dies in 1917, it seems that he was succeeded (perhaps reluctantly) by Tau Théophane (Léon Champrenaud). The details are murky, and there are conflicting accounts, but it looks as if Theophane held the patriarchate of the Église Gnostique de France until 1921, when Patrice Genty Tau Basilide) took up the mantle until 1926, when the Église Gnostique de France was put permanently to rest. At some point, though, it seems that Chamuel (Lucien Mauchel – Tau Bardesanes), one of Doinel's original bishops, instituted an Église Gnostique Universelle that was distinct from Bricaud's church of the same name.

Teder dies in 1918, just two years after succeeding Papus as Grand master of the Martinist Order. Teder is succeeded by Jean Bricaud (who is already Patriarch of the EGU) as Grand Master of the Martinist Order, Memphis-Misraïm, and the OTO for France. Theodor Reuss shows his approval of this succession by making Bricaud "Delegate General" of the OTO for France, and issuing him a warrant for a French Sovereign Sanctuary of Memphis-Misraïm. Bricaud reciprocates by naming Reuss "Gnostic Legate for Switzerland." Also, this year, Bricaud consecrates Blanchard as Tau Targelius.

After the death of Péladan in 1918, his Ordre de la Rose+Croix Catholique fractured into several branches. One of the more prominent branches, headquartered in Belgium, was carried on by Emile Dantinne (1884-1969). Dantinne, also known as Sâr Hieronymus, reorganized the Rose+Croix Order into l'Ordre de la Rose+Croix Universelle, l'Ordre de la Rose+Croix Universitaire, and l'Ordre de la Rose+Croix Interieur. R+C Universelle and R+C Universitaire served essentially the same purpose, and were each composed of 9 degrees, but the R+C Universitaire was reserved for only those who had received University training. The R+C Interieur served as an inner Order of 4 degrees. These additional developments were implemented in 1923.

The FUDOSI Years: 1930s-1940s

The next major developments occurred in 1934; but there are a number of meaningful events in the interim that should probably be mentioned. In America, H. Spencer Lewis' Ancient Mystical Order Rosæ Crucis (AMORC) was gaining some popularity domestically and internationally, but still lacked the sort of "validation" from the European Orders that Lewis desired. In the early '20s he tried to work with Theodor Reuss (who had issued Lewis an honorary VII° OTO charter) and Heinrich Traenker (1880-1956), who had worked with Reuss, Krumm-Heller, and Karl Germer, among others. Neither of these contacts seemed to pan out for Lewis. But Lewis would soon find the European contacts he so earnestly sought.

Lewis' Rosicrucian contacts in Europe were initially facilitated by the Belgian Freemason and historian, François "Frans" Wittemans. Through Wittemans, Lewis made contact with Jean Mallinger, who was a member of the Belgian Memphis-Misraïm Rite (which had broken away from the French Obedience of Bricaud), and Emile Dantinne in 1932. Dantinne had been trying to organize a congress similar to that of 1908. Dantinne had also contacted Victor Blanchard, and the three of them - Dantinne, Lewis, and Blanchard (who was secretary of the '08 Congress) - would go on to organize a legendary collaboration known as FUDOSI. This collaboration seems to have strengthened the Belgian orders, and Belgium begins to emerge as a new hub for esoteric activity. It is in Belgium, in 1932, that Palaprat's Ordre du Temple is reorganized as the Ordo Supremus Militaris Templi Hierosolymitani, or, Sovereign Military Order of the Temple of Jerusalem (OSMTH/SMOTJ).

1934 would be an historic year for the Traditional Orders and Societies. Sadly, this is also the year of Jean Bricaud's death. The succession of Grand Master of the Martinist Order passes to Victor Blanchard, but he declines and is replaced by Constant Chevillon (1890-1944). Chevillon (Tau Harmonius) also becomes Patriarch of Bricaud's EGU, as well as inheriting the leadership of the French M-M, OTO, etc. One of the reasons Blanchard refused the Grand Mastership of the Ordre Martiniste is because he had been more or less operating his own Martinist activities independently of the Order. This is because Bricaud had led the Order away from its founding principles, requiring Masonic prerequisites, and denying full membership to women. It was not until Bricaud's death, though, that Blanchard would "officially" constitute the Ordre Martiniste et Synarchique. The OM&S, then, would be the first real branching off of the Martinist Order. However, the practice of "Free Initiators" ensured that there were many practicing Martinists that may have operated outside the bounds of any Lodge or official Order. And of course there were the many Russian Martinists, whose practices were largely isolated from Western Europe, and developed along slightly different lines.

In Belgium, 1934 would see the realization of the Fédération Universelle des Ordres et Sociétés Initiatiques, or Federatio Universalis Dirigens Ordines Societatesque Initiationis. The first FUDOSI convention occurred in Brussels, Belgium from August 8 through August 16, 1934. The Federation was headed by 3 "Imperators": Sâr Hieronymus (Emile Dantinne); Sâr Alden (H. Spencer Lewis); and Sâr Yesir (Victor Blanchard). The Orders and Societies represented at the 1934 convention are as follows:

1. Ordre de la Rose+Croix Universelle (Sâr Hieronymus Dantinne)
2. Ordre de la Rose+Croix Universitaire (Sâr Hieronymus Dantinne)
3. Ordre Kabbalistique de la Rose+Croix (Sâr Yesir - Blanchard; representing Lucien Mauchel)
4. Confrerie des Freres Illumines de la Rose+Croix (Sâr Artemis - August Reichel)
5. AMORC (Sâr Alden - Lewis; Sâr Emmanuel - Many Cihlar; Sâr Johannes - Hans Grueter)
6. Militia Crucifera Evangelica (Sâr Alden -Lewis)
7. Ordre R+C de Suisse - AMORC Switzerland (Sâr Artemis - Reichel)
8. Société Alchimique de France (Sâr Artemis - Reichel)
9. Ordre des Samaratains Inconnu (Sâr Artemis - Reichel)
10. Ordre Hermetiste Tetramegiste et Mystique / Ordre Pythagoricien (Sâr Succus - François Soetewey; Sâr Helios)
11. Ordre Martiniste et Synarchique (Sâr Yesir - Blanchard)
12. Fraternité des Polaires (Sâr Yesir - Blanchard)
13. Ordre Maçonnique Oriental de Memphis-Misraïm - Stricte Observance (Sâr Iohannes - Grueter; Sâr Ludovicus – Luis Fitau)
14. Co-Masonic Order of Memphis-Misraïm (Sâr Laya; Sâr Fulgur - Maurice de Seck)
15. Église Gnostique Universelle (Tau Targelius - Blanchard, representing Tau Bardesanes - Lucien Mauchel)

There are many interesting stories and facts concerning the various Orders and Societies of the FUDOSI. However, we shall not get bogged down with too many of the finer details, which can be easily discovered by the interested student in many books, documents, and internet sites. We only want to examine some of the major events that would significantly impact the future of the Gnostic Church and its related initiatic movements. It is remarkable that so many Orders were able to come together in fraternal union. Blanchard, who was Secretary to the 1908 Congress in Paris, must surely have seen the FUDOSI as the realization of the dream set forth by Papus years prior. One of the down sides of the whole thing, though, was that in declaring the FUDOSI members "the authentic Initiatic Orders and Societies," every other Traditional Order must therefore be *inauthentic*.

Émile Dantinne

There were two individuals who were particularly outraged. The first, as one might expect, was Constant Chevillon who, as stated before, was Bricaud's successor to the French Orders. From Chevillon's perspective, the FUDOSI members were undoubtedly seen as apostates. Memphis-Misraïm, Martinism, and the Gnostic Church had all formed "schismatic" branches which had all united in Belgium to claim the initiatic throne of authenticity. One may well imagine that Chevillon must have been livid. The second individual to whom I have referred is the American, Reuben Swinburne Clymer (1878-1966). Clymer was an American Martinist S∴ I∴ (though he never seems to have affiliated with the Martinist Order) who founded the Fraternitas Rosæ Crucis, which he claimed was a perpetuation of P.B. Randolph's "Brotherhood of Eulis." Clymer and Lewis had been bitter rivals since the '20s, each claiming that the other was a fraud; a situation that unfortunately has been all too common within fraternities of "enlightenment."

Clymer and Chevillon began working together toward the development of an organization to rival the FUDOSI. With the help of August Reichel (Sâr Artemis), who left the FUDOSI after the first convention, and others, such an organization came into being as the Federation Universelle des Ordres, Sociétés et Fraternités des Initiés, or FUDOFSI. The first (and only) meeting of the FUDOFSI occurred in 1939 in Paris. In addition to those individuals already mentioned, other members present included: Charles-Henri Dupont (1877-1961); Raoul Fructus (who had been a member of FUDOSI); Camille Savoire (famous Freemason and head of the Rite Écossais Rectifié, or Scottish Rectified Rite); Alfred Sharp; Count Jean de Czarnomsky; Henri Dubois; Antoine Fayolle; Hans Rudolph Hilfiker-Dunn (Swiss OTO); Arnoldo Krumm-Heller (Fraternitas Rosicruciana Antiqua); and others. In all, the following Orders were represented:

1. Église Gnostique Universelle
2. Ordre des Chevaliers Maçons Élus-Coëns de l'Univers
3. Ordre Martiniste-Martinèsist de Lyon (as Chevillon's reformed Martinist Order was now known)
4. The Ancient and Primitive Rite of Memphis-Misraïm
5. Ordre du Saint Graal
6. Ordo Templi Orientis (French and Swiss sections)
7. Fraternitas Rosicruciana Antiqua
8. Fraternitas Rosa: Crucis
9. Ordre Kabbalistique de la Rose+Croix Gnostique
10. Rite Écossais Rectifié
11. Confrèrie des Freres Illuminés de la Rose+Croix

The year 1939 saw other rivalries as well. Apparently, Victor Blanchard had had some sort of vision, and informed his fellow FUDOSI brethren that he had been designated the "Universal Grand Master of the Rose+Croix and all of the Initiatic Orders of the World." This outrageous claim earned him expulsion from the FUDOSI, and several OM&S members defected as well, including George Lagrèze (Sâr Mikael). Lagrèze associated himself with another Martinist Order that had been founded in 1931 by Victor-Emile Michelet and Augustin Chaboseau (co-founder, with Papus of the original Ordre Martiniste), the Ordre Martiniste Traditionnel. The OMT had been founded by those who accepted neither Chevillon's Ordre Martiniste-Martineziste de Lyon, nor Blanchard's Ordre Martiniste et Synarchique. So, when Blanchard was expelled from FUDOSI, he was replaced as Imperator by Augustin Chaboseau, and the OM&S was replaced by the OMT.

George Bogé de Lagrèze

Shortly before the '39 convention, Imperator H. Spencer Lewis dies. His son, Ralph M. Lewis, replaces him as Imperator of AMORC. At the FUDOSI convention, he is also installed as an Imperator of FUDOSI to replace his late father. Emile Dantinne remained as the only original Imperator of FUDOSI. At this time, Ralph Lewis, who had already received Martinist Initiation in the OM&S in 1936 by Blanchard, received as well the S:::I::: Initiateur of l'Ordre Martiniste Traditionnel from Lagrèze, under the authority of Chaboseau. Lewis receives a charter authorizing him as "Sovereign Delegate and regional Grand Master of the OMT for the United States." In the US, the OMT is known as the Traditional Martinist Order (TMO), and functions under the direction of AMORC.

The Spiritual warfare waging among the occult societies has its parallel on the geopolitical scene. The very month of the '39 conference (September), Germany invades Poland and the War is in full swing. The Second World War soon spreads across Europe, driving the esoteric Orders, Societies, and Churches underground. Mussolini's ban on Freemasonry, and Hitler's complete intolerance of all esoteric and fraternal Orders and Societies, would bring scrutiny, imprisonment, and even death upon many prominent occultists. Several FUDOSI dignitaries died during the War, and Constant Chevillon was brutally murdered on March 23, 1944, by French Nazi sympathizers. The Gestapo did not seem to discriminate between the "authentic" or "inauthentic" Orders and Societies.

Post-War Reconstruction and the Emergence of the American Gnostic Churches

With the death of Chevillon, the group of "Lyon" organizations is left in relative chaos. Charles-Henri Dupont succeeded Chevillon as Grand Master of the OM de Lyon; and M-M was carried on by George Lagrèze (who invoked the rights of his 1909 charter from John Yarker) and Camille Savoire (of the Scottish Rectified Rite). Although Lagrèze had been a rival of Chevillon throughout the 1930s, he was now working closely with Chevillon's people in an attempt to repair some of the damage caused by Nazi occupation. Perhaps the War put things into a different perspective; perhaps the petty squabbles of years past didn't seem quite so threatening.

Lagrèze had conferred the S∴ I∴ Degree on Robert Ambelain in December, 1940, and made him a Delegate of the M-M Rite (95°) after Chevillon's death. Ambelain had been a close friend of Chevillon. So, the fact that he was working closely with Lagrèze, who was still a FUDOSI member, I think is very telling of the spirit of fraternal cooperation inherent in Ambelain's character. Ambelain became, through the M-M rite, and, as we shall see a bit later, the Gnostic Church and Martinist Order, a great force for the unifying of disparate branches of the French esoteric tradition.

The matter of Chevillon's EGU is a much more messy matter. The fact is, there was no clear successor. Chevillon had not appointed a successor, and there were no other bishops in his church at the time. Some sources suggest that Rene Chambellant succeeded Chevillon in 1945 (when the War ended), who then passed the Patriarchate to Dupont in 1948. It is unclear, though, whether or not (or if so, when) Chambellant was ever consecrated as a bishop. Though it appears that he may have been consecrated by Edouard Gesta of Blanchard's EGU. Another source has Antoine Fayolle as Chevillon's successor. Fayolle seems to have received consecration by a Marcel Cotte, of the original Doinel succession. This, of course, raises the question of valid apostolic succession. If Cotte's succession came from one who had received Fabré-Palaprat's Johannite succession, which seems plausible, then it is a non-issue. It is said then that Charles-Henri Dupont succeeded Fayolle. So, either way, it seems clear that Dupont, ultimately, was considered as the legitimate successor of Chevillon by 1948.

In 1945 Blanchard's EGU was still active, and he (who had been consecrated by Bricaud himself, remember, in 1917) consecrated Robert Amadou, Edouard Gesta, and Roger Ménard as Tau Eon II. Ménard, in turn, consecrates Ambelain in 1948 as Tau Jean III. Just after the dreaded War ends, the Light of Gnosis is able to peek through once more; no, not a peek, but a full ray of Holy Illumination, for it is then that 13 volumes containing over 50 Gnostic texts are discovered near Nag Hammadi, Egypt. Although it will be another 30 years before a full translation is made available to the public, it is nevertheless a hugely significant discovery - both academically and spiritually - and a symbol of Gnostic rebirth.

A year later, in 1946, Augustin Chaboseau dies, and the Grand Mastership of the OMT/TMO passes to Lagrèze. Lagrèze's reign would be short-lived, however, as he himself died just a few months later. He would be succeeded by Jean Chaboseau, Augustin's son, as Grand Master. That summer, the FUDOSI held its first convention since the onset of WWII. Apparently, the mood was still that of reconciliation, as Victor Blanchard was once again a member of FUDOSI, though he would never again become Imperator. So now the OMT and the OM&S were both present within the FUDOSI. For some reason or other, Jean Chaboseau is not recognized by the FUDOSI council as Grand Master of the OMT. This causes schisms within the OMT. Chaboseau resigns a year later, in '47, and many other members leave for other Martinist obediences. The only branch left functioning was the American TMO, operating within AMORC.

After WWII it becomes increasingly difficult to follow all of the sub-branches of the Martinist Order and the Gnostic Church. We shall not try to trace the myriad permutations, but only those which are most pertinent to the development of our own Apostolic Church of the Pleroma. Therefore, the next year that we are going to look at is 1953. In January of this year it is said that Hector-François Jean-Maine (1924-1984), son of Lucien- François Jean-Maine, is consecrated into the episcopate by his father, with Robert Ambelain (Tau Jean III) and Charles-Henri Dupont (Tau Charles-Henri) as co-consecrators; thus uniting the Bricaud/Chevillon and Chamuel/Blanchard lines with the original Doinel/Synésius line, within the Ecclesia Gnostic Spiritualis. H-F Jean- Maine takes the episcopal nomen of Tau Ogdoade Orfeo III. He also, at this time, receives Ambelain's Martinist lineage.

Victor Blanchard dies a few months later, and is succeeded as Grand Master of the OM&S by Edouard Bertholet (Sâr Alkmaion). There doesn't seem to have been a clear successor to his EGU, but after Blanchard's death, Ambelain founds his own branch: l'Église Gnostique Apostolique.

One last event of 1953 that is significant, is the consecration of the Australian Ronald Powell (Richard Duc de Palatine) by Mar Georgi.us (Hugh George de Wilmott-Newman). The Duc de Palatine forms the Pre-Nicene Gnostic Catholic Church in England. This branch will later come to the United States as the Ecclesia Gnostica, which we will address a bit further on.

Philippe Encausse

In 1958, a Federation of Martinist Orders is created to unite the bodies headed by Ambelain, Dupont, and Philippe Encausse, son of Gerard Encausse. In 1960, the Orders of the Federation merge into the Ordre Martiniste de Paris, also known as the Ordre Martiniste de Papus. Philippe Encausse is chosen to head up the newly re-formed Martinist Order, with Ambelain leading Élus-Coëns activities. Also this year, Dupont's EGU and Ambelain's EGA unite under Ambelain as the Église Gnostique Apostolique Universelle. This branch will go through further permutations, and its branches will ultimately be declared "autocephalous"; that is, independent, without a central Patriarchate.

On April 30, 1960, Lucien-François Jean-Maine dies while visiting students in Boston, Massachusetts, USA. Two years later, his son, Hector-François, is elevated to the Patriarchate of the Ecclesia Gnostica Spiritualis (EGS) by Lucien's Spanish successor, Martin Ortiere de Sanchez y Marraga (Tau Ogdoade Orfeo II). Not long after this, Hector-François takes on a young American student with a background in Martinism: Michael Paul Bertiaux. In 1963, while on a teaching consignment for the Episcopal Church of Haiti, Michael Bertiaux was consecrated as Tau Ogdoade Orfeo IV by H-F Jean-Maine, Luc Guzzotte (whose work Bertiaux would use later in his *Voudon Gnostic Workbook*), and two other Haitian Gnostics whose names he was not given. This consecration to the Gnostic episcopate occurred on August 15, at Petionville, Haiti, at about 4:00 pm. Bertiaux helps to further develop Jean-Maine's system, and is appointed heir to the Patriarchate of the EGS, as well as to the Grand Mastership of the OTOA, Memphis-Misraïm, La Couleuvre Noire, and other associated rites, such as the Monastery of the Seven Rays.

In 1967, Forest Ernest Barber and Dr. Stephan A. Hoeller are consecrated by Richard Duc de Palatine into the Pre-Nicene Catholic Church. Hoeller's American branch is known as the Ecclesia Gnostica, and still thrives (mostly in the western United States) under the Patriarchate of Tau Stephanus (Hoeller) as of the time of this writing. Dr. Hoeller has done much to bring an academic respectability to the modem Gnostic Church through his writings and lectures.

Fr. Roger St. Victor-Herard of Haiti, Apostolic Prefect of North America for the Église Gnostique Catholique Apostolique, is consecrated in 1970 as Tau Charles, Primate of the West Indies, by Willer Vital-Heme (Tau Guillaume). Vital-Heme had been consecrated in 1967 by Roger Pommery who, in turn, had been consecrated by Robert Ambelain in 1958.

During the 1970s, since Ambelain's Church had abolished the patriarchate and declared all branches "autocephalous," it seems that René Chambellant decided to "take back" the title of "Primate of the Gauls," and declare himself Patriarch of the EGA according to the Constitution of Synésius of 1906. I really don't want to spend too much time on this convoluted claim, but we shall look briefly at these puzzle pieces and attempt to untangle them a bit. First, the title of "Primate of the Gauls" as used by Synésius, referred only to the Patriarchate of the Église Gnostique (de France), whose last Patriarch, Patrice Genty (Tau Basilide) put the church "to sleep" permanently in 1926. Therefore, although there were spiritual successions from the EG (such as the Jean-Maine line, received from Synésius himself), there were no successors to the Patriarchate of this church. The only Patriarchal seat held by Chambellant was that of Bricaud's EGU, which Synésius himself declared a "schism" and a "heresy." Therefore, the Patriarchate of the EGU would in no way carry any legitimate succession of "The Primate of the Gauls" of the church of Synésius, and thus, there would be nothing to "take back." In addition, Chambellant had not held the Patriarchal seat of the EGU in decades. Back in 1960, the legitimate Patriarch of the EGU, Charles-Henri Dupont, personally authorized the absorption of the EGU into Ambelain's EGA (EGAU). So, unless the current successor of the Patriarchate were to empower Chambellant, which does not seem to have happened, there is actually nothing for him to reclaim; especially anything having to do with Synésius! We see, then, that if we look at these puzzle pieces, we realize that they are pieces of different puzzles that have been forced together in order to give the illusion of a cohesive whole. This is not to say that Chambellant's work was in any way illegitimate, only that his church was in fact a new church that drew upon the older traditions. 1bis new EGA was legally incorporated in France in April of 1982, then dissolved and reincorporated again in 1993. Chambellant died the same year without naming a successor.

Back in the United States, Michael Bertiaux received sub-conditione consecration from F.E. Barber in 1979, thus uniting the English Gnostic succession (Due de Palatine) with his own Franco-Haitian succession. A few years later, in 1984, Hector-François Jean-Maine dies. The EGS, OTOA, LCN, etc., are inherited by Bertiaux who, at the time of this writing, remains the Patriarch of the EGS, though many other activities (LCN, OTOA, etc) have been delegated to his heir-apparent, Courtney Willis (Tau Ogdoade Orfeo VIII).

1984 was also the year that another Haitian succession was introduced to the United States. The aforementioned Roger St. Victor-Herard was a Haitian expatriate living in the United States. On November 4, 1984, he consecrated Robert Cokinis, Tau Charles Harmonius II, as bishop of Wisconsin for the autocephalous EGCA. In the following January, Herard consecrates Jorge Rodriguez-Villa as Tau Johannes XIII, Primate of Columbia and Latin America. Rodriguez was the only Primate ever consecrated by Herard and thus the only successor of Herard having any claim to the Primacy of his North American Jurisdiction.. Rodriguez also received several sub-conditione consecrations from bishops such as Michael Bertiaux and Roberto de la Caridad Toca y Medina. Later that year, Herard conferred some new episcopal dignities upon bishop Cokinis, naming him "Diocesan Bishop of Bellwood, Illinois and consequently Auxilliary of the Metropolitan of Chicago, *sine nulle jure successionis*." Here is the document in full:

Eglise Gnostique Catholique Apostolique
Primatie Des Etats Unis D'Amerique Du Nord

Ecclesia Gnostica
Apostolica
U.S.A.

PRIMATIE DE L'EGLISE GNOSTIQUE APOSTOLIQUE DE L'AMERIQUE DU NORD.

Au Nom de l'Essentiel existant par SOI et en SOI, unis de coeur et d'esprit avec toutes les Intelligences qui peuplent les Saints Eons qui prient avec Nous et nous assistent Amen.

A tous ceux qui ces presentes liront, SALUT, PAIX et BENEDICTIONS APOSTOLIQUES, au Nom tres Saint du PANTOKRATOR, le KRISTOS SOTHER, Mediateur pour l'union de tous dans la splendeur du Divin Plerome Amen.

Nous, ROGER SAINT VICTOR-HERARD, in ecclesia TAU CHARLES, Eveque de Bethanie par la grace de Dieu, Metropolitain de Chicago, Illinois. Primat de l'Eglise Gnostique Catholique Apostolique Autocephale de l'Amerique du Nord, Detenteur de la Filiation Apostolique selon EVODUS, premier Patriarche de l'Eglise d'ANTIOCHE DE SYRIE, consacre par l'Apotre PIERRE, Faisons savoir a tous ceux qui ces presentes liront qu'usant de nos pouvoirs primatiaux a nous conferes par la Succession de la Cathedre Apostolique de France, Nous designons Mgr ROBERT COKINIS a la fonction d'Eveque Diocesain de BELLWOOD, ILLINOIS et par consequent AUXILIAIRE DU METROPOLITAIN DE CHICAGO, sine nulle jure successionis,

Nous demandons a nos Eveques, Pretres, Diacres, aux Membres de nos diverses Fraternites et Communautes Religieuses en communion avec l'Eglise Gnostique Catholique Apostolique de reconnaitre la position de Mgr Robert COKINIS Eveque Titulaire de SARDES, Eveque du Wisconsin en ses nouvelles attributions d'Eveque de BELLWOOD, ILLINOIS, Assistant du METROPOLITAIN DE CHICAGO, sine nulle jure successionis.

Donne de nous, sous nos Sceau et Signature en Notre Cathedre primatiale de CHICAGO, ILLINOIS, le 1er DECEMBRE MilNeuf CentQuatre Vingt Cinquieme de l'An du Seigneur.

Tau CHARLES, Primat
ROGER VICTOR-HERARD

Supplement: A Brief History of the Gnostic Church

In can be seen in the above document that toward the end, it again references "…his new attributions of Bishop of Bellwood, Illinois, Assistant of the Metropolitan of Chicago, *sine nulle jure successionis*." So, we see twice in the same document that these appointments are *"without any right of succession."* In other words, not only were his "new attributions" limited to "Bishop of Bellwood" and "Auxiliary/Assistant of the Metropolitan of Chicago," they were "without any right of succession" to those offices, much less the office of Primate. This is mentioned only because of a falsehood that has been perpetuated in recent years that would have bishop Cokinis as the Primatial successor to Herard. Now, there had been a coadjutor appointed by bishop Herard, Mgr. Gaspard Mervilus. But Mgr. resigned from the Church before Herard's death, leaving bishop Rodriguez as the highest ranking clergy. Now, some have maintained that Rodriguez's ministry was more along the Old Catholic lines than strictly Gnostic. This may be the case, but the fact remains that he was the only Primate ever consecrated by Herard, and he never renounced his Gnostic Primacy, although he did appoint a successor in bishop Valdiveso Matthews. At any rate, the case is laid out convincingly in "A Concise History of the EGCA – Primatial See of North America and Columbia" by Tau Guillaume II.

Gnosis in the 21ˢᵗ Century

The Apostolic Church of the Pleroma derives its apostolic succession from multiple sources. While its primary episcopal source is through the "Bertiaux" lineage, the ACP holds successions from Herard (via lines from Rodriguez and Cokinis), Hoeller, and virtually every other major line of both Gnostic and Orthodox Apostolic lineages due to sub-conditione consecrations of its Patriarch, Tau Phosphoros, as outlined in the Appendix G. In addition, the ACP maintains the Christian Knights of Saint-Martin as an appendant body, preserving the historical link between Martinism and the Gnostic Church; and the Order of Asiatic Architects, a fraternity of *Haut-Grade Maçonnerie* and Hermetic Initiation. The CKSM holds multiple French and Russian lineages derived principally from the lineages of the Ordre Martiniste des Chevaliers du Christ. The OAA maintains a number of charters authorizing its various degrees, though the OAA itself is independent of any other Masonic or initiatory body.

The ACP works quietly and resolutely, always striving to put quality over quantity. The ACP Is not isolationist, though. The Church is always willing to maintain fraternal relations with those who share the goal of universal regeneration and reintegration. Consequently, the ACP is in full ecclesiastical inter-communion with several Gnostic and Apostolic jurisdictions.

This paper has barely skimmed the surface of our rich and varied tradition, but hopefully it gives a glimpse of some of the ideas and movements that have persisted throughout the ages; in various places and under different names, but always maintaining a link to the Masters of the Past, and always to the Greater Glory of the Eternal, and the Benefit of Mankind.

The Folly of Peter

Anonymous

Let Sabaoth in the seventh heavenly sphere bear witness. These are the true and exact words sent from the Holy Spirit and revealed to her faithful bridegroom, a veiled prophet of the Light, concerning the folly of Peter, and the victory of the Children of the Light in their triumphant restoration of gnosis in the Body of Christ.

In the years of our Lord Jesus Christ there were those who followed him called Apostles, or messengers. They are said to have been twelve in number, but do not be fooled or misled. For there were those of the twelve who were not true messengers, and there were those not of the twelve who proclaimed His gospel clearly and truly. Among those who were called "messengers" was one Simon, called Peter because of his steadfast devotion to the Savior. Jesus loved Peter, but also pitied him for his lack of understanding; for Peter was enamored with Jesus, but was deaf in one ear, thus unable to comprehend the fullness of the Master's message.

When the Master had returned to the Eternal Aeon from which He had descended, His students would meet often to remember Him, and to partake of His Body and Blood, and to discuss the meaning of His teachings, and to prepare themselves to deliver His gospel to the world. On one such occasion, the students were gathered, as was typical, around the Savior's most beloved companion Mary. One of the students asked her, "What did the Master tell you of the last days, and the coming of the kingdom of God?"

Mary said to them, "These are the words the Savior said to me regarding these matters: 'The end is also the beginning, as the beginning is the end. The new Aeon you seek is an Eternal Aeon. It has always been, though you have not known it. The kingdom of God is without, and it is within; just as I am in the Father and He in me. Do not seek for the treasure at the end of days. Seek, rather, your beginnings in the Light of the Pleroma. In that search will you find the treasure. And in that beginning will you find the end.'"

As the Apostles paused to consider these words of the Master, Peter grew furious. The words confounded Peter because he was deaf in one ear, as a senile old man. And he was jealous of Mary and hated her because Jesus loved her, and kissed her on the mouth as an equal, while Peter received his kisses on the cheek and forehead as a child. Peter's love for the man had blinded him to the message. Peter collected himself and began formulating a plan whereby Mary would, by her own mouth, discredit herself by virtue of her being a woman. Peter rose and asked of Mary, "Sister, you, a woman, has told us of many strange and fantastic teachings of the Savior. You speak to us in riddles of beginnings and endings, but can you remind us of how it was, in the beginning, that Adam was expelled from Paradise?"

Mary frowned at hearing this, sensing immediately the trap he had laid for her. She replied to him, "Oh Peter! Have you heard nothing that Savior has said to us? You are truly as a crippled old man in his dotage! But as our Lord loved you, and took pity on you, so will I remind you of the Master's instruction. Jesus said, 'I am the Eagle and I am the Serpent. As the Tree of Knowledge is of my Mother, the Holy Spirit, so am I the Fruit of that Tree. The paradise of Eden was a false paradise of ignorance and illusion. It was I in the garden that led Eve to the Tree and induced her to partake of its Fruit, which is my Flesh, so that she might be free from the fetters of the archons and their ruler; and that she might also share the Fruit, which is my Flesh, with Adam, her companion; and that together they might turn to the original Light, the fragments of which reside within them, and guided by Sophia, be reunited into the Fullness of God and the Holy Aeons. But darkness was to fall over the minds of humans once again. That is why I have been sent to you now; to once again bring the Light of gnosis into the world, and into the hearts of men.'"

When Mary finished saying these things, a profound silence spread across the room. Peter, in his fury, denounced Mary as a liar and a whore, and a child of a whore, and strode angrily into the courtyard. A number of the men followed Peter outside, while a smaller number remained to console Mary, who was now weeping quietly into her hands. Through her tears she cried out, "Why does he speak so? Let him hate me, but he damns himself denouncing the words of the Savior. Thomas, my brother, you are called the twin. Surely Peter will listen to your wisdom about the Savior."

Thomas said to her, "Mary, my beloved sister, you know that I have recorded the words of the master that he gave to me. Of those words, our brother Peter hears only half; half of half. He hears only that which he chooses, and is convenient for him. For the rest of it, it is as if the Savior never spoke them at all. I cannot remain with him. My journey is upon another road."

Then she turned to Philip and said to him, "Philip, my brother, you loved our Lord and you have deep and profound insights into his teachings and parables. Can you bring our brother Peter to the Light of gnosis that our Master wishes for us?"

Philip looked softly and sadly into her eyes and said, "My dear sister Mary, most loved and companion, Christ came down from the Aeons bearing that Light of which you speak. He released us from our prisons, and absolved us of our sin, which is ignorance. If our brother has refastened his own shackles, then his soul is truly lost. But have faith my sister. Our Lord has chosen Peter for His own reasons, and though our brother may be in soul-ignorance, yet he has the blessings of the Master, and is the keeper of the seed of spiritual goodness. I must, therefore, leave him to succeed or fail as is the Will of God."

Mary now wept more; no longer for herself, but for the soul of Peter, and those he would lead astray. She at last looked to John, and asked him, "John, oh my brother John, most beloved of men by the Savior, what are we to do?"

John said to her, "Mary, my wise and lovely sister, our Master was not ignorant of these things. Those who Know will preach the Truth, but few have ears to hear or eyes to see. Those who do not Know will also preach. Their falsehoods will fall upon the ears of the multitudes, who also do not Know, and will be taken as truth, though it is not. For this reason, the Lord has instructed me to remain and to follow and aid Peter in all ways, and to not openly contradict the words of Peter. My testament will be heard by many, but to those who have received the seeds of gnosis, that same testament will contain a key to the mystery of salvation, invisible to the blind, but gleaming as a brilliant jewel to those who have eyes to see. I this way will the seed of gnosis follow the seed of Peter until such time as the seed of Peter is received and purified by the children of the Light, who will have received also the seed of gnosis and recognized it for what it is. And my name will come to be known as a symbol of the hidden knowledge by those who are the servants of the Light. Do not despair then Mary, for the Savior has foreseen these events, and will continue to guide the elect. Go from here now, away from Peter, and seek out those peoples and places where the Truth of the Savior may be received and flourish."

Then they each embraced and departed to do what they were each called to do. And events transpired as our Lord Jesus Christ had foreseen. Peter, and the children of Peter perverted the message of the Master in every way. That which is good, they called evil. And that which is evil, they praised as the good. The archons and their ruler, Samael, god of the blind, were upheld as the assembly of the Most High, and the True God of Light was forgotten all together. They have denied the Wisdom of the Mother, and loathed every woman. Jesus said that, "whoever has come to know the world has discovered a carcass." But the children of Peter have discovered a carcass and taken it for the living Christ. They fornicate with decay, yet they do not understand death. Death is theirs, but the wisdom of death eludes them. Their sacraments are but shadowy substitutes. They have, in word and deed, denounced Christ, the bringer of the Light of Gnosis, as Satan, the adversary.

And so the children of Peter continued from generation to generation, seeking to extinguish the Light wherever they found it. Countless atrocities did they commit in the name of our Lord. But the Light persisted and grew, as the seed of gnosis was passed down through successive generations. Then, after seemingly countless generations, the Aeon Christ came in a vision to one of His elect. In this vision, Christ instructed His faithful disciple that the time had come to gather the children of the Light and to establish the True Church, as was intended by the Savior.

The servant of the Lord set out to accomplish this monumental task, gathering Light's children from the hidden bodies dedicated to preserving the Holy Secret. This was a great blow to the archons, their ruler, and the children of Peter who served them. The Realms of Light rejoiced, and caused some of the hidden fragments of Gnostic wisdom to be unearthed. The archons then plotted and rose up, and stirred a great commotion, causing chaos and turmoil to dominate the earth for a time.

The Light was gaining strength, though, and would not be thwarted. For in the years that followed the great chaos, the seed of Peter would find the keepers of the seed of gnosis, and at long last become purified by the children of the Light. Thus was another great blow struck to the archons and their blind god. And again did the archons retaliate, and stir hatred in the hearts of men, and cause another great wave of chaos and destruction to ripple across the face of the earth, the likes of which had not been known since the days of Noah.

But again, though the destruction was great, even greater was the resolve of the children of the Light. And the Eternal Realms again rejoiced, and the earth shook in resonance with the heavenly song, and in her ecstasy delivered up body upon body of lost and hidden wisdom. In the ages to follow, the children of the Light would multiply and come to explore and know the varied and wondrous nature of the Aeons of Light. And the sacraments of the Church of the children of the Light would become perfect vehicles of the living gnosis.

Concerning the children of Peter, it would be wrong to say that they had been dealt a death blow, having never been alive. Still they feast, as vultures upon a rotting corpse, while the children of the True Seed partake of the living Flesh and Blood of our Lord and Savior Jesus Christ. And the children of Peter have lost their mastery upon the earth. Even the archons themselves, and their angels, tremble and bow to the will of the children of the Light. And Samael, the blind, curses himself in his hell. And the Lord in his Aeon laughs at the foolish, and glorifies the Father and the Mother, and so is glorified Himself.

Here ends the revelation of the folly of Peter and the victory of the children of the Light.

APPENDICES

Appendix A

The Tetragrammaton as the Tetractys of Pythagoras

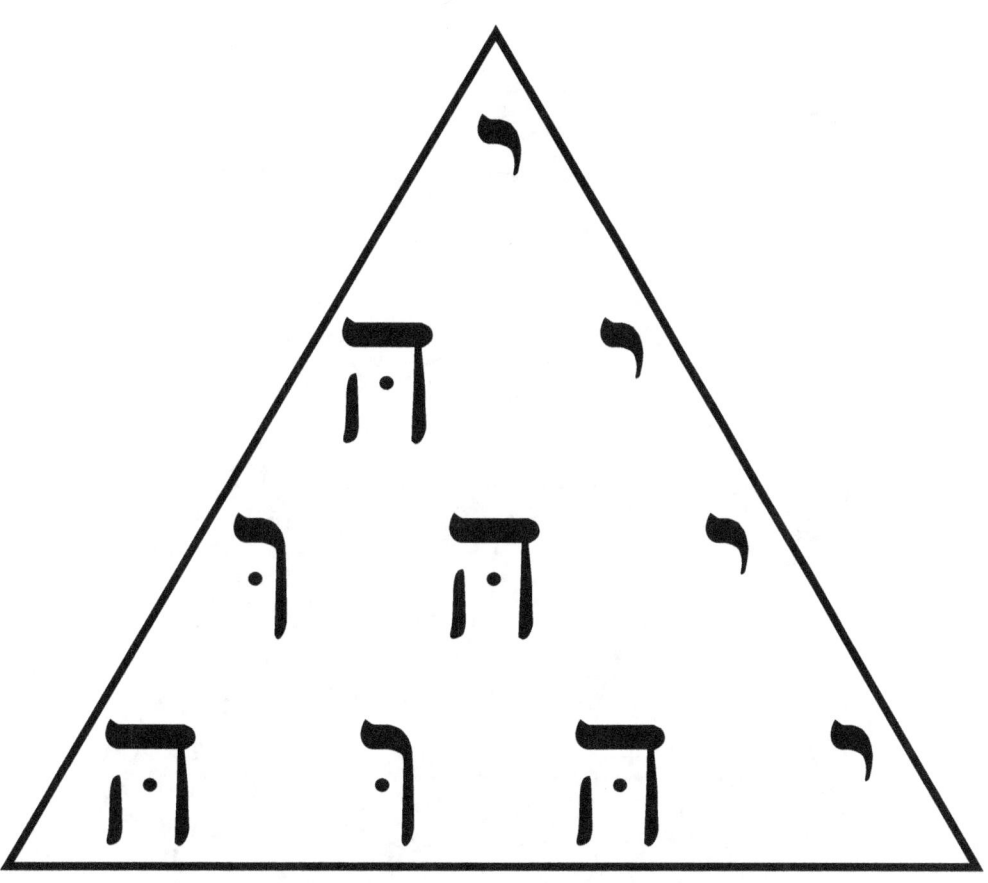

```
    I    = 10
   H I   = 15
  V H I  = 21
 H V H I = 26
           ──
           72
```

Appendices

Appendix B

Qabalistic Tree of Life

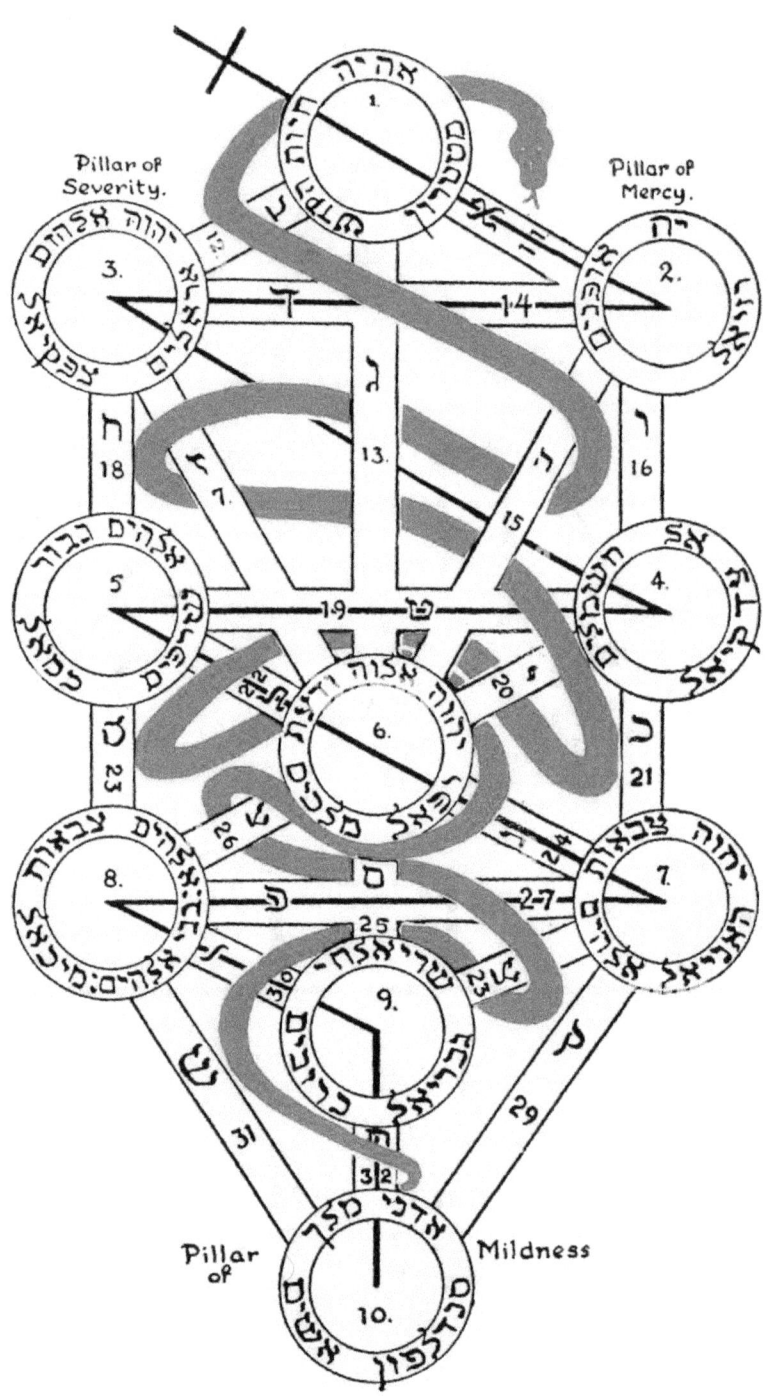

ACP Clergy Handbook

Appendix C

Key to the Sephirotic Correspondence

1. Hebrew: כתר - KThR
   Transliteration: Kether
   Meaning: Crown, corona, Equilibrating Providence
   God Name: Eheieh
   Archangel: Metatron
   Universe: Primum Mobile

2. Hebrew: חכמה - ChKMH
   Transliteration: Chokhmah
   Meaning: Wisdom, Divine Wisdom
   God Name: YOD-HE-VAV-HE (or Yah)
   Archangel: Raziel
   Universe: The Zodiac

3. Hebrew: בינה - BINH
   Transliteration: Binah
   Meaning: Understanding, Ever Active Intelligence
   God Name: YOD-HE-VAV-HE Elohim
   Archangel: Tzaphkiel
   Universe: Saturn

4. Hebrew: חסד - ChSD
   Transliteration: Chesed
   Meaning: Infinite Mercy, Magnificent Benignity
   God Name: El
   Archangel: Tzadkiel
   Universe: Jupiter

5. Hebrew גבורה - GBVRH
   Transliteration: Geburah
   Meaning: Strength, Severity, Absolute Justice
   God Name: Elohim Gibor
   Archangel: Khamael
   Universe: Mars

6. Hebrew: תפארת - ThPARTh
   Transliteration: Tiphareth
   Meaning: Ineffable Beauty
   God Name: YOD-HE-VAV-HE Eloah Va Da'ath
   Archangel: Raphael
   Universe: Sun

7. Hebrew: נצח - NTzCh
   Transliteration: Netzach
   Meaning: Victory of Life over Death
   God Name: YOD-HE-VAV-HE Tzabaoth
   Archangel: Haniel
   Universe: Venus

8. Hebrew: הוד - HVD
   Transliteration: Hod
   Meaning: Splendor, Glory, Eternity of Being
   God Name: Elohim Tzabaoth
   Archangel: Michael
   Universe: Mercury

9. Hebrew: יסוד - ISVD
   Transliteration: Yesod
   Meaning: Foundation, Generation, Cornerstone of Stability
   God Name: Shaddai El Chai
   Archangel: Gabriel
   Universe: Moon

10. Hebrew: מלכות - MLKVTh
    Transliteration: Malkuth
    Meaning: Kingdom, Dominion, Principle of Forms
    God Name: Adonai Melekh
    Archangel: Sandalphon
    Universe: Elements

Appendix D

Hebrew Letter Values and Correspondences

Tree of Life	Hebrew	Transliteration	Value	Name	Meaning
11	א	A	1	Aleph	Ox / Plow
12	ב	B	2	Beth	House
13	ג	G	3	Gimel	Camel
14	ד	D	4	Daleth	Door
15	ה	H	5	He	Window
16	ו	V	6	Vav	Peg / Nail
17	ז	Z	7	Zain	Sword / Weapon
18	ח	Ch	8	Cheth	Fence / Wall
19	ט	T	9	Teth	Coild Serpent
20	י	I, Y	10	Yod	Right Hand / Fist
21	כ	K	20	Kaph	Left hand / Palm
22	ל	L	30	Lamed	Ox goad / Prod
23	מ	M	40	Mem	Water
24	נ	N	50	Nun	Fish / Sea Creature
25	ס	S	60	Samekh	Ouroboros
26	ע	O	70	Ayin	Eye / Face
27	פ	P	80	Pe	Mouth / Tongue
28	צ	Tz	90	Tzaddi	Fishhook
29	ק	Q	100	Qoph	Back of Head
30	ר	R	200	Resh	Head / Face
31	ש	Sh	300	Shin	Tooth / Fang
32	ת	Th	400	Tav	Sign of Cross
	ך	K (final)	500	Kaph final	
	ם	M (final)	600	Mem final	
	ן	N (final)	700	Nun final	
	ף	P (final)	800	Pe final	
	ץ	Tz (final)	900	Tzaddi final	

Appendix E

Greek Letter Values

Greek	Trans.	Value	Name
Α α	A	1	Alpha
Β β	B	2	Beta
Γ γ	G	3	Gamma
Δ δ	D	4	Delta
Ε ε	E	5	Epsilon
Ϝ ϝ	(archaic / not in use)	6	Digamma
Ζ ζ	Z	7	Zeta
Η η	Ē	8	Eta
Θ θ	Th	9	Theta
Ι ι	I	10	Iota
Κ κ	K	20	Kappa
Λ λ	L	30	Lamda
Μ μ	M	40	Mu
Ν ν	N	50	Nu
Ξ ξ	X	60	Xi
Ο ο	O	70	Omicron
Π π	P	80	Pi
Ϙ ϙ	(archaic / not in use)	90	Qoppa
Ρ ρ	R	100	Rho
Σ σ ς	S	200	Sigma
Τ τ	T	300	Tau
Υ υ	U	400	Upsilon
Φ φ	Ph	500	Phi
Χ χ	Ch	600	Chi
Ψ ψ	Ps	700	Psi
Ω ω	Ō	800	Omega

Appendix F

The Chakras

Chakra	Position in Body	Planet	Alchemical Metal
Muladhara	Base of Spine	Saturn	Lead
Svadhisthana	Genitals	Mars	Iron
Manipura	Navel/ Solar Plexus	Jupiter	Tin
Anahata	Chest / Heart (Alt.)	Sun (Mercury)	Gold (Mercury)
Vishuddha	Throat	Venus	Copper
Ajna	Forehead / Brow	Moon	Silver
Sahasrara	Crown of Head (Alt.)	Mercury (Sun)	Mercury (Gold)

Appendices

Appendix G

Tables of Apostolic Succession

Among these Tables could be shown dozens, if not hundreds, of permutations due to various subconditione and cross consecrations. Some of these will be demonstrated at length early on in the lists, but may be omitted if they would be repeated further on. Bishops often hold successions from multiple Apostolic sources, and often several lines within each of the Apostolic lineages. For example, you will see that Tau Phosphoros holds successions from St. Peter, St. Andrew, St. John, and so on. And within the Petrine succession he holds lines from Antioch, Roman Catholic, Anglican, etc. And within the Antiochian succession his lines descend from more than a dozen sources, and this is not even a complete accounting. To give a complete rendering of the extant lines would require a volume larger than this *Clergy Handbook*, and would be needlessly redundant. A fair amount of redundancy has been preserved within these Tables for the benefit of the ecclesiastical researcher, but the Tables presented here cannot be considered anywhere near to complete. Note too that within each Apostolic line the Tables are given chronologically, so that all of the lines that come through William Behun and Martin Jacobs are listed first, followed by those from James Foster, and finally those from Valdiveso Matthews, which occurred on 27 April, 2002; 22 December, 2002, and 22 March, 2003 respectively. We would also mention that this Appendix has been augmented from that given in the 3rd edition. Several typos have likewise been corrected, as well as some corrections provided by bishop Bertiaux and from our own additional research. Perfect accuracy cannot be guaranteed, since at times different respected sources relate different dates, places, etc. These discrepancies have been rectified as best as possible, but further research is always needed and welcomed on this topic.

Antiochian-Jacobite Succession from St. Peter:

1. Peter
2. Evodus 40
3. Ignatius I 43
4. Aaron 123
5. Cornelius 123
6. Eodos 142
7. Theophilus 157
8. Maximinus 171
9. Seraphim 179
10. Astlediaes 189
11. Philip 201
12. Sebinus 219
13. Babylos 237
14. Fabius 250
15. Demetrius 251
16. Paul I 259
17. Domnus I 270
18. Timotheus 281
19. Cyrilus 281 (291?)
20. Tyrantus 296
21. Vitalius 301
22. Philognius 318
23. Eustachius 323
24. Paulinius 338
25. Philabianus 383
26. Evagrius 386
27. Phosphorius 416
28. Alexander 418
29. John I 428
30. Theodotus 431
31. Domnus II 442
32. Maximus 450
33. Accacius 454
34. Martyrius 457
35. Peter II 464
36. Philadius 500
37. Serverius 509
38. Sergius 544
39. Domnus III 547
40. Anatasius 560
41. Gregory I 564
42. Paul II 567
43. Patra 571
44. Domnus IV 586
45. Julianus 591
46. Athanasius I 595
47. John II 636
48. Theodorus I 649

49. Severus 668
50. Athanasius II 684
51. Julianus II 687
52. Elias I 709
53. Athanasius III 724
54. Evanius I 740
55. Gervasius 759
56. Joseph 790
57. Cyriacus 793
58. Dionysius I 818
59. John III 847
60. Ignatius II 877
61. Theodosius 887
62. Dionysius II 897
63. John IV 910
64. Basilius I 922
65. John V 936
66. Evanius II 954
67. Dionysius III 958
68. Abraham I 962
69. John VI 965
70. Athanasius IV
71. John VII 1004
72. Dionysius IV 1032
73. Theodorus II 1042
74. Athanasius V 1058
75. John VIII 1064
76. Basilius II 1074
77. Abdon (Abdoone) 1076
78. Dionysius V 1077
79. Evanius III 1080
80. Dionysius VI 1088
81. Athanasius VII 1091
82. John IX 1131
83. Athanasius VII 1139
84. Michael I 1167
85. Athanasius VIII 1200
86. Michael II 1207
87. John X 1208
88. Ignatius III 1223
89. Dionysius VII 1253
90. John XI 1253
91. Ignatius IV 1264
92. Philanus 1283
93. Ignatius Baruhid 1293
94. Ignatius Ismael 1333
95. Ignatius Basilius III 1366
96. Ignatius Abraham II 1382
97. Ignatius Bacalius IV 1412
98. Ignatius Behanam I 1415
99. Ignatius Kalejih 1455
100. Ignatius John XII 1483
101. Ignatius Noah 1492
102. Ignatius Jesus I 1509
103. Ignatius Jacob I 1510
104. Ignatius David I 1519
105. Ignatius Abdullah I 1520
106. Ignatius Naamathalak 1557
107. Ignatius David II 1577 (1576?)
108. Ignatius Philathus 1591
109. Ignatius Abdullah II 1597
110. Ignatius Cadhai 1598
111. Ignatius Simeon 1640
112. Ignatius Jesus II 1661 (1653?)
113. Ignatius Messiah 1661
114. Ignatius Cabeeb (or Cabeed) 1686
115. Ignatius Gervasius II 1687
116. Ignatius Isaac 1708
117. Ignatius Siccarablak 1722
118. Ignatius Gervasius III 1746
119. Ignatius Gervasius IV 1768
120. Ignatius Mathias 1781
121. Ignatius Behanam II 1810
122. Ignatius Jonas 1817
123. Ignatius Gervasius V 1818
124. Ignatius Elias II 1839
125. Ignatius Jacob II 1847
126. Mar Ignatius Peter III (Mutran Boutros ibn Salmo Mesko) 1872
127. Paulose Mar Athanasius (Kadavil Kooran) 3 Nov. 1876 (1877?)
128. Mar Julius I (Antonio Francis Xavier Alvares) 28 July 1889
129. Mar Timotheos (Joseph Rene Vilatte) 29 May 1892 or 5/25 per Ambelain)
130. Paolo Miraglia Gulotti 6 May 1900
131. Frederick E. Lloyd 19 December 1915
132. Samuel Gregory Lines 21 July 1923
133. Justin Joseph Andrew Boyle (aka Robert Raleigh / Justin II)1927 (21 December? Or August?)
134. Lowell Paul Wadle 31 August 1930
135. Herman Adrian Spruit 22 June, 1957
136. Forest Ernest G. Barber 15Jun. 1971
137. Michael Paul Bertiaux Tau Ogdoade Orfeo IV / Tau Orfeo Bardesens I) 16 June 1979
138. Geoffrey Lantz 1995
139. Louvel Delon 1997
140. William A. Behun Tau Thomas / Mar Thomas) 1998
141. Reginald M. Freeman (Tau Valentinus / Tau Phosphoros) 27 April 2002

Also via:

126. Mar Ignatius Peter III (Mutran Boutros ibn Salmo Mesko) 1872
127. Jules Raymond Ferrette (Mar Julius) 2 June 1866
128. Richard Williams Morgan (Mar Pelagius I) 6 March 1874
129. Charles Isaac Stevens (Mar

Appendices

Theophilus I) 6 March 1879
130. Leon Chechemian (Mar Leon) 1890
131. Charles Albert McLaglen (Mar Andries I) 2 November 1897
132. Herbert James Monzani Heard (Mar Jacobus II) 4 June 222
133. William Bernard Crowe (Mar Basilius Abdullah III) 13 June 1943
134. Hugh George de Willmott Newman (Mar Georgius) 10 April 1944
135. Ronald Powell (Richard Jean Chretien Duc de Palatine) 25 September 1953
136. Forest Ernest Gregory Barber 9 April 1967
137. Michael Paul Bertiaux Tau Ogdoade Orfeo IV / Tau Orfeo Bardesens I) 16 June 1979
138. Geoffrey Lantz 1995
139. Louvel Delon 1997
140. William A. Behun Tau Thomas / Mar Thomas) 1998
141. Reginald M. Freeman (Tau Valentinus / Tau Phosphoros) 27 April 2002

Also via:

130. Leon Chechemian (Mar Leon) 1890
131. James Martin (Mar Jacobus I) 1890
132. Benjamin Charles Harris 1916
133. Charles Leslie Saul (Mar Leofric) 17 November 1944
134. Thomas Tollenaar

8 January 1950
135. Joseph Marie Thiesen (Mar Justinos) 4 April 1951
136. Johann Maria Bloom Van Assendelft-Altland (Mar Joannes Maria) 24 January 1954 (or 25 January 1953 per Anson)
137. Christopher C.J. Stanley 1958
138. Francis H. Roebke 21 June 1964
139. Forest E.G. Barber 7 March 1965
140. Michael Paul Bertiaux Tau Ogdoade Orfeo IV / Tau Orfeo Bardesens I) 16 June 1979
141. Geoffrey Lantz 1995
142. Louvel Delon 1997
143. William A. Behun Tau Thomas / Mar Thomas) 1998
144. Reginald M. Freeman (Tau Valentinus / Tau Phosphoros) 27 April 2002

Also via:

131. Frederick E. Lloyd 19 December 1915
132. John Churchill Sibley 28 August 1929
133. John Sebastian Marlow Ward (Mar John) 6 October 1935
134. Hugh George de Willmott Newman (Mar Georgius) 25 August 1945
135. Ronald Powell (Richard Jean Chretien Duc de Palatine) 25 September 1953
136. Forest Ernest Gregory Barber 9 April 1967

137. Michael Paul Bertiaux Tau Ogdoade Orfeo IV / Tau Orfeo Bardesens I) 16 June 1979
138. Geoffrey Lantz 1995
139. Louvel Delon 1997
140. William A. Behun Tau Thomas / Mar Thomas) 1998
141. Reginald M. Freeman (Tau Valentinus / Tau Phosphoros) 27 April 2002

Also via:

131. Frederick E. Lloyd 19 December 1915
132. Axel Zacharias Fryxell 24 June 1924
133. Arthur Edward Leighton 17 April 1927
134. William Albert Nichols (Ignatius) 4 June 1929
135. George W. Plummer (Georgius) 8 May 1934
136. Arthur Wolfort Brooks (Mar John Emmanuel) 22 June 1934
137. Charles W. Keller (Mar Carolus) 16 September 1934
138. Hugh George de Willmott Newman (Mar Georgius) 25 August 1945
139. Ronald Powell (Richard Jean Chretien Duc de Palatine) 25 September 1953
140. Forest Ernest Gregory Barber 9 April 1967
141. Michael Paul Bertiaux Tau Ogdoade Orfeo IV / Tau Orfeo Bardesens I) 16 June 1979
142. Geoffrey Lantz 1995
143. Louvel Delon 1997

144. William A. Behun Tau Thomas / Mar Thomas) 1998
145. Reginald M. Freeman (Tau Valentinus / Tau Phosphoros) 27 April 2002

Also via:

130. Paolo Miraglia Gulotti 6 May 1900
131. William Whitebrook 27 December 1908
132. Basil Maurice Stannard 7 April 1912
133. Aloysius Stumpfl (Mar Timotheos) 27 July 1947
134. Joseph Marie Thiesen (Mar Justinos) 17 April 1949
135. Johann Maria Bloom Van Assendelft-Altland (Mar Joannes Maria) 24 January 1954 (or 25 January 1953 per Anson)
136. Christopher C.J. Stanley 1958
137. Francis H. Roebke 21 June 1964
138. Forest E.G. Barber 7 March 1965
139. Michael Paul Bertiaux Tau Ogdoade Orfeo IV / Tau Orfeo Bardesens I) 16 June 1979
140. Geoffrey Lantz 1995
141. Louvel Delon 1997
142. William A. Behun Tau Thomas / Mar Thomas) 1998
143. Reginald M. Freeman (Tau Valentinus / Tau Phosphoros) 27 April 2002

Also via:

129. Mar Timotheos (Joseph Rene Vilatte) 29 May 1892
130. Paolo Miraglia Gulotti 6 May 1900
131. Julien Houssay (Abbé Julio) 4 December 1904
132. Louis François Giraud (François) 21 June 1911
133. Jean Bricaud (Tau Jean II) 21 July 1913
134. Victor Blanchard (Tau Targelius) 5May 1918
135. Roger Menard (Tau Eon II) 7 January 1945
136. Robert Ambelain (Tau Jean III) 10 June 1946
137. Hector- François Jean-Maine (Tau Ogdoade Orfeo III) 25 January 1953
138. Michael P. Bertiaux (Tau Ogdoade Orfeo IV) 15 August 1963
139. Geoffrey Lantz 1995
140. Louvel Delon 1997
141. William Behun (Tau Thomas) 1998
142. Reginald Freeman (Tau Valentinus. Tau Phosphoros) 27 April 2002

Also via:

130. Paolo Miraglia Gulotti 6 May 1900
131 Joseph Zielonko 1908 (or 16 November 1913?)
132. Joachim Souris 2 June 1951
133. Walter M. Propheta 3 October 1964
134. Francis H. Roebke 1965
135. Forest E.G. Barber 7 March 1965

136. Michael Paul Bertiaux Tau Ogdoade Orfeo IV / Tau Orfeo Bardesens I) 16 June 1979
137. Geoffrey Lantz 1995
138. Louvel Delon 1997
139. William A. Behun Tau Thomas / Mar Thomas) 1998
140. Reginald M. Freeman (Tau Valentinus / Tau Phosphoros) 27 April 2002

Also via:

132. Louis François Giraud (François) 21 June 1911
133. Pierre Gaston Vigué 28 December 1921
134. Aloysius Stumpfl (Mar Timotheos) 3 June 1924
135. Charles Leslie Saul (Mar Leofric) 22 June 1947
136. Hugh George de Willmott Newman (Mar Georgius) 14 July 1947
137. Ronald Powell (Richard Jean Chretien Duc de Palatine) 25 September 1953
138. Forest Ernest Gregory Barber 9 April 1967
139. Michael Paul Bertiaux Tau Ogdoade Orfeo IV / Tau Orfeo Bardesens I) 16 June 1979
140. Geoffrey Lantz 1995
141. Louvel Delon 1997
142. William A. Behun Tau Thomas / Mar Thomas) 1998
143. Reginald M. Freeman (Tau Valentinus / Tau Phosphoros) 27 April 200

Appendices

Also via:

132. Louis François Giraud (François) 21 June 1911
133. Bernard-Isidore Jalbert-Ville 2 February 1930
134. Louis-Jean-Marie-Fournié 24 July 1951
135. Jean-René Malvy 12 August 1951
136. Johann Maria Bloom Van Assendelft-Altland (Mar Joannes Maria) 11 July 1954
137. Christopher C.J. Stanley 1958
138. Francis H. Roebke 21 June 1964
139. Forest E.G. Barber 7 March 1965
140. Michael Paul Bertiaux Tau Ogdoade Orfeo IV / Tau Orfeo Bardesens I) 16 June 1979
141. Geoffrey Lantz 1995
142. Louvel Delon 1997
143. William A. Behun Tau Thomas / Mar Thomas) 1998
144. Reginald M. Freeman (Tau Valentinus / Tau Phosphoros) 27 April 2002

Also via:

134. Victor Blanchard (Tau Targelius) 5 May 1918
135. Roger Menard (Tau Eon II) 7 January 1945
136. Robert Ambelain (Tau Jean III) 10 June 1946
137. Roger Pommery Tau Jean IV) 26 May 1958
138. Willer Vital-Herne (Tau Guillaume) 16 September 1967
139. Roger St. Victor-Herard (Tau Charles) 7 September 1970
140. Robert Cokinis (Tau Charles Harmonius II) 4 November 1984
141. James Foster (Tau Iohannes III) July 2002
142. Reginald Freeman (Tau Valentinus / Tau Phosphoros) 22 December 2002

Also via:

134. Victor Blanchard (Tau Targelius) 5 May 1918
135. Robert Amadou 28 January 1945
136. Nils Bertil Persson 1988
137. George Boyer 1990
138. Lewis Keizer July 12, 1993
139. Alberto La Cava (Tau Ignatius of Alexandria VII) 1995
140. Robert Cokinis (Tau Charles Harmonius II) 2000
141. James Foster (Tau Iohannes III) 2002
142. Reginald Freeman (Tau Valentinus / Tau Phosphoros) 2002

Also via:

134. Victor Blanchard (Tau Targelius) 5 May 1918
135. Robert Amadou 28 January 1945
136. Nils Bertil Persson 1988
137. Barwin 1989
138. William George Spaeth Jr. (Yuri) 1990
139. Valdiveso Matthews (Hermas Apollos / Tau Mikael III Basilides) 30 October 1998
140. Reginald Freeman (Tau Phosphoros) 22 March 2003

Also via:

132. Louis François Giraud (François) 21 June 1911
133. Constant Chevillon (Tau Harmonius) 5 January 1936
134. Arnoldo Krumm-Heller (Tau Huiracocha) 1939
135. Johannes Muller Riders
136. Roberto de la Caridad Toca y Medina 1982
137. Jorge Rodriguez-Villa (Tau Johannes XIII) 16 February 1986
138. Valdiveso Matthews (Tau Mikael III Basilides) 30 October 1999
139. Reginald Freeman (Tau Valentinus / Tau Phosphoros) 22 March 2003

Roman Succession from St. Peter (Old Catholic):

1. Peter
2. Linus 67
3. Ancletus 76
4. Clement 88
5. Evaristus 97
6. Alexander I 105
7. Sixtus I 115
8. Telesphoros 125
9. Hygimus 136
10. Pius I 140
11. Anicetus 155
12. Soter 166
13. Eleutherius 175
14. Victor I 189
15. Zephyrinus 199
16. Callistus I 217
17. Urban I 222
18. Pontian 230
19. Anterus 235
20. Fabian 236
21. Cornelius 251
22. Lucius I 253
23. Stephen I 254
24. Sixtus II 257
25. Dionysius 259
26. Felix I 269
27. Eutychian 275
28. Caius 283
29. Marcellinus 296
30. Marcellus I 308
31. Eucebius 309
32. Melchiades 311
33. Sylvester I 314
34. Marcus 336
35. Julius I 337
36. Liberius 352
37. Damasus I 366
38. Siricius 384
39. Anastasius I 399
40. Innocent I 401
41. Zosimus 417
42. Boniface I 418
43. Celestine I 422
44. Sixtus III 432
45. Leo I 440
46. Hilary 461
47. Simplicius 468
48. Felix III 483
49. Gelasius I 492
50. Anastasius II 496
51. Symmachus 498
52. Hormisdus 514
53. John I 523
54. Felix IV 526
55. Boniface II 530
56. John II 535
57. Agapitus 535
58. Sylberius 536
59. Vigilus 537
60. Pelagius I 556
61. John III 561
62. Benedict I 575
63. Pelagius II 579
64. Gregory I 590
65. Sabinianus 604
66. Boniface III 607
67. Boniface IV 608
68. Deusdedit 615
69. Boniface V 619
70. Honorius 625
71. Severinus 640
72. John IV 640
73. Theodore I 642
74. Martin I 649
75. Eugene I 654
76. Vitalian 657
77. Adeodatus II 672
78. Donus 676
79. Agatho 678
80. Leo II 682
81. Benedict II 684
82. John V 685
83. Conon 686
84. Sergius I 687
85. John VI 701
86. John VII 705
87. Sisinnius 708
88. Constantine 708
89. Gregory II 715
90. Gregory III 731
91. Zachary 741
92. Stephen II 752
93. Paul I 757
94. Stephen III 768
95. Adrian I 772
96. Leo III 795
97. Stephan IV 816
98. Paschal I 817
99. Eugene II 824
100. Valentine 827
101. Gregory IV 827
102. Sergius II 844
103. Leo IV 847
104. Benedict III 855
105. Nicholas I 858
106. Adrian II 867
107. John VIII 872
108. Marinus I 882
109. Adrian III 884
110. Stephan V 885
111. Formosus 891
112. Boniface VI
113. Steven VI 897
114. Romanus 897
115. Theodore II 897
116. John IX 898
117. Benedict IV 900
118. Leo V 903
119. Sergius III 904
120. Anastasius III 911
121. Landus 913
122. John X 914
123. Leo VI 938
124. Stephan VII 928
125. John XI 931
126. Leo VII 936

Appendices

127. Stephen VIII 939
128. Maginus II 942
129. Agapitus II 946
130. John XIII 955
131. Leo VII 963
132. Benedict V 964
133. John XIV 965
134. Benedict VI 973
135. Benedict VII 974
136. John XV 983
137. John XVI 985
138. Gregory V 996
139. Sylvester II 999
140. John XVII 1003
141. John XVIII 1004
142. Sergius IV 1009
143. Benedict VIII 1012
144. John XIX 1024
145. Benedict IX 1032
146. Sylvester III 1045
147. Benedict IX 1045
148. Gregory VI 1045
149. Clement II 1046
150. Benedict IX 1047
151. Damasus II 1048
152. Leo IX 1049
153. Victor II 1055
154. Stephan IX 1057
155. Nicholas II 1059
156. Alexander II 1061
157. Gregory VII 1073
158. Victor III 1087
159. Urban II 1088
160. Paschal II 1099
161. Gelasius II 1118
162. Callistus II 1119
163. Honorius II 1124
164. Innocent II 1130
165. Celestine II 1143
166. Lucius II 1144
167. Eugene III 1145
168. Anastasius IV 1153
169. Adrian IV 1154
170. Alexander III 1159
171. Lucius III 1181
172. Urban III 1185
173. Gregory VIII 1187
174. Clement III 1187
175. Celestine III 1191
176. Innocent III 1198
177. Honorius III 1216
178. Gregory IX 1227
179. Celestine IV 1241
180. Innocent IV 1243
181. Alexander IV 1254
182. Urban IV 1261
183. Clement IV 1265
184. Gregory X 1271
185. Innocent V 1276
186. Adrian V 1276
187. John XXI 1276
188. Nicholas III 1277
189. Martin IV 1281
190. Honorius IV 1285
191. Nicholas IV 1288
192. Celestine V 1294
193. Boniface VIII 1294
194. Benedict XI 1303
195. Clement V 1305
196. John XXII 1316
197. Benedict XII 1334
198. Clement VI 1342
199. Innocent VI 1352
200. Urban V 1362
201. Gregory XI 1370
202. Urban VI 1378
203. Boniface IX 1389
204. Innocent VII 1389
205. Gregory XII 1406
206. Martin V 1417
207. Eugene IV 1431
208. Nicholas V 1447
209. Callistus III 1455
210. Pius II 1458
211. Paul II 1464
212. Sixtus IV 1471
213. Innocent VIII 1484
214. Alexander VI 1492
215. Pius III 1503
216. Julius II 1503
217. LeoX 1513
218. Adrian VI 1522
219. Clement VII 1523
220. Paul III 1534
221. Julius III 1550
222. Marcellus II 1555
223. Paul IV 1555
224. Pius IV 1559
225. Pius V 1566
226. Gregory XIII 1572
227. Sixtus V 1585
228. Urban VII 1590
229. Gregory XIV 1590
230. Innocent IX 1591
231. Clement VIII 1592
232. Leo XI 1605
233. Paul V 1605
234. Gregory XV 1621
235. Urban VIII 1623
236. Innocent X 1644
237. Alexander VII 1655
238. Antonio Barberini 1655
239. Michael le Tellier 1668
240. Jaques Benign de Bousseut 1670
241. James Coyon de Matignon 1693
242. Dominicus Marie Varlet 1719
243. Cornelius Van Steenhoven 15 Oct. 1724
244. Johannes Van Stiphout 11 July 1745
245. Gaultherus Michael Van Niewenhuizen 7 February 1768
246. Adrian Brockman 21 June 1778
247. Johannes Jacobus Van Rhijin 5July 1787
248. Gilbertus de Jong 7 November 1805

249. Wilibrodus Van Os 24 April 1814
250. Johannes Bon 12 April 1819
251. Johannes Van Santen 13 Nov. 1825
252. Hermanus Heijkamp 17July 1864
253. Casparus Johannes Rinkel 11 Aug. 1873
254. Geraldus Gul 11 May 1892
255. Arnold Harris Matthew 28 April 1908
256. Fredrick Samuel Willoughby 28 October 1914
257. James I. Wedgewood 13 February 1916
258. Irving S. Cooper 3 July1919
259. Charles Hampton 13 September 1931
260. Herman A. Spruit 22 June 1957
261. Forest E. Barber 15 June 1971
262. Michael P. Bertiaux (Tau Ogdoade Orfeo IV) 16 June 1979
263. Geoffrey Lantz 1995
264. Louvel Delon 1997
265. William Behun (Tau Thomas) 1998
266. Reginald Freeman (Tau Phosphoros) 27 April 2002

Also via:
254. Geraldus Gul 11 May 1892
255. Jean-Marie Michael Kowalski 5 October 1909
256. Marc-Marie-Paul Fantome 4 September 1938
257. Paulus Helmut Norbert Maas 9 October 1949
258. Ephem Maria Mauro Fusi 24 May 1953
259. Clemente Alfio Sgroi Marchese 26 May 1954
260. Hugh George de Wilmott-Newman (Mar Georgius)
261. Richard Due de Palatine (Ronald Powell) 25 September 1953
262. Forest E. Barber 9 April 1967
263. Michael P. Bertiaux (Tau Ogdoade Orfeo IV) 16 June 1979
264. Geoffrey Lantz 1995
265. Louvel Delon 1997
266. William Behun (Tau Thomas) 1998
267. Reginald Freeman (Tau Valentinus / Tau Phosphoros) 27 April 2002

Also via:
254. Geraldus Gul 11 May 1892
255. Arnold Harris Mathew 28 April 1908
256. Rudolph Francis Edward St. Patrick Alphonsus Ghislain de Gramont Hamilton de Lorraine-Brabant, Prince de Landas Berghes et de Rache 29 June 1913
257. Carmel Henry Carfora 4 October 1916
258. Mather W. Sherwood 19 March 1931
259 Michael Bertiaux (N.D.)
260 Geoffrey Lantz 1995
261. Louvel Delon 1997
262. William Behun (Tau Thomas) 1998
263. Reginald Freeman (Tau Valentinus / Tau Phosphoros) 27 April 2002

Also via:
257. Carmel Henry Carfora 4 October 1916
258. Edwin Wallace Hunter 11 February 1924
259. Wallace David de Ortega Maxey 24 March 1929
260. Hugh George de Wilmott-Newman (Mar Georgius) 6 June 1946
261. Richard Due de Palatine (Ronald Powell) 25 September 1953
262. Forest E. Barber 9 April 1967
263. Michael P. Bertiaux (Tau Ogdoade Orfeo IV) 16 June 1979
264. Geoffrey Lantz 1995
265. Louvel Delon 1997
266. William Behun (Tau Thomas) 1998
267. Reginald Freeman (Tau Valentinus / Tau Phosphoros) 27 April 2002

Also via:
259. Wallace David de Ortega Maxey 24 March 1929
260. Charles Leslie Saul (Mar Leofric) 5 June 1946
261. Thomas Tollenaar 8 January 1950
262. Joseph Marie Thiesen (Mar Justinos) 4 April 1951
263. Johann Maria Bloom Van Assendelft-Altland (Mar Joannes Maria) 24 January 1954 (or 25 January 1953 per Anson)
264. Christopher C.J. Stanley 1958
265. Francis H. Roebke 21 June

Appendices

1964
266. Forest E.G. Barber 7 March 1965
267. Michael Paul Bertiaux Tau Ogdoade Orfeo IV / Tau Orfeo Bardesens I) 16 June 1979
268. Geoffrey Lantz 1995
269. Louvel Delon 1997
270. William A. Behun (Tau Thomas / Mar Thomas) 1998
271. Reginald M. Freeman (Tau Valentinus / Tau Phosphoros) 27 April 2002

Also via:

257. Carmel Henry Carfora 4 October 1916
258. Earl. Anglin James 17 June 1945
259. Grant Timothy Billet 25 December 1950
260. Christopher C.J. Stanley 1957
261. Christopher C.J. Stanley 1958
262. Francis H. Roebke 21 June 1964
263. Forest E.G. Barber 7 March 1965
264. Michael Paul Bertiaux Tau Ogdoade Orfeo IV / Tau Orfeo Bardesens I) 16 June 1979
265. Geoffrey Lantz 1995
266. Louvel Delon 1997
267. William A. Behun Tau Thomas / Mar Thomas 1998
268. Reginald M. Freeman (Tau Valentinus / Tau Phosphoros) 27 April 2002

Also via:

256. Rudolph Francis Edward St. Patrick Alphonsus Ghislain de Gramont Hamilton de Lorraine-Brabant, Prince de Landas Berghes et de Rache 29 June 1913
257. William Henry Francis Brothers 3 October 1916
258. William Montgomery Brown 24 June 1925 (assisted by Zielonko)
259. Wallace David de Ortega Maxey 21 January 1927
260. Charles Leslie Saul (Mar Leofric) 5 June 1946
261. Thomas Tollenaar 8 January 1950
262. Joseph Marie Thiesen (Mar Justinos) 4 April 1951
263. Johann Maria Bloom Van Assendelft-Altland (Mar Joannes Maria) 24 January 1954 (or 25 January 1953 per Anson)
264. Christopher C.J. Stanley 1958
265. Francis H. Roebke 21 June 1964
266. Forest E.G. Barber 7 March 1965
267. Michael Paul Bertiaux Tau Ogdoade Orfeo IV / Tau Orfeo Bardesens I) 16 June 1979
268. Geoffrey Lantz 1995
269. Louvel Delon 1997
270. William A. Behun (Tau Thomas / Mar Thomas) 1998
271. Reginald M. Freeman (Tau Valentinus / Tau

Phosphoros) 27 April 2002

Also via:

255. Arnold Harris Matthew 28 April 1908
256. Frederick Samuel Willoughby 28 October 1914
257. James Bartholomew Manks (Mar James) 9 July 1922
258. Sidney Ernest Page Needham (Mar Theodorus) 28 May 1940
259. Hugh George de Wilmott-Newman (Mar Georgius) 4 January 1945
260. Richard Due de Palatine (Ronald Powell) 25 September 1953
261. Forest E. Barber 9 April 1967
262. Michael P. Bertiaux (Tau Ogdoade Orfeo IV) 16 June 1979
263. Geoffrey Lantz 1995
264. Louvel Delon 1997
265. William Behun (Tau Thomas) 1998
266. Reginald Freeman (Tau Valentinus / Tau Phosphoros) 27 April 2002

Also via:

259. Hugh George de Wilmott-Newman (Mar Georgius) 4 January 1945
260. Charles Dennis Boltwood 6 July 1956
261. Emmett Neil Enochs 31 August 1958
262. Demetrius F.C. King 9 May 1963

263. Francis Homer Roebke 1 January 1965
264. Forest E.G. Barber 7 March 1965
267. Michael Paul Bertiaux Tau Ogdoade Orfeo IV / Tau Orfeo Bardesens I) 16 June 1979
268. Geoffrey Lantz 1995
269. Louvel Delon 1997
270. William A. Behun (Tau Thomas / Mar Thomas) 1998
271. Reginald M. Freeman (Tau Valentinus / Tau Phosphoros) 27 April 2002

Also via:
254. Geraldus Gul 11 May 1892
255. Jean-Marie Michael Kowalski 5 October 1909
256. Marc-Marie-Paul Fantome 4 September 1938
257. Paulus Helmut Norbert Maas 9 October 1949
258. Jean Prevost 9 August 1953
259. Robert Bonnet 1956
260. Patrick Truchemotte 4July 1970
261. Jaques Bersez 26 February 1985
262. Joel Duez 1 April 1985
263. Philippe Pissier 20 October 1993
264. Massimo Mantovani (Tau Sokaris) 5 June 1998
265. Phillip A. Garver (f au Vincent II) 2001
266. James Foster (Tau Iohannes III) July 2002
267. Reginald Freeman (Tau Phosphoros) 22 December 2002

Roman Catholic Succession via Scipione Cardinal Rebiba:

223. Paul IV (Gian Pietro Carafa)
224. Scipione Cardinal Rebiba 14 May 1541
225. Archbishop Santorio 3 March 1566
226. Mgr. Bemerio 7 September 1586
227. Archbishop Sanvitale 4 April 1604
228. Mgr. Judovisi 2 May 1621
229. Mgr. Gaetani 12June 1622
230. Mgr. Carpegna 7 October 1630
231. Mgr. Altieri 2 May 1666
232. Benedictus PP XIII (Pietro Francesco Vincezno Maria Orsinide Gavina) 3 Feb. 1675
233. Melchior de Polignac 19 March 1726
234. Antonius Petrus de Grammont II 11 September 1735
235. Josephus Guilemus Rink Von Baldenstein
236. Josephus Nicolaus de Montenach 1 April 1759
237. Jean Baptiste Gobd 22 March 1772
238. Antoine-Adrien Lamourette 27 March 1791
239. Jean Baptiste Royer 4 April 1791
240. Guillaume Mauviel 3 August 1800
241. Bernard Raymond Fabre-Palaprat 29 July 1810
242. Jean Machault 29 July 1810
243. François-Ferdinand Toussaint Chatel 20 February 1831
244. Michel Henri d'Adhemar 24June 1836
245. Manuel Lopez de Brion (Orfeo V) 2 February 1857
246. Paul Pierre de Marraga (Orfeo VI) 2 February 1860
247. Lucien-François Jean-Maine (Tau Ogdoade Orfeo I) 15 August 1899
248. Hector-François Jean-Maine (Tau Ogdoade Orfeo 1111) 25 January 1953
249. Michael Paul Bertiaux (Tau Ogdoade Orfeo IV) 15 August 1963
250. Geoffrey Lantz 1995
251. Louvel Delon 1997
252. William Behun (Tau Thomas) 1998
253. Reginald Freeman (Tau Valentinus / Tau Phosphoros) 27 April 2002

Also via:

241. Bernard Raymond Fabre-Palaprat 29 July 1810
242. Bernard Clement
243. Jean Bricaud (Tau Jean II)
244. Victor Blanchard (Tau Targelius) 5 May 1918
245. Robert Amadou 28January 1945
246. Nils Bertil Persson 1988
247. George Boyer (Tau Georgius de Landres) 1990

Appendices

248. Lewis Keizer 12 July 1993
249. Alberto La Cava (Tau Ignatius of Alexandria VII) 1995
250. Robert Cokinis (Tau Charles Harmonius II) 2000
251. James Foster (Tau Iohannes III) July 2002
252. Reginald Freeman (Tau Valentinus / Tau Phosphoros) 22 December 2002

Also via:

246. Nils Bertil Persson 1988
247. Barwin 1989
248. William George Spaeth Fr. (Yuri) 1990
249. Valdiveso Matthews (Hermas Apollos/ Tau Mikael III Basilides) 30 October 1998
250. Reginald Freeman (Tau Valentinus / Tau Phosphoros) 22 March 2003

Also via:

232. Benedictus PP XIII (Pietro Francesco Vincezno Maria Orsinide Gavina) 3 Feb. 1675
233. Benedictus PP XIV (Prospero Lorenzo Lambertini) 16 July 1723
234. Clement PP XIII (Carlo della Torre Rezzoni) 19 March 1743
235. Cardinal Bemardinus Giraud 15 (or 26) April 1767
236. Cardinal Alexander Matthaeus 23 February 1777
237. Cardinal Petrus Franciscus Galeffi 12 September 1819
238. Cardinal Iacobus Philippus Fransoni 8 December 1822
239. Cardinal Carolus Sacconi 8 June 1872
240. Cardinal Eduard Howard 30 June 1872
241. Cardinal Mariano Rampoolla Marchese del Tindaro 8 December 1882
242. Cardinal Joaquin Arcoverde de Albuquerque-Cavalcanti 26 October 1890
243. Archbishop Sebastiao Leme de Silbeira Cintra 4 June 1911
244. Archbishop Carlos Duarte Costa 8 December 1924
245. Luis Fernando Castillo-Mendez 3 May 1948
246. Forest Ernest Barber 30 January 1985
247. Michael P. Bertiaux (Tau Ogdoade Orfeo IV) 16 June 1979
248. Geoffrey Lantz 1995
249. Louvel Delon 1997
250. William Behun (Tau Thomas) 1998
251. Reginald Freeman (Tau Valentinus / Tau Phosphoros) 27 April 2002

Also via:

244. Archbishop Carlos Duarte Costa 8 December 1924
245. Dom Antido Vargas
246. Pedro Friere (Tau Petrus) December 17 1970
247. Fermin Vale Amesti (Tau Valentinus III)
248. Willer Vital-Herne (Tau Guillaume)
249. Roger St. Victor-Herard (Tau Charles)
250. Robert Cokinis (Tau Charles Harmonius II)
251. James Foster (Tau Iohannes III)
252. Reginald Freeman (Tau Valentinus / Tau Phosphoros)

Also via:

253. Roger St. Victor-Herard (Tau Charles)
254. Jorge Rodriguez-Villa (Tau Johannes XIII)
255. Valdiveso Matthews (Tau Mikael III Basilides)
256. Reginald Freeman (Tau Valentinus / Tau Phosphoros)

Succession from St. Peter (Anglican):

1. Nicholas I 858
2. Formosus 864
3. St. Plegmund 891
4. Althelm 909
5. Wulfhelm 914
6. Odo 927
7. St. Dunstan 957
8. St. Aelphege 984
9. Elfric 990
10. Wulfstan 1003
11. Ethelnoth 1020
12. Eadsige 1035
13. Stigand 1043
14. Siward 1058
15. Lanfranc 1070
16. Thomas 1070
17. St. Anselm 1094
18. Richard de Delmeis 1108
19. William of Corbeuil 1123
20. Henry of Blois 1129
21. St. Thomas Becket 1162
22. Roger of Cloucester 1164
23. Peter de Leia
24. Gelbert Glanville 1185
25. William of St. Mere l'Église 1199
26. Walter de Gray 1214
27. Walter Kirkham 1249
28. Henry 1255
29. Anthony Beck 1284
30. John of Halton 1292
31. Roger Northborough 1322
32. Robert Wynil 1330
33. Ralph Stratford 1340
34. William Edendon 1346
35. Simon Sudbury 1362
36. Thomas Brentingham 1370
37. Robert Braybrooke 1382
38. Roger Walden 1398
39. Henry Beaufort 1398
40. Thomas Bourchier 1435
41. John Morton 1479
42. Richard Fitzjames 1497
43. William Warham 1502
44. John Langlands 1521
45. Thomas Cranmer 1533
46. William Barlow 1536
47. Matthew Parker 1559
48. Edmuch Grindal 1559
49. John Whitgift 1577
50. Richard Bancroft 1597
51. George Abbot 1609
52. George Mantaigne 14 December 1617
53. William Laud 1621
54. Brian Duppa 1638
55. Gilbert Sheldon 1660
56. Henry Compton 1674
57. William Sancroft 1678
58. Jonathan Trelawney 1685
59. John Potter 1715
60. Thomas Herring 1738
61. Frederick Cornwallis 1750
62. John Moore 1783
63. William White 1787
64. John Henry Hopkins 1832
65. Leon Chechemian (Mar Leon)
66. Andrea Carlo MacLagen (Mar Andries) 2 November 1897
67. Herbert James Heard (Mar Jacobus II) 4 June 1943
68. William Bernard Crow (Mar Basilius Abdullah III) 13 June 1943
69. Hugh George de Wilmott-Newman (Mar Georgius) 10 April 1944
70. Wallace de Ortega Maxey (Mar David I) 8 June 1946
71. Lowell Paul Wadle (1951?)
72. Herman Adrian Spruit 22 June 1957
73. Forest E. Barber 15 June 1971
74. Michael P. Bertiaux (Tau Ogdoade Orfeo IV) 16 June 1979
75. Geoffrey Lantz 1995
76. Louvel Delon 1997
77. William Behun (Tau Thomas) 1998
78. Reginald Freeman (Tau Valentinus / Tau Phosphoros) 27 April 2002

Also via:

69. Hugh George de Wilmott-Newman (Mar Georgius) 10 April 1944
70. Richard Due de Palatine (Ronald Powell) 25 October 1953
71. Forest E. Barber 9 April 1967
72. Michael P. Bertiaux (f au Ogdoade Orfeo IV) 16 June 1979
73. Geoffrey Lantz 1995
74. Louvel Delon 1997
75. William Behun (Tau Thomas) 1998
76. Reginald Freeman (Tau Valentinus / Tau Phosphoros) 27 April 2002

Also via:

63. William White 1787
64. Thomas John Claggett 17 September 1792
65. Edward Bass 17 May 1797
66. Abraham Jarvis 18 October

Appendices

67. John Henry Hobart 29 May 1797
67. John Henry Hobart 29 May 1811
68. Henry Ustick Onderdonk 25 October 1827
69. Samuel Allen McCoskry 7 July 1836
70. William Edward McLaren 8 December 1875
71. William Montgomery Brown 24 June 1898
72. Wallace de Ortega Maxey 2 January 1927
73. Nils Bertil Persson 7 November 1986
74. Karl J. Barwin 5 August 1989
75. William George Spaeth Jr. (Yuri) 1990
76. Valdiveso Matthews (Tau Mikael III Basilides) 30 October 1998
77. Reginald Freeman (Tau Valentinus / Tau Phosphoros) 22 March 2003

Coptic Succession from St. Peter via St. Mark the Evangelist:

1. St. Mark 61
2. Inianos 64
3. Mielou 94
4. Kerdonou 107
5. Epriemou 120
6. Iostos 132
7. Oumenios 143
8. Markianos 154
9. Kalavtianos 163
10. Aghreppinios 177
11. Yulianos 189
12. Demetrios 199
13. Yaraklas 233
14. Dionesios 244
15. Maximos 270
16. Theona 282
17. Petros I 293
18. Archelaos 303
19. Alexanderos I 303
20. Athanasios I 326
21. Petros II 372
22. Timotheos I 378
23. Theophelos 384
24. Kyrillos I 412
25. Dioscoros I 443
26. Timotheos II 458
27. Petros III 480
28. Athanasios II 489
29. Yoannis I 496
30. Yoannis II 505
31. Dioscoros II 516
32. Timotheos III 519
33. Theodosios I 536
34. Petros IV 567
35. Damianos 571
36. Anastasios 606
37. Andronikos 619
38. Benjamin I 625
39. Aghatho 664
40. Joannis III 68 1
41. Isaac 689
42. Simeon I 682
43. Alexanderos II 703
44. Kosma I 728
45. Theodoros 729
46. I<hail I 743
47. Mina I 766
48. Yoannis VI 775
49. Markos II 798
50. Jacob 818
51. Simeon II 829
52. Yousab I 832
53. Khail II 849
54. Kosma II 852
55. Shenouda I 858
56. Mikhail I 869
57. Gabriel I 908
58. Kosma III 919
59. Macarios I 932
60. Theophelios 951
61. Mina II 956
62. Abraham 976
63. Philotheos 979
64. Zacharias 1004
65. Shenouda II 1032
66. Khristosolos 1047
67. Kirellos II 1078
68. Mikhail II 1092
69. Macarios II 1102
70. Gabrial II 1130
71. Mikhail III 1144
72. Yoannis V 1146
73. Markos III 1165
74. Yoannis VI 1188
75. Kirellos III 1234
76. Athanasios II 1250
77. Gabriel III 1269
78. Yoannis VII 1271
79. Theodosios III 1294
80. Yoannis VIII 1300
81. Yoannis IX 1320
82. Benjamin II 1327
83. Petros V 1340
84. Marcos IV 1350
85. Yoannis X 1369
86. Gabriel IV 1370
87. Matheos I 1378
88. Gabriel V 1409
89. Yoannis XI 1428
90. Matheos II 1453
91. Gabriel VI 1466
92. Mikhail IV 1477
93. Yoannis XII 1480
94. Yoannis XIII 1483
95. Gabriel VII 1555
96. Yoannis XIV 1573

97. Gabriel VIII 1590
98. Marcos V 1610
99. Yoannis:XV 1621
100. Matheos III 1631
101. Marcos VI 1650
102. Matheos IV 1660
103. Yoannis XVI 1676
104. Petros VI 1718
105. Joannis XVII 1727
106. Marcos VII 1745
107. Yoannis XVIII 1770
108. Marcos VIII 1797
109. Petros VII 1810
110. Kyrillos IV 1854
111. Demetrios II 1862
112. Kyrillos V 1874
113. Yoannis XIX 1929
114. Macarios III 1944
115. Yousab II 1946
116. Kyrillos VI 10 May 1959
117. Ahuna Basiliyos 28 June 1959
118. Gabre Mikael Kristos 12 July 1959
119. David William Worley 28 November 1972
120. Patrick J. Healy 20 January 1973
121. Charles Richard. McCarthy 30 April 1977
122. Charles David Luther 25 September 1977
122. Francis Jerome Joachim Ladd 9 August 1982
123. Forest Ernest Barber 2 March 1985
124. Peter Paul Brennan 14 March 1987
125. Alberto La Cava (Tau Ignatius of Alexandria VII) 1997
126. Robert M. Cokinis (Tau Charles Harmonius II) 2000
127. James Foster (Tau Johannes III) 2002
128. Reginald Freeman (Tau Valentinus / Tau Phosphoros) 2002

Also via:

125. Alberto La Cava (Tau Ignatius of Alexandria VII) 1997
126. Emanuele Coltro Guidi (Tau Sebastos Athanasius Sokaris)
127. Phillip A. Garver (Tau Vincent II)
128. Valdiveso Matthews (Tau Mikael III Basilides)
129. Reginald Freeman (Tau Valentinus / Tau Phosphoros)

Succession from St. John via Polycarp (Apostolic See of Smyrna):

1. Polycarp
2. Pothinus
3. Irenaeus
4. Zaccharius
5. Elias
6. Taustinus
7. Verus
8. Julius
9. Ptolemy
10. Vocius
11. Maximus
12. Tetradus
13. Verissimus
14. Justus
15. Albinus
16. Martin
17. Antiochus
18. Elpidius
19. Licarius
20. Eucherius I
21. Pateius
22. Lupicinius
23. Rusticu
24. Stephanus
25. Viventiolus
26. Eucherius II
27. Lupus
28. Licontius
29. Sacerdos
30. Nicetus
31. Priscus
32. Aetherius
33. Augustine
34. Laurentius
35. Mellitus
36. Justus
37. Honorius
38. Deusdedit
39. Theodore
40. Brithwald
41. Tatwine
42. Nothelm
43. Cuthbert
44. Bregwine
45. Lambrith
46. Aethelhard
47. Wulfred
48. Theogild
49. Ceolnoth
50. Ethelred
51. Wereferth
52. Athelm
53. Wulfhelm
54. Odo
55. Dunstan
56. Aelphege
57. Elfric

Appendices

58. Wulfstan
59. Ethelnoth
60. Eadsige
61. Stigand
62. Siward
63. Lanfranc
64. Thomas
65. St. Anselm
66. Richard de Delmeis
67. William of Corbeuil
68. Henry of Blois
69. St. Thomas Becket
70. Roger of Gloucester
71. Peter de Leia
72. Gilbert Glanville
73. William of St. Mere l'Eglise
74. Walter de Gray
75. Walter Kirkham
76. Henry
77. Anthony Beck
78. John of Halton
79. Roger Northborough
80. Robert Wyvil
81. Ralph Stratford
82. William Edenfon
83. Simon Sudbury
84. Thomas Brentingham
85. Robert Braybrooke \
86. Roger Walden
87. Henry Beaufort
88. Thomas Bourchier
89. John Morton
90. Richard Fitzjames
91. William Warham
92. John Langlands
93. Thomas Cranmer
94. William Barlow
95. Matthew Parker
96. Edmund Grindal
97. John Whitgift
98. Richard Bancroft
99. George Abbot
100. George Montaigne
101. William Laud
102. Brian Duppa
103. Gilbert Sheldon
104. Henry Compton
105. William Sancroft
106. Jonathan Trelawney
107. John Potter
108. Thomas Herring
109. Frederick Cornwallis
110. John Moore
111. William White
112. John Henry Hopkins
113. Leon Chechemian (Mar Leon)
114. Andrea Carlo MacLagen (Mar Andries)
115. Herbert James Heard (Mar Jacobus II)
116. William Bernard Crow (Mar Basilius Abdullah III)
117. Hugh George de Wilmott-Newman (Mar Georgius)
118. Wallace de Ortega Maxey
119. Lowell Paul Wadle
120. Herman Adrian Spruit
121. Forest Ernest Barber
122. Michael Paul Bertiaux (Tau Ogdoade Orfeo IV)
123. Geoffrey Lantz
124. Louvel Delon
125. William Behun (Tau Thomas)
126. Reginald Freeman (Tau Valentinus / Tau Phosphoros)

Succession from St. Thomas (Assyrian) / Nestorian:

1. Thomas (Toma)
2. Bar Tulmay 33
3. Addai 33
4. Agai 45
5. Mari 48
6. Abris 90
7. Graham I 130
8. Yacob I 172
9. Ebid M'shikha 191
10. Akhu d'Awu 205
11. Shakhlupa of Kashkar 224
12. Papa Bar Gaggai 247
13. Shimun Bar Sabbai 328
14. Shahdost 345
15. Bar Bashmin 350
16. Tumarsa 383
17. Qaiyma 393
18. Eskhaq 399
19. Akhkhi 411
20. Yoalaha I 415
21. Maana 420
22. Qarabukht 421
23. Kakishu 421
24. Bawai (Babu) 457
25. Aqaq 484
26. Bawai 496
27. Sheela 505
28. Marsai 524
29. Elisha 524
30. Polos 539
31. Yosip 552
32. Khazqiyil 570
33. Eshuyow I Arzunaya 581
34. Soreshu I Garmaqaya 596
35. Greghor Partaya 605
36. Eshuyow II
37. Mar Immeh 647
38. Eshuyow III Kdayawaya 650
39. Gewargis I 681
40. Yokhannan I Bar Marta 684

41. Khnaishu I 686
42. Yokhannan II, Garba 693
43. Sliwazkha 714
44. Pethyon 731
45. Awa 741
46. Surin 752
47. Yacob II 754
48. Khnanishu II
49. Timotheus I 780
50. Esho-barnon 820
51. Gewargis II 825
52. Soreshu II 832
53. Oraham II Margaya 837
54. Teadasis 850
55. Sargis, Suwaya 860
56. Annush d'beth Garmay 873
57. Yokhannan III Bar Narsai 884
58. Yokhannan IV 892
59. Yokhannan V 900
60. Orham III, Abraza 906
61. Ammanoel I 937
62. Esrail Karkhaya 961
63. Odishu Garmaqaya 963
64. Mari Aturaya 967
65. Yokhannan VI 1001
66. Yokhannan VII 1013
67. Eshuyow IV 1023
68. Elea I 1028
69. Yokhannan VIII 1049
70. Soreshu III (Bar Zanbur) 1057
71. Odishu II (Bar Ars) Aturaya 1072
72. Makkikha I (Bar Shlemon) 1092
73. Elea II 1111
74. Bar Soma (of Suwa) 113
75. Bar Babbara 1138
76. Odishu III 1138
77. Eshuyow V (from Beth Zodai, Baladaya) 1148
78. Elea III (Abukhalim) 1176
79. Yoalaha II (Bar Waiyuma) 1191
80. Soreshu IV 1222
81. Soreshu V (from Baghdad) 1226
82. Makkikha II 1257
83. Dinkha I, Arbilaya (from Arbil) 1265
84. Yoalaha III, Bar Turkaye 1281
85. Timotheus II, Arbilaya 1318
86. Dinkha II 1329
87. Dinkha III 1359
88. Shimun III 1369
89. Shimun IV 1403
90. Elia IV 1407
91. Shimun V 1420
92. Shimun VI 1448
93. Elia V 1491
94. Shimun VII 1505
95. Eshuyow Shimun VIII 1538
96. Dinkha Shimun IX (Bar Mama) 1552
97. Yoalaha Shimun X 1558
98. Dinkha Shimun XI
99. Elia Shimun XII
100. Eshuyow Shimun XIII 1653
101. Yoalaha Shimun XIV 16990
102. Dinkha Shimun XV 1692
103. Shlemon (Sulaiman) Shimun XVI 1700
104. Mikhail (Muukhattis) Shimun XVII 1740
105. Yonan (Yuna) Shimun XVIII 1740
106. Oraham Shimun XIXI 1820
107. Ruwil Shimun XX 1860
108. Anthony Thondetta (Mar Antonius Abd-Isu) 17 December 1862
109. Luis Mariano Soares (Mar Basilius) 24 July 1899
110. Ulric Vernon Herford (Mar Jacobus) 30 November 1902
111. William Stanley McBean Knight (Mar Paulus) 28 February 1925
112. Hedley Coward Barlett (Mar Hedley) 18 October 1931
113. Hugh George de Wilmott-Newman (Mar Georgius) 23 October 1938
114. Richard Due de Palatine (Ronald Powell) 25 October 1953
115. Forest Ernest Barber 9 April 1967
116. Michael Paul Bertiaux (Tau Ogdoade Orfeo IV) 16 June 1979
117. Geoffrey Lantz 1995
118. Louvel Delon 1997
119. William Behun (Tau Thomas) 1998
120. Reginald Freeman (Tau Valentinus / Tau Phosphoros) 27 April 2002

Appendices

Succession from St. James the Less, Bishop of Jerusalem:

1.	James the Less	43.	Hilary	85.	Ivor
2.	Simeon	44.	John II	86.	Morgeneu I
3.	Justus I	45.	Praglius	87.	Nathan
4.	Zacceus	46.	Juvenal	88.	Jenan
5.	Tobias	47.	Anastacius	89.	Arwystl
6.	Benjamin	48.	Martyrius	90.	Morgeneu II
7.	John I	49.	Salutis	91.	Ervin
8.	Matthias	50.	Elias	92.	Trahacam
9.	Philip	51.	St. John of Jerusalem	93.	Joseph
10.	Seneca	52.	St. David	94.	Bleiddud
11.	Justus II	53.	Cynog	95.	Salien
12.	Levi	54.	Teilo	96.	Abraham
13.	Ephraim	55.	Ceven	97.	Rhyddmarch
14.	Joseph	56.	Morfall	98.	Wilfrid
15.	Judas	57.	Haerwneu	99.	Bernard
16.	Marcus	58.	Elwaed	100.	D. Fitzgerald
17.	Cassianus	59.	Gwrnwen	101.	Peter de Leia
18.	Publius	60.	Llumverth	102.	G. Camb
19.	Maximus I	61.	Gwrgwyst	103.	G. de Henelawe
20.	Julian	62.	Gwgan	104.	Jowert
21.	Caius	63.	Eineon	105.	Gross
22.	Symmachus	64.	Clydawg	106.	de Carew
23.	Caius II	65.	Elfod	107.	T. Hech
24.	Julian II	66.	Ethelman	108.	D. Martin
25.	Maximus II	67.	Elane	109.	H. Gower
26.	Antonius	68.	Magelsgwyd	110.	J. Thorsby
27.	Capito	69.	Made	111.	R. Brian
28.	Valius	70.	Cadell	112.	F. Fastolfe
29.	Daleanus	71.	Sadwrnfen	113.	H. Doughton
30.	Narcissus	72.	Novis	114.	J. Gilbert
31.	Dius	73.	Sulhaithnay	115.	G. de Mona
32.	Germanio	74.	Idwall	116.	Henry Chichele
33.	Gordius	75.	Asser	117.	John Stafford
34.	Alexander	76.	Arthwael	118.	Joseph Kemp
35.	Nazabancus	77.	Samson	119.	Thomas Bouchier
36.	Hymenacus	78.	Reubin	120.	John Morton
37.	Zamboas	79.	Rhydderch	121.	Henry Dean
38.	Herman	80.	Elwin	122.	William Warham
39.	Marcarius I	81.	Morbiw	123.	Thomas Cranmer
40.	Maximus III	82.	Llunwerth	124.	Reginald Pole
41.	Cyril	83.	Hurbert	125.	Matthew Parker
42.	Herenius	84.	Enerius	126.	Edmund Grindal

127. John Whitgift
128. Richard Bancroft
129. George Abbot
130. William Laud
131. William Juxon
132. Gilbert Sheldon
133. William Sancroft
134. Jonathan Trelawney
135. John Parker
136. Thomas Herring
137. Frederick Cornwallis
138. John Moore
139. William White
140. John Henry Hopkins
141. Chechemian
142. Andrea Carlo MacLagen (Mar Andries)
143. Herbert James Heard (Mar Jacobus II)
144. William Bernard Crow (Mar Basilius Abdullah III)
145. Hugh George de Wilmott-Newman (Mar Georgius)
146. Wallace de Ortega Maxey
147. Lowell P. Wadle
148. H. Adrian Spruit
149. Forest E. Barber
150. Michael P. Bertiaux (Tau Ogdoade Orfeo IV)
151. Geoffrey Lantz
152. Louvel Delon
153. William Behun (Tau Thomas)
154. Reginald Freeman (Tau Valentinus / Tau Phosphoros)

Succession from St. Andrew:

1. St. Andrew
2. Stachys 38
3. Onesimus 54
4. Polycarpus I 69
5. Plutarch 89
6. Sedecion 105
7. Doigenes 114
8. Eleutherius 129
9. Felix 136
10. Polycarpus II 141
11. Athendodorus 144
12. Euzois 148
13. Laurence 154
14. Alypius 166
15. Pertinax 1169
16. Olympians 187
17. Mark I 198
18. Philadelphus 211
19. Ciriacus I 217
20. Castinus 230
21. Eugenius I 237
22. Titus 242
23. Dometius 272
24. Rufinus I 284
25. Probus 293
26. Metrophanes 306
27. Alexander 314
28. Paul I 337
29. Eusebius of Nicodemia 339
30. Macedonius I 342
31. Eudoxius of Antioch 360
32. Demophilus 370
33. Euagrius 379
34. Maximus 380
35. Gregory I 381
36. Nectarius 381
37. John I Chrysostom 398
38. Arascius of Tarsus 404
39. Atticus 406
40. Sisinius I 426
41. Nestorius 428
42. Maximianus 431
43. Proclus 434
44. Phlabianus 446
45. Anatolius 449
46. Gennadius I 458
47. Acacius 471
48. Phrabitas 488
49. Euphemius 489
50. Macedonus II 495
51. Timotheus I 511
52. John II of Cappadocia 518
53. Epiphanius 520
54. Anthimus I 535
55. Menas 536
56. Eutychius 552
57. John III Scholasticus 565
58. John IV Nesteutes 582
59. Cyriacus 596
60. Thomas I 607
61. Sergius I 610
62. Pyrrhus I 639
63. Paul II 641
64. Peter 654
65. Thomas II 667
66. John V 669
67. Constantine I 675
68. Theodore I 677
69. George I 679
70. Paul III 687
71. Callinicus I 693
72. Cyrus 705
73. John VI 712
74. Germanus I 715
75. Anastasius 730
76. Constantine II 754
77. Nicetas 766
78. Paul IV 780
79. Tarasius 784
80. Nicephorus I 806
81. Theodotus I Cassiteras 815
82. Antony I 821
83. John VII Grammaticus 836
84. Methodius I 843
85. Ignatius I 847
86. Photius I the Great 858

Appendices

87. Stephanus I 886
88. Antony II K.auleas 893
89. Nicholas I Mysticus 901
90. Euthymius I 907
91. Stephanus II 925
92. Tryphon 928
93. Theophylactus 933
94. Polyeuctus 956
95. Basil I Skamandrenus 970
96. Antony III Studites 974
97. Nicholas II Chrysoberges 984
98. Leo Michael 991
99. Leonti.us 1004
100. John I 1015
101. Theopemptus 1037
102. Hilarion 1051
103. George 1072
104. John II 1080
105. John III 1096
106. Ephraim 1096
107. Nicolas 1098
108. Nicephorus I 1108
109. Nicetas 1124
110. Michael II 1127
111. Clement 1147 154.
159. Frank Dyer
112. Constantine 1154
113. Theodore 1160
114. John IV 1164
115. Constantine II 1167
116. Nicephorus II 1185
117. Matthew 1201
118. Cyril I 1205
119. Joseph 1237
120. Cyril II 1240
121. Maximus 1283
122. Peter 1305
123. Theognostes 1328
124. Alexis 1254
125. Cyprian 1381
126. Photius 1408
127. Isadore 1436
128. Johnah 1448
129. Theodosius 1462
130. Phillip I 1467
131. Gerontius 1472
132. Zosimus 1491
133. Simon 1495
134. Barlaam 1511
135. Daniel 1522
136. Joasaph 1539
137. Macarius 1542
138. Germanus 1564
139. Phillip 1565
140. Cyril III 1568
141. Anthony 1572
142. Dionysius 1582
143. Job 1589
144. Hermongenes 1606
145. Philaret 1619
146. Joasaph I 1633
147. Joseph 1642
148. Nikon 1653
149. Joasaph II 1667
150. Pitrim 1672
151. Joachim 1674
152. Adrian 1690
153. Metropolitan Stephen (Yavorsky), of Rostov, Guardian of the Patriarchate 1701
*** From 1721-1918 the Patriarch of the Russian Orthodox Church was replaced with the Most Holy Synod.
154. Nikon (Metropolitan of Moscow?)
155. Macarius II (Makary II) Michael Nevsky 12 February 1884
156. Evdokim Basil Mikhailovich Meschersky 4 January 1904
157. Aftimios Ofiesh 13 May 1917
158. Ignatius William Albert Nichols 27 September 1932
159. Frank Dyer
160. Matthew Nicholas Nelson 16 March 1947
161. Lowell P. Wadle 27 July 1947
162. H. Adrian Spruit 1957
163. Forest E. Barber 1971
164. Michael P. Bertiaux (Tau Ogdoade Orfeo IV) 16June 1979
165. Geoffrey Lantz 1995
166. Louvel Delon 1997
167. William Behun (Tau Thomas) 1998
168. Reginald Freeman (Tau Valentinus / Tau Phosphoros) 27 April 2002

Also via:

154. Nikon (Metropolitan of Moscow?)
155. Ivan Nikolaevich Stragorodsky, Metropolitan of Nizhni-Novgorod, afterward Sergij (Patriarch Sergius I), Patriarch of Moscow) 1901
156. Henry Joseph Kleefisch 1918 (1917?)
157. Odo Acheson Barry (Mar Columba) 29 July 1946
158. Hugh George de Willmott Newman (Mar Georgius I) 17 July 1955
159. Charles Dennis Boltwood 6 July 1956
160. Emmett Neil Enochs 31 August 1958
161. Demetrius F.C. King 9 May 1963
162. Francis Homer Roebke 1 January 1965
163. Forest E.G. Barber 7 March

1965
164. Michael Paul Bertiaux Tau Ogdoade Orfeo IV / Tau Orfeo Bardesens I) 16 June 1979
165. Geoffrey Lantz 1995
166. Louvel Delon 1997
167. William A. Behun (Tau Thomas / Mar Thomas) 1998
168. Reginald M. Freeman (Tau Valentinus / Tau Phosphoros) 27 April 2002

Also via:

156. Henry Joseph Kleefisch 1918 (1917?)
157. Antoine Aneed 23 August 1945
158. Lowell P. Wadle 23 August 1945 (Wadle, Aneed, & Kleefisch exchanged consecrations on this date along with Hampton and Maxey)
159. Herman Adrian Spruit 22 June, 1957
160. Forest Ernest G. Barber 15Jun. 1971
161. Michael Paul Bertiaux Tau Ogdoade Orfeo IV / Tau Orfeo Bardesens I) 16 June 1979
162. Geoffrey Lantz 1995
163. Louvel Delon 1997
164. William A. Behun Tau Thomas / Mar Thomas) 1998
165. Reginald M. Freeman (Tau Valentinus / Tau Phosphoros) 27 April 2002

Also via:

159. Antoine Aneed
160. Franklin B. Robinson 1945 (with Kleefisch, Wadle, & Edgar R. Verostek)
161. William C. Conway
162. Cecil F. Russell
163. Franklin Thomas Jr.
164. Roland Merritt-Shreves (Tau IX)
165. Marc Lully (Tau IV)
166. Michael P. Bertiaux (Tau Ogdoade Orfeo IV) 25 December 1967
167. Geoffrey Lantz
168. Louvel Delon
169. William Behun (Tau Thomas)
170. Reginald M. Freeman (Tau Valentinus / Tau Phosphoros) 27 April 2002

Succession from Thaddeus & Bartholomew (Armenian):

1. St. Thaddeus
2. St. Bartholomew
3. St. Zadaria 68
4. St. Zementus 76
5. St. Atirnerseh 81
6. St. Mousche 97
7. St. Schahen 128
8. St. Schavarsch 154
9. St. Ghevondius 175
10. St. Mehroujan 230
11. St. Gregory the Illuminator 301
12. St. Aristakes I Parthian 325
13. St. Vertanes I Parthian 333
14. St. Houssik I Parthian 341
15. Paren I Aschtischat 348
16. St. Nerses I the Great 353
17. Sahak I of Manazkert 373
18. Zaven I of Manazkert 377
19. Aspourakes of Manazkert 381
20. St. Sahak I the Great 387
21. St. Hovsep I of Hoghotzim 440
22. Melitus I of Manazkert 452
23. Movses I of Manazkert 456
24. St. Gut I of Araheze 461
25. St. Hovhannes I Mandakoune 478
26. Babken I of Othmous 490
27. Samuel I of Ardzke 516
28. Mousche I of Ailaberk 526
29. Sahak II of Ouhki 534
30. Kristapor I of Tiraritch 539
31. Ghevont I of Erast 545
32. Nerses II of Bagrevand 548
33. Hovhannes II Gabeghian 557
34. Movses II of Eghivart 574
35. Abraham I of Aghbatank 607
36. Comitas I of Aghtzil 615
37. Kristapor II Apahouni 628
38. Yezer I of Parajcnakert 630
39. Nerses III of lschkhan 641
40. Anastasius I of Akori 661
41. Israel I of Othmous 667
42. Sahak III of Tzorapor 677
43. Eghia I of Ardjcsch 703
44. St. Hovhannes III of Otzoun 717
45. David I of Aramonk 728
46. Tirdat I of Othmous 741
47. Tirdat II of Dasnavork 764

Appendices

48. Soin I of Bavonk 767
49. Yessai I of Eghipatrousch 775
50. Stepanos I of Douinc 788
51. Hovab I of Douinc 790
52. Soghomon I of Garni 791
53. Gueorg I of Oschakan 792
54. Hovsep II of Parpi 795
55. David II of Gagagh 806
56. Hovhannes IV of Ova
57. Zakaria I of Tzak 855
58. Gueorg II of Garni 878
59. St. Maschtotz I of Eghivart 898
60. Hovhannes V of Draskhonakert 899
61. Stepanos II Rischtouni 931
62. Theodoros I Rischtouni 932
63. Yeghische I Rischtouni 938
64. Anania I of Moks 943
65. Vahan I Suni 967
66. Stepanos III of Sevan 969
67. Khatchik I Arscharouni 972
68. Sarkis I of Sevan 992
69. Petros I Guetadartz 1019
70. Khatchik II of Ani 1054
71. Grigor II Vikaiasser 1065
72. Barsegh I of Ani 1105
73. Grigor III Pahlavouni 1113
74. St. Nerses N Schnorhali 1166
75. Grigor N Tegha 1173
76. Grigor V Karabege 1193
77. Grigor VI Apirat 1194
78. Hovhannes VI Medzabaro 1203
79. Constantine I of Bartzrberd 1221
80. Hacob I of Kla 1267
81. Constantine II Pronagortz 1286
82. Stepanos N of Thomkla 1290
83. Grigor VII of Anavarza 1293
84. Constantine III of Caesarea 1307
85. Constantine N of Lambron 1322
86. Hacob II of Tarsus 1327
87. Mekhitar I of Gmer 1341
88. Mesrob I of Ardaze 1359
89. Constantine V of Sis 1372
90. Poghos I of Sis 1374
91. Theodoros II of Cilicia 1377
92. Karapet I of Keghy 1393
93. Hacob III of Sis 1408
94. Grigor VIII Khantzoghat 1411
95. Poghos II of Garni 1416
96. Constantine VI of Vahka 1429
97. Grigor IX Moussabeguian 1439
98. Grigor I Moussabeguian 1441
99. Garabed Yevtogatsi 1446
100. Stepanos Saratsortsi 1475
101. Hovhannes I Andioktsi 1483
102. Hovhannes II Tulgurantsi 1489
103. Hovhannes III Kilistsi
104. 1525
     Simeon Zeitountsi 1539
105. Ghazar Aeitountsi 1545
106. Taros Sisetsi 1578
107. Khachadour I Chorig 1553
108. Khachadour II Zeitountsi 1560
109. Azaria I Jughayetsi 1584
110. Hovhannes N Aintabtsi 1602
111. Bedros I Gargaretsi 1584
112. Minas Gonnetsi 1621
113. Simeon II Sebastiatsi 1648
114. Nerses Sebastiatsi 1648
115. Toros II Sebastiatsi 1654
116. Khachadour III Sebastiats 1657
117. Sahak I Meykhaneji 1677
118. Axaria II Gargaretsi 1688
119. Grigor II Adanatsi 1686
120. Asdvadzadour Sasuntsi 1695
121. Madteos Gesaratsi 1703
122. Hovhannes V Hajentsi 1705
123. Grigor III Gesaratsi 1721
124. Ghougas Sisetsi Atchabahian 1731
125. Abraham Peter Ardzivian 1737
126. Jacob Peter Hovsepian 1749
127. Michael Peter Kasparia 1753
128. Basil Peter Avakadian 1780
129. Gregory Peter Kupelian 1788
130. Gregory Peter II Djeranian 1812
131. Jacob Peter II Holassian 1841
132. Gregory Peter III Derasdvazadourian 1843
133. Anthony Peter Hassoun 1866
134. Leon Chorchorunian 7 April 1861 (this is the actual consecration date; the above dates refer to the Armenian Patriarchate)
135. Chechemian 23 April 1878
136. Andrea Carlo MacLagen (Mar Andries) 2 Nov 1897
137. Herbert James Heard (Mar Jacobus II) 4 June 1922
138. William Bernard Crow (Mar Basilius Abdullah III) 13 June 1943
139. Hugh George de Wilmott-

Newman (Mar Georgius) 10 April 1944
140. Richard Due de Palatine (Ronald Powell) 25 October 1953
141. Forest E. Barber 9 April 1967
142. Michael P. Bertiaux (Tau Ogdoade Orfeo IV) 16 June 1979
143. Geoffrey Lantz 1995
144. Louvel Delon 1997
145. William Behun (Tau Thomas) 1998
146. Reginald Freeman (Tau Valentinus / Tau Phosphoros) 27 April 2002

Succession from St. Paul the Apostle:

1. St. Paul
2. St. Timothy 62
3. St. Onesemus 91
4. St. John the Elder 113
5. Demetrius 131
6. Lucius 156
7. St. Polycrates 175
8. St. Irenaeus 177
9. St. Nicomedian 180
10. Maximus 203
11. Philip Deoderus 341
12. St. Matthias 276
13. Gregory Antilas 276
14. Andrew Meletius 283
15. Pious Stephenas 291
16. Mark Leuvian 312
17. Paul Anencletus (the Elder) 330
18. St. Christopher 394
19. James 413
20. Basil 415
21. Clement of Lyons 436
22. Timothy Eumenes 468
23. Christopher II 472
24. Christopher III 485
25. St. Evarestus 502
26. Linus 532
27. Gregory II 547
28. John 562
29. St. Mark Pireu 581
30. Maximus Lyster 587
31. Aetherius 591
32. St. Augustine 601
33. Laurentius 604
34. Justus 635
35. Deusdedit 652
36. Theodore 668
37. Ethelburh 712
38. Egbert 749
39. Herefrid 788
40. Cuthbert 814
41. Rufus 859
42. Phlegmund 890
43. Odo 941
44. Dunstan 959
45. Ethelgar 988
46. Segeric 990
47. Aelfric 995
48. Elphege 1006
49. Edmund 1012
50. Wulfstan 1064
51. St. Anselm 1093
52. Ralph d'Escures 1109
53. William de Corbeuil 1122
54. Theobald 1139
55. Thomas Becket 1162
56. Richard 1170
57. Baldwin 1178
58. Reginal 1183
59. Ritz-Jocelin 1191
60. Hubert Walter 1197
61. Stephen Langton 1205
62. Richard Weathershed 1230
63. Edmund 1234
64. Boniface of Savoy
65. Robert Kilwardby 1269
66. John Peckham 1279
67. Robert of Winchelsea 1293
68. Walter Reynolds 1313
69. Simon Langham 1327
70. Simon Sudbury 1367
71. James Abingdon 1381
72. Henry Chichele 1413
73. Cardinal Kemp 1452
74. Cardinal Bourchier 1469
75. Cardinal Morton 1488
76. William Warham 1503
77. Thomas Cranmer 1533
78. Philip Barlow 1536
79. Dr. Parker 1559
80. Steven Grendall 1575
81. Mark Whitgift 1577
82. Richard Bancroft 1604
83. Kyle Abbot 1610
84. William Laud 1633
85. William Joxon 1660
86. Gilbert Sheldon 1662
87. Henry Compton 1674
88. William Sancroft 1678
89. Jonathan Trelawney 1685
90. John Potter 1715
91. Frederick Cornwallis 1750
92. John Moore 1783
93. William White 1787
94. John Henry Hopkins 1832
95. George David Cummins 15 November 1866
96. Charles Edward Cheney 14 December 1873
97. William Rufus Nicholson 24 February 1876
98. Alfred Spencer Richardson 22 June 1879
99. Leon Chechemian 4 May 1890 (with Charles Isaac

Stevens)
100. Andrea Carlo MacLagen (Mar Andries) 2 November 1897
101. Herbert James Heard (Mar Jacobus II) 4 June 1922
102. William Bernard Crow (Mar Basilius Abdullah III) 13 June 1943
103. Hugh George de Wilmott-Newman (Mar Georgius) 10 April 1944
104. Richard Due de Palatine (Ronald Powell) 25 October 1953
105. Forest E. Barber 9 April 1967
106. Michael P. Bertiaux (Tau Ogdoade Orfeo IV) 16 June 1979
107. Geoffrey Lantz 1995
108. Louvel Delon 1997
109. William Behun (Tau Thomas) 1998
110. Reginald Freeman (Tau Valentinus / Tau Phosphoros) 27 April 2002

Other Apostolic Lines:

American Greek Melchite:

1. Cyril VI
2. Athanasius Savoya (Sawaya)
3. Antoine Aneed 9 October 1911
4. H. Adrian Spruit
5. Forest E. Barber
6. Michael P. Bertiaux
7. Geoffrey Lantz
8. Louvel Delon
9. William Behun
10. Reginald Freeman

Orthodox Patriarchate (Constantinople):

1. Patriarch Sergius (Ivan Nikolayevich Stragorodsky)
2. Henry Joseph Kleefisch 1 January 1918
3. Ignatius Peter Aneed 29 June 1927
4. Lowell P. Wadle 23 August 1945
5. H. Adrian Spruit
6. Forest E. Barber
7. Michael P. Bertiaux
8. Geoffrey Lantz
9. Louvel Delon
10. William Behun
11. Reginald Freeman

Order of Corporate Reunion:

1. Richard Williams Morgan (Mar Pelagius I) 1874
2. Charles Isaac Stevens (Mar Theophilus) 1879
3. Leon Chechemian (Mar Leon) 1890
4. Andrea Carlo MacLagen (Mar Andries) 2 November 1897
5. Herbert James Heard (Mar Jacobus II) 4 June 1922
6. William Bernard Crow (Mar Basilius Abdullah III) 13 June 1943
7. Hugh George de Wilmott-Newman (Mar Georgius) 10 April 1944
8. Wallace de Ortega Maxey 8 June 1946
9. Lowell Paul Wadle 23 April 1948
10. Herman Adrian Spruit 23 May 1957
11. Forest Ernest Barber 15 June 1971
12. Michael P. Bertiaux (Tau Ogdoade Orfeo IV) 16 June 1979
13. Geoffrey Lantz 1995
14. Louvel Delon 1997
15. William Behun (Tau Thomas) 1998
16. Reginald Freeman (Tau Valentinus / Tau Phosphoros) 27 April 2002

Ukrainian, Albanian, & Greek Orthodox:

1. Metropolitan Heirotheos
2. Theophan Noli 21 November 1923
3. Arsenias Saltas 25 August 1934
4. Joseph Klymowycz 1935
5. Peter Andrew Zhurawetzky 15 October 1950
6. Metropolitan Nikloaus Ilnyckyj 2 March 1978
7. William George Spaeth Jr. (Yuri) 13 May 1989
8. Valdiveso Paschal Matthews (Hermas Apollos/Tau Mikael III Basilides) 30 Oct 1998
9. Reginald Freeman (Tau Valentinus / Tau Phosphoros) 22 March 2003

Gnostic & Esoteric Lines of Succession:

Église Gnostique:

1. Jules-Benoit Stanislas Doinel (Tau Valentin II) 1890
2. Gérard Encausse (Papus / Tau Vincent) 1893
3. Lucien-François Jean-Maine (Tau Ogdoade Orfeo I) 1899
4. Hector-François Jean-Maine (Tau Ogdoade Orfeo III) 25 January 1953
5. Michael P. Bertiaux (Tau Ogdoade Orfeo IV) 15 August 1963
6. Geoffrey Lantz 1995
7. Louvel Delon 1997
8. William Behun (Tau Thomas) 1998
9. Reginald Freeman (Tau Valentinus / Tau Phosphoros) 2002

Also via:

1. Jules Doinel (Tau Valentin II) 1890
2. Fabre des Éssarts (Tau Synésius) 27 September 1894 (Elected 18 Sept.1892)
3. Jean Bricaud (Tau Jean II) 1901
4. Victor Blanchard (Tau Targelius) 5 May 1918
5. Roger Menard (Tau Eon II) 7 January 1945
6. Robert Ambelain (f au Jean III) 10 June 1946
7. Hector-François Jean-Maine (Tau Ogdoade Orfeo III) 1953
8. Michael P. Bertiaux (Tau Ogdoade Orfeo IV) 1966
9. Geoffrey Lantz 1995
10. Louvel Delon 1997
11. William Behun (Tau Thomas) 1998
12. Reginald Freeman (Tau Valentinus / Tau Phosphoros) 2002

Also via:

6. Robert Ambelain (Tau Jean III) 10 June 1946
7. Roger Pommery (Tau Jean IV) 26 May 1958
8. Willer Vital-Heme (Tau Guillaume) 16 September 1967
9. Roger St. Victor-Herard (Tau Charles) 7 September 1970
10. Robert M. Cokinis (Tau Charles Harmonius II) 4 November 1984
11. James Foster (Tau Iohannes III) July 2002
12. Reginald Freeman (Tau Phosphoros) 22 December 2002 Also via:
9. Roger St. Victor-Herard (Tau Charles) 7 September 1970
10. Jorge Rodriguez-Villa (Tau Johannes XIII) 6 January 1985
11. Valdiveso Matthews (Tau Mikael III Basilides) 30 October 1999
12. Reginald Freeman (Tau Valentinus / Tau Phosphoros) 22 March 2003

Vintrasian Carmelite:

1. Eugene Vintras
2. Marius Breton
3. Jean Bricaud (Tau Jean II)
4. Victor Blanchard (Tau Targelius)
5. Roger Menard (Tau Eon II)
6. Robert Ambelain (Tau Jean III)
7. Hector-François Jean-Maine (Tau Ogdoade Orfeo III)
8. Michael P. Bertiaux (Tau Ogdoade Orfeo IV)
9. Geoffery Lantz
10. Louvel Delon
11. William Behun (Tau Thomas)
12. Reginald Freeman (Tau Phosphoros)

Gnostic Therapeutic Sempiesta:

1. Jean Sempé
2. Jules Houssay (Abbé Julio / Mar Julius)
3. Louis François Giraud (François) 21 June 1911
4. Jean Bricaud (Tau Jean II) 21 January 1913
5. Victor Blanchard (Tau Targelius) 5 May 1918
6. Roger Menard (Tau Eon II) 7 January 1945
7. Robert Ambelain (Tau Jean III) 10June 1946
8. Hector-François Jean-Maine (Tau Ogdoade Orfeo III) 25 January 1953
9. Michael P. Bertiaux (Tau Ogdoade Orfeo IV) 15 August 1963
10. Geoffery Lantz 1995
11. Louvel Delon 1997

12. William Behun (Tau Thomas) 1998
13. Reginald Freeman (Tau Valentinus / Tau Phosphoros) 27 April 2002

Gnostic Kabbalistic of Memphis-Misraïm:

1. Manuel Lopez de Brion (Orfeo V)
2. Paul-Pierre de Marraga (Orfeo VI) 2 February 1860
3. Lucien- François Jean-Maine (Tau Ogdoade Orfeo I) 15 August 1899
4. Martin Ortier de Sanchez y Marraga (Tau Ogdoade Orfeo II) 27 December 1918
5. Hector- François Jean-Maine (Tau Ogdoade Orfeo III) 1962
6. Michael P. Bertiaux (Tau Ogdoade Orfeo IV) 15 August 1963
7. Geoffery Lantz 1995
8. Louvel Delon 1997
9. William Behun (Tau Thomas) 1998
10. Reginald Freeman (Tau Valentinus / Tau Phosphoros) 27 April 2002

Ecclesia Gnostic Spiritualis:

1. Lucien-François Jean-Maine (Tau Ogdoade Orfeo I) 1899
2. Martin Ortier de Sanchez y Marraga (Tau Ogdoade Orfeo II) 1918
3. Hector-François Jean-Maine (Tau Ogdoade Orfeo III) 1962
4. Michael P. Bertiaux (Tau Ogdoade Orfeo IV) 1963
5. Geoffery Lantz 1995
6. Louvel Delon 1997
7. William Behun (Tau Thomas) 1998
8. Reginald Freeman (Tau Valentinus / Tau Phosphoros) 2002

Église Gnostique Universelle:

1. Jean Bricaud (Tau Jean II)
2. Constant Chevillon (Tau Harmonius)
3. Heinrich Arnold Krumm-Heller (Tau Huiracocha)
4. Johannes Muller Riders
5. Roberto de la Caridad Toca y Medina
6. Jorge Rodriguez-Villa (f au Johannes XIII)
7. Michael P. Bertiaux (Tau Ogdoade Orfeo IV)
8. Geoffery Lantz
9. Louvel Delon
10. William Behun (Tau Thomas)
11. Reginald Freeman (Tau Valentinus / Tau Phosphoros)

Also via:

6. Jorge Rodriguez-Villa (f au Johannes XIII)
7. Valdiveso Matthews (Tau Mikael III Basilides)
8. Reginald Freeman (Tau Valentinus / Tau Phosphoros)

Ecclesia Gnostica (Pre-Nicene Catholic Church):

1. Richard Due de Palatine
2. Forest E. Barber
3. Michael P. Bertiaux (Tau Ogdoade Orfeo IV)
4. Geoffery Lantz
5. Louvel Delon
6. William Behun (Tau Thomas)
7. Reginald Freeman (Tau Valentinus / Tau Phosphoros)

Also via:

1. Richard Due de Palatine
2. Stephan A. Hoeller (Tau Stephanus)
3. Phillip A. Garver (Tau Vincent II)
4. James Foster (Tau Iohannes III)
5. Reginald Freeman (Tau Valentinus / Tau Phosphoros)

Ecclesia Gnostica Apostolica - American Rite:

1. Joan Marie Zolna Asturrizaga (Tau Abrielle Valentina Magdalena)
2. Valdiveso Matthews (Tau Mikael III Basilides)
3. Reginald Freeman (Tau Valentinus / Tau Phosphoros)

Ecclesia Gnostica Antiqua:

1. Tau Ignatius V of Antiochia and Tau Vladimir di Magdala
2. Alberto La Cava (Tau Ignatius of Alexandria VII)

3. Robert M. Cokinis (Tau Charles Harmonius II)
4. James Foster (Tau Iohannes III)
5. Reginald Freeman (Tau Valentinus / Tau Phosphoros)

Ecclesia Gnostica Mysteriorum:

1. Rosamonde Miller (Tau Rosamonde) 18 Jan. 1981
2. Manuel Cabrera Lamparter 25 December 1982
3. Luis Asensio Cristobal
4. Emanuele Coltro Guidi (Tau Sebastos Athanasios Sokaris)
5. Phillip A. Garver (Tau Vincent II)
6. James Foster (Tau Iohannes III)
7. Reginald Freeman (Tau Valentinus / Tau Phosphoros)

Apostolic Church of the Third Age:

1. William Behun (Tau Thomas) & Martin Jacobs (Tau Philip-Markos)
2. Reginald Freeman (Tau Valentinus / Tau Phosphoros)

Nouvelle Alliance:

1. Roger Caro
2. Denis Claing
3. Jean-Marie Pomerleau
4. Ronald V. Cappello
5. Phillip A. Garver (Tau Vincent II)
6. James Foster (Tau Iohannes III)
7. Reginald Freeman (Tau Phosphoros)

Apostolic Johannite Church:

1. James Foster (Tau Iohannes III)
2. Reginald Freeman (Tau Valentinus / Tau Phosphoros)

Thelemic Gnostic Church of Alexandria:

1. Gerald del Campo (Tau Apollonius)
2. Reginald Freeman (Tau Valentinus / Tau Phosphoros)

Église Gnostique Catholique Apostolique - Catholicate de la Croix de Rose (Oriental Apostolic Church of Damcar):

1. Valdiveso Matthews (Tau Mikael III Basilides)
2. Reginald Freeman (Tau Valentinus / Tau Phosphoros)

Appendices

Appendix H

Alphabetical listing of the Gnostic, Catholic, and Orthodox lines of succession currently within the Apostolic Church of the Pleroma

1. African Orthodox Catholic Church
2. Albanian Orthodox
3. American Catholic Apostolic Church
4. American Catholic Church
5. American Greek Melchite
6. American Orthodox Church
7. Ancient British Church
8. Ancient Catholic Church of France
9. Ancient Orthodox Catholic Church
10. Anglican
11. Anglican – Celtic
12. Anglican Universal Church
13. Antiochian- Jacobite
14. Apostolic Church of the Third Age
15. Apostolic Episcopal Church
16. Apostolic Johannite Church
17. Armenian Uniate
18. Assembly of the Knowledge & Wisdom of Solomon
19. Brazilian National Catholic
20. British Orthodox Church (Catholicate of the West)
21. Byzantine American Church
22. Byzantine Orthodox Catholic
23. Catholic Apostolic Church (Catholicate of the West)
24. Catholic Apostolic Church of Antioch – Malabar Rite
25. Catholic Apostolic Orthodox
26. Catholic Church of India
27. Chaldean Uniate
28. Coptic Orthodox
29. Coptic Uniate
30. Dutch Old Catholic
31. Ecclesia Apostolica Rosae et Aurae Crucis
32. Ecclesia Apostolica Synarchica Universalis
33. Ecclesia Gnostica (Pre-Nicene Catholic Church)
34. Ecclesia Gnostica Antiqua
35. Ecclesia Gnostica Apostolica -American Rite
36. Ecclesia Gnostica Catholica Apostolica Latina
37. Ecclesia Gnostica Catholica Hermetica
38. Ecclesia Gnostica Hermetica
39. Ecclesia Gnostica Mysteriorum
40. Ecclesia Gnostica Pravus
41. Ecclesia Gnostica Spiritualis
42. Église Catholique Apostolique Primitive d'Antioche Orthodoxe et de Tradition Syro-Byzantine
43. Église Catholique Française (Église Gallicane)
44. Église Constitutionelle
45. Église Gnostique
46. Église Gnostique Apostolique
47. Église Gnostique Catholique Apostolique
48. Église Gnostique Universelle
49. Église Johannite des Chretien Primitifs
50. Ekklesia Agia Sophia
51. Ethiopian Orthodox
52. Free Protestant Episcopal Church in England
53. Free Swiss Church
54. Gnostic Apostolic Church of the Holy Grail
55. Gnostic Kabbalistic of Memphis-Misraïm
56. Gnostic Rosicrucian
57. Gnostic Therapeutic Sempiesta
58. Greek Orthodox
59. Haitian Independent
60. Iglecia Expectante (Gnostic Expectant)
61. Iglesia Gnostica Catolica Apostolica
62. Igreja Catolica Apostolica Brasileira

63. Independent Catholic Church of Ceylon, Goa, & India
64. Independent Catholic Church of Italy
65. Indian Mellusian Church
66. Irish
67. Liberal Catholic Church
68. Neo-Pythagorean Church
69. Non-Celtic Irish
70. Non-Juring Bishops of Scotland
71. North American Old Roman Catholic Church
72. Nouvelle Alliance
73. Old Armenian
74. Old Catholic Church in America
75. Old Catholic Church (Utrecht communion)
76. Old Catholic – Mariavite (Polish Mariavite)
77. Old Catholic Orthodox
78. Old Gnostic Eleusinian
79. Old Greek Melchite (Byzantine)
80. Old Roman Catholic Church in England
81. Old Templar Church
82. Order of Corporate Reunion
83. Oriental Apostolic Church of Damcar
84. Orthodox Catholic Church in England
85. Orthodox Church in America
86. Orthodox Patriarchate (Antioch)
87. Orthodox Patriarchate (Constantinople)
88. Polish Mariavite (Old Catholic)
89. Polish National Catholic
90. Pre-Nicene Catholic Church (Ecclesia Gnostica)
91. Q.B.L. Alchemist Church
92. Restored Apostolic Church of Jesus Christ of Immaculate Latter-Day Saints
93. Roman Catholic
94. Russian Orthodox
95. Soviet Living Church
96. Spanish Albigensian Gnostic
97. Syrian-Gallican
98. Syrian-Malabar
99. Syrian Orthodox
100. Syro-Chaldean
101. Thelemic Gnostic Church of Alexandria
102. Ukrainian Orthodox
103. Vintrasian Carmelite
104. Welsh
105. Western Orthodox Catholic Church

Appendices

Appendix I

Documents

Included in the appendix are a sampling of various documents pertaining either to the establishment of the ACP or to the establishment of ecclesiastical and/or initiatic authority of its Patriarch. The inclusion of these documents is for informational and historical purposes, and does not imply any current formal connection with the issuing bodies or persons. Many initiation certificates, patents and charters have been omitted, but may be inspected by our clergy upon request. The following documents are included:

Certificate of Appreciation – Document issued under the authority of the late EGCA regionary bishop +Robert Cokinis for the assistance of Reginald Freeman in establishing the Parish of St. Michael the Archangel, EGCA in Kenosha, WI. Signed by Kenneth J. Canterbury in his capacity of Priest-in-Charge of St. Michael's

Ordination Charter: Minor Orders ordination document. Issued by +Cokinis and signed by him and Kenneth Canterbury in his capacity as Chancellor of Athenea Theologica.

Bull of Election: Issued by bishop +William Behun, in ecclesia Tau Thomas, Patriarch of the Apostolic Church of the Third Age, announcing the election of Fr. Reginald Freeman to the order of the Episcopate. Signed by Patriarch Behun and bishop Martin Jacobs, in ecclesia T Philip- Μαρκος.

Consecration Instrument: Issued by Patriarch William Behun, announcing the consecration of Reginald Freeman to the sacred order of the Episcopate. Signed & sealed by +Behun.

Consecration Instrument: Issued by bishop +Valdiveso Matthews, in ecclesia Tau Mikael Basilides III, announcing the subconditione consecration of Reginald Freeman. Assisting Clergy listed. Signed by bishop +Matthews.

Charter for the Parish of St. Michael the Archangel, Ecclesia Gnostica Catholica Hermetica: Issued by the Sovereign Triad of the EGCH to bishop +Reginald Freeman, in ecclesia Tau Valentinus. Signed by the members of the Sovereign Triad.

Official Ecclesiastical Pronouncement: Announcing the creation of the independent jurisdiction of the Apostolic Church of the Pleroma by bishop +Reginald Freeman. Signed by bishop +Freeman.

Initiation Certificate: Announcing the initiation of Reginald Freeman into the degree of Associate in the Traditional Martinist Order. Signed by Freeman, Samuel G. Akpan, Christian Bernard.

Initiation Certificate: Announcing the initiation by Valdiveso Matthews, S.I.I.L. of Reginald Freeman as a Free Initiator in the lineage of l'Ordre Martiniste des Chevaliers du Christ. Signed by Matthews.

Knighthood Certificate: Announcing the installation of Reginald Freeman as a Knight of the Order of the Temple, Sovereign Military Order of the Temple of Jerusalem, Priory of the United States, Grand Priory of Portugal, at the hands of Ronald V. Cappello and Alberto La Cava. Signed by Cappello and La Cava.

Primatie Des Etats Unis D'Amerique Du Nord
Eglise Gnostique Catholique Apostolique

Certificate of Appreciation

The Priest, and the parishioners of St. Michael the Archangel, Gnostic Catholic Apostolic Church, do offer to GOD prayer and thanksgiving in grateful appreciation to:

Reginald Freeman

For his outstanding work in helping to establish St. Michael's Parish. Let it be known that The Ecclesia Gnostica Apostolica appreciates all the hard work involved. He has demonstrated generous and faithful service in God's work. Issued this 2nd Day Of October, 2000 A.D.

Fr. Kenneth J. Canterbury, C.S.M
Archpriest-Chancellor
Diocese of the Midwest
Priest in Charge, St. Michael's

Primatie Des Etats Unis D'Amerique Du Nord
Eglise Gnostique Catholique Apostolique
Charte D'Ordination

Au Nom de l'Essentiel, Existant par SOI et en SOI Dieu Tout-Puissant, Eternel, Uni de Coeur et d'Esprit à toutes les Intelligences qui peuplent les Saints Eons, qui prient avec Nous et Nous assistent, Amen! Nous Most Rev. Robert M. Cokinis in Ecclesia Tau Charles Harmonius II Evêque de Sardis, par la grâce de Dieu, faisons savoir à tous ceux qui ces présentes liront que le 25 Novembre 2000.

Nous avons conféré à **Reginald Merl Freeman**

l'ordre du **Minor Ordres et Acolyte**

Nous certifions qu'il a été procédé à cette Ordination selon notre Pontifical. Nous demandons à nos Evêques, Prêtres et Diacres et a tous les Frères de nos diverses Fraternités et de toutes les Communautés Religieuses en union avec notre SAINTE EGLISE GNOSTIQUE CATHOLIQUE APOSTOLIQUE *de reconnaître les Pouvoirs qui ont été accordés par Notre Sainte Eglise à Notre Freré Reginald Freeman donné de Nous en notre chapelle de* SAINT MONSALVAT, *situé à* Villa Park, ILLINOIS *le l'An de Grâce du Seigneur 25 Novembre 2000.*

HOLY APOSTOLIC CHURCH OF THE THIRD AGE

BULL OF ELECTION

FOR THE CONSECRATION
OF
THE VERY REVEREND REGINALD M. FREEMAN
TO THE SACRED ORDER OF THE EPISCOPATE

HIS EXCELLENCY, THE MOST REVEREND WILLIAM BEHUN
IN ECCLESIA, TAU THOMAS
PRIMATE AND PATRIARCH OF THE HOLY APOSTOLIC CHURCH
OF THE THIRD AGE (JOACHIMITE)

UNTO ALL THE FAITHFUL IN CHRIST AND THE HOLY GNOSIS
THROUGHOUT THE WORLD

PEACE SALVATION AND BENEDICTION

WE, THE HUMBLE SERVANTS OF GOD, HEREBY ALLOW THE CONSECRATION BY THE HOLY SPIRIT OF THE PRIEST, FATHER REGINALD M. FREEMAN ELECTED FOR THE EPISCOPAL DIGNITY FOR THE ECCLESIA GNOSTICA CATHOLICA HERMETICA IN THE NAME OF THE FATHER, OF THE SON AND THE HOLY SPIRIT, AMEN. WE STAND UP BEFORE GOD'S MAJESTY, AND RAISING OUR HANDS TOWARD HIS GRACE, PRAY, THAT THE HOLY SPIRIT MAY DESCEND UPON HIM, AS HE DID UPON THE APOSTLES AT THE TIME OF THE ASCENSION OF OUR LORD JESUS CHRIST, BY WHOM THEY WERE MADE PATRIARCHS, BISHOPS, AND PRIESTS, AND WERE AUTHORIZED TO BIND AND LOOSE, AS WRITTEN BY ST. MATTHEW.

WE, THEREFORE, BY VIRTUE OF OUR APOSTOLIC AUTHORITY, AUTHORIZE HIM TO BIND, TO LOOSE, TO MAKE BISHOPS, PRIESTS, DEACONS, AND ALL HOLY ORDERS AS ORDAINED BY THE HOLY AND APOSTOLIC GNOSTIC CATHOLIC HERMETIC CHURCH. ELEVATING OUR VOICE, WE OFFER THANKS TO GOD. WE PRAY TO GOD TO GRANT HIM CHEER OF FACE BEFORE HIS THRONE OF MAJESTY, AND THAT AT ALL TIMES FOREVER AND EVER

GIVEN ON 2ND OF MARCH, OF THE YEAR OF OUR LORD, TWO-THOUSAND AND TWO, FROM THE PATRIARCHAL SEE.

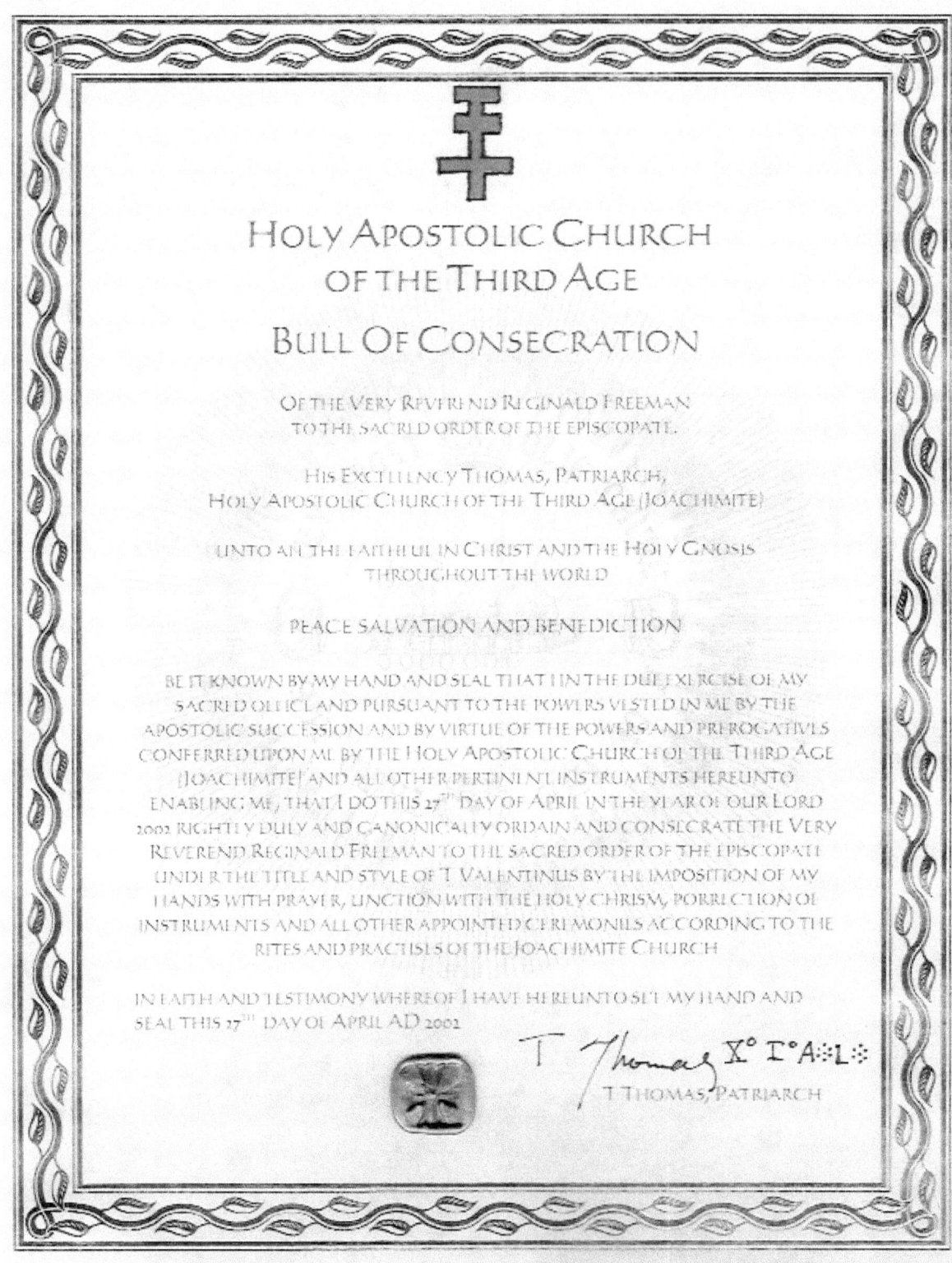

Iglesia Gnostica Apostolica

Eglise Gnostique Catholique Apostolique
Catholicate de la Croix de Rose

Chancery
THE MOST REVEREND MSGR. VALDIVESO MATTHEWS
PMB #362, 528 S. STATE ST, ANN ARBOR, MI 48104-2473 • U.S.A.
(734) 677-6180

CONSECRATION INSTRUMENT

In the name of the Essential, All Powerful God, existing by HIMSELF, bound in heart and spirit with all the Holy Aeons that inhabit the Divine Pleroma, who pray with us and assist us. AMEN.

TO THOSE WHO SHALL READ THESE PRESENTS:

GREETINGS, PEACE, and APOSTOLIC BLESSINGS, in the name of the Very Holy PANTOKRANTOR, the KRISTOS SOTHER, their Mediator, for the unity of all in the Splendor of the Divine Pleroma. AMEN.

HENCEFORTH LET IT BE KNOWN BY ALL WHO READ THESE PRESENTS THAT:

We, VALDIVESO MATTHEWS, in ecclesia, TAU MIKAEL III BASILIDES, by the Grace of GOD, Titular Bishop of Edessa, Metropolitan of Ann Arbor, Catholicos of the SELF-GOVERNING, SOVEREIGN Gnostic Catholic Apostolic Church, Steward of the Apostolic Filiation according to EVODUS, First Patriarch of the Church of ANTIOCH, consecrated by Peter the Apostle,

DO HEREBY ANNOUNCE

That on Saturday, March 22, 2003 A.D., Vigil of the Feast of Holy Gabriel the Archangel, in the presence of a Gnostic Christian Assembly at a private chapel at 6501 Third Ave, Kenosha, WI 53140, by virtue of the Episcopal powers granted to us by the succession of Apostolic See of Antioch, in Syria, having invoked with our prayers the PNEUMA HAGION, The Divine Holy Ghost, We, Valdiveso Matthews, in ecclesia, MIKAEL III BASILIDES, with the assistance of my esteemed brothers in the Holy Gnosis, +Gerald del Campo, in ecclesia, Tau APOLLONIUS, + David Louis Kennedy, in ecclesia Tau IGNATIUS DAVID III and + Philip Otto Kirsch, in ecclesia, Tau IGNATIUS SIMEON II, did impose our hands upon

The Most Reverend Father Reginald M. Freeman

We have consecrated him, with the Holy Chrism in the title of Bishop according to the ancient and traditional Pontifical Rite in use in the Holy Catholicate of the Rose Croix, and recognize him in the name, in ecclesia, of

TAU VALENTINUS

We have recognized his authority to ordain minor orders, to ordain to the Diaconate and the Presbyterate, to consecrate bishops, the Churches, the Holy Vessels, the Altars, the Cemeteries, and to carry out all of the functions inherent of the Episcopal dignity.

We ask that Our Bishops, Priests, Deacons, the Members of our Various Fraternities and Religions in communion with The Holy Catholicate of The Rose Croix, to respectfully recognize the powers and authorities granted to him by our Holy Church.

Given from us, under our Signature, in the Fifth Year of our Episcopate, on the day of the consecration, the Twenty-Second day of March, The Two-Thousand and Third Year of Our Lord, Jesus Christ, AMEN.

The Consecrator
The Most Reverend Valdiveso Matthews, in ecclesia, Tau Mikael III Basilides
Metropolitan Catholicos

Ecclesia Gnostica Catholica Hermetica

In the Name of IAO!

To all whom these Presents Shall Come, Greetings!

Whereas, THE PARISH OF SAINT MICHAEL THE ARCHANGEL is granted a Charter of Operation by Ecclesia Gnostica Catholica Hermetica, incorporated under the Laws of the State of Wisconsin, is granted said Charter on this 28th day of April, in the year of our Lord 2002.

Now Therefore, We, the members of the Sovereign Triad of The ECCLESIA GNOSTICA CATHOLICA HERMETICA by virtue of the powers vested in us, do hereby issue this Charter to THE MOST REVEREND REGINALD M. FREEMAN of the operation of said parish in Kenosha, Wisconsin.

In Testimony Whereof, thereto set our hands and cause to be affixed the Seal of the Church, at the city of Kenosha, this 28th day of April 2002. e.v.

The Very Reverend
Karatah J. Cerneck, Ep. Gn.

The Very Reverend
Andrew J. Angelo, Ep. Gn.

The Most Reverend
Reginald M. Freeman, Ep. Gn.

OFFICIAL ECCLESIASTICAL PRONOUNCEMENT

In the Name of the Unknown Father, Invisible, Ineffable Light; and of the Son, Alone-Begotten of the Father, Christos, Soter, Logos; and of the Holy Spirit, First Thought of God, Mother of All Worlds. AMEN.

Apostolic Greetings To All Brothers and Sisters In the Light of Gnosis!

LET IT BE KNOWN that I, the Most Rev. Mgr. +Reginald Freeman, Ep. Gn., in ecclesia Tau Valentinus, on this 31st day of May, in the Year of our Lord, 2009, at the celebration of Holy Pentecost, do formally and officially institute the Apostolic Church of the Pleroma, for the purpose of the administration of the Holy Sacraments; most especially the Eucharist of our Lord Jesus Christ; and for the dissemination of the ancient and sublime teachings of the Holy Gnosis.

WHEREAS this Gnostic and Apostolic jurisdiction has been instituted under the authority of Tau Valentinus, whose valid Apostolic lines of succession may be attested to by many leaders in the Gnostic Apostolic community, and,

WHEREAS the greater Gnostic community may benefit from the unique rites and liturgies offered by the Apostolic Church of the Pleroma, thus necessitating the creation of this jurisdiction.

WE THEREFORE respectfully request that the Patriarchs, Primates, Metropolitans, Exarchs, Eparchs, and all other bishops and clergy of the authentic Gnostic and Apostolic jurisdictions in North America, and worldwide, recognize and accept the Apostolic Church of the Pleroma, and her validly ordained clergy.

May the Almighty look favourably upon His Church, and may the Grace and Comfort of the Holy Spirit be upon all those serving at her altars.

Through our Lord Jesus Christ, Saviour and Logos, So Mote It Be!

T Valentinus Ep. gn.

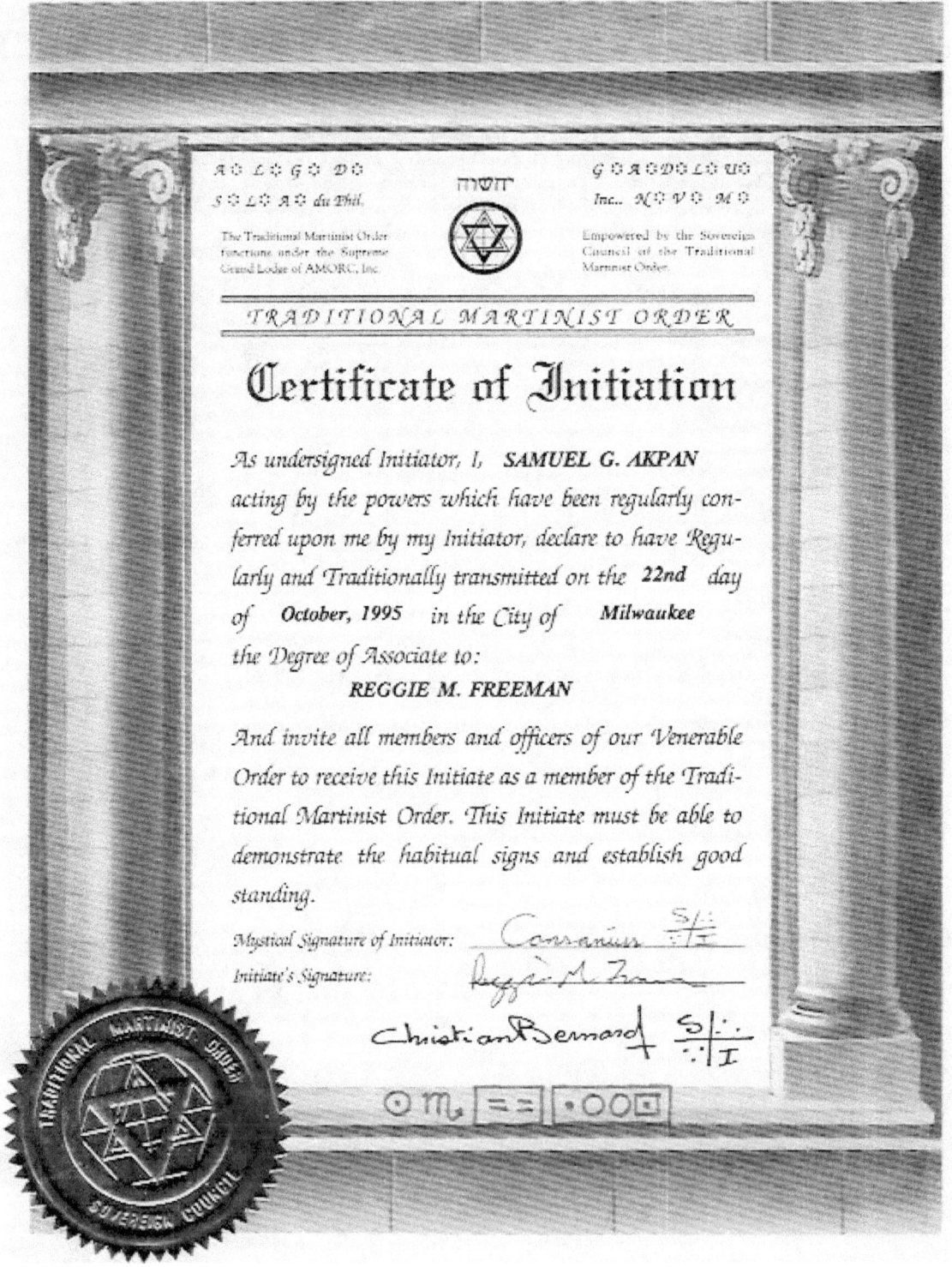

A la Gloire du Souverain Architecte des Mondes

Sous les Auspices du Philosophe Inconnu Notre Vénérable Maitre

FREE MARTINIST LODGE OF THE INLAND SEAS

Charter of Initiation

In the Name of the Sovereign Architect of All Worlds, and under the auspices of the Unknown Philosopher, our Venerable Master,

We, the Free Initiators and Sovereign Grand Inspectors General of the FREE MARTINIST LODGE OF THE INLAND SEAS, under the direction of the Sovereign Grand Commander of the Order, do hereby affirm that our Brother, Reginald M. Freeman, has been properly initiated as a Martinist Free Initiator in the lineage of L' Ordre Martiniste Chevaliers du Christ for the FREE MARTINIST LODGE OF THE INLAND SEAS, and is known to us by the Nomen Mysticum, Sâr Phosphoros.

In accordance with the wishes of the Supreme Council and the Sovereign Grand Commander, this Charter of Initiation is issued to Sâr Phosphoros for the purpose of holding regular meetings, conducting initiations as authorized by the Supreme Council, and delivering the communications of the Sovereign Grand Commander to the Brethren.

Given by us on the 19th day of June, 2004 A.D., under the Signature of the Sovereign Grand Commander, Brother Valdiveso Paschal Matthews, in Nomen Mysticum Sâr Leo Viridis.

Sâr Leo Viridis

KNIGHTS TEMPLAR
ORDER OF THE TEMPLE

In Hoc Signo Vinces

To all Illustrious Knights and Dames of the Noble and Magnanimous Order of the Temple

In Cruce Salus

This Is To Certify That

Sir Knight

Sir Reginald M. Freman

Has been regularly passed through the Orders pertaining to Knighthood and has been dubbed a Novice, Squire and has been installed as a

Knight of the Order of the Temple

on the 13th day of the month of October in the year of Our Lord, 2000, and of the Order 882; and has been made a member of Order of the Temple Stationed at Yonkers, New York; Under the Jurisdiction of The Grand Priory of Portugal of the Sovereign Military Order of the Temple Of Jerusalem, and of the Priory of the United States of America. According to the Ancient formulas of Chivalry and Knighthood. And is now entitled to exercise all rights and privileges as a

Knights Templar of the Order of the Temple

In Witness Whereof we hereunto subscribe our names and affix the Seal. Given this the 30th day of the month of October in the Year of Our Lord 2000, at the Priory and Grand Commandery for the United States of America.

U.S. ARCHIVIST

U.S. LEGATE O.S.M.T.H

"Non Nobis Domine Non Nobis Sed Nomine Tuo da Gloriam"

ACP Clergy Handbook

Appendix J

Glossary of Liturgical and Ecclesiastical Terms

ABSOLUTION: The formal remission of sin imparted by a priest. The ACP does not require its members or clergy to participate in an individual confession of sins to a priest in the sense of the Roman Catholic Penance; but Absolution is offered within the context of the Mass to all who are truly desirous of receiving this special purification. (Latin, *absoluere*, to absolve; *absolutio*, acquittal.)

ALB: A long white linen robe that is worn by all levels of clergy during Liturgical services, Theurgic Operations, or Martinist activities. (Latin, *alba*, white.)

ANAPHORA: The most solemn part of the Christian liturgy, particularly in the celebration of the Eucharist. It is the prayer of consecration and thanksgiving during which the bread and wine are offered and transformed into the Body and Blood of Christ. (Greek, *anaphora*, offering, lifting up.)

ASPERGES: The ceremony of sprinkling the Altar, clergy, and congregation with Holy Water. The instrument used for the sprinkling is called an Aspergillum, or Aspergill. (Latin, *aspergere*, to sprinkle.)

BENEDICTUS QUI VENIT: Part of the Sanctus prayer in the Christian liturgy, specifically within the Eucharistic celebration. It is often sung or recited during the Anaphora or Consecration as an expression of praise and welcome to Christ. (Latin, blessed is he who comes; cf. Matt. 21:9, Psalm 118:26.)

BURSE: A flat cloth case for carrying the corporal that is used in celebrating the Eucharist. (Latin, *bursa*, purse, pouch.)

CANDELABRA: (Also called Candelabrum) A large multi-armed candlestick. (Latin, *candelabrum*.)

CASSOCK: An ankle-length ecclesiastical garment with a close-fitting waist and sleeves. (French, *casaque*, long coat.)

CATECHUMEN: Someone who is undergoing formal instruction in the Christian faith in preparation for baptism. (Greek, *katechoumenos*, one being instructed.)

CHASUBLE: A long sleeveless vestment worn over the alb by a priest. (Latin, *casubla*, hooded garment.)

CIBORIUM: A liturgical vessel designed to hold the consecrated hosts (the Eucharistic bread) during the celebration of the Eucharist or for reservation in the tabernacle. Typically, a ciborium resembles a chalice but has a lid, which differentiates it from the open chalice used for wine. The lid helps protect the consecrated hosts and ensures reverence. (Latin, *ciborium*, Greek, *kiborion*, drinking cup, goblet.)

CINCTURE: A belt, sash, or cord worn with an ecclesiastical vestment. Also called the Cordelier. (Latin, *cingere*, to gird.)

CONFITEOR: A prayer in which confession of sins is made. (Latin, *confiteri*, to acknowledge.)

COPE: A long cloak-like ecclesiastical vestment worn over an alb or surplice. (Latin, *capa*, cloak.)

CORPORAL: A white cloth on which the consecrated elements are placed during the celebration of the Eucharist. (Latin, *corporalis*, of the body.)

CREDO: A declaration of the core beliefs. (Latin, *credo*, I believe.)

CROZIER: A ceremonial staff carried by bishops and some abbots in Christian liturgical traditions. It is shaped like a shepherd's crook, symbolizing the pastoral role of the bishop as a spiritual shepherd guiding their flock. Typically, it is carried during processions or other significant ecclesiastical ceremonies. The symbolism ties back to Christ's depiction as the Good Shepherd. (Old French, *crosier*, Latin *crocia*, *crociare*, crook, curved staff.)

DALMATIC: A wide sleeved vestment worn over the alb by a deacon, priest, or bishop at the celebration of the Mass. (Latin, *dalmaticus*, of Dalmatia, present-day Croatia.)

DIACONATE: The office, or rank, of a deacon. (Latin, *diaconus*, deacon.)

EPARCH: A diocesan bishop or metropolitan. (Greek, *eparkhein*, to rule over.)

EPARCHY: A diocese of the Church. (Greek, *eparkhia*, provincial government.)

EPICLESIS: A term used in Christian liturgy, referring to the specific prayer invoking the Holy Spirit to sanctify the elements of bread and wine in the Eucharist. This prayer is a pivotal moment in the Eucharistic liturgy, as it emphasizes the role of the Holy Spirit in transforming the bread and wine into the Body and Blood of Christ. (Greek, *epiclesis*, calling upon, invocation.)

EPISCOPATE: The office, or rank, of a bishop. (Greek, *episcopos*, overseer.)

EUCHARIST: A sacrament and the central rite of the ACP, which was instituted at the Last Supper, and in which bread and wine are transubstantiated into the Body and Blood of Christ. (Greek, *eukharistos*, grateful, thankful.)

EXARCH: A bishop ranking immediately below a patriarch. (Greek, *exarkhos*, from *exarkhein*, to lead.)

EX OPERE OPERANTIS: From the work of the one working. This concept is discussed by Br. A.D.A. in his excellent treatise, *The Magic of Catholicism: Real Magic for Devout Catholics*. This is the principle at work in operations of Theurgy, wherein the efficacy is determined, in the words of Br. A.D.A., "by the virtue and merit of the operator." (Latin.)

EX OPERE OPERATO: From the work done. This phrase is found in Roman Catholic theology in reference to the validity of sacraments performed by priests or bishops considered heretical or otherwise out of communion with the R.C.C. It refers specifically to the principle that a sacrament is utterly independent of the person celebrating, the faculty of man being unable to limit (or augment) God's action or agency.

GENUFLECT: To bend, touching one knee to the floor, at which time the sign of the cross is made upon the self. (Latin, *genu*, knee + *flectere*, to bend.)

GLORIA: The hymn of praise and worship known as the Gloria in Excelsis Deo ("Glory to God in the Highest").

GRADUAL: A biblical text between the Epistle and the Gospel of the Mass. (Latin, *gradus*, step.)

HOST: The consecrated bread or wafer of the Eucharist. (Latin, *hostia*, sacrifice.)

ICON: An image or representation of a sacred or sanctified personage in the Church. (Greek, *eikenai*, to be like.)

INTROIT: The opening part of the Mass or service, traditionally consisting of a short antiphon, psalm verse, and doxology (a short hymn of praise to God). (Latin, *introitus*, entrance.)

Glossary

KYRIE: A brief petition and response used in various liturgies of several Christian churches, including the ACP. (Greek, *kurios*, lord + *elein*, to show mercy.)

LAVABO: The ceremonial washing of the hands by the celebrant before the Eucharist. (Latin, *lavare*, to wash.)

LECTIONARY: A book of Scriptural passages to be read at church services during the year. (Latin, *lection*, a reading.)

LITANY: A liturgical prayer consisting of a series of petitions and responses. (Greek, *lite*, supplication.)

MANIPLE: A narrow strip of fabric, often richly decorated, that hangs over the left arm of the celebrant during Mass. The maniple is typically made to match the other vestments, such as the chasuble and stole, in both color and design. (Latin, *manipulus*, small bundle.)

MITER: A ceremonial headdress worn by bishops, abbots, and some other clergy in certain Christian traditions. The miter typically consists of two pointed peaks, one in the front and one in the back, with two lappets (long strips of fabric) hanging down from the back. (Greek, *mitra*, headband, turban.)

MONSTRANCE: A receptacle in which a consecrated host ts contained. Also known as an ostensorium. (Latin, *monstrare*, to show.)

MUNDA COR MEUM: Latin, "cleanse my heart." This phrase is part of a prayer recited by the priest, specifically before proclaiming the Gospel.

OBLATION: The offering of the bread and wine during the Eucharist, which are later consecrated as the Body and Blood of Christ. (Latin, *oblatio, oblatum*, an offering.)

OFFERTORIUM: One of the principal parts of the Eucharistic liturgy at which bread and wine are offered to God by the celebrant. (Latin, *offere*, to offer.)

ORATE FRATRES: A call to prayer addressed by the priest to the faithful in the Roman Catholic Mass, just before the Prayer over the Offerings, inviting them to pray that the sacrifice and their own may be acceptable to God. (Latin, pray brethren.)

OSTENSORIUM: see *Monstrance*.

PALL: A linen cloth or a cloth-covered square of cardboard used to cover the Chalice. (Latin, *pallium*, cloak, covering.)

PATEN: A plate, usually of gold or silver, that is used to hold the host during the celebration of the Eucharist. (Greek, *patane*, platter.)

PATER NOSTER: The Lord's Prayer. (Latin, *pater*, father + *noster*, our.)

PRESBYTERATE: The office, or rank, of a presbyter or priest. (Greek, *presbus*, elder.)

PURIFICATOR: A cloth used to clean the chalice after the celebration of the Eucharist. (Latin, *purns*, clean.)

PYX: A small, round container, often made of metal, used to carry the Eucharist (or consecrated host) to those who cannot attend Mass or are otherwise unable to receive Holy Communion. (Greek, *pyxis*, box.)

RELIQUARY: A container used to hold and display sacred relics, which are objects of religious significance, such as body parts, clothing, or possessions associated with saints or religious figures. (French *reliquaire*, from Old French *relique*.)

ROCHET: A white linen vestment resembling a surplice with close-fitting sleeves worn especially by bishops. (Latin *rochettum*, an ecclesiastical vestment.)

STOLE: A long scarf of silk or linen, worn over the left shoulder by deacons and over both shoulders by priests and bishops while officiating. (Greek, *stole*, garment.)

SURPLICE: A loose-fitting, white ecclesiastical gown with wide sleeves, worn over a cassock. (Latin, *super*, super + *pellicum*, fur coat.)

TAPER: A slender candle that should be made of bee's wax or liturgical wax. (Old English, *tapor*.)

THURIBLE: A censer used in ecclesiastical ceremonies or liturgies. The bearer of the Thurible is called the Thurifer. (Latin, *thur*, incense; from the Greek, *thuein*, to sacrifice.)

TRANSUBSTANTIATION: The transformation of the bread and wine of the Eucharist into the Body and Blood of Christ. (Latin, *trans*, + *substantia*, substance.

TRISAGION: An ancient Christian hymn of praise to God. (Greek, *trisagion*, thrice holy.)

TUNICLE: A liturgical vestment worn in certain Christian traditions, primarily by subdeacons and, on rare occasions, by bishops. It is similar in appearance to the dalmatic, which is worn by deacons, though the tunicle is often slightly simpler in design. (Latin, *tunicula*, tunicle.)

WORKS CITED AND SELECTED BIBLIOGRAPHY

ADA, Brother. *The Magic of Catholicism: Real Magic for Devout Catholics.* n.p. CreateSpace, 2015.

Achad, Frater. *Q.B.L.* York Beach, ME: Red Wheel / Weiser, 2005

Aland, Kurt, Matthew Black, Carlo M. Martini, Bruce M. Metzger, and Alan Wikgren, eds. *Greek New Testament*, Fourth Corrected Edition. United Bible Societies, 1993.

Amadou, Robert. *Documents martinistes: Martinisme.* France: Editions Rosicruciennes, n.d.

Ambelain, Robert. *Martinism: History & Doctrine.* Paris: Niclaus, 1946. Trans. Piers A. Vaughn, 2002.
- *Abbé Julio: His Life, His Work, His Doctrine.* Fox Lake, IL: Triad Press, 2021.
- *The Practical Kabbalah.* Paris: Niclaus, 1951 (1990 reissue). Trans. Piers A. Vaughan.
- *Sacramentary of the Rose+Croix.* 1963. Trans. Ronald V. Cappello, 1992.
- *Spiritual Alchemy: The Inner Path.* 1961. Trans. Piers A. Vaughan, 2005.

American Heritage Dictionary of the English Language, Fourth Edition. Boston: Houghton Mifflin Co., 2006.

Anson, Peter F. *Bishops at Large.* Berkley: Apocryphile Press, 2006

Apiryon, Tau (David Scriven). "History of the Gnostic Catholic Church." 1995. (electronic version accessed 28 Sept. 2013 from http://hermetic.com/sabazius/history_egc.htm)

Aquinas, Thomas. *Summa Theologica*, volume two. Chicago: Encyclopedia Britannica, Inc., 1990.

Barnstone, Willis, and Marvin Meyer, eds. *The Gnostic Bible.* Boston: New Seeds, 2003.
- Barnstone, Willis, trans. "The Song of the Pearl."
- Bethge, Hans-Gebhard, and Bentley Layton, trans. "On the Origin of the World."
- Grant, Robert M., trans. "Letter to Flora." Layton, Bentley, trans. "Reality of the Rulers."
- Meyer, Marvin, trans. "The Secret Book of John." Meyer, Marvin, trans. "The Gospel of Thomas."
- Turner, John D., and Charles W. Hedrick, trans. "Valentinian Liturgical Readings."
- Wisse, Frederik, trans. "The Paraphrase of Shem."

Bate, Alistair, ed. *A Strange Vocation: Independent Bishops Tell Their Stories.* Berkley: Apocryphile Press, 2009.

Bauer, W., F.E. Danker, W.F. Arndt, and F.W. Gingrich, eds. *A Greek-English Lexicon of the New Testament and Other Early Christian Literature*, Third Edition. Chicago: University of Chicago Press, 2000.

Bibliography

Bertiaux, Michael. *Voudon Gnostic Workbook*. York Beach, ME: Weiser, 2007.

Betz, H. trans. *Greek Magical Papyri in Translation*. Chicago: University of Chicago Press, 1984.

Binz, Stephen J. *Conversing with God in Scripture: A Contemporary Approach to Lectio Divina*. Frederick, MD: The Word Among Us Press, 2008.
- *Conversing with God in Lent: Praying the Sunday Mass Readings with Lectio Divina*. Frederick, MD: The Word Among Us Press, 2010.
- *Conversing with God in the Easter Season: Praying the Sunday Mass Readings with Lectio Divina*. Frederick, MD: The Word Among Us Press, 2013.

Blitz, Edouard. *Ritual & Monitor of the Martinist Order*. n.p., 1896.

BMG MS 4123: Extract of What is Contained in the Grades of the Ordre of the Élus Coëns. Austin: Ordre Martinistes Souverains, 2020.

Bogaard, Milko. *Of Memphis and of Misraïm: The Oriental Silence of the Winged Sun*. n.p., 2013.
- "Ecclesia Gnostica." 2000. (Web. 21 July 2009)
- "F.U.D.O.S.I." 2001. (accessed 24 February 2010 from http://hermetics.org/fudosi.html)
- "Martinism." 2001. (accessed 24 February 2010 from http://hermetics.org/fudosi.html)

Bois, Jules. *The Little Religions of Paris*. Fox Lake, IL: Triad Press, 2022.

Bowen, Anthony, and Peter Garnsey, trans. *Lactantius: Divine Institutes*. Liverpool: Liverpool University Press, 2003.

Boyer, Rémi. *Mask, Cloak, Silence: Martinism as a Way of Awakening*. Bayonne, NJ: Rose Circle Publications. 2021.

Brenton, Sir Lancelot C.L. *The Septuagint With Apocrypha: Greek and English*. Peabody, MA: Hendrickson Publishers, 1986.

Caillet, Serge. *Arcanes & rituels de la Maçonnerie Egyptienne*. n.p., Guy Trédaniel, 1994.
- *La Franc-maçonnerie égyptienne de Memphis-Misraim*. n.p., Dervy, 2003

Charles, R.H., trans. *The Book of Enoch*. Mineola, NY: Dover Pub., 2007.

Chatel, Ferdinand-François. *Catéchisme À L'usage de L'église Catholique Française*. Paris, 1833.

Churton, Tobias. *Gnostic Philosophy*. Rochester, VT: Inner Tradition, 2005.
- *Invisible History of the Rosicrucians*. Rochester, VT: Inner Traditions, 2009.

Clark, Katherine. *The Orthodox Church*. London: Kuperard, 2009.

Conybeare, F.C., trans. "The Testament of Solomon." *Jewish Quarterly Review*. October, 1898.

Copenhaver, Brian P., trans. *Hermetica*. Cambridge: Cambridge University Press, 1992

Crowley, Aleister. *Agape vel Liber C vel Azoth*. Privately issued.
- *The Book of the Law - Liber AL vel Legis*, centennial edition. San Francisco: Red Wheel/ Weiser, 2004.
- *Liber DCCCLXXXVIII- The Gospel According to Bernard Shaw*. 1953. (electronic version accessed 28 Sept. 2013 from http://hermetic.com/crowley/libers/lib888.html)
- *Liber XV - The Gnostic Mass*.
- *The Worlds Tragedy*. Paris, 1910. (electronic version accessed 3 Oct. 2013 from http://hermetic.com/crowley/worlds-tragedy/)
- *The Holy Books of Thelema*. York Beach, ME: Weiser, 1983.
- *Magick in Theory and Practice*. New York: Dover, 1976.
- *Book 4*. York Beach, ME: Weiser, 1980.
- *The Vision and the Voice*. Dallas: Sangreal Foundation, Inc., 1972
- *The Equinox*: Vol. III, No. I. San Francisco: Red Wheel/Weiser, 2007.

Darlison, Bill. *The Gospel and the Zodiac: The Secret Truth About Jesus*. London: Duckworth Overlook, 2007.

Dehn, Georg, and Steven Guth, trans. *The Book of Abramelin*. Lake Worth, IL: Ibis Press, 2006.

Dubois, Genvieve. *Fulcanelli and the Alchemical Revival*. Rochester, VT: Destiny Books, 2006.

Duez, Joël. *Rituels Secrets des Hauts-Grades de la Franc-Maçonnerie Égyptienne: Rite de Memphis-Misraim, Arcana Arcanorum*. Thot-Hermes, 2009.

Ehrman, Bart D. *The Lost Gospel of Judas Iscariot: A New Look at Betrayer and Betrayed*. Oxford: Oxford University Press, 2006

Bibliography

Elias, Rev. Nicholas M. *The Divine Liturgy Explained*. Athens, Greece: Papadimitriou Publishing, 1966.

Evola, Julius. *The Hermetic Tradition*. Rochester, VT: Inner Traditions, 1995.
- *Revolt Against the Modern World*. Rochester, VT: Inner Traditions, 1995.

Ferguson, Kitty. *The Music of Pythagoras*. New York: Walker & Co., 2008

Flowers, Stephen. *Lords of the Left-Hand Path*. Rochester, VT: Inner Traditions, 2012.

Fortune, Dion. *The Mystical Qabalah*. San Francisco: Red Wheel / Weiser, LLC, 2000. (Originally published in 1935 by Williams and Norgate, Ltd.)

Gerosa, Libero. *Canon Law*. New York: Continuum, 2002.

Graeb, James. Correspondence to William Breeze. 19 March 2004.

Grant, Kenneth. *The Magical Revival*. London: Frederick Muller Ltd., 1972.

Guaïta, Stanislas de. *Le serpent de la génèse: Le temple de Satan*. Paris, 1915.

Guillaume II, Tau. "A Concise History of the EGCA: Primatial See of North America and Columbia." (electronic version accessed 3 March 2025 from https://l-egca-panc.org/a-concise-history-of-the-egca-primatial-see-of-north-and-south-america/)

Hall, Manly P. *The Secret Teachings of All Ages: An Encyclopedic Outline of Masonic, Hermetic, Qabbalistic, and Rosicrucian Symbolic Philosophy*: Diamond Jubilee Edition. Los Angeles: The Philosophical Research Society, 1988.

Hoeller, Stephan A. *Gnosticism: New Light on the Ancient Tradition of Inner Knowing*. Wheaton, IL: Quest Books, 2002.
- "Ecclesia Gnostica Position Paper Concerning the Thelemite or Crowleyan Gnostic Churches." N.D., cir. Early 1980s. (electronic version accessed 28 Sept. 2013 from http://parareligion.ch/hoeller.htm)
- *A Gnostic Catechism*. Los Angeles, 1998.

Holy Bible, King James Edition. Wichita: Heirloom Bible Publishers, 1991.

Julio, Abbé. *Grand Marvelous Secrets*. Fox Lake, IL: Triad Press, 2022.
- *Liturgical Prayers*. Fox Lake, IL: Triad Press, 2025.

- *The Secret Book of Grand Exorcisms and Benedictions.* Fox Lake, IL: Triad Press, 2025.

Kalisch, Rev. Dr. Isidor, trans. *Sepher Yetzirah: A Book On Creation.* New York: L.H. Frank & Co., 1877. (AMORC reprint, 1943.)

Kasser, Rodolphe, Marvin Meyer, Gregor Wurst, and François Gaudard, eds. *The Gospel of Judas*, Second Edition. Washington: National Geographic, 2008.

Laurence, Richard, trans. *The Book of Enoch the Prophet.* N.D. (reprint, Bensenville, IL: Lushena Books, Inc.)

Law, William, trans. *The 'Key' of Jacob Boehme.* Grand Rapids, MI: Phanes Press, 1989.

Leadbeater, Charles W. *Ancient Mystic Rites.* Wheaton, IL: Theosophical Publishing House, 1986. (Originally published in 1926 as Glimpses of Masonic History.)
- *The Science of the Sacraments.* Adyar: Theosophical Publishing House, 1929.

Le Forestier, René. *L'Occultisme en France aux XIXème siècles: L'Église Gnostique.* Milano: Archè, 1990.
- *Occultist Freemasonry in the 18th century and the Order of Élus Coëns.* Fox Lake, IL: Triad Press, 2023.

Mackey, Albert Gallatin. *History of Freemasonry: Its Legends and Traditions, Its Chronological History*, vols. 1-4. New York & London: The Masonic History Company, 1898, 1906.

Mathers, S.L. MacGregor, trans. *The Key of Solomon the King.* London: G. Redway, 1889. (Dover fac. 2009.)

Mead, G.R.S., trans. *Pistis Sophia.* Mineola, NY: Dover Publications, Inc., 2005

Meyer, Marvin, ed. *The Nag Hammadi Scriptures*, International Edition. New York: HarperCollins, 2007.
- Funk, Wolf-Peter, trans. "The Second Revelation of James."
- Meyer, Marvin, trans. "The Gospel of Philip."
- Meyer, Marvin, trans. "The Gospel of Truth." Meyer, Marvin, trans. "The Revelation of Peter."
- Meyer, Marvin, trans. "The Second Discourse of Great Seth." Pearson, Birger A., trans. "The Testimony of Truth."

Nestle, Eberhard & Erwin, Barbara & Kurt Aland, Johannes Karavidopoulos, Carlo M. Martini, and Bruce M. Metzger, eds. *Novum Testamentum, Graece et Latine*, Editio XXVII. Stuttgart: Deutsche Bibelgesellschaft, 1994.

Bibliography

New Revised Standard Edition, New Testament. National Council of the Churches of Christ, 1990.

Olivet, Fabre d'. *The Secret Lore of Music: The Hidden Power of Orpheus*. Rochester, VT: Inner Traditions International, 1987. (Trans. J. Godwin.)

Pagels, Elaine H. *The Gnostic Paul: Gnostic Exegesis of the Pauline Letters*. Philadelphia: Fortress Press, 1975.
- *The Johannine Gospels in Gnostic Exegesis*. Atlanta: Scholars Press, 1989.

Palamas. *Coalescence*. Cobb, CA: Transmutation Publishing, 2018.
- *Enkrateia*. Redding, CA: Transmutation Publishing, 2019.
- *The Homeromanteion*. n.p., Society of Spiritual Stoics, 2024.
- *Lux Occulta*. Redding, CA: Transmutation Publishing, 2021.
- *Spirit Builders: A Free Illuminist Approach to the Antient & Primitive Rite of Memphis+Misraïm*, Vol. 1 & 2. Fox Lake, IL: Triad Press, 2025.
- *Sympatheia: A Liturgical Guide to Esoteric Stoicism*. n.p., Society of Spiritual Stoics, 2023.
- *Syzygy: Reflections of the Monastery of the Seven Rays*. Cobb, CA: Transmutation Publishing, 2015.

Papus (Gerard Encausse). *The Qabalah: Secret Tradition of the West*. York Beach, ME: Samuel Weiser, Inc., 1977.
- *Exegesis of the Soul: Three Treatises on the Nature, Origin, & Destiny of the Human Soul*. Fox Lake, IL: Triad Press, 2022.
- *How to Read Hands: First Elements of Chiromancy*. Fox Lake, IL: Triad Press, 2023.
- *Martinès de Pasqually: His Life, His Magical Practices, His Work, His Disciples*. Fox Lake, IL: Triad Press, 2024.
- *Traité élémentaire de science occulte*. Paris: Chamuel, 1898.
- *What a Master Mason Ought to Know*. Fox Lake, IL: Triad Press, 2022.
- *What is Occultism?* Fox Lake, IL: Triad Press, 2022.

Pasqually, Martinès de. *Treatise on the Reintegration of Beings*. Fox Lake, IL: Triad Press, 2024.

Perschbacher, Wesley J., ed. *The New Analytical Greek Lexicon*. Peabody, MA: Hendrickson Publishers, 1990.

Petersson, Joseph H., ed. *The Lesser Key of Solomon: Lemegeton Clavicula Salomonis*. York Beach, ME: Weiser, 2001.
- *The Sixth and Seventh Books of Moses*. Lake Worth, FL: Ibis Press, 2008.

Phosphoros, Tau, trans. *The Baylot Manuscript in Translation*. Fox Lake, IL: Triad Press, 2020.
- *Degrees of Wisdom: A Compendium of Rituals from the Rites of Memphis and Misraïm*. Fox Lake, IL: Triad Press, 2025.

- *The Gnosis Restored: Essays from the Masters of the French Gnostic Renaissance.* Fox Lake, IL: Triad Press, 2025.

Phosphoros, Tau. *Apostolic Church of the Pleroma Lectionary for Mass.* Fox Lake, IL: Triad Press, 2025.
- *The Pleromic Light Unveiled: An Instructive Monograph on the Holy Gnostic Liturgy of the Pleromic Light.* Fox Lake, IL: Triad Press, 2018.

Phosphoros, Tau and Tau Bruno II. *Light Beyond Shadows: A Collection of Gnostic Homilies from the Apostolic Church of the Pleroma.* Fox Lake, IL: Triad Press, 2025.

Pierce, William. "A Brief Gnostic Interpretation of the Gospel According to Matthew, part one: Chapters 1-12." 2013. (http://pleromachurch.org)

Plummer, John. *The Many Paths of the Independent Sacramental Movement.* Berkley: Apocryphile Press, 2005.

Polychronis, Demetrius G., trans. *An Anthology of Theurgic Operations of the Rose+Croix of the Orient.* Athens, Greece, 2008. (Privately published by "Omega Chapter.")

Ragon, J.-M. *Masonic Orthodoxy: Followed by Occult Masonry and Hermetic Initiation.* Fox Lake, IL: Triad Press, 2023.

Ravignat, Mathieu G. *The Original High Degrees and Theurgical System of the Masonic Elect Cohen Knights of the Universe.* n.p., 2019.

Robinson, James M. ed. *The Nag Hammadi Library.* San Francisco: HarperCollins, 1988.
- Attridge, Harold W., and George W. MacRae, trans. "The Gospel of Truth."
- Isenberg, Wesley W., trans. "The Gospel of Philip."
- MacRae, George, trans. "The Thunder: perfect Mind."
- Parrott, Douglas M., trans. "Eugnostos the Blessed."
- Turner, John D., and Orval S. Wintermute, trans. "Allogenes."

Sadhu, Mouni. *Theurgy: The Art of Effective Worship.* London: George Allen & Unwin, 1965.

Scriven, David. (see Apiryon, Tau.)

Saint-Martin, Louis-Claude de. *Theosophic Correspondence.* Pasadena: Theosophical University Press, 1982. (Trans. & ed. By Edward Burton Penny. Originally published by William Roberts, 1863.)

Bibliography

Saint-Yves d'Alveydre, Marquis Alexandre. *The Kingdom of Agarttha*. Rochester, VT: Inner Traditions International, 2008. (Originally published in 1886 as The Mission of India in Europe.)

Sibley, Ebenezer. *The Clavis or Key to the Magic of Solomon*. Lake Worth, FL: Ibis Press, 2009.

Smith, Andrew Phillip. A Dictionary of Gnosticism. Wheaton, IL: Quest Books, 2009.

Smith, Andrew Phillip, ed. *The Gnostic 3: A Journal of Gnosticism, Western Esotericism and Spirituality*. Dublin: Bardic Press, 2010.
- Casey, Robert Pierce, trans. "Excerpts from Theodotus."
- Freeman, Reginald. "The Gnostic Gospel of Luke: A Gnostic- Hermetic Exegesis of the Tenth Chapter of the Gospel According to Luke."

Stavish, Mark. *Egregores: The Occult Entities that Watch Over Human Destiny*. Rochester, VT: Inner Traditions, 2018.

Stenring, Knut, trans. *Sepher Yetzirah*. London: William Rider & Son, Ltd., 1923

Synésius, Tau. *The Gnostic Tree*. Fox Lake, IL: Triad Press, 2024.

Teder (Henri-Charles Détré). *Rituel de l'Ordre Martiniste*. Paris: Dorbon-Aîné, 1913.

Wagner, Wynn. *A Catechism of the Liberal Catholic Church*. Dallas: Mystic Way Books, 2010
- *The Complete Liturgy for Independent, Mystical, and Liberal Catholics*. Dallas: Mystic Way Books, 2010.

Waite, Arthur Edward. *A New Encyclopedia of Freemasonry*. New Hyde Park, NY: University Books, 1970.
- *The Holy Kabbalah*. New York: Carol Publishing Group, 1995.

Ware, Timothy (Metropolitan Kallistos). *The Orthodox Church*. London: Penguin Books, 1997.

Welling, Georg Von. *Opus Mago-Cabbalisticum et Theosophicum*. York Beach, ME: Red Wheel / Weiser, LLC, 2006.

Wirth, Oswald. *Tarot of the Magicians*. San Francisco: Red Wheel/Weiser, 2012.

Yarker, John. *The Arcane Schools*. Zion, IL: Triad Press, LLC, 2006.

Zerwick, Max, and Mary Grosvenor. *A Grammatical Analysis of the Greek New Testament*, Fifth Edition. Rome: Editrice Pontifico Instituto Biblico, 1996.